Palgrave Studies in Agricultural Economics and Food Policy

Palgrave Textbooks in Agricultural Economics and Food Policy

Series Editor

Christopher B. Barrett, Department of Applied Economics and Management, Cornell University, Ithaca, NY, USA

This book series provides instructors and students with cutting-edge textbooks in agricultural economics and food policy.

William A. Masters · Amelia B. Finaret

Food Economics

Agriculture, Nutrition, and Health

palgrave
macmillan

William A. Masters
Friedman School of Nutrition
and Department of Economics
Tufts University
Boston, MA, USA

Amelia B. Finaret
Department of Global Health Studies
and Department of Business
and Economics
Allegheny College
Meadville, PA, USA

ISSN 2662-3889 ISSN 2662-3897 (electronic)
Palgrave Studies in Agricultural Economics and Food Policy
ISSN 2662-5474 ISSN 2662-5482 (electronic)
Palgrave Textbooks in Agricultural Economics and Food Policy
ISBN 978-3-031-53839-1 ISBN 978-3-031-53840-7 (eBook)
https://doi.org/10.1007/978-3-031-53840-7

Cover photo by W. A. Masters (2011), showing a farmer's granary in Uganda. Corn (maize) can be boiled, roasted or baked into a variety of foods, used as animal feed, processed into ethanol for fuel, or transformed into vegetable oil, liquid sugar, refined starch, and other products.

This Palgrave Macmillan imprint is published by the registered company Springer Nature Switzerland AG
The registered company address is: Gewerbestrasse 11, 6330 Cham, Switzerland

Paper in this product is recyclable.

William A. Masters: For Diane, who makes all of us better.

Amelia B. Finaret: For people who eat and are fed in all kinds of ways. You deserve a good food life.

Preface

Welcome. If you are interested in food and curious about economics, this book is for you. Our approach starts by recognizing your expertise: every reader comes to this book with a lifetime of eating, making choices and thinking about food. Your intimate familiarity with food gives you a head start on our topic, ready to use the language and toolkit of economics for dialogue with others about the causes and consequences of everyone's daily meals and snacks.

Economics about food offers a new way of talking and learning about something that everyone shares, to learn from what past food economists have discovered and add new insights of your own. Economics provides a research method—a toolkit for understanding—to help explain everyday choices, predict the consequences of change and evaluate alternative outcomes so that people can make better choices in the future. Thank you for joining us through use of this book.

You Know More Than You Think, but This Book Offers Surprising New Insights

When thinking about food, each of us brings many years of trial-and-error practice as well as reading, watching and hearing from others. This book will help you add one more type of thinking to your toolkit, using economics to help interpret what you see. Economic thinking can help you avoid common misunderstandings, build your own critical thinking and communication skills, and help guide change in agriculture, food and health for your community and around the globe.

The book is designed to be understood with no prior training in economics and no prior subject-matter knowledge regarding agriculture, food or nutrition. We introduce food economics through a sequence of twelve chapters, each with two main sections. Students and instructors could sprint through all twelve topic areas in a single semester or use the book for a two-semester sequence. There is more material here than can typically be taught or learned in just one semester, with the intention that instructors can focus on the sections of greatest relevance to their students. Readers can also use the book independently and skip around to the topics of interest to them. Many ideas in the book are cumulative, so if you encounter something unfamiliar you can search for its definition and first use earlier in the book.

The book's chapter structure will help you learn and practice using the toolkit of economics to analyze each part of the food system, from production of crops and livestock through food processing and distribution to final consumption. Each chapter features a main narrative with analytical diagrams that explain causal mechanisms, and data visualizations that summarize available observations of key variables. Readers who are already familiar with one aspect of the story will see how that relates to other aspects of agriculture, food and nutrition, using economics to provide a unifying framework through which to achieve many different goals.

Your background and interests will echo what you have learned elsewhere, while some parts of the book will be new and challenging. When learners, including ourselves as authors, encounter material that is puzzling or difficult, one strategy that we have found particularly useful is to slow down and pursue *deliberate practice*. The hardest parts for many readers are the analytical diagrams, each of which is a kind of puzzle whose pieces fit together in surprising and meaningful ways. To see how each puzzle works, you will need to sketch each diagram yourself, using pencil and paper, screen and stylus, or any kind of whiteboard. At first, you will not see why the lines and curves fit together as they do, or why the observed points are where they are. But as you erase and redraw to make your diagrams look like those in this book, the logic will come into focus and you will have a powerful new way of understanding the world around us.

The book begins with individual choices: the economics of consumption and of production. Then, we explore social interactions, in markets, trade and government policies. We start our analysis of interactions using a kind of frictionless benchmark thought experiment: just as high school physics asks you to imagine forces interacting in a vacuum with no friction or other complications, we begin with a sequence of thought experiments contrasting perfectly competitive markets with extreme monopolies and other benchmarks. That gives us a vocabulary with which to describe differences among markets, including topics such as market structure, elasticity and externalities. Next, we examine how differences among people influence the food economy, such as behavioral barriers to eating high-quality diets, and poverty. Finally, we explore the food system in the context of the economy as a whole, showing long-term trends and global comparisons in employment, agricultural development, and food consumption and health outcomes. Notes below each chart provide links to data sources.

Boston, USA
Meadville, USA
April 2024

William A. Masters
Amelia B. Finaret

Acknowledgments

We are grateful for the inspiration, guidance and support provided by the many people who made this book possible. The book itself began with an invitation from Chris Barrett, series editor for the Palgrave Studies in Agricultural Economics and Food Policy, who has given his time so generously to this and other pioneering projects advancing the field of food economics. We are grateful to him and the Palgrave Macmillan team at Springer Nature for the opportunity to turn our teaching materials into this finished product.

The book's content draws on everything we learned from our own undergraduate and graduate-school instructors, of whom we will name only two: Wallace Huffman (1943–2020) and Walter Falcon (1936–2023). Both were born on farms in Iowa, attended one-room schoolhouses and went on to contribute mightily to agricultural economics all around the world. They taught us how to learn from others through fieldwork and conversation, reading from diverse sources, and collaboration with colleagues whose skills and knowledge complement our backgrounds. This book brings together findings from our own work with dozens of research partners, building on thousands of other studies involving millions of farmers, food businesses and consumers. The common knowledge summarized in this book rests on their uncommon efforts.

Once we became classroom teachers, we discovered how students shape our courses by driving the evolution of class materials over time, semester after semester, as we experimented in response to new conditions and changing interests. We are grateful for every puzzled or skeptical look when we explained things poorly, questions and comments pointing out what we had omitted, and the bored silences that showed where delivery was dull. We hope that any past students who might read this book will be happy to see how much better we present things now, thanks to their feedback. This book has also been shaped by our mentors and colleagues teaching other courses, and the many students who served as teaching assistants over the years. Specific individuals who contributed greatly to our recent teaching and to this manuscript include Steve Block, Sean Cash, Leah Costlow, Amy Deng, Nancy Fox, Beatrice Masters, Ken Pinnow, Jerry Shively, Vesta Silva, Caryl Waggett and Parke Wilde.

Most of all we thank our spouses and children for their support and patience as we devoted weekend after weekend to this project—and we thank you, using this book now, for bringing it to life in your own work.

Praise for Food Economics

"*Food Economics* is much more than just another textbook in agricultural economics. It provides an easily-accessible and exciting economics perspective to food systems, including agricultural production, food markets and value chains, consumer choices, and nutrition and health outcomes. Written by international leaders in their fields, this book combines theoretical rigor with up-to-date empirical insights about trends and challenges for sustainable food systems development."

—Matin Qaim, *Director of the Center for Development Research and Professor of Agricultural Economics, University of Bonn, Germany; President, International Association of Agricultural Economists*

"In what is sure to become a leading standard text, Masters and Finaret's *Food Economics* provides a broad, accessible introduction to the economics of food and agriculture."

—Jayson Lusk, *Dean of Agriculture and Professor of Agricultural Economics, Oklahoma State University, USA; former President, Agricultural and Applied Economics Association*

"*Food Economics* is a unique thoughtful synthesis of the economics of food, nutrition and agriculture. It's written to be accessible to undergraduate students. The book is particularly noteworthy for its extensive use of data visualizations that will be illuminating to the student and teacher alike."

—Bharat Ramaswami, *Professor of Economics, Ashoka University, India*

This Book in Verse

Some years ago, William was asked by the authors of the *Freakonomics* series of books, blogs and podcasts to help explain why kiwifruits in New York City were sold at three for a dollar. That seemed weirdly inexpensive, even cheaper than a postage stamp. Their question prompted the following answer which they published in 2009. This silly poem remains a fun summary of food economics, and we'll return to it in the book's epilogue.

Why Are Kiwis So Cheap?

Damn supply and damn demand:
Why cheap hogs and costly ham?
Bargain wheat, expensive flour,
The oldest villain's market power.

Just one seller makes us nervous,
Like that U.S. Postal Service:
They may offer bargain prices,
But who disciplines their vices?

Middlemen have long been blamed
For every market that's inflamed,
Yet better explanations come
From many a Hyde Park alum.

Modern views from Chicago-Booth
Give a nuanced view of truth,
Steven Levitt and John List
Made each of us a freakonomist.

We let data speak its mind
No matter what Friedman opined
And find the price of fruit and veg
To be driven by the market's edge.

Like the tail that wags the dog,
Marginal thinking clears the fog:
Sellers, buyers, traders too,
Interact and prices ensue.

A kiwi costs 33 cents
Simply because no one prevents
Another farm or New York store
From entering and selling more.

In contrast apples may be dear,
For reasons that will soon be clear:
Picking them's below our station,
To lower costs we need migration.

Bananas have a different story,
Seedless magic, breeder's glory,
Cheap to harvest and to ship,
Who cares if workers get paid zip?

Each crop's method of production,
Where it grows and how it's trucked in,
Satisfies some needs quite cheaply
While other costs will rise more steeply.

A buyer's choices matter too,
For nonsense stuff like posh shampoo,
Prices are not down to earth,
The more you pay the more it's worth.

Behavior is as behavior does,
Maybe some things are just because
Much of life's a mystery,
A habit due to history.

For prices, though, it's competition
Plus tariffs set by politicians,
That determines whether we see
Such delightfully cheap kiwi.

Contents

List of Figures

List of Tables

CHAPTER 1

Introduction

1.1 From Farming to Eating, Research and Teaching

Each reader of this book brings its pages to life, using your own history and insights to interpret and apply what we have written. Before writing this book, Amelia and William were students then researchers and teachers in a variety of places. We worked in agricultural schools, liberal arts colleges and health-science campuses in the U.S., Europe and Africa, and conducted workshops and fieldwork in Latin America and Asia. In each place, we have found students interested in agriculture, food and health coming from many different backgrounds, and going on to a wide range of career paths in the public and private sectors.

The topic of agriculture, food and nutrition offers common ground, and economics offers a shared vocabulary and toolkit of analytical methods. Putting the two together makes food economics a broad field of active dialogue among diverse people seeking a shared understanding of the world. Many people care about and participate in decisions about the food people eat, and everyone can use economic principles to improve decision-making. This book captures the intersection of *food* and *economics*, to discover new facts, explain what we see, and help people improve outcomes from agriculture to health.

W. A. Masters and A. B. Finaret, *Food Economics*,
Palgrave Studies in Agricultural Economics and Food Policy,
https://doi.org/10.1007/978-3-031-53840-7_1

1.1.1 Using Food Economics, for Professional Life and as Consumers and Citizens

The food economy involves people in every kind of profession as well as commercial businesses, community organizations and advocacy groups, government agencies and other institutions. One of the most common goals for our students is to fix global problems and improve global health, especially with the looming threats of climate change and income inequality which would stifle humanity's impressive progress in health improvement over the last hundred years. Our students want to make meaningful contributions to improving global health through the food system. People everywhere also want to make well-informed food choices for themselves and their families.

This volume is intended to be a core textbook for advanced undergraduate and master's or doctoral courses that help students gain insights and skills from economics to improve agriculture, nutrition and health around the world. Economic aspects of food and health are important for all kinds of careers in health care and policy, food production and agriculture, nutrition assistance and other domains. Economics provides a powerful toolkit for understanding how different individuals' decisions interact and lead to many unintended but sometimes predictable outcomes that can be improved with strategic intervention. The book shows how people can use economics to guide practical decisions, such as what to eat for dinner today, in ways that add up to large-scale choices facing humanity, such as how best to address persistent poverty and inequity, climate change and other threats.

1.1.2 The Origins of This Book

Much of economics originated in the study of agriculture and food policy, such as the British trade restrictions that favored landowning aristocrats and motivated Adam Smith to write *The Wealth of Nations* (1776), and the link between population growth and famine that led Thomas Malthus to his *Essay on Population* (1798). The word *economics* itself derives from the ancient Greek word for household management, extended in the eighteenth, nineteenth and twentieth centuries to study interactions between people and societal outcomes.

One precursor to this textbook is *Food Policy Analysis*, published in 1983 by Peter Timmer, Walter Falcon and Scott Pearson. That book was among the first to use just analytical diagrams, instead of more complicated mathematical models, to show how the principles of economics can help explain, predict and guide change in all kinds of agriculture and food systems worldwide. When *Food Policy Analysis* first appeared, the world was in a deep recession after the commodity boom and then the food price crises of the 1970s. Massive famines in both Africa and South Asia dominated the headlines, and many countries still faced the high food prices and trade restrictions that motivated

Adam Smith, as well as the rapid population growth and persistent poverty that motivated Thomas Malthus' analysis of humanity's future crises.

In the four decades since *Food Policy Analysis* was published, the world has changed dramatically. Large-scale investments in agricultural research and the rollout of new farm technologies known as the Green Revolution lifted over a billion farmers out of poverty and sharply lowered real food prices, while dietary transition led to the global obesity epidemic and unchecked use of fossil fuels drove climate change. Many people face terrible threats to their food lives, but our toolkit for action is bigger and more powerful than ever and we can use food economics to guide decisions.

This textbook aims to cover decision-making about the food people eat, from crops and livestock through food manufacturing to nutrition and health, with examples from many different settings. We summarize what's been learned in recent years by thousands of food economists asking age-old questions about how best to feed ourselves and the world. What's new is to present that material in a unified, accessible and compact manner, with a balanced perspective on all aspects of the food system from commodity agriculture to urban gardens, and the latest evidence on dietary transition and rising obesity rates alongside continued food insecurity and undernutrition.

The economics of food helps explain deeply rooted facts and trends, such as the persistence of self-employed family farmers even as input supply and food distribution is done by ever-larger companies with many employees. Some of these insights are surprising even to insiders. For example, we observe that total farmland remains roughly constant even as prime farmland is converted to nonfarm uses, because urban sprawl happens around towns and cities while farmers elsewhere bring land into agricultural use. The work of food economists, like other scientists or practitioners, is to use logical inference from all the available data to see what others might miss, and contribute the new insights needed to address our evolving challenges. We're excited to explore these ideas with you through this book.

1.1.3 Supplementary Materials

This book is intended to be a standalone resource, primarily for use as the primary textbook for courses on economic aspects of agriculture, food and nutrition. For that purpose, we invite readers to visit the book's accompanying website at http://sites.tufts.edu/foodecon.

1.2 Why Study Food Through Economics, and Economics Through Food?

1.2.1 Learning Objectives of the Book

This book is a study of economics about food, including the sustainability of agricultural production, equity in the food system and health outcomes from food consumption. Through this book, students will learn how to apply the economics toolkit to major policy questions around the world. Our methods are presented graphically using analytical diagrams and data visualization, building skills that are widely used in professional life and a foundation for more advanced study.

The beginning of each section will tell you what you should expect to learn on that topic, to guide your reading and explain the purpose of the material we present. The book also has overarching learning objectives. After reading this book and practicing your use of the economics toolkit described here, you will be able to:

1. Describe causal mechanisms behind observed production, consumption, market and trade outcomes using analytical diagrams that illustrate economic principles;
2. Apply economic principles to assess the consequences for wellbeing of market failures, government policies, regulations and external shocks to the global food system;
3. Obtain, use and explain available data on food, agriculture, nutrition and health;
4. Imagine, describe and analyze the effects of individual actions and systemic changes in agriculture, food and nutrition, taking account of resource constraints, available technologies and how people respond to incentives.

1.2.2 Why Study Food Through Economics, and Economics Through Food?

Food is life. Food systems span the entire range of human experience, and economics give us sharp insights into how food production and consumption works within the larger universe of individual experience, societal interactions and our physical environment. Humanity evolved to live almost everywhere on earth, catching or growing and eating an astonishing variety of foods. Our choices for what to eat, and how to obtain the foods we want, are among our most frequent and important decisions, both individually and for each household, community and country.

The ancient Greek definition of 'economics' was household management, and the modern economics of food still begins there: we focus on individuals and families, to explain and predict decisions about who does what within the home. We then turn to interactions between households, as people buy and sell things that would be more difficult or impossible for each family to do on their own.

The first modern economics textbook is Alfred Marshall's *Principles of Economics*, published in 1890. That book provides some of the earliest sketches of what became the analytical diagrams and other research methods presented in this and other modern economics writing. The first sentence of Marshall's *Principles* remains a valuable definition of what we do, explaining that '*Economics is a study of mankind in the ordinary business of life; it examines that part of individual and social action which is most closely connected with the attainment and with the use of the material requisites of wellbeing*'.

That opening sentence defines economics in a remarkably powerful way that remains accurate today, and is worth repeating to comment on each part of the definition. What Marshall wrote is that:

- *Economics is* ***a*** *study* (not the only one),
- *of* ***mankind*** (today we would say humankind, but Marshall was already emphasizing universality),
- *in the* ***ordinary*** *business of life* (focusing on everyday decisions, such as farming and eating)*;*
- *it examines* ***that part of*** *individual and social action* (again, not all aspects of every action, but their commonalities that link individual choices and actions by whole societies),
- *which is most closely connected with the* ***attainment*** *and with the* ***use*** (in other words, how and why things are made, distributed and consumed),
- *of the* ***material requisites*** *of wellbeing* (not wellbeing itself, but the material things that are needed for people to meet their broader life goals).

Using economics to understand choices reveals how individual decisions and social interactions are constrained by what is physically possible to do, and what the rules of society allow. Nature and technology determine the universe of physical possibilities, and people's choices are further constrained by societal norms, institutional rules and government policies of all kinds. Many people have few options, or only bad options. Environmental conditions may fluctuate wildly, and often degrade over time as we all use up the natural resources around us. But investments in new technology can open new possibilities, and people can change the rules of social interaction to improve outcomes.

The economics toolkit described in this book shows how individual and social choices about food have evolved over time and are changed by the actions of each successive generation in every country. Our work draws on and contributes to almost every other domain of research and practice in the health, environmental and social sciences, or the humanities. For many readers, a primary motivation is human health. We all want our food to sustain a healthy and active life for everyone, to overcome societal disparities and inequity. Agriculture and food also play a crucial role in the climate crisis and in addressing many concerns about sustainability and the environment. Food economics can help address each of these challenges through a wide range of careers. People everywhere also have an intrinsic interest in food as such: the challenge and opportunities of eating well every day and the unique joys of meals on special occasions.

Economists study people, explaining behavior in terms of how nature and technology shape each choice people make. To understand how food affects human health, we can all use many results from *nutritional biochemistry and physiology*, showing how we metabolize bioactive compounds and other attributes of food to build our bodies and fuel our lives. We also draw heavily on *nutritional epidemiology,* revealing how diets affect health outcomes over the life course. To understand where food comes from, and how our food choices affect the world around us, we draw heavily on *agronomy and agroecology* for plant production, and *veterinary or animal science* for animal-sourced foods, as well as *food science* for the study of how packaging and processing affects the food people eat. We are also attentive to more specialized work about specific aspects of the food system, such as *fisheries and aquaculture* and many subfields of the *environmental sciences*.

The economics of food borrows from the natural sciences to understand how food is produced, and from the health sciences to understand how it affects health, but the topic itself is about people: this textbook draws heavily on findings from *demography* that measures how the size and composition of each population changes over time, as well as *sociology and anthropology* to study how groups of people relate to each other, *political science* to study how governments and other institutions make decisions, and especially *history and the humanities* to tell the story of each community's relationship to food.

The many disciplines that inform food economics, like economics itself, have deep internal debates that drive change in the frontier of knowledge. New facts are discovered, and then we develop new theories to explain them and predict future observations. For this textbook, we aim to describe exactly how recent scientific knowledge, whether in nutrition or agronomy or other fields, can inform economic decision-making and analysis, in ways that can be updated as new discoveries are made.

Why Use Economics to Study Food?

Economics is particularly well suited to understanding agriculture and nutrition, with a long history of using national statistics and household surveys to understand and address rural poverty and food scarcity. The quantities and prices of food produced, traded, delivered and consumed are among the first and most important kinds of data available since the beginning of recorded history, and have been used to explain, predict and assess links to a wide range of outcomes that people care about. Having available data about important choices has allowed generations of economists to test hypotheses, build the toolkit described in this book and use those methods and results to guide individual choices, program interventions and government policies.

Why Use Food to Understand Economics?

People everywhere care about food as such, but food-related choices are also profoundly revealing about human behavior and societal concerns more generally. For example, how nutrition assistance programs use cash, vouchers or physical deliveries and advice about what to eat reveals more general truths about the use of social insurance and safety nets to address inequities, how policymaking works and how program participants respond to each kind of intervention. Food is a fascinating lens through which to learn about people and society, offering endless variation on the common themes described in this book. Each situation is unique and unprecedented in some ways, but we can use that variation to reveal underlying principles that drive the outcomes we see.

Economics as a Science

Economics is a science in the sense of using systematic methods to record observations, make predictions and test hypotheses about what is observed. The resulting methods and data, shared among a community of researchers and practitioners, form a discipline that offers a specific toolkit and way of knowing about the causes and consequences of our actions and reactions. For use in diverse cultures the words in this book might need to be translated, but the analytical diagrams and data visualizations would remain intact and would be understood by academic economics trained in any country of the world. The explanations and predictions made by economists, like the work of other scientists, come from building simplified models that capture some, but not all, of the forces behind the outcomes we observe. Each model represents specific aspects of our infinitely complex world, omitting everything that is not needed for each particular set of explanations and predictions.

Like other disciplines, economics offers many different models, each tailored to specific circumstances and designed to guide particular decisions. Some researchers may aspire to producing a universally applicable holistic model that describes everything, but such a model would be as complex and unwieldy as the world itself. No single model can be all-encompassing, so we need a variety of models, each designed to explain and predict specific outcomes in particular settings. The development of this economics toolkit, like any other kind of research, is driven by curiosity about the causes of things, but also the need for structural models of causal relationships to solve practical problems, guiding our actions in each situation to improve future outcomes for ourselves and society as a whole.

Economics as a Social Science

Like other social sciences, economics differs in important ways from physical or biological sciences. One key difference is that the subject of economics is our own lives and human society. Every student, researcher and practitioner brings their own rich set of experiences and prior beliefs to their work, informing how we do economics. As scientists, we follow the evidence. As human beings, we all have other concerns including family and friends, religious faith and social or political commitments. All those social factors influence each economist and the field as a whole as we seek to improve outcomes in our individual lives and professional careers. The economics toolkit presented in this book is itself the product of past choices, and how we use and adapt that toolkit depends on decisions we make today, as you read and use this book.

A particularly interesting aspect of social science is that things we study may be directly influenced by our research. For example, if a food economist publishes results describing 'shrinkflation', whereby companies reduce package size instead of raising prices, news coverage of that study could lead consumers to read the fine print about quantity and focus on cost per unit instead of just the item price. That change in awareness would remove the incentive for companies to practice shrinkflation, thereby eliminating the phenomenon described in the research. Media coverage of economics research, like other scientific findings, can influence what people do, and of course there are many other sources of variation and change over time. For that reason, economists need an increasingly complex and diverse toolkit of different models, each one matched to decision-making needs in a particular setting.

How Economics Differs from Other Social Sciences

Economists explain variation in observed outcomes as the result of peoples' choices under various circumstances. This kind of research draws on many other fields of social science and the humanities, such as psychology and cognitive sciences to understand individual decision-making, sociology, anthropology and history to understand the cultural and societal context of our actions, as well as management and government to understand institutional structures, power and control in businesses, social organizations and political life. Economics also involves explicit constraints representing what nature and technology allow, which draws heavily on knowledge from the physical sciences and engineering, natural and environmental sciences, as well as biological and health sciences. People in other fields also use economic methods and data, so the boundaries between disciplines are fundamentally blurry, but the economics toolkit retains a distinctive identity relative to other social sciences.

A first signature feature of economics is to focus on individuals' choices, interpreting their actions as having been the best (or the least bad) of the options available to them. By focusing on peoples' choices, economics focuses our attention on situations where improvements are possible, and by interpreting observed actions as each person's best (or least bad) option, economics focuses our attention on peoples' circumstances and what their choices reveal about their goals and aspirations. In situations where people have only one option or our actions are predetermined, economics is not applicable—economists would just move on to questions for which people do have choices. And where what appear to be choices are random, controlled by outside forces or otherwise not revealing anything about the person's needs and wants, economists again would just move on to questions where analysis and prediction could be used to improve outcomes. Our concern in this book is situations in which we observe people consistently choosing one thing instead of another, in ways that allow us to infer something from people's actions about their preferences and desires.

The mathematical jargon for economists' way of interpreting choices is that each individual person's actions reveal some degree of *optimization*, meaning that they chose the option that was best (or least bad) for them, given the limitations imposed by their circumstances. In everyday life, the term 'optimization' is used to mean improvements on what would otherwise happen, but in economics the word is used as a way of explaining why people did what we observe them to have done. Economics is concerned with peoples' choices, using the idea of optimization to distinguish peoples' constraints and options from their goals and preferences. Economics is about choice under scarcity, for use in situations where people have a limited set of options, and our actions reveal what matters most to us. Under extreme scarcity, people choose the least bad of their options. In better times, people may get almost all of what they desire. Observing many choices under various conditions can reveal similarities and differences in the priorities revealed by each person. Interpreting observed behavior as having been optimal allows us to infer something about peoples' preferences and gain insight into how far a population was able to get towards their goals and aspirations.

A second signature feature of economics is to focus on interactions between people, where the rules of interaction determine the degree to which a whole population can achieve its goals. The options available to each person depend in part on choices made by others, so individuals' decision-making cannot be understood in isolation. By interpreting each person as having done the best they can, economics avoids blaming an individual and focuses on ways to improve outcomes by changing peoples' circumstances. Economics uses a systems approach to the social determinants of health, explaining each outcome as a simultaneous interaction between multiple forces. Each set of goals and constraints is represented by a system of simultaneous equations represented as lines on a diagram, explaining observed outcomes as points of tangency or intersection that result from interaction among all of the various factors taken into account by any particular economic analysis.

The mathematical jargon for economists' view of societal interactions is that observed outcomes are seen as an *equilibrium* between people, meaning a balance between multiple forces whose outcome may be better or worse. In everyday life, the term equilibrium is used to mean something stable and calm, and things in equilibrium are generally good. But within economics, the word 'equilibrium' does not mean stable or good—something being an economic equilibrium just means it is the predicted outcome of interaction between different people under the circumstances described in a specific scenario. Most importantly, in economics an equilibrium need not be itself an optimum. For example, in an apartment with three housemates who prepare their own meals, each might do the best they can, but the group might not get along, experiencing conflict and missed opportunities for joint meals. This situation might persist for weeks or months until someone suggests a change in house rules, such as a fixed roster for chores or a new way of cooking that makes cooperation easier and leads to a better equilibrium. Both the initial outcome and the later improvement are equilibria, and revealed preference tells us that the second is better than the first. In this case, what economics reveals is how the improvement can be sustained only if all housemates agree to live by those rules or to chip in and share the cost of new kitchen equipment.

Like any scientific activity, economic analysis begins with observation and description, leading to explanations and predictions about what might be observed under different circumstances. In this textbook, we draw each model graphically and then use charts of data to see patterns and trends. Each prediction is a potentially testable hypothesis. Decades of research have led to the rejection of many plausible hypotheses, leading to the retention and refinement of the models in this textbook. Over time, each model in our toolkit has been validated and calibrated to fit observed data in various settings. This chapter focuses on that aspect of economics as a ***positive social science***, so called because researchers 'posit' theories to be tested and refined with additional data. Later chapters will focus on the ***normative implications*** of each model, in the sense of identifying desirable 'norms' to improve societal outcomes.

Economics about agriculture, food and health is always an ***interdisciplinary*** activity. Production and supply depend on the physical environment, natural resource management and available technologies, while consumption and demand depend on biological needs as well as cultural and other forces shaping food choice, and the interaction between them is shaped by many social, institutional and political as well as geographic and technological factors. The analytical diagrams derived in this and later chapters are ***stylized models*** designed for generality so that each student, researcher and practitioner of food economics can draw them around specific scenarios reflecting their own knowledge and interests. For example, the diagrams in this book could be used to focus on climate change, water use, antibiotic resistance or other aspects of farm production, as well as food manufacturing and marketing or other food businesses. Others might use these diagrams to focus on weight, diabetes, nutrition and health. In each case, the causes and effects shown in each diagram depend on individual choices and business activity, but also policy choices and government interventions.

In summary, economics explains observed outcomes as resulting from individuals' choices that were optimal for them, under circumstances where the societal equilibrium could potentially be improved through changes in policy or technological innovations. This approach to social science can be applied to many questions, at any scale of analysis. For example, when commodity prices start rising as they did during the world food price crises of the 1970s, and then again in the mid-2000s and the 2020s, exporting countries often respond by restricting outbound shipments. Their reactions make the price spike even worse, responding to a period of scarcity by holding back sales. Similar problems affect buyers who respond by stocking up in fear of further price rises. Agreements among buyers and sellers can help stabilize the market but may be difficult to introduce and enforce. Economics starts with individual households but quickly scales up to the world as a whole, helping guide decisions in many different settings.

What Economics Is Not

The economics toolkit described in this book may surprise you, because economics itself is often described in misleading or confusing ways.

One confusion is between economics and 'the economy'. When economists describe and measure 'the economy', we mean the circular flow of all goods and services exchanged among households or individuals, companies and the government. That flow of goods and services adds up to national income, as described in Chapter 9. But as you will see in this book, only some of what we study counts as income. Alfred Marshall's original definition explained that economics is concerned with the material requisites of wellbeing in general, so this book is also concerned with nonmarket factors such as pollution and climate change, and the many decisions about food and health that do not involve market transactions such as meal preparation within the home.

Another confusion is between economics and business or finance. Many people who want to work in private enterprises study economics, and some businesses have employees with 'economist' in their job title, but most of the economics discussed in this book is conducted in academic institutions or the public sector. This kind of economics research takes business practices as given, and our primary research question is what governments should do. Our findings are published in the public domain and investigate how changes in public policy might alter outcomes. The use of economics as training for a business career is particularly widespread in U.S. liberal arts colleges that do not have undergraduate business schools, but when people actually study how to manage a business their courses often focus on other topics such as accounting and finance, marketing and advertising, personnel management and entrepreneurship. Those aspects of business administration all have some links to academic economics, but business schools focus primarily on other aspects of enterprise management.

A third area of confusion concerns the role of specific schools of thought within economics. As defined in this book, economics as a whole is a scientific discipline that explains observed outcomes as resulting from individuals' choices that were their best options at the time, under circumstances where the societal outcome of interactions between people could be improved with better government policies. Some economists focus on ways in which governments intervene too much, ultimately leading to a libertarian or small-government approach to politics. Other economists focus on ways that interventions could be extended, leading to a more activist or progressive approach to politics. Individual economists often engage in advocacy for or against specific policies, and schools of economic thought often form around a political ideology: for example, from the 1960s through the 1980s a 'Chicago School' of economists successfully sought to reduce the size of government, while competing groups of 'saltwater' economists at coastal universities favored a larger role for the public sector. The size and influence of each group varies over time as the discipline evolves, but the slow and uneven pace of change can be frustrating especially regarding gender dynamics and racial disparities, underscoring the need for each generation of new economists to bring their goals and ambitions to the profession.

Questions About Food and Nutrition that Economics Can Answer
Below are some broad questions that can be answered using economics, using the example of vegetable consumption as an important determinant of individual and population-level health. To feasibly work on questions like these for a research project, the questions would need to be focused on particular contexts (e.g., places, people, time periods) and be specific (e.g., which vegetables, which rules, which policies).

- Why do so many people eat less vegetables than nutritionists advise?
- Which households, and which people within those households, consume more than others?
- What technologies or policies might make it easier and more appealing to eat vegetables?
- How do food safety, food waste or time use and meal preparation relate to vegetable use?

Nutritionists and health scientists generally avoid characterizing individual foods as healthy or unhealthy, since the impact of a given food on health depends on what else is being consumed. Instead we focus on a healthy diet, meaning an overall dietary pattern balanced among food groups with a mix of attributes that meet the needs of a given individual or population. The degree to which any given set of foods provides a balanced diet is measured using metrics described in the text including the Healthy Eating Index (HEI) and the Cost and Affordability of Healthy Diets (CoAHD) indicators. Individual foods that tend to be insufficiently consumed can be described as healthful, because they bring attributes for which additional quantities are needed for health.

Amelia is a practicing dietitian, and knows from working with patients that predominant narratives about food can perpetuate harm through eating disorders, undesired weight loss or weight gain, dietary restriction and nutrient deficiencies. One of Amelia's favorite principles from nutrition and dietetics is that there are no 'good' or 'bad' foods, and that finding the right foods for each person at each time and place can be a lifelong challenge. Food economics as presented in this book can be a helpful approach to meeting health needs in more sustainable and equitable ways at home and worldwide.

Economic Thinking as a Useful Skill for Any Profession
Studying food economics will help you build all kinds of skills for professional life, regardless of your career path. We use familiar examples to learn about the impacts of our own actions and societal choices and learn how to improve outcomes in practical ways. The theories and data analysis methods presented in this book can be helpful for any situation where people need to make decisions. Our goal is to build models that are useful in the real world to explain, predict and evaluate human choices.

This book focuses on data about agricultural production, food distribution and dietary intake. We describe how the world's farming, marketing and eating activities are measured, and provide data analysis methods and data visualizations to help make sense of the results. Modern computing and communications have given us unprecedented access to information, almost all of which is filtered and distorted by other people for their own purposes. Learning how to find and interpret the data you need is especially important in a world of algorithms and artificial intelligence. As new tools become available, each of us needs even more advanced analytical skills to use them for our own purposes. Building up your own logic and intuition about data analysis is also important for self-protection, to avoid being misled by other people who might not share your goals. All these important skills can be used directly in a wide range of jobs and underlie research that would test the validity of economic models, estimate relationships and quantify impacts and cost-effectiveness of actual choices.

1.2.3 Intended Audiences for This Book

The economics toolkit used in this book is presented graphically in two dimensions, using analytical diagrams and data visualizations. The book spells out the *principles of economics* using terminology, diagrams and visualizations that have evolved over decades of practice, summarizing the findings of economic research and practice using only natural language and basic geometry. The book is written primarily for students with no previous knowledge of economics, as a first introduction to economic principles. The book can also be used by readers familiar with economics from other fields, using those principles to explain and predict changes in agriculture and natural resource use as well as food-related businesses, nutrition and health outcomes.

The book is intended for advanced undergraduates, graduate students and professionals working in agriculture, food and health. We provide many concrete examples from diverse settings, but our focus is on the general principles discovered by decades of economic research as summarized in graphical models of human behavior and societal outcomes. More advanced economic models use multivariate calculus to explore many dimensions at once, and specialist graduate courses use even more general analysis of all possible real numbers. The simplifications used for this book flatten the world to just lines and curves on a page, leaving you to imagine how these economic principles play out in your own experience and for other people in different circumstances.

Researchers and practitioners using economics draw on the theories and data in this book, simplifying the infinitely complex world to explain, predict and evaluate change. The analytical diagrams used in economics are in some ways like how physical processes are drawn in chemistry or physics, where letters and arrows illustrate theories about underlying structures that explain and predict what we see. Likewise, the charts and tables through which we visualize observed data are also like how data are communicated in other fields. Just as travelers use a variety of standard kinds of maps for different kinds of navigation, economists and other scientists use different kinds of two-dimensional pictures to describe the infinitely complex world.

The Models Used in This Book

Economic models all use similar principles but take different forms when representing any particular research or policy question, for any particular population and their circumstances. Economists have developed a variety of models suited to different places and people. In each model, peoples' objectives and constraints have a mathematical structure with specific parameters that are predetermined in each scenario, as a set of options from which the observed or predicted outcomes are just one of several potential outcomes.

At the introductory 'principles' level of economic analysis, all models are shown in just two dimensions as a choice between two kinds of things. The same logic extends in all other dimensions, with increasingly abstract mathematics needed to show more than just two variables at once. The relatively simple two-dimensional analytical diagrams used in this book have evolved greatly since Alfred Marshall's textbook in 1890, through generations of researchers studying agriculture and food choice as well as other topics. The resulting models provide stylized but rich descriptions of human behavior, in a form whose predictions and implications are remarkably useful.

The first part of our journey consists of thought experiments, systematically building up our explanations and predictions in a series of *analytical diagrams* that illustrate causal mechanisms behind observed outcomes. Each diagram is a *qualitative model*, representing a thought experiment that yields predictions about the nature and direction of change in response to what-if scenarios that you can imagine and apply to your own life. To study the economics of food, we show a subset of the diagrams shown in more general textbooks and adapt them to focus on agriculture and health. A key feature of our diagrams is consistent notation throughout the book, with the main thing of interest shown along the horizontal (X) axis and other things on the vertical (Y) axis.

The second part of our journey explores the real world, summarizing data from thousands of surveys and other observations in two-dimensional *data visualizations* that summarize patterns and trends in agriculture, food and nutrition around the world. These visualizations present *quantitative results* of empirical studies, summarizing what was observed in a way that might be useful for predictions and assessment. By definition, these charts show only actual observations and not the other possibilities that might have been. To imagine alternatives, we need to think about why those observed outcomes were chosen, using insights from the analytical diagrams.

In economics, the outcomes we see are explained as the result of several variables whose simultaneous interaction forms a system of equations representing a relationship between multiple objectives and multiple constraints. These relationships could be written mathematically, but for this textbook we will show each equation as a line or curve on an analytical diagram. Economics uses diagrams in much the same way as biology or chemistry, with lines and symbols showing interactions that could potentially be measured to estimate magnitudes of response and test the statistical significance of each model's predictions.

To understand observed choices, economists analyze people's decisions *on the margin*. What this means is that economic models aim to understand decisions about consuming *the next unit* of a given good, by analyzing whether the benefit of consuming the next unit of the good outweighs the cost of doing so. Marginal thinking is different from *either-or* thinking, because analyzing decisions on the margin is inherently asking *how much* of the good you are going to consume, not just whether you will consume it at all. Economists analyze decisions on the margin for all types of decisions, and in this section, we will focus on consumption decisions. This is another example where terminology in economics differs from ordinary language. In everyday usage, 'marginal' means unimportant, for example when people are 'marginalized' and excluded from the center of social and economic or political life. In economics, the 'marginal' unit is the most important one, because it sets the total quantity consumed and the price at which other items are bought and sold. These and other concepts are clearly illustrated by the analytical diagrams.

All parts of the book fit together, as the economic theory in our analytical diagrams guides what is measured and how to interpret each observation. Economists see observed outcomes as the result of individual choices, with each person having learned from their own and others' experiences, leading to outcomes that depend on our natural environment, available technologies and government policies. That kind of explanation leads to systematic predictions that are tested empirically using *econometrics*, the toolkit of advanced statistical methods developed for causal inference, experimental tests and estimation of the relationships shown in our analytical diagrams and data visualizations.

Two-Dimensional Diagrams Show a System of Simultaneous Equations

On each diagram we draw multiple lines and curves, each a different equation between the two variables. The resulting system of simultaneous equations illustrates how people might interact with each other and the world around them, leading to a specific outcome shown as a point on the diagram. Changes in circumstances are shown as shifts in the position of each line or curve, causing people to move along a given line or curve to a different outcome. This kind of systems thinking permits economists to trace each observation back to its possible causes, generate predictions and hypotheses to test using new observations, and imagine alternatives that might improve the outcomes we see.

How to Learn These Models

This book explains each diagram in words, and we could try to teach and learn all the economics using only words. But sketching the diagrams is hugely valuable because the lines and curves lead to specific points on the axes. Tracing each line or curve according to its definition leads to a specific conclusion, using the logic of geometry to augment human intuition. Each point represents an observable fact in the world, such as the quantity of ice cream that a person eats in a day. Each line or curve represents a relationship between two numbers that is based partly on observable facts, such as the market price of ice cream that day, and partly on the scenario or situation that the model is designed to represent, such as the temperature and how ice cream is made, packaged and sold. Each diagram is built to explain a set of observed facts, predict how those facts would change under different conditions and assess whether those changes would be good or bad for the people we care about.

On the Philosophies of Modeling

The everyday work of economists consists of making and testing predictions using models like the analytical diagrams shown in this textbook. Economists build and calibrate models to fit specific observations, and then validate those models against other evidence. Our own personal experience plays a large role in how we use each model. Your own past experiences give you intuition and skills, and working with the models builds further intuition and skills. 'Thinking like an economist' means seeing how economic models might be relevant to any given situation. The shape and position of each curve captures underlying biophysical, natural and social conditions, and the interaction between curves leads to outcomes that we could observe.

The models developed in economics, as in many other fields, result from use of *Occam's Razor* to explain what we see using the least complicated plausible mechanism. In the famous phrase attributed to Albert Einstein, 'models should be as simple as possible, but no simpler'. When we reduce each model to just two-dimensional diagrams or data visualizations, all other dimensions are left out, and we can focus on a specific set of interactions that are themselves infinitely rich and complex. Much is omitted, but the remaining content provides powerful explanations and predictions about the world around us.

Another central aphorism to guide our work is due to statistician George Box, who famously said 'all models are wrong, but some are useful'. Models are helpful when used under specific conditions, for particular scenarios. Outside those circumstances, the model would be misleading or simply irrelevant. To be clear about the situations described by a particular model, economists aim to be as explicit as possible about the logical premises or mathematical assumptions used to derive each prediction. Like other scientific theories, economic models may be precisely accurate only under very narrow circumstances, and yet also approximately true and broadly useful over a wider set of conditions, up to the point where a different model might be more useful. An important aspect of training in any discipline is to learn when each tool is most useful, and when to adopt a different tool. This textbook presents the models we have found most useful for economics about food, in ways we will explain. Each model provides only a part of the story, but taken together they provide a powerful toolkit to understand, predict and improve food systems for health.

Ways of Knowing in This Book

This book tells a story, using three ways of describing what we see:

First, we use *analytical diagrams* introduced in Chapters 2 through 6 to summarize economic theory, showing how economists explain and predict outcomes in terms of points, lines and areas on a graph. Each point on an analytical diagram is a *potential* outcome, joined together in a causal framework illustrated with geometry. The goal of the analytical diagrams is to explain why people choose the observed points rather than other options, and how changes would lead to different outcomes. More complex versions of these diagrams use more advanced math such as calculus and statistics, but retain the same economics principles and draw similar conclusions.

Second, we use *data visualizations* in Chapters 7 through 12 to represent observed outcomes, showing patterns and trends over many observations. These are usually either *scatterplots* made up of individual points, *line graphs* that trace change over time or *bar charts* that compare magnitudes. A few data visualizations involve specialized ways of arranging each observation, such as a Lorenz curve that shows the degree of inequality in a population so as to calculate the resulting Gini coefficient. In each chapter, analytical diagrams and data visualizations will complement your learning about a particular concept.

Third, we use *written explanations* throughout the book to connect the dots, asking what-if questions and describing a variety of examples. We will specify when particular words are used by economists in unusual ways, such as the terms 'optimization' and 'equilibrium'. To follow the story, you can read the text in sequence from chapter to chapter, but you can also use the book more interactively, drawing the mechanisms behind current events in your own versions of our analytical diagrams, and making your own data visualizations from downloadable data of interest to you. As you proceed in economics, you will pick up a new way of thinking, and a new vocabulary. Familiar terms will gain new meanings, and you can be increasingly intentional about learning to think like an economist, conduct research and write like an economist, and potentially even become an economist if that turns out to be an attractive career path for you.

One topic omitted from this book is *causal inference*, meaning the use of observed data to infer causality about why things happened as they did, in contrast to other potential outcomes that might have occurred instead. The branch of statistics used to test economic theories is known as econometrics. We expect that some readers of this book might go on to do research of their own, using statistics and econometrics to advance the scientific literature in food economics, but the main audience for this book is students who need insights, knowledge and skills other than advanced statistics. Instead of statistical hypothesis tests, we will use charts and tables to show as much data as possible, and briefly describe what we see in the text below each set of data. Interpreting what we see using insight from economics helps us explain why people experienced what they did, and what changes might help lead to better outcomes in the future.

1.3 Understanding Charts of Economic Data

Visualizing data is an increasingly important skill, requiring practice beyond the traditional tools of writing and computation. A picture can reveal and communicate relationships that would be much harder to explain in words or statistics.

Understanding data visualization starts with what's on the axes. Each chart or figure flattens our multidimensional world onto a page or screen. For most charts of data, your first step is to know what variables are arrayed along the horizontal and vertical axes. These should be clearly labeled in the chart's title and labels for each axis, communicating what was observed and how those observations were transformed into a number and a position along an ordered list or number line. Explanations of what is meant by each symbol, line or area on the chart should be provided in the chart's legend and notes below the figure, describing each variable in terms of what was observed and their units of measure.

After you know what variables are being shown, you can compare the data, looking for patterns or changes over time that make the chart worth reading as a compact way of communicating what was observed. Colors and shapes used to differentiate regions of the world, demographic groups or time periods will provide visual clues. A skillfully made chart will attract your attention with a main message that is immediately visible and reward you with more subtle variation that may take some time to see.

One aspect of data visualization that is especially important for economics is the use of a logarithmic scale for some variables, instead of a linear scale. *Linear scales* are like the numbers on a ruler or yardstick, in which each unit of physical distance corresponds to the same change in the level of a particular variable. For example, equally spaced tick marks might be labeled 0, 1, 2, 3 and so forth. Our analytical diagrams almost always use linear scales, but data visualizations sometimes use *logarithmic scales* instead, using each unit of physical distance to show an exponential change in the level of that variable. On a logarithmic scale, equally spaced tick marks might be labeled 1, 10, 100, 1000 and so forth, raised to the tenth power showing orders of magnitude with each step.

Data visualizations in economics often use logarithmic scales because the underlying relationship is exponential. This is no accident: exponential relationships arise whenever each thing makes more of itself, for example when people use buildings and tools to make more buildings and tools, allowing production and income to grow over time. Historically, growth rates of 2–4% per year can sometimes be sustained for many decades, so that production and income doubles every 18 to 36 years. Any given exponential process must have started somewhere and cannot continue forever, so a key task for economists is to detect points of inflection when each particular rate of change accelerates or slows down. When comparing data across countries, their levels of income per person is often put along the horizontal axis using a log scale because the outcome of interest, along the vertical axis, has some kind of exponential relationship to income. Converting these scales to logarithmic terms makes it possible to see the data much more clearly.

A central idea for all sciences is the difference between correlation and causation, and the difference between purely descriptive or 'positive' analyses of what we observe versus prescriptive or 'normative' analyses of what we think should occur. In this textbook, we will use data visualization to show correlations in our descriptive work, and use analytical diagrams to show the conditions under which we can infer changes in wellbeing for normative assessments of what should be. When describing things, all human beings make judgments: we look at data and want to say why things are and how they should be different. As you read this book, we hope you will be surprised and interested by what you see, and find that knowledge useful to guide action.

CHAPTER 2

Individual Choices: Explaining Food Consumption and Production

2.1 Consumer Choices: Food Preferences and Dietary Intake

2.1.1 Motivation and Guiding Questions

People choose what to do from a limited set of options. What determines those options, and how does each person decide which of them to choose? Why do people at the same place and time often eat similar foods, while others have very different dietary patterns? And most importantly, to guide intervention, what can an outside observer infer from observed choices about a person or population's level of wellbeing, in a way that might guide intervention to improve outcomes?

In the health sciences, researchers and practitioners often answer these questions using psychology and a social-ecological approach to health behavior. Nutritionists and dietitians draw on the health sciences to explain food choice as the result of each person's individual response to their circumstances, based on the individual's biological needs, psychological needs or social condition in the context of their household, community and broader environment. Nutritional epidemiologists often refer to a person being 'exposed' to certain foods, in the same way that they might be exposed to other factors influencing their health such as viruses or air pollution.

The health behavior approach can be very helpful in clinical practice or other settings, but it is focused on providing guidance towards healthier choices. The economics approach to food choice aims to explain and predict observed food choices, whatever they may be, in a way that allows us to infer something about the population's preferences. Both health behavior and economics research start with the dignity and agency of each individual,

W. A. Masters and A. B. Finaret, *Food Economics*,
Palgrave Studies in Agricultural Economics and Food Policy,
https://doi.org/10.1007/978-3-031-53840-7_2

recognizing that every person responds to their circumstances in their own unique way. Both then observe that human biology and other factors introduce enough commonality that whole populations often behave somewhat similarly in response to different circumstances.

In economic models of consumer behavior, the underlying structure behind food choice is the idea that people have selected what we observe from a limited set of available options, in pursuit of their individual goals. In economic terms, goals are represented as preferences. These preferences are sometimes described as a population's *utility function*, meaning the usefulness of each thing in pursuit of the population's various goals and aspirations. A person's preferences describe how, in terms of Alfred Marshall's original definition of economics mentioned in Chapter 1, a person uses 'material requisites' to form their 'wellbeing'.

Some things may be consumed for their own sake, while others may be instrumental for some other purpose such as future health. The options from which a person can choose are constraints on their wellbeing. For food choice, economists illustrate those options in terms of relative prices (meaning the cost of choosing one thing instead of other things) and total income (meaning the sum of all things that a person could afford to choose). Health behavior interventions generally aim to alter preferences, while economic interventions often target prices or income.

In the graphical approach to consumer choice, each person's preferences are shown as indifference curves, where higher levels of those curves represent a more preferred outcome. The person's constraints are shown as budget lines, where higher levels of that budget line represent a larger total income or potential level of expenditure, while the slope of that budget line shows the relative price or cost of each unit along the X axis in terms of the number of units required along the Y axis. That 'rise over run' of the budget line is constant, whereas the slope of the corresponding indifference curve can vary. This section presents a unified economic framework for understanding food consumption decisions, to analyze how preferences shape food consumption when prices or incomes change and explore the evidence on what people actually eat around the world in response to differences in preferences, prices and income.

Our eating decisions are among the most frequent choices we all make. Most people eat multiple times per day, under different circumstances over time. The resulting dietary patterns are a major determinant of cardiometabolic disorders including diabetes and hypertension as well as several types of cancer. The severity of infectious diseases is also affected by dietary patterns, as poor nutritional status can limit immune response and worsen outcomes from all kinds of illness. Children are affected by their parents' diets, not only during pregnancy but throughout life, and poor dietary quality at any age can have personal, societal and intergenerational health consequences.

Every person has their own unique food preferences, with strong links to our psychological and moral or cultural wellbeing. Some food preferences depend on the biology of taste and texture, but people may also seek out food that is thought to be healthier for us and others, and contribute to other goals involving climate change and the environment, or community and social justice. Readers of this book will include people who follow many different special diets such as vegetarians or vegans that are chosen for reasons involving health, sustainability and social justice, while others will follow low-fat diets that focus on protein and carbohydrates, paleo diets that limit carbohydrates or diets that avoid specific compounds such as gluten-free and lactose-free diets. Each of those dietary practices can be represented in the economics framework as an aspect of the person's preferences guiding their day-to-day choices among all the options they might otherwise have chosen.

In this section, we will examine how to explain diets as peoples' choices from among their options, and thereby investigate why food choices might differ between individuals. Even when people face similar food prices at their local grocery outlets they will choose different items, in part due to different levels of total income, but also due to different preferences at a given level of income and prices. Explaining and predicting those choices is possible only to the extent that preferences are stable to some degree, over time for the same person and among people in the same population. Economists aim to observe a sufficient range of choices under diverse conditions for whatever set of preferences is revealed. For example, if a population consistently chooses to eat an average of 5% more avocadoes when the price of avocadoes falls by 10%, that information would be used to characterize the *revealed preferences* of that population.

All observations are subject to measurement error, and even if choices and circumstances were perfectly measured, we would expect some unexplained variation in any set of choices. But when enough high-quality data are available, populations often reveal consistent preferences that allow economists to make predictions about their average response to changes in income or prices. For example, if a population with options A and B typically choose A, and when they have options B and C they typically choose B, economists predict that they would typically prefer A over C if given that choice. Consistency in this sense has been observed in a very wide range of settings. People do sometimes behave inconsistently by choosing C over A, but that would be the part of behavior that cannot be explained by past choices using revealed preferences.

The purpose of explaining behavior in terms of revealed preferences is not just for predictions about what people will choose when they have different options, but also to permit a kind of inference from those choices about the population's level of wellbeing. In the example above, circumstances that remove option A can be inferred to have reduced the population's wellbeing, in the sense of their own revealed preference for A over B or C. The population's own preferences may not be what other people would want for them.

For example, young children might choose to drink soda every day instead of water or juice, while their parents might know that the child would later regret that. In such cases, observers can see that the child's long-term best interests are best served by having parents who restrict their beverage options. Even adults might make food choices that do not reflect their own interests, if only because consumers cannot see and are sometimes misled about the healthiness of different options.

Revealed preferences serve a population's own long-term wellbeing only to the degree that people have experienced the impact of each option on their lives and choose among their options in a way that serves their lifetime goals. Since the impact of food choices on future outcomes may be unknown or misleading, food policies often prohibit false claims and require labeling to disclose what's inside each food. Labeling and education may not be sufficient to align choices with lifelong interests, so populations may prefer to have some ingredients or types of food be banned entirely. In any case each person's observed choices reveal something about how each thing serves their wellbeing, as described in this chapter.

In the section below, we will see how any set of consistent preferences can be described as having pursued the individual's highest available level of subjective wellbeing from their own perspective. In that sense, people can be said to have chosen the best or least bad of their options, based on what they have experienced or know about the consequences of each option. In other words, people make choices that are 'optimal' for them, 'maximizing' the utility or usefulness of their available resources in pursuit of wellbeing. This terminology is one of the several cases where economics differs from everyday language. In normal life, an 'optimal' outcome is the best it could possibly be, whereas in economics it is just the best of the available options for that person. None of the options may be good, so the optimal choice we expect to observe is the least bad of each person's options. And economists expect those choices to reflect all the person's goals, whereas everyday language might focus on just one goal. For example, a most medical professionals might think of an 'optimal' diet as maximizing health, whereas an economist would use the term to mean a diet that best achieves all the person's goals including health but also convenience and other aspirations.

By the end of this section, you will be able to:

1. Describe the economic determinants of food consumption choices;
2. Sketch indifference curves and budget lines to explain choices as points on a diagram;
3. Use the analytical diagrams to explain and predict change in food choices in response to change in prices, incomes and preferences; and
4. Describe strengths and limitations of the economics approach to explaining food choice.

2.1.2 Analytical Tools

The toolkit of economics is a set of mathematical models that we can build using lines and curves on a two-dimensional diagram. Each line or curve shows a relationship between two things, drawn with a shape and position that represents an equation between the two variables shown in the graph, holding constant all other variables.

A Model of Consumer Choices

The shape and position of each line or curve represents a set of facts about the world. For example, we will start with diagrams about an individual person's food choices in which preferences are shown with curves that always slope down and are bowed in, like the bottom-left corner of a circle O, or the bottom half of an opening parenthesis. The set of all such curves parallel to each other forms a nest like (((. We then draw the options among which they choose using a downward sloping straight line, whose position represents the person's income, and the slope represents the price they pay to consume one more unit of the variable shown on the horizontal axis. When different people shop at the same grocery store and face the same prices, their incomes are shown as parallel lines like \\\. The points where a curve just touches a line is a possible choice, and we use that system of simultaneous equations to explain observed choices, and predict the outcome of changing incomes, prices and preferences.

Notation and Specification of Variables on Each Axis

In this section we start our formal analysis by defining *goods* as anything for which more is better and less is worse. Most foods are goods in that sense, meaning that each additional unit adds something to the consumer's wellbeing. As we will see, increasing quantities are eventually subject to diminishing returns, and too much of a good thing can be bad, but the quantities consumed that we observe in practice are usually within a range over which additional (or 'marginal') units are desired in some way. Our analytical diagrams refer to the use of goods not because more is always better, but because people incur costs to obtain things, and those costs imply that people usually stop buying something when additional units are no longer desirable. Exceptions to that rule, when some people consume too much of a good thing, turn out to be an important aspect of food choice. That is one of many reasons why it is helpful to have a specialized textbook in food economics.

In this textbook, we begin building the toolkit of economics by representing individual behavior using the kind of diagram shown in this section. And in diagrams throughout this textbook, a solid black dot near the center represents the observed combination of things actually observed, while variables such as Q_X servings of product X are charted along the horizontal axis, and Q_a quantity of another things are charted along the vertical axis. Our goal is to explain why that quantity was chosen, predict what other choices might have been observed under other circumstances or a policy change, and evaluate whether such a change would improve or worsen this person's subjective well-being given their individual needs. Each food choice is made from a limited set of options shown by an area, line or curve, and changes in circumstances or policies shown by shifts in a line or curve lead to movements along another line or curve to a new food choice or other outcome.

The diagrams in this section of the book refer to quantities consumed by an individual person and have the observed quantities near its center because that gives us plenty of space along the axes with which to consider what other options might have been observed, under other circumstances. To show these comparisons visually must flatten the world into just two dimensions, so analysis using these diagrams begins by defining what is shown on each axis. For example, food economists and nutritionists are often interested in the total quantity of vegetables consumed along the horizontal axis, in contrast to other things along the vertical axis.

Indifference Curves for Consumption of Each Good

Analysis of food choice begins with the concept of an *indifference curve*, aiming to explain and predict consumption of something whose quantity is shown along the horizontal axis. Quantities of a food such as vegetables might be measured in servings (one tomato, two carrots or half an onion might all be considered one serving of a vegetable) or units of weight (such as ounces or grams) or volume (cups or liters). Nutritionists in the U.S. often measure fruits and vegetables in cup-equivalents, a hybrid unit that aims to capture just the solid dry matter in each food, while any kind of food can also be measured in terms of total dietary energy (in calories or joules) or grams of each macronutrient (carbohydrates, protein and fats). Quantities of something else along the vertical axis could refer to a particular thing, such as the quantity of fruit, and could be counted using the same units of measure as vegetables along the X axis.

For the diagrams in this section of the book, it is helpful for the vertical Y axis to add up the quantity of *all other goods and services* that a person might consume. The reason for this will be clear later when we consider how much of what's on the X axis a person can afford to obtain, which will be shown using the person's total income and the price of what's on the X axis relative to the prices of all other things. Adding the quantities of disparate things such as groceries and school supplies, restaurant meals and concert tickets cannot be done with physical units like cups or kilograms, but it can be done in terms of their monetary value. For that reason, one can think of all other things along the vertical axis as a stack of money, where more represents a larger quantity of all other things that could be obtained as shown in Fig. 2.1.

The purpose of Fig. 2.1 is to show all options that a person might find as desirable as the observed point labeled **O**, where they consume Q_X and Q_a. This observation might have come from a household consumption survey or dietary recall, in which the person reported having that many servings of

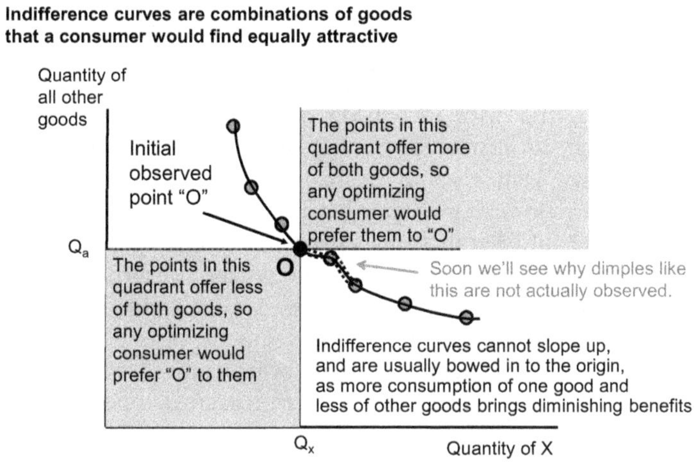

Fig. 2.1 Definition of the indifference curve

vegetables and that amount of total spending on all other things. To explain why the person chose this instead of some other possible combination of things, we must draw all possible alternatives to the observed point that could have been chosen instead.

Figure 2.1 shows how economists draw the foundations of food choice, using a curve to illustrate general principles about each person's needs and wants. The diagram shows all possible quantities that would provide this person with the same level of subjective wellbeing, using different combinations of Q_x (e.g., servings of vegetables) and Q_a (spending on other things). Each set of equally attractive options is called an *indifference curve* (IC), because the person whose preferences are shown in this diagram would be indifferent between all the points along that curve. The curve's specific location and shape will differ, but all indifference curves used in economics have two fundamental attributes:

First, indifference curves *always slope down* from left to right, to show that person would generally require additional quantities of the X good to compensate for less of all other things, if they are to maintain the same level of subjective wellbeing. This holds true as long as X is a good for which more is better. At extreme levels of X or Y, the curve might conceivably slope up, but we would not observe consumption choices in that region if X and Y are costly to obtain. Indifference curves that draw observed preferences will not slope up, but food economists understand that people may not choose quantities that are in their own long-run interests. Later we will compare the indifference curves that are revealed by a person's present choices with the preferences of their future self who might regret what was chosen. We will also discuss the consequences of being exposed to things that people themselves have not chosen, such as air pollution or contaminants in food, but the diagrams are designed to illustrate quantities of things that people have chosen to obtain.

Second, indifference curves typically slope down *with a decreasing slope*. The line becomes flatter with increasing quantities of what's on the X axis, reflecting how each additional unit of X is less valuable for this person's subjective wellbeing. That kind of decreasing returns in consumption gives indifference curves a bowed-in shape that mathematicians would call convex. As shown in Fig. 2.1, indifference curves may have regions that are not bowed in. The curve may have a bowed-out dimple where consuming a small quantity drives desire for more, so people are observed to consume either small or zero quantities to the left of the bowed-out segment, or large quantities to the right of the bowed-out segment. That idea was captured by a famous advertisement for potato chips, saying people 'can't eat just one', because eating one is likely to lead to eating more until some limit is reached.

Another example is how learning to cook at home builds skill that offers increasing returns up to a point, as practicing a few times makes future meals even better. At some quantity any person's subjective wellbeing from each additional unit will decline, resulting in a flatter indifference curve as quantities increase. Once people have experimented, their usual diets are such that additional quantities would yield diminishing returns, leading to a bowed-in shape for the indifference curves we draw around each point actually observed or predicted.

The downward sloping, bowed-in shape of each indifference curves follows from the fact that, around each observed point, the shaded region above and to the right of the observed point would have more of both things, so would have already been chosen if that had been possible, while the shaded region below and to the left of the observed point would have less of both things, so would not have been chosen instead of the observed point. Redrawing such quadrants around any potentially observed point reveals why the whole curve must slope down, as people's trial-and-error experiences with each food lead to the preferences we observe.

Having drawn one indifference curve through the observed point, we can see how other outcomes would provide different levels of wellbeing, as illustrated in Fig. 2.2.

Figure 2.2 has many indifference curves, each one representing different combinations of Q_x and Q_a that a person would find equally desirable. Higher levels of wellbeing are shown by points along a higher indifference curve, on which there might be more of everything that this person desires. Figure 2.2 shows how each level of wellbeing is illustrated by a curve that never crosses a lower or higher indifference level, unless the person has changed their mind to a different set of preferences as shown by the dashed curve. Along the solid curve all circles are equally attractive, but if this person's preferences change they might decide that the hollow triangle is as good as the solid dot, instead of the hollow circles which were their previous preferences.

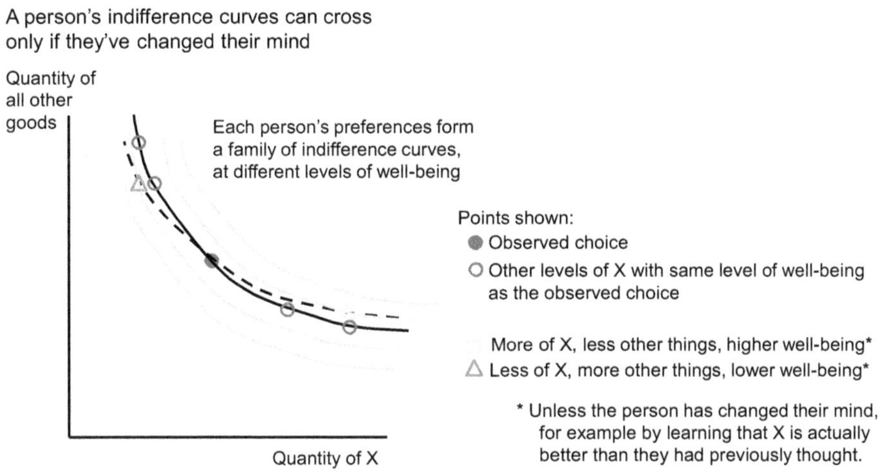

Fig. 2.2 Each person has many possible indifference curves

The purpose of economic models like Fig. 2.2 is to capture the predictable aspects of behavior. Having a stable set of preferences requires that a person's indifference curves not cross each other, so that each successive level of wellbeing is unambiguously higher or lower. If indifference curves were to cross, the person's preferences would lead to seemingly random switching for example from a circle to the triangle. In reality we observe some random behavior, for example when a person wants unexpected variety, but then we would draw quantities along the X axis as the fraction of time they want that thing.

A person's set of indifference curves can be imagined as topographic lines showing altitude on a map, or the lines of constant temperature on a weather map. The curvature of each line is important because it shows how rapidly the person's level of wellbeing changes as they increase consumption of each product. A gently curved indifference level implies that about the same quantity of all other things could substitute for the item of interest along the X axis, while a sharply curved indifference level leads to a narrower range of observed consumption. In extreme cases a person might have an L-shaped indifference level, implying that a fixed quantity of what's on the X axis is needed for each level of wellbeing, and any deviation from that leads to a different level of wellbeing. The meaning and use of indifference curves become intuitive as you practice sketching them, for example conducting imaginary thought experiments about your own food preferences.

Having established that a person's needs and preferences can be drawn as successively higher indifference curves, what level of wellbeing can a person reach? To answer, we need a different kind of line that shows the options from which they choose. Such a line illustrates all the possibilities that this person could afford, based on the money and time or other resources available to

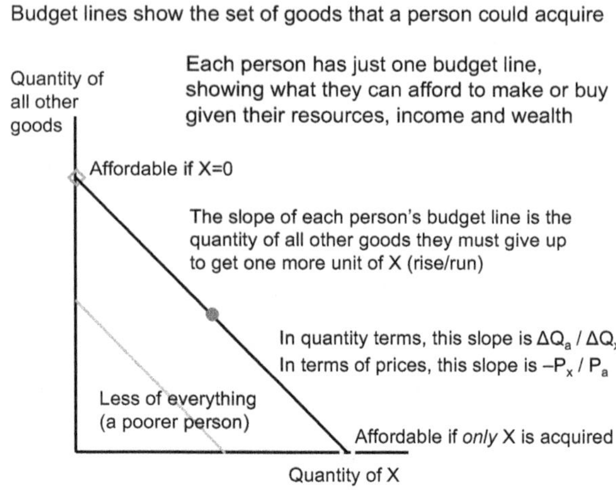

Fig. 2.3 Definition of the budget line

them. The set of all options that a person could afford is known as a budget line, showing their possible total expenditure as drawn in Fig. 2.3.

The budget lines shown in Fig. 2.3 are drawn on the same axes used for indifference curves, but now the lines show all options that are equally affordable whereas indifference curves show the combinations that would be equally desirable. The difference is that budget lines have a constant slope. The slope of any line or curve is its rise over run, in this case denoted $\Delta Q_a/\Delta Q_X$ where Δ (delta) means difference from one point to the next, or change in Q_a for each unit of change in Q_X. In other words, the slope of a budget line is the quantity of all other things that must be given up to obtain one more unit of the thing along the X axis. If we imagine the quantity of all other things to be represented by a stack of money, then that slope is simply the price of X. We can also use 'price' metaphorically to mean everything that must be given up to obtain the thing of interest. Or, if the things on each Y axis also had their own price, we would need to divide the price of X by the price of Y to obtain the *relative price* of X. For that reason, the budget line's slope is generally written as $\frac{-P_x}{P_a}$. A negative sign appears before price because that is the amount of other things that must be given up to get a larger quantity of X, and a steeper budget line implies a higher cost of X. The slope of each budget line represents prices paid, while the level of each line represents the person's total income or expenditure. A budget line that is closer to zero shows how that person has fewer options, due to lower income so they can afford less of each thing. The vertical intercept of each budget line shows the person's income before buying any of the item along the X axis, and the budget line's horizontal intercept shows the quantity of X they could buy if they spent all of their resources on that item.

Fig. 2.4 What we observe is each person's preferred choice from the options they can afford

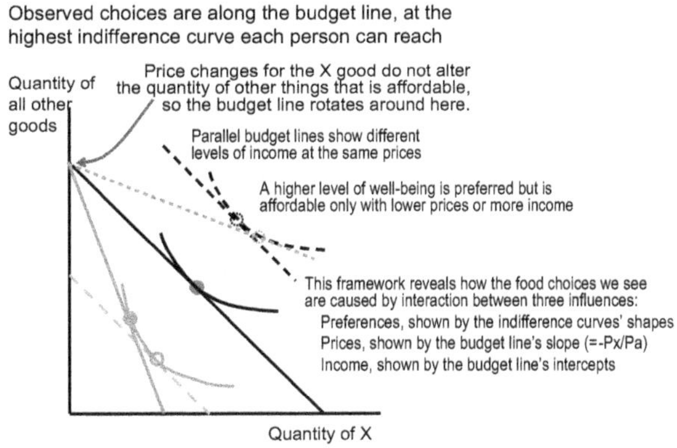

Having defined how budget lines show the options that are available and affordable for each person, and indifference curves show that person's preferences, we can now put together a complete model to explain what we observe and predict how changes in each causal factor would alter food choice. In the causal framework used by economists, each potential observation results from the individual having experienced different options and chosen what they prefer from their set of affordable options as shown in Fig. 2.4.

Figure 2.4 shows four possible points that differ from the observed solid dot in the middle, revealing how a higher level of wellbeing along the dashed indifference curve could have been reached with a lower price of X or a higher level of income, and similarly a higher price of X or a lower income could lead to lower wellbeing as shown by the lower indifference curve.

The general principle underlying each point we might observe is that the person's choices are based on their own experiences and knowledge of how each option might affect their wellbeing. Economists might say that the person has already optimized, choosing the best (or least bad) of their options, based on their own preferences. This way of explaining behavior is based on recognizing the limited agency of each individual, as they respond to the socioecological conditions around them. A change in the price paid for each X good, shown in Fig. 2.4 as rotation of the budget line around its Y intercept, would be the result of community factors such as the food environment, while a change in the person's level of income is generally a household characteristic.

In Fig. 2.4 the slope and curvature of the indifference curves have stayed the same for all four alternatives to the observed point, illustrating a situation in which the person's preferences have not changed. Later we will see how advertising, behavior-change programs and other interventions might alter preferences. Before that, it is important to note that most foods are not actually consumed at all, and when affordability or preferences change people switch from zero to significant quantities as part of an overall dietary pattern. That aspect of food choice and preferences is illustrated using Fig. 2.5.

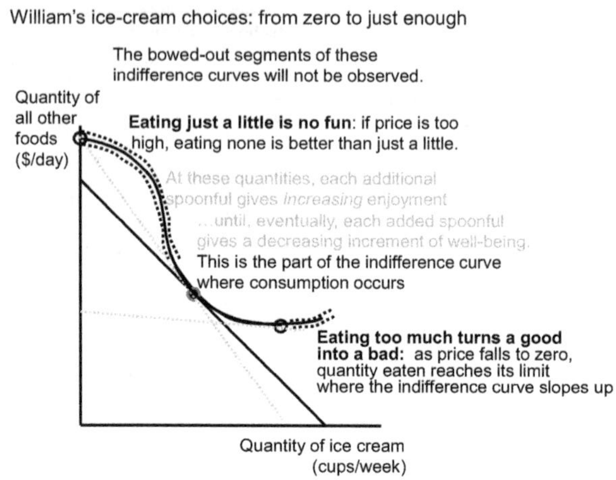

Fig. 2.5 What we observe is along a bowed-in portion of each indifference curve

Figure 2.5 has a large bowed-out segment on the left, whereas our initial indifference curve in Fig. 2.1 had a small dimple in the middle of the diagram. Both are possible. Having seen that people choose along their budget lines the combination that gives them the highest level of indifference, we can appreciate why bowed-out segments are not observed, and people often jump from zero or lower to higher quantities along a bowed-in segment of their indifference curve. The reason is that observers see only the outcome of each person's choices. By the time consumption is measured, the person has already experienced or imagined different options and chosen the best of what they can afford.

The example in Fig. 2.5 relates to William's high school job scooping ice cream. Now, as an adult, if ice cream were very expensive he would probably not eat any at all, because eating just a little makes the next bite all the more satisfying as shown by the steeper slope of the indifference curve when moving from zero to the right. William's experience with ice cream includes a time when it was basically free, so the price line was very flat but there was still a limit on how much he consumed. In other words, William's consumption of ice cream is always observed along the bowed-in and downward sloping of his indifference curves, precisely because he has experience with other quantities that led to the choices he now makes.

So far we have discussed consumption choices for an individual person. To clarify the story, it is helpful to imagine using one diagram to explain the different choices of multiple shoppers in the same supermarket as shown in Fig. 2.6.

The diagram in Fig. 2.6 shows the choices of nine different people, all of whom face the same market prices shown by the slope of their budget lines. Each of the shoppers has their unique level of wellbeing shown by their own indifference curve. The quantity of X that we observe shoppers having purchased is interpreted as having been chosen by them because it was the

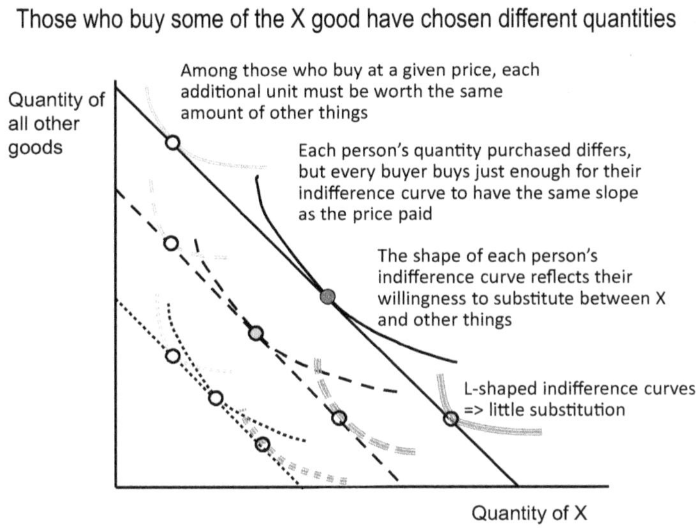

Fig. 2.6 People differ in their preferences and incomes, but face similar prices

best (or least bad) of their options on that day. For that reason, each indifference curve touches the person's budget line just once, because it shows the highest level of wellbeing they can reach. For simplicity we show only three levels of income, so all other variations are due to preferences. On the left of the diagram we see higher incomes corresponding to more purchase of other things, but no change in consumption of X, and in the middle we see higher income corresponding to more purchase of both things. All these outcomes are possible, with the economics framework allowing us to distinguish between income and preferences as a cause of the variation we observe.

An important observation from Fig. 2.6 is that each person has a different indifference curve, but at the observed quantities purchased all of those curves have the same slope. The reason is that people have moved along their budget line to their highest available indifference level, which is known in mathematical terms as a point of tangency between the person's budget line and their highest attainable indifference curve. As with any line or curve, the indifference level's slope is always its rise over run, which in this case would be written mathematically as $\Delta Q_a/\Delta Q_X$. At the highest attainable level of indifference, that slope is exactly equal to the relative price of X. If the indifference curve were steeper or flatter than the product's market price, the person would go back and adjust their purchase to where each additional unit purchased has a *marginal rate of substitution* with other things along the indifference curve that is just equal to the price paid.

Now that we have a model of consumer behavior in the form of indifference curves and budget lines, we can use this model to understand how a population's consumption behavior might adjust to change in prices, incomes or

Fig. 2.7 A price increase for the X good has both substitution and income effects

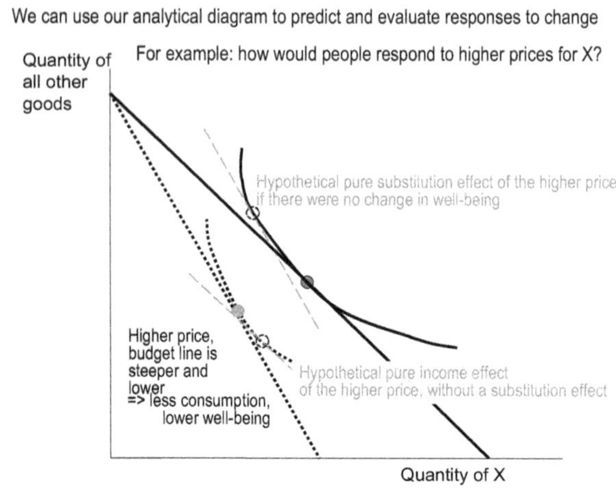

preferences. In these thought experiments we will change only one thing at a time, and then combine multiple changes in more realistic scenarios. To illustrate this we show a change in prices from the solid to the dotted or dashed lines in Fig. 2.7.

Figure 2.7 shows how, when the price of food goes up, the budget line rotates inwards along the horizontal axis, towards the origin, because less of X can be purchased at the same level of income. The Y intercept stays the same, since the price of all other goods has not changed and therefore, if none of X were being consumed, the amount of other things that could be consumed is unchanged. How do we know in which direction to rotate the budget line? Remember that the slope of the budget line is the price of X, so when that increases the budget line gets steeper and the consumer can no longer reach their original level of wellbeing. They are reduced to a lower budget line, along which their best (or least bad) option is at a new point of tangency, between the new (dotted) indifference curve and the new (dotted) budget line. Remember that the lower-level indifference curve is part of the same preference mapping as the original indifference curve, so the two curves cannot cross.

The change in consumption due to a lower price is just one change but it can be understood as having two components. A first change is a reduction in the consumer's purchasing power. When prices rise, consumers cannot purchase as much as before if income stays the same. This is the *income effect* of a price change. It represents a reduction in what the person can afford. The second change is due to the new price ratio between goods. Even if the consumer were offered compensation for their loss of real income to the same level of wellbeing, they would still move along their indifferent curve because the relative price of X has changed. This is the *substitution effect* of the price change, as people adjust away from good that has become relatively more expensive.

Later in this book we will see how the framework used in these diagrams can be applied to explain, predict and evaluate the outcomes of many different changes in circumstances, including a wide range of government policies. You may want to start sketching different diagrams yourself now, to see how the logic works in various scenarios.

2.1.3 Conclusion

Nutritionists focus on measuring what people eat and how it affects their health, while economists focus on explaining and predicting changes or differences in dietary patterns. Actual events are an infinitely complicated mix of interacting forces, which economists represent as elements of each analytical diagram that distinguish between prices, incomes and preferences. In each community, the prices of available foods are likely to be similar for everyone, while incomes will differ between households and preferences will differ between individuals. In economics, we disentangle complex changes by examining one factor at a time, in a system of simultaneous equations through which everything is interconnected. So far we have seen only the drivers of food choice. In the next section we look at food production and distribution, to address actions of farmers and food sellers, before we turn to societal outcomes and government policies.

2.2 Producer Choices: Agriculture and Food Manufacturing

2.2.1 Motivation and Guiding Questions

So far, we have seen how economists explain food consumption choices. What determines food production, and how does food production interact with consumption?

In this section we analyze farming and production decisions using the same type of diagram as the previous section's analysis of food choice and consumption, building up towards a unified approach to the economics of agriculture and food systems. In this view, economists explain production choices as the best (or least bad) choice from the available options for each individual producer. We observe a bewildering variety of choices around the world, and we interpret each one as the point where a line meets a curve, at the person's highest attainable level of wellbeing. As with consumption, this framework helps explain why people do similar things when in similar circumstances, while allowing us to predict and evaluate producers' response to changes in underlying conditions and government policies.

Economists explain production with the same underlying principles as consumption, based on the observation that people have unique experiences with their own situation over time. This insight is especially important when trying to understand farmers' choices, as they are often members of multigenerational families who have farmed their lands together for decades. Farmers typically have more information about their situation, options and the consequences of each choice than any outside observer. Economists take that information into account by interpreting the actions we observe as having been chosen from among the person's limited options as the best way for them to achieve their objectives, given the difficult, often dangerous, weather-dependent and risky circumstances under which food is produced.

This textbook aims to cover all interlinked aspects of the food system, from agriculture to health. Interest in the work of farmers and food producers goes beyond their role in meeting nutrient needs. Farming is by far the most common occupation for low-income people in Africa, Asia and Latin America, and food production jobs play a similar role for many low-income people in the U.S. and other countries. These livelihoods are universally important as entry-level jobs for younger workers, as well as recent immigrants and other people who lack the formal qualifications and connections needed for employment in higher wage sectors. Farming and food production also has an outsized impact on the natural world, high vulnerability to extreme weather and climate change, and important cultural resonance as the main work for almost everyone's ancestors.

One important aspect of food systems is that farmers often consume at least some of what they produce, linking production and consumption even more directly than would be the case for other people. Another key factor is that over 90% of farms worldwide are family enterprises, owned and operated by close relatives, with almost no outside investors or salaried employees. Family farms may borrow money and rent some of the land they farm, and may hire seasonal or part-time workers, but management decisions are typically made by trusted family members. This ensures that farm sizes are typically limited by the area of land that one family can manage, whether the land is owned or rented. Only a few types of agricultural operations such as greenhouses and wineries or sugar or tea plantations attract investors and salaried managers, typically in situations where operations require less of the place-specific, weather-dependent day-to-day decision-making done by independent family farmers who live where they work.

The persistence of family farming is among the most surprising facts about the economics of food. In the U.S. and elsewhere most farms do not sell directly to consumers but operate behind the scenes, selling their produce in bulk to specialists for transport and distribution, often for use as ingredients in packaged and processed foods. Unlike farms, the food companies with whom consumers usually interact are typically owned by investors and run by hired managers. They buy ingredients from various sources, often combining produce from many different farms. Consumers everywhere in the world often seek out opportunities to buy directly from individual farmers, but that is special in part because it is relatively rare.

The reason why most farms are family owned and use mostly family labor is not because consumers prefer to buy from family farms, but because family farming is a more efficient and lower-cost way of producing most agricultural products. One underlying reason is that field crop operations require quick decisions based on location-specific information each day throughout the season. A farmer's skill and effort in planting, weed or pest control and harvesting is visible to them but very difficult for a supervisor to observe, because outcomes are heavily influenced by many intervening factors. Only someone very close to the action can distinguish skill from luck, so self-motivated family members consistently outperform hired workers.

The fact that most farms are family operations does not mean they are small in terms of land area or quantity produced. In high-income settings, farms remain in operation only if they can cover their costs and justify the management effort they require, so family operators may cultivate thousands of acres using equipment that costs several million dollars. Whether a family farm is small or large, its efficiency typically relies on workers being highly self-motivated, making efforts and making decisions based on information they observe in the fields every day. The exceptions to this rule provide important insight into the problem, as nonfamily operations tend to dominate where production is concentrated spatially and easier to supervise, such as livestock operations or sugarcane, cut flowers, and some kinds of fruit or vegetable production.

In this chapter, we will develop and use analytical diagrams to explain and predict changes in food production, to understand how production can be made more resilient, sustainable and inclusive while also meeting consumer needs for safe and nutrient dense foods in sufficient quantities for a supportive, high-quality diet. Just as our analytical diagrams for consumption began with indifference curves that are bowed in to show diminishing returns to each additional unit consumed, our diagrams in this chapter begin with production possibility frontiers that are bowed out to show diminishing returns from each additional unit produced. Those diminishing returns interacting with the relative price or value of each thing lead people to choose the quantities we observe.

You experience diminishing returns in production activities within your own life too. Think about the number of hours you might study for an exam in food economics. The first hour that you study might be hugely productive in terms of your grasp of the material. The second hour that you study would still be very productive, but not quite as productive as the first, and so on. Once you understand the concept of diminishing returns, you will start to see it everywhere.

In this chapter, you will learn how to understand farmer decisions through three difference glances into their marginal decision-making: the choice between two outputs (the *production possibilities frontier*, or *PPF*), the choice of input and output level (the *input response curve*, or *IRC*), and the choice between two inputs (the *isoquant*, or *input substitution curve*). The effects of price changes and farmer choices between these dimensions will allow us to derive supply curves and elasticity.

By the end of this section, you will be able to:

1. Describe the economic determinants of food production choices;
2. Sketch production possibilities frontiers and revenue lines, input response curves and profit lines, and isoquants and cost lines, to explain choices as points on a diagram;
3. Use the analytical diagrams to explain and predict change in agricultural production in response to change in prices, available technologies and the natural environment; and
4. Describe differences and similarities between farming and other activities in the economy.

2.2.2 Analytical Tools

The diagrams used by economists to explain production are similar to the diagrams for consumption, but in reverse. Previously we explained food choice as the point along their budget line that reaches the highest attainable indifference curve, while this section explains production as the point along a curve that reaches the highest attainable revenue or profit line. In each case, the line's slope is fixed by relative prices, explaining movements along each curve to reach a point of tangency where the curve's varying slope just equals the fixed slope of each price line. As we will quickly see, actually sketching these diagrams provides visual insights that are much clearer than any explanation in words, and are generally applicable to a wide range of specific examples.

The Production Possibilities Frontier (PPF)
In a mirror image of logic to consumer decision-making, we begin with producer choices between the quantities of two outputs: the quantity of X on the horizontal axis and the quantity of all other goods on the vertical axis. Each point on this two-dimensional diagram represents one possible choice we might observe, along a curve that shows the frontier of other production possibilities as shown in Fig. 2.8.

In Fig. 2.1 we identify the amount produced using the letter Q for a variable quantity along each axis, with a subscript to say which quantity we are talking about. In this case, along the vertical axis we show the quantity of all other goods labeled Q_a, and along the horizontal axis we show the specific product of interest that could be anything so its quantity is labeled Q_x. The combination of Q_a and Q_x we observe is the point labeled **O**, along a curve that maps out the production possibilities frontier (PPF) of all points that would be equally feasible for our farmer to grow, based on the natural conditions and technology available to her. As before, we derive this curve from the observation that farmers will do the best they can with what they have, and sketch the result in two dimensions at a given level of all other variables. With this producer's same amount of labor and other resources, the other points

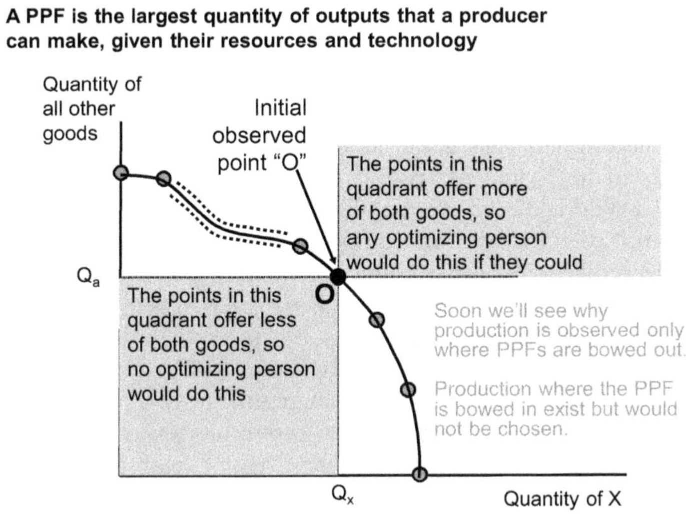

Fig. 2.8 Definition of the production possibilities frontier (PPF)

she might have chosen could not be in the top-right shaded quadrant because those would have been better and therefore chosen instead of the observed point if that were feasible for this producer, and cannot be in the lower-left shaded quadrant for the opposite reason that they produce less output and are less desirable than the observed point.

As implied by its name, the PPF is the frontier of feasible production, but unlike everyday use of the term 'frontier', economists expect all observed production to be along that curve. In other words, the frontier is defined as the feasible region for ordinary producers, who are expected to have learned from experience to do the best they can with what they have. Like an indifference curve, the PPF must be downward sloping, but in this case the curve's slope captures the incremental cost of making each additional or marginal unit of the product shown on the X axis, in terms of all other things the producer might have made with the same resources, under a given set of circumstances dictated by nature and the technologies available to this producer. As the quantity of X that she produces is increased from zero to the observed level, resources such as land and labor must have been reallocated from making other things into production of X. At some point there could be increasing returns, shown as a bowed-in portion of the PPF, where and when allocating more resources to production of X makes each additional unit more productive, but the actual observed point will be at a point along the PPF where the producer experiences diminishing returns along a bowed-out segment of the curve.

For example, in William's childhood his family kept a few chickens in a backyard shed. Going from zero to just three or four open-air scavenging chickens was very easy and took almost nothing away from other family activities such as gardening. That would yield one or two eggs each day, and feeding them grain might yield up to three eggs per day, but additional work yielded diminishing returns in terms of fewer additional eggs until the family put enough effort into properly housing, protecting and also feeding a whole flock of at least a dozen chickens. Once the shed was fenced and care practices learned, the additional work came at relatively little cost in terms of other activities and led to a yield of around ten eggs per day. Beyond that, additional efforts would again encounter diminishing returns, shown as a steeper PPF along which each incremental egg produced comes at an increasing cost in terms of other activities. As the household varied its daily egg production from zero to twenty or more, the family's PPF for eggs versus all other activities would have had some bowed-in segments, but the actual observed quantity of eggs produced was usually at a point where the PPF's curvature was bowed out or concave in shape as shown in the diagram.

Like indifference curves, the PPF is an economist's way of explaining and predicting human behavior. Producers may have explored some alternative uses of their own land and labor, but they will also have learned from neighbors and others about how best to use the resources available to them. Much of the learning process is unconscious, as people shift resources from other activities into production of X they would naturally move to the frontier of possibilities and shift along their PPF to a point of diminishing returns. In William's childhood his family kept a vegetable garden as well as the backyard chickens, and after a few years his parents had learned about the right placement and timing of operations for each type of plant. The household's PPF for vegetables, like the family PPF for eggs, had some increasing returns that made it worthwhile to take the garden seriously, with features like fencing against deer and rabbits, raised beds and a trellis for climbing beans, but also diminishing returns that limited the garden's total size to what the family could manage. Producing along the family's PPF did not require unusual skills or resources, just the typical degree of learning achieved by an average vegetable producer at that place and time. Each PPF describes the production possibilities available to a specific individual producer, but the curve's shape would be similar for other people who have the same resources and technologies available to them.

As with observed consumption along each indifference curve, explaining the producer's choice along their PPF calls for additional information about the price or value of X relative to other things. From the previous chapter we saw that a consumer's options were described by a budget line, along which she chooses the point of consumption that gives the highest attainable level of wellbeing, illustrated as the highest of many parallel indifference curves. For production, the person's options are drawn as a PPF, along which she chooses the point of production that gives the highest attainable level of income or revenue as shown in Fig. 2.9.

The straight, negatively sloped line in Fig. 2.9 is the *revenue line* of total income, showing the set of goods that a producer could obtain by exchanging X for other things in trade with other people. Starting at the observed point

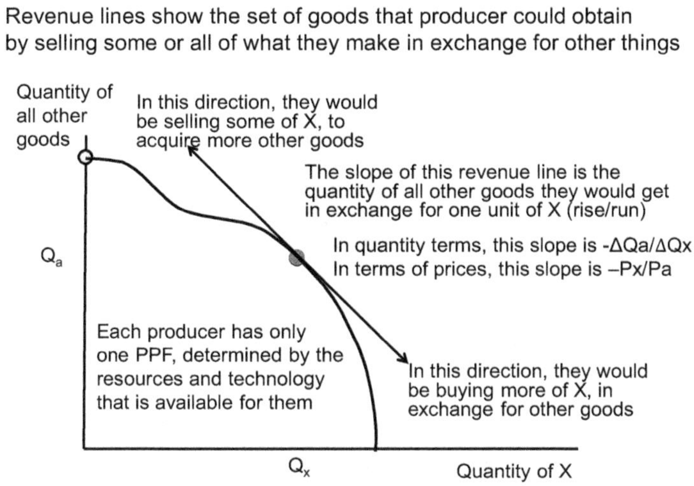

Fig. 2.9 Definition of the revenue line

of production (Q_x, Q_a), the producer might acquire more of other goods by selling some X and moving along the arrow up and to the left, or they might acquire more X than they produced by selling other things along the arrow down and to the right.

The producer's revenue line is also their income for use in consumption. The slope of that line is the rise in quantity of all other goods per unit of X that is traded with other people. If no trade with other people were possible, the producer's revenue and income would be their PPF curve itself, but when transport and storage make it possible to exchange with other people, consumption can occur along a straight line whose slope is the quantity of all other things traded for one unit of X. That slope, defined as rise/run or $-\Delta Q_a/\Delta Q_x$, is the price of X relative to all other things or $-P_x/P_a$. As with consumption, observed production is at a point of tangency along the curve where its slope just equals the price of X. The PPF's slope is the producer's *marginal rate of transformation* of all other things into production of X, while the revenue line's slope is the price of X available in trade with other people.

The PPF diagram for production, like other analytical diagrams, illustrates the fundamental principle that people have learned from experience, so when we observe their choices they have done the best they can, given what they have. This principle leads to the result that observed production is at a point of diminishing returns, where the producer's marginal rate of transformation from other things is just equal to the relative price they receive, as shown in Fig. 2.10.

Figure 2.10 shows the producer's PPF again as the curved black line, along which various possible levels of X might be produced. Straight lines whose slope is the relative price of X show levels of revenue that the producer could

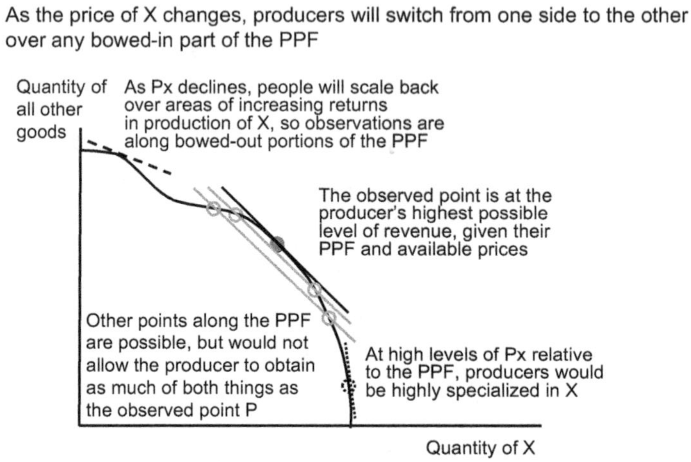

Fig. 2.10 Production we observe is each producer's choice from the options they have

obtain from each point of production. The hollow dots show various possibilities that might be observed, with the observed point being at the highest level of revenue or income that the producer's PPF would allow. As illustrated by the dashed line, at a lower price of X the producer might cut back to a lower quantity produced, potentially bypassing the bowed-in section of the PPF. Similarly at higher prices illustrated by the dotted line, the producer might increase production of X despite diminishing returns.

Over time, innovations may offer new technologies with increasing returns to additional production. The simplest kind of increasing returns comes from use of an indivisible thing like an entire machine or production method. If the relative price of X makes using or doing that thing worthwhile, producers can be expected to switch resources out of other things and use the new method up to the point where its marginal rate of transformation of other things into X is again just equal to the relative value of X compared to other things. That process is illustrated on the right side of Fig. 2.11.

Figure 2.11 shows a situation with two kinds of change in the PPF, both illustrated with no change in prices. To the right of the previously observed point, an innovation might allow farmers to adopt new equipment or other technology that offers increasing returns to greater specialization in producing more X and less of other things. To the left of the previously observed point, we show the effects of environmental degradation or climate change that reduces the production potential of this producer's resources. Both kinds of shift in producers' PPF curves occur from year to year, with growth or declines in output even when there is no change in prices. When prices change, as seen later in this book, producers would move along their PPF curves. In so doing, economists explain and predict observed points as the result of

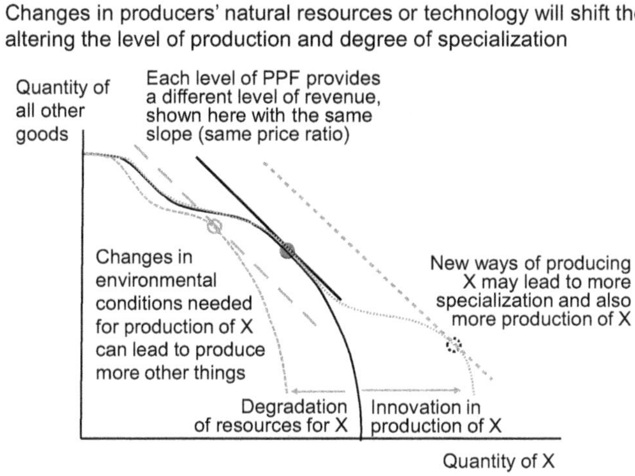

Fig. 2.11 Each producer has one PPF that shifts over time

producers having learned from experience, but any actual set of observations includes measurement error and noise or temporary adjustments to unanticipated events. It is only the average shape and location of PPFs and revenue lines that can be used for explanation and prediction with these analytical diagrams.

Each analytical diagram flattens our complex world into just two dimensions, at given levels of all other variables. The indifference curve and PPF diagrams can be drawn with the same axes as consumption decisions, with an output of interest along the horizontal axis. To complete the story, we can look at production decisions with the quantity of an input along the X axis. Economic analysis of how inputs are used in production looks somewhat similar to choices about how products are used for consumption, but there is an important difference: consumers use their income to achieve the highest attainable level of subjective wellbeing based on their own personal preferences, whereas producers use inputs to make outputs that can potentially be exchanged with other people. The options from which consumers choose are dictated by income and prices, and are shown by a budget line along which they move to reach their highest possible indifference curve. In contrast for producers, the options from which they choose are dictated by nature and technology, drawn as curves along which producers move to reach their highest level of earnings. The PPF curve explains a producer's choices between two outputs, while the curves introduced below show their choices about use of inputs.

The Input Response Curve (IRC)

Explaining a producer's use of inputs begins with the *input response curve* (IRC), showing the frontier of an output that can be produced at each level of an input. Farmers use inputs such as labor and equipment, land and fertilizer whose quantity can be shown along the horizontal axis, to produce an output whose quantity can be shown along the vertical axis as shown in Fig. 2.12.

Just like the PPF, an IRC is a frontier of technical efficiency, showing the highest possible level of output along the vertical axis that would be attainable at each point along the horizontal axis, at the same level of all other factors that might influence production such as weather and available resources. These frontiers are dictated by nature and technology available to the producer. If they have learned from experience, they would always be along these frontiers, because any higher point would be infeasible and any lower point would be undesirable.

A key fact about production that can be captured in both a PPF and an IRC is the possibility of increasing returns, highlighted in Fig. 2.12 using a dotted border around the curve. In the range of increasing returns, the IRC's slope is rising as additional inputs are applied. For example, going from zero to ten hours of labor on a strawberry field might yield zero fruit, because that is just enough time for planting and not enough time for harvesting. Reaching twenty hours might allow both planting and harvesting of some fruit, but adding another ten or more hours for weeding and pest control would make the planting and harvesting even more productive. To the extent that farmers have learned from experience they will prioritize the most important steps first, encountering diminishing returns as they add hours beyond the steepest region of the IRC.

As with the PPF, an IRC shows the producer's constraints set by nature and technology, offering a limited set of options from which to choose. Again, we expect producers to move along that curve to their preferred point, based

Fig. 2.12 Definition of the input response curve (IRC)

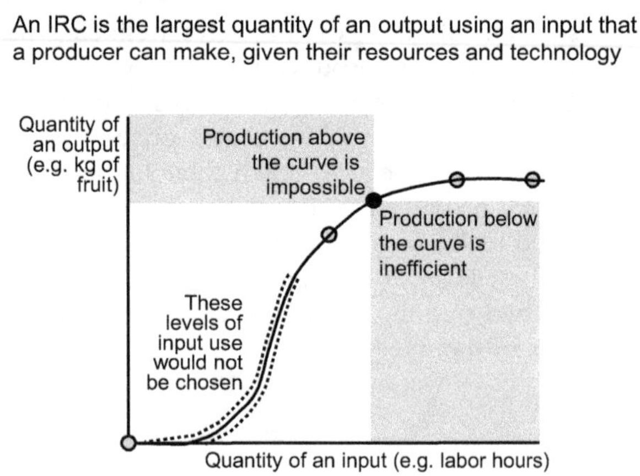

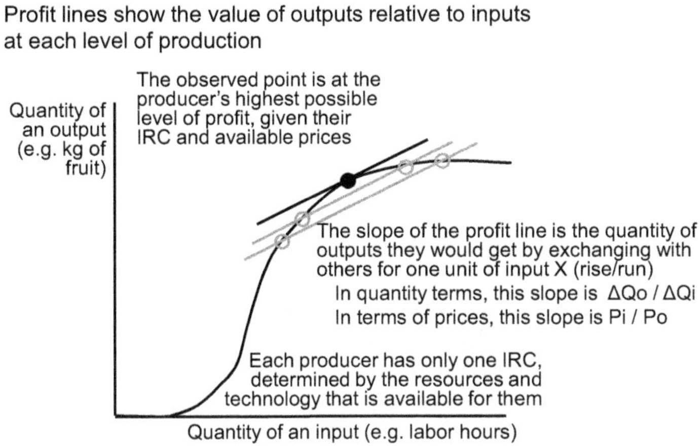

Fig. 2.13 Definition of the profit line

on the highest level of earnings they can attain. In the case of an IRC, the producer's earnings come from *profits,* defined as the value of output minus the cost of inputs, shown graphically using *profit lines* to find the most valuable level of input use as shown in Fig. 2.13.

The profit lines used with the IRC in Fig. 2.13 are similar to the revenue lines used to explain choices along the PPF in previous figures. Both are *price lines* whose slope shows the relative cost of what's on the horizontal axis, in terms of what's on the vertical axis. For example in this case, if the output were fruit that is worth \$50 per bushel and the input is labor worth \$10 per hour, then one bushel of fruit is worth five hours of labor, and the profit line's slope is 0.20 bu/hr (\$10 per hour divided by \$50 per bushel). Farmers who have learned from experience would move along their IRC until they reach the highest level of profit, at which point the IRC's slope just equals that same cost of labor in terms of fruit. Other points along the curve would all be technically efficient but are less desirable for the producer, simply because they produce a lower value of output after accounting for the value of inputs used.

The slope of each price line could reflect market prices paid or received when buying or selling, but might also reflect other costs incurred or values received. For labor use along the horizontal axis, only some farm work is paid by the hour. Most agricultural labor is done by self-employed members of a family enterprise, working to maintain their farm and earn a share of whatever the farm can produce. The family may grow barely enough to survive and avoid losing their land or other assets, but each worker would still be choosing the best of their limited options along an IRC.

Even when things are bought and sold at a market price, the economic definition of something's value is its full *opportunity cost*, referring to the best available alternative. For example each hour of family labor would be valued at that person's opportunity cost of time, including whatever else they would be doing such as caring for others or oneself. Opportunity costs vary throughout the day and among people, and may actually switch between positive and negative values. For example an activity like gardening is done by some people for enjoyment, even as others do similar work for their livelihood.

The entire opportunity cost of something that is bought or sold includes not only its market prices, but also any other *transaction costs* that must be incurred when trading with other people. Transaction costs play a large role in food systems. For example, in farm production the cost of hiring a worker is not just the wages paid but also time and effort required for supervision. Work on crop fields can be especially difficult to monitor when operations occur out of sight and affect output in ways that are not easily measured. More generally, whenever transportation or other barriers make it difficult to exchange something with others, people have to do things for themselves. When transactions are easier, people can trade with each other to provide options beyond what each person can do with their own limited resources.

The slope of each price line is set by often unknown levels of market prices, opportunity costs and transaction costs, while the shape and position of each PPF and IRC is set by highly variable environmental conditions and available technologies. Our analytical diagrams are typically impossible to quantify, but they are still very useful to provide qualitative explanations, predictions and assessments of whether, how and why outcomes might change. The lines and curves on our diagrams lead to useful insights into how people respond to change, as illustrated in Fig. 2.14.

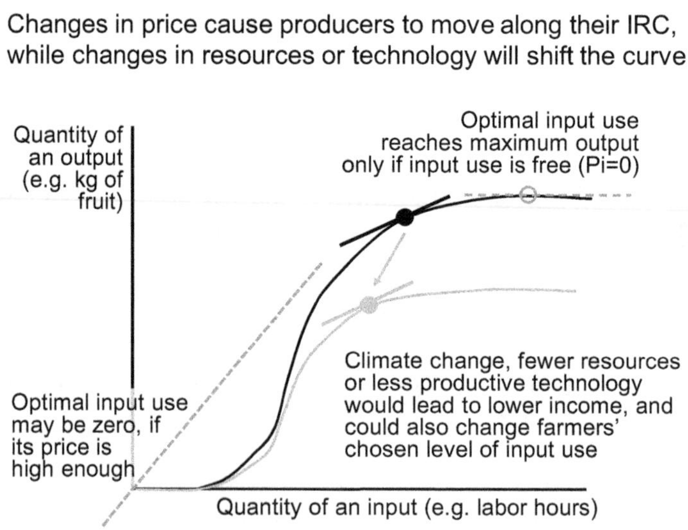

Fig. 2.14 Input use and output level will vary with prices, resources and technology

In Fig. 2.14, the initial observed point resulting from a producer's previous experience is shown as usual by the dark solid point. One kind of change would be caused by variation in prices of the output or the input, leading to movements along the same IRC. If the output becomes more valuable relative to the input, a producer would seek out higher production levels, moving up along the IRC with additional input use. The farthest extreme we could observe, if the price of the input fell to zero, is the round O at the highest possible level of output beyond which additional inputs would not add to profits. Conversely if the relative price of the input were to rise, a producer would cut back on input use, moving to the left along the IRC, and as the price line gets steeper eventually the farmer's best option would be to shut down or choose zero input use, as shown at left of the IRC. Intermediate levels of input use along the bowed-up region of the IRC would not typically be observed, because producing nothing at all would be better than that. Any production that is worthwhile would have exhausted any available increasing returns and be observed along a region of diminishing returns. This aspect of the IRC in Fig. 2.14 is similar to choices along the PPF in Fig. 2.10, which showed how producers move along their production possibilities to specialize in activities that offer economies of size or scale, up to a region where incremental changes have diminishing returns.

Another kind of change away from the observed point could be caused by nature and technology, shifting the IRC itself in ways that alter production at each price. That kind of change was presented for the PPF in Fig. 2.11, where the diagram illustrated both degradation of natural resources which reduces output at each level of input use, and also innovation towards new technologies which increase output at each level of input use. The existing PPFs and IRCs along which farmers produce is the net result of both kinds of change in the past, with some environmental harms that have reduced output and some innovations that have increased it, each of which alters the level of profits and alters farmers' decisions about input use.

The changes shown in Fig. 2.14 illustrate the consequences of climate change or other worsening of input response. These typically alter not only the level of output at each input level, but also the slope of the IRC. A worsening of input response implies a flatter as well as lower IRC at the original level of input use, shifting from the black to the gray curves. The producer would soon discover that, under their new circumstances, the old level of input use is no longer the best they can do.

As drawn in Fig. 2.14, the highest profit along the gray curves calls for a lower level of input use than before. In some cases, environmental change would make the IRC steeper at the old input level, driving producers to increase input use. Changing input levels can also be caused by innovations and new technologies that alter the IRC, including new mechanical equipment that changes the use of labor, and new agronomic techniques or biochemical inputs that can reduce fossil fuel use and hence greenhouse gas emissions.

Fig. 2.15 Average versus marginal product per unit of inputs

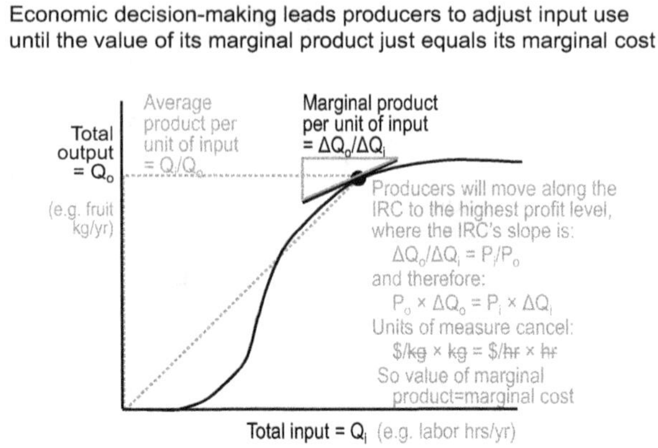

The economics approach to explaining and predicting decisions is that choices are made based on the incremental value of each unit. The average or total value is important to see the person's level of revenue, cost or profit, but change is driven by differences in the ***marginal product*** of each additional unit as shown in Fig. 2.15.

The marginal product of an additional input is the IRC's slope, and at the producer's best available option that slope is also the cost of inputs in terms of the output. Figure 2.15 shows how the marginal value of an input differs from its average value. Quantities chosen are based on marginal values, yielding the average value that drives the producer's income or level of profits. Without randomized experiments an outside observer cannot observe the slope of the IRC, but economists can infer from observed behavior of producers that their expected marginal product is the marginal cost they pay for inputs. In other words, the marginal physical product of inputs along the IRC ($\frac{\Delta Q_o}{\Delta Q_i}$) would just equal the relative price paid ($\frac{P_i}{P_o}$) and is similar among producers who face similar prices, while each producer may have very different levels of average product ($\frac{Q_o}{Q_i}$) based on their resources and technology.

The Isoquant *or Input Substitution Curve (ISC)*

So far, we have examined producers' choice among their options for which outputs to make along a PPF, and then how much of each input to use along an IRC. The third possible way of looking at a producer's options is their choice among inputs, along an ***input substitution curve*** (ISC). This third view completes our set of two-dimensional diagrams showing the producer's multi-dimensional ***production function***, tracing the boundaries of technical efficiency allowed by nature and available technology. The boundary on production of all outputs using all inputs can be imagined as a continuous surface, playing out all possible variations of the three curves. We could redraw these curves for every aspect of production, considering every possible pair of inputs and outputs, and all such curves would have one of the three possible shapes: either a PPF between outputs, an IRC for an input and an output, or an ISC between two inputs. In each case, economic analysis reveals how a producer might move along the curve in response to a change in prices or other circumstances towards their best available option.

Historically the curve between two inputs was called an *isoquant,* to emphasize that it traces all possible combinations for the *iso* (same) *quant*ity of all outputs. That traditional name remains in widespread use, but might be confusing in the context of this book because all two-dimensional curves in this section are all *isolines*. The PPF and IRC, like the ISC and the consumer's indifference curve, are all drawn at a constant level of all variables other than those on the two axes. Referring to the curve between two inputs as an ISC is helpful because it more specifically describes what is shown, and also complements the term IRC which shows responsiveness of output to an input. While the IRC slopes upward, the ISC or isoquant slopes downward as shown in Fig. 2.16.

To draw the ISC shown in Fig. 2.16, we can start with the observed combination of two inputs at the solid black dot. As before, if the producer has learned from experience and done the best they can at the given level of all other variables, then we can infer that it would be impossible for them to have produced the same output with less of both inputs, and undesirable or inefficient for them to have produced the same output with more of both inputs. That is why the ISC must slope down. The ISC shows the different techniques that a producer might adopt, substituting between the resource shown along the horizontal axis (such as their own labor effort, in hours of person-power per year) and the resource shown along the vertical axis (such as machinery time, in hours of horsepower or kilowatt-hours of electricity use).

Fig. 2.16 Definition of the isoquant or input substitution curve (ISC)

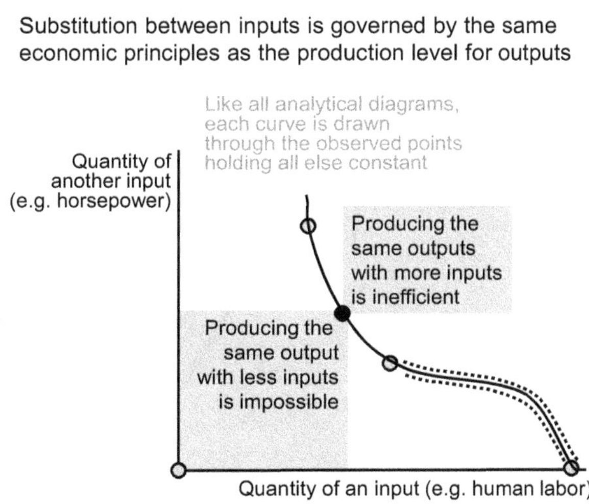

The downward sloping ISC could have segments that are bowed out or in. For example, as drawn in Fig. 2.16 there might be a bowed-out segment on the right when the producer first adopts some equipment instead of working entirely by hand. In this example, over the region highlighted by dotted lines, each increment of machinery up from zero offers increasing returns, working together with other mechanical parts to substitute for more and more labor as shown by a flatter slope when moving along the ISC from right to left. As with the IRC and PPF, however, that region would not actually be observed. To identify the combinations of labor and machinery that a producer might choose, we need relative prices and the resulting cost lines shown in Fig. 2.17.

Choices along an ISC are explained using the same economic principles as along the PPF and IRC, except that a producer's preferred option would have the lowest total cost, instead of the highest revenue or profit. In mathematical terms, the *cost minimization* problem shown in Fig. 2.17 mirrors the *profit maximization* used to explain levels of output, as well as *utility maximization* when consumers choose what combination of products to use in pursuit of overall wellbeing. Each diagram shows a form of *constrained optimization,* revealing the implications of people having chosen the best of their available options, as illustrated graphically in our analytical diagrams.

At this point in the text it is helpful to revisit how terms like 'optimization' have a specific meaning in economics that differs from their use in everyday life. When economists explain observed behavior as having been an *optimal choice*, shown in our diagrams as the point with the lowest available cost or the highest available revenue and profit, we are using the term 'optimal' to mean only that the action was best for that person at that time, given their options and constraints such as opportunity costs and transaction costs. In everyday use, the word 'optimal' is often used for an imagined world with fewer constraints and lower costs than in real life. Similarly, within economics

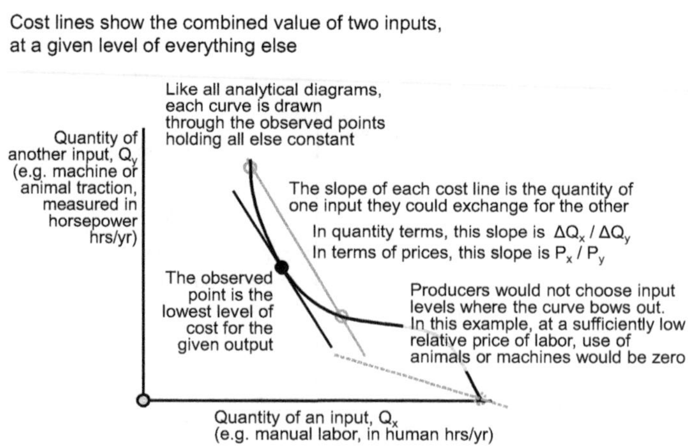

Fig. 2.17 Definition of cost lines and choice among inputs

we explain the level of things using the *marginal value* of each additional unit, and we place that quantity in the middle of our diagrams so as to explain why that was chosen instead of alternatives. In other settings, the word 'marginal' means peripheral to the main story, whereas in economics the marginal thing is central to our explanations and predictions.

In the context of Fig. 2.17, we explain the combination of inputs used by a producer as having their lowest total cost of production, shown by a *cost line* whose slope is the price of the input along the horizontal axis, divided by the price of the input along the vertical axis. That rise over run is the quantity of the input on the vertical axis that could be exchanged with other people for one more unit of the input on the horizontal axis. The available options are dictated by nature and technology, which leads to the ISC between these two inputs at a given level of all other variables. When producers have learned from experience, the best of their options is the point along that ISC with the lowest total cost.

Using the example shown in Fig. 2.17, if the price or opportunity cost incurred by the producer for each hour of labor is extremely low, production might occur with only human labor and zero animals or machinery on the right of the ISC. The cost line's slope is the relative price of labor, so if opportunities to use animals or machinery become available at lower cost per hour of work, a producer could adopt technologies that use increasing amounts of horsepower or kilowatts to replace each hour of human labor. The process of mechanization is shown here as movement along the ISC, illustrating how there is typically a region of increasing returns where adopting each additional unit of horsepower or kilowatts saves an increasing number of human labor hours. At relative prices shown by the slope of the solid cost line, mechanization offers cost reduction along the ISC only up to the observed point, due to diminishing returns that make further mechanization less attractive to the producer than their observed choice.

The economic principles that help explain technology adoption along an ISC provide important insights into how incentives guide innovation over time. When there are trends in the relative cost of things, for example rising wages compared to the cost of machinery, production can be expected to use less of the inputs that are increasingly expensive, and more of the inputs that are increasingly abundant. These trends drive the adoption of new techniques and also guide the invention of entirely new technologies, as illustrated in Fig. 2.18.

The example in Fig. 2.18 shows how a higher cost of labor, for example due to higher opportunity costs of a farmer's time or transaction costs when hiring workers, would lead producers to choose a higher level of mechanization along the solid ISC to the open circle. Furthermore, the invention of entirely new technologies could offer options to produce at even lower costs as shown by the dashed price line, saving even more labor using newly invented production methods along the dashed ISC.

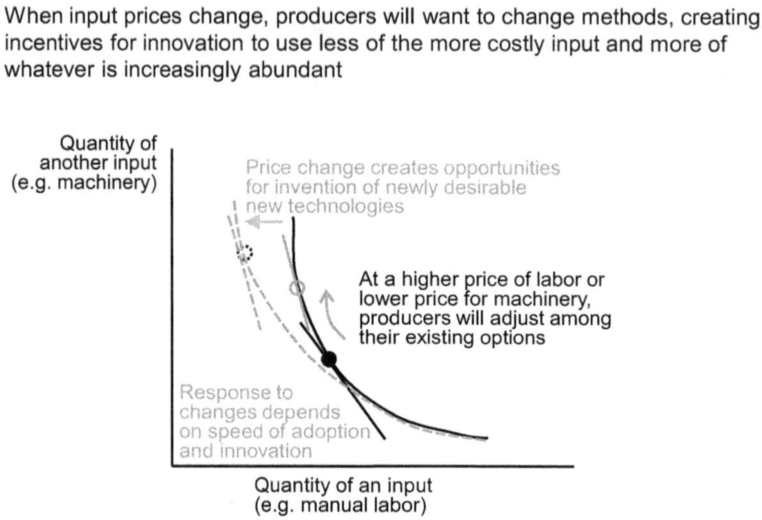

Fig. 2.18 A change in price can induce invention as well as adoption of new techniques

Differences or changes in the relative cost of inputs are sometimes predictable, driving the direction of technological change in a process known as ***induced innovation***. The example of induced innovation shown in Fig. 2.18 is how higher labor costs relative to other inputs lead to not only adoption of known techniques to use less labor, but also innovations that create new options to go even further in that direction. The dashed gray price line has the same slope as the solid gray price line, but the new dashed ISC offers a flatter slope than the solid ISC at previously observed levels of labor use, leading producers to replace even more labor with machinery.

The process of induced innovation shown in Fig. 2.18 is among the most important forces affecting agriculture and food systems, driving change over time and differences between regions. Induced innovation shapes not only mechanization and employment but also use of energy and other resources. Through most of the twentieth century, steady declines in cost of fossil fuels, inorganic fertilizers and crop chemicals drove a seemingly endless trend towards use of petrochemicals, for both intensification to higher yields on existing fields and also cropland expansion. In the late twentieth century the direction of change shifted away from fossil fuels, with a rapid but not yet sufficient race towards electricity powered by renewable energy sources, and many other shifts in agriculture and food systems described in Chapters 10, 11 and 12.

2.3 Economics of Size and Scale

The means of production available at each place and time have been shown by PPF, IRC and ISC curves, tracing all possible two-dimensional perspectives on the multidimensional functions by which people could potentially convert inputs into outputs. Each production process might offer a region of increasing returns along which increasing quantities is increasingly attractive, and we expect producers to learn about those opportunities and choose options that yield the lowest available cost and highest available revenue or profit at the relative prices they face. These principles help explain why observed outcomes have diminishing returns to further changes, and also minimum and maximum quantities that are likely to be observed.

In economics, changes in the *scale* of an activity or enterprise refer to proportional changes in all inputs and other resources used. An enterprise that is 10% larger in scale would use 10% more of each thing, including 10% more hours for each type of labor as well as 10% more land and 10% more equipment and also 10% more energy. In contrast, the *size* of an enterprise refers to altering resources per worker, for example with more machinery or a larger land area. The observed scale and size of each enterprise is limited by diminishing returns to adding more of each variable input, given the enterprise's fixed factors that do not change.

The phrase *economies of scale* refers to the possibility that increasing returns to scale allow expansion to lower cost or increase revenue and profit per unit of production, while *diseconomies of scale* arise when diminishing returns impose a limit on further expansion. The intermediate case is *constant* returns to scale, where for example a proportional increase in all inputs yields that same proportional increase in all outputs. With constant returns, cost per unit is the same for enterprises of different scales.

A limiting factor determining the scale of each individual enterprise is often its management and the transaction cost of expanding operations across more different settings. For example, a given city will have various kinds of restaurants and cafeterias, each with a different number of seats and meals served per day. Owners and managers of independent restaurants serving individual customers may start with just one location, and then try to replicate or diversify their operations at different locations, but even the most successful restaurant owners and managers cannot effectively supervise more than a small fraction of all restaurants in a typical city. In contrast, large-scale institutional food service at schools, hospitals and other facilities is more suited to centralized management, so cities may have just a few big commercial food service providers.

The economics of size and scale concerns both the magnitude of each individual enterprise and also the cost per unit sold for an entire sector of production. Management challenges limit the size and scale of individual enterprises, but an ecosystem of many enterprises can often expand with constant or even increasing returns to scale until the whole sector encounters its own diminishing returns. For example, a city might have a wide range of restaurants that serve various meals at different prices, and that entire ecosystem of restaurants might expand or shrink over time. Enterprises often benefit from each other's presence, leading to agglomeration in geographic clusters of similar activities. The benefits of agglomeration are often visible in the restaurant sector, as establishments choose to locate near each other and neighborhoods with many similar restaurants often have higher quality and lower prices. Agglomeration effects occur between sectors as well. The initial start of a cluster may be influenced by transportation routes or other geographic factors, but then various kinds of activities will benefit from proximity to each other, leading to urbanization and the growth of each individual town or city even as the surrounding rural area remains cultivated by dispersed family farmers in rural areas.

Scale economies for individual enterprises and for entire sectors play a crucial role in agriculture and food systems, determining the size and structure of organizations that can sustainably undertake each kind of activity. The smallest restaurants we typically see have enough tables or take-out business to keep several people busy for much of the day. It may be operated by an owner who lives near the premises, but almost all restaurants have multiple employees and many are run by salaried managers. In contrast, most farms have zero salaried employees, even in the U.S. or other industrialized countries. Most farms are owned and operated by family members who live on site, often hiring part-time workers only for specific operations where supervision and transaction costs are low. Year-round employees are observed mainly in concentrated livestock operations, production of fruits and vegetables, or crops that require on-farm processing such as sugar or tea, where there are scale economies derived from equipment and facilities and tasks for which workers can be hired and supervised relatively easily. As technologies change, the number of workers as well as the area of land or number of animals that can effectively be managed in each individual operation, as well as the number of such operations in each area, changes with shifts in production technology and relative prices.

The enterprises we actually observe in each part of the food system are big enough to have survived, somewhere between the minimum and maximum size of feasible operation for each activity. A helpful way to describe economies of size and scale is to distinguish between ***fixed costs*** of big, lumpy or indivisible capital investments, in contrast to ***variable costs*** of applying increasing quantities of a continuous input. Fixed costs include buildings and facilities as well as management skills and other assets that are specific to an enterprise but can be used repeatedly over time, while variable costs include all materials and other inputs that are used up in production. Fixed costs are often the source of increasing returns that determine the minimum scale typically observed, while variable costs often encounter diminishing returns that limit the size of each operation.

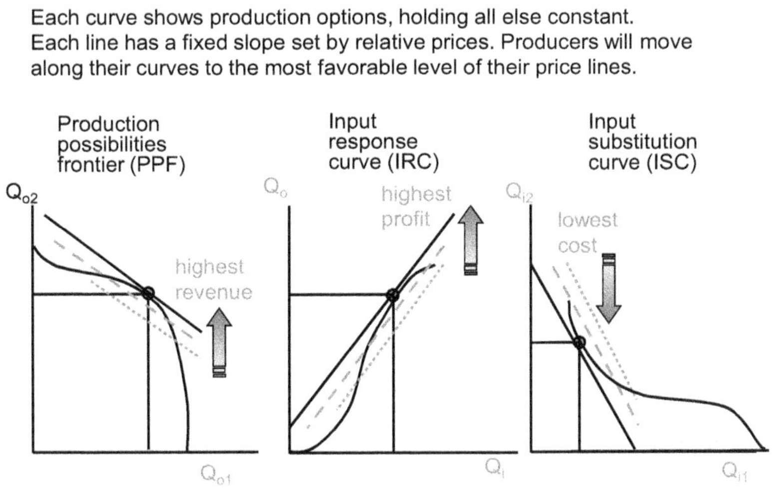

Fig. 2.19 Summary of all three two-dimensional perspectives on production

To explain the size and type of operations we are likely to see at each place and time, it is helpful to keep all three of our production diagrams in mind as shown in Fig. 2.19.

The trio of analytical diagrams in Fig. 2.19 shows how the observed point of production is chosen as the best option for that producer, offering their highest level of revenue or profit and also their lowest cost per unit of output. The slope of each price line is the relative value or cost of incremental units along the curve, where prices include all opportunity costs and transaction costs of transaction with other people. Meanwhile the shape and position of each curve are dictated by nature and technology, embodying all past investments that determine what can be made with additional inputs at each place and time.

More advanced classes in economics represent production choices mathematically using multivariate calculus and real analysis, generalizing the graphical approach illustrated in our two-dimensional diagrams. Advanced methods are helpful to explore special cases and details not covered in this introductory textbook, but the principles of economics can readily be summarized as the consequences of people having chosen the best of their available options. Redrawing these diagrams around any given decision will reveal how these principles play out in each situation, as producers choose among inputs to obtain outputs. The diagrams could be redrawn for specific people making particular things, using concrete numbers of each input and output, but the important thing is to recall the definition of each line and curve in terms of the variables shown in each axis. Once you have practiced sketching these diagrams, starting with the axes then curves and lines leading to the observed points, you will see that there is need to memorize examples because you can always redraw a new diagram for each situation.

A key feature of our individual-choice diagrams in this chapter is that the axes show quantities, measured in natural units of something such as weight, volume or servings of food, land area and labor time or energy use. Prices are used here only in relative terms, showing the relative value or cost of each thing when exchanging it for other things. The diagrams used in this chapter can help explain individual choices in food system decisions that may not involve any market transactions at all, as shown in Fig. 2.20.

The diagrams in Fig. 2.20 begin our analysis of the entire food system, showing the interaction between production and consumption for an individual person. The diagram allows us to imagine the choices of a farmer who is entirely self-sufficient, and does not exchange anything at all with other people. The diagram focuses on one of their foods they grow and eat, for example beans. Their production options between beans and all other things are limited by their PPF, along which the highest level of wellbeing is at the hollow O based on their consumption preferences shown by the dotted indifference curve. Other points along their PPF are equally possible but would be less preferred in consumption. The left side diagram shows this farmer in a situation where other people offer to buy beans from them in exchange for other things, while the right diagram shows a situation where other people offer to sell beans to them in exchange for other things.

Starting with the left diagram in Fig. 2.20, if other people offer to buy some beans along a steeper price line than the slope of the farmer's PPF at their self-sufficient level of production, the farmer could reach a higher level

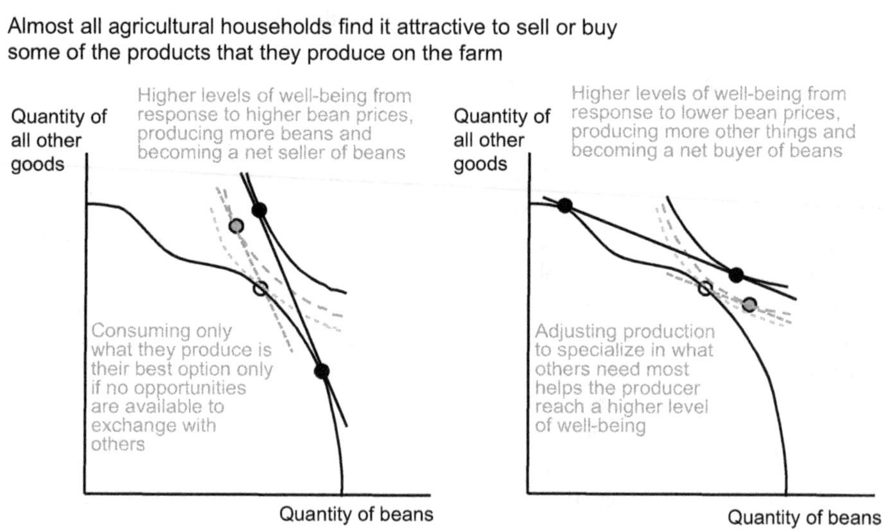

Fig. 2.20 Production and consumption for the farming household

of wellbeing by selling some of the beans they produced leftward along the price line up to the gray dot which reaches the dashed indifference curve. Learning from experience, however, the farmer would soon discover that they can reach even higher wellbeing by moving production along their PPF to the right, increasing production of beans so as to sell a larger quantity and reach the solid indifference curve which turns out to be the best of their available options, given their production options and consumption preferences.

Now turning to the right side of Fig. 2.20, we see the identical farmer in a situation where other people offer to sell them some beans at a lower price than the slope of their PPF in self-sufficiency. Again we can see that the farm could improve their wellbeing by accepting the offer, selling some of their beans from the original point of production rightward along the price line down to the gray dot which reaches the dashed indifference curve. Again, however, we would expect them to learn from experience, and soon discover that they can reach an even higher level of wellbeing by moving production along their PPF to the left, reducing production of beans so as to make more other things which they sell to others and reach the solid indifference curve, which in this case is the highest they can reach given their production options and consumption preferences.

Taken literally, the diagram refers to an individual farmer living alone, but we can also use the diagram to describe a farm household that pools their resources and makes joint decisions in service of the whole family's wellbeing. In later chapters we will address some of the ways in which households do not act like individuals, for example due to differences between household members in their preferences and bargaining power. Gender and age disparities within each household can be extremely important for nutrition and health, and for the wellbeing for women and children generally. We will return to that topic but for now we can imagine the benchmark case of a unified household that is either one individual or a family that acts together as if they were a single farmer who consumes some or all of what they grow.

Comparing the two sides of Fig. 2.20 is the foundational discovery of economics, showing how exchanging goods with other people helps each person or joint household reach a higher level of wellbeing for themselves and their children. The magnitude of gain depends on the details of each line and curve, but the qualitative discovery is that gains from trade exist whether other people want to buy from us or sell to us. In either case, remaining entirely self-sufficient is possible but undesirable and therefore unlikely to be observed. Exchanging with others, whether buying or selling, helps farmers overcome diminishing returns on their own farm in both production and consumption. This observation helps explain why even the most ancient archeological sites show evidence of food trade, and even the most remote people who value self-reliance choose to exchange with other people at least some of what they produce and consume.

The final analytical diagram to complete this chapter shows how economists can use PPFs and indifference curves for an individual farmer to explain and predict response to change. Students can redraw these diagrams for any imaginable scenario, identifying cause and effect for changes in nature or technology and hence production possibilities, changes in market conditions and hence relative prices, or changes in preferences and hence the shape of each indifference curve. The example shown is the impact of a lower relative price of beans than was used to draw the farmer's previous choice, as illustrated in Fig. 2.21.

The impact of a lower price of beans on the farmer's wellbeing depends on whether they are buying or selling beans to other people. As shown in Fig. 2.21, the farmer is always producing and consuming some beans, with the left diagram showing a *net seller* who produces more than they consume, and the right diagram showing a *net buyer* who consumes more than they produce. In this picture, the only reason for the difference is what others are willing to do. The left diagram shows a net seller because others have offered to buy their beans at a relatively high price, and the right diagram shows a net buyer because others have offered to sell them beans at a relatively low price. For the net seller, a lower price of beans reduces the gains from trade and lowers their wellbeing, as shown by the switch to the dashed price line, gray dots and dashed indifference curve. For the net buyer, a lower price of beans increases the gains from trade and raises their wellbeing.

Figure 2.21 clearly reveals how the initial direction of trade drives our qualitative conclusions about the direction of cause and effect, while the shapes of each curve influence magnitudes. On the right diagram, the initially low price of beans had led this farmer to specialize in other things, and the quantity of beans they produce is not much affected by further reduction in market price.

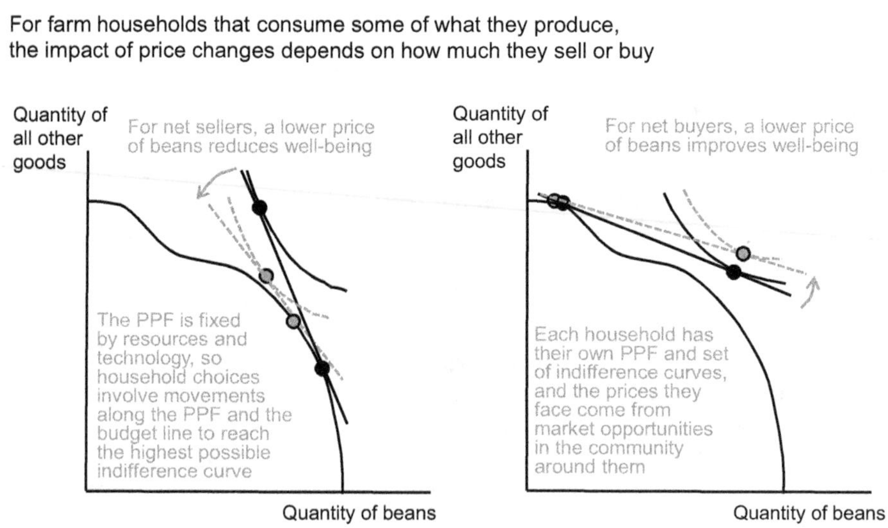

Fig. 2.21 Impact of a lower price on net sellers and net buyers

For example, they might have just a small backyard garden, and the lower price of beans allows them to buy more beans and also spend more money on other things. Meanwhile the left diagram showed the farmer putting more variable costs into moving along their PPF towards production of beans for sale to others, and the lower price leads them to cut back on that. In either case the farmer's consumption preferences is such that the quantity of beans consumed changes relatively little, and the price alters wellbeing mostly through income available to consume other things.

2.3.1 Conclusion

This long chapter spells out the economic principles used to explain and predict changes in an individual person's choices for production and consumption. Our analytical diagrams reveal how the quantities we observe being produced and consumed are the result of choices, as each person selected actions to meet their needs given their options. This approach focuses our attention on understanding and improving those options. We also recognize that some aspects of behavior may have been random and unpredictable, or preordained and unchangeable. Our focus is on the kind of behavior that was described by Alfred Marshall in 1890 at the start of his *Principles of Economics* textbook as 'the ordinary business of life', regarding 'the material requisites of wellbeing'. The underlying first principle of economics, underlying all else in this textbook and other work in economics, is that people might have chosen what we observe because it was the best of their options. The result of each person's everyday choices can be sketched graphically in two dimensions, leading to a set of causal models that make clear predictions about how people will respond to a change in production possibilities, prices and income, or preferences. The resulting theory of change is an abstract simplification of the infinitely complex world, but it sets economists on a profoundly human journey of exploration to understand and improve societal outcomes.

By design, economics is not a single complete theory of everything, but a way to create customized models suited to answering various questions about everyday living standards. Each analytical diagram is a different model, suited to different circumstances and scales of observation. Our goal in this textbook is to spell out a toolkit of interconnected models used in the economics of food, linking agriculture and natural resource use to human nutrition and health. This chapter provides a first set of modeling tools, using analytical diagrams to explain and predict individual choices in food consumption and production, as people learn from experience and move among their available options along each line or curve towards their preferred choice shown by the observed point. In the next chapter we connect the dots between each person's choices to explain and predict societal outcomes, meaning the prices and quantities produced or consumed by an entire population.

CHAPTER 3

Societal Outcomes: Predicting Food Market Prices and Quantities

3.1 Market Equilibrium with Perfectly Competitive Interactions

3.1.1 Motivation and Guiding Questions

The previous chapter described how individual behavior is influenced by prices, but where do prices come from? Why are some foods expensive while others are cheap, and how do prices relate to quantities produced or consumed?

To answer these questions and predict how prices and quantities might change in response to different government policies or other circumstances, we derive analytical diagrams that provide qualitative insights, offering simplified models to explain the direction and relative magnitude of differences or changes in price and quantity. A wide range of theories about prices and quantities have been tested by successive generations of economists, leading to the causal framework described here. These diagrams guide how prices and quantities are measured and interpreted. Testing hypotheses about predicted outcomes under different circumstances leads to further refinement of the models, altering their focus to capture the most important aspects of behavior for each situation.

Our focus is on interactions between people in what economists call a *market,* meaning any in-person or electronic environment in which people exchange things. In most markets, whether transactions occur online or in physical places, people exchange things for money and we track prices paid or received as well as the quantities bought and sold. The same analytical models can also be used for *nonmarket transactions* such as volunteering and use of donated things, for example to explain, predict and assess services provided in food pantries or meal services.

W. A. Masters and A. B. Finaret, *Food Economics*,
Palgrave Studies in Agricultural Economics and Food Policy,
https://doi.org/10.1007/978-3-031-53840-7_3

The market diagrams in this chapter use lines and curves to identify a *market equilibrium*. This is one of many instances where terminology in economics can be confusing. Economists use the word 'equilibrium' to mean any predictable outcome of interactions between people. In everyday usage, an equilibrium is a stable or desirable condition, but the balance between economic forces that predict market outcomes can lead to terrible outcomes such as price spikes, hunger and deprivation. Predicting these outcomes as an equilibrium between forces allows economists to identify how changing policies or technologies might lead to different outcomes.

The conditions under which transactions occur is known as *market structure*. For example, some markets involve interactions only within a community, while other markets are open to trade with people elsewhere. This section of our first chapter on market equilibrium concerns the simplest kind of market, in which a community of people has many buyers and sellers exchanging a uniform product at a single price. Markets of this type are *perfectly competitive*. Like any kind of perfection, a market with entirely perfect competition cannot exist in reality, but the resulting model provides a useful benchmark against which to compare outcomes from various kinds of *market failures* addressed in later chapters such as monopoly power, externalities and lack of information about product quality. Food markets are often subject to market failures, but can also be shaped by policy and technology to have more buyers and sellers, fewer externalities and greater transparency about product quality, thereby reducing imperfections and moving towards the benchmark model of perfect competition introduced in this chapter.

The toolkit of analytical diagrams in this and later chapters uses different market structures to predict different outcomes, all following the same economic principles. In the previous chapter, we explained individual behavior as each person's choice from their limited options, drawn as points of tangency between a line and a curve. In this chapter, we explain societal outcomes as an interaction between individuals, drawn as a point of intersection between two curves. For individuals, the optimal choice may be the least bad of their options, and for societies even a perfectly competitive equilibrium can be very undesirable. The toolkit of economics allows us to build market models tailored to observed conditions and identify how changes in policies and technologies could lead to market outcomes with greater sustainability, equity and health for the populations we serve.

By the end of this section, you will be able to:

1. Derive supply curves from PPFs and revenue lines;
2. Derive demand curves from indifference curves and budget lines;
3. Describe how movements along supply and demand curves differ from shifts in those curves, and lead to observed outcomes; and
4. Identify predicted prices and quantities produced and consumed in markets with imports, exports or without trade, in settings with many buyers and sellers for a standard product of known quality.

3.1.2 *Analytical Tools*

The models for societal outcomes used in this book are all derived from the theory of individual choice developed in the previous chapter. Like those individual-choice diagrams, market models are drawn by first defining the variables on each axis, and then tracing lines and curves that show a particular relationship between those two variables. The definition of each line or curve leads to its position and shape, and the predicted outcome is the point of intersection between two of the lines. As always, each diagram corresponds to a specific scenario with a given level of all other variables.

Every market model refers to a specific community, adding up the choices of all individuals in that community. Market models refer to a specific set of people, often all of the residents of a city, state or the world as a whole, and may also distinguish between subpopulations especially regarding equity between groups. The horizontal X axis always shows the total quantity of a good or service, added up over a specific period of time, while the vertical Y axis shows its price or cost per unit at that time. Quantities are measured in weight or volume which might add up to millions of liters or tons per year, while prices are those facing each individual such as cost per serving.

For quantitative research, market models would correspond to actual data published by someone, such as the price and quantity of all apples each year in the U.S. which is estimated by the USDA based on surveys of apple growers and distributors. In this book we use diagrams only for qualitative analysis, to see causal relationships and relative magnitudes based on geometric relationships. This allows us to make diagrams about something for which quantitative information is not available, such as the cost and quantity of home-made bread produced and consumed in a neighborhood each month. We could try to estimate that, but we can also obtain useful insights through qualitative analysis.

To build our market models we begin with production, deriving a community's supply curve from the production possibility frontiers (PPFs) and price lines faced by each individual farmer or food producer. We then derive that same community's food demand curve from each individual consumer's budget lines and indifference curves, and explain outcomes as the interaction between people in the benchmark case of a perfectly competitive market, with many sellers and buyers who face a single price for a uniform product. We draw each market diagram first for a community in isolation, leading to a single quantity produced and consumed, and then for a community that might also export or import the product by trading with other people. The resulting predictions can be surprising and provide useful insights about the real world, even before we explore market failures and policy interventions in later chapters.

The Supply Curve

Total production in any community is the sum of each person's quantity produced. Here we show how that level of supply is derived from each individual's production possibilities, moving along their PPF towards additional output of things whose price has increased. For simplicity we derive the community's supply curve from each individual's production possibilities at a fixed level of all input used, but similar decisions underlie choices based on input response and input substitution curves. Because individuals have moved to points where each curve's slope just equals the relative price received, the price received always equals the *marginal cost* of additional production.

The relationship between substitution among outputs along a PPF and the marginal opportunity cost of production is shown for an individual producer with example numbers in Fig. 3.1.

The diagram in Fig. 3.1 uses concrete numbers between 1 and 4, allowing you to verify each calculation in the transformation of individual choices on the left to a supply curve on the right. As shown in the previous chapter, each individual will try to produce at a point of tangency between their PPF and a price line, so in this case they might produce one unit at a price of 1/3, three units at a price of 1 and four units at a price of 3. We use pesos as the name of the monetary unit in this diagram only because it is a short and familiar word for money in several countries. More generally we would use whatever currency can be exchanged for the set of all other goods along the vertical axis of the right panel, which can be imagined as a vertical stack of all other things measured in monetary terms. To simplify comparison between the two panels, they are drawn to scale so you could verify these slopes using a ruler.

The data in Fig. 3.1 are shown with example numbers of kilograms and pesos for a single person. That allows you to check unit conversions and thereby build your intuition about how the variables on each axis relate to

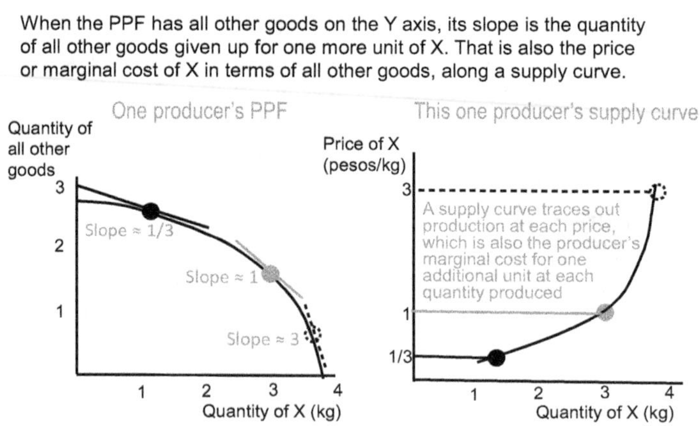

Fig. 3.1 We can derive an individual producer's supply curve from their PPF

each other. Even without numbers you can use the name of each measurement unit to see how individual choices underlie the supply curve. Once we see the quantity of all other things along the vertical axis of the PPF as a vertical stack of money, in this case pesos, so the rise-over-run slope of the frontier is measured in pesos per kilogram. The slope of each price line used to identify producers' choices along their PPF is also measured in pesos/kg, and that price is also the unit of measure for the supply curve's vertical axis.

Verifying unit conversions, with or without concrete numbers, can be extremely helpful to confirm that abstract concepts like price and quantity are being used as intended in each situation. The structure of models like Fig. 3.1 can be explained in words and mathematical symbols, and then you can check how the variables relate to each other by replacing each variable name with its unit of measure. For example you can replace price with P in pesos/kg, and replace quantity with Q in kg, to verify that P times Q would be measured in pesos. Every variable in our models has an implicit unit of measure, and making those units explicit can be very helpful to check the validity and meaning of the model. In the case of Fig. 3.1, the units are specified as pesos and kg for one individual person, but there is no mention of time or location. Models used in practical applications should be labeled with the time, place and other identifying information.

Each producer's PPF and supply curves reflect their individual circumstances and are drawn on our analytical diagrams in the simplest form needed to show the qualitative direction of effect. The individual supply curve in Fig. 3.1 happened to be bowed upwards but that was an accident driven by the arbitrary numbers used for ease of calculation. For visual clarity it is easiest to draw supply curves as straight lines, and we can imagine a variety of similar individual producers in a community whose market supply curve is shown in Fig. 3.2.

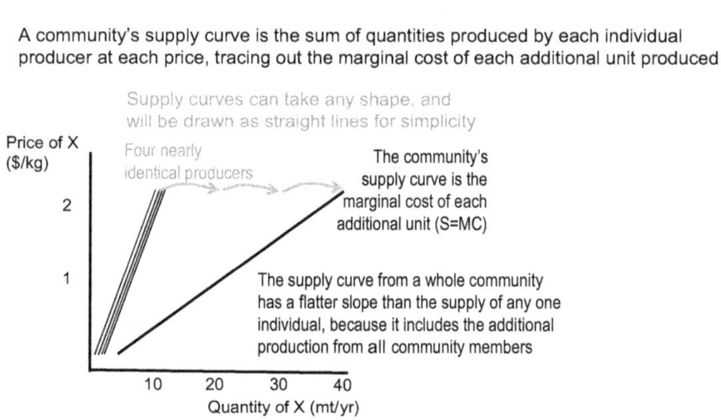

Fig. 3.2 Definition of the supply curve

Market supply in Fig. 3.2 is shown with numbers along the axes to illustrate how the quantities from each individual are added up to obtain the whole community's supply curve at each price. In this case we use the abbreviated dollar sign for monetary price per kilogram ($/kg) along the vertical axis, and to show large quantities over a long period time the horizontal axis is in metric tons per year (mt/yr).

Supply curves are drawn as straight lines here and throughout this book partly for visual clarity, and also to differentiate supply curves from the indifference curves, PPFs, IRCs or ISCs each of which has a specific curvature. Using a set of straight lines reveals how the horizontal sum of quantities at each price has a flatter slope than each individual line. That qualitative insight would remain true for supply curves of different shapes. When supply curves are estimated statistically they take a variety of mathematical forms, but in all cases the definition of supply is the quantity produced at each price, or equivalently the price required for each quantity produced. Price always equals marginal cost, so supply curves can always be labeled S = MC.

Models like Fig. 3.2 help us distinguish clearly between *supply*, meaning the entire curve of quantities produced at each price, and *production* which is a particular quantity produced along the curve. A larger community or changes in circumstances would bring *shifts in supply*, to a different quantity at the same price. Those would be caused by external factors not shown in this diagram, sometimes called *exogenous* changes originating outside the model. In contrast, a change in price from people moving along their supply curves is *endogenous* to the model. Those terms use the Latin prefixes exo- and endo- to mean outside or inside, and -genous to mean where the change comes from. Exogenous changes are sometimes called 'shocks' to the model, whether or not they happen suddenly because they come from outside, whereas endogenous changes are results that the diagram aims to explain and predict. Some examples are shown in Fig. 3.3.

The points in Fig. 3.3 show six different quantities produced, from around 12 to over 40 mt/yr. Initial observations might be either of the two solid black dots, at a low or high price, but then resource depletion might shift supply leftward leading to the gray dashed line, or technological innovation might shift supply rightward leading to the gray solid line. Actually estimating any of these lines would require advanced techniques for data collection and analysis. The qualitative model in each diagram provides helpful vocabulary, tells us what to look for and generates hypotheses that could be tested to distinguish among possible causal mechanisms behind the outcomes we see.

The changes shown in Fig. 3.3 use linear supply curves only for simplicity. The only attribute of all supply curves is that they never slope down. Where available technologies offer increasing returns to size or scale, producers might switch up to larger operations at higher prices and shut down entirely to produce zero when prices are below a minimum threshold. Available technologies might also allow expansion at constant returns and hence horizontal

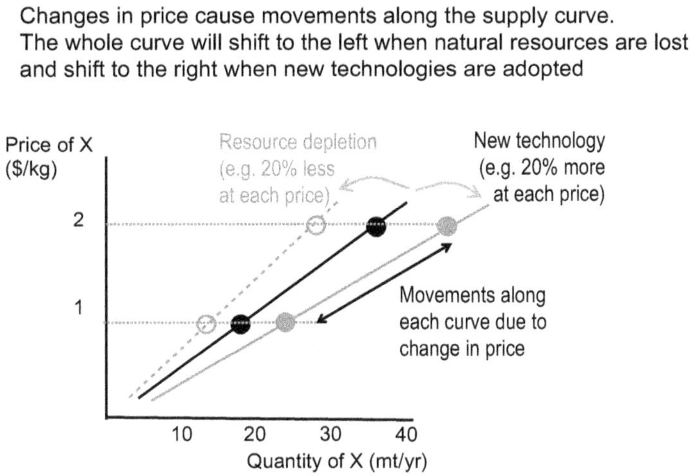

Fig. 3.3 Price change leads producers to move along their supply curve, which can shift

supply curves until some limiting factor is reached, beyond which producers face diminishing returns and upward sloping supply.

Drawing supply curves yields remarkable insights about production, showing how people's choices select from all possible options in systematic ways. Due to human selection, the range of things we might actually observe in any situation is only a subset of potential outcomes. Economic principles reveal qualitative similarities in what might be observed, point to the subject-matter knowledge we would need for empirical work in specific situations, and suggest causal mechanisms that might explain, predict and allow improvement in observed results. For example, in Fig. 3.3, there are two possible points on each supply curves. What explains which point we might observe? For that we need additional information, starting with consumer demand.

The Demand Curve

Like supply, we can derive demand using each person's choices from their available options. Just as supply was defined as the quantity produced at each price, derived from producers choosing among production possibilities based on price received, demand is defined as the quantity consumed at each price and is derived from consumers choosing along budget lines to reach their highest level of wellbeing.

The derivation of an individual's demand curve from their budget lines and indifference curves is illustrated in Fig. 3.4.

The left and right panels of Fig. 3.4 show how demand curves relate to each person's subjective wellbeing, reflecting their individual goals and constraints. The left panel shows how a higher price for the product of interest, for example shifting from one to two pesos per kilogram, might reduce their quantity

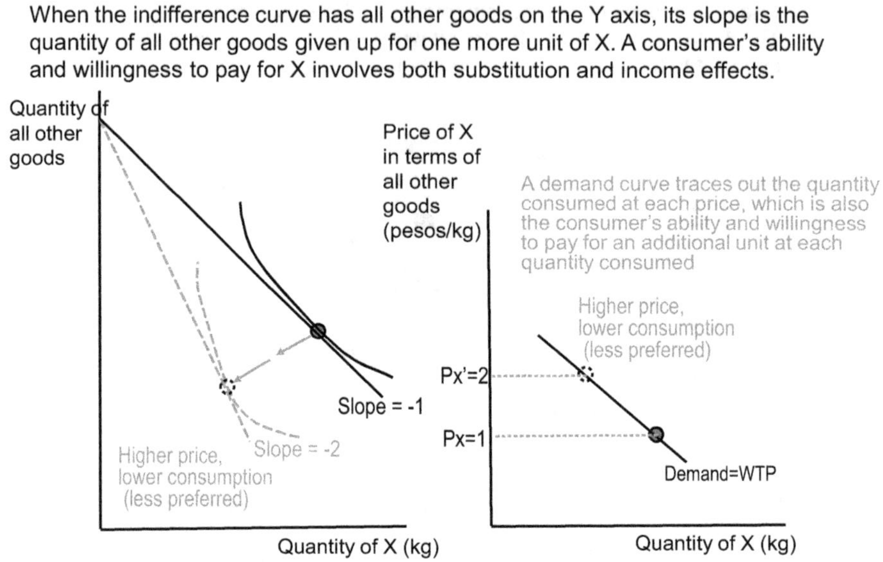

Fig. 3.4 We can derive an individual's demand curve from their indifference curve and budget line

consumed. The consumer's choices along their budget lines lead to level of wellbeing where the price paid for something just equals the slope of their indifference curve for it, meaning the additional quantity of all other things they would accept for one more unit of it. The right panel shows that price as the consumer's willingness to pay (WTP) at each quantity, or equivalently the quantity that they would be willing and able to consume at each price paid.

In the same way that production choices traced out a curve labeled S = MC, demand curves can be labeled D = WTP. In that notation, the S = MS and D = WTP both refer to a price along the vertical axis, for the quantity shown on the horizontal axis. Some sources refer to these as ***inverse supply*** and ***inverse demand*** curves, when referring to equations where quantity is a function of price. In practice, however, price and quantity are determined simultaneously so the two curves can simply be called supply and demand.

The individual's demand curve in Fig. 3.4 is shown as a straight line only for visual clarity, joining the solid black dot and the dashed gray dot in the simplest possible way. That simplification makes the demand curve on the right look superficially like the budget line on the left, but their definitions and interpretation are completely different. The budget line is always drawn linearly to show the price paid for additional units, just as the indifference curve is always bowed-in to show the degree of diminishing marginal benefits or rates of substitution in consumption of things. Meanwhile the demand curve could take any shape, and is usually shown as a straight line only to make each market diagram easier to interpret.

As shown by the two panels of Fig. 3.4, higher prices generally lead to lower quantities consumed. That is the net result of two changes, the loss of purchasing power and lower real income shown by the lower indifference level, and a substitution effect along each indifference curve. The combination of income and substitution effects is such that moving from solid black to dashed gray almost always reduces quantity consumed along the horizontal axis, so demand curves almost always slope down.

The unusual cases where demand curves might sometimes slope up are so rare that they are named after the researchers who first described them. In the 1890s, at the same time as Alfred Marshall's *Principles of Economics* popularized the use of demand curves to explain consumption, the British statistician Robert Giffen described how the poorest people in Britain were sometimes forced by rising price of the cheapest foods such as potatoes to buy even more of them, because higher costs left them able to afford even less of their preferred but more expensive foods such as milk or vegetables. Soon thereafter, in 1899 the American sociologist Thorstein Veblen noted that richer people in the U.S. were buying expensive things as a signal of wealth and taste, thereby creating both high prices and high quantity for some items. We will return to both Giffen goods and Veblen goods later in this book, but both are relatively rare and limited to a subset of the population. In general for entire societies, the 'Marshallian' demand curve for each good slopes down.

As with supply, a community's demand curve is the horizontal sum of each person's quantity at each price. For demand we add up the community's consumption, tracing quantity consumed at each price, or equivalently the price that consumers would be willing to pay for each quantity as shown in Fig. 3.5.

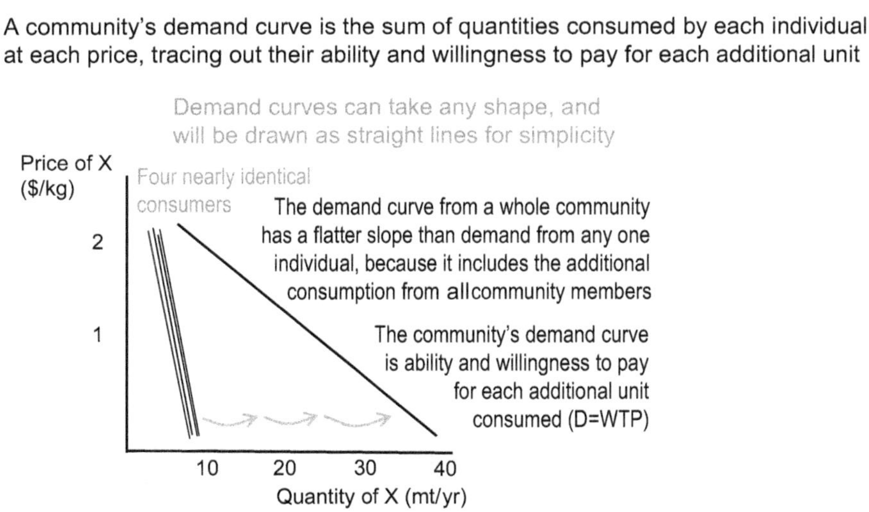

Fig. 3.5 Definition of the demand curve

Each community's demand curve, like their supply curve, reveals how *movements along the curve* involve variation in both price and quantity under a given set of circumstances, while *shifts in the curve* represent a change in circumstances. For the supply curve, shifts are caused by changes in the natural environment or available technology, whereas demand curve shifts are caused by changes in population size, income or preferences. For production, the two kinds of shift go in opposite directions: changes in environmental conditions typically reduce supply, while new technologies that are adopted typically increase supply. For consumption, income and preferences can shift demand in either direction, as illustrated in Fig. 3.6.

Food demand curves generally shift to the right over time due to growth in the size of each population, expanding quantities demanded at each price. Another factor that often shifts demand to the right is income growth per person, but richer people do not always have higher willingness to pay at each quantity. For some foods, known as *inferior goods* for the population of interest, higher income shifts demand down and to the left. Changes in preferences and other factors can also shift demand in either direction, to the left or to the right.

In recent decades there have been large changes in global food consumption known as the *dietary transition*, typically towards more packaged and processed food as well as food consumed away from home. Some of these changes could be due to movements along the demand curve for each type of food, but observed price changes have been insufficient to explain the magnitude, direction and timing of quantity changes discussed in Section 10.2 of this book. Beyond price-induced movements along each curve, some of the dietary transition must have been caused by shifts in the curves as shown in Fig. 3.6.

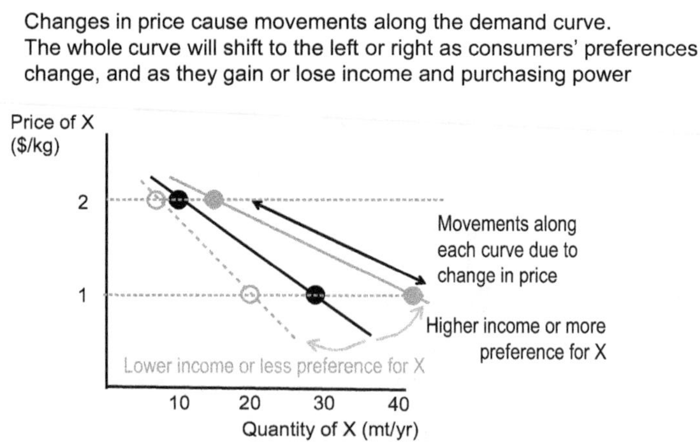

Fig. 3.6 Price change leads consumers to move along their demand curve, which can shift

The extent of movements along and shifts in demand curves for different foods in different places has been difficult to measure precisely, but analytical diagrams like Fig. 3.6 suggest what to look for and how to interpret observed data. Some shifts in demand curves at each price have been associated with changes in employment, urbanization and preferences about time use. Other shifts in demand could be caused by changes in how foods are produced and marketed, as well as changes in public perceptions and news coverage that influence the attractiveness of different foods.

To begin seeing how we might distinguish among the possible causes of change in consumption, we need to describe how producers and consumers interact. When we put supply and demand together, we will see that some markets are for products that are exchanged only within the community of interest, while others involve trade with other people outside the community. These interactions determine the prices we observe and quantities produced or consumed.

In later chapters of this book we will look beyond price and quantity to address other kinds of market outcomes and different market structures. For example, in the next chapter we will address inequity and social welfare, using the example of a market composed of distinct individuals. Then Chapter 5 addresses market power, and the ways in which a monopoly business might influence outcomes. To start, we use the benchmark case of a perfectly competitive market in which there is a very large number of similar buyers and sellers as described below.

Interaction in Markets Between Local Producers, Local Consumers and Trade with Others

Market models use supply and demand curves to explain and predict changes in price and quantity. Each curve traces all possible points that producers and consumers might have chosen, so only the *intersection of two curves* is a point that could be sustained by interaction between producers, consumers and other people. Those intersections are a potential *market equilibrium* that might be observed, if it persists long enough to be measured before the next shift in supply or demand leads to a different equilibrium.

Readers of this book can use market models directly, just by following the definition of each line to each point of intersection. Geometry will lead us to the logical outcome of each scenario. But it is easy to misinterpret one or more elements of the diagrams, and thereby draw incorrect conclusions. Building your own understanding of the diagrams, by sketching them yourself and explaining them in your own words, is the only way to be sure that you have used each element as intended. Practicing economists sketch these diagrams repeatedly, over and over again, with slight variations to see how the elements interact and build intuition about the logic.

For some readers, many or all of the logical steps using each diagram will seem familiar, and the results will be intuitively plausible. Some of the most valuable moments, however, will be when a sequence of plausible steps leads to an unexpected conclusion, with results that seem completely implausible. That's helpful when it prompts readers to retrace their steps, which might reveal an error and improve understanding of how economic models work. But the best moments of all are when retracing each step confirms that the story is correct, and leads to a new understanding of the world itself. Readers might go from bored to puzzled, or from 'duh' to 'huh?', with the goal being to reach those elusive 'aha!' moments of unexpected insight.

If you have not yet encountered a surprising aspect of economics, you are likely to find one by working through the logic of market interactions shown in Fig. 3.7.

The three market diagrams in Fig. 3.7 are drawn around real-life examples with which many students might be familiar. All three diagrams refer to the entire population of Massachusetts in a recent year. In the left panel is the state's market for hot pizza, sold in every community around the state in restaurants or for home delivery. In the middle is the market for cranberries, a fruit grown for centuries in coastal wetlands, and on the right is the market for apples, a fruit that grows in many temperate environments. To be clear that we are talking about real things consumed by actual people, the units of measure shown are slices of pizza, pounds (lbs) of cranberries and bushels (bu) of apples, and it turns out that Massachusetts has about 7 million people, served by about 2000 registered pizzerias, about 375 cranberry growers and roughly 400 apple growers. The state's demand and supply curves could be estimated empirically, but for this textbook we focus on qualitative insights about how people would respond to change.

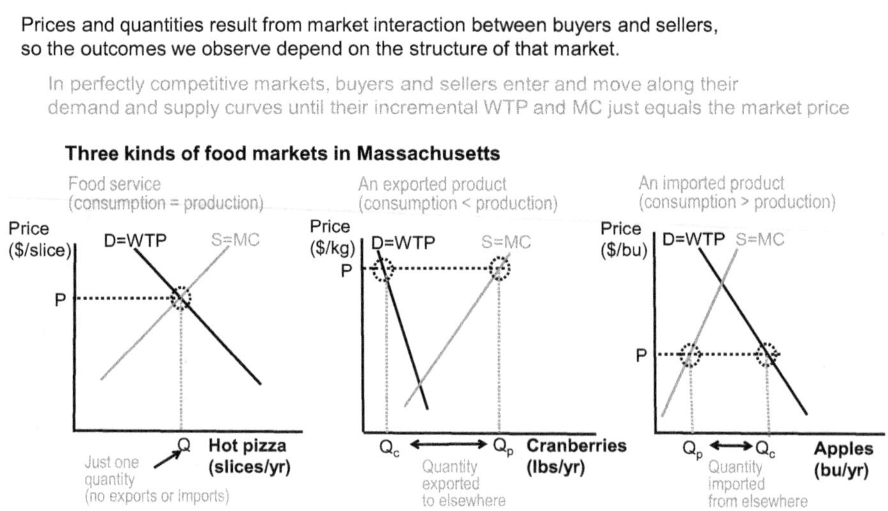

Fig. 3.7 Interactions between supply, demand and trade

Starting with the supply of pizza, cranberries and apples, every potential seller will produce along their own production possibilities, building new facilities and hiring the staff needed to sell each quantity. For pizza the first units along the state's supply curve might be sold from low-rent storefronts with low-cost ingredients by low-wage workers, and building more pizzerias would require bidding for additional space and workers with other options. The pizza supply curve might actually be horizontal if the pizza sector has scale economies that reach lower or constant costs at greater quantities sold, but at some point expansion would encounter diminishing returns and the supply curve would slope up. A similar logic applies to the supply curve for cranberries, which are grown on suitable wetlands in coastal areas that might also be used for recreation and other purposes, as well as the supply curve for apples that are grown in orchards all around the state. All of the supply curves could be horizontal or upward sloping, and are drawn as straight lines for simplicity.

Switching to the demand for pizza, cranberries and apples, we can trace downward sloping demand curves for each food as consumers with the greatest willingness and ability to pay for the items buy the first units, and successive consumers enter to buy each additional quantity if sold at a lower price. We could have a very enjoyable discussion of what determines those quantities consumed at each price, including product quality and convenience as well as cultural and historical factors, healthiness and so forth, but the demand curves would still almost always slope down, drawn straight for simplicity.

Turning to the predicted outcome for each product, the definition of a perfectly competitive equilibrium is the price and quantity that follows if many buyers and sellers can easily find each other and exchange a known product of uniform quality. Perfect competition implies that producers move along their supply curve until they run out of willing buyers, and consumers move along their demand curve until they run out of willing sellers.

The model's prediction about pizza is our first main result. It may seem intuitively plausible that supply equals demand, but this diagram is supposed to illustrate all production and consumption for the entire state, so that the entire state's lowest willingness to pay for one additional unit just equals the entire state's highest marginal cost of production. In fact Massachusetts extends almost 190 miles in length, and the feasible distance for pizza delivery or pickup might be up to 5 or 10 miles, so there cannot be competition between all producers for delivery to all consumers. It would be more realistic to draw separate supply and demand curves for each place, leading to the possibility that prices differ by location. There might also be separate supply and demand curves for pizza of different qualities, and many other refinements.

The model's prediction about cranberries is also surprising. One might think that supply equals demand, but Massachusetts ships most of its production out of state. Generic processed cranberries can readily be put on a truck or train and shipped thousands of miles at very low transport costs, and products from each region are of similar quality, so there is in effect a national market and a single U.S. price for that product at any one time. Massachusetts producers can sell to any buyer so move along their supply curve up to that price paid for shipments out of state, and Massachusetts consumers find nothing to buy below that price, so the horizontal price line from the U.S. as a whole dictates both production and consumption. Within Massachusetts, demand and supply do not meet, and local prices come from the supply-demand balance in the entire U.S.

The model's predictions about apples is the mirror image of cranberries. While Massachusetts was once an exporter of apples to other states, other regions of U.S. now produce much larger volumes at prevailing prices, and Massachusetts is a net importer. Again, the result of relatively low shipping costs is that local prices come from the balance of supply and demand to and from all other locations. Consumption in Massachusetts can extend along its demand curve all the way down to that price, while production in Massachusetts extends along its supply curve only up to that cost. In fact a few additional apples may be sold at a premium for being locally grown, but that would be drawn as separate markets for apples of different types.

Despite the limitations of these three simple models, the central insight of Fig. 3.7 is that the perfectly competitive benchmark provides a useful starting point, revealing that only local services such as pizza delivery in each town have markets where local production equals local consumption. For products that can transported at low cost relative to product value, prices are set over the whole market area such as the entire U.S., and each community is likely to be either exporting or importing to other regions.

The purpose of each market diagram is to provide qualitative insights that explain and predict responses to change. It is helpful to draw a separate set of diagrams for service such as hot pizza in each neighborhood where supply equals demand, in contrast to products such as cranberries or apples that can be traded with people elsewhere. We start with the nontraded services for which each location is said to be in ***autarky***, from the Greek word for self-sufficiency. In this context, autarky and self-sufficiency refer only to the absence of trade in this specific product, and does not imply autonomy or self-reliance in general. As we will see, being self-sufficient in one thing may come at a cost in terms of vulnerability and limited access to other things, so can reduce a community's degree of overall autonomy and self-reliance. That question is addressed in the next chapter when we address social welfare. For now we focus on how price and quantity respond to change as shown in Fig. 3.8.

The left side of Fig. 3.8 reveals how shifts in supply trace out the market's demand curve, while the right side shows how shifts in demand trace out the market's supply curve. This figure also introduces a new aspect of our analytical diagrams, which is to use the prime (') and double-prime (") symbols to denote different scenarios. On the left panel drawing shifts in supply, the initial price and quantity observed in this market are P and Q at supply curve S, and then when supply improves the new outcome is P' and Q' at S', or when supply worsens the outcome becomes P" and Q" and S". A similar trio of scenarios is shown in the right panel, with the initial price and quantity, then a prime and a double-prime.

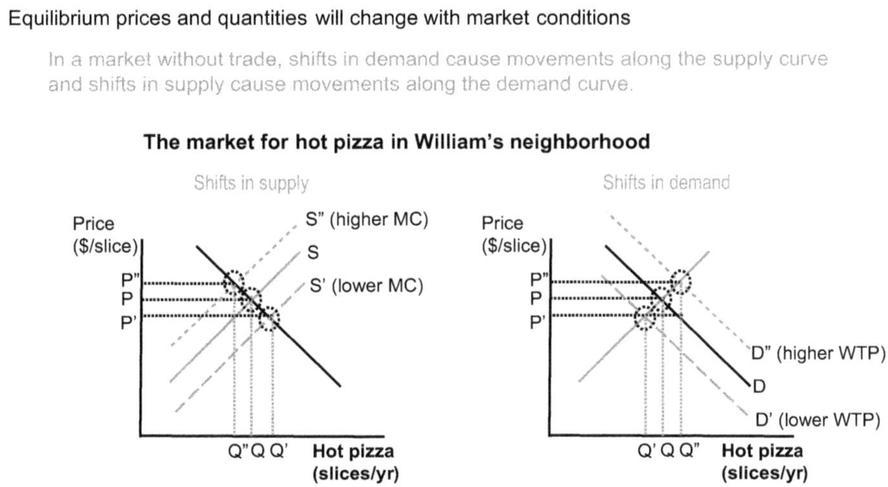

Fig. 3.8 Supply and demand shifts in a market without trade

In each case, only one of the curves shifts and the other doesn't. Movements along the curve that stays in place are ***endogenous*** changes generated inside the model, while shifts in the other curve are ***exogenous*** events arising from other variables. Example scenarios might be a supply-enhancing innovation that causes the shift from S to S', or damage to the environment that shifts supply to S", each of which is drawn as an exogenous shock which the model predicts would cause endogenous demand response through consumers' movement along the demand curve.

Behavioral responses within the simplified model of Fig. 3.8 are all drawn as straight lines with similar slopes for visual clarity, but supply may in fact be quite horizontal due to expansion at roughly constant costs, while demand may be quite steep due to consumer preferences. The role of differences in slope will be addressed in the following section, where slope is measured as the elasticities of supply and demand.

For market diagrams about products in communities that are traded with people elsewhere, shifts in local supply and demand affect only local production and consumption. Price is set in the larger market outside of any given community. With trade, local production does not equal local consumption but the difference is the quantity traded and not a 'surplus' or 'shortage'. Market structure depends not just on characteristics of the item but also the community whose producers and consumers are shown in the diagram. For example, Massachusetts is an importer of apples from elsewhere, but the U.S. as a whole is an exporter of apples to other countries. Whether importing or exporting, trade ensures that shifts in demand and supply affect only one side of the market, because price is set elsewhere as shown in Figs. 3.9 and 3.10.

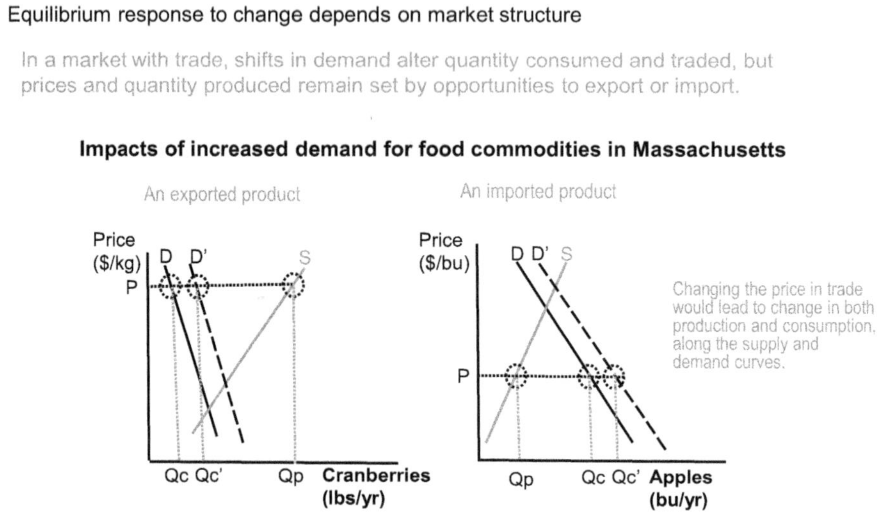

Fig. 3.9 Response to shifts in demand for products that are traded with others

The consequences of shifts in demand for a traded product are shown in Fig. 3.9. In these markets, when foreign buyers offer higher prices than our community would have in self-sufficiency, our sellers choose to export (as shown for cranberries on the left panels), or when foreign sellers offer lower prices, so our buyers choose to import (as shown for apples on the right panels). In either case, shifts in demand affect only consumption and the quantity traded, which adjusts to the price set in the rest of the world.

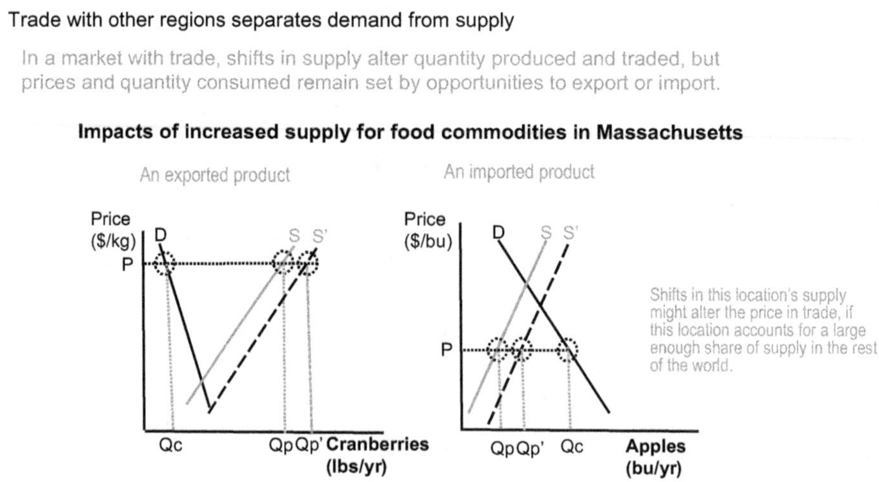

Fig. 3.10 Response to shifts in supply for products that are traded with others

Shifts in demand shown in Fig. 3.9 are mirrored by shifts in supply shown in Fig. 3.10, where exogenous shocks to production conditions affect only quantities grown, and quantities traded adjust to prices set by the rest of the world. In each of these cases, researchers might ask whether the shift in demand or supply shown in each diagram is large enough to affect prices in the entire market elsewhere. That depends on relative sizes of regions where the change occurs, and the elasticities of market response as discussed in the following section.

3.1.3 Conclusion

Market diagrams explain observed outcomes using lines that show quantities chosen at each price, or equivalently the price at which each quantity would be chosen. Each diagram shows production, consumption and all transactions in a given community for a specified product over some period of time. Outcomes that could persist long enough to be observed are at the intersection of two lines, because that is the point where all transactions that people would have chosen already occurred. In each diagram, the points of intersection between two lines are called an ***equilibrium*** because they result from a balance of forces. Different outcomes might be better, at least for some people, but further transactions towards a different point would not be chosen unless circumstances change.

For restaurant food and local services such as hot pizza, each unit is consumed near the place and time of production, so market diagrams explain outcomes as the intersection of supply and demand in each neighborhood. For food products like cranberries or apples that can readily be shipped by truck, train or boat, the cost of transportation and storage is typically low enough that prices are set by supply and demand over large areas. Since people in each community can trade with people elsewhere, market outcomes are where supply and demand meet the price observed for trade with others, and each community's quantity produced differs from its quantity consumed.

Any supply, demand and trade diagram can provide useful insights only to the degree that it reflects the actual decision-making of people in each community. The initial benchmark model shown in this chapter would arise in perfectly competitive situations, with no obstacles to transactions between many buyers and many sellers for a uniform product. Later chapters will introduce models for situations with a variety of market failures and imperfect competition. Economics consists of choosing among models and tailoring them to fit the analyst's subject-matter knowledge, including magnitudes of response as described in the following section.

3.2 Market Elasticities: Measuring How People Respond to Change

3.2.1 Motivation and Guiding Questions

The previous section showed how to construct analytical diagrams for perfectly competitive markets in any given situation. Those were purely qualitative models, designed to show causal mechanisms behind observed outcomes, but economists often need to estimate quantitative magnitudes of likely response to a change in circumstances. When shifts in supply, demand or trade opportunities occur, how much change will we see in prices and quantities? When governments introduce taxes or regulations, how much change will we see in production and consumption?

Market diagrams can be drawn for transactions using many different units of measure, such as servings per day or tons per year. Prices may be measured in any currency, such as pesos or dollars whose value differs at each place and time. Quantifying how much change to expect calls for subject-matter knowledge, including familiarity with many kinds of data about the factors that influence behavior. To compare findings across settings, it is very helpful to report results as *elasticities* of change in quantity.

Elasticities of response are the percent change in quantity observed due to a one percent change in something else. Discussing change in terms of elasticity is helpful not only to measure and compare magnitudes of change, but also to make qualitative predictions such as whether an intervention will have any effect at all on buyers or sellers.

So far, we have seen how individual choices lead to societal outcomes within a market. Introducing elasticities of response allows us to begin discussion of other factors that affect outcomes, including government interventions or environmental, technological and other shifts. Later chapters will show data visualizations of how much change has actually occurred and the magnitude of differences observed in populations around the world.

By the end of this section, you will be able to:

1. Describe the relationship between price elasticity and supply or demand curves, and between income elasticity and Engel curves;
2. Use supply and demand diagrams, with and without trade, to show how price elasticities shape the impact of taxes and regulations on producers and consumers;
3. Describe the factors influencing magnitude of price and income elasticities; and
4. Describe and use diagrams to show how government trade policies differ from domestic interventions in their effects on producers and consumers.

3.2.2 Analytical Tools

Elasticities are needed to collect and compare results of observed changes for different things in different places, translating the results of our analytical diagrams into magnitudes of response in quantities and prices. Changes in anything can be reported in percentage terms.

In economics, the term 'elasticity' always refers to the percentage change in quantity that would follow from each percentage change in something else. *Price elasticities* are a percent change in quantity for each percent change in price and would be computed for both supply and demand. A product's *price elasticity of supply* is always positive (or more precisely it is never negative, because supply curves never slope down), and its *price elasticity of demand* is almost always negative (and would be positive only for Giffen goods and Veblen goods discussed in the previous section).

For demand we can also calculate *income elasticities,* which are the percent change in quantity consumed for each percent change in personal or household income of a population. A product's income *elasticity of demand* is usually positive but can be negative for inferior goods consumed more at lower incomes. Demand and supply curves can shift due to prices of other things, so economists also refer to the *cross-price elasticity* for consumption or production of something with respect to the price of something else. When two products are *complements* typically consumed together, such as tomato sauce and pasta, a rise in the price of tomato sauce might cause a decline in quantity sold of pasta, meaning a negative cross-price elasticity of demand. Most foods are substitutes for each other, leading to positive cross-price demand elasticities.

Elasticities are a ratio between two percentages, providing a unit-free measure that can be measured and compared across different settings. In some situations, analysts use a *semi-elasticity,* which is the percent change in quantity associated with a specific increment of change in something else. For example, to study soft drink demand, we might report the *elasticity* of demand for each one percent change in income or price, but the *semi-elasticity* of demand for each one degree change in temperature.

Using elasticities helps build intuition in applying economic principles to any given situation, by converting the bewildering array of different units into a ratio of percentage changes. Whether elasticities are positive or negative, and greater or less than one, corresponds to qualitative differences in the direction of change for variables of interest that we can discuss verbally and show graphically, even without numerical data.

To see how and why to convert natural units such as pesos and kilograms into elasticities, we start with the mathematical notation that underlies our diagrams. That math could also be used to see how supply and demand elasticities are all interconnected, using algebra in a multivariate system of equations that reflects the world's multidimensional food system. Readers can also skip the math and go directly to using elasticities for qualitative analysis of how people respond to change.

Mathematical Notation and the Definition of Elasticities

In Chapter 2, we showed individual choices along lines and curves whose slopes are always ($\frac{Rise}{Run}$). Price lines have a constant slope, showing the relative cost of one more unit along the X axis ($\frac{-Px}{Py}$), while curves have varying slopes showing the quantity of things along the Y axis given up for each increment along the X axis ($\frac{\Delta Qy}{\Delta Qx}$). Individual-choice diagrams explain each point as having tangency between their lines and curves, meaning that $\frac{-Px}{Py} = \frac{\Delta Qy}{\Delta Qx}$. The slope of a curve on any market diagram, ($\frac{\Delta P}{\Delta Q}$), might vary at different points (P, Q) and it has very awkward units of measure as explained below. We therefore convert change along each curve to unit-free elasticities, such as the percent change in quantity ($\frac{\Delta Q}{Q}$) for each percent change in price ($\frac{\Delta P}{P}$), expressed as a ratio: ($\frac{\Delta Q}{Q}$)/($\frac{\Delta P}{P}$).

Why do we need all that notation? To understand any computation we can do *analysis of units*, in which a variable's units of measure are treated as if it were itself a number. For example, the price of apples might be measured as dollars per pound ($\frac{\$}{lb}$), and its quantity might be measured in tons per year ($\frac{mt}{yr}$). The slope of its supply or demand curve, ($\frac{\Delta P}{\Delta Q}$), would then be measured in terms that make no sense ($\frac{\$/lb}{mt/yr}$). This unit conversion reveals that the slopes of our diagrams are not interpretable in themselves, but must be converted to unit-free percentage terms:

$$\varepsilon = \frac{percent\ change\ in\ quantity}{percent\ change\ in\ price} = \frac{\Delta Q/Q}{\Delta P/P} = \frac{\Delta Q}{\Delta P} \cdot \frac{P}{Q}. \tag{3.1}$$

Writing the definition of elasticity in mathematical terms confirms that elasticities are related to run-over-rise ($\frac{\Delta Q}{\Delta P}$) which is the inverse of slope, multiplied by ratio of price to quantity ($\frac{P}{Q}$).

Elasticities Summarize Complex Interactions in Production and Consumption

Readers can skip over our use of mathematical notation, but seeing it can help everyone recognize that each number is also a variable, that there can be many variables in a model, and that each model specifies just one of the many possible relationships between variables. Elasticities are a two-dimensional relationship within a larger theory of change, summarizing behavioral responses that reflect complex interactions in production and consumption.

The principles of economics, presented graphically and verbally in this or other introductory textbooks, are all derived from more complex models that have evolved over a century of experimentation and practical experience. Each two-dimensional diagram and its resulting elasticities summarize systems of simultaneous equations. For production, the three kinds of curve (PPF, IRC and ISC) represent all kinds of *production functions* between all inputs and all outputs, from which observed choices come from *profit functions* that link quantities and prices. Similarly for consumption, the indifference curves and budget lines represent *demand systems* of interaction between all requisites of wellbeing such as food, housing, education and so forth.

Supply or demand curves and their elasticities are bivariate summaries of deeper multivariate models that can and should consider variation over time, space and other dimensions. Real-life work by professional economists includes the use of two-dimensional models like our diagrams, or multivariate versions of those models that are written in algebraic notation and solved using calculus or other techniques to analyze all possible real numbers. Modern ways of formulating and estimating these models were advanced in the 1980s and 1990s by Angus Deaton, the use of which led to his being awarded the economics Nobel Prize in 2015. The statistical toolkit used to test and estimate economic relationships, known as econometrics, generates estimated elasticities often used in computational models for projections and policy simulations.

In each case, the practical work of economists begins with data in natural units and converts relationships into elasticities for ease of communication. Elasticities show the connection between two variables of a model, but the elasticity itself depends on other factors and could vary when other things change. For food systems one of the most important results of multidimensional models is that elasticities depend on the passage of time. A common finding, named *Le Chatelier's principle* after the nineteenth-century scientist who found a similar phenomenon in chemistry, is that quantity change in response to a given shock is often small at first and then rises as more adjustments occur.

Le Chatelier's principle arises whenever responses happen slowly, and is extremely important for food policies such as soda taxes and agricultural policies such as crop insurance. In many situations, quantity consumed or produced will respond very little at first, but the long-run effect is large. Le Chatelier's principle can be seen in individuals, if each person responds gradually, and is particularly common for populations where each person responds at a different time. For example soda taxes might have zero effect on some people whose habits are formed, while causing others to cut back as they gradually discover alternatives, and leading future cohorts of people to acquire different habits as they grow through childhood and adolescence. Similarly, crop insurance might lead to no change in just one year followed by experimentation and expansion of riskier activities that are protected by insurance in future years.

Elasticities do not always increase over time, because not all adjustments are costly and slow. In the food system there are often big but temporary jumps in quantity or price that later revert to long-term trends. We often see spikes or dips in quantities of specific things when a news story, price fluctuation, income shock or product introduction lead people to try something new, but then gradually return to their long-term trajectory. For storable products, price elasticities are heavily influenced by stockholding. In normal times inventories may be adequate to absorb shocks, but when inventories are low or shocks are high we see price spikes as consumers, producers, distributors and traders hold on to supplies or build up stocks which they later sell, driving prices back down to long-term levels.

Each elasticity summarizes just one two-dimensional relationship in a dynamic, multidimensional world. Describing relationships in elasticity terms is extremely useful, giving us a clear way to compare responsiveness of quantity to price, income or other factors, but the numerical value of each elasticity is not necessarily fixed. Indeed, an important policy priority may be to increase price elasticities, and thereby make the food system more flexible and resilient.

Price Elasticity and Behavioral Responses Along Supply and Demand Curves

We can see the range of price elasticities graphically and compare them to the slopes of supply and demand in Fig. 3.11.

Figure 3.11 shows three curves for supply and for demand, illustrating how quantity can be more or less responsive to changes in price. The right side of the figure also lists how elasticities are classified for qualitative analysis. Less response to price means a larger slope and steeper curve, with an elasticity closer to zero.

When describing different levels of elasticity for alternative products in various scenarios, we compare elasticities to each other and also focus on whether the elasticity is above or below zero (0) and one (1). The terms used to compare elasticities describe use their magnitude in absolute value, denoted $|\varepsilon|$. A *unit-elastic* curve has $|\varepsilon| = 1$, so the percentage changes in quantity and price are equal. With unit-elastic demand, they offset each other and total consumer spending on that product is fixed. For example, a 5% price rise might lead to a 5% quantity decline, and no change in spending. More commonly, we

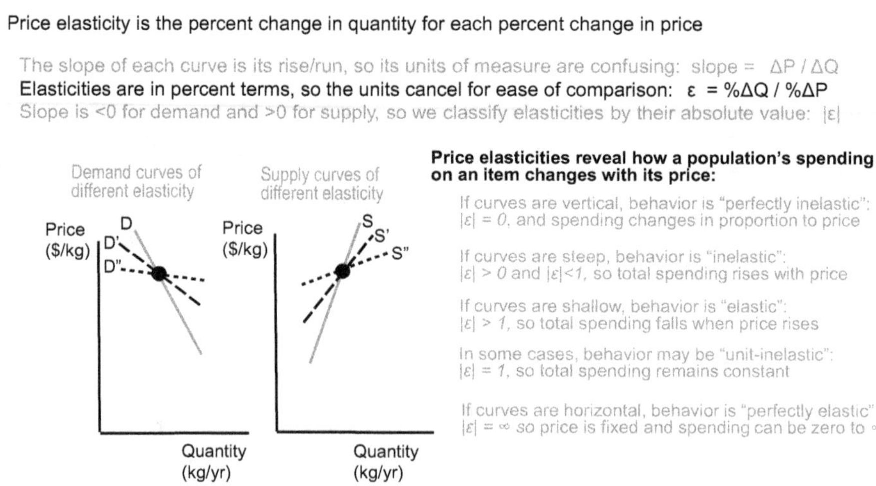

Fig. 3.11 Definition and terminology for price elasticities of demand and supply

are interested in whether a curve is relatively steep and *inelastic*, so that $|\varepsilon| < 1$, or relatively flat and *elastic*, meaning that $|\varepsilon| > 1$. If the curve is *perfectly inelastic* it would be vertical so $|\varepsilon| = 0$ and quantity remains unchanged when price changes. A curve could also be *perfectly elastic* and horizontal so $|\varepsilon|$ is infinitely large and price remains unchanged even if quantity changes.

The three scenarios in Fig. 3.11 could show adjustment over time, as short-, medium- and long-run demand and supply curves for products such as eggs or liquid milk. Quantities adjust slowly because of how these products are produced and consumed, and also because they are difficult to transport and store. At any given place, a permanent but one-time expansion in supply would cause movement down the demand curve. In the short run, within one or two months, we might see a big price decline along a steep, inelastic demand curve like D. But then in the medium run after one or two years we expect less price change along D', and in the long run almost all of the shock might be absorbed by increased quantity along D'. Similarly for supply, if there were a permanent but one-time rise in demand, for example building a cake factory that uses a fixed quantity of milk and eggs each month, the initial price change would be large along S, but as farmers respond the price change would be smaller along S' and then S".

The three different levels of price elasticity could also correspond to the product category, for example whether the shock affects all dairy products, all kinds of cheese, or just cheddar. For demand, a broader category typically has larger income effects on each consumers' budget lines and less substitution along indifference curves, leading to differences in the slope of their demand curve. For supply, broader categories generally have fewer substitution possibilities along the producer's PPF and IRC, and hence more inelastic supply curves. Cheddar is a narrow category with a small share of all spending and close substitutes among other cheeses, so consumers and producers might quickly adjust quantity in response to a shock. In contrast, all dairy is a broad category with larger income effects and fewer substitution possibilities, so quantity would change less quickly and the shock would be absorbed by prices.

The range of elasticities that might be observed in any given situation reveals the need for domain experts with local knowledge about the product and market situation being analyzed. Elasticities are not a fixed characteristic of things, but a behavioral response in each community of interest. To offer just one more example, a population of office workers who receive lunch vouchers worth $10 per day and usually spend that mostly at restaurants near the office would have a close to unit-elastic price elasticity of demand for restaurant lunches, with very price-inelastic demand for all beverages if they usually want one drink with their meal, but highly price-elastic demand for any specific food or beverage as they switch between items on the menu. Those elasticities might not have previously been measured in any empirical study, but a domain expert or qualitative researcher might know what to expect, using the concept of elasticity to explain and predict change.

Elasticity is important for economics because it gives us useful terminology with which to discuss the behavior of individuals and populations, and opportunities to measure whether an external shock is absorbed by change in quantities, prices or some of both. Elasticities are also useful to discuss and measure quantity change in response to other factors, especially income.

Income Elasticity, Engel's Law and Bennett's Law

Income drives food choice because it sets the level of each consumer's budget constraint, and incomes of other people influence the food environment around us. Like price response, each person or population's ***income elasticity of demand*** is context-dependent, so the concept offers an extremely useful way of discussing and measuring behavioral responses. The relevant diagrams for individual behavior are presented in Chapter 2, for example Fig. 2.6 that shows how people with different preferences would have different expansion paths of increased consumption for each thing of interest as their income rises. On a market diagram, income changes would be shown as a shift in the demand curve. In each case, the concept of income elasticity converts confusingly jumbled units of measurement into proportional terms, as the percentage change in quantity consumed for each one percent change of income as shown in Fig. 3.12.

Income elasticities, denoted *e,* are classified and discussed in the same way as price elasticities that are denoted ε. In both cases, we can focus on absolute value which is ***inelastic*** when close to zero and ***perfectly inelastic*** when exactly zero. Income elasticity can never be perfectly elastic because quantities consumed cannot be infinitely large, but income elasticities vary widely and are mostly but not always positive. Important thresholds include $e = 1$ and $e = 0$, leading to specific terms used only for income elasticity.

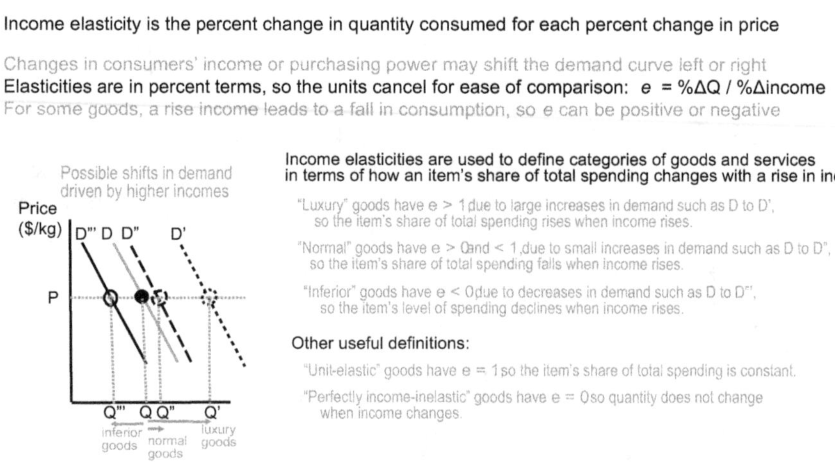

Fig. 3.12 Definition and terminology for income elasticities of demand

Income elasticity is 'normal' when between zero and one ($0 < e < 1$), meaning that increased income causes a less than proportional increase in quantity consumed. Most goods are almost always normal in this sense, including food. For normal goods, higher incomes lead to a higher level of consumption but a smaller share of total spending, because some of that higher income is spent on other things instead. Those 'luxury' goods have an income elasticity above one ($e > 1$), so that higher-income people spend a larger fraction of their income on luxuries. At the other extreme, some goods for some people are 'inferior', meaning a negative income elasticity ($e < 0$) as higher-income people reduce the quantity consumed.

Figure 3.12 shows how a higher income might shift demand differently for different people, or for different products, causing them to be classified as a normal, luxury or inferior good. For example, the diagram might show how demand shifts in response to a 10% higher income, with no change in price because supply is infinitely elastic, due to ease of expanding production or transport from elsewhere. Some things might be luxuries, so the demand shift to D' moves to quantity Q' more than 10% higher, while most are normal so demand at D' raises quantity Q' less than 10%, and some things are inferior so demand at D'' lowers quantity to Q''.

Whether a product is inferior, normal or a luxury good depends on its context. For many readers of this book, a familiar food that would be classified as inferior in income elasticity is packets of instant noodles. These are commonly consumed as a backstop or fallback meal, so higher incomes lead to lower consumption. But in other settings those same instant noodles might be a normal or even a luxury good, for which higher incomes lead to more consumption or even a larger share of income, because the alternatives are less preferred.

The two main observations about income elasticities of food are known as *Engel's Law* and *Bennett's Law*. Ernst Engel came first, writing in German in 1857 that '**the poorer a family, the greater is the share of their total expenditure spent on food**', which he illustrated with data from two different surveys of wage-earning households published in French by others two years earlier. Engel's law refers to the income elasticity of demand for everything, adding up every type of food or beverage, so that a 10% difference in income causes a less than 10% difference in food spending.

Engel's law is primarily about the quality of each family's diet, observing that the switch to or from more expensive items like meat, fish and milk was less than proportional to income. The total quantity of food was already known to vary in a narrow range. Long before in 1776, Adam Smith had written in *The Wealth of Nations* that 'the rich man consumes no more food than his poor neighbour', because both are 'limited by the narrow capacity of the human stomach'. Adam Smith was referring to quantity in the sense of weight or volume, and shortly thereafter, in the 1780s, Antoine Lavoisier discovered dietary energy could be measured in units of heat. All three ways of measuring quantity (weight, volume or calories) vary with income much less than variation in quality, which was originally measured just as cost per day.

Bennett's law came later, first observed by Merrill K. Bennett in 1941 from international data compiled during World War II about total quantities of food available in each country. Bennett added up all calories estimated to have been consumed from all foods and from cereal grains like rice or wheat together with starchy roots like potatoes and cassava. Bennett's estimates suggested that, as of 1935, about half of the world's population had 80–90% of their calories from the cereals-potato group, while the richest tenth of the world population had only 30–40% of their calories from it. Bennett's observation concerned just cereal grains plus starchy roots, to which modern observers would add plantain bananas in a category called starchy staples. In other words, Bennett's law is that **the poorer a country, the greater is its share of total calories from starchy staples**.

Bennett was writing soon after the discovery of essential nutrients and wrote that 'the function of the cereal-potato group of foodstuffs in human diets is mainly to provide energy for the body', while other foods were needed to provide protection from disease 'in the form of protein, vitamins, and minerals'. That observation led Bennett to write that 'ratios of cereal-potato calories to total food calories may be regarded as an indicator of relative qualitative adequacy'. Bennett also noted that cereals and potatoes were typically the least expensive source of calories at that time, so shifting to other sources represented a shift to more expensive diets.

Since Bennett's 1941 study many others have investigated how shifts in spending alter diet quality, and also followed up on Bennett's observation that starchy staples differ in taste and ease of preparation. For example, Bennett noted that some people 'regard rice so highly - so greatly enjoy eating it' that the share of rice in their diet does not decline as income rises. Recent studies have also revisited Bennett's observation about price per calorie, as the cost of vegetable oils and raw sugar have declined to be about the same as the cheapest starchy staples, and the least expensive calories are now from mixtures of starchy staples with oil and sugar.

Ongoing studies related to Engel's law focus on all the changes in food spending associated with income, and new work related to Bennett's law focuses on calorie shares from different kinds of food. Modern terminology refers to these patterns as *dietary transition*, as higher incomes and associated trends bring different dietary patterns as discussed with data visualizations in Chapter 10. To facilitate that and other discussion of actual data on changes over time and differences among populations, it is helpful to see a schematic illustration of how quantities consumed might vary with income across a wide range of conditions.

The lines shown in Fig. 3.13 trace out two possible expansion paths of spending on each type of food, in response to changes in income. The food categories for which spending is shown on the vertical axis could be defined broadly (such as all kinds of fish) or more narrowly (such as all kinds of rice).

The term 'income' along the horizontal axis refers to *full income*, meaning the person or population's income from all sources, not just labor earnings but also other sources of purchasing power such as income from assets, gifts and program benefits. Full income in this sense is difficult to measure, so in practice the horizontal axis is measured as the sum of total expenditure on all goods and services, while the vertical axis shows a subset of the total.

Figure 3.13 is not an analytical diagram like our previous figures, because each point is an observation without controlling for other factors. The analytical diagrams explained why the observed outcome was chosen instead of other options. When people experience income growth the underlying factors causing that income growth might also affect food consumption. The impact of income as such might not be causal, but the patterns of correlation are nonetheless important for understanding how food consumption varies in the population.

The two Engel curves shown in Fig. 3.13 reveal how consumption of each food category usually begins only after people reach some threshold level of full income. For people moving from A to B along curve 1 and also curve 2, consumption of each kind of food is a luxury in the sense that they take an increasing share of income, even though these things might be basic necessities from the perspective of other people. When moving from B to C, the product shown in curve 1 remains a luxury with an increasing income share, while the product shown in curve 2 has 'unit-elastic' demand with a constant share of spending, indicated by a double line that points outward at a constant slope from the origin of zero income and zero consumption. From C to D, the top Engel curve is similarly unit elastic, shown by a double line that is not parallel to the lower double line, but both expand outward at a constant rate from the origin. The Engel curves eventually turn down to become 'normal' goods

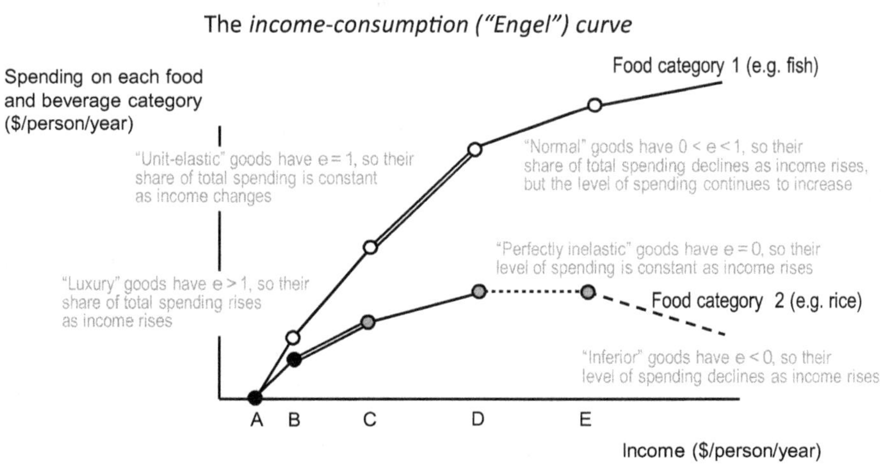

Fig. 3.13 Visualization of all possible income elasticities along two Engel curves

for which spending rises with a declining income share, and the lower curve shows a good for which demand growth with rising income slows to zero, so the Engel curve is 'perfectly inelastic' and turns negative for an 'inferior' good.

Engel curves like Fig. 3.13 can be drawn with actual data from cross-sectional surveys at one point in time to capture income differences, or a series of observations for the same population year after year to capture income changes over time. Higher or rising income is both cause and consequence of structural changes in society ranging from time use and paid employment to infrastructure and urbanization. Food technology also plays a big role, for example adopting an electric rice cooker to prepare rice unattended or switching from raw to parboiled rice for faster cooking time at home. For all these reasons, observed Engel curves and dietary transitions can be seen as a function of income as shown in Fig. 3.13 but they also trace the passage of time in terms of technological innovation, cultural shifts and many other factors that are correlated with each other over time and space.

Engel's original observation in 1857 was that richer families spend a smaller share of their total expenditure on all foods and beverages, but their total spending of food and beverages continues to rise as they get richer. Engel's law continues to hold for almost all populations today, but only if we include spending on restaurants and other food away from home, food delivery, the cost of kitchens and even private chefs for the very wealthy. Much of the variation in spending we observe is for processing, packaging, distribution and other food-related services, even with the same food ingredients. As we will see in later chapters, the dietary transition suggested by Engel's law is largely about changes in what we will call *value added*, which is the cost of facilities, labor and other inputs used to transform ingredients before final consumption, along each *value chain* which is the sequence of steps by which farm products are transformed, transported and ultimately delivered to the consumer.

Bennett's law refers to the share of calories obtained from starchy staples, noting that it is usually smaller at higher incomes. To show that we would need to redraw Fig. 3.13 for its vertical axis to show the percent of all calories derived from cereal grains, potatoes or other starchy plant roots such as plantain bananas. Bennett's original observation was a very sharp decline for his cereal-potato grouping from 80–90% on the left to 30–40% on the right, using national averages observed in 1935. A downward slope of that type would still hold for most populations today, but as Bennett noted in 1941, some forms of starchy staples are very attractive especially in processed, precooked and packaged form.

Income elasticities observed historically and today reveal how only some of the rise in food spending involves changing from the least expensive ingredient categories, which are now cereal grains, vegetable oils and sugar, to more expensive food groups such as meat and fish, dairy and eggs, or vegetables and fruits. When we observe Engel's law today, some of the change is towards more expensive ingredients within food groups, such as a shift from vegetable oil to olive oil, or from sardines and other small fish to large fish consumed without bones, but most of the shift concerns how those foods are processed, packaged and distributed. Elasticities of demand for both raw ingredients and also food transformation and meal preparation have important effects on both health and the environment, and relate closely to the work of food businesses along each value chain towards final consumption as discussed in Section 11.2.

Elasticities Determine the Impact of Intervention on Market Outcomes

Economists use elasticities not just to describe observed changes, but because elasticities can tell us how people will respond to interventions. Later in this book we will look more deeply into the interventions themselves, including the very wide range of policies and programs adopted by governments and other institutions. We will describe the economic principles that help explain why the policies and programs we observe are adopted, what factors might help explain changes in those policies and programs, and how policy analysts can help decision-makers improve outcomes.

In this section we describe how market outcomes are altered by interventions, using elasticities to show how people adjust and respond to policy change. Even without numerical estimates of each elasticity, we can use the concept to guide our qualitative understanding of policy impacts, as illustrated for taxes and government restrictions starting with Fig. 3.14.

Taxes and licenses of the type shown in Fig. 3.14 are some of the oldest, most widely used and important interventions in the food system. Taxes and licenses are used by national governments, local jurisdictions and even non-governmental organizations to influence outcomes in ways that are driven by elasticities in predictable but often surprising ways.

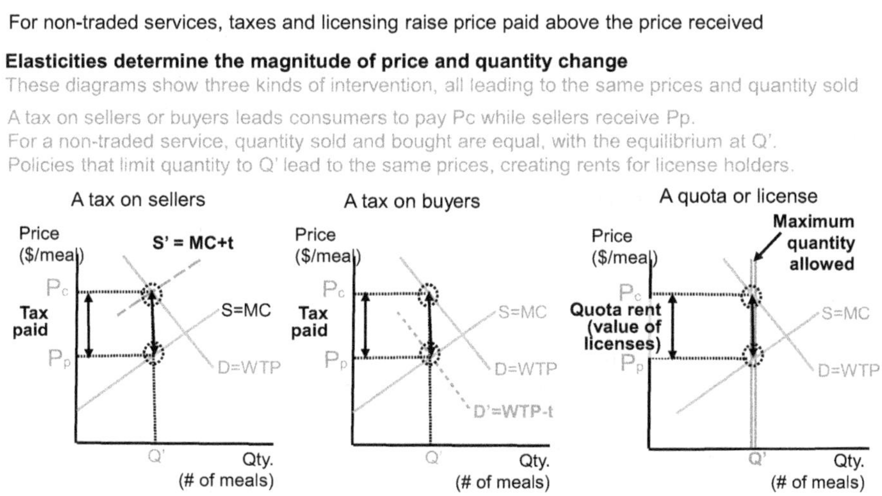

Fig. 3.14 Elasticities describe response to policy change

The context for intervention shown in Fig. 3.14 is a market for goods and services that are not traded with people outside the community shown. For example, these diagrams could show taxes or licensing of bars and restaurants in a city or state, as well as products like liquid milk or fresh eggs that are difficult to transport long distances or store over time. Where Amelia lived in Kinshasa, people would carry 10 or more cardboard cartons that held 30 eggs each on their heads for transport which took serious skill. Later we will see how the possibility of trade with other people alters the effect of a policy. As in all our market diagrams, the supply curves show production by people in a given community of interest, for example all of the restaurant operators in your town; the demand curves show consumption by all the people in your town, for example all restaurant customers in your town.

In the left panel we see the example of a tax paid by sellers. For these diagrams, a tax is a payment to the government per unit sold. That tax, labeled t, must be added by each producer to their marginal cost of production before each sale which creates the new market supply, S' = MC + t. Consumers can no longer buy at the old supply curve, S = MC, but must move along their demand curve to where D meets S' which is Q', at which point consumers are paying P_c of which producers receive P_p.

In the middle diagram we see a different policy, which is a tax that must be paid by buyers when they purchase each unit. That tax is the same height, again labeled t, but now it must be paid by each consumer to the government out of their willingness to pay, so the producers receive only the new market demand, D' = WTP − t. Producers can no longer sell to consumers at D but must now move along their supply curve to where S meets D' which is Q', at which point consumers are paying P_c of which producers receive P_p.

It may be surprising that two very different policies point to the same outcome. Whether governments levy the tax on producers or consumers, our analytical diagrams show peoples' own decisions about how much to produce and consume lead to a shared burden of the tax, with the same quantity sold at a lower price for sellers and a higher price for buyers. Economic principles guide us towards explanations and predictions that take account of people having learned from experience and made their own choices. We represent each person's complex circumstances using lines and curves that abstract from other factors and focus on how diversity in circumstances leads people to adjust along upward sloping supply and downward sloping demand, resulting in the outcome we see in Fig. 3.14.

The example of restaurant prices shown in Fig. 3.14 was chosen in part because it is familiar to anyone who has traveled between the U.S. and elsewhere. The middle diagram corresponds to restaurants in the U.S., where menu prices are lower than what customers ultimately pay due to taxes and tips that are added to the bill after each meal. The left panel shows restaurants in Europe and other places where menu prices include all taxes and almost all wages for the staff. Visitors to the U.S. may be confused at first, but soon learn how taxes and tips are done and take those costs into account when deciding what to buy. Likewise, travelers from the U.S. to Europe may be surprised by high menu prices, but soon learn that taxes are included and that tips are a smaller fraction of worker earnings than in the U.S., so they can take that into account in their choices.

Redrawing each diagram to tell the story of real people making choices under different conditions often leads to a sequence of discoveries. The first puzzle to solve is how the diagram actually works, and how economic principles are captured by lines and curves that point to each outcome. That takes time and is aided by a second kind of discovery which is how the diagrams relate to personal experiences and observations. The diagrams can be seen as abstract puzzles, but they represent real people, with lines and curves designed to help us take a population's various interests into account when predicting their behavior. Finally, a third discovery is how to interpret and perhaps modify the diagram for different circumstances. People learn from experience and make their own decisions, but not everyone learns the same way. For example, many Americans traveling abroad tip more than locals, because the use of tips to pay restaurant workers is such a deeply rooted practice in American culture. Different structures for our diagrams may also be needed to capture the real-life market failures discussed later in this book.

Drawing and comparing the first two panels in Fig. 3.14 uses economic principles to guide and build intuition about behavior, showing the qualitative direction in which people will move as they learn from experience. The left and central panels show how people move towards the same outcome in the two cases, whether governments impose taxes on consumers or on producers. That is surprising in part because, until we use supply and demand curves to take account of behavioral responses among diverse people, we might think of policies in terms of the stated intentions of government officials. Policy statements might say that a tax will be paid by producers as in the left panel, or by consumers as in the right panel. The stated goals and specific instruments used by policies and programs are important, but outcomes depend on how people respond.

The right side panel of the diagram shows a third and very different kind of policy, which is a license or quota restriction on the number of meals that can be served. Governments do not control meals directly, but they commonly restrict the size and number of restaurants and regulate them in other ways which limit the number of meals served. If that number is Q', restaurant operators will be unable to open beyond that number, so they move along their supply curve to rent, maintain and renovate new premises only up to there. Likewise, consumers will be unable to go beyond Q', so they will move along their demand curve only up to there. Consumers' D = WTP up to Q' is above producers' S = MC at that point, and it is restaurants who set menu prices. They will be able to charge at or near D = WTP, for premises that cost only S = MC to operate and maintain, and they will be willing to pay up to the entire difference between P_c and P_p for the license to open an additional restaurant. Those potential licensing fees are known as a *quota rent* and can be very large especially in cities that issue relatively few liquor licenses in popular neighborhoods.

The similarity and differences between licenses on the right and taxes at left and center can be investigated at length using Fig. 3.14 and a reader's contextual knowledge of different market environments. Some readers will have worked or managed restaurants and might even have participated in decisions about where and how to expand or reduce the number of tables, including whether to buy or sell a license to operate. Others will simply have been customers in different towns and cities, and either known or wondered why places differ in terms of the number, size and location of establishments, as well as the quality and pricing of meals and service. Many of those differences are deeply rooted in food culture and other aspects of each place, but visitors can also ask or read about how city and state policies govern restaurant operations. Most often, the impact of taxes and licenses is most visible when they change, and people observe short-run movements along whichever side of the market is more inelastic.

The analysis above reveals how the effects of a tax do not depend very much if at all on how the tax is collected, but depends on relative elasticities as explained below.

Price Elasticities and the Incidence of a Tax or Regulation

Elasticities reflect the flexibility of buyers and sellers. When a government introduces a tax or regulation, the more flexible or elastic side of the market can escape to other activities, so a larger share of the cost is borne by those with a lower price elasticity. The *incidence* of a tax or regulation is the burden paid by each type of participant, which depends on their price elasticities. Each panel of Fig. 3.14 was deliberately drawn so that demand and supply had the same price elasticity, and the burden of each tax or regulation was borne equally by buyers and sellers. The more general case, in which one side of the market pays a larger share, is shown in Fig. 3.15.

In Fig. 3.15 we introduce squares and triangles around the different points of intersection, to emphasize that the same quantity can now have two different prices. The earlier example of a tax was a fixed amount of money (t) per unit sold, added to producers' cost or subtracted from consumers' payments the seller, so that the market supply and demand curves (S' and D') were parallel to their underlying marginal costs and willingness to pay (S and D). That was done only for visual clarity and simplicity. More commonly, taxes are a fixed percentage of the price for each unit sold, which implies a proportional rotation of the S or D curve.

Our example in Fig. 3.15 is the restaurant tax in Massachusetts, which happens to be 6.5%. In practice that is usually added to the bill after each meal, but because consumers know that it is coming we can draw the diagram as an addition to costs so the new market supply curve (S') is 6.5% higher than S, to S' = MC × 1.065. This proportional increase is known as an *ad-valorem* tax, whereas a fixed amount such as $0.65 per meal is known as a *specific* tax.

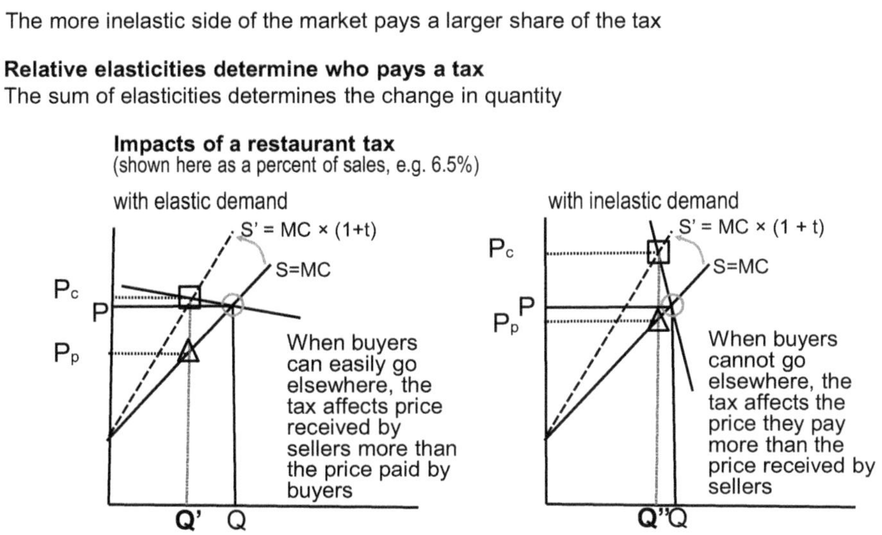

Fig. 3.15 Elasticities tell us who pays a tax

Curious readers can verify by sketching the diagram that drawing Fig. 3.15 with a specific tax makes no difference to the results, just as it would make no difference to show the tax as paid by consumers.

In reality, as shown in Fig. 3.15, the group of people who pay the tax is whichever side of the market happens to be more inelastic in response. If consumers can easily go elsewhere or eat at home, the demand curve will be relatively elastic demand curve with a low slope, and sellers will have no choice but to absorb the tax in a lower price received at Q'. In contrast, if consumers insist on going out to eat in this area, the demand curve is steeper so sellers can charge higher prices and quantity sold declines only to Q'.

Elasticities determine who pays taxes, and elasticities also affect how regulation affects prices and quantities. Understanding elasticities can help clarify the policy similarities and differences between taxes and rules, as shown for a place that restricts restaurant supply with licenses as shown in Fig. 3.16.

How rules are implemented makes a big difference to the experience of restaurant operators and their customers, so contextual knowledge plays a big role in policy analysis in any specific setting, but the general economic principles illustrated here show analysts what to look for. As revealed by Fig. 3.16, when regulators allow only Q' to be provided, sellers and buyers must cut back from Q to that new quantity. Sellers will discover that it is unprofitable to invest beyond where their community's supply curve reaches Q' at P_p, and also discover that they can charge consumers along their demand curve D reaches Q' at P_c.

The qualitative insight here is that, for a given degree of supply response, inelastic demand makes restrictions more costly to consumers. Redrawing

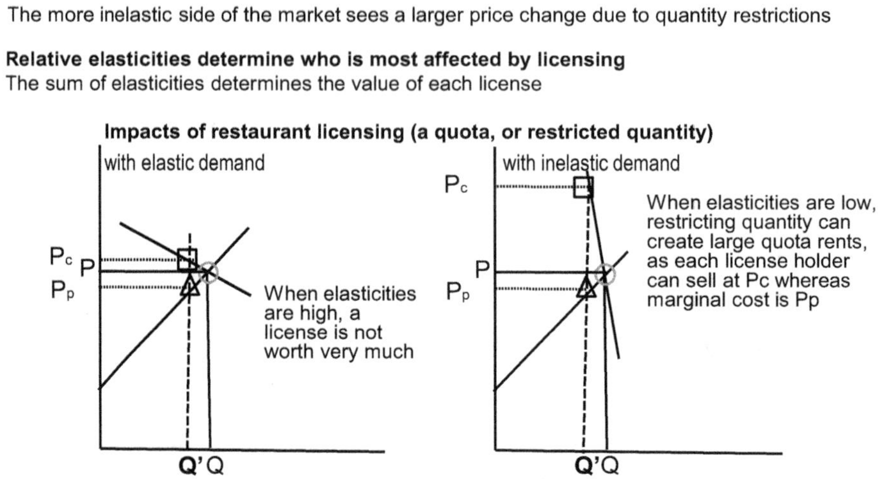

Fig. 3.16 Elasticities tell us how a quota affects prices paid and received

Fig. 3.16 with steeper supply curves would show that licensing at Q' would then cause even greater price gaps, because the quota rent depends on adding up the effects of both elasticities as sellers and buyers interact towards the lower quantity allowed. For government decision-makers who might want to limit quantity at Q' but also want to keep prices down, an important priority could be to promote greater elasticity of demand in the sense of more different options for consumers.

Trade Policy: Tariffs and Quotas on Imports or Exports

In communities that import goods from outsiders, governments often seek to restrict imports. Later we will see the effect of these policies on wellbeing, and how economic principles help explain why governments adopt these and other policy choices in Chapters 4 and 5. That helps explain why import restrictions are among the oldest and most widely used kind of tax, called an *import tariff*, and how import tariffs are different or similar to restrictions on the quantity imported, known as an *import quota*.

Our only earlier diagram with imports was Fig. 3.7 in the previous section, showing the market for apples in Massachusetts. Each state in the U.S. cannot restrict imports from other states, so that diagram showed how free trade works: distributors can move apples into Massachusetts where consumers have the option of buying imported apples at prices prevailing in other states, so producers can sell along their supply curve only up to that price in trade. Apple growers in Massachusetts can try to differentiate their apples to sell them at a higher price, and transport or storage costs will lead to small price differences across space and time, but the quantities observed are where supply and demand meet the price prevailing for trade with other places. Unlike individual states within the U.S., national governments can require importers to stop at the border for inspection and compliance with trade rules, and the mechanisms by which tariffs and quotas affect outcomes are both illustrated in Fig. 3.17.

The left panel of Fig. 3.17 shows an import tariff, illustrated as the specific amount t paid to the government of the place shown in the diagram, per unit of the product imported. The right panel shows an import quota, which is a specific quantity q allowed over a specific period of time.

With free trade, distributors can import the product at its prevailing price in trade from elsewhere, P, so consumers can move along their demand curve to where D meets P at Q_c, and producers move along their supply curve to where S meets P at Q_p, so consumption exceeds production by the quantity imported which is $Q_c - Q_p$. This outcome is a useful benchmark against which to compare the effects of different policies.

When a tariff is charged, distributors who wish to import must pay P for the product plus t for the tariff. Consumers can then move along their demand curve only to Q_c', where D meets P' = P + t, and that higher price allows producers to move along supply curve to Q_p' where S meets P'. There is still separation between production and consumption, but the quantity imported is now $Q_c' - Q_p'$.

When a quota is imposed, distributors who wish to import can do so only up the fixed limit q, in addition to quantities produced locally along the supply curve. We can find the new predicted outcome by adding q to S which generates a new curve for local supply plus the quota, shown as S'. Consumers can then move along their demand curve only to Q_c', where D meets S' = S + q.

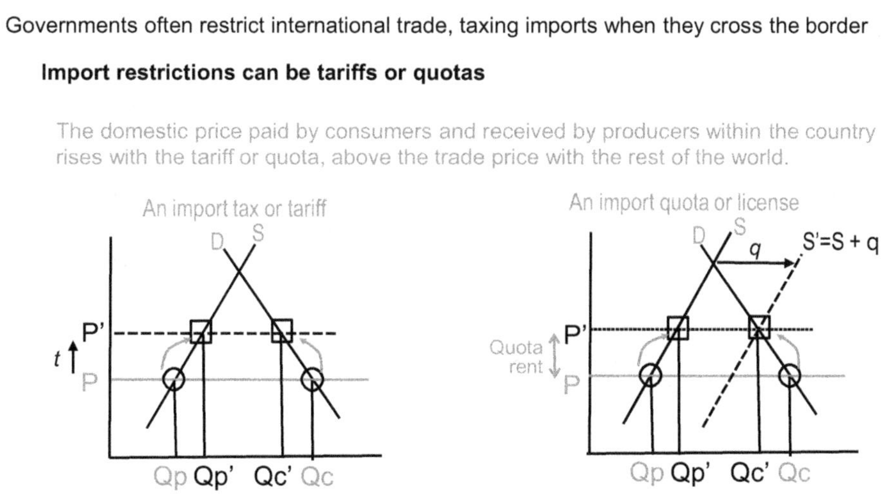

Fig. 3.17 Import restrictions raise domestic prices, reducing quantity consumed

The price paid where D meets S' is P', so producers can sell at that price too and move along supply to Q_p'. The mechanism of adjustment differs, but the quantity imported is again Q_c'$-$$Q_p$'.

As with the previous comparison of taxation and licensing, the diagrams are constructed so results are identical, to show how two instruments can lead to the same outcome due to behavioral response by market participants. The difference is that taxes are paid to the government, while licensing creates 'rents' paid to people who are allowed by government to do the restricted activity. In Fig. 3.17, those *quota rents* are the difference between the price obtained, P', and the price paid for imports, P, over the quantity imported which is Q_c'$-$$Q_p$'. The different outcomes are driven by different mechanisms of adjustment. With a tariff, the local price is where D meets the prevailing price of imports, P, so shifts in local supply or demand will alter price only if they cause a change in that price of imports. With a quota, the local price is where D meets S' = S + q, so shifts in local supply and demand directly alter price, as if this location was in autarky.

Contrasting the two policies highlights the key role of elasticity along demand, supply and trade lines in how policies affect vulnerability or resilience to shocks. With free trade or tariffs, consumers are insulated from fluctuations in local supply, and producers do not experience changes in local demand, because both face the foreign price directly. Shifts in local S and D are absorbed in quantity imported at the import price P for which consumers pay P + t. With quotas, quantity is fixed at q and hence shifts in local S' = S + q and D are reflected directly in the local price P'. That distinction makes a very big difference in practice, because for most products in most places the rest of the world is larger and more diverse than local own supply and demand. That makes the rest of world a more elastic provider of each product at a more stable price than each location would have in autarky, and a tariff will lead to more stable local prices than import quota.

Trade policy affects local conditions through either imports or exports. The import tariffs and quotas shown in Fig. 3.18 tend to be long-lasting, widely used policies that remain in place for decades. Corresponding restrictions on exports are sometimes long-lasting but are more often responses to a temporary spike in world prices when global stocks are low, or highly targeted efforts to keep supplies within the country. As for imports, our only earlier diagram with exports was Fig. 3.7 showing the market for cranberries in Massachusetts, and now we show the effect of a government policy to restrict such trade as shown in Fig. 3.18.

With exports, as with imports, a population that can trade freely with the rest of the world faces the prevailing price in trade, *P*, so produces at that price along its supply curve at Q_p and consumes at that price along the demand curve at Q_c. The resulting quantity traded is the difference, Q_p-Q_c.

When an export tax (t) is imposed, people in the country seeking to export receive only P' = P–t. Producers adjust along their supply curve to Q_p',

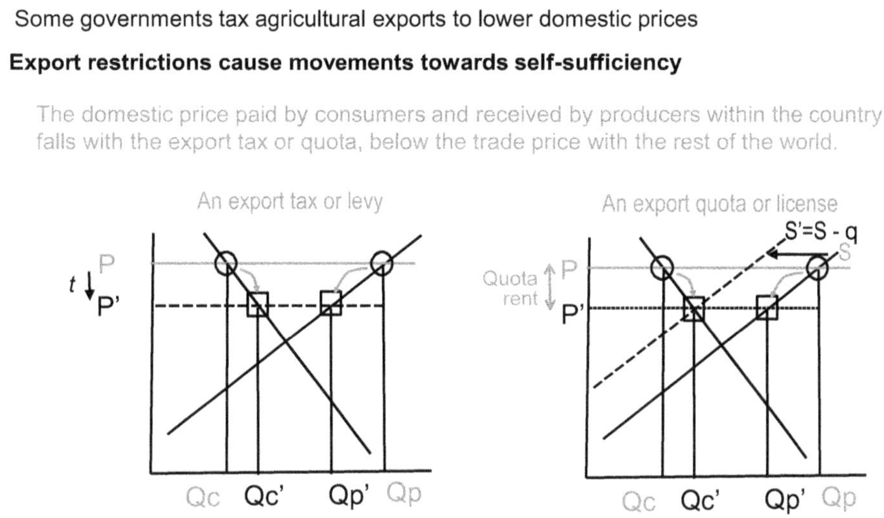

Fig. 3.18 Export restrictions lower domestic prices, reducing quantity produced

consumers adjust to Q_c', and the tax reduces the quantity exported to Q_p' – Q_c'.

When an export quota (*q*) is used, people seeking to export can sell only up to a limited quantity. The resulting price can be found by subtracting only that quota from local production, so the restricted market supply is S' = S – *q*. Participants in the local market then adjust along S' and D to P', the price at which buyers are willing to pay for the quantity that producers can supply, after accounting for the fixed quantity exported.

As with import restrictions, the export taxes and quotas shown in Fig. 3.18 can be drawn to have identical outcomes in terms of peoples' responses along their supply and demand curves. As before, one difference is that taxes are paid to the government, while licensing creates quota rents paid to whoever is allowed to buy locally at P' and export at P, over whatever share of the quota is given to them by the government. And as before, another difference concerns instability and adjustment. Export restrictions are usually a temporary policy, imposed during brief periods of world price spikes, unlike the import tariffs and quotas discussed earlier. These interactions between local conditions and trade opportunities greatly influence resilience and response to change, in ways that are especially visible when we go beyond the trade to consider 'domestic' policies affecting local producers and consumers.

Domestic Policies and Separability Between Supply and Demand

Government interventions within a country's borders are known as domestic interventions, in contrast to trade policies that operate at the border. We have already seen domestic regulations like restaurant licensing, and now turn to a

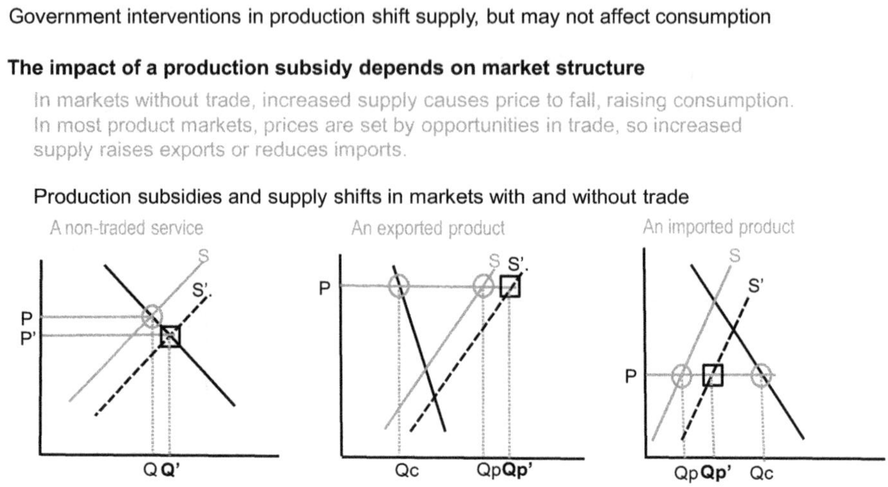

Fig. 3.19 Domestic policies affect outcomes differently without and with trade

broader set of policies that might shift supply or demand. As before, once we take account of producer and consumer responses the impact of intervention can be surprising, as shown first for supply shifts supply shown in Fig. 3.19.

Production subsidies that increase supply, shown in Fig. 3.19 as a shift from S to S', could be payments from government to producers or their input providers that reduce the marginal cost of selling one more unit, or equivalently to increase the quantity sold at each level of marginal cost. Examples include low-cost loans and crop insurance, assistance with fuel or machinery and other inputs, or direct payments to farmers in proportion to area or quantity produced. If the government simply provides a cash payment of s per unit sold, then S' would be $S = MC - s$, but actual subsidies usually shift supply in other ways.

Many agricultural subsidies do not actually increase supply, in some cases because they are designed explicitly to be 'decoupled' from output and help farmers without raising quantity produced. In other cases, payments to farmers may be intended to reduce output, such as a set-aside or buyout program, or they aim to address other concerns such as climate change, biodiversity or animal welfare. Some of these payments might have little effect on supply or shift it to the left, from S' to S. Examples of supply-reducing payments to farmers include programs for land conservation, tree planting and carbon sequestration, avoidance of water use or less intensive livestock production. Those are payments for services or things other than output, and would be analyzed with other kinds of diagrams.

The purpose of Fig. 3.19 is to show how the left panel, for supply shifts in a market without trade, differs from the same supply shifts in a market with exports or imports. In the market for a nontraded product like fresh eggs or liquid milk, a shift in supply causes movement along the demand curve from Q to Q', lowering price to P' and affecting consumers as well as producers. In contrast, for products exported to or imported from a large and diverse rest of the world, the prevailing price in trade at P is often not affected by local events, so a shift in supply from S to S' does not alter price and does not affect consumers.

The finding that supply shifts affect consumers only where people cannot trade with others is known as *separability*. Readers can easily sketch a version of Fig. 3.19 in which it is the demand curve that shifts, leading again to separability as demand shifts affect producers only where people cannot trade with others. The reason for separability is that the rest of the world is usually so large and diverse that their prevailing price is almost unaffected by the policy or other shift we are analyzing in a given community of interest.

Trade with others creates the possibility of separation between supply and demand for a whole community, just as our individual diagrams in Chapter 2 showed that exchange with others created separability between consumption and production for an individual farmer who consumes some of what they produce. This reinforces how supply and demand is the sum of all individual choices, reflecting the diversity of individuals within one community and also the differences between one community and the rest of the world.

3.2.3 Conclusion

Analytical diagrams like those presented in this chapter will be used again throughout this book to explain and predict response to policy interventions, environmental shocks, technological innovations and other events. So far we have focused on prices and quantities in places with many buyers and sellers, so that producers move along an upward sloping supply curve and consumers move along a downward sloping demand curve, to the predicted point where no further adjustment would be chosen. Where a community of buyers and sellers can trade with people in the rest of the world, quantities produced and consumed are where supply and demand curves meet that prevailing price.

The diagrams summarize people's choices among many options as movements along a curve, and we summarize the slopes of those curves using elasticities that convert price and quantity data into percentage changes. The concept of elasticities gives us a clear vocabulary with which to discuss a group's responsiveness as their percentage change in quantity for each one percent change in price, income or other factor. Elasticities are helpful for measurement and empirical analysis, but we can also use them directly for qualitative analysis based on contextual knowledge of a specific product in a particular community.

A central finding of this chapter is that having larger price elasticities, meaning that people can more freely adjust quantities in response to shocks, can be an important source of resilience to external factors that might otherwise cause large changes in price. One important source of highly elastic response to local shocks is trade with others, as shifts in local supply or demand can be absorbed by changes in quantity exported or imported. Elasticities along each curve of our diagrams, and the model structures through which we predict how people will adjust along those curves, provide useful insights into price and quantity responses. In the next chapter we introduce a measure of social welfare that links prices and quantities, greatly expanding the analytical toolkit to explain and predict policy choices, consider many forms of market failure and analyze the empirical data discussed later in this book.

CHAPTER 4

Social Welfare: Evaluating Change in Food Markets

4.1 Economic Surplus: Who Gains from Market Transactions?

4.1.1 Motivation and Guiding Questions

So far we have focused on changes in quantities and prices, which could affect different people in society to different degrees. How much does each person gain or lose from a change? Can we add up different peoples' gains and losses, to compute the change in total welfare for society as a whole? And how do market outcomes affect other people in society, for example the victims of climate change caused by greenhouse gas emissions?

Our economic principles explain observable quantities and prices as the result of each person having made consistent choices from their limited options. Systematic analysis of those choices allows us to draw diagrams showing how people will adjust along lines and curves towards potentially predictable points, based on attributes of each line such as its degree of curvature, slope and elasticity.

The lines used to predict outcomes in our analytical diagrams all result from people having chosen the option that was best for them. We can now use that to infer something about the population's preferences, and what movements along each line or curve reveal about how far towards their goals they can get in each market outcome.

To quantify improvements or worsening in how far each person could get towards their goals, we will interpret the areas between curves as a measure of *economic surplus*, and use changes in the area of economic surplus to compare gains and losses for each person in the society of interest. The concept of economic surplus is a measure of wellbeing only for the people making

W. A. Masters and A. B. Finaret, *Food Economics*,
Palgrave Studies in Agricultural Economics and Food Policy,
https://doi.org/10.1007/978-3-031-53840-7_4

transactions in a given market. Each society's economic surplus from those transactions consists of *consumer surplus* from willingness to pay along the demand curve, producer *surplus* from marginal cost along the supply curve, and the gains or losses incurred by other actors such as government agencies or traders who hold licenses and quotas.

Having defined economic surplus for market participants, we can compare that to the unintended side effects of a change in production or consumption, which we call *externalities*. Among the most important negative externalities is greenhouse gas emissions, but other external harms include water pollution and antimicrobial resistance, and there are also many external benefits from expanding healthier and more sustainable activities. The term externality is used to signal that these costs and benefits are felt by other people, and therefore not already counted in economic surplus of decision-makers in production or consumption. In some cases externalities harm or help the decision-maker's own future self, for example when consumers are unable to take account of how their current food choices affect their long-term health. Adding or subtracting externalities to the economic surplus of market participants gives us a more complete measure of societal wellbeing and is the first of several market failures to be addressed throughout this book.

By the end of this section, you will be able to:

1. Derive producer and consumer surplus from supply and demand curves;
2. Use economic surplus to identify who gains and who loses from changing opportunities to make market transactions, and the relative magnitudes of those gains and losses, in markets with and without trade;
3. Distinguish a population's total gains or losses from the gains or losses per person that might be caused by a policy change, and identify how that difference influences policy choice; and
4. Describe how separability between production and consumption affects the impact of a policy change in markets with and without trade.

4.1.2 Analytical Tools

The analytical diagrams drawn so far in this book use only symbols such as S and D for the curves or P and Q for the axes. The elements of each diagram are a set of smooth lines and curves leading to points, providing qualitative insights about these elements relative to each other. Drawing each diagram without numbers is confusing at first but very helpful later, because the same diagrams can be reused for a wide range of examples.

The definition of each element on each diagram leads to a distinctive shape, such as PPFs being bowed out and S being upward sloped. Contextual knowledge allows us to draw each element on diagrams tailored to particular situations. Individual diagrams in Chapter 2 refer to a person, and the market diagrams derived from that in Chapter 3 refer to a type of product in a population, such as apples in Massachusetts. The distinctive shape of each element follows from people having chosen what they do, from a limited set of options. Those choices involve production and consumption of each product, and also exchange of that product between people.

Economics consists of using contextual knowledge to construct an appropriate model for each situation, selecting from the modeling toolkit described in this book. The book provides a large number of examples, but every student can and should redraw the diagrams around their own examples to see how the same logic of economics plays out similarly or differently in each situation.

The new element introduced in this section is *economic surplus,* defined in terms of areas between lines and curves in each market. Economic surplus is remarkably useful as a measure of social welfare derived from economic models of any market, yielding deep insights into questions such as why governments adopt the policies we observe, and how those observed policies might be improved to help people get farther towards their goals. Later we will use economic surplus in its general form, labeling areas on each diagram with letters and shading. Drawing each element without numbers reveals the qualitative principles of economics that would hold for any example.

In this chapter we introduce a new way of explaining individual choices and market outcomes, switching from abstract diagrams to a specific case study with actual numbers and the names of people. This concrete example allows us to derive the population's economic surplus from each person's choices, along supply and demand curves whose slope and position comes from their individual circumstances. Results of the model follow from each person's choices for how much to produce and consume, exchange within the community and trade with others.

The concrete example in this section reveals how economic principles follow from a universal observation about human behavior, which is that each person has chosen from limited options. The results we obtain come from the diversity of those options. Diversity among people leads to gains from exchange within a community, and also gains from trade with others, but also inequities and market failures that could be addressed by government policies.

A Toy Model: Introducing the Alphabet Beach Fish Market

The example community we introduce in this section is Alphabet Beach, an imaginary place with specific features that are easy to explain. Playing with this toy model can be fun, and useful to see how the principles of economics unfold in each scenario.

The Alphabet Beach fish market involves eight people, each with their own circumstances. Five are potential buyers of fish, and three are potential fish sellers. Each potential seller could sell up to two fish per day, of which each potential buyer would want only one. All fish are identical and cannot be stored so the market for fish repeats anew on the beach each day.

Alphabet Beach is a useful toy because we can easily imagine breaking the rules. For example, what if people live in households? What if we add other foods, or different details? We could spend hours playing out any scenario. Later in this book we will look at real data, and return to all possible scenarios that fit those data using more abstract diagrams, but for now let's go to the beach shown in Fig. 4.1.

Our diagrams refer to just one aspect of life, which is the market for fish. In Fig. 4.1 the vertical axis shows the price of each fish, which could be expressed in any unit of currency. For example, a more elaborate toy model would introduce another food, such as coconuts, and the price of fish could be coconuts per fish. Then we could draw indifference curves for consumption between these two foods, and production possibilities for harvesting coconuts or catching fish, all with relative prices that involve no money at all. For now we focus on just one thing so do not need to specify the units of price, but can use any familiar word such as pesos or dollars.

What matters in our toy model is the number of fish, shown along the horizontal axis for each individual and for the village as a whole. Market demand and supply comes from adding up quantities bought or sold by each person. In this toy model, each potential consumer can buy only one fish, and each potential producer can sell up to two fish. The quantity for each buyer or seller is fixed, so the slopes of demand and supply come only from diversity among people.

In our toy model each person's name signals their interest in fish. In the left of each panel in Fig. 4.1 we see each individual's own demand and supply curve for one person, and then we add those up horizontally to obtain demand

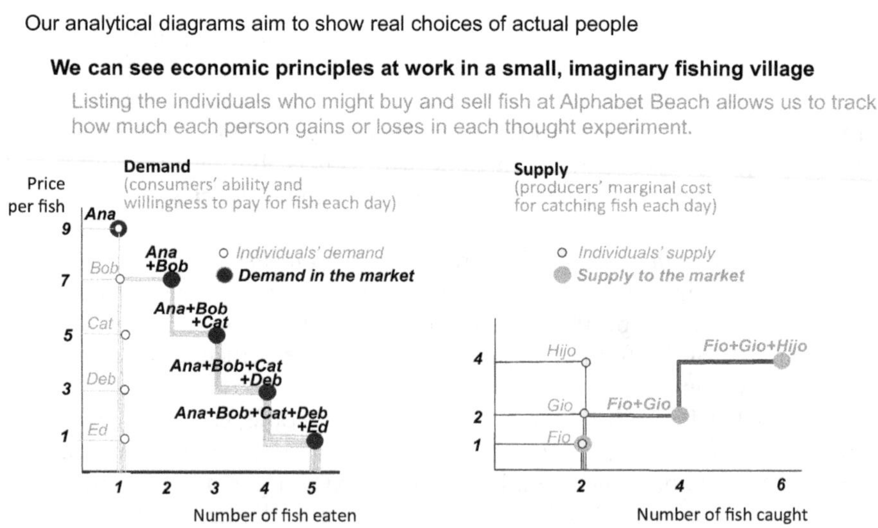

Fig. 4.1 Demand and supply of fish at Alphabet Beach

and supply in this whole market. If we allowed each person to buy or sell a varying number of fish, there would be some slope for their individual demand or supply curves, but in this simplest case the demand curve is sloped down only because people differ.

For demand, each buyer's circumstances are shown by their willingness and ability to pay for one more fish. Ana would pay up to 9 pesos or dollars per fish, Bob up to 7, Cat up to 5, Deb up to 3 and Ed up to 1. Each person could have a different fish demand for many reasons, such as differences in their wealth and income, cooking skills or food preferences. If we wanted to change demand, we would need a lot of other data about each person to see what lies behind their willingness to pay, but to predict market outcomes and evaluate economic surplus it is sufficient to observe their revealed preferences and effective demand.

For supply, each seller's circumstances are shown by their marginal cost of bringing one more fish to the market. For Fio, fishing comes easily and he can catch his couple of fish at a cost of just one peso or dollar per fish. For Gio and especially Hijo, production is more costly. Each potential supplier could have a different cost of production for many possible reasons, such as differences in travel time, the other opportunities they have and their fishing skills or preferences for other kinds of work. If we wanted to change supply, we would need a lot of other data about each person to see what lies behind their cost of production, but to predict market outcomes and evaluate economic surplus it is sufficient to observe the quantity they are willing and able to sell at each price.

The staircase shape of supply and demand in Fig. 4.1 could lead to some ambiguity about the exact price or quantity of things. Smooth curves in our general models lead to a specific point that we can label as the predicted quantity or price. When things are lumpy and indivisible, like a whole fish, we leave room for negotiation about that last incremental unit. That aspect of this toy model is more realistic than the point predictions derived from smooth curves, but takes some explaining. As shown below, the outcome of our toy market comes down to negotiations between one seller and one buyer, and the result is a range of possible prices.

Market Equilibrium Between Buyers and Sellers

In previous chapters we derived supply and demand from individual decisions, based on all potential choices we might observe from all possible options people might have. Now we have a concrete example of eight individuals, each with only one choice to make. The five potential buyers decide whether or not to buy at the offered price, and the three potential sellers decide whether or not to go fishing based on the price they would receive. Ana, Bob, Cat, Deb and Ed would all like to buy a fish each day at any price up to their willingness to pay, while Gio, Fio and Hijo would like to go fishing if they receive a price of at least their marginal cost.

There are many possible ways that the people of Alphabet Beach could interact, each of which is a specific *market structure*. Market structures come from the technologies and institutions through which people buy and sell. For example, Gio might introduce an app through which buyers bid for home delivery, Ana might build a shop with a refrigerator to sell fish later in the day or the whole group might form a government that sets policies. The institutional aspects of market structure are themselves influenced by technology, making it easier or more difficult for people to communicate and sustain each type of organization.

The market structure we introduce first is known as *perfect competition*. The use of 'perfect' in that name conveys the idea of a benchmark extreme case. Reality always falls short of perfection, and later in this book we will present models for *market failures* such as monopoly power (when there is only one seller or only one buyer that controls the entire quantity) or information asymmetries (when buyers or sellers cannot see product quality, so they expect low quality even if it could be high). Those are forms of *imperfect competition* that yield systematically different outcomes from the benchmark found here, and any type of activity could generate *externalities* that are yet another kind of market failure. Many different potential outcomes can be analyzed with our toy model, each based on a different scenario.

To reach a *perfectly competitive* outcome, a product of known quality must be exchanged among enough different sellers and buyers for none to influence total quantity. Under those conditions, interactions between people lead to a price and quantity with the distinctive feature that no other quantity could yield a greater sum of all economic surplus for the society as a whole, and is economically *efficient* in the sense of taking fullest possible advantage of the society's resources to generate wellbeing for all market participants. But economic surplus is mostly useful to measure whether a change is *equitable*, based on the distribution of benefits and costs within society.

All principles of economics, including predictions about each market structure and changes in economic surplus, rely on the idea that observed outcomes result from each person having done the best they can. Economics is most useful for situations where people have learned from experience, perhaps through their own trial and error, and avoided repeating their mistakes. If that has happened, the choices we observe were selected from the person's limited options, as the actions that were best for them. We all are used to thinking of our own choices that way, as the best of our options to pursue our goals, and the toy model of Alphabet Beach Village helps us imagine a group of other people each with their own objectives.

Later in this book we will return to predicted outcomes of different market structures in various circumstances, focusing on how policy and program interventions might alter the efficiency and equity of each outcome, and also the vulnerability and resilience of societal outcomes to shocks over time. For now, we can use the example of Alphabet Beach to understand what we mean by a perfectly competitive market, and the economic surplus that each person

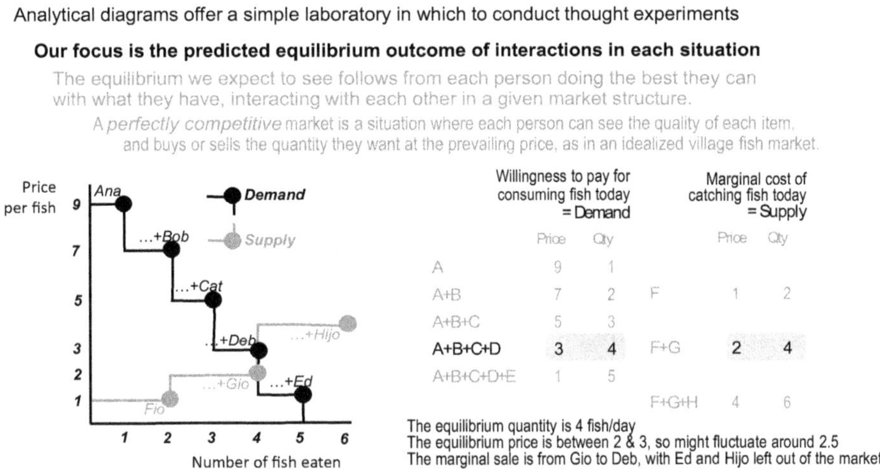

Fig. 4.2 The equilibrium price and quantity of fish sold at Alphabet Beach

obtains from it, beginning with the decisions of each individual interacting with each other as shown in Fig. 4.2.

To see how markets work, it may be tempting to look at Fig. 4.2, observe the two lines and conclude that the outcome must be where they cross. That would be a mistake. Competitive markets would move towards that outcome, but different market structures would lead to different outcomes. The model is not the market, just like a map is not the land. The purpose of imagining Alphabet Beach fish market is to remind us that economics is about people, and having a toy model of imaginary people allows us to play out the consequences of many different scenarios.

For example, we can imagine Ana, Bob and the other potential buyers walking down to the beach to see what's offered each day, while Fio, Gio and other potential sellers show off their catch. There could be fascinating details of how transactions might work, and we can use our toy model to imagine all kinds of things that might vary from day to day and place to place. As economists, we are interested in what Alfred Marshall called 'the ordinary business of life', looking to predict the average outcomes we might typically observe over a wide range of circumstances. To make that prediction, we need to imagine all eight people having experienced enough different outcomes to avoid doing things that are not the best they can do.

The curves on Fig. 4.2 and the table to the right of that diagram specify what each person is willing and able to do. Ana would buy from any seller offering a price at or below 9, while Bob would buy from any seller at or below 7, and so forth down to Ed who would buy only at or below 1. The demand curve and the first two columns of table at the right show the cumulative number of fish that would be bought for each price from 9 to 1. Similarly, among sellers, Fio would sell to any buyer paying a price at or above 1, while

Gio would sell to any buyer paying at or above 2, and Hijo would sell to any buyer paying at or above 4. That is the supply curve, and also the last two columns of the table at the right.

A first question about equilibrium is whether a predictable outcome even exists. Quantities and prices might be random, or predetermined by factors outside the market. And if the model does predict outcomes, the equilibrium could involve more than one price (for example, a different price for each buyer), or prices that fluctuate within a range. We can use our toy model to see how, as people learn about the market, their behavior might cause convergence towards predictable outcomes. Playing with the example of Alphabet Beach reveals economic mechanisms by allowing us to explicitly say how each person might learn from experience, and what alternative outcomes might have arisen in the past but are not repeated enough to be frequently observed.

Starting with price, all potential buyers (Ana, Bob, Cat, Deb and Ed) might sometimes discover that they paid more than another buyer for the same kind of fish. They would learn that to reach their various objectives, it would be better to make at least some effort to keep shopping and buy at the lowest prevailing price. Similarly, each potential seller (Fio, Gio and Hijo) might sometimes find that they had sold for less than another seller, and they would learn how to sell at the highest available price.

As each person learns about the market, prices will converge but the outcome depends on market structure. All buyers and all sellers see the same price only when there are many of them, seeing what each other pays for a product of uniform quality. We have already seen how taxes can create a gap between prices paid by buyers and sellers, and we will soon see what happens when there is only a single buyer or a single buyer for each type of product who sets the quantity. In that case we might see *price discrimination* with different prices for each unit, sometimes through *product differentiation* with different qualities of each unit so as to get different prices for it. Market models to explain those outcomes are based on additional constraints, such as barriers to entry or limited information, each of which creates a different market structure. With no such constraints, in the perfectly competitive benchmark model prices converge to a single value, or range of values.

Learning about market opportunities causes convergence not only in price, but also in quantity. Having a toy model allows us to tell imaginary stories about each individual person in the market. For example, one day there might be just Fio catching a single fish, which they give to Ana because she is the person who can pay the most. But Fio would soon learn that a second fish to Bob is worthwhile, even though Ana would not pay as much. Gio might then discover what Fio had learned, which is that he too could sell one fish to Cat, and that in fact it's even better for him to sell one to Cat and one to Deb. Gio's choice drives down the price received by Fio, so both receive the same price.

In the toy model of Alphabet Beach, our prediction is that a quantity of exactly 4 fish will be sold at an equilibrium price that could be anything between 2 and 3. Competition among sellers leads to a single equilibrium quantity, but leaves uncertainty about the equilibrium price because the marginal unit is a whole fish sold by Gio to Deb. That is a one-to-one negotiation, in which Gio will sell if the price is at or above 2, and Deb will buy if the price is at or below 3. The actual outcome will depend on a bargaining process that would depend on factors outside this simple model, from which we know only that quantity will be 4 and price will be in the range of 2 to 3.

Economic Surplus for Consumers and Producers

Our market model is useful not only to explain and predict outcomes, but also to infer from each person's choices something about how far they got towards their goals. That inference about wellbeing is done using the concept of *economic surplus*.

Economic surplus is defined in terms of each market model, adding up the area between different lines and curves. We start with economic surplus of market participants, and in the next section we include external costs and benefits that are unintended side effects of production or consumption. Later chapters include change in the value of government services, and ultimately, the entire society's changes in economic surplus are the sum of changes lost or gained by everyone in the community, including market participants plus those affected by externalities and the government. The change in overall total economic surplus available for an entire society is important, but as we will see, much of the action comes from changes in the *distribution of economic surplus* and equity within societies.

Economic surplus for consumers, known as *consumer surplus*, is defined as the area between their demand curve and the price paid. Likewise, *producer surplus* is defined as the area between producers' supply curve and their price received. The definition of economic surplus is area on a diagram and is not any kind of 'surplus' amount of goods in the sense of excess quantity along the horizontal axis. Areas on our diagrams are measured in terms of height (price) times length (quantity), so economic surplus is a value measured in local currency terms.

Consumer surplus is related to each person's income and expenditure, while producer surplus is related to their revenue and profit, but economic surplus is not the same thing as income or profit. Economic surplus is an inference about wellbeing that we draw from the model. It is not a variable we could potentially observe outside the context of each market diagram. To the extent that each person chose whether and how much to buy or sell, we infer that each individual making a market transaction must have gained something from it, and the total economic surplus available for the entire society is the sum of what each individual gained from transactions in the market we are analyzing.

In practice we will focus on *change in economic surplus*, as a way of measuring changes in wellbeing based on the difference in outcomes from each scenario. The absolute level of economic surplus for an entire society can be calculated but that is not our focus, because the shape of each line or curve is actually measurable only in the vicinity of observable points. As we have seen, the elasticity of response to change can be empirically estimated from actual data, or derived from contextual knowledge about the market of interest, but extensions of each line or curve beyond the region of potentially observed points is poorly defined and has no practical value.

Using our toy model of Alphabet Beach helps explain economic surplus, because it allows us to see very clearly how a change in policy or other factors affects each individual's wellbeing. Producer and consumer surplus are shown on our diagrams as shaded areas that could be added up as shown in Fig. 4.3.

Showing economic surplus in terms of each individual on Alphabet Beach reveals how the concept works, in terms of both strengths and limitations.

For consumer surplus, in this example we know that Ana, Bob, Cat and Deb were potentially willing to pay up to 9, 7, 5 and 3 respectively, but in the end they all paid between 3 and 2, so the economic surplus they obtained is the dark-shaded area between demand and price paid. Four fish were purchased, generating a total consumer surplus of 14. We can imagine how this measure of wellbeing might be related to wellbeing, but we do not actually know why Ana was willing to spend more than Deb. Without additional data we cannot know how a change in consumer surplus actually affects each person, but we can infer that the transaction has helped them achieve whatever goals they have for how to use their income and other resources.

For producers, in this model we know that Fio and Gio could have caught and sold fish for just 1 and 2 respectively, and in the end they both received a price between 2 and 3, so the shaded economic surplus they obtained adds up to a total producer surplus of 4. Again we can imagine how this number might

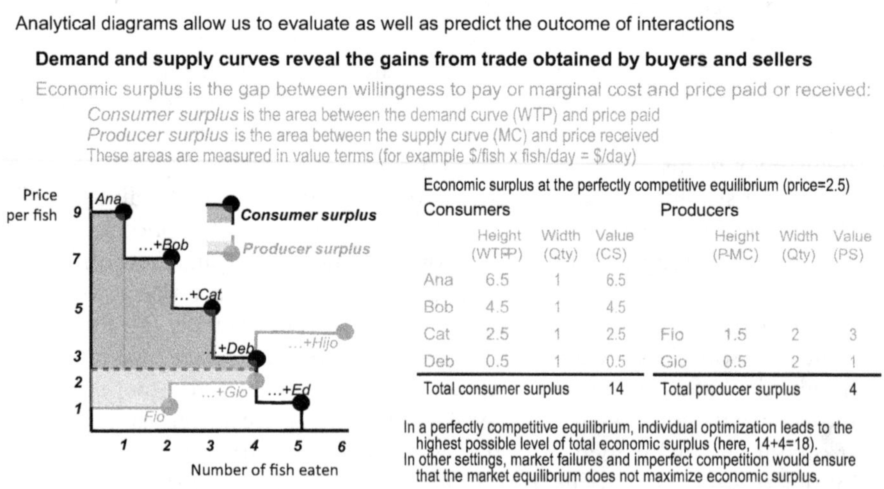

Fig. 4.3 Definition and calculation of economic surplus for consumers and producers

be related to Fio and Gio's livelihoods, but from the potentially observable facts we can only know that being able to sell fish helped them use their limited resources to achieve their goals.

Using our toy model allows us to see how and why Ed and Hijo are excluded from the market. Ed would like to buy fish but is able and willing to pay less than it would cost to produce, while Hijo would like to sell fish but that would cost him more than buyers would be willing and able to pay. For that reason, Ed and Hijo gain none of this market's economic surplus. In real societies, market participants often use some of what they gain from it to help others, through either charitable donations or government services, and economic surplus analysis helps us understand the role and need for those non-market activities. The diagram also reveals how different participants gain different degrees of benefit from the market. Those differences will turn out to play a decisive role in how economists explain, predict and assess the impacts of policy.

In our toy model we know exactly what each person has gained from the market, because we specified each producer's marginal cost and each consumer's willingness to pay. In reality those are not observable. All we have is empirical estimates or prior knowledge about prices, quantities and scenarios to be analyzed. We may have estimated elasticities from observational and experimental studies, or contextual knowledge about how people might adjust to a change. That information is enough to consider changes in economic surplus, ignoring the part of economic surplus that is difficult to measure and does not change.

Focusing on *change in economic surplus* due to a change in policy or other conditions reveals who gains and who loses from the change, and shows the relative magnitude of those gains or losses. To quantify the impact of change in policy on economic surplus available for an entire society, we begin with changes among consumers and producers, and then include externalities and transfers to or from government. Those changes in economic surplus give us additional insight into the mechanisms that lead to a change in equilibrium price and quantity, as shown by comparing market outcomes with and without trade.

Gains and Losses from Allowing Trade for Producer and Consumer Surplus

We have previously seen how and why individuals might gain from transactions with others, at Alphabet Beach or other settings. Our general analysis of how an individual is affected by trading with others within their own community was shown in Chapter 2, when we considered the options for a farmer who consumes all or some of their own production. We drew their PPF, budget lines and indifference curves in Fig. 2.15, revealing how a person can reach the same or higher level of indifference if they are willing to make trades with other people, instead of remaining isolated. But what happens when a whole community begins to trade with others?

Changes in economic surplus caused by opening to trade with other people provide a clear picture of who gains and who loses, in ways that help explain and predict policy responses. Later we will see changes in very general models drawn to show a wide range of circumstances, but it is useful to start with change for each person in our toy model as shown in Fig. 4.4.

With our toy model we can imagine that the fish market on Alphabet Beach was isolated for decades, perhaps on the far side of a remote island, and then suddenly connected to the outside world by boat or other ways to buy or sell fish across long distances. We can then use the diagram to predict how each person in the Alphabet Beach fish market is likely to respond, and see how economic surplus helps measure the change in each person's ability to meet their personal objectives.

The left panel of Fig. 4.4 shows the outcome when foreigners offer to buy at a price of 5. We draw this as a horizontal dashed line showing export demand for fish shipped to foreigners. The export demand line is drawn horizontal for simplicity, despite being slightly downward sloping like any demand line, to avoid the need for separate diagrams showing trade between the rest of the world and Alphabet Beach. If we drew those diagrams, we would see that the rest of the world is so much larger than Alphabet Beach that it can absorb any quantity of fish exports at an approximately constant price. The downward slope of demand for exports is imperceptible, for example when Alphabet Beach begins to export the price received might fall from 5.00 to 4.99, and we can greatly simplify our diagram by drawing a thick dashed line at 5.

When foreigners offer to buy at a price of 5, Hijo is now able to catch and sell fish, which raises total production to 6 fish each day. Fio and Gio can

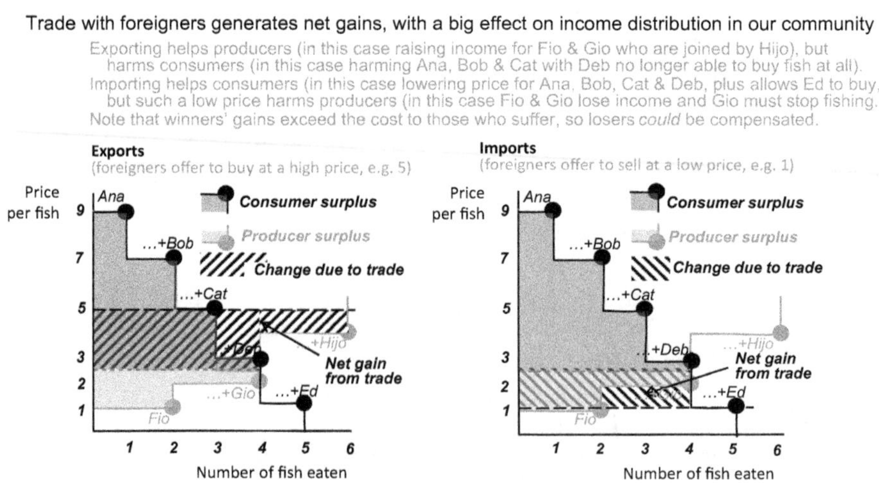

Fig. 4.4 Gains and losses from trade at Alphabet Beach, with exports and imports

now also sell at that price. Producer surplus is the area between price received and the supply curve up to the quantity sold of 6, so at the new price of 5, the entire producer surplus rises to 4 for each fish sold by Fio, 3 for each fish sold by Gio, plus 1 for each fish sold by Hijo. But if we focus only on the observable facts when Alphabet Beach opens to trade, we are interested only in the change in price from between 2 and 3 up to 5. That is the area shaded with stripes, ////, sloped forward to remind us that change in producer surplus is the area between the two prices from zero out to the upward-sloping supply curve.

Because foreigners have offered 5, consumers are no longer able to buy at the lower price between 2 and 3. Deb no longer buys any fish so is excluded from the market, like Ed. Cat can still buy, but the price of 5 is all that she was willing and able to pay, so she also no longer gains any consumer surplus from market. Bob and Ana also lose from the price rise up to 5. The remaining consumer surplus is the area between price paid and the demand curve up to the quantity of 3, shown as the dark gray area between price and the demand curve, but again our focus is just the change in consumer surplus, which is the area between the two prices out to the demand curve. On this diagram that is part of the area previously shaded with forward stripes (///), but only the part of it up to the demand curve which is shown as the area that has stripes and is also shaded dark gray.

The result of our economic surplus analysis is that the three producers (Fio, Gio and Hijo) have together gained more economic surplus than the four consumers (Ana, Bob, Cat and Deb) must have lost. That difference is called the *gains from trade*, recognizing that there is a net increase in the whole society's economic surplus, in the specific sense that the three sellers together have gained more from opening to trade than the four buyers lost from it. This fact may or may not be surprising, because we are often told that exports are good. What is more surprising is the symmetry with imports shown on the right side of the same diagram.

On the right panel of Fig. 4.4, foreigners offer to sell us fish at a price of 1. Again we draw this as a heavy-dashed horizontal line, for the same reason as before. In this case, the line shows the foreign market's supply of exports to us. Their export supply curve might be slightly curved up, so for example when Alphabet Beach begins to import, the price paid might rise from 1 to 1.01, but the rest of the world is relatively large so they are willing and able to provide whatever Alphabet Beach will buy at an approximately constant price.

When foreigners now offer to sell at 1, it is possible for Ed to buy fish and all other consumers gain from the lower price. It is the producers who lose, as Gio can longer sell anything and Fio receives a lower price. The consumer surplus area gained by consumers is between the two prices up to the demand curve, shaded with backward stripes, \\\\, sloped downward way to remind us that change in consumer surplus goes out to the downward-sloping demand curve. The producer surplus loss to Gio and Fio is the lightly shaded part of that. Because demand and supply curves have some slope, the gains to the five consumers (Ana, Bob, Cat, Deb and now also Ed) must be larger than the losses for the two producers (Fio and Gio). The net gain is the striped area with no shading.

Both imports and exports offer a net gain for the community as a whole. Imports help the community by benefiting consumers more than they harm producers, while exports help producers more than they harm consumers. Those comparisons rely on equally weighting the economic surplus gains and losses to each person, reflecting the same symmetry we saw for individuals in Fig. 2.15 but now there are gains and losses for different people. In the community context, the fact that imports create some gains from result is surprising because we are often told that imports are bad. Our diagram for Alphabet Beach reveals why societies often dislike imports but appreciate exports, based on differences in who is affected, how much each person has gained or lost and the visibility of those gains or losses.

When Alphabet Beach opens to imports, the gains are divided among five consumers (Ana, Bob, Cat, Deb and Ed), each of whom gains the amount of price change for one fish each. In contrast, the losses are experienced by just two producers (Fio and Gio), each of whom has lost the price change for two fishes. There is twice as much loss per producer as there is per consumer, simply because each producer has a larger quantity at stake than each consumer. Furthermore, Gio has lost their entire fishing business, which is a highly visible and potentially devastating harm to them, their family and the community. The two producers' losses are far more visible than the five consumers' gains, and the producers themselves are more likely to respond with political efforts than the consumers.

In contrast when Alphabet Beach opens to exports, the losses are spread among four consumers (Ana, Bob, Cat and Deb), while gains go to three producers (Fio, Gio and Hijo). Again, each producer experiences twice as much gain as each consumer, and there is one producer whose entire livelihood has changed: exports allow Hijo to start fishing, which is a highly visible and attractive event for the whole community. The four consumers who lose from exports include Deb who can longer buy any fish, but notice that Deb's economic surplus gain from buying a fish had been relatively small. This could be because Deb has a very low income and hence ability to pay, or because Deb does not care very much about fish. In either case the new unaffordability of fish for Deb, and the higher cost paid by Cat, Bob and Ana, is not as visible or important in politics as the new profitability of fishing for Hijo, and the higher profits earned by Gio and Fio.

The difference between opening to exports and to imports comes from the distribution of gains and losses. Each producer (Fio, Gio or Hijo) experiences a larger gain or loss than each consumer (Ana, Bob, Cat, Deb or Ed), and the marginal producer goes in or out of business (which is visible to everyone), whereas the marginal consumer just starts or stops buying (which is a private decision others might not care about). This asymmetry in distribution helps explain why societies mobilize against imports while encouraging exports, even though the whole society gains from trade in both cases.

The total gains from trade, whether exporting or importing, are real benefits. We can see that both gains from trade exist in our toy model, and in real life people have experienced and observed the gains from imports as well as exports everywhere in the world, since the dawn of humanity. Opening to imports is valuable economically, just like opening to exports, but it is much more difficult politically. In each case the winners could pool their gains to compensate the losers, and we do observe some government policies that provide safety net compensation directly tied to trade. For example, in the U.S. since 1974 the Federal government provides payments called Trade Adjustment Assistance to compensate workers who can show job loss due to imports, expanding an earlier program introduced in 1962 called Trade Adjustment Assistance for Firms that provides payments and services to company owners harmed by imports. There is no such compensation for those who lose from exports, and in both cases most governments respond to harm from trade by restricting trade itself. Those restrictions are extremely important to protect farm and food businesses affected by imports, and also a few brief export restrictions to keep prices lower for food businesses and consumers during world price spikes.

Later in this book we will see the data and examples of these policies and their effects. Knowing what to look for, and how to interpret the data and stories we see, is much easier when we have stylized models in mind about the mechanisms behind each change. Our toy model of the Alphabet Beach fish market is helpful to play out different scenarios, but real life is much more complicated. For example, each person does not have a fixed quantity they would buy or sell. In our toy model, supply and demand response came only from change in the number of people buying or selling, and the gains from trade arose only from diversity among people in their willingness to pay and cost of production for fish. Real-life markets involve both diversity among people in each community and variation in the quantity that each person is willing to buy or able to sell at each price.

In this book, all market models use linear supply and demand curves for market participants and horizontal prices for trade with the rest of the world as a simplification to show more clearly each mechanism behind the equilibrium outcomes. In any specific instance, actual supply and demand could take many different forms as long as supply never slopes down and demand almost never slopes up. Similarly, the price in trade would not actually be fixed, but the rest of the world is usually much larger than a given community and can absorb relatively small quantities traded at almost infinite elasticity shown by an almost horizontal line. We draw supply with an upward slope, demand with a downward slope and trade prices as a horizontal line because the resulting shapes are easy to draw and redraw, and lead to the same qualitative results as more complicated shapes.

Real-life applications of economic modeling rarely use linear supply and demand curves, and models that focus on international trade need not specify those prices as horizontal, because each application uses contextual knowledge and empirical data to tailor the model for that situation. Model specifications often involve smooth curves that can be estimated statistically, and may be designed for computational simulation as in more realistic versions of our toy model for Alphabet Beach. All models are 'stylized' to some degree, in the sense that they blur away any background variation that might be distracting, and each type of line and curve is stylized in specific ways to show how mechanisms interact to produce each outcome. The distinguishing feature of economic models is that each person in the model has chosen from limited options what is best for them. This foundation of individual optimization distinguishes economic models from other approaches to social science, and leads to equilibrium outcomes illustrated most clearly using linear supply, demand and trade lines. We will return to the toy model of Alphabet Beach, with named people and numerical values, but for most of the book we use a stylized model with linear supply and demand as in Fig. 4.5.

The stylized model of Fig. 4.5 shows how we may not need specific labels along the axes, and need not give names to each line and curve, because we are focused on qualitative implications of interaction between people shown by elements of the diagram that are now familiar to us. To use the diagrams accurately, we should just remember that the slopes of each supply and demand come from changes in quantity at each price for individual people, with the possibility of change in the number of people who participate in the market shown, and the area between curves and prices represents economic surplus

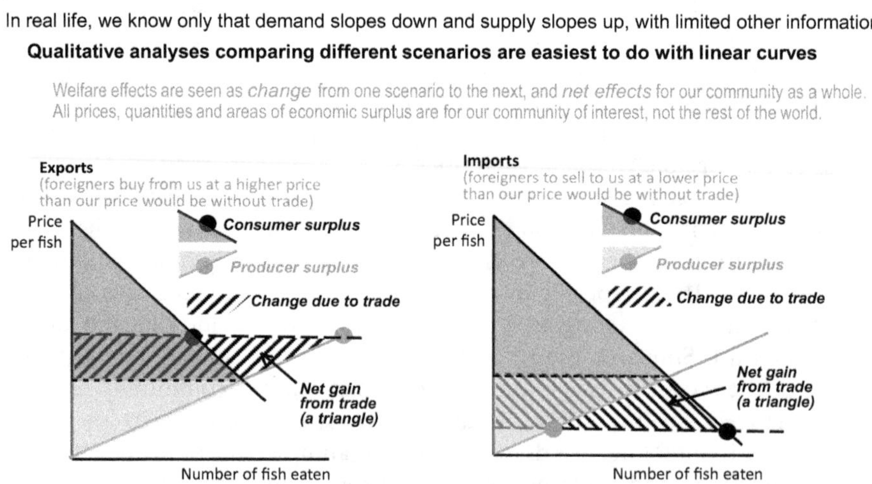

Fig. 4.5 Perfect competition and gains from trade with linear demand and supply

gained or lost from transactions over a specific product among the specific group of people shown on the diagram.

When drawing a stylized model like Fig. 4.5 for any particular situation, we would want to give it a specific title such as 'Fig. 4.1. The market for apples in Massachusetts', and note the time period to which that model applies. For this textbook, the figure's title instead shows the principle being illustrated. In this case, perfect competition without trade would drive price and quantity to the intersection of supply and demand, while opening to free trade would drive equilibrium price and quantity to the intersection of the price in trade with supply (for production) and demand (for consumption). The surprising outcome shown in Fig. 4.6 is that, in general for any community that opens to trade, there is symmetry between imports and exports in terms of economic surplus, with a clear asymmetry in the identity of who gains or loses.

The symmetry in economic surplus from exports and imports is the triangular net gains from trade, shown as the triangle between supply, demand and the price received or paid. On the left, net gains from exporting come from foreigners whose demand for our exports (their price line) is more than our own community's cost of production (along our supply curve) and our willingness to pay (along our demand curve). On the right, triangular net gains from importing are received from foreigners who provide imports at a cost to us that is less than our cost of production and willingness to pay.

The asymmetric political response to exports and imports comes from who gains and loses within each community. Opening to exports helps producers at the expense of consumers, while opening to imports helps consumers at the expense of producers. Production is almost always more concentrated among fewer people than consumption, so each producer has much more at stake than

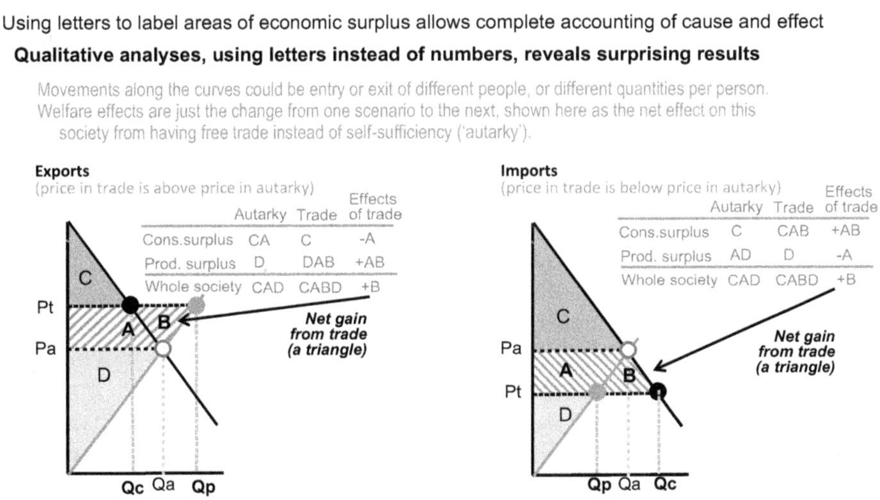

Fig. 4.6 Adding up economic surplus and the gains from trade

each consumer. Producers also have assets at stake, for example the entire value of their fishing boats or apple orchards which cannot easily switch to make other things, while consumers are spending just a few dollars on fish or apples each month and can easily switch to other foods.

Asymmetry in the magnitudes of impact, where each producer cares more while consumers are more numerous, is translated into observed policies through political mobilization of each community with common interests. Producers are typically concentrated geographically, often know each other personally and may be sociologically similar, which helps them form specialized groups that have political representation. As we will see, this asymmetry provides a powerful political and social force against imports in favor of exports, thereby missing out on the gains from trade. Sustaining openness to trade allows a country's population to gain more overall economic surplus for their society as a whole, but trade's impact on equity and the political feasibility of remaining open to trade may depend on workers having diverse job opportunities and also a strong social safety net for those who lose from imports.

In our stylized two-dimensional models for one thing at one place and time, and especially in numerical models with many foods in many places over time, it is challenging to keep track of each change. A key feature of this textbook is use of consistent notation across all of the analytical diagrams, as illustrated in Fig. 4.6.

The qualitative results of our stylized models are easiest to discuss using letters for each potentially observed outcome, such as P_a and P_t for prices in autarky or with trade, then also Q_a for quantity in autarky and Q_p or Q_c for quantities with trade that are produced or consumed. As before we can use different shadings to denote areas of economic surplus, and it is helpful to use other letters for each area gained or lost from a change. Figure 4.6 shows the exact same scenarios as our previous Fig. 4.5, but with the diagrams made narrower to leave space for a table that adds up those letters, showing their relative magnitudes and net changes for this entire society.

The use of Fig. 4.6 reveals how focusing on changes, in this case from autarky to trade, implies a focus only on the difference between two scenarios. The areas of economic surplus denoted C and D are unaffected by trade and play no role in the analysis, which is important because we actually have no data and little confidence in our model beyond the range of observed points. The areas A and B that we infer from the model are traced out by potentially observable changes in price from P_a to Pt, and changes in quantity from P_a to Q_p and Q_c, so we can be confident that areas A and B exist. Beyond the potentially estimated elasticities of response shown by slopes between potential outcomes, the shape of each supply and demand curve beyond the observable range has no role in our results. Using straight lines with specific intercepts along the axes is done only for visual convenience.

Models of real-world markets often trace many changes at once, each of which can be quantified, providing many different numerical estimates for each value shown on the right 'effects of trade' column of each panel. The letters in that column correspond to areas measured in the currency units of each price change, over all the quantities along the horizontal axis. Area AB is our society's entire benefit from trade shown as a positive (+) gain to our community, which is the difference between P_a and P_t with forward stripes (///) to show gains for our community's producers up to their supply curve when foreigners buy our exports, and with backward stripes (\\\) to show gains for our community's consumers up to our demand curve when foreigners sell us imports. Area A is the offsetting loss to some people within our community, which must be subtracted (−) to compute the net gain to this society as a whole which is area B.

In practical applications and analysis of current events, changes can go in either direction. Instead of gains from trade shown by area B, a society may experience a loss of trade opportunities. Opening to trade often happens gradually with innovations and investments that lower transport costs, while loss of trade opportunities often happens abruptly such as the sudden closure of a river or ocean port due to natural disaster, conflict or a policy choice. When describing each change it is important to be explicit about the direction of change, and to think about the time period of response being described, as well as the place and population of interest that would be responding to the change along their supply and demand curves. When describing policies or loss of transport that restrict trade, triangles of net loss like area B are known as ***deadweight losses***. Throughout this book we will see many changes that create net gains to society, and many changes that create net losses, each with their distributional effects.

The net economic surplus from changes like those shown in Fig. 4.6 can seem miraculous when societies experience big net gains, and darkly mysterious when societies experience big deadweight losses. Gains from trade can be particularly important when they sustain and reward investment in innovations that allow a country to do more with less. The mechanisms behind those gains often happen slowly, and rely on the government policies and public investment as well as private investments and adoption of innovations needed for advances to occur. Meanwhile, other societies may fall behind through inaction or obstruction, especially under climate change and other environmental changes that shift production possibilities and supply inward, either slowly or abruptly. As shown in our diagrams, these outcomes rarely have one single cause. Economic models show how everything is interconnected, with each exogenous change engaging several endogenous responses.

Economic Surplus in Perfect Competition: The First Theorem of Welfare Economics

The concept of economic surplus used to measure social welfare in our analytical diagrams is well-defined only for one set of exogenous changes at a time. More advanced, multidimensional economic models use generalized versions of economic surplus, based on multidimensional versions of our indifference curve diagrams. The link between economic surplus for a community and indifference curves for each individual in the community is discussed below. Those generalized models lead to a mathematical finding known as the *first theorem of welfare economics*, which says that **perfectly competitive market structures lead to the highest attainable sum of all individuals' welfare in that market**. That result is derived using advanced math in multidimensional models. In economic surplus terms for each individual market, it can be demonstrated geometrically as in Fig. 4.7 where free trade within and between communities yields the highest attainable total economic surplus. The practical application of this theorem is through its corollary, which is that **imperfections in market competition ensure that highest attainable social welfare has not been reached**, pointing to opportunities for improvement.

The exact definition of 'perfect' competition refers to the mathematical structure of a model, but the kinds of perfection required can readily be seen from our graphical models. In general, **'perfect' competition requires that (a) many different producers and consumers can freely enter or exit the market with infinitesimally small units of additional production and consumption, and also that (b) no barriers limit exchange among them of a product whose uniform quality is known to everyone.** Because any real situation involves imperfections, economics consists of discovering how real-world market structures create opportunities to improve social welfare.

A first concern is whether different producers and consumers can freely enter and exit, moving along supply and demand curves with infinitesimally small changes in quantity. As we have seen, individual choices may span regions of increasing returns that create discontinuities, so activities shut down or jump up in size and scale when prices cross specific thresholds. In the toy model of

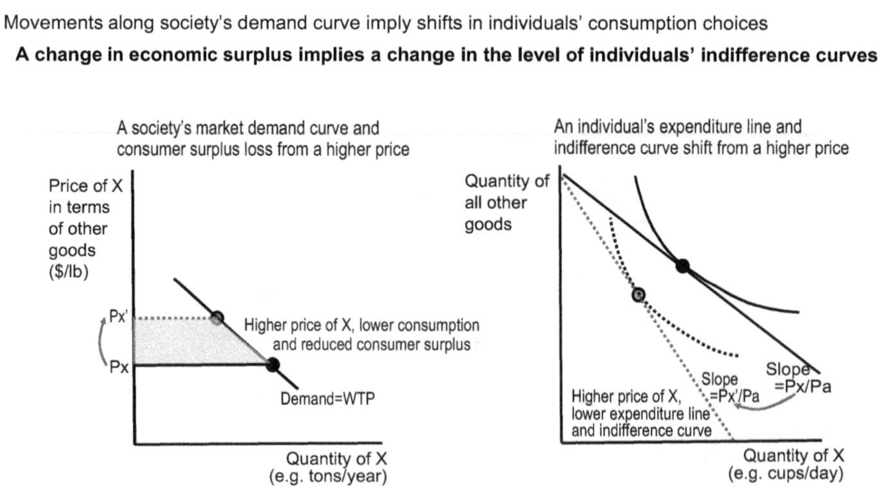

Fig. 4.7 Linking society's economic surplus to individuals' indifference curves

Alphabet Beach, where each producer can catch two fish but each consumer wants only one, the only consequence of this imperfection is that prices for the sixth fish could vary between 2 and 3. In markets where just a single company sets the quantity, the result is market power of the type presented in the next chapter. Innovations and policies that facilitate small increments from new producers or consumers generally help move towards the highest attainable total welfare, although other imperfections might cause unintended side effects such as externalities discussed in the next section.

A second kind of imperfection concerns barriers to exchange of a product whose uniform quality is known to everyone. As we have seen there can be many barriers to exchange, including both policy decisions such as licensing that could be reduced through political mobilization, and also technology or infrastructure that could be reduced through innovation and investment in less expensive ways of making transactions. Many of these barriers are obstacles to information flow, as the underlying attributes of something may be unknown or misleading. As we will see, differences in both visible and invisible attributes of each item are central to food economics, including especially the impact of each item on the consumer's future health discussed throughout the later chapters of this book.

Using economic surplus to investigate market failures such as externalities and market power is useful, but in so doing it is important to keep in mind that the model shows only one specific market at a time. The interests of other people are not shown on the diagram, unless they are included in assessments of a specific externality such as greenhouse gas emissions. And the diagram shows conditions at a given level of all other things, which could change and therefore shift the lines and curves. Economists using these diagrams are typically well aware of these limitations and redraw the diagrams differently around each decision, much as maps used when traveling are redrawn around each step in navigation. As with travelers using maps for navigation, economists using models must also look up and out to experience the world itself more directly, providing the contextual knowledge needed to use the model appropriately for decision-making in the real world.

Linking Economic Surplus to Consumers' Interest in Policy Change

Economic surplus is defined as the area between prices up to a society's demand and supply curves, which in turn are derived from each person's indifference curves and production possibilities. Focusing on the links between the population's consumer surplus and each individual's indifference curves provide helpful insight into the meaning of economic surplus, as shown in Fig. 4.7.

The illustration in Fig. 4.7 links societal response in each market to individual wellbeing. In this example, an exogenous rise in price from P_X to P_X' traces out the shaded loss of consumer surplus on the left panel for the market as a whole and for each person on the right panel. Each individual in the population will have their own indifference curve and level of income, but everyone using the same marketplace will face the same food price change that rotates their budget downward. As shown on the right panel of Fig. 4.8, the price change reduces each person's purchasing power for everything and also induces substitution away from this specific product towards other things. Those two effects were first noted in Chapter 2. Now we can see how a price change's income and substitution effects matter for decision-making, by creating a difference between how a change in food prices is experienced after it has occurred and how it is anticipated beforehand. The distinction between how a change is experienced and anticipated can be quantified by comparing the *compensating variation* in real income after a change has occurred to the anticipated *equivalent variation* in real income before the change, as shown in the two panels of Fig. 4.8.

The two panels of Fig. 4.8 show the experience of a price change after it has occurred (on the left) and the anticipation of a price change before it has occurred (on the right). The difference has practical importance because the compensation needed to restore equity after a price change differs from each person's interest in a policy change before it occurs. On the left each person's *compensating variation* experienced from the change is shown as the vertical gap in real income from the dotted to the dashed budget lines, measuring the compensation needed to restore their earlier level of wellbeing. In contrast, the right panel shows the *equivalent variation* in real income anticipated before the price change occurs, shown as the vertical gap from the solid to the dashed budget line.

As shown on the right panel of Fig. 4.8, each person's anticipated effect of a price change, as measured by their equivalent variation in real income, depends on the anticipated curvature of their indifference curve when their real income is lowered by the price rise. If the double-line indifference curve

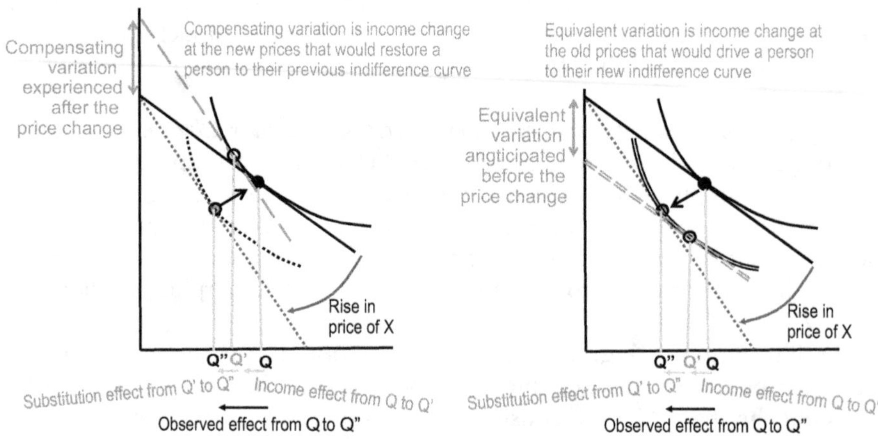

Fig. 4.8 Definition of compensating and equivalent variation in wellbeing

were anticipated to be highly bowed, there would be little ability to substitute away from the product with a higher price, and the vertical intercept of the dashed budget line would be lower. That would indicate a larger equivalent variation and greater anticipated harm. In contrast, as shown on the left panel, each person's experience of harm after the price change depends on their actual degree of substitution.

For any actual price change, both compensation required after the change and anticipated effects before it occurs are determined primarily by the magnitude of price rise and the initial budget share of the item whose price has risen, as shown by the shift from solid to dotted budget lines. Curvature of the two indifference curves also matters for the magnitude of both compensating variation and equivalent variation, especially if the anticipated curvature of the lower indifference curve differs from its actual curvature after people have adjusted. In situations where people anticipate that they will have fewer other options and hence less flexible response at the new higher prices than they would really have after the change occurs, they will have greater interest in the price change and hence more political engagement to influence proposed changes in policy.

Linking Gains from Trade to Wellbeing, Separability and Comparative Advantage

The link between societal outcomes and each person's wellbeing is reflected in how gains from trade in a market relate to choices among production possibilities, which in turn determines the level of each budget line and the highest level of indifference they can reach. Comparing the analytical diagrams used for markets and for individuals is especially helpful to revisit the concept of *separability* that was introduced earlier in Chapter 3, and to define and use the concept of *comparative advantage* as shown in Fig. 4.9.

The three scenarios shown in Fig. 4.9 are all drawn with the same prices and the same demand curve, to illustrate how differences in market supply and individual PPFs determine differences in *comparative advantage* for that society and for each individual. **A society or person's 'comparative advantage' is the relative value to them of doing one thing, relative to the value of doing other things.** Comparative advantage affects decision-making in ways that may seem obvious and intuitive in some ways, but closer examination reveals the concept's surprising implications.

In the left panel of Fig. 4.9, this community's initial supply curve S meets their price in trade at point ***A***, which corresponds to the individual's point ***a*** on the right panel. At the prevailing price in trade, the whole society exports this product and the individual is a net seller, as shown by how their quantity produced exceeds quantity consumed. The changes shown are declines in quantity produced at the given price in trade, for example due to worsening environmental conditions. One decline could be to point ***B*** for society which corresponds to point ***b*** for this individual, and a further decline could lead to point ***C*** for the community and point ***c*** for this person.

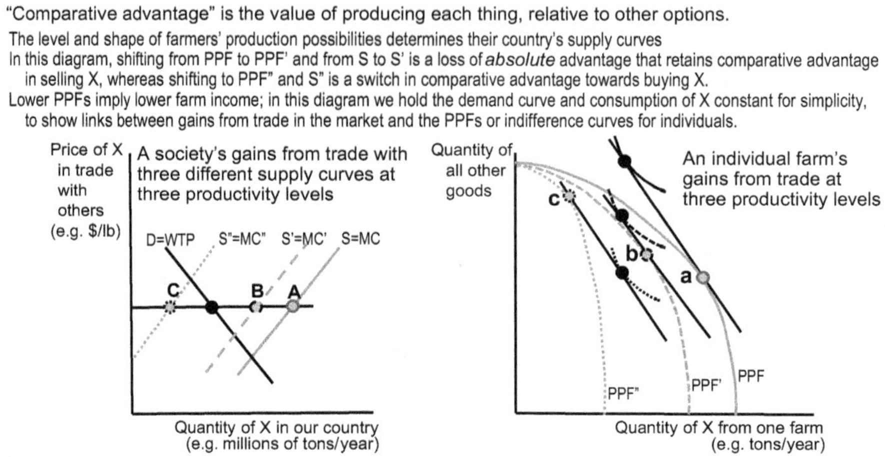

Fig. 4.9 Definition of comparative advantage and separability, for societies and individuals

These scenarios illustrate the concept of *separability* between production and consumption that was introduced in Section 3.2. Separability in a market and for a person is the difference between quantities produced and consumed that arises for things traded or exchanged with others. In the case shown on Fig. 4.9, there is no change at all in quantity consumed. On the left panel, the environmental degradation that shifts the supply curve in this market leftward causes no change in the trade price, which is our familiar representation of how changing the quantity traded of a small community has small and often imperceptible effects on the price they pay or receive from the large rest of the world. On the right panel, the leftward shift in PPFs and hence budget lines cause no change in quantity consumed, which arises because this person's preferences happen to leave the quantity of this product unchanged at each level of real income. In real-world applications, a more advanced version of this model could allow for both trade price changes and income effects on consumption, without altering the results of separability and comparative advantage.

The scenarios in Fig. 4.9 show how people might initially have a strong comparative advantage in the product shown, leading to large exports from the initial point ***A***. Environmental degradation or other changes that cause a leftward shift in supply and each individual's PPF might reduce the degree of comparative advantage and exports at ***B***, and further shifts in that direction could eliminate and then reverse their comparative advantage, leading to imports at ***C***. The corresponding change for each farm is their shift from being a large net seller of this product at point ***a***, to a smaller quantity sold at point ***b***, and reversal to becoming a net buyer at point ***c***. In each case, separability means that production and consumption have different causes, resulting in the degree or direction of comparative advantage for the product shown.

The example shown in Fig. 4.9 is designed to be readily understood, as an example of comparative advantage and separability that is typically consistent with intuition formed by personal experience and stories about other people. In this case, environmental factors reduced a community's comparative advantage and even reversed it, with little or no change in consumption. A typical example might be apple production in Massachusetts, if local weather shifts production and hence quantities shipped in or out, with little impact on consumption. Later in this book we will see many other applications of these models which lead to more surprising results, building intuition about how to take account of causal mechanisms behind observed outcomes.

Conclusion

This section introduced the concept of economic surplus as a measure of social welfare, and demonstrated its relationship to each individual's wellbeing and interest in policy change. The sum of those interests drives whether a group of people experiences improvements or worsening over time in their ability to achieve their goals, as measured by economic surplus in each market and the corresponding equivalent or compensating variation in each individual's wellbeing.

Analyzing social welfare in economic terms helps explain, predict and assess changes in the living standards of entire societies. This section showed how some of those changes are due to gains from trade with other people, but those gains are unevenly distributed with systematic differences in who gains and who loses. Those distributional effects drive not only the equity outcomes of each change, but also determine how changes are experienced or anticipated, and hence each person's interest in mobilizing efforts to influence policies. The analytical models presented in this chapter provide clear qualitative predictions about relative magnitudes, guiding application of economic principles to empirical analysis of food system change.

The growing toolkit of economic models presented so far in this book reflect the underlying principle that observed outcomes are selected from a limited set of options by each person, and that they have learned from experience and chosen the actions that are best for them. Our market diagrams use a variety of elements to explain, predict and assess those choices, with different market structures that specify the shape and position of each line and curve that leads to individual points of price and quantity, tracing out areas of economic surplus from each change. Subsequent chapters show how alternative market structures lead to different outcomes, and affect the impacts of policy intervention, environmental change or technological innovation.

Before we turn to the impacts of policy or other changes in alternative market structures, it is helpful to introduce how economists take account of the unintended side effects of choices in each market. Those side effects are captured by adding a new element to our diagrams that does not alter the predicted outcome of each market, but does affect the total economic surplus and wellbeing that results from that outcome, with important implications for decision-making.

4.2 Externalities: Unintended Side Effects of Market Activity

4.2.1 Motivation and Guiding Questions

The previous sections of this book have shown how economic principles help explain observed outcomes within each market, tracing how individual choices drive response to changes in production and consumption. But what if each person's choices have unintended side effects? Almost every activity causes some kind of pollution or depletion of environmental resources, and food choices can have large impacts on a person's future health. How can we account for those impacts on societal wellbeing, and how do these side effects of market activity affect decisions about policy intervention?

The unintended side effects of market activity are known as *externalities*. By definition, an externality is unintended, meaning that it was not accounted for in the decisions of the person choosing how much to produce or consume. Side effects typically involve a different dimension of life not shown on each market diagram, such as climate change or health and longevity. In many situations we know that some such effect must exist but we do not know its magnitude. In other settings we can estimate the magnitude of external costs or benefits from each unit of production or consumption, and take that into account. Whether or not the magnitude of an externality is measurable, we can see its qualitative implications for societal welfare by including externalities as an additional area of economic surplus loss or gain from each unit produced or consumed.

When economists account for externalities in our market diagrams, we are taking an outside view of society that includes market failures. We are identifying gains or losses that market decision-makers do not consider in their own decisions, and we can add those external costs or benefits to construct our own measure of total social welfare. Including the costs or benefits of externalities allows us to determine the specific market failure caused by those unintended side effects, and identify that choices that would have generated the highest level of social welfare if the externalities were taken into account. Throughout this book we will label those socially optimal outcomes with an asterisk, for example Q^*, to show its special status as a benchmark to which policy interventions can aspire.

The actual value of Q^* in a real-world market cannot be observed directly and is usually not even estimated, precisely because externalities are unintended consequences not counted by anyone in society. For example, when farmers apply manure and fertilizers to their fields, only some of the nutrients are taken up by crops to increase yield. Some nutrients will be taken up by plant roots or residues and remain in the soil as organic matter, while other nutrients are lost into the air or leach down into groundwater and run off into surface water used by other people. Each farmer's choice of how much fertilizer to use is based on their observations of how it affects their crop growth and soil profile, but nutrients flowing through the air and water are not typically observed by anyone. Farmers and water users know some flows exist because their effects are plain to see in local rivers and ponds, and some flows from fields to specific destinations have been quantified by soil scientists and hydrologists, but mapping all flows and their impacts on all water users is not feasible. Our goal in this section is to gain qualitative insights, identifying how externalities affect socially optimal outcomes such as ***Q**** relative to observable quantities such as market equilibrium ***Q*** and potential outcomes with policy interventions such as ***Q'***.

Externalities occur all around us. Once we start thinking about them it can be hard to stop, because every activity has some degree of unintended side effects. Many externalities are positive, for example when farming and farmers' markets enhance a community's appeal, while other externalities are negative. The impact of externalities on each person depends on that person's preferences, and may be difficult to define let alone to measure. For example, William worked for many years at Purdue University, near a corn processing plant that often emitted a strong sweet odor. Visitors were surprised and many local people objected, but when asked about the odor some locals would smile and say it was the smell of money. Eventually, air-quality regulations led the company to pay for a new kind of thermal oxidizer that reduced pollution without reducing production, thereby revealing how externalities can sometimes be addressed directly so each activity has less side effects. As shown in this section, regulation and innovation to address externalities directly can be much more cost-effective than altering the level of the activity itself, because interventions that alter market outcomes have their own unintended side effects.

Many externalities involve relatively small effects like occasional noise outside a restaurant, but other externalities pose existential threats such as greenhouse gas emissions. A variety of policy interventions may be used to address each one. In this section we focus on policy interventions in each market that aim to 'internalize' the externality, showing how producers and consumers can be induced to take side effects into account so the new quantities, denoted ***Q'***, are closer to the socially optimal quantities, ***Q****. In Chapter 6 we will address decisions by governments and organizations to address externalities and other market failures through their own actions. Those are called collective actions delivering a public good, in contrast to the individual actions for private goods and services discussed in this section. When we get to Chapter 6, we will distinguish between two different aspects of externalities: first that they are *non-excludable*, meaning that their creator cannot exclude some people from experiencing them, and second that they are *non-rival*, meaning that each person who experiences them does not stop others from also experiencing that same externality. The distinction between non-excludability and non-rivalry affects decisions about how public goods are provided, but for this section the relevant observation is that most externalities are both non-excludable and non-rival in the affected community.

By the end of this section, you will be able to:

1. Define and provide examples of marginal external costs and marginal external benefits caused by food production and consumption activities;
2. Draw the total marginal social costs and marginal social benefits of production or consumption activities, and show how those affect socially desirable quantities produced and consumed in markets with and without trade;
3. Draw and describe consequences of externalities in terms of economic surplus; and
4. Use diagrams to show how a policy change that takes account of externalities could intervene to alter quantities and change the population's total economic surplus.

4.2.2 Analytical Tools

Externalities are unintended side effects of market activity that harm or help specific people. In the case of odor and air pollution from processing plants or manufacturing facilities, there may be significant harm to nearby residents downwind of the facility. Introducing pollution to a neighborhood worsens quality of life and lowers property values. New activities that might harm local residents are often placed where people are unlikely or unable to object, and low-income people with few other options may move to places that are affordable in part because of negative externalities that lower housing costs at that location. Understanding externalities helps us see how income distribution and equity is related to environmental justice based on impacts of the externality itself, in addition to the externality's role in society's total economic surplus. The magnitude of externalities discussed in this section may be difficult to quantify but our analytical diagrams are helpful to see the relative direction of their effects.

Externalities and the Full Social Cost or Benefit of Each Activity

Externalities can arise from either production or consumption, and can involve both negative and positive side effects. When production activities generate harmful externalities such as air or water pollution, the *marginal external cost* of each unit produced can be added to the producers' own marginal costs along their supply curve, to show the *marginal social cost* of each addition unit in production. When it is consumption that generates a harmful side effect, such as higher medical costs for an insured population, those marginal external costs are subtracted from willingness to pay along the demand curve, to show the ***marginal social benefit*** of each additional unit consumed. In both cases, the social cost or social benefit curves are not observable in the marketplace, but are constructed for the purpose of identifying policy goals regarding both market efficiency for total economic surplus, and social equity regarding economic surplus and environmental justice.

Similarly when production activities generate beneficial side effects such as attractive businesses that improve the quality of life for others in a neighborhood, those ***marginal external benefits*** would be subtracted from the company's own private marginal costs along their supply curve to show the marginal social cost of each additional unit. And when consumption generates beneficial side effects, such as one's own education that helps other people, those benefits are additional to each person's willingness to pay along their demand curve to show the marginal social benefit of additional learning.

For local services where quantities produced are immediately consumed, there may be no need to distinguish whether externalities come from production or consumption, because the quantity supplied is exactly equal to the quantity demanded. For example, if we are concerned about the negative externalities from late-night alcohol service at bars and restaurants, we could draw those harms as a higher marginal social cost of selling drinks above the supply curve, or a lower marginal social benefit of buying drinks below the demand curve, as shown in Fig. 4.10.

The example shown in Fig. 4.10 provides two perspectives on the same market failure, which is the external costs of a local bar's late-night service. On the left panel, external costs experienced by neighbors and others are added vertically to the bar's supply curve, while the left panel shows the same external costs subtracted vertically from the drinker's demand curve. Both ways of analyzing the problem lead to the same conclusion, which is a socially optimal amount of late-night drinking (Q*) below the free-market equilibrium quantity (Q). On the left panel that social optimum is found by showing where the entire population's marginal social cost curve (MSC), composed of the supply

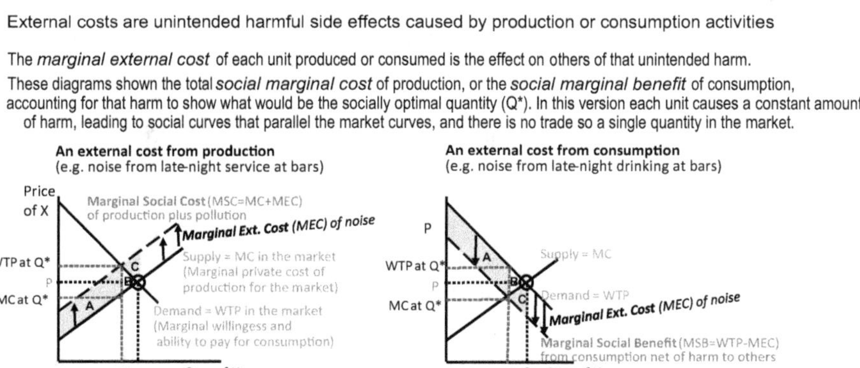

Fig. 4.10 Definition of external costs from production or consumption

curve (S) plus the marginal external cost (MEC) of supply to other people, just equals the population's demand curve (D). On the right panel, the same result is found by showing where S meets the entire population's marginal social benefit curve (MSB), which is composed of D plus the MEC of demand for other people.

Externalities are shown in Fig. 4.10 using dark vertical arrows whose height is magnitude of MEC, representing the cost to other people (not the sellers or the drinkers) of each additional late-night amount of bar service. In this example, for visual clarity those vertical arrows have the same height for each unit, starting at zero out to Q that would be observed in a free market. It would be difficult or even impossible to measure the harm to other people of late-night drinking, but we might imagine some kind of market experiment or observational analysis among the neighbors and other affected members of this society to estimate the height of MEC. Tracing that vertical cost over each unit along the horizontal axis, from zero out to Q, is the environmental harm to others in society shown here as area ABC.

A first surprising finding from Fig. 4.10 is that the social optimum is not necessarily to have zero late-night drinking. For the value of Q* to be zero, the height of the MEC would need to be the entire gap between S and D at their vertical intercepts. This result occurs because the social optimum considers not only the negative side effects of late-night drinking, but also the interests of sellers and buyers in the market for drinks. Both panels of the figure show how a reduction in late-night drinking from Q towards Q*, if it could be achieved, would trace out area C of societal gains. Every step away from Q opens up area B where demand exceeds supply. The social optimum can be found where further reductions in quantity no longer add to area C, so it forms a triangle similar to our gains from trade.

A second finding from Fig. 4.10 is that at the social optimum, there may still be a lot of negative external cost shown by area A. Those magnitudes are difficult to measure, but they are evident to anyone who has lived in the vicinity of neighborhoods with many late-night bars and are sufficient to mobilize local property owners to have their city governments impose noise ordinances and strict licensing of bars and restaurants, including limits on late-night opening. Such policies would need to be enforced using fines or police action because at any quantity below Q, the drinkers' willingness to pay exceeds the bars' marginal costs, so they would want to keep drinking back to Q.

A third result from these findings is that policies or innovations to shrink the height of the MEC could yield much more total benefit to society than regulating the quantity sold. For example, if the externality is just noise, then ordinances that require noise-proofing the space might sharply reduce all of area A, and be a preferable solution than any effort to reduce drinking. Noise is just one of several possible externalities from late-night drinking, however, and it might be impossible to address each one directly. Real-life policymaking involves a combination of interventions, each responding to the political interests mobilized for or against each intervention.

Finally, a fourth insight from Fig. 4.10 is that reaching the social optimum involves tradeoffs between the interests of different groups. When quantity is reduced from Q to Q*, the further pursuit of one group's interests delivers gains to them that are just equal to costs imposed on others. In this diagram, Q* is the intersection of lines accounting for all three interest groups, counting the MEC as well as S and D. If policymaking represented all interests proportionally to their economic surplus in monetary terms, then governments would routinely guide societies towards their Q* outcomes. But as we have already seen from the contrast between imports and exports, individuals in different constituencies have very different degrees of motivation to mobilize politically. Economic analysis can help reveal which groups are getting more favorable policies and can help amplify the interests of groups with less influence on observed policies.

The example above focused on a simple kind of external harm in food systems. Other externalities involve beneficial side effects, which would be drawn by subtracting the marginal external benefit from sellers' marginal costs to obtain a social marginal cost curve below the supply curve, or adding the marginal external benefit to buyers' willingness to pay to obtain social marginal benefit above the demand curve. An example is shown in Fig. 4.11.

The two panels of Fig. 4.11 tell the same story as the previous diagram, but with external benefits instead of external costs. Compared to Fig. 4.10, the only difference is that we scale the price axis slightly differently in the two panels just to give space for the labeling.

Many different examples of externalities could be discussed around the diagrams in Figs. 4.10 and 4.11. That same market structure applies to any product without trade. An example of an externality in a market with trade is shown at the end of this section, in Fig. 4.16. We introduce that later

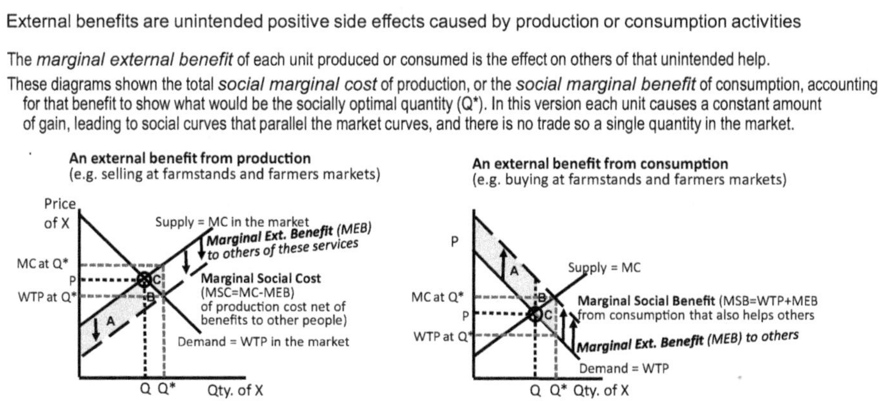

Fig. 4.11 Definition of external benefits from production or consumption

because trade can be imports or exports, so there would potentially be an additional eight diagrams to show each kind of externality, in addition to the four externality diagrams shown so far. The eight diagrams would show two kinds of activity (production and consumption) each having two kinds of side effects (harms and benefits) in each of two kinds of markets (exports and imports). Fortunately there is no need to enumerate all twelve kinds of externality diagrams, because the principles of economics play out similarly in each one.

When introducing trade to markets in autarky, our central insight was that supply and demand become separated from each other. Production is where supply meets the price in trade, and consumption is where demand meets the price in trade. For that reason, drawing externalities with trade in the diagrams is straightforward. If there is an externality in supply, then *socially optimal production* would be where our community's MSC meets the price in trade, but socially optimal consumption is still the market equilibrium quantity. Conversely, if there is an externality in demand, then *socially optimal consumption* would be where our community's MSB meets our price in trade, but socially optimal production is still the market equilibrium quantity.

For example, using the left panel of Fig. 4.11, we have space to imagine drawing a horizontal price line for imports somewhere below the lines' intersections, so that the price in trade meets demand at a high quantity consumed. The presence of the MEB so that MSC is below supply has no effect on the level of consumption that would be socially optimal, but does imply that socially optimal production would be where the MSC meets the price in trade. Areas A, B and C of the diagram then trace out the difference between private and social cost curves, up to the horizontal supply of imports line, which replaces the demand curve in determining production.

We could also introduce the role of trade to the right panel of Fig. 4.11, where we have space to imagine drawing a horizontal price line for exports somewhere above the lines' intersections. Again, separability would ensure that the externality in consumption affects only the socially optimal quantity consumed, as socially optimal production remains where the supply curve meets the price in trade. It is preferable not to enumerate all twelve of these externality diagrams with trade, because nothing is learned from each additional one, and privileging just a few might misleadingly suggest that externalities are found only under certain market structures. In fact they exist in all kinds of markets, and our one representative example in a market with trade is Fig. 4.16 at the end of this section.

Related Terminology: Pecuniary Externalities, Network Effects and Congestion

The term externality can mean any side effect of market activity on other people, leading to a variety of special cases with specific uses of the term.

A first kind of 'externality' that is already captured in our diagrams, operating through market prices, is *pecuniary externalities* from additional sales or purchases that alter the market price for that person and all other market participants. For example, as we saw in Alphabet Beach village, the entry of Gio to sell one fish to Cat drove down the price received by Fio when selling to Ana and Bob, and then Gio's sale of the second fish to Deb further reduced the price paid and received. That side effect of market activity was historically called a pecuniary externality, because it reduces the monetary price received and paid to others. The change in price has a large effect on equity and the distribution of income or wealth, but those gains and losses offset each other and have no impact on the society's total economic surplus.

Another specific use of the term is *network externalities*, in which one person's use of something makes it more valuable for others. In food systems a simple example is popular bars and restaurants, where people want to be seen by others all enjoying the same thing. This is a kind of scale economy in which popularity is difficult to predict because it might depend on just a few influencers on social media. The reverse is *congestion costs*, in which one person's presence uses up space and makes the thing less valuable for others. Both give rise to opportunities for coordination, and use of shared signals about what certain kinds of people are likely to do in the future. The push and pull of networking and congestion was beautifully captured long ago by Yogi Berra, a quick thinker who famously said of a popular bar he no longer liked that 'Nobody goes there anymore, it's too crowded'.

The balance between network effects that bring people together and congestion costs that spread people apart was transformed by the internet, which reduces the importance of physical movement and hence congestion costs, while opening new opportunities for attracting people through network externalities. The result has been to concentrate users on just one or a few providers for each type of online service, even as congestion effects remain important when physical travel or transport is needed. For example, in the food system there is profound concern that online ordering for home delivery will have network externalities and other scale economies, leading to just a few platforms to match buyers with sellers. To the extent that occurs, these platforms could exercise market power against both buyers and sellers on their platform as shown in Chapter 5.

Long before the internet, the main example of network externalities and congestion costs was urbanization. For centuries, rural people have migrated into cities, attracted by network effects and scale economies in many activities. Those forces of agglomeration attract people until diminishing returns and congestion costs make it unattractive for additional migrants to move. That kind of internal migration plays a major role in the agricultural transformation and associated dietary transition discussed in the final chapters of this book.

Equity and Sustainability Effects of Externalities in the Food System
As we have seen, each externality is a kind of market failure in which observed outcomes differ from socially optimal quantities. This is important for understanding how policy interventions might raise a society's overall average living standards by moving from the equilibrium Q towards the socially optimal Q*. Understanding externalities also offers important insights about the distribution of wellbeing, inequities and social or environmental justice. These issues arise in all kinds of markets, many of which have exports or imports, but it is visually convenient to focus on markets without trade as in Fig. 4.12.

The four panels of Fig. 4.12 differ from previous externality diagrams only in that each activity's marginal external cost or benefit is drawn as a proportional addition or subtraction from the supply and demand curve, rotating each MSC or MSB curve away from its corresponding S or D curve. Representing externalities as a proportion of price is a plausible representation of some externalities, but as noted earlier the actual magnitude of externalities is difficult or impossible to measure. The purpose of our analytical diagrams is to see their qualitative implications, which are the same whatever their size and whether the externality per unit is proportional to quantity as shown in Fig. 4.12, or is a specific constant per unit as shown in other diagrams.

Putting four externality diagrams in one figure is helpful to see what they have in common and to begin discussion of how interventions might lead to improved outcomes. In all cases the dashed MSC and MSB curves are not themselves any kind of supply or demand. Externalities are non-market side effects that do not influence decisions until policy interventions lead to a new Q' that might approach Q*. In later diagrams, we will see a variety of such interventions and show how they alter the distribution of economic

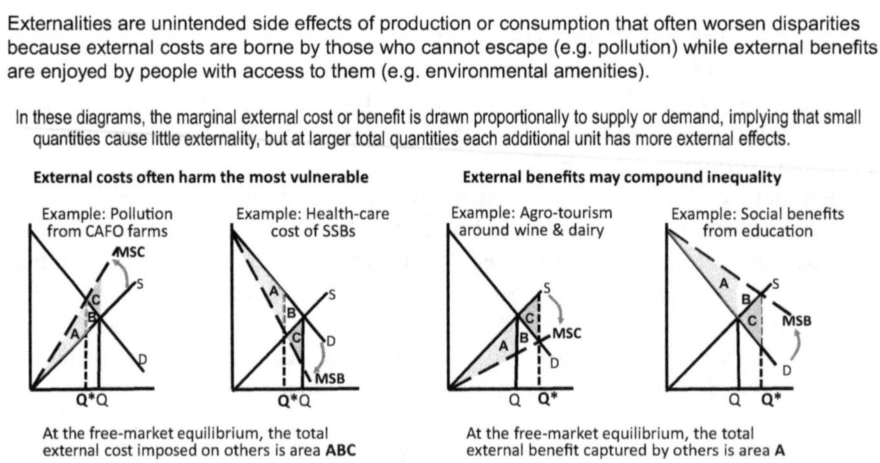

Fig. 4.12 Externalities can cause inequity as well as inefficiency

surplus among buyers and sellers. Some interventions change the extent of externalities by changing the quantity of the product shown, while other interventions alter the process by which that product is made or consumed thereby addressing each externality directly. Intervening to change how a product is produced or consumed can shrink external costs over the entire quantity, thereby improving equity and sustainability as shown in each of these four examples.

On the left of Fig. 4.12, the example of pollution from concentrated animal feeding operations, known as CAFOs, shows how the socially optimal quantity Q* would be to the left of the observed quantity produced if people were to choose their own production and consumption in a free market whose observed outcome would be Q_{free}. The externalities that make social costs higher than the supply curve include air pollution that harms people downwind of the CAFO, and water pollution that harms people who are downstream or use the groundwater affected by CAFOs. Those side effects can potentially be observed directly and have clear impacts on identifiable populations. Other externalities that are even harder to quantify include fostering antimicrobial resistance that makes it harder to control infectious disease in the future and worsening animal welfare that is valued by many people in society. Each of those externalities could be addressed directly by regulations which would shrink the height of area ABC. If we were to draw these regulations, compliance would raise the cost of production to a new supply curve denoted S' which would meet D at a new Q' to the left of Q, while lower social costs be shown as a lower MSC' curve and a smaller ABC' area of harm to other people. Sketching different versions of this diagram around each kind of livestock operation, and talking with stakeholders about the relative magnitudes of each effect, can help analysts participate in the many contentious debates about each of these interventions.

The next diagram in Fig. 4.12 shows the example of healthcare costs from sugar sweetened beverages (SSBs). There may be production externalities involved in making SSBs, but the main harm comes from consuming them which can lead to earlier and more severe diabetes and other metabolic disease over time. Each consumer takes their own future health into consideration only to some degree, first because the effects of SSBs on disease are visible only through epidemiological and clinical studies, and then even if people are told about those effects in dietary guidelines or other advice, there are many limits on how consumers might act on that knowledge. An externality that affects the consumer themselves is sometimes known as an *internality*, but even if people did take their own future health fully into account, there would still be important harms to other people. One group that might experience harm is family and friends, employers and others who have a personal interest in the SSB consumer's future health. More generally, at least some of each person's health care costs are paid by other people through health insurance and public services. Each individual's disease risk can have significant external costs, and in the case of SSBs those costs may be directly proportional to quantity consumed leading to interventions such as restrictions on sales to children or in schools, warning labels, soda taxes and other efforts to reduce consumption.

A third diagram in Fig. 4.12 illustrates how farms might provide multi-functional benefits beyond the outputs they produce. The clearest example is how wine and dairy or cheese creates opportunities for tourism, as an attractive amenity that helps whole regions create employment and manage their local economic development. Almost everyone appreciates the landscape and connection to the natural world as well as local history offered by well-managed farms and farmers markets, including roadside farmstands and urban gardens, which can provide a variety of ecosystem services such as pollination and biodiversity. These positive externalities in production exist even for people who do not consume the produce itself, so they are often addressed directly in ways that focus on the services provided instead of just the output produced. For example, many peri-urban areas have educational farms which bring together a wider range of species in one location than would be chosen by commercial farms, supported by philanthropy and government. Other places have various kinds of community-supported agriculture that customers can visit personally in addition to buying their produce. All of these benefits are shown as area ABC on the diagram, and generate a wide variety of efforts to support beneficial farming activities in addition to commercial production along the supply curve.

The fourth example in Fig. 4.12 is shown regarding this book and education more generally. When people spend their time and money to be students, the resulting demand for education is met by a supply of schools and other services. Purely commercial activity might lead to an equilibrium number of semesters and other measures of quantity at Q, but throughout history people have recognized than at least some of the benefit from schooling are externalities so its MSB is above the demand curve. Those benefits include internalities that help the student and their own family, especially because students with high potential but low wealth cannot pay as much as education would be worth to them. More generally there are externalities that help other people, including family and friends, employers and others who have a personal interest in student's future skills. Historically, these externalities were especially big in rural education for farm families, but even in urban areas today there are many missed opportunities to expand education. Almost all countries do this partly through regulation as compulsory schooling for example through age 16, complemented by government and philanthropic funding as well as subsidized lending. It is difficult for students to know ahead of time whether any given program is worthwhile for them, so there are situations where people have enrolled in programs that they subsequently wish they had not done, but much of economic and social development consists of increased schooling towards personally and socially optimal levels of education.

Each of the examples shown could be investigated in many different ways, at any scale of observation. The diagrams could be drawn for a small community over a single year, or for the world as a whole over an entire century. In markets for products that are traded with others, then externalities in production involve only producers and do not alter socially optimal consumption, while consumption externalities involve only consumers and do not alter socially optimal production. These general principles provide a valuable framework in which to see causal mechanisms behind the inequities and unsustainability of some activities and guide intervention to improve outcomes.

Internalizing Externalities: Regulation, Taxation and Allocation of Legal Rights

Externalities are a type of market failure that affects almost all activity to some degree, creating opportunities for intervention to improve production and consumption in many different ways. Some externalities are minor local nuisances, regulated through social conventions and local ordinances such as litter or noise, but the main focus of economics research and practice is externalities that threaten survival through climate change, pollution and other determinants of human health.

Addressing externalities is among the oldest concerns of government. About 1600 years ago the Greek philosopher Plato described an imaginary 'philosopher-king' who somehow discovered what people should do, using the idea of a benevolent dictator to discuss how governments might compel people to do the right thing. Even today many activities are governed by direct regulation, by which some authority sets standards and requirements for specific products. In 1920, the English economist Cecil Pigou published *The Economics of Welfare* which established modern terminology around externalities, and showed that governments could reach socially optimal quantities by setting taxes or subsidies equal to their marginal external cost or benefit. Later in 1960, the American economist Ronald Coase published an article titled 'The Problem of Social Cost', showing how externalities could sometimes be addressed by policing the harm, giving rights to people so that externalities occur only with the consent of all those affected.

Policies to address an externality can be said to 'internalize' it, leading decision-makers to take each side effect into account. The three types of policy described above serve as a useful framework to catalog interventions, as either direct regulation, 'Pigouvian' taxes and subsidies, and 'Coasian' rights. All three approaches can be used to address beneficial externalities, but we start with their use to address harmful side effects of various activities as illustrated in Fig. 4.13.

The diagrams in Fig. 4.13 show the same kinds of intervention that we first introduced in Chapter 3, focusing on how intervention alters the quantity of each thing, potentially leading society closer to optimal outcomes. Later diagrams in this section will focus on equity, using areas between the curves to show how interventions would alter the distribution of economic surplus and external harms. Other diagrams could address sustainability by showing

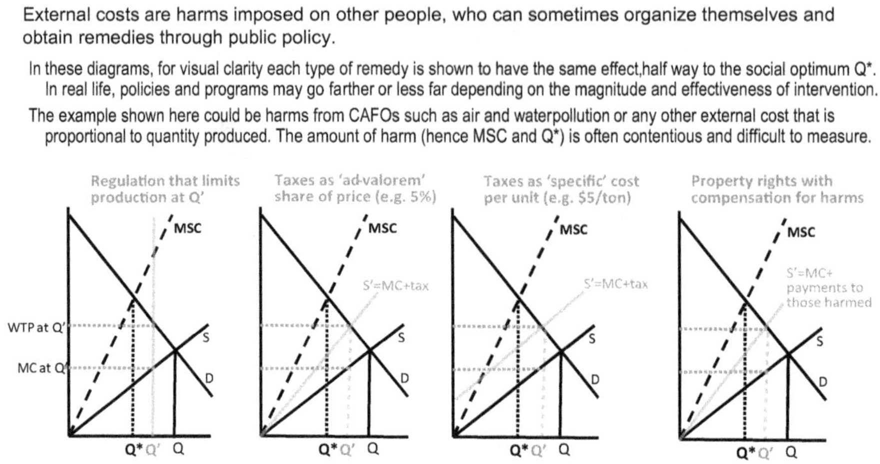

Fig. 4.13 External costs can be limited by direct regulation, taxation or legal rights

shifts in each curve over time. Here we begin with the mechanism by which interventions act on producers and consumers to alter their decisions.

On the left of Fig. 4.13, we draw a scenario like licensing of bars and restaurants, in which governments set quantity directly. Direct regulations might be informed by scientific evidence about the location of Q*, but the actual regulatory process involves political representatives of each constituency mobilizing to influence legislation, executive actions, judicial decisions and enforcement mechanisms. The result is that a regulator might specify the total number of units allowable at Q' and find some way to prevent additional sales despite the gap between demand and supply. People who have a quota or license for their share of Q' can charge along the demand curve and earn more than their cost of supply, creating strong incentives for quota or license holders to maintain those restrictions. Some of the most impactful rules in the food system include building permits, zoning and land use regulation, as well as occupational licensing, visas for immigration and labor law. These and other regulations on total quantity of land and labor typically also regulate how each license can be used, ideally bringing the MSC curve closer to S in addition to any movement of Q' closer to Q*.

In the center diagrams, we show two different kinds of Pigouvian taxes. Both show an external cost that is proportional to quantity so MSC is a line rotated above S. The left shows an ***ad valorem tax*** that is a fixed proportion of price, such as 5%, while the left shows a ***specific tax*** that is a fixed amount per unit, for example $5/ton. Pigou's insight was that government officials could move society towards Q* based only on information about the externality itself, and imposing a tax that equals the harm to society. This can be especially important for equity, as the tax revenue can be used to compensate people who might be harmed by the externality, or harmed by intervention itself.

'Sin taxes' whose revenue has targeted uses can be helpful for city, state and even some national governments, for example when governments introduce a soda tax whose revenue is to be spent directly for the communities affected. These interventions are controversial, however, partly because of the clearly identifiable losses that they cause, but also because the magnitude of market failure that they are intended to remedy is so difficult to measure.

The right side panel in Fig. 4.13 shows the example of *Coasian transactions* from the initial Q to Q' which could potentially approach Q*. Coase's insight was that some side effects from production were historically or could potentially be remedied with a rights-based approach. One of his examples was the relationship between ranchers and farmers, or more generally any livestock producers operating near crop growers, in places where animals might enter fields before harvest and harm the crop. In Fig. 4.13, the diagram would show output from livestock, and the external cost is experienced by crop growers. In reality, there are potential benefits of livestock for nearby crops and many different ways of managing crop-livestock interactions. Coase set aside the details of agricultural production, and focused on the insight that governments can improve outcomes, even without direct regulation or taxation.

The Coasian approach is potentially the most confusing of the three policy remedies for an externality. One reason for confusion is that Coasian ideas were introduced as philosophical arguments with anecdotes or parables but little empirical data. Another cause of confusion is that Coase focused only on property rights, whereas the same arguments would actually apply to the rights of workers or other citizens. Coase was awarded the Nobel Prize for economics in 1991, after which computerized data allowed economists in Chicago and elsewhere to become much more empirical, and economics itself expanded to become more diverse and global. The economics toolkit in this textbook includes Coasian mechanisms as they have been used since the 1990s, as a way to address external harms in a rights-based approach generally, including worker protection and civil rights.

Coasian mechanisms as illustrated in Fig. 4.13 could involve legal rights for farmers to keep livestock off their fields. The government would need to actively monitor and defend farmers' rights, perhaps sending police to enforce the law. Coase's insight was that farmers might be willing to allow livestock damage in exchange for compensation from the livestock owner. Coase saw that in a frictionless world, where farmers can get livestock owners to pay for damages with no transaction costs, and the government can monitor and defend farmers with no enforcement costs, legal rights for farmers might lead them to accept damages all the way to Q*. In that hypothetical thought experiment, the compensation payments would become costs of livestock production that raise S all the way to the MSC curve. In real-life settings with some transaction costs the improvement might stop at Q', but the basic idea is that external side effects become a market of their own.

Real life offers various examples of Coasian mechanisms, as people offer and accept compensation for help or harm. For example, in agriculture there are payments for the positive externality between farmers and beekeepers. Plants feed the bees which make honey, and in exchange the bees pollinate the crop. Which person should pay the other? A payment might not be needed if the benefits to each are roughly equal. In practice we observe farmers paying beekeepers for pollination services. If honey were extremely valuable we might imagine beekeepers paying farmers for the right to use their fields, but either way the equilibrium quantity of both honey and crops moves from Q towards Q*.

The idea that legal rights and private transactions could address externalities long predated Coase's writing. What Coase did was to focus on external harms and notice the potential symmetry between a farmer's right to keep livestock away, and a rancher's right to let animals graze freely. Coase noted that when ranchers have those rights, farmers might pay them to stay away. In terms of Fig. 4.13, ranchers would be paid by farmers to reduce quantity supplied, and move from Q to Q'. In a frictionless world with costless enforcement from the government and no transaction costs between farmers and ranchers, farmers would pay ranchers to stay back all the way to Q*.

The potential symmetry in compensatory payments between farmers and ranchers is the *Coase theorem*, which states that if enforcing and trading rights were costless, initial assignment of rights to either party would lead to transactions towards the same outcome that yields the highest level of total or average income. Whether farmers are given the right to keep livestock off their fields, or ranchers are given the right for their animals to graze freely, frictionless transactions would lead to the quantity we call Q*.

One corollary to the Coase theorem is that rights are valuable and shape the distribution of income and wealth. If farmers have the right to keep livestock off their fields, payments from ranchers to let them in becomes an additional source of income beyond crop sales. Conversely, if ranchers have the right for their animals to graze freely, they receive payments from farmers and become richer. Assigning rights to the community with lower initial income or wealth can therefore improve both equity and efficiency.

Another corollary to the Coase theorem is that frictions matter, so assigning rights in ways that lower enforcement and transaction costs will make a big difference to the outcome. Regarding disputes between farmers and ranchers, it is easy to imagine how protecting the land use rights of farmers would work. Farmers can readily see which animals are on their fields and then ask government for help in forcing livestock owners to pay compensation for that, but the reverse is not feasible in practice. Giving ranchers the right to graze freely and expecting farmers to pay them to stay away would not work, if only because that would give ranchers an incentive to extract payments by repeatedly threatening the farmer's fields with additional animals.

In practice, the Coase theorem provides guidance for how governments might use a rights-based approach to externalities, by focusing attention on opportunities to protect people who suffer from external harms. Doing so can improve both equity and efficiency, up to the limit of enforcement and transaction costs. One of the most fundamental examples is worker protection through employees' civil rights. If enforced through lawsuits and criminal penalties, those rights can stop exploitation and create high-wage opportunities for the few who are willing to do dangerous work. A food system example is higher wages offered to the waitstaff in smoking clubs. Those are Coasian transactions between workers and customers, by which the staff accept the harms of second-hand smoke in exchange for pay.

Coasian transactions involve payment for what would otherwise be a nonmarket harm or benefit, often raising ethical questions about the nature of consent or entitlement. Many societies today ban smoking in public places, but allow private smoking clubs in which workers are paid to accept second-hand smoke. Do others in society agree to allow that type of work? Consent is often tied to the age of the worker, as all kinds of child labor are increasingly banned, but are farm families allowed to have their own children work on their own farms? Ongoing ethical debates about what should be allowed are ultimately settled in legislatures or the courts, where economic analysis can be helpful to track who gains and who losses from regulation.

The interventions to address externalities discussed so far focus on limiting external harms, but there are equally important opportunities for intervention to expand activities that create external benefits. We have already mentioned the Coasian example of beekeepers being paid to make honey near orchards and fields, and other instruments can be illustrated using Fig. 4.14.

In Fig. 4.14, the quantity chosen by buyers and sellers when deciding for themselves and interacting in a competitive market would be Q, but there is an external benefit to each unit consumed that makes socially optimal

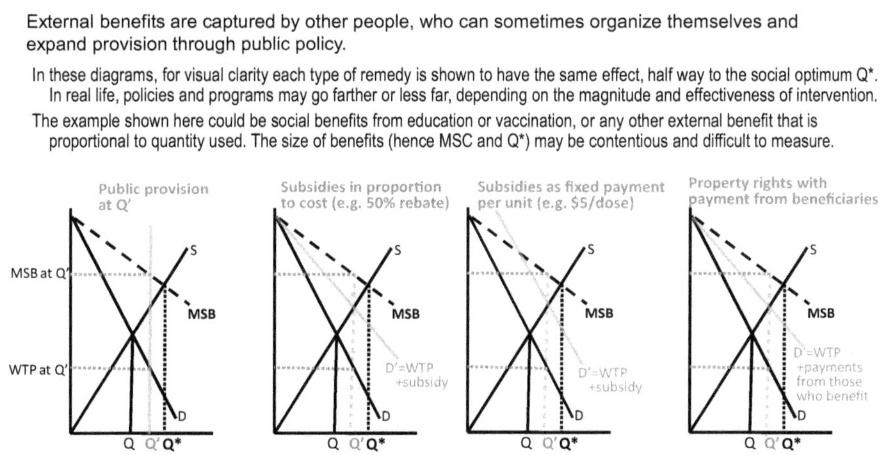

Fig. 4.14 External benefits can be expanded by direct provision, subsidies or property rights

quantities Q*. Each diagram in the figure shows a different kind of intervention that could potentially increase average wellbeing per person in this society. The actual policy-induced outcome at Q' is determined by the interaction of market responses with government interventions, which in turn are determined by many factors other than the limited available evidence about externalities. In any real-life application of these models, Q' might be very far from Q*, and the purpose of economic analysis is to support improvements in how governments intervene. We will return to each kind of intervention in more detail, but it is helpful to see different policy instruments to address positive externalities all together here.

The first diagram shows direct public provision by government, using funds obtained from taxation as well as money creation and borrowing from investors. The government's sources of funds are discussed later in Chapter 9, and its spending on the food system is done through multiple agencies that conduct research, provide education and information as well as public infrastructure and institutional arrangements which underpin markets. These goods and services are public because they have benefits to people in society above market demand, as shown by MSB above D, as the value created by each unit helps people other than the buyer and seller. We have already referred to these external benefits as potentially *non-excludable* and perhaps also *non-rival*, and we will return to those concepts in Chapter 6 which focuses on the provision of public goods.

The next two diagrams contrast direct provision by government with subsidies to individual buyers and sellers, first as a proportional payment (for example, an agency might pay 50% cost-sharing to farmers who make environmentally favorable investments, or a 50% rebate that doubles the quantity of fruits and vegetables a shopper can buy), and then as a fixed payment (for example, paying $5/dose to vaccinate livestock, or a voucher for $5 of fruits and vegetables). The three diagrams on the left of Fig. 4.14 illustrate the many ways that governments can boost use of externally beneficial activities. In each case, public provision or assistance raises the society's total or average wellbeing per person as long as the MSB of each additional unit exceeds its marginal cost along the supply curve, and that requires public intervention because private buyers have a lower willingness and ability to pay along their demand curve as shown in each diagram.

The various ways that public agencies intervene to expand use of beneficial goods and services can be illustrated by all the meals purchased each day with U.S. government funds. The exact number of such meals is unknown, but could be at least 50–80 million meals each day. Some of these are served by government employees in public schools, military facilities and other institutions, while other meals are prepared by private company staff under grants and contracts to different government agencies. Many such meals are made by individuals for themselves using foods bought with benefit cards from the U.S. Supplemental Nutrition Assistance Program (SNAP) and the related program for Women, Infants and Children (WIC) as well as overseas food aid delivered through the United States Agency for International Development (USAID). Each of those programs provides food tailored to support the relevant agency's mission, intervening in ways that take account of different needs to differing degrees. Some meals prepared with U.S. government funds aim to improve health and are mandated to follow the latest Dietary Guidelines for Americans, while other meals are designed for different objectives, with frequent debate about the magnitude and nature of the beneficial externalities that justify public provision and subsidies from government agency.

The fourth diagram in Fig. 4.14 shows how Coasian transactions can sometimes address externalities without government payments, as in the example of how beekeepers are paid directly by farmers for pollination services. In that situation the diagram's horizontal axis might show the number of commercial hives in a country, and the vertical axis shows the price received and costs incurred by beekeepers for maintaining each hive. Consumers' demand for honey does not take the benefits of pollination into account, and the MSB of additional beehives can be quite high. Farmers who benefit from those externalities are willing and able to pay beekeepers for bringing hives onto their farmland, signing pollination agreements that provide additional revenue above the demand for honey. If the entire value of pollination by beehives were captured by local farmers, these Coasian transactions could fully internalize the side effects of producing honey, but in practice pollination promotes biodiversity desired by other people beyond the one farmer who paid for their field to be pollinated. Other landowners might contract for pollination of wildflowers and trees, but there are clear limits to how far Coasian contracts can go to internalize the side effects of each activity.

So far we have analyzed externalities in terms of production and consumption quantities that would take account of their side effects, in addition to the total economic surplus from market transactions. The toolkit of economics is designed so that analysts can draw diagrams tailored to many different kinds of intervention, in the context of many different market structures. To see how changes in economic surplus and external costs or benefits can be altered by policy, we must choose a specific example and draw the corresponding diagram as in Fig. 4.15.The example of Fig. 4.16 is well-known to agricultural policy analysts in the U.S., because it reflects a large and longstanding policy debate. The U.S. first restricted sugar imports in 1789 using tariffs, as one of the few available ways for the new government to raise revenue. Over time sugar production within the U.S. increased, first using the forced labor of enslaved people and later with mechanized production. During the twentieth century the government developed more cost-effective ways of taxing property and income instead of tariffs on trade, and the rising influence of domestic producers and sugar refiners, as well as the reduced need for tax revenue, led to a policy switch from tariffs to quotas in 1934. The switch of import restriction instrument from tariffs to quotas occurred as one of many agricultural policy changes at that time, and ever since then sugar companies

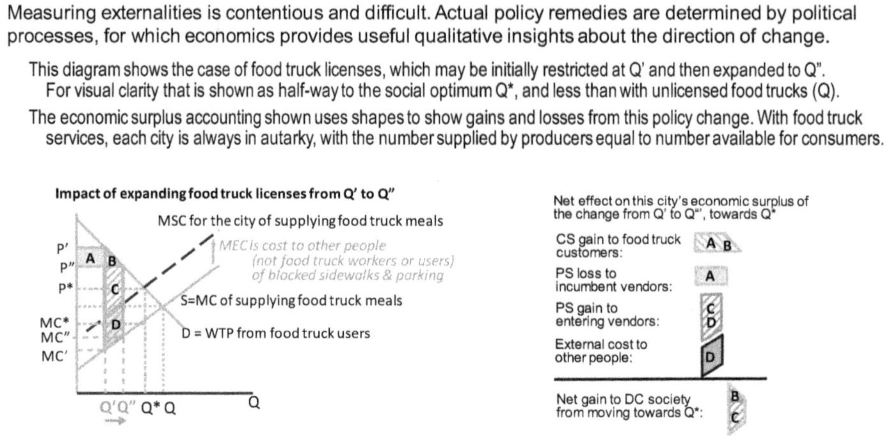

Fig. 4.15 Economic surplus can be used to add up gains and losses from policy intervention

have been allocated import licenses for fixed quantities which drive the market outcomes shown in Fig. 4.16.

The case study shown in Fig. 4.15 is a common real-world example, showing municipal licenses for street food vendors to use public space in potentially congested areas of a town or city. Almost all cities have such vendors, and they are almost always regulated to some degree. The diagram refers to food trucks that have their own small kitchen for hot meals. The same diagram could also be used for food carts, sidewalk vendors, or even the use of street space by nearby restaurants.

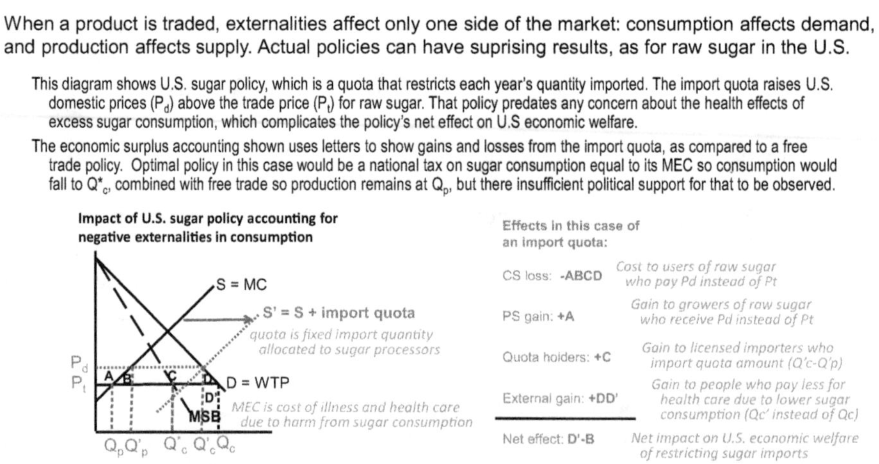

Fig. 4.16 Policy effects depend on market structure, as in the example of U.S. sugar policy

If there were no government restriction on the number of food trucks, they would be parked during the day at many locations around the city at Q, where demand for meals meets their marginal cost of supply. The side effects of having so many food trucks parked around town would lead to complaints from other people, driving city government to pass ordinances regulating where the food trucks can park and how they can operate thus limiting their quantity to Q'. Cities differ in the restrictiveness of their regulations, but historically in many cities automobile drivers and local businesses were more influential than pedestrians, leading to a low or even zero number of food trucks allowed despite high demand by food consumers. In those settings, Q' might be below the socially optimal Q*, and popular demand might lead a government to relax their restrictions and allow more food trucks up to Q".

In the scenario of Fig. 4.15, policy changes to allow more food trucks provide a helpful example of how change alters income distribution and the population's overall average wellbeing. Analysis of these changes in equity and effect focus entirely on the change from one potentially observable price and quantity to another. The remainder of the diagram outside the boundaries of observed Q' and Q" is shown in Fig. 4.15 for visual clarity, but plays no role in our analysis which focuses only on the shaded areas labeled as A, B, C and D.

When government issues additional licenses, new vendors enter bringing in additional units at the same or higher cost along their supply curve, allowing consumers to buy more along their demand curve. When the limited number of licensees operate competitively, as quantity rises from Q' to Q" the market price per meal falls from P' to P", and consumer surplus expands by the gap between those two prices out to the demand curve which is area AB. Producers who had licenses before the change lose from the lower price up to their quantity supplied which was Q', so they lose area A. Meanwhile the entering food truck vendors gain the area between their selling price at P" and their supply curve, so they gain area BCD. Area D is also a harm experienced by the other people who would have used the public space. Putting all the pieces together, the city's population experiences a net gain of BC and important distributional changes in equity and employment.

The results of Fig. 4.15 provide qualitative insights that can help decision-makers anticipate political mobilization of each interest group around any given policy change, based on any available information about the magnitudes of gains and losses per person. For example, if there were about ten new entrants and ten thousand customers who gain from the policy change, but a hundred existing vendors and a hundred other local businesses who lose from it, some research into likely changes in price or profitability would quickly reveal the politics of the situation. To know how much each group might gain or lose, analysts would need to consider not only the baseline situation, but also the plausible elasticities of response. This kind of contextual knowledge may be difficult to assemble but is often hiding in plain sight as revealed by our Fig. 4.16.

The case study of sugar policy is useful here partly because it offers a national-scale contrast to the local food policy example in Fig. 4.15, and partly because it illustrates the difference in outcomes and welfare effects caused by market structure. Sugar is easily stored and transported, so it is commonly traded over long distances. For simplicity we draw its price in trade as a fixed horizontal line at P_t, recognizing that changes in the quantity imported by the U.S. might alter that price slightly with no effect on the qualitative results of our analysis. The external effect of sugar on health is a negative externality in consumption, so we draw the MSB curve below the demand curve. The socially optimal level of consumption, Q_c*, is where MSB curve meets the opportunity cost of buying or producing sugar, which is its price in trade. There might be externalities in production, for example when cane fields are burned or processing plants emit air pollution, but for simplicity the diagram shows only sugar's health effects on consumption. Many other subtleties about sugar policy are also omitted, such as differences between cane and beet sugar, but none of those refinements would alter the basic results shown here.

Figure 4.16 is drawn to show the effects of the quota relative to a hypothetical policy of free trade, as a way of explaining why the U.S. government instituted its import quota in 1934 and has continued to maintain that restriction each year since then. Due to the policy, instead of the free trade quantity imported between Q_c and Q_p, only the gap between Q_c' and Q_p' is allowed into the country. The observed quantity sold is domestic production along S plus the quota, and the resulting price is where that market supply S' meets D at the observed domestic price P_d which sustains quantities Q_c' and Q_p'.

The impacts of U.S. sugar policy on economic surplus and social welfare are shown as letters for each of the differences between the without-policy benchmark and the with-policy observed outcomes. The policy comes at the expense of U.S. consumers who lose area ABCD, which is the price difference out to their demand curve. The policy benefits U.S. producers who gain area A, which is the price difference out to their supply curve, and also benefits sugar companies issued import licenses, who gain C from buying at P_t and selling for P_d over the quantity imported from Q_p' to Q_c'. Taking account of health externalities, to the extent that those could potentially be measured, would be a gain to the U.S. of DD', because consumption has fallen from Q_c to Q_c', resulting in lower rates of diabetes or other metabolic disease. Since D was a loss in consumer surplus but a gain in health, the net effect to U.S. welfare is the gain of D' minus the loss of B.

The results of Fig. 4.16 offer a powerful example of how sketching an analytical diagram can reveal economic mechanisms behind the headlines, in ways that are readily understood once we have practiced drawing these lines and curves. Empirical estimates of each slope and position would be needed to calculate magnitudes, but economic principles are sufficient to see how basic contextual facts about the policy and numbers of people involved help explain policy choices and societal outcomes. These principles play out as visible features of the food policy landscape, illustrated vividly by the example of U.S. sugar policy.

First, the impact of policy on consumers often goes unnoticed by the general public. In this case, their loss of area ABCD is spread over more than 300 million people, whose quantity per person is small enough for the slightly higher price to be of little interest, even each person were told everything about the policy. Even more strikingly, the health gains of DD' are typically not known even to public health nutritionists. Many other factors intervene to influence sugar consumption and disease, and demand for raw sugar is probably quite inelastic so area DD' is relatively small. That fact that health advocates in the U.S. have recurring debates over sugar taxes, without needing to know or mention that U.S. policy already raises the price of raw sugar using trade policy, clearly demonstrates that policies towards retail products like sugar sweetened beverages are formed in very different ways than policies around agricultural commodities like sugar.

Second, the policy's net impact on efficiency for the country as a whole is much smaller than its distributional effects. To explain why the U.S. instituted this policy in 1934 and has maintained it for almost a century, one must look to how much those who benefit are gaining from the policy, and hence their willingness and ability to mobilize political support. In the U.S., the annual gain of areas A and C go to small number of sugar growers and refiners who are geographically concentrated, each of whom sells a large quantity and is highly motivated to maintain the import quota, so they maintain very active engagement with legislators targeting this narrow issue.

Finally, existing policies may have long histories and be supported by powerful interests, but also come to be challenged by new groups that form political coalitions in surprising ways. Legislation to relax the import quota and lower the price of raw sugar is frequently introduced in the U.S. Initiatives to allow more imports are promoted by the confectionery and dairy industries that buy sugar as an ingredient, and are opposed by sugar growers and refiners who sell raw sugar. Environmental groups sometimes join to support reform and reduce harm to the Everglades and other places in Florida where sugar is grown. Understandably, public health groups have other priorities and do not typically participate in these debates.

Conclusion

This section summarized how the toolkit of economic analysis can be applied to account for unintended side effects of market activity. These externalities are a kind of market failure, by which even a perfectly competitive market is inefficient in the sense of not reaching the society's highest potential total economic surplus or other metrics of wellbeing.

Almost all activity generates externalities, ranging from minor nuisances to fundamental drivers of societal wellbeing, including greenhouse gas emissions that threaten all life on earth. Externalities are generated by the ways food is produced and consumed, affecting both sustainability and health, and can be either beneficial or harmful. The harms from negative externalities often disproportionately affect those who are least able to prevent or escape their effects, while the benefits of positive externalities are amenities sought out by those who can afford to take advantage of them. The resulting environmental injustice and health disparities compound the inefficiency caused by externalities, creating opportunities for intervention to improve both equity and efficiency.

Interventions that lead decision-makers to take externalities into account involve regulation, taxes or subsidies and legal rights. Policies often combine multiple interventions and vary greatly in the distribution of their effects among groups in society. The interventions we actually observe are those that attracted sufficient support to be implemented. Altering policies to addressing externalities is contentious in part because those unintended side effects of each activity are not normally quantified as part of anyone's decision-making. Scientific efforts to measure each kind of beneficial or harmful externality would be needed to quantify their magnitude, and then they could be taken into account in economic models.

In this section we analyzed the qualitative effects of externalities on society, showing how interventions could alter those outcomes in ways that could potentially improve economic efficiency as well as equity and sustainability. Each market model is a slightly different analytical diagram, drawn around a specific type of externality in a specific market structure based on contextual knowledge of the situation. The relevant market model can then be used to show the impact of each kind of intervention being considered, revealing how economic principles help explain the diversity of experiences and potential for change to improve outcomes.

CHAPTER 5

Market Power: Imperfect Competition and Strategic Behavior

5.1 Monopoly and Monopsony: When One Seller or Buyer Sets Total Quantity and Price

5.1.1 *Motivation and Guiding Questions*

The market diagrams used so far in this book have many buyers and sellers, but what happens when a single enterprise controls the market? Our individual-choice diagrams show what drives the size and scale of each individual enterprise, suggesting the possibility that one might grow large enough to be the only seller or the only buyer at some place and time.

We use the term *market power* to mean the potential ability of just one seller or buyer to control the entire quantity sold in a particular market. Agriculture and food systems are vulnerable to market power because manufacturing and distribution enterprises have much greater economies of size and scale than family farms and individual households. In many places around the world, whole communities have just one buyer or seller for some important goods and services. Why does market power arise? What outcomes can we expect from this kind of imperfect competition, and how might the resulting market failure be addressed through policy interventions?

Our economic analyses refer to individual markets, each showing a specific community or population interacting at one place and time. Every analytical diagram is drawn based on prior knowledge of that situation, which then determines how supply, demand and trade opportunities are specified. The term *monopoly* refers to markets with just one seller, and *monopsony* refers to markets with just one buyer. The two are symmetrical: both types of market power rely on being just one enterprise buying or selling in a community. As

W. A. Masters and A. B. Finaret, *Food Economics*,
Palgrave Studies in Agricultural Economics and Food Policy,
https://doi.org/10.1007/978-3-031-53840-7_5

we will see, opportunities to trade with others and thereby increase quantities can eliminate market power. The ability of one seller or buyer to control quantity depends on their own scale relative to the market, so market power can arise with just one enterprise in a small town, a larger company in a region or country or a multinational entity serving the whole world.

By the end of this section, you will be able to:

1. Describe how scale effects and innovation create opportunities for market power;
2. Derive marginal revenue curves from demand curves faced by a monopoly seller, to show what quantities they would choose to gain the highest possible level of profit;
3. Derive marginal expenditure curves from supply curves faced by a monopsony buyer, to show what quantities they would choose to gain the highest possible level of profit; and
4. Use diagrams to show how differences in elasticities of supply and demand affect the markup and profits obtained when using market power to restrict quantity.

5.1.2 *Analytical Tools*

The underlying source of market power is increasing returns to size or scale of individual enterprises discussed in Chapter 2. Increasing returns often involve lumpy or indivisible inputs, such as one person or one machine, which fit together with other people and machines in ways that benefit from close coordination within an enterprise. The result is a high fixed cost of setting up the enterprise relative to its marginal cost of expanding, leading to differences between that marginal cost and the enterprise's total cost of operation, and hence its average cost per unit bought or sold. When a single enterprise serves the entire market at lower average cost than if there were multiple enterprises, it is called a *natural monopoly*.

Natural monopolies arise where and when it is more efficient to concentrate production in a single enterprise, using one set of fixed costs to reach many customers at low marginal costs. As we will see, natural monopolies are often regulated as public utilities or provided directly by government as public goods addressed in Chapter 6. In this chapter, we focus on private enterprises, using economic principles to see how their choices affect their own revenue, expenditures and profits.

The scale effects that create market power involve equipment and personnel working together in a single enterprise, often using some kind of specialized knowledge or trade secrets. Every enterprise involves learning from experience, building skills and information over time. The spread of that knowledge is among the most important externalities in agriculture and food systems. Knowledge spillovers help other people adopt valuable innovations, and government funding can help discover and share the most helpful kinds of knowledge, but some innovations arise only through learning by doing within an enterprise. The inventions and specialized knowledge of private enterprises have long been protected by governments using a rights-based approach, using legal restrictions on how ideas can be used. These instruments include privacy protections and labor laws that protect trade secrets, as well as patents and trademarks that confer specific *intellectual property rights*.

Intellectual property is the glue that holds together many enterprises, providing 'intangible' assets that complement their equipment and personnel. Some enterprises hold patents, through which they disclose a specific invention that they can then prevent others from using for a fixed period of time, typically 20 years. Many more enterprises keep trade secrets that may not ever be disclosed, and use trademarks to establish a brand identity that can last for centuries. All intellectual property is a kind of fixed cost, allowing large enterprises to grow and prevent the entry of competitors who might erode their market power.

Relative Scale of Enterprises in Agriculture and the Food Sector

Food purchase decisions are made by individual households, and farming is predominantly a family enterprise, but scale effects often lead to a few large enterprises around them. The resulting hourglass shape in the number of enterprises is illustrated in Fig. 5.1.

The hourglass in Fig. 5.1 illustrates how there are often just a few input suppliers selling to many farm households, and those farm households then sell their output to a few enterprises that trade, transform and distribute food to consumers. The names listed are modern examples with global operations, but the diagram could be used to help understand local agriculture and food systems at any place and time.

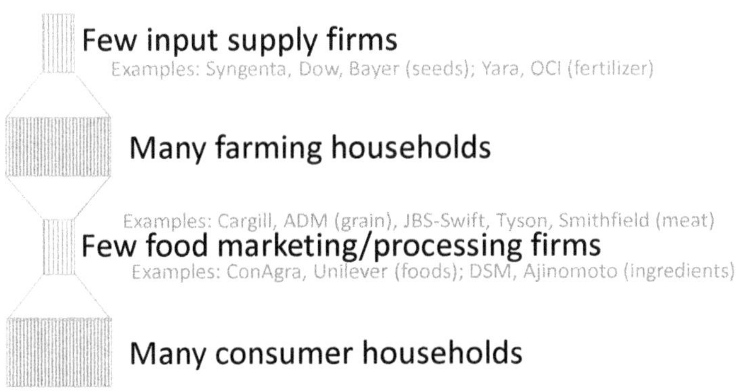

Fig. 5.1 Scale economies in agrifood systems create opportunities to exercise market power

Each enterprise that buys from or sells to farmers, which we can call an *agribusiness*, typically specializes in a specific kind of input in particular locations. The earliest agribusinesses in human history include grain mills, powered by water or wind and sometimes donkeys or horses walking in circles, grinding cereals into flour to serve dozens or hundreds of farmers in their vicinity. Other ancient kinds of agribusiness described in historical records include specialized makers and distributors of tools and equipment, and transport or storage providers in rural areas. Over time, enterprises grew to supply increasingly specialized seeds and other inputs. In each case, local farmers decide whether to do each thing within their own household or to buy that service from an agribusiness which might serve many farmers in their area.

Enterprises that serve consumers, which we might collectively call food businesses, have similar specializations. Food businesses operate at various scales. They often start small as family operations that grow and change as they discover sources of increasing returns and ways to expand. The names shown in Fig. 5.1 are food manufacturers like Unilever and ingredient makers like Ajinomoto, but retailers, restaurants and food service providers can also grow to enormous scale. Grocery chains and restaurants sometimes grow under a single brand name like Walmart or McDonald's, and sometimes grow as a conglomerate of multiple brands. Enterprises can grow through licensing as well as ownership, as for example Starbucks licenses its name and trade secrets to local operators and also directly manages some outlets for which it is both owner and operator.

The hourglass shape of Fig. 5.1, showing a small number of enterprises serving many farmers and many consumers, could be drawn at any geographic scale. Historically, small areas would be served by local enterprises, with agribusinesses serving a few dozen or hundreds of farmers, and food businesses serving hundreds of thousands of individual customers. Over time, increasing specialization and declining costs of transport has expanded the geographic scale of many enterprises. Whether their market is a small village or the entire world, one or more enterprises can potentially use their scale to exercise market power.

We use the term *monopoly* to describe a market with just one seller and the less common term *monopsony* when there is just one buyer. The two are symmetrical, so both kinds of market power are sometimes called monopoly power. But distinguishing between monopoly and monopsony is useful because food businesses can potentially exercise both at the same time. For example, a large dairy processor and distributor might become a monopsonist in buying raw milk from farmers and a monopolist in selling dairy products to consumers. Their potential market power is 'two-sided', similar to online platforms for food delivery that could potentially become the only intermediary between restaurants and customers. It is also possible for two large enterprises with market power to face each other, for example if an ingredient is made by just one seller and sold to just one food manufacturer, which would be a strategic interaction of the kind analyzed in the next section of this chapter. For now we turn to monopoly and then monopsony, showing how each can be understood using a similar kind of analytical diagram.

Monopoly Sellers, Marginal Revenue and Price Discrimination
To see how monopolies decide their quantities produced, we can go back to our toy model of the Alphabet Beach fish market. In this setting we know the names and details of each producer and consumer so can readily imagine what a monopolist would do using Fig. 5.2.

The stepwise supply and demand curves of Fig. 5.2 allow us to consider what would happen if Fio and Gio merged into a single enterprise. They might form a household that pools their resources, or be siblings in a family business, or just meet regularly to agree on what to do. Because this pooled Fio-Gio fishing enterprise controls set the entire quantity sold and earns all of the revenue from sales, their joint decisions differ from when Fio and Gio decided individually, when they did not take into account how their sales affected the other.

The earnings of the combined Fio-Gio enterprise from each unit sold are shown in the table on right of Fig. 5.2. In this initial scenario we consider the usual case in which the Fio-Gio enterprise cannot distinguish among buyers and prevent them from exchanging with each other. Each fish is identical so there is only one price, based on the community's marginal willingness to pay along the demand curve. For example if the monopolist sells just one fish, they can post a price of 9 and Ana will buy, but if they want to sell two fish they would have to reduce the price to 7 so that Bob will buy as well. The monopolists cannot prevent Ana from buying at the same price they offer to Bob, however, so the marginal revenue that a monopolist receives from additional sales is much less than the price received.

Monopolists like the Fio-Gio enterprise take account of the reduced price they get from a given customer like Ana when they decide to seek additional

In Alphabet Beach Village, if Fio and Gio merged into one fishing enterprise, what would they do?

Monopolists choose the total quantity produced, and typically sell at the same price to everyone.

A monopolist's total revenue is quantity times price. They maximize profits by expanding until *marginal revenue* from each additional unit sold falls below its marginal cost of production.
In this case, the unified Fio-Gio enterprise would stop at selling two fish and use only Fio's boat, since using Gio's boat to sell more fish yields marginal revenue (MR) below its marginal cost (MC).

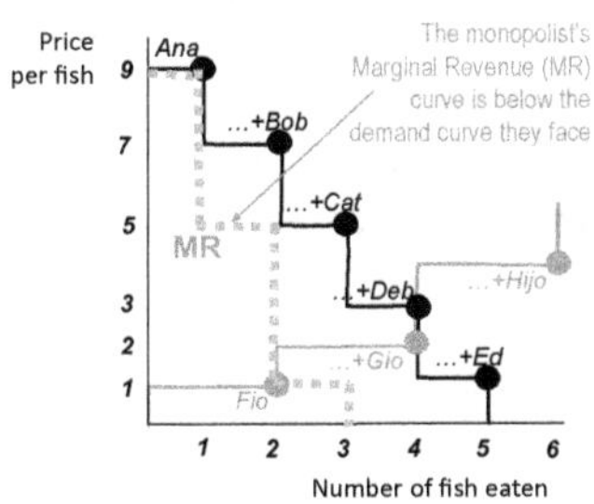

	Demand		A monopolist's perspective		Supply	
	Qty. sold	*WTP*	Total Revenue	Marginal rev. (MR)	*MC*	Producer
A	1	9	1x9 = 9	9-0 = 9	1	Fio
A+B	2	7	2x7 = 14	14-9 = 5	1	Fio
A+B+C	3	5	3x5 = 15	15-14 = 1	2	Fio+Gio
A+B+C+D	4	3	4x3 = 12	12-14 = -2	2	Fio+Gio
A+B+C+D+E	5	1	5x1 = 5	5-12 = -7	4	F+G+H

When Fio and Gio merge and control the whole market, adding the 3rd fish has a marginal cost of 2 but a marginal revenue of only 1, so they would prefer to sell only Fio's catch.

Fig. 5.2 Monopolists can earn excess profits by restricting production sales to customers like Bob. Selling one fish gave the Fio-Gio enterprise total revenue of 9, and selling two fish gave them total revenue of 14. The marginal revenue of the second fish was therefore 5. Raising quantity sold to three allows Cat to buy as well, but the price they can get falls to 5 and total revenue is 15, so the marginal revenue from their third fish is only 1. The marginal cost for the Fio-Gio enterprise to catch that third fish is 2. Monopolists who seek the highest level of total revenue minus total cost would produce only up to the quantity where marginal revenue is above marginal cost. If the Fio-Gio enterprise did catch a third fish, they would soon realize that was a mistake, and cut back to only two. They would use only Fio's fishing gear and share the resulting income.

The astonishing arithmetic of market power shows why a joint enterprise with both Fio and Gio would choose to produce less than if Fio and Gio worked independently. By merging with Fio, it is possible for Gio to make more by not fishing at all, as long as Fio shares the proceeds from the two fish they sell. The dynamics of their partnership is addressed in Section 5.2 where we introduce strategic interactions between two people. For now we focus on the unexpected logic of how and why monopolists sell less together than if they were separate enterprises along their supply curve.

To see market power graphically, we plot the incremental earnings from each fish on the seller's *marginal revenue* (MR) curve in Fig. 5.2. That curve is much steeper than the demand curve, and the monopolist's highest total income is where MR meets S. The marginal revenue curve is steep because each additional unit sold reduces the price received on all the items sold. Marginal revenue determines the income received by the monopolist but is not itself a demand curve. At the quantity selected by the monopolist where their marginal revenue meets or falls below their marginal cost, they can sell along the D curve at the consumer's willingness to pay.

The scenario shown in Fig. 5.2 is the baseline scenario for most monopolists, but only because they cannot distinguish well enough among buyers to charge each one a different price. Competitive sellers have no incentive or opportunity to differentiate among buyers, because they receive the entire price paid by the marginal buyer. Once an enterprise gains market power, however, they have a very strong incentive to find a way to sell at a higher price to buyers with a higher willingness to pay as shown in Fig. 5.3.

In the extreme benchmark case shown in Fig. 5.3, the Fio-Gio combined enterprise offers a differentiated fish to each buyer, and is somehow able to charge them the consumer's entire willingness to pay. One might imagine, for example, that Fio and Gio have prior knowledge that Ana is wealthy and would pay up to 9 for fish cut a certain way and delivered at a particular time, they might do that and sell one fish at 9. If they also knew that Bob would pay 7 for fish cut a different way, they might do that and thereby sell one at 9 to Ana and also one at 7 to Bob.

The result of charging each customer their entire willingness to pay is that marginal revenue equals demand (MR = D), and the monopolist can keep

Monopolists can sometimes charge higher prices to customers with greater demand

Successful price discrimination requires segmenting the market, charging each type of customer a different price based on their own willingness to pay.
Completely perfect price discrimination would allow monopolists to expand production to the perfectly competitive level, collecting all available consumer surplus as monopoly profits.

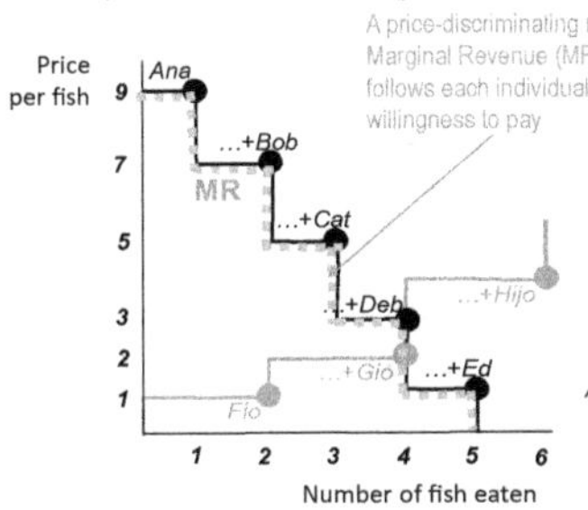

	Demand		A perfectly price-discriminating monopolist		Supply	
	Qty. sold	*WTP*	Total Revenue	Marginal rev. (MR)	*MC*	Producer
A	1	9	9 = 9	9-0 = 9	1	Fio
A+B	2	7	9+7 = 16	9-16 = 7	1	Fio
A+B+C	3	5	16+5 = 21	21-16 = 5	2	Fio+Gio
A+B+C+D	4	3	21+3 = 24	24-21 = 3	2	Fio+Gio
A+B+C+D+E	5	1	24+1 = 25	25-24 = 1	4	F+G+H

Perfect price discrimination requires selling the same fish for a different price to each buyer, *and* knowing exactly how much that buyer is willing and able to pay.

Fig. 5.3 Monopolists can earn even more excess profits through price discrimination

selling to each additional buyer until demand equals their marginal cost (MC) along their supply curve. On Alphabet Beach the Fio-Gio enterprise catches both of Gio's two fish, because the marginal cost of each is 2, and they can sell one to Cat for a price of 5 and another to Deb for a price of 3. This restores the perfectly competitive quantity of 4, but it is not worth expanding further. If Hijo were to join with Fio and Gio, their additional fifth fish would have a marginal cost of 4 but a maximum price of 1 from Ed.

The benchmark cases shown in Figs. 5.2 and 5.3 show the two mechanisms by which enterprises with market power can take advantage of becoming the only seller of something to a group of buyers. The first mechanism is quantity restriction, as they cut back on quantity sold to where MR meets S, and sell at the community's marginal WTP for that quantity along D. The second mechanism is price discrimination, as they try to sell each unit for that individual buyer's WTP, in which case they can sell a larger quantity out to where WTP meets S.

Total revenue for the Fio-Gio enterprise is shown in each table, and their total cost is readily seen by adding up marginal costs of each fish. With quantity restriction, the enterprise's total income is 12 (total revenue of 14 minus total cost of 2). With perfect price discrimination, by charging each buyer their entire willingness to pay, the enterprise's income is 19 (revenue of 25 minus total cost of 6). Both levels of total revenue for the Fio-Gio enterprise are far above their combined earnings prior to merging. When working independently, the competitive market led to a price between 2 and 3. Fio sold two fish and had producer surplus between 2 and 4 (total revenue of 4 to 6, minus total cost of 2), while Gio also sold two fish and had producer surplus between 0 and 2 (the same total revenue as Fio, but total cost of 4), so their combined revenue in the competitive market ranged from 2 to 6.

The results of Figs. 5.2 and 5.3 show clearly how every producer would like to be the only seller of their product for a particular market. In the Fio-Gio example, they go from combined earnings in the range of 2 to 6 when competing with each other, to joint earnings of 12 when they practice quantity restriction, and joint earnings up to a maximum of 19 when they achieve price discrimination. The field of *marketing* is devoted to understanding how companies can gain and exercise some degree of market power, which they call *pricing power*, and perhaps also achieve some degree of price discrimination. From an economics perspective, when companies become monopolies and restrict quantity, there is clear inefficiency because quantity is below the point where marginal costs just equal marginal benefits. If companies begin as a monopoly, their ability to price discriminate enables a larger quantity to be sold, although they also use that to take a larger share of the available consumer surplus.

Many businesses are able to achieve some degree of market power, for at least some of their products, in specific settings where they have few competitors. They would then have an opportunity to raise profits by restricting quantity, but an even stronger incentive to raise profits more through price discrimination. To see these decisions it was helpful to use our toy model of Alphabet Beach. For more general cases it is preferable to draw straight supply and demand curves in our stylized diagrams, which allow us to see the symmetrical case of monopsonies.

Monopsony Buyers and Marginal Expenditure

What if there is only one buyer, instead of only one seller? Markets with a single buyer are called a *monopsony*, and the buyer in a monopsony is called a *monopsonist*. As illustrated by the hourglass in Fig. 5.1, monopsony power can sometimes be exercised by agribusinesses that buy from farmers. This is especially common for products like raw milk that have significant scale economies in processing, and high transport costs for farmers to reach competing processors in other locations. Switching to stylized diagrams with straight lines for visual clarity, we can compare monopoly and monopsony in Fig. 5.4.

The left panel of Fig. 5.4 shows the same story as Fig. 5.2, but with linear MR and demand curves. The diagram shows how we can derive the exact MR curve from demand, with notation showing how one could use algebra and calculus to show that a linear demand curve leads to a linear MR curve whose slope is exactly twice that of the demand curve, as each additional unit sold reduces price received by the monopoly seller.

The right panel introduces the mirror image of MR, which is the marginal expenditure (ME) curve for price paid by the monopsony buyer. When the monopsonist buys each incremental unit along the sellers' supply curve, they raise the price they pay for the other units as well. In the case of a dairy monopsony, for example, they might be able to buy some raw milk from a few nearby farmers for a low price, but if they want to buy more they must offer a higher price to everyone.

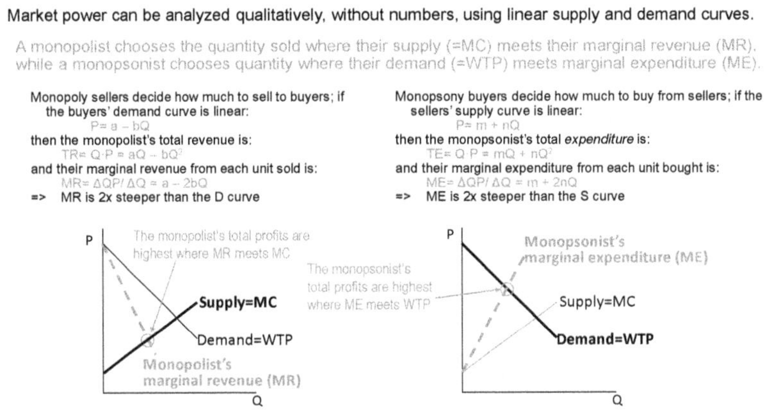

Fig. 5.4 Monopolies and monopsonies with simplified linear demand and supply curves

The circled points in Fig. 5.4 indicate where enterprises with market power stop adding additional units of quantity, because their S = MR for monopolists, and D = ME for monopsonists. The price at which they can sell that quantity, in the simple case without price discrimination, is shown in Fig. 5.5.

The symmetrical panels of Fig. 5.5 show how each kind of market power permits the charge or enterprise to earn higher profits than would be possible with a competitive market structure. Both show the simple case where only one price prevails, so the monopoly seller restricts quantity to Q_m so they can sell at P_m despite an additional unit costing only MC_m, and similarly the monopsony buyer restricts quantity to Q_m so they can buy at P_m despite having a willingness to pay for an additional unit of WTP_m. In both cases, if they were able to use price discrimination, they could increase quantity beyond Q_m and earn even more profits. Perfect price discrimination would potentially

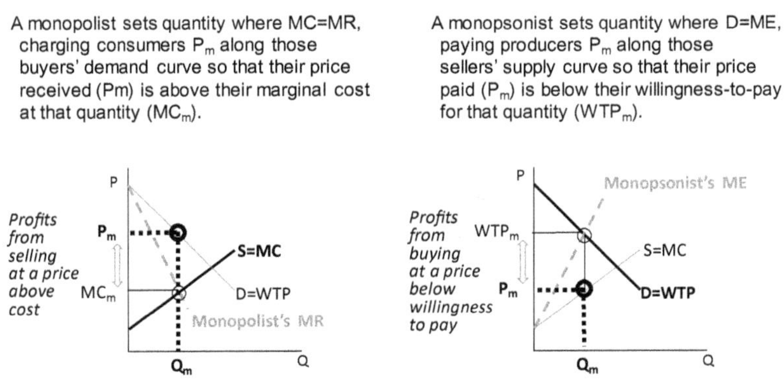

Fig. 5.5 Monopoly and monopsony both allow firms to raise profits by restricting quantity

allow them to sell all the way to where S meets D, capturing all of the profits shown for each unit.

Like all of our two-dimensional diagrams, this analysis of market power illustrates only general principles. In addition to the marginal costs shown here, a more complete analysis would take account of the fixed costs that create scale effects in the first place, and also take account of the complex detail around any particular case study. Before introducing two specific examples, it is helpful to add the areas of economic surplus gain or loss to the diagram.

Impacts of Market Power on Economic Surplus, Equity and Efficiency
Market power benefits enterprises that have it, at a cost to society. A monopoly seller's profits come at the expense of consumers along their demand curve, and a monopsony buyer's profits come at the expense of people who sell to it along their supply curve. We can see the relative magnitudes of these changes in Fig. 5.6.

The shaded areas and letters shown in Fig. 5.6 are gained and lost from market power relative to the perfectly competitive benchmark. In markets with scale economies, there is typically no actual policy instrument that could achieve perfect competition, but showing the effects of enterprises that restrict quantity in this way reveals what is at stake.

On each panel of Fig. 5.6, quantity restriction opens up area A that is gained by the enterprise at the expense of others, so that is purely an equity effect. In contrast, areas B and C measure the efficiency loss of producing less than this market's potential to generate economic surplus through additional units for which willingness to pay exceeds demand. The entire areas AB is lost by the population facing the monopolist or monopsonist. Area C is the additional loss of economic surplus when the enterprise cuts back on quantity. As in our previous analyses of market response, elasticities of S and D determine the

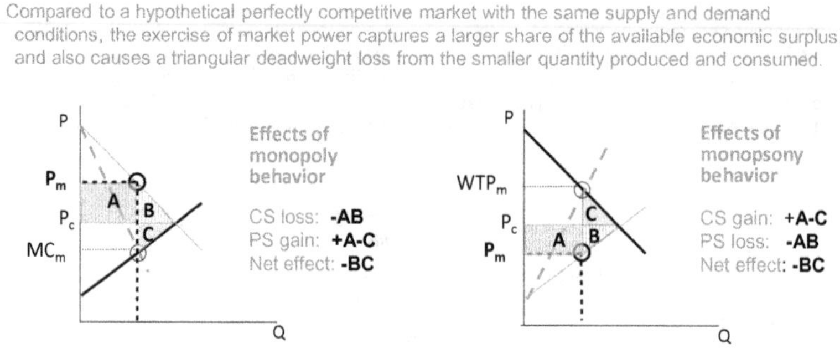

Fig. 5.6 Market power alters income distribution and also reduces total economic surplus

relative sizes of these areas, and especially the magnitude of deadweight loss BC relative to the equity effect A.

Market power can arise for a variety of reasons and might allow an enterprise to make high profits on some products in some locations, while other parts of the business are highly competitive. Each opportunity to be the only seller or buyer might be temporary, as others notice the high profits to be made and enter the market. Whether any particular enterprise actually has significant market power is difficult to determine, but it is useful to see two examples from recent U.S. history to illustrate specific aspects of how monopolies might arise and operate.

Market Power Can Be Obtained by Innovation: Walmart in the 1970s and 1980s

The first example is chosen to illustrate how an enterprise might gain economies of scale over time, using the example of Walmart as sketched in Fig. 5.7.

Walmart is a useful example because the roots of its initial success can be described in terms of a few familiar technologies that offered clear scale economies for retailing across the U.S. As shown on the left side of Fig. 5.7, Walmart was founded in 1962 grew into a chain at the start of the computer era, establishing one of the first interconnected systems of electronic inventory control in the 1970s. That network allowed inventories at all locations to be centrally monitored in real time, while competitors were still using much more expensive methods including periodic closure to physically count everything on the shelves. Walmart then became among the first users of several new

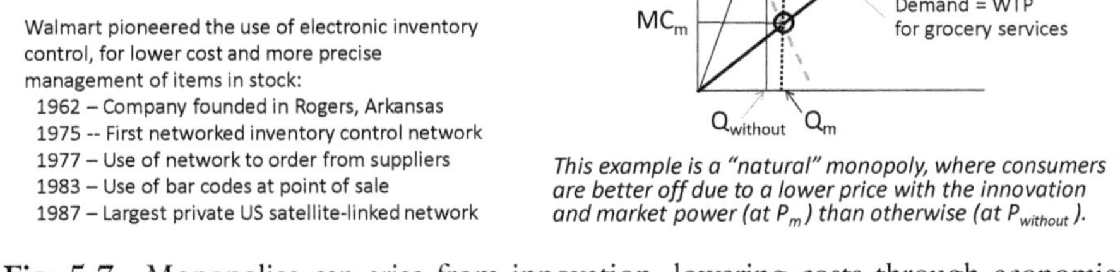

Fig. 5.7 Monopolies can arise from innovation, lowering costs through economies of scale *Source*: Timeline extracted from Jianfeng Wang [2006], "Economies of IT systems at Wal-Mart: an historical perspective." *Journal of Management Information and Decision Sciences*, 9[1]: 45–66

techniques for store management, each with high fixed cost but low marginal cost of expanding to new locations throughout the 1980s and 1990s.

The actual cost and pricing structure of any real business is enormously complex, but the basic principle of innovation and scale economies is drawn on the right of Fig. 5.7. One might imagine an initial competitive market of many small but expensively operated enterprises, operating at the high initial price and low total quantity. If an innovator successfully drops the marginal cost of supply low enough, it can be attractive to consumers even if it restricts quantity to Q_m and charges at P_m. In the case of Walmart, quantity restriction is seen in the way that its new stores were initially located relatively far apart across rural America. If Walmart were a public utility like the post office, they might have rolled out a larger number of stores closer to each other, as long as the marginal cost of each location was lower than willingness to pay and the enterprise could cover its fixed costs. Adding new locations would help customers reduce their travel time, but would have reduced the profitability of existing locations so Walmart had a smaller number of locations in the 1990s than its cost advantages might have allowed.

Market Power Can Be Obtained Legally, Including Through Protection from Trade

The second example is chosen to illustrate the potential role of government in allowing or preventing producers from joining together to operate as a monopoly. This example is particularly instructive because international trade is involved. Markets with trade usually cannot be monopolized, so creating market power in this case was possible only because the government could control trade in support of its efforts to help producers, as shown in Fig. 5.8.

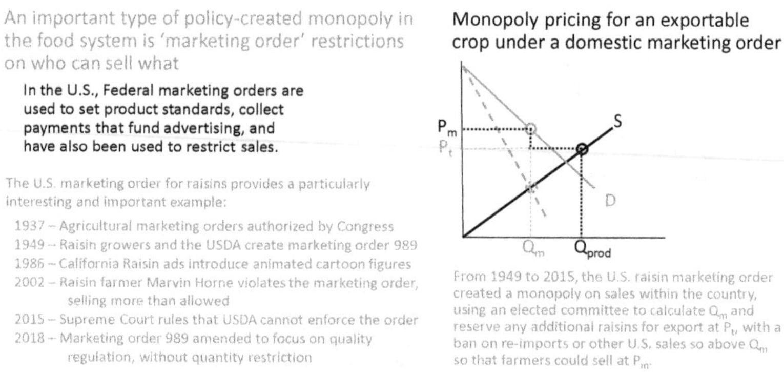

Fig. 5.8 Monopolies can arise from legal protections, as in a marketing board *Source*: Timeline adapted and extended from Dean L. Lueck [2016], "The curious case of Horne v. Department of Agriculture: good law, bad economics?" *NYU Journal of Law & Liberty*, 10: 608–625

The timeline sketched on the left side of Fig. 5.8 describes how the U.S. Department of Agriculture (USDA) is authorized by the law to help producers of a specific crop join together to regulate sales. These marketing orders allow registered growers to form an organization whose governing board is empowered to set standards and in some cases also limit quantities sold. In this case, from 1949 to 2015, marketing order number 989 allowed the raisin board to decide the total quantity allowed to be sold inside the U.S. each year. Each year the board would estimate demand, take account of production costs and attempt to find the quantity Q_m at which the price P_m would yield the highest total income for the farmers they represent, accounting for the fact that they could also export raisins at price P_t. The board also took into account fluctuations in supply and trade prices by managing storage, building up or drawing down their stockholding to provide additional control over Q_m to earn the highest possible farm income over time. Given the possibility of exports, farm income is shown in Fig. 5.8 as the entire producer surplus from the supply curve up to the U.S. price P_m for quantity Q_m, and then between the supply curve and the export price P_t for the quantity exported between Q_m and total production Q_{prod}.

For the USDA-supported raisin board to maintain higher prices inside the U.S. than elsewhere, for example across the border in Canada, they needed to restrict reimports of the quantity exported. That aspect of enforcement was administratively easy to accomplish, as import restrictions are a routine aspect of trade law. A more difficult challenge was to allocate shares of Q_m among farmers to sell at P_m, given that any additional quantities could be sold at the lower P_t. In practice, like many organizations in this situation, the raisin board allocated each farmer a share of Q_m based on their past production. If just one farmer were to sell more than their allotted share of Q_m at P_m, there might not be much decline in price along the demand curve. If multiple farmers did so, the price for all growers would eventually fall to P_t.

As shown in the timeline, raisin farmers generally obeyed the marketing order for many decades. Growers elected the board which decided Q_m and obtained P_m, using government regulation to prevent other farmers from entering which would have reduced the price. Over time, individual farmers might seek to increase their share of Q_m, and in 2002 one grower decided to do so on the grounds that a government-supported restriction on quantity sold was unacceptable to them. The case attracted the attention of people who wanted to limit government regulations in general, and they appealed the case all the way to the U.S. Supreme Court which ultimately ruled in favor of the farmer's right to sell as much as they wished. Thereafter the marketing board could no longer set quantities to raise prices, so its work is limited to quality standards and other functions.

The higher income earned by operating as a monopolist allows the group of farmers to behave as if it were a single enterprise, for example by advertising to promote the brand. The example of U.S. raisin farmers and their marketing board is famous in part because in the late 1980s, the board paid for an advertising campaign with cartoon figures known as California Raisins who formed a band playing popular songs. The fictional band's animated music videos were wildly successful, and although actual raisin sales did not rise enough to justify continuing the campaign in the 1990s, the idea of cartoon raisins remains vivid in American popular culture.

The economic aspects of the raisin board's story is worth telling in this book for many reasons. First, there is the human drama of organizing people for any collective purpose, because each individual then has an incentive to break away and take advantage of others having followed the rule. We will return to that in the next section of this chapter. Second, there is the way that our raisin example shows the role of trade restriction in making market power possible. Third, there are important aspects of the story involving human health and government decision-making, as policies adopted for one purpose can work against other interests, sometimes in ways that may remain unknown even to well-informed people but could be revealed by economic analysis.

The nutrition and health aspect of the marketing board story is important because raisins (among other fruits) are promoted in the USDA's own Dietary Guidelines for Americans. During much of the period shown in Fig. 5.8, the nutrition services of USDA were actively promoting fruit consumption for health reasons, even as the quantity sold was actively being restricted by the marketing arm of the USDA. Different political forces drive the two arms despite them being housed in the same agency. Even if higher-level decision-makers in government were aware that one arm of the USDA was restricting sales even as another arm sought to increase them, there might have been little they could do about that contradiction. The political balance of forces driving each policy was in a kind of equilibrium between the government's diverse constituencies, and there was little reason for anyone to devote the time and effort it might take to alter the outcome.

For economics generally, an important aspect of the marketing board story helps us understand that actions by individuals and groups have unintended consequences, and that economic analysis reveals those effects without needing to know anything about what people are thinking, or how they use what they earn in pursuit of their own objectives. In writing this section of the book we do not have or need any particular knowledge about the motivations of the raisin farmer and his supporters who financed the lawsuit that ended the board's quantity restrictions. They may have believed that government restrictions were harming them, or they may have been willing to sacrifice future earnings in pursuit of other goals. Economic analysis is useful only to show what decisions provide the largest total gains relative to costs in a particular setting, recognizing that each person can and will have multiple motivations for what to do with the income they might earn.

Finally, the raisin story brings us back to the analysis of market power, and whether the board's most important concerns actually involved quantity restriction at all. As we have seen, an even more valuable source of pricing power would have been price discrimination. Even before the marketing board was formed, raisin farmers had formed a cooperative called Sun-Maid to provide joint marketing services, one aspect of which was to differentiate branded raisins from the same food in generic packaging. Then in the late 1980s a major focus of the marketing board was to invest in advertising for all kinds of raisins. Building a generic California Raisins campaign might have aimed to shift the demand curve outward to raise Q_m, but it could also have aimed to make the demand curve steeper so as to reach a higher P_m even with no change in quantity.

Profits from Market Power Depend on Price Elasticities

The role of consumers' demand elasticities in allowing monopolists to charge high prices is illustrated in Fig. 5.9.

The two panels of Fig. 5.9 show two monopolists with identical supply curves and an identical quantity sold. The two monopolists differ only in the demand curves they face, and consumers' elasticities of response to their choice of quantity sold. Comparing the two figures shows how the steeper, more inelastic curve on the left offers greater potential pricing power. With linear curves the slope of each MR curve is exactly twice the slope the corresponding demand curve, so the difference between the two MR slopes is exactly twice as large as the difference between the two demand curves. When consumers have relatively inelastic demand on the left, the monopolist can charge P_m and earn a much larger markup over their marginal costs MC_m than the otherwise identical monopolist on the right who has the same monopoly position but faces more elastic demand, and hence lower profits based on the smaller gap between P_m' and MC_m'.

The comparison shown in Fig. 5.9 helps explain why enterprises invest heavily in trying to become monopolists for things whose demand is always price-inelastic, and also helps explain why enterprises with some market power

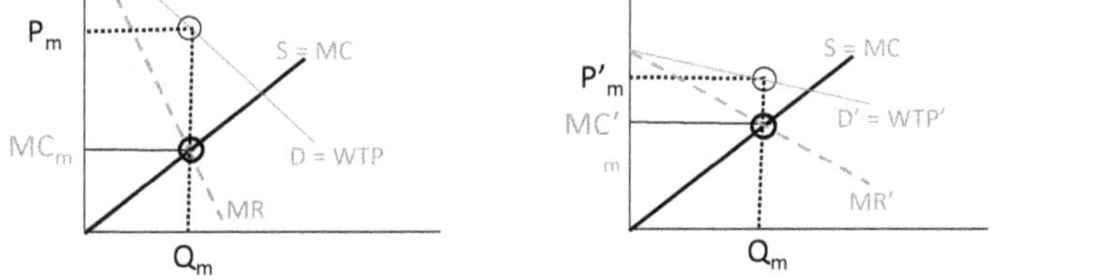

Fig. 5.9 Inelastic demand raises a monopolist's pricing power

often seek to make demand for their products as inelastic as possible by focusing their advertising and other business practices on brand loyalty and repeat purchases. In contrast, advertising that is targeted towards expanding quantities sold is more widely used in more competitive settings, and can make elastic demand curves even flatter by attracting purchasers who have more other options.

Figure 5.9 can also be used to see the demand curve along which a price-discriminating monopolist could charge, if they successfully differentiated their product to sell at high prices for consumers with high willingness to pay. More inelastic demand raises the potential profits from price discrimination, creating strong incentives for enterprises with some degree of market power to find ways of selling otherwise similar items to different people at different prices. For example, a food manufacturer could sell the same product under a premium brand with expensive packaging and advertising, while simultaneously selling it under a generic label at a lower price. Similarly, a grocery store could charge more to online shoppers who value convenience, and restaurants charge higher margins on alcohol and prestige items for diners who are willing to pay for that.

The economic mechanisms by which enterprises with market power can sometimes earn high profits also reveal how competition can work to bring those profits back down, as challengers see opportunities to enter and compete in newly profitable market segments. Product differentiation can attract other enterprises specializing in premium brands, leading to segmented markets for each kind of product. With market segmentation, enterprises aiming for the high value-added segment compete along their supply curve with high costs of marketing, packaging and other services, while enterprises aiming for the high-volume segment compete with low prices of that same product in generic form. Every market is defined spatially as well, as a monopolist's quantity restrictions in one location will attract a larger volume of sales from competitors elsewhere, creating geographic patterns of spatial competition. And competition also occurs over time, with the pricing power of monopolists is limited not only by existing competitors at each place and time, but also by the threat of future entry. Even longstanding monopolies might eventually be disrupted, and some monopolies are in contestable markets with few barriers to entry so they must behave competitively to deter competition that would displace them entirely.

Measuring Market Power

Each market diagram shows quantity and price for a specific product quality, at a particular place and time. When applying these models to any real-life situation, economists must specify the extent of the market being analyzed in terms of the product characteristics, time period and population whose supply, demand and trade opportunities are shown in the model.

In this textbook we show economic principles graphically in two dimensions, so our models in this section are limited to monopoly and monopsony.

By definition, real-life examples of just one buyer or seller arise only when the market is defined narrowly around one enterprise's specific product, place and time. For example, we might draw the market for groceries in a given neighborhood, helping to explain how a single big supermarket might behave differently from many small shops when serving the same population with a given demand curve. Studies can sometimes measure market power at that level of granularity, but the available data usually defines markets more broadly to include a whole sector or segment of the food system, for example as the number of different grocery chains that might potentially compete with each other over a given region.

The number of enterprises serving a market segment or sector is often reported directly, but enterprises differ greatly in size. For example, a given city might be served by one to three superstores or chains, and then a larger number of small and medium-sized enterprises. The likelihood that an enterprise can exercise market power in any part of the sector or segment that it serves could depend on its geographic scale or range of products offered. For example, if one large grocery chain serves a whole region, it might have monopoly power only in a few neighborhoods or product categories where smaller chains and independent shops cannot compete. Instead of counting enterprises, analysts typically use data on volume sold to compare market shares.

The market share of an enterprise is its fraction of sales. For sufficiently uniform products this can be defined in quantity terms, such as a dairy processor's share of all raw milk sold in a state each year. Every gallon of raw milk is similar enough in quality that volume could be measured in weight (pounds or kilograms) or volume (gallons or liters). In other markets, different enterprises sell a variety of differentiated products so their volume is measured by the value of sales in monetary terms. Having defined a market category, for example all dairy products, analysts compare the value of sales by each enterprise to the sum of sales by all enterprises in the market as a whole.

Market shares are often expressed as *concentration ratios*, focusing on the few largest enterprises that might be able to monopolize some part of the market. The largest market share is the C1 ratio, and sum of shares over the two or three largest enterprises would be the market's C2 or C3 ratio. A typical approach is to focus on C4. For example, in Britain during the 2010s the four largest supermarket chains by market share were Tesco (31%), Sainsbury's (17%), Asda (17%) and Morrisons (13%), for a combined C4 share around 78% in 2011. Then the expansion into Britain of two small-format chains from Germany, Aldi and Lidl, and also a new online-only retailer, Ocado, reduced the shares of all top-four retailers, bringing the C4 ratio to 66% in 2023. This kind of data typically comes from private firms that specialize in marketing strategy such as Kantar or Nielsen.

Market power can potentially be exercised within market segments, so economists are often interested in degrees of concentration across the entire distribution of enterprises. For example, two markets may have the same C4 ratio, but very different degrees of concentration among the top four, and potentially also different concentration among the other smaller enterprises. To capture that aspect of concentration, analysts can use the sum of squared market shares which is the same method used in environmental sciences to measure lack of biodiversity over a whole population of organisms. Among economists, the sum of squared market shares for each firm is known as the *Hirschmann-Herfindahl index*, while measuring biodiversity using the sum of squared shares of each species in a population is known as the *Simpson index*. With just a single monopolist this index has a value of 1, and increasing competition or diversity drives the index towards zero. When all have equal shares, then the sum-of-squares index simply returns that share. For example, with two equal shares, the squared value of each share is $0.25 = 0.5 \times 0.5$, and the sum-of-squares returns $0.50 = 0.25 + 0.25$. From that baseline, increasing concentration raises the index. For example, 80–20 shares have an index of 0.68, and 90–10 shares have an index of 0.82 which is beginning to approach the monopoly status of a single seller. The magnitude of a Hirschmann-Herfindahl index depends on whether shares are reported in decimal form or as percentage points (0.25 or 25) and also depends on the number of enterprises included in the index, so values may be rescaled for use in different contexts.

Measuring concentration is only a first step to inform policy response. Whether concentration actually leads to the exercise of market power and profits at the expense of consumers or other enterprises depends on all the factors shown in our models, such as elasticities of response. Our diagrams could be drawn in two dimensions, for example using the MR and ME curves to identify quantity sold, because they focus on a single monopolist or monopsonist facing a market of many others who adjust along their demand or supply curves. The next section of this chapter shows interactions between just two decision-makers, with the resulting outcomes shown in a table of payoffs from each choice. More advanced game theory considers an even wider range of possible interactions among two or more actors, with each kind of interaction corresponding to a different market structure in the field of economics known as industrial organization, with great relevance to agricultural input supply and food businesses.

Policies to Address Market Power

A first kind of policy concerns mergers or acquisitions, which is the initial example used in this section when Fio and Gio joined together to raise price. That scenario involved no innovations to reduce cost. The only source of market power was the agreement between Fio and Gio to merge operations and raise both of their incomes by either quantity restriction (ending Gio's catch and sharing the profits) or price discrimination (selling each unit at the buyer's willingness to pay).

In the U.S., rules against otherwise legal businesses gaining market power are known as *antitrust* law, because they were introduced in the late nineteenth century specifically against merged businesses that were then known as trusts. In other countries, similar legislation is known as competition policy. Many antitrust efforts aim to limit mergers or break up existing enterprises, through administrative review and legal proceedings to assess whether larger size operations would generate sufficient cost savings to offset the dangers of market power. The primary focus of legal cases is usually whether larger enterprises can manipulate their own prices and quantity. Antitrust policy can also be used to address whether large enterprises actively stop others from competing with them, for example by preventing workers from switching employers. Criminal law also plays a role in antitrust policy, through rules that prohibit enterprises from making agreements with each other to manipulate prices or quantities and limit competition. That kind of price-fixing through cartels is a criminal offense in many sectors, but antitrust regulations are commonly waived for organizations designed to help farmers such as cooperatives and marketing boards.

A second kind of policy concerns the flow of innovations that might affect market power and enterprise scale. Innovations often have high fixed costs for invention and adoption, but then low marginal cost to deploy over each unit of production, thereby introducing a new source of increasing returns that reaches lowest total cost at a larger scale of operations than earlier enterprises. Some innovations allow many small enterprises to be formed, such as online platforms or shared kitchens and co-packers that help individuals start new food businesses, but then the facilitating platform itself could begin to exercise market power against those businesses. Policies to encourage innovation also introduce some kinds of market power deliberately, using patents to give inventors a temporary monopoly over their invention in exchange for disclosing it, as well as other protections to encourage research and discovery within private enterprises. These factors make market power dynamic and temporary, where the best remedy against market power by one enterprise may be to encourage formation of other companies using different techniques at different scales over time.

A third category of actions to address market power involve the institutions, infrastructure and policies that influence whether enterprises can be insulated from competition. Market power comes from enterprise scale relative to the extent of each market. One aspect of market size is geographic area. The evolution of food systems often involves a transition from competition among enterprises for local market power (for example, a country might have a hundred dairy processors but only two or three in each place, seeking monopsony power when buying milk from local farmers and monopoly power when selling to local consumers), to competition among larger enterprises serving a greater geographic extent (for example, two or three enterprises competing with each other over the entire country). Enterprises with local market power are often challenged by entrants from neighboring places, in ways that can be helped or hindered by government action.

A fourth category of policies about market power concerns product differentiation and demand for higher-quality products. If the only way for an enterprise to signal quality is their own brand identity, then they will have to invest heavily in marketing, packaging, advertising and other ways to convince people that their product actually has the desired quality attributes. Price itself can be a signal of quality, if people expect that low prices imply low quality, and expect that high prices and high incomes provide the seller an incentive to maintain high quality over time. Both marketing costs and price as a signal of quality make high-quality products unnecessarily expensive, especially when there are scale effects and inelastic demand that give a monopolist some pricing power on top of all their actual high costs of maintaining product quality.

Product standards enforced by governments and private associations have been an important aspect of food systems since the earliest historical records, driven by the fundamental problem that people can actually observe only a few aspects of food quality such as color, odor and taste. Some of the first recorded food standards in European history focused on preventing use of nonfood ingredients in bread and beer that would increase their weight or volume, soon followed by rules to maintain food safety of products such as milk and meat. The minimum quality regulations for all foods sold were soon complemented by quality standards to differentiate higher-priced versions of similar products, such as the first pressing of olive oil at mills that also extract lower-quality oil. Labeling then allows consumers to see what they could not otherwise detect for themselves, making it possible for markets to sustain competition for high-quality products.

Introducing and enforcing quality standards can help new entrants compete with established enterprises, lowering the cost to consumers of items at or above each level of quality. Establishing new standards is politically challenging in part because established businesses that already meet the standard do so with brand identities and high prices signaling their own high quality, while other businesses might need to incur significant added costs to meet the standard. By definition the attributes that need to be signaled cannot be seen or experienced directly, allowing critics to sow doubt about the scientific basis for each standard.

Establishment of organic product standards is a particularly important example in the U.S. and many countries, aiming to create a larger and more competitive market for items that meet those requirements. Introducing a separate standard for organic products leaves open the question of quality standards for conventional products. Each market segment, the policy options for quality signaling range from disclosure requirements such as the back-of-package nutrition facts panel, to requiring more visible marks such as front-of-pack warning labels, and direct regulation of product contents and advertising such as bans on harmful ingredients or rules against deceptive marketing.

5.1.3 *Conclusion*

Market power can potentially be used in ways that raise an enterprise's own profits at the expense of the society as a whole, in ways that can be remedied by policies to facilitate entry of competitors meeting sufficiently high-quality standards. This section shows how barriers to entry allow existing enterprises to increase their own profits in non-competitive ways, either restricting quantity to earn higher margins on the uniform product at the same price or by product differentiation and price discrimination. Exercising market power can be done by enterprises that are the only seller (a monopoly) or the only buyer (a monopsony). In either case, exercising market power yields higher profits when quantity response is more inelastic. When monopolies or monopsonies exist, an effective way to limit the resulting harm is to make response more price-elastic by ensuring that people have other options.

The fundamental source of market power in the food system is scale economies in activities other than farming and household food consumption, such as farm input provision or food manufacturing and distribution. Agricultural production is done mostly by owner-operated family farms, and food choices are made by individuals and households, while agribusinesses and food enterprises can often gain market power through larger scale relative to the extent of the market they serve. Markets are defined in terms of a specific product, place and time period, and power over that market can be exercised only as long as it remains protected from competitors through high barriers to entry. New competitors, if they arise, could begin as startups within the monopolized market, but when scale economies make total cost lower at larger volumes, competitors can also enter and compete across a wider range of products and larger geographic areas. One of the most important sources of competition and elasticity of quantities to limit market power is trade with other places, limiting ability of existing enterprises in any one place to profit at the expense of other people in their own society.

Once an enterprise has market power, they can use it to earn additional profits through either quantity restriction or product differentiation and price discrimination. In the food system some products have uniform quality, often because a government agency or voluntary organization has set and enforced the specifications for that type of product. Crops such as wheat or rice are generic commodities bought and sold competitively, but each bag or truckload can be substituted for another only to the extent that they all meet a written standard published by the government or some other organization. In the absence of such standards, each enterprise must try to signal quality through expensive branding and high prices, often allowing price discrimination by large enterprises or the emergence of segmented markets whose costs of signaling quality could be reduced through uniform standards. Any food attribute that cannot be seen or experienced by end-users, including many aspects of nutrition and health, contributes to market failure that can potentially be remedied by quality standards and certification for more competitive markets.

5.2 Strategic Behavior: Game Theory for Two-Person Interactions

5.2.1 Motivation and Guiding Questions

The choices we have seen so far explain and predict outcomes by looking at each individual's options, identifying the actions that would best achieve their goals. Can we generalize these insights to interactions between two people, where each takes the other's decision-making into account? What determines whether two people will cooperate with each other towards a common goal? Can we predict what circumstances might lead them to stop cooperating, or even harm the other person?

The choices we address in this section are *strategic* behavior, used in the same sense as '*strategic*' moves in chess or other settings. The predicted equilibrium outcome of such interactions requires a kind of analysis known as *game theory*, used in economics to address industrial organization and other topics where just two or a few actors interact with each other. In this book we introduce strategic behavior in its simplest context, which is a single interaction between two individuals each choosing from the same two options. That simplicity allows us to draw a *payoff matrix* of four possible outcomes, and shows how modeled choices respond to incentives in ways that are surprisingly informative about real-life interactions.

Our analysis of game theory, like the rest of this book, focuses on general principles applied to the food system, using analyses that can be presented graphically with almost no formal mathematics. For strategic interactions, we focus on the simplest possible framework, reduced to just two decision-makers choosing between two options. Understanding how and why people in different circumstances would choose to cooperate in a joint activity, or go it alone against the other person's interests, is deeply revealing about human behavior in general and especially in the food system.

By the end of this section, you will be able to:

1. Describe how game theory and Nash equilibrium are used to explain and predict the outcome of strategic interactions;
2. Use a 2 × 2 payoff matrix to identify the predicted outcome of an interaction between two people choosing between two options;
3. Describe how altering the payoff matrix influences behavior, as in the prisoner's dilemma created by police to elicit confessions, or a positive-sum game that elicits cooperation; and

4. Describe how social norms and commitment mechanisms can alter payoffs and influence outcomes, with examples such as climate policy and natural resources in agriculture.

5.2.2 *Analytical Tools*

Previous sections have explained outcomes in terms of each person's choice, with everyone else's choices shown by their willingness to pay along the demand curve, marginal cost along the supply curve or opportunities for trade with others. In perfectly competitive markets, each individual is a *price taker*, adjusting their quantity whether or not that alters prices paid or received by others. In a monopoly or monopsony, one individual sets the entire quantity and can be seen as a *price maker*, choosing whatever prices will meet their own goals. In this section, we ask what if an individual faces just one other individual and can take into account that both of them are making choices?

As we will see, game theory models of strategic behavior have many concrete applications to the real world with clear relevance to food systems. Game theory yields useful insights at many different scales, from relationships within a household to bargaining between enterprises and country governments. To help us follow how human decision-making leads to the outcomes we see, it is helpful to start with our toy model of Alphabet Beach, and then introduce a variety of other scenarios.

When we first saw the perfectly competitive model of Alphabet Beach fish market, an additional seller such as Gio entered as long as the additional buyers such as Cat and Deb could cover their costs of production. Gio's entry directly benefited Cat and Deb who got to eat Gio's fish and also lowered costs for Ana and Bob. The price reduction caused by competitive entry came at the expense of the other seller, Fio, leading us to model a scenario where Fio persuaded Gio to join together in a merged Fio-Gio enterprise. The result was a monopoly with a clear interest in either ending Gio's catch entirely to sell at a single higher price to both Ana and Bob, or differentiating among buyers to sell at a higher price to Ana than to Bob and also to Cat and Deb.

In this section we can look more closely at the relationship between Fio and Gio. They have a strong interest in collaborating, but what circumstances make them more likely to agree on a shared strategy and act as one, and what would make them more likely to compete with each other? The actual example of Fio and Gio is not well-suited to introduce game theory, because they have an unequal starting place. Fio is the low-cost supplier who will choose to catch fish whether or not Gio goes fishing. In the toy model, that gives Gio a strategic advantage in bargaining with Fio: Gio can credibly threaten to catch and sell fish which would reduce Fio's price, whereas Fio has no similar way to threaten Gio's income. Also we know that Fio earns more from fishing than Gio, but that might be because Gio has better options for other employment, further strengthening Gio's strategic advantage in their negotiation over a potential partnership.

Game theory models with asymmetric payoffs could potentially be used to predict the outcome of bargaining between Fio and Gio. We might discover, for example, that Fio is likely to voluntarily give Gio a majority vote in decisions and larger share of profits from the Fio-Gio enterprise, because that is the only way for Fio to ensure that Gio remains in their joint enterprise. To see how bargaining unfolds, however, it is far easier to start with the case of symmetrical bargaining, in which the two actors face the same choice between two options. Modeling strategic interactions between two equal partners ensures that we are focusing on when and how cooperation emerges spontaneously, without one person being forced by circumstances to accept the other's conditions.

The Payoff Matrix for a Symmetric Two-Person Interaction

The payoff matrices we analyze in this textbook are the simplest case, with the same two choices being made by two people, for whom the potential outcomes can all be arrayed in a two-by-two matrix. To distinguish between rows and columns we will call the two people X and Y, and each chooses yes or no. The consequences of each choice for the X person are shown in rows, and consequences for the Y person are shown in columns, forming the payoff matrix in Table 5.1.

In each cell of the payoff matrix there will be two numbers, separated by a backward slash \, denoting that the first number is the payoff to person X from their choice in that row, and the second number is the payoff to person Y from their choice in that column. Using the backward slash can be a useful reminder of which payoff goes to which person, as person X's choice is labeled on the left side of each row, and person Y's choice is listed at the top of each column.

In Table 5.1, person X's choices are shown in two rows, and Y's choices are in two columns. In the first row if X says yes, Y might say yes or no, and in the second row if X says no, person Y might say yes or no. In this simplest version of their interaction, there is only one time period, the two people choose simultaneously, and each person knows that both of them face identical payoffs. This setup is valuable because it isolates the core question of how each person's choices are influenced by the payoff to each outcome.

Table 5.1 Example of variables in a payoff matrix

		Person Y	
		Says yes	*Says no*
Person X	Says yes	$X_{yes} \setminus Y_{yes}$	$X_{yes} \setminus Y_{no}$
	Says no	$X_{no} \setminus Y_{yes}$	$X_{no} \setminus Y_{no}$

The economic principles used to predict choices in this context are known as *Nash equilibrium*, named after the American mathematician John Nash who characterized the problem as part of his PhD dissertation in 1950. Nash's insight was that even if each person chooses simultaneously, we can imagine that they have learned from experience in other contexts and want to avoid choices they might regret. The resulting 'no regret' equilibrium techniques then have very wide applicability to many other problems, and allows us to see how the payoff matrix drives the outcomes we are likely to observe as each person decides on their best choice given what they know about the other person's options.

Payoffs and Predicted Outcomes of the Prisoner's Dilemma
The idea of Nash equilibrium in a two-by-two payoff matrix is often described as a *prisoner's dilemma*, because that is how the interaction was first explained by mathematicians and economists in the 1950s. They chose this example in part for its realism, because it helps explain how detectives learned to solve crimes and how those accused of crimes have learned to respond, in situations described by Table 5.2.

The prisoner's dilemma shows a situation where the police have set the penalties and rewards for each action in a way that helps them solve crimes quickly. The dilemma they create for each prisoner starts with arresting two suspects who the policy believe might have been involved in a crime, and placing the suspects in separate cells. Each is offered the same options: a favorable outcome if they confess and explain the crime, or a heavy penalty if they deny involvement and are convicted. The payoff matrix in Table 5.2 shows the two prisoners' options. If both deny involvement then the police have no evidence, and neither can be convicted so they both walk free. If both confess their penalty might be −2, but longstanding police practice is to make a favorable offer such as +1 for the first to confess, and a harsh penalty such as −3 to suspects who deny involvement and are later convicted.

By setting these penalties, the police have created a dilemma by which each prisoner knows they would both be better-off if neither confessed, but each prisoner has no way of ensuring that the other does not choose to confess. John Nash provided the algorithm to solve this and many other game theory problems by identifying the best option for X depending on what Y does in each column, and the best option for Y in each row, then ruling out options that would be regretted.

Table 5.2 The payoff matrix in a prisoner's dilemma is designed to elicit confessions

		Suspect Y	
		Confess	*Deny*
Suspect X	Confess	−2 \ −2	+1 \ −3
	Deny	−3 \ +1	0 \ 0

With the example payoffs in Table 5.2, person X knows that if Y confesses, their own choices in the first column are between −2 and −3, and if Y denies involvement their choices are between +1 and 0. The payoffs created by the police thereby ensure that X has a clear incentive to confess no matter what Y does. The situation is symmetrical, so suspect Y is choosing between −2 and −3 if suspect X confesses, or between +1 and 0 if suspect X denies involvement. Both suspects have been given an incentive to confess, no matter what the other does. Police set payoffs in this way to make it more likely that prisoners will confess, because it is the only Nash equilibrium outcome of the situation.

The payoffs in Table 5.2 are just the smallest whole numbers in the simplest scenario needed to illustrate the idea of Nash equilibrium in the prisoner's dilemma context. In reality, this kind of interaction gets repeated many times, and the penalties or rewards actually offered vary widely depending on the context. Potential prisoners who might be detained and rewarded for confessing will evolve a strong norm of silence in these situations, including severe retaliation against anyone who they think might have cooperated with the police. Countless stories could be told about how people try to alter the payoff matrix to elicit the behaviors they want, and some of the best examples come from real-life situations in the food system.

Price Fixing in the Global Lysine Market: Ajinomoto and ADM in the 1990s

A famous historical case for which our two-by-two symmetrical payoff matrix provides helpful insights occurred in the 1990s, when the leaders of Archer Daniels Midland (ADM) in the U.S. and Ajinomoto in Japan decided jointly to restrict quantity and raise prices for lysine, an amino acid that they manufactured in large volumes as an ingredient for animal feed around the world, and also citric acid, an important ingredient in soft drinks and other products. These are standardized commodities so no price discrimination was involved. ADM and Ajinomoto were the two leading global suppliers, and a few other companies also had significant market share but were not in a position to quickly increase output if prices rose.

In October of 1996, ADM was convicted of colluding with Ajinomoto to limit quantity sold in the U.S., leading to a large fine and ultimately also prison sentences for three officials of the company when they were found to have agreed on how much each would sell at what price in the U.S. and elsewhere. Price fixing was determined to have begun in June 1992 for lysine and January 1993 for citric acid, and ended when the scheme was exposed in June 1995. The details of the case are fascinating, in part because it was unusually well-documented by an informant who was himself also convicted of defrauding the company. The story clearly reveals how incentives to limit quantity can tempt company managers into illegal activity as illustrated in the payoff matrix of Table 5.3.

The payoffs in the matrix in Table 5.3 are very roughly scaled to potential revenue gains from restricting supply of lysine and citric acid to the

Table 5.3 The hypothetical payoff matrix for two participants in a price-fixing conspiracy

		Company Y	
		Compete	*Restrict supply*
Company X	Compete	50 \ 50	200 \ 0
	Restrict supply	0 \ 200	150 \ 150

U.S. market, in millions of dollars per year during the 1990s. In this case 'compete' means to produce additional lysine until price received just meets marginal cost, while 'restrict' means to hold back on sales to where their jointly estimated marginal revenue meets their marginal cost.

Solving for the Nash equilibrium is done in the same way for these payoffs as for the prisoner's dilemma. For company X, the first column shows their payoffs if company Y chooses to compete, so their options are 50 or 0 and it is better for them to compete. Likewise if company Y chooses to restrict, the options for company X are 200 or 150 and again it is better for them to compete. This example is symmetric so company Y faces the same choice. For both companies, it would be better to compete than to restrict production, unless it is possible for company leaders to agree that they will both restrict supply.

In the historical case of ADM and Ajinomoto, it was ADM leadership that first contacted Ajinomoto and persuaded them to cut back on sales. In this and similar conspiracies, there were large profits to be made from jointly restricting supply, but also temptation to violate the agreement and return to competition, taking advantage of the other having temporarily restricted supply. Because these conspiracies are illegal, the agreement to restrict supply can only be enforced privately. For example, X might persuade Y to restrict supply by threatening to sell at a loss until Y is forced into bankruptcy. The two companies might also credibly guarantee that they will both restrict supply by inviting observers from the other company into their factories.

In the case of ADM and Ajinomoto, the conspiracy was undone by an employee of ADM who rebelled against his own company. Governments provide large incentives to individual informants who are willing to come forward, because company leadership could potentially sustain their conspiracy for many years. Eventually the payoff matrix would change, for example due to the entry of other companies, making it less profitable to maintain the criminal conspiracy, or one company might violate the agreement for other reasons such as a change of personnel. Then the market might return to competition without the need for antitrust action, but in the meantime consumers would have suffered great losses. In the ADM-Ajinomoto case, the reduced quantity of lysine led to a loss of efficiency due to slower livestock growth around the world.

Influence of the Payoff Matrix on Cooperative Behavior

The classic examples of a prisoner's dilemma and a price-fixing conspiracy might give readers the impression that the payoff matrix to strategic interactions always or often leads to unfortunate outcomes. In fact those two examples are used precisely because of the drama involved. Everyday interactions often involve payoff matrices that reward positive or pro-social acts of collaboration and cooperation. These are sometimes called positive-sum games, because the sum of values from acting together exceeds the value of not doing so, as illustrated in Table 5.4.

The example of Table 5.4 shows how a parent with two children might offer incentives that encourage collaboration between siblings, for example by setting up games that reward nicer play. In this scenario, the payoffs to child X are higher if they play nicely no matter how child Y responds, and similarly for child Y, the payoffs are higher if they play nicely no matter how child X responds. In a payoff matrix like Table 5.4, collaboration can be sustained without the need for external enforcement, as long as each child understands the situation and realizes that playing nicely is their best choice from the available options.

Many examples of self-sustaining cooperation arise every day, in workplaces and public interactions where people help each other simply because pro-social behavior is their best option, whether or not other people return the favor. The concept of Nash equilibrium helps us understand how a payoff matrix like that of Table 5.4 leads each person to play nicely even if the other acts selfishly. In experiments where people are given incentives of this type people occasionally deviate from the predicted Nash equilibrium, because they misunderstood their options or just had a bad day, but most people return to cooperative pro-social behavior once they realize it is preferable for them to do so.

The influence of payoffs on expected outcomes can be seen by anticipating the consequences of a small reduction in the payoff to playing nicely when the other is selfish. That change can tip the equilibrium away from pro-social behavior, for example when payoffs are as shown in Table 5.5.

The only change from Tables 5.4 to 5.5 is the reduction from 6 to 4 in the payoff to playing nicely when the other child is selfish. That small difference creates a situation where if Y plays nicely, X would also want to play nicely, while if Y is selfish, X would also want to be selfish. In this situation there are two Nash equilibria, and each might be equally likely. An equilibrium where both play nicely, and both children experience their highest payoff,

Table 5.4 A payoff matrix for self-sustaining collaboration

		Child Y	
		Play nicely	*Be selfish*
Child X	Play nicely	8 \ 8	6 \ 7
	Be selfish	7 \ 6	5 \ 5

Table 5.5 A payoff matrix with two Nash equilibria

		Child Y	
		Play nicely	*Be selfish*
Child X	Play nicely	8 \ 8	4 \ 7
	Be selfish	7 \ 4	5 \ 5

would arise when each understands and expects the other to do the same. But if one expects the other to be selfish, then children might choose to protect themselves so both would act selfishly.

Parents and others who can influence the payoffs might be able to shift incentives in ways that reward cooperation, but changes in the payoff matrix can also tip the balance away from cooperation as in Table 5.6.

The change illustrated by Table 5.6 is a lower payoff in the top-left corner. When the rewards to both playing nicely declines from 8 to 6, the payoff matrix is such that when Y plays nicely there is an incentive for X to be selfish, and when Y is selfish there is also an incentive for X to be selfish. That makes it likely that each would choose to protect themselves and act selfishly. With a payoff matrix of this type, some pairs of children might play nicely and experience the payoff in the top-left corner, but the situation is such that each will be tempted to act selfishly no matter what the other does, leading them both to the less favorable anti-social outcome in the lower-right corner.

Applying economic principles to strategic behavior using a payoff matrix reveals surprising truths about human behavior. We are used to thinking about our own choices as having been the best we could do under the circumstances. Economic analysis allows us to think that way about other peoples' behavior, revealing how incentives might be altered to improve outcomes. Understanding behavior as a Nash equilibrium is especially helpful for agriculture and the food system, where real-life payoff matrices are heavily influenced by nature and technology, limiting our options but also providing new insights about the causes of each outcome we observe.

When people work together in farming, fishing, hunting, cooking or other food-related activities, they are working in nature, using tools that reward cooperation to differing degrees. For example plowing with oxen requires two people, irrigation from a river requires upstream and downstream farmers to agree on water use and kitchen operations may be suited to working together

Table 5.6 A payoff matrix that discourages cooperation

		Child Y	
		Play nicely	*Be selfish*
Child X	Play nicely	6 \ 6	4 \ 7
	Be selfish	7 \ 4	5 \ 5

or alone. Nature and technology shape behavior in ways that have been richly documented by anthropologists, economic historians and other observers, but the examples in this book also show how payoffs can potentially be modified by other people who influence the setup of each interaction, such as the police who set penalties to elicit confessions in the prisoner's dilemma, or parents who set up games that encourage their children to play nicely together.

The strategic behavior elicited by each kind of interaction often becomes a habit or a cultural norm, especially when the same type of payoff matrix appears repeatedly in a person's life. It is impossible and also unnecessary for people to use John Nash's algorithm for everyday decisions. In real life people just learn from experience, including both our own experiences and the experiences of other people as communicated to us in stories and advice. Using economic principles to explain these habits and cultural norms is useful to help us change, by understanding why each kind of behavior arises and how we might alter incentives to elicit different behaviors in the future.

Repeated Games, Commitment Mechanisms and Incomplete Contracts

Most interactions do not take place just once, but occur in the context of repeated opportunities to cooperate or compete. In the food system, producers and consumers are interacting with a small number of other people every year near the location where they live and work. Farmers and family members need to help each other to survive, and workers everywhere need to collaborate for their enterprise to thrive.

In settings where pairs or groups of people have repeated interactions, patterns emerge that differ slightly from the simple two-by-two example. One important finding is the emergence of intertemporal *commitment mechanisms*. It can be extremely valuable for people to make credible commitments that they will in fact do something in the future, whatever the circumstances when the time comes. Farmers in small, isolated communities often commit to helping each other in the event of hardship, and share many things as a way of demonstrating their commitment. Food consumers can also benefit from advance commitments, for example by subscribing to an entire season of regular food deliveries from a community-supported farm, instead of buying only the items they want each week, as a way of ensuring that the farmer can start the season in confidence.

A related aspect of repeated games is the prevalence of *incomplete contracts*. When we first learn how incentives affect behavior, it is tempting to think that offering additional incentives for each specific kind of effort is usually helpful, but in the food system and other sectors many important relationships are left vague. Important contracts such as land rental agreements for farmers or employment contracts for restaurant workers, are often little more than a handshake and a price. These contracts are 'incomplete' in the sense that they do not specify much about what will be done in exchange for payment. Economists have often run experiments to test whether additional incentives such as pay-for-performance contracts yield better results and sometimes they do, but actual businesses typically revert to incomplete contracts when the experiment ends. One reason is that spelling out everything needed for a successful outcome is very difficult, and over time people find it is preferable to use a strategy that relies on self-motivation. Farmland owners and tenant farmers choose contracts that reward mutual trust, as do restaurant managers and employees, and incomplete contracts are helpful for that purpose.

Finally, a common finding of research on repeated interactions is known as the *folk theorem*, so called because it emerged as a common understanding in the field before studies demonstrated its general validity. The folk theorem states that repeated interactions tend to elicit more pro-social cooperative behavior than interactions that are limited in time. Versions of the folk theorem have been shown using game theory, and similar results have been found in experiments and field studies. The basic mechanism behind the folk theorem is that repeated interactions can offer greater rewards to cooperation and stronger options for retaliation against anti-social behavior. The prospect of repeated interactions is not always sufficient to elicit cooperation, in part because real-life interactions are not actually infinite in duration, but this insight helps explain how and why the duration of relationships is related to their outcomes.

Multi-person Games and the Tragedy of the Commons

The symmetric two-by-two payoff matrices shown in this book are the simplest kind of game with which to model strategic interactions. Extensions to asymmetric bargaining and a very wide range of special cases have been explored and solved mathematically for their Nash equilibria, and used to test how different people respond to incentives in experimental settings or real-life observations. One of the most difficult and important kinds of extension is towards multi-person games, such as all people in a household, every worker in a restaurant or ultimately all people in society.

Early explorations of multi-person games used computer simulations, for example evolutionary models for a population of individuals each of whom is of a fixed type that always plays the same strategy. These simulations can be repeated to assess how different strategies perform under diverse conditions, simulating the process of natural selection among different types of individuals. Simulations of this type are also known as agent-based models, because each person is an 'agent' in the sense of playing out a fixed strategy. The development of these simulation models traces the history of computing, towards increasingly complex models and also convenient user interfaces. Insights from such models are sometimes used in economics, but they differ from standard economics in that each individual's strategy is predetermined. In other words, the agents in evolutionary models lack the 'agency' we associate with actual people who make their own choice among multiple options.

Solving for a Nash equilibrium in settings where multiple people take account of each person's responses to other people's choices can be mathematically impossible. To describe different kinds of situations, game theorists have developed a large toolkit of various specifications designed around specific forms of interaction. In each model, introducing just a few additional actors or different options can be sufficient to yield predictions that are similar to the outcomes of a competitive market with many participants. Our toy model of Alphabet Beach fish market had only eight people in it, but the interactions between them give insights into outcomes for a village of eight hundred, a country of eight million or a planet of eight billion people.

An especially famous and important kind of multi-person interaction for agriculture and the environment is known as the *Tragedy of the Commons*, after the title of a 1968 essay in *Science* magazine by the American biologist Garrett Hardin. In that essay, Hardin uses the example of herders whose animals graze on public pastures, using the term 'commons' to mean land open to all in a community. Hardin explained how each herder would gain the full benefit of putting one more animal on the commons, while experiencing only a fraction of the cost imposed when the animal eats plants that would otherwise keep growing and be available for others to graze. Mathematically, each herder can be seen as gaining $+1$ for the value of each animal they add, while experiencing costs of n/N where n is the number of animals they own, out of the community's total of N animals on the commons. Hardin's essay spells out the human tragedy as each herder chooses to add one more animal to their own n, despite imposing a cost of n/N on every other member of their community, relentlessly driving down the available commons until no grass is available for anyone.

The tragedy of the commons that prompted Hardin's essay was human population growth, which was the subject of widespread concern in the 1960s. Garrett's essay ended with a call to restrict people's 'freedom to breed'. Similar ideas contributed to a campaign of forced sterilization in India during 1976–77, and China's one-child policy introduced in 1979. Garrett's arguments about population control were popular at the time but have since been discredited. As we will see in Chapter 10, human demographics did not turn out to be a fixed path to tragedy or to require forced reductions in fertility, in part because incentives changed leading to smaller family size as women gained more schooling and employment opportunities outside the home as well as other changes associated with economic development.

The most important tragedy of the commons today is undoubtedly greenhouse gas emissions and climate change. Warnings were issued but not heeded for decades, in part because emissions cause a global externality where each individual, company or country bears only a small fraction of its cost to all of humanity in future years. Innovations that sharply reduce the cost of generating and storing renewable energy now offer a path to rapidly decreasing use of fossil fuels, but only if existing equipment is rapidly replaced and new installations adopt the lower-cost new technologies. Changing incentives plays a large role in that energy transition, along with changes in net emissions of carbon and methane from agriculture or other aspects of sustainability and health in the global food system.

5.2.3 Conclusion

This section of the book introduced game theory and its applications to the economics of agriculture, food and nutrition. The toolkit of game theory shows how strategic behavior emerges and is sustained in different settings, based on the payoffs to each action. Using this framework, observed outcomes can sometimes be predicted and explained as an economic equilibrium between people.

In a strategic interaction, equilibrium behavior is the set of actions by each person that would be the best of their options, no matter what the others decide. This is an equilibrium in the sense that each person would not regret their choice. Many empirical studies have shown that people do indeed often choose the predicted strategies in both experimental and real-life settings.

The central question addressed in this section is how pro-social, cooperative behaviors that lead to the most efficient use of available resources can be sustained voluntarily. In many interactions people might act selfishly, missing out on opportunities for more favorable outcomes available if people collaborate. Joint efforts are often needed in agriculture and the food system, for example among farmers who need to cooperate when using a shared irrigation system, or restaurant workers who need to cooperate in the kitchen.

The examples in this section focus on choices where two people select between two options. That is the simplest possible kind of strategic interaction, allowing us to see how the equilibrium depends on relative payoffs to each action. When people see that their interactions will have payoffs similar to those of the prisoner's dilemma or a tragedy of the commons, they can anticipate the outcome and alter the terms of interaction to promote collaboration. The main finding of this section is that changes to the payoff matrix can lead to different behaviors. In real life, actions become habits and norms that people experience as personality and culture. To the extent that those behaviors evolved in response to past incentives, a change in payoffs can lead people to learn from experience and eventually adopt different habits, adding up to different norms for their entire community.

The example of changing incentives used in this section is a parent who oversees different games played by their children. Some games have relative payoffs whose equilibrium is for each child to play nicely, and some have relative payoffs whose equilibrium is for each child to be selfish. Parents who want children to play nicely often provide games that encourage cooperative play, and avoid games that encourage selfishness. We also saw the example of a game in which both equilibria are equally possible, in which case parents can set norms that nudge children towards nicer play.

The use of two-by-two games in this section, like our toy model of Alphabet Beach and all of the analytical diagrams in other chapters, aims to provide a toolkit of stylized models in which economic principles play out differently in different contexts. Economists can then choose the most suitable model for each situation, based on prior knowledge or research about which model would be the best fit to explain, predict and guide choices.

In real-world applications to the food system, specifying each economic model relies on contextual knowledge of how nature, technology and society determine the available options for agriculture and health. The next chapter completes our introduction to the economics toolkit by developing the main models used to understand changes in government policy, then the second half of this book turns to empirical data about those facts.

CHAPTER 6

Collective Action: Government Policies and Programs

6.1 Public Goods and Social Choice: Property Rights, Taxes and Subsidies

6.1.1 *Motivation and Guiding Questions*

The story so far has been about individuals interacting with each other in voluntary transactions, under a variety of market conditions. We have seen how a benchmark perfectly competitive market would deliver the most economic surplus, providing a framework in which to diagnose each real-world market failure away from that benchmark such as externalities, monopolies, hidden quality differences and other societal objectives not met by existing markets in the real world. No we turn to policy remedies for those market failures. What determines the extent and impact of policy interventions? Can we use economic principles to understand government policies and programs?

Previously in this textbook we treated government interventions as external factors that influenced market outcomes. Here we address the role of government directly, introducing the toolkit of *public economics* and the *political economy* of how policies and programs arise and persist. This reveals how missed opportunities for societal gains can arise from both too little and too much government intervention. When public-sector activity is insufficient, we observe persistent market failures due to collective inaction or inattention. In other settings, we observe opportunities for societal gains by reducing or removing government-mandated obstacles to transactions whose benefits would outweigh their costs. Both kinds of policy failure coexist as the public-sector counterpart to private-sector market failures. *Social choice* is the process by which communities obtain the mix of government and market activities that determine their collective wellbeing over time.

W. A. Masters and A. B. Finaret, *Food Economics*,
Palgrave Studies in Agricultural Economics and Food Policy,
https://doi.org/10.1007/978-3-031-53840-7_6

Governments are sovereign entities with authority over a specific geographic region. There may be disputes over the borders of their jurisdiction, and limits to the extent of their control within those borders, but the distinction between governments and markets derives from the potential for a single entity to gain ultimate authority over all people within their territory. The instruments used by each national or local authority to create and govern markets include policies that establish property rights and enforce laws to regulate private activity, and programs that directly provide public goods and services. Private voluntary groups also take *collective action* to govern their members, but membership in a non-governmental organization is a choice and each person can join or help create multiple nonprofit groups and associations, just as we form new commercial enterprises.

Governments come to power in many ways, and may or may not act in the best interests of the people in each place. The history of each population shapes its governance, and there is abundant research focusing directly on politics, law and other aspects of how governments operate. Economics about government, known as public economics or political economy, focuses on the relationship between governments and markets in the places they control.

By the end of this section, you will be able to:

1. Define and use the concepts of non-excludability and non-rivalry to distinguish between private and public goods, and the role of common property or gated club goods in society;
2. Identify how a population's willingness to pay for a public good affects the quantity that would lead to the highest possible level of economic surplus;
3. Describe how each person's gain or loss from public action, including their expectations about what others will do, affects their incentives to engage in collective efforts; and
4. Describe and provide examples of policy processes that influence government choices in the food system.

6.1.2 *Analytical Tools*

The government of a country is a singular entity, typically subdivided into sub-regional and local governments with authority over distinct parts of their territory, and also subdivided into branches and agencies with control over distinct aspects of government. Democracies use elections and other mechanisms to make government officials more accountable to the people of their country, with diverse levels of success in having their government serve the public's interests.

Economists typically use the term *public sector* to mean all activities of government, while the *private sector* consists of both commercial enterprises and nonprofit organizations as well as individual activities. The two sectors are intertwined from the start, when governments create the legal framework for each enterprise to be formed and governed with specific rights and responsibilities. For example, in the U.S. about ten percent of private-sector employment is in nonprofit organizations whose registration status entitles them to pay fewer taxes, governed by boards that elect their successors. In contrast, commercial enterprises have owners who elect or appoint the directors and managers of the enterprise, or self-employed people such as many farmers who work independently as an individual or a partnership.

Terminology about both government and private-sector enterprise varies around the world, but in this book, we use the term *policies* to mean rules and institutional arrangements that govern other activities, while *programs* deliver goods and services to conduct those policies. For example, a country's agricultural authorities might have diverse programs to implement and enforce their policies about land use, irrigation and water rights, and the country's food and nutrition services might have diverse programs to implement and enforce policies about school meals or product labeling.

Decisions about each policy and program are a *collective action*, also known as a *social choice*, in the sense that one choice affects a whole community. Collective actions occur at every scale and in all kinds of social organization, from a small partnership to a global enterprise, but we are especially interested in choices that involve governments due to their potential *monopoly of force,* meaning their ability to make and enforce rules that apply to everyone within their territory.

Government decisions in agriculture and food systems often involve flows between countries, for example to govern international trade, migration and investment, or foreign aid. Governments also undertake regional or global collective actions through *international organizations,* whose member states agree to the organization's rules in exchange for the benefits of participating. The largest grouping is the United Nations (UN) whose specialized agencies such as the Food and Agriculture Organization (FAO), the World Food Program (WFP) and World Health Organization (WHO) implement programs on behalf of member countries.

The UN and its agencies are not a global government, because they operate in each place only at the invitation of that country's national authorities. Country governments have also created various international groupings alongside the UN such as the World Trade Organization (WTO), the Organization for Economic Cooperation and Development (OECD), the World Bank and others that play major roles in global agriculture and food systems. International organizations jointly owned by multiple governments are known as *multilateral* agencies, in contrast to *bilateral* programs of one country's agencies working elsewhere such as the U.S. Agency for International Development (USAID) or the Japan International Cooperation Agency (JICA).

Governments and their various agencies often work through *implementing partners* that receive grants and contracts to provide public goods and services on the governments' behalf. For example, in the fiscal year ending

October 2023, USAID used contracts, grants and other arrangements to award about $37 billion for its implementing partners around the world, managed by agency staff and operational expenses costing less than $2 billion. Implementing agencies may be international or local non-governmental organizations licensed to operate in each country where they work.

Collective actions are the result of political processes in and between countries, influenced by the extent to which individuals and organizations join together in groups that invest their time and efforts in pursuing their common interests. These interest groups may try to influence elections by contributing time and money to candidates or advocacy groups, and participating directly in outreach, activism and lobbying of government officials. The economics of public decision-making, often known as ***political economy***, concerns the incentives for people to devote time and resources to influencing government.

Economics about government seeks to understand policies in terms of peoples' choices among limited options, doing two kinds of analysis in parallel: *positive* political economy seeks to explain and predict government actions, and *normative* political economy that seeks to assess the degree to which government actions help people reach their goals. Positive analyses are descriptive about *what is*, while normative analyses are prescriptive about *what should be*, and in economics both rest on the same framework as described in this chapter.

To begin our analysis of political economy and policymaking, we return to the four types of goods and services that we introduced in Chapter 4. At that point we introduced externalities, which are ***non-excludable*** and often also ***non-rival*** costs or benefits affecting people as an unintended side effect of market activity. Here we focus on collective action to manage things that are done insufficiently or excessively by voluntary private activity, shaping the market through public-sector intervention.

Public Goods are Non-excludable, and May Also be Non-rival

One role of governments is to provide ***public goods***. These are goods or services that would be provided insufficiently or not at all by the private sector, because sellers cannot capture a sufficient fraction of the benefits to cover the cost of supplying those goods and services. An agricultural example is the underlying data and methods used for weather forecasts. Meteorological information is of immense value to both end-users and the media companies that repackage and deliver weather forecasts for specific audiences. Once someone creates the underlying information, its value is ***non-rival*** because additional people can use it at the same time without reducing its value to others, and also ***non-excludable*** if the provider cannot stop people from copying the information. The two attributes create the four-way classification of all goods and services shown in Fig. 6.1.

The top-left and bottom-right corners of Fig. 6.1 show the two extreme cases, with purely private goods in the top left and purely public goods in the bottom right. Private goods can be exchanged in markets without government intervention, as in the example of Alphabet Beach fish market. Public goods

	Demand is *rival* (if one person uses it, they displace other users)	**Demand is *nonrival*** (if one person uses it, other people can use it too)
Supply is *excludable* (provider controls who can use it)	*Private goods & services* *such as food & fuel*	*Gated goods & services* *such as software & content*
Supply is *non-excludable* (once provided, anyone can use it)	*Common property* *such as public roads*	*Public goods & services* *such as climate & air quality*

Fig. 6.1 Definition of four types of goods and services, from private to public

are like the information behind weather forecasts, or more importantly the actual weather and air quality that affects everyone. Those are the cases where private provision is minimal, and if the government does not do something then it is not done.

The other two corners of Fig. 6.1 are intermediate cases, with important roles for collective action to influence the extent and impacts of market activity. The top-right corner shows examples of things that are non-rival but potentially excludable, such as software and media content. These 'gated' services include the media companies that repackage government weather forecasts in distinct ways, for example with more entertaining meteorologists or customized versions of the public data. The bottom-left corner shows things that are non-excludable but may be subject to congestion when too many people use them at once such as public roads, sidewalks and other facilities. Everyone in a given area could potentially try to use that common property at the same time, reducing its value for everyone. In these settings governments can improve market outcomes by allocating property rights, regulating use and taxing or subsidizing market activity.

We introduced the role of property rights to address externalities in Chapter 4, where the government's role in allocating rights to people was shown to be a major determinant of how income and wealth are distributed, as well as the efficiency of resource use. Earlier in Chapter 3, we also saw the same thing for regulations or taxes and subsidies, which have big impacts equity as well as the total economic surplus available for each society. To achieve more efficient as well as more equitable outcomes, collective action to address each kind of market failure is needed such as antitrust policy to limit monopoly power.

In discussions of public policy observers often use shorthand descriptions of a country's economy as being more or less market-oriented, with more or less focus on public goods. The term *capitalism* typically refers to governments giving greater property rights for owners of commercial enterprises, who are 'capitalists' in the sense of using financial investments and physical assets as 'capital' in the production of things for sale in private markets along the top row of Fig. 6.1. The opposite term *communism* typically refers to governments giving more limited rights to enterprise owners, so that people buy and sell fewer things in private markets. Ideological debates around capitalism and communism were influential in twentieth-century politics, but other shorthand descriptions of policy orientation are more common today. Policy debate in the twenty-first century is more often described as between a conservative movement that wants things to be as they were, and a progressive movement that wants change towards something new. Other axes of debate focus on the demographic composition and origins of interest groups, the role of government in enforcing morality and cultural norms or the personalities of political leaders.

Over time, modern economics research has become increasingly empirical, using the increasing availability of data and computing power to focus research efforts on the challenge of making accurate predictions and providing practical advice. Economists test, adapt and apply the models presented in this book for both positive description and normative prescription. The interests of economists themselves undoubtedly play a role in their work, driving topic selection and choice of methods towards the kind of research that people want to have done. Researchers who are interested in the benefits of something are more likely to look for and find evidence of gains, while researchers who are interested in the harms from something might look for and find its costs. Schools of thought emerge around specific questions, for example the prospects for plant-based alternatives to animal-sourced foods, but modern economics involves a diverse set of debates about different topics instead of polarization between two political ideologies.

Economics about the public sector uses the market models presented earlier in this book to show how government intervention affects private-sector activity, and adds methods designed specifically around the supply and demand of public goods and services. Economists explain the resulting models with the analytical diagrams shown in this section, and apply them to practical questions using the empirical methods in the second section of this chapter.

The Scale and Scope of Public Goods Provision: Local, National and Global

Governments deliver a variety of goods and services, providing nonmarket complements to market activity. What determines the scale and scope of decision-making by each public sector institution?

Data and analysis of public-sector policies typically starts with national governments. As of 2023 the world had about eight billion people governed by the 193 member states of the United Nations, ranging in size from China and India to microstates like the city of Monaco or the island of Palau. Whatever the country's size, its national policies and programs cover their entire territory for example trade policy implemented at the country's borders and monetary policies affecting the macroeconomy, while other kinds of intervention are decided upon by local or regional governments within countries, or by international organizations.

When comparing countries economists usually focus on data per person in each territory, but that can be ambiguous. Borders may be disputed and can change over time, and the population of each place may include travelers, migrants and displaced people. International agencies often revise their statistics to account for changes in how people are counted, and country governments do the same for subnational data.

The highest level of decision-making for most policies and programs is the country's national government. They routinely delegate local decisions to subnational authorities such as towns and regions, and countries also participate in international organizations such as UN agencies or the World Bank. Every institution has a history of its own, as for example city governments may have been formed by people who lived there well before the establishment of the national government, and accidents of history often dictate geographic borders.

Economists use non-rivalry and non-excludability to help explain the scale and scope of many government functions. The *subsidiarity principle* of delegation suggests that public-sector decisions are typically most cost-effective when made at the geographic scale within which their costs and benefits are contained. In some cases, the actual scale and scope of government functions follows that principle. For example, food safety and licensing of restaurants is usually run by local governments, because the costs and benefits of that service are mostly contained within their jurisdiction. In contrast, food safety and licensing of food manufacturers is usually done by state or national governments, because those products are bought and sold throughout their territory.

The principle of subsidiarity provides only very loose guidance about the most cost-effective scale and scope of each agency, and factors other than cost-effectiveness influence their operations, but the geographic area within which effects are contained provides useful insights into the evolution of many public institutions. Irrigation systems in agriculture, for example, may have been built through collective action of a few farmers and their local governments, but then changing scarcity drives demand for water management over a larger geographic area, leading to intervention by the state or national government. Similarly, transboundary disputes over irrigation water have traditionally been settled through negotiation between two countries, but larger regional initiatives are increasingly used to monitor river basins and lakes, and global agreements increasingly govern the use of the oceans and the atmosphere.

The Value of a Public Good Is the Sum of Willingness to Pay at Each Quantity

The value of public goods and services cannot be shown using a market demand curve, because each unit provided benefits multiple people at the same time. Every person in the population potentially experiences the same quantity provided, so that quantity's value to society is the vertical sum of each individual's willingness to pay as illustrated in Fig. 6.2.

In the example shown in Fig. 6.2, we can return to Alphabet Beach village and imagine that Ana, Bob and Cat want to use some of the shoreline for a public park. Again, we can imagine that Ana has the highest willingness to pay

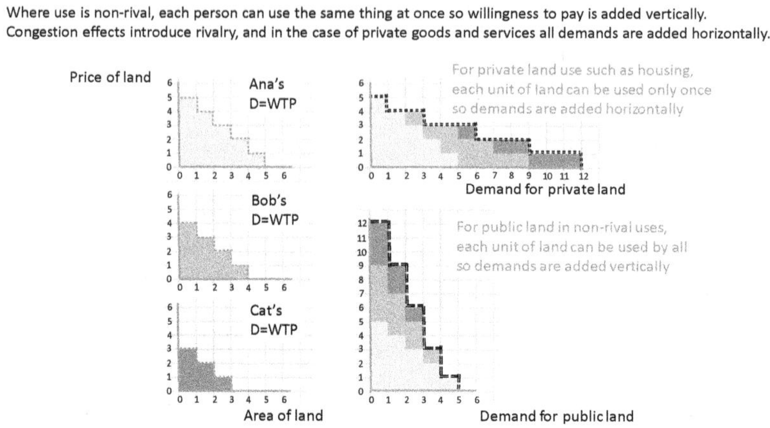

Fig. 6.2 The value of public goods to a community is a vertical sum of private demands

for land to be used as a park, perhaps because she really loves the idea and would like the park to be as big as possible. Bob has intermediate demand, and Cat has the lowest willingness to pay because she cares about other things, while others in this community might have no desire at all for a public park.

In this context, the value to each person could be scaled in different ways depending on how we are using the term 'value'. If we want to compare the value of parkland to other public services such as a new sewage system that would cost money, we might want to use a concept like economic surplus. We would count each person's monetary willingness to pay for land in the park, and differences between people might be partly due to their income or wealth. We might also want to make comparisons using another metric such as time use, measuring their willingness to invest time in creating the park or using it afterwards. We could also assign to Ana, Bob and Cat a metric of value that is derived from observations of other people, for example if studying parks elsewhere revealed that each additional unit of parkland yielded the number shown of additional life years for other people like Ana, Bob and Cat.

Whatever measure of willingness to pay we might use, the sum of Ana, Bob and Cat's valuation of land in the park is shown in the bottom-right corner of Fig. 6.2. The first unit of parkland would have a total value of twelve for the community as a whole, composed of five for Ana, four for Bob and three for Cat. The next unit would be worth only nine and then six to the three of them. The fourth unit of land in the park is of value only to Ana and Bob, and the fifth unit helps only Ana. In contrast, when land is used as private property, quantities are added horizontally as shown in the top right of Fig. 6.2. Because each unit can be used privately by only one person or household, a much larger total area of private space is needed, while total willingness to pay for the small area of public parkland is very high.

In real-life valuation of public goods and services, analysts might take account of congestion and rivalry in the use of the public amenity, modeling how each person's willingness to pay is modified by the number of other people using it. Many other challenges arise for measurement and comparison of cost-effectiveness among public activities, but the basic contrast shown in Fig. 6.2 remains the central distinction between public and private goods.

When collective action can mobilize resources to provide public goods, each unit provided can have extremely high total value when many people have high willingness to pay, and additional quantities have lower value to the community due to diminishing marginal value for each person. Empirical modeling can estimate the socially optimal level of public good provision, based on a corresponding study of the fixed and marginal costs of government provision. The highest possible level of total or average value created per person would be where the marginal social cost of providing one more unit meets its marginal social value, but providing public goods at any level is challenging due to the difficulty of collective action.

Barriers to Collective Action: Inattention, Free Ridership and Voting
Using the example of Fig. 6.2, we can imagine how Ana, Bob and Cat might hold meetings and pool their efforts to obtain a public park for Alphabet Beach. They might be able to hire people to persuade others that the community needs the park, for example by conducting studies and forming advocacy groups. They could proceed within the private sector as a philanthropic initiative, forming a nonprofit organization to achieve their goals, but could they persuade their whole community to create the park? More generally, what determines the quantity of public goods provided by governments?

Who has what influence over government decisions is the topic of political science, and also studied in law schools and by policy specialists in diverse fields. Those researchers use the economics toolkit and add details about the options available in each setting, focusing on how policymaking differs from the market for private goods. In the markets seen earlier, outcomes follow from individual transactions between sellers and buyers. Each transaction is motivated by the opportunity to close a gap between price received and marginal cost (for sellers) or between price paid and willingness to pay (for buyers). Markets emerge whenever transaction costs are low enough for individuals to act on their own interests. Collective actions are much more difficult to obtain. The economics toolkit about collective action is often framed in terms of three concepts that had long been understood intuitively but were formalized for empirical research purposes in the mid-twentieth century.

A first constraint on collective action is the problem of *inattention*, stemming from the fact that political effort depends on the stakes per person, not just the number of people, and many people have such low stakes that even learning about the issue is not worthwhile for them. We have already seen the issue in action when discussing trade policy, where producers who sell large quantities are very attentive to policy and invest heavily in persuading people to restrict imports and thereby raise price, with little pushback from consumers each of whom buys a small quantity and often has an insufficient stake to even bother learning about the issue. In our toy model, there are three people who want the park (Ana, Bob and Cat) and we know that the village has at least five other residents (Deb, Ed, Fio, Gio and Hijo). The three advocates could potentially pool their efforts and obtain a park, even if all five of the others are indifferent or potentially opposed, simply because the five are focused on other issues and inattentive to the question. More importantly, even Cat may have an insufficient interest in the park to justify any effort at all.

Using time as the unit of valuation in Fig. 6.2, Cat's willingness to pay for the first unit of parkland was 3 hours of work. If she expected that advocating for the park would cost 3 or more hours, she would realize that acting on her interest in the park is not cost-effective for her. She might still work on the issue, but that would be for some other reason such as altruism towards Ana and Bob, and economists analyzing that motivation would want to have included altruism in Cat's estimated willingness to pay. More generally, learning about any issue is itself costly, and Cat would realize that even learning about an issue would not be cost-effective for anything whose value to her ultimately turns out to be below the cost of advocating for it. The time cost of political action ensures that for most individuals it is not worthwhile to even learn about the issues they might care about, so only those with a high stake in the matter will pursue it. The inattention constraint was formalized in the book *An Economic Theory of Democracy* by Anthony Downs, published in 1957, showing how the cost of political engagement and of acquiring information can pose big barriers to having collective action, leading to advocacy groups formed only by people with high stakes in that specific issue, and more effective public goods provision in settings that have low costs of political engagement and easy access to accurate information about each policy.

A second big constraint on collective action is *free ridership*, popularized in a book entitled *The Logic of Collective Action* by Mancur Olson published in 1965. Free ridership is the same mechanism as the Tragedy of the Commons and limits collective action even when people know that they care enough about an issue to take action. In our toy model the total value to Ana, Bob and Cat of a one-unit park is 12 hours of fun, and if it costs each person 3 hours of work to obtain it, Cat might decide to drop out of the effort. If Ana and Bob succeed, they would have a net gain of 3 and 1 respectively, but they would also know that Cat is getting the park for free. Bob might then realize that Ana really wants the park and will pursue it no matter what, leading Bob to drop out leaving Ana to pursue the effort alone. The incentives for people to free ride on others' efforts depend on each person's expectations about the behavior of others, and strongly rewards efforts to establish social norms and other mechanisms to enforce participation of each person likely to gain from the collective action.

The economic obstacles of inattention and free ridership both limit the incentives for each individual to contribute their full willingness to pay in pursuit of public goods, but even among those who do invest there is an important limitation to the concept of a socially optimal level of public goods. That obstacle was first formalized by Kenneth Arrow in his doctoral dissertation published in 1950, using an *impossibility theorem* to show that aggregating preferences among people cannot produce the kind of consistent ranking that characterizes an individual person's preferences. In other words, there is no voting scheme that can prevent preference reversals such as a community having voted for a park instead of a library, a library instead of a garden and then also for a garden instead of a park. Even if each individual in the community has consistent preferences between the three options, the community as a whole may have inconsistent preferences. The Arrow impossibility theorem does not mean that voting is ineffective. To the contrary, the study of voting systems shows how different electoral systems have very large impacts on the way in which popular preferences are represented, including the relative influence of interest groups in agriculture and food policy.

The three economic limits to collective action described here all refer specifically to the way that economics compares benefits to costs as a guide to decision-making. Many other factors outside the economics toolkit affect public-sector decisions. In fact, a core implication of inattention, free ridership and Arrow's impossibility theorem is that successful collective action involves not just economic incentives for individuals but also social psychology, political institutions and attention to accidents of history. Keeping both economic and non-economic influences in mind can be helpful to understand the dynamics of collective action in any given setting. The problem of inattention leads us to focus on the gains and losses per person, relative to the cost of political participation and obtaining accurate information. The problem of free ridership leads us to focus on social norms about participation, and the study of voting leads us to focus on how public interests are aggregated to guide public policy.

Agricultural and food policies have long provided big opportunities for initiatives that overcome obstacles to collective action and improve outcomes. In the 1960s and 1970s, a professor of political science named Elinor Ostrom built a research program to record how people around the world have in fact created social norms and institutions that successfully overcome the tragedy of the commons, free ridership and costly information, and come closer to socially optimal levels of public goods provision over time. Ostrom's most influential book, *Governing the Commons: The Evolution of Institutions for Collective Action,* published in 1990, was almost entirely about how groups of farmers, herders and others manage natural resources and develop governments literally from the ground up, as small self-governing communities who develop commitment devices to elicit cooperative behavior around local public goods like irrigation and grazing. Ostrom was awarded the Nobel Prize for economics in 2009, recognizing her achievements in expanding the toolkit of economic analysis from individual to social action.

Policy Processes: Veto Players, Rent-Seeking and Median Voters

Each policy or program that governments actually implement must pass through a long sequence of political processes, each of which imposes a different political constraint. Useful terminology about policy processes includes the role of *veto players* who can stop things and *rent-seeking* by actors who see opportunities to influence policy in ways that restrict competition and make their activities more profitable. Advocacy groups pursuing their own preferred outcomes must overcome opposition by potential veto players, and to limit rent-seeking by those who might alter policies to their advantage.

Policy processes often include steps where voting occurs. The general public may elect its leaders, often through a sequential processes that lead to policies by votes among those representatives. When elections or other voting specifies that actions require a majority vote, a change needs only 50% plus one vote to pass, giving political leaders strong incentives to adjust policies until they are just sufficient to reach that threshold. When voters are arrayed on a scale from strongly opposed to strongly in favor of the change, so majority-rule decisions rest on persuading the *median voter* to switch sides. Similarly, in elections that require a supermajority such as two-thirds (66%) of the voters to approve, the deciding vote would be at the 66th percentile of those voting. Most political processes evolve such that the outcome of voting comes down to the marginal or 'swing' decision-maker favoring or opposing the change.

Observed policies are those for which leaders were able to build coalitions with just enough support to pass through each step of the political process, navigating through veto players and rent-seeking efforts to stop or modify the policy, and attracting the median voter at each stage of policymaking. Economic principles can help us understand how a given set of political institutions shapes the policies that decision-makers will actually enact. Decision-making at each stage depends not only on whether or not a person favors a change, but the intensity of their preferences and their willingness to sacrifice other things to attain that goal.

6.1.3 Conclusion

Public policy and programs for agriculture and the food system operate at diverse scales, with varying scope to address each kind of market failure and achieve societal goals for sustainability, equity and health.

This section introduces the economics toolkit to understand how public action differs from private transactions. Economic analysis of the public sector begins with the costs and benefits experienced by individuals, and the incentives they must engage in collective action to obtain government-provided goods and services. For example, a small group of farmers might build a shared irrigation system, while another group of herders might set rules for grazing. The governing bodies of those local institutions might then collaborate with others over a larger geographic area, expanding to address regional issues like watershed management and animal disease control. Their scope of operations can also vary to combine different kinds of public goods, such as joint governance of crops and livestock to improve all of agriculture.

Economic analysis of the public sector typically begins with national governments. Countries are the main unit of analysis due to their sovereignty over all the people in the territory they control. Each government has branches and specialized agencies for each public function, with nested subnational governments of states or regions, counties or districts, and towns or cities to provide public goods and services at each scale of operation. Many aspects of agriculture and food systems cross country borders, so national governments often join international organizations with specialized regional or global agencies to perform public functions of varied scale and scope. The principle of subsidiarity calls for tailoring the scale and scope of each governing body to the problems it solves, making organizations as small as possible to maintain accountability, while achieving the economies of scale and scope needed to provide the nonmarket public goods and services that can overcome market failures in each situation.

Priorities for change and opportunities for collective action evolve over time, requiring each successive group of people to work together in new ways. Incentives for individuals create dilemmas where cooperation can help others but be costly for oneself, leading to the intentional creation of social norms and commitments to sustain cooperative behavior and overcome free ridership. Groups can then build institutions with low cost of participation and easy access to accurate information, overcoming the problem of inattention and allowing government to take costs and benefits into account when setting policies and providing programs. The following section describes how data on those costs and benefits are obtained and used in the actual practice of government for agriculture, food and health.

6.2 Cost-Effectiveness and Nonmarket Goals in Food and Agriculture

6.2.1 *Motivation and Guiding Questions*

The previous section showed how economists use each person's incentives to understand collective action, helping government agencies and other large organizations meet goals that individuals cannot achieve through market transactions. These nonmarket goals drive policy interventions that shape the economy, potentially providing remedies for market failure and delivering public goods and services. What determines which interventions would best help each population meet its goals? In other words, how can we know if an intervention is cost-effective?

Government decisions can be seen as yes/no choices, often among multiple options. Each choice will help or harm different people in different ways. Economics can help decision-makers predict those impacts and compare their relative magnitudes. As we will see, the cost-effectiveness of each policy or program depends not only on what it does, but also the extent or magnitude of each action. Helpful interventions can become harmful when they are too much of a good thing. Some policy actions involve choices like the menu at a restaurant with predetermined portion sizes, while other decisions are like a grocery store where people choose between things first, and later decide how much to use.

For each decision, economic analyses compare costs to benefits. As we have seen, net gains or losses for each person help explain individual choices, market outcomes and our own willingness to spend time and money on collective action, but incentives for each individual do not fully determine what governments do. The actual policies and programs we see were created in the past, influenced accidents of history, and ongoing changes are driven by social norms and beliefs about other people. Those beliefs can be self-perpetuating, as we saw in the example of a two-person strategic game where expecting others to act nicely makes it in each person's interest to do so. Social activists and political leaders shape common narratives and beliefs, while policy decisions change actual payoffs to the options among which people can choose, potentially aligning costs and benefits so that outcomes improve over time.

The role of history and beliefs in collective action ensures an ongoing need for creative leadership, whenever individuals in society see opportunities for improvement. Throughout human history, governments have sometimes done too much, taking actions whose costs exceed benefits, and sometimes done too little, or what they have done is too late for the populations that could potentially have been helped with actions whose benefits exceed their costs. Public-sector actions or inactions that harm the public interest are known as *policy failures,* in the same way that private interactions' failure to achieve a population's full potential are known as *market failures*.

Economists use the same kind of cost-effectiveness analysis to assess both policy failures and market failures. In each case, understanding the value of each option calls on subject-matter knowledge about the environmental conditions, available technologies and human factors that determine production possibilities and consumption needs, as well as economic techniques to add up and compare costs and benefits. Professional economists sometimes craft policy proposals, but more often they volunteer or are employed to analyze options proposed by others, and economic techniques can readily be used by anyone to assess the net gains or losses from any initiative.

By the end of this section, you will be able to:

1. Explain how to convert market prices and monetary values from one time and place to another, accounting for inflation and differences in purchasing power;

2. Describe how economic and social valuation of something is affected by how far in the future it will occur, as well as risk and uncertainty about whether it will occur, using interest rates and discounting;
3. Describe how economists elicit a population's valuation and willingness to pay for things that they are not currently buying; and
4. Explain how cost–benefit and cost-effectiveness analysis can be used to inform decisions relating to agriculture, food and nutrition.

6.2.2 *Analytical Tools*

The previous section showed how the benefits of a change in public goods or services can be added up over the population it serves, drawn as the vertical sum of each person's valuation. In this section we turn to how those benefits can be compared to their costs. Both benefits and costs can be counted in their natural units, for example hours of time or kcals of energy or years of life lost. Monetary comparisons refer to things that could be bought and sold and therefore valued at market prices, in terms of economic surplus based on whatever currency units are used for transactions. Other things are counted in natural units and can be compared to each other only in that same unit of measure.

In this section we use the term *cost-effectiveness analysis* broadly, to include all comparisons of gains and losses experienced by a population that might be attributed to changing a policy or program. Specialized terminology can be helpful to identify the technique used to quantify gains or losses. For example, *cost–benefit analysis* usually refers to comparisons between different things that are measured in monetary terms. When studies focus on probabilities, they are often called *comparative risk assessments*, or risk-benefit analysis. This section introduces the economic principles used for these cost-effectiveness studies, for both market and nonmarket objectives of policy.

Comparing Monetary Values: Adjusting for Inflation and Purchasing Power

Comparing monetary costs or benefits such as economic surplus requires adjusting currencies for inflation and differences in purchasing power. The *nominal prices* that are observed at each place and time, and also the *real prices* that adjust for inflation, refer to what money can buy in terms of all other goods and services. Nominal prices are also known as prices in 'current' terms, while real prices are in 'constant' terms.

Inflation over time is typically measured and reported as the average rate for an entire country, so that real prices have constant buying power for the quantities of all goods and services that people report buying in nationally representative surveys. Similarly, international comparisons are made in *purchasing power parity* terms, with constant buying power for average of all goods and services available in each country. Subnational comparisons are also possible, for example with separate inflation rates and purchasing power comparisons for rural or urban populations.

Adjusting for inflation and purchasing power can be very confusing and is a common source of misleading information about costs and benefits. To avoid errors, it is helpful to do the ***analysis of units*** that was introduced in Section 3.2 on elasticities. In an analysis of units, the descriptive name of each number's measurement units, for example 'pesos in 2024' is used as a variable in a mathematical expression to confirm that numerical conversions are done consistently. Nominal data might show a value of 20 pesos in 2023 and 21 pesos in 2024.

Consumer price indexes to monitor inflation are typically shown as one hundred in the base year to see percentage differences since then and might have shown that the national average level of prices rose from 100 in 2023 to 105 in 2024. Analysis of units reveals how the real value of the 21 pesos in 2024 must be divided by 1.05 = 105 in 2024/100 in 2023, because that divides 'in 2024' by itself so those words cancel out. The result in this case is that 21 nominal pesos in 2024 equals 20 real pesos in 2023 terms.

Similar analysis of units can be used to ensure that any other unit conversion is done accurately, to avoid misleading comparisons of costs and benefits. Logical consistency can be checked by using variable names in a sentence, or using variable names in an equation to confirm that ratios cancel, or using numerical examples to verify magnitudes. In each case it is helpful to remember the original definition of each term. For example, when monetary values in Japanese yen or Mexican pesos are converted to real purchasing power parity terms in U.S. dollars, by definition each real dollars should have the same average purchasing power over all goods and services in Japan as in Mexico, and only the relative prices of different things within Japan and Mexico would differ.

When we introduced externalities in Section 4.2, we showed their costs and benefits in monetary terms. Using a common denominator such as real dollars is needed whenever cost-benefit analyses seek a common unit of measurement. Comparing market and nonmarket benefits using economic surplus, expressed in real monetary terms, is helpful to make comparisons in terms of all things that money can buy.

The material requisites of wellbeing sometimes have an observable price, for example in the form of higher rents and house prices near public amenities like a park, or lower rents and house prices in places with more pollution. Analyses could use those monetary values to quantify questions of environmental justice and efficiency, adding up gains and losses from parks or pollution for different populations. Similar analyses could potentially be done for social conditions such as worker protections and occupational safety, but analysts may also prefer to use natural units such as years of life lost from disease or disability, or biophysical measures of change in the environment.

Risk and Uncertainty: Use Values, Option Values and Existence Values

Environmental and natural resource economists study how people interact with the ecological and geographic conditions around us. Ecosystem services are the benefits provided by the natural environment such as carbon sequestration, clean air, pollination, education and recreation. Many cost-benefit studies involving ecosystem services focus on their *use value*, based on the average level of each attribute employed by people in production or consumption.

Risk ensures that people place an additional value on environmental attributes or ecosystem services they might need, which is known as an attribute's *option value*. Option values are computed based on known probabilities, for example the option value of groundwater might be calculated based on historical risks of low rainfall leading to the probability that groundwater will be needed. Systemic shifts such as climate change alter those probabilities, and different people will have different ideas and models in mind about what the environment is worth to them. *Risk assessment* is the standard term for estimating probabilities, and *risk aversion* is a person's willingness to pay to avoid riskier things.

Adding up the population's subjective valuation of potential needs or intangible benefits of environmental attributes or ecosystem services is known as their *existence value*. As we have seen, all valuations in economics are ultimately subjective, capturing how much people value each thing for their overall wellbeing. Nonmarket valuations are contentious in part because of limited data about both quantities and values, especially for option values and existence values. But economists can elicit those valuations using a variety of techniques, and often find somewhat predictable patterns. For example, diminishing returns ensures that existence values depend greatly on the level of something, and the risk that it will be lost forever, leading to very high valuation of species at risk of extinction or rare natural amenities.

Comparing Costs and Effects over Time: Interest Rates and Discounting

Many studies involve projects whose benefits are felt long after the costs are incurred. Decisions today often have consequences at different points in the future, for example after one month, one year, one decade or one century.

People reveal their relative valuation of things that are experienced sooner rather than later in many ways. For things that people can buy with money, *interest rates* reflect the price paid or received for delaying costs and benefits, and economists use *discount rates* to mean a person's willingness to pay for that delay. A higher rate means more discounting of future benefits and costs. For example, something now worth a hundred dollars but received after ten years would now be worth about $82 today at a discount rate of 2% per year, or about $56 at a discount rate of 6% per year. Longer time periods greatly increase the importance of interest and discount rates, for example after twenty years the difference between 2 and 6% per year is a present value of \$67 or \$31.

Because delays involve risk, interest rates and discount rates are always affected by differences in risk assessment and risk aversion. For example, private lenders offer lower interest rates for auto loans than for student loans, in part due to less risk that the loan will not be repaid when lenders can repossess the vehicle and sell it if loan payments are missed. The value created by student loans is more difficult for lenders to capture, and those externalities help explain government support for educational investments.

Adding up a whole population's discount rate for public goods in the future leads to very different results than the discount rates revealed by individual transactions today. Many people have discount rates for long-run benefits experienced by a whole community or the global population that are much lower than the rates we apply to the short-term needs of individuals today. These differences are revealed by both nonmarket behavior and thought experiments, for example when people borrow or lend for short-term loans at high interest rates that imply a high degree of impatience, even as we all protect land and resources for our children and grandchildren at near-zero discount rates. The difference arises in part because overlapping generations create a potentially infinite time horizon for the group, and population growth means that collective assets like land or public goods could potentially be shared among a larger number of people.

Potentially larger population sizes over potentially long time horizons lead many people to place a much higher value on the future of their whole community than on their own future consumption. But attitudes towards the future are also shaped by beliefs about future living standards. If people expect or arrange for incomes to grow over time, then diminishing returns in consumption make an additional dollar in the future less valuable than it is today. On the other hand, if people expect or fear that living standards might be lower in the future, we all would be more willing to sacrifice things today. These beliefs are difficult to quantify but have a very large effect on people's discount rates and willingness to save and protect resources for the future. We will return to each person's risk assessment and risk aversion in Chapter 7, and then to our intertemporal comparisons in Chapter 8, to keep the focus in this chapter on collective action among groups of people.

Social Welfare and Inter-personal Comparison of Costs and Benefits

Any decision about collective action involves adding up impacts among people. Cost-effectiveness analyses usually aim to count each gain or loss equally, without regard to other attributes of that person. One reason is the practical difficulty of making those distinctions, because we often know the magnitude of total gains or losses but we do not know which person in society experienced how much gain or loss. For example, economic surplus is defined relative to supply or demand curves and then measured using observed prices, total quantities and elasticities of response, usually with no way of knowing which person sold or bought each unit of the product.

Even if a cost-effectiveness analysis had data on which person experienced each gain or loss, counting them differently based on a person's observed characteristics would require a weighting scheme that decision-makers would find attractive. For example, a study of health impacts might count gains only when experienced only by people in certain demographic groups, but the centuries-old trend in many societies has been towards counting all people equally. For the English-speaking world, a first step in that direction was the Magna Carta adopted over 800 years ago in 1215 granting a very limited set of rights for each citizen, and then almost 250 years ago in 1776 another step was the U.S. Declaration of Independence from Britain which claimed additional rights because 'all men are created equal'. That was followed eventually by the Emancipation Proclamation of 1863 ending the U.S. government's enforcement of slavery, the 19th Amendment to the U.S. constitution adopted in 1920 granting women the right to vote, and similar steps towards equal counting of all people when making collective decisions. Not all societies aspire to counting people equally, and each step towards greater equality is often followed by steps back, but the effort to count gains and losses more equally over time is a deeply rooted tradition.

An important use of cost-effectiveness analysis that counts each person equally is to identify how actual policy decisions favor some groups over others. For example, we have seen how import restrictions and licensing arrangements favor producers over consumers. Economic surplus analysis can then show which groups gain or lose, revealing the relative strength of each group when influencing policy. Similarly, comparative effectiveness studies in health service provision can show which groups gain more from an intervention, and which gain less. In other words, equal counting often reveals unequal treatment, in ways that would not be possible if the cost-effectiveness accounting used differential weights on gains and losses of different groups.

Counting each person equally does not mean that each person experiences equal costs and benefits. Different metrics count different impacts, so their magnitude differ in systematic ways. For example, comparative effectiveness in health can be calculated based on either lives saved, or years of life saved. An intervention saving a child might extend their life by many years, while an intervention saving an older adult might contribute only a few additional years. Further weighting is often done by ***quality-adjusted life years*** (QALYs) or ***disability-adjusted life years*** (DALYs) which account for improvements in living standards. When counting disability, improving vitamin A status through better diet, supplementation or fortification often ranks as one of the world's most cost-effective health interventions because it reduces blindness (which has a high weight in QALYs and DALYs), and often does so for preschool children (and hence many years per life).

Selection of the outcome metric in each cost-effectiveness study typically aims to reflect both the kind of data available for the study and the policy or program questions being asked. Environmental policies and projects often involve a wide range of outcomes that are compared in cost–benefit terms, whereas health programs all target human longevity and years of disease-free life, so they are evaluated using cost-effectiveness methods in units such as QALYs or DALYs. In some cases, health programs are compared to each other without cost data, which is known as *comparative effectiveness*. In health care, efforts to standardize and improve the metrics and methods chosen often make use of *reference case* guidelines, a term coined in the 1990s to help adapt the economic principles of cost-effectiveness analysis to the needs of health care providers.

Ecosystem Services and Environmental Analyses of Costs and Benefits
The climate crisis has made greenhouse gas emissions the single most important environmental outcome of recent years, but ecosystem services are extremely diverse in whether and how they can be measured. To facilitate comparison, the European Environment Agency defines and characterizes different ecosystem services in a uniform way, regularly updating the Common Classification of Ecosystem Services (CICES) as illustrated in Table 6.1.

Table 6.1 Types of ecosystem services

Category	*Type*	*Ecosystem service examples*	*Benefit received by humans*
Regulation and maintenance	Biotic	Decomposing and filtering of wastes, noise reduction, reducing smells, disease control	Mitigation of the effects of daily life on the environment
	Abiotic	Diluting chemicals, filtration, sequestration, storage, flows of gases and liquids	Dissolving silica in soil runoff, reducing the cost of disposal of chemical wastes
Provisioning	Biotic	Cultivated and wild plants and fibers, livestock for work or food for humans, wild animals for food or materials	Sources of fuel, food, clothing, medicines, building materials
	Abiotic	Water for energy, drinking, and lubrication; minerals; wind energy, solar energy, geothermal energy	Hydration, cleaning, energy production, manufacturing capabilities
Cultural	Biotic	Direct outdoor interactions, education about nature, research about ecology	Happiness, mental and emotional wellbeing, a feeling of purpose
	Abiotic	Geological features, rocks	Recreation, exercise, identity

Source Authors' adaption of definitions and examples from the European Environment Agency, whose updated infographics are at https://www.eea.europa.eu/ds_resolveuid/INF-169-en

The actions that government take to improve ecosystem services sometimes use regulation that restricts what people can do. Compliance can be costly so restrictions are resisted, and it may be easier for governments to use incentive payments instead. For example, the U.S. Clean Water Act of 1972 sharply reduced pollution into navigable rivers from identifiable point sources such as industrial factories but did not cover surface water through which agricultural runoff often flows. In 2015 the government proposed a new regulation that would extend Federal protection from navigable rivers to seasonal streams and wetlands, known as the Waters of the U.S. (WOTUS) rule. That proposal would have limited what many farmers and others could do, prompting counter-pressure that was ultimately resolved in 2023 by restricting protection to year-round streams and lakes with surface connection to navigable rivers that cross state boundaries.

In contrast to the difficulty of implementing WOTUS, since 1996 the U.S. Federal government has run a popular Environmental Quality Incentives Program (EQIP), which generally pays for up to 75% of farmers' costs of actions to reduce runoff and provide other ecosystem services. Farmers apply for cost-sharing of investments for changes in crop residue management and cover cropping, irrigation and nutrient management or other improvements to their farm. Much of EQIP aims to reduce negative externalities, using payments for voluntary actions instead of regulations like WOTUS, providing additional support shaping how production occurs to complement other payments to help farmers such as subsidized crop insurance.

Cost-Effectiveness of Optimal, Second-best and Politically Feasible Actions

Economic principles provide helpful guidance for using cost-effectiveness to improve collective action. As shown in Chapters 2, 3 and 4, attaining the highest possible level of wellbeing requires that actions are adjusted until their social marginal costs just equal their social marginal benefits. Marginal costs and benefits differ from average or total costs and benefits, and scale effects imply that analysts must consider different scales of intervention to find the highest level of wellbeing. Adjusting until marginal costs just equal marginal benefits is known as *the first equimarginal principle*. The same idea also applies to equalizing marginal costs among different resources used, and equalizing marginal benefits among different benefits created, which is known as the *second equimarginal principle*.

The optimality conditions needed to maximize societal wellbeing imply that different strategies would be pursued in a coordinated manner. For example, regarding fertilizer use and other runoff into public water supplies, there might be a combination of actions like WOTUS and EPIC, each of which would be pursued until the overall gains reached their maximum. Decision-makers would keep expanding helpful actions and reducing harmful ones until the marginal social cost of each change just equals its marginal social benefit.

Economic models provide guidance about the direction and magnitude of changes that would improve outcomes, but this chapter also shows the political economy constraints on collective action. Economists use the term *second-best* to mean the most cost-effective policies and programs given political constraints. Second-best interventions differ from socially optimal actions in systematic ways. For example, in U.S. agricultural policy, extending Clean Water Act protections to smaller streams through WOTUS has been more difficult to implement than payments to farmers through EQIP, so the second-best policy is to do more EQIP than would be socially optimal if the two policies were equally easy to implement.

Eliciting Willingness to Pay and to Accept in Market and Nonmarket Settings

Goods and services that are traded in markets can be valued at their social opportunity cost, meaning the best available alternative. The social opportunity cost of traded products is typically the price paid by or received in trade, while nontraded goods have social opportunity costs that depend on both supply and demand. Opportunity costs can sometimes be estimated based on computerized models, but estimating a population's willingness to pay for a given change requires specialized set of economic or *nonmarket valuation* techniques.

The methods used to elicit willingness to pay begin with *revealed preferences* shown by actual choices. As seen in Chapter 3, for market transactions economists use can estimate demand systems from the population's variation in supply, but for nonmarket goods and services economists must use artificial experiments to elicit willingness to pay. In some settings researchers also elicit *stated preferences*, which are surveys that might include hypothetical choices designed to capture how much a person would value each good or service.

A central challenge for preference elicitation is to obtain robust estimates of willingness to pay that can predict observed behavior over time. As we know from Chapters 2, 3 and 4, each person's willingness to pay and hence the society's demand curve depends on what else is available or needed, at what price. A person's willingness to pay for health interventions, for example, can range from their entire wealth when faced with an immediate life-or-death choice, to almost nothing when the benefits are uncertain and long delayed. How an analyst frames each question can also affect preference elicitation. A purely hypothetical question such as 'how much would you be willing to pay' is unlikely to predict actual future behavior, but specialists in preference elicitation have developed a large toolkit of empirical methods used to guide both private-sector marketing of new products and economic valuation of public-sector actions.

We will return to the psychological factors that influence individual decisions in Chapter 8, but for cost-effectiveness of collective actions a particularly important aspect of decision-making is known as *status-quo bias,* also known as *loss aversion*. That idea creates a gap between a person's willingness to pay (WTP) to acquire something and their *willingness to accept* (WTA) compensation for giving up that same thing when they already have it. People consistently put a higher value on things they have, so a population's WTA for something is consistently above its WTP for that same thing. A typical example involves land use, where individuals and communities place a very high value on avoiding change. The entire toolkit of preference elicitation includes both WTP and WTA, using methods like those listed in Table 6.2.

The methods listed in Table 6.2 aim to overcome a variety of challenges in eliciting a population's valuation of nonmarket goods and services. These concerns may be common to all surveys, starting with problems of *selection bias* in who is contacted and who is willing to respond. Careful sampling and testing for differences between respondents and the target population is an essential starting point, along with appropriate use of rewards to ensure that a representative sample completes the survey.

Even if people agree to start a survey, results are often influenced by respondents choosing the most convenient way to finish. Respondents' inattention or fatigue during the survey can be addressed to some degree with careful questionnaire design, and testing to detect various systematic biases. For example, survey responses are subject to *heaping* on round numbers, to *priming* when the sequence of questions influences responses, and to *framing* effects when people choose intermediate values in any range because they expect that to be the appropriate preference. There can also be important selection bias within the survey, when respondents skip questions that they prefer not to answer.

An important kind of risk in valuation research is that respondents will answer in accordance with preferences they want to project or believe they should have, instead of the preferences they actually have. That *social desirability bias* appears in all kinds of survey responses, reflecting how people want to be seen. Social desirability bias can arise even with real stakes and when responses are anonymous, helping a person see themselves as they want to be. A related problem is *strategic response bias*, when a respondent wants to influence the survey result. Social desirability bias and strategic responses can be seen as kind of hypocrisy, but there can also be genuine differences between what a person wants for their community and what they do for themselves.

One example of differences between valuation for collective action and for individual choice concerns the effect of food system regulations that alter the cost of production, such as animal welfare rules. Survey results consistently show populations placing higher value on animal welfare than their purchase behavior suggests. The survey data could be misleading due to social desirability or other biases, but purchase behavior could also be affected by market failures such as asymmetric information when buyers don't trust animal welfare labels, or by free ridership when buyers are not willing to be the only people who pay higher prices, in which case it is survey responses that are closer to the population's true willingness to pay for public intervention.

Table 6.2 Examples of methods for preference elicitation and economic valuation

Method	*Description*	*Benefits*	*Drawbacks*	*Typical use*
Revealed preference methods				
Demand system estimation	Uses market prices and quantities to estimate elasticities	Corresponds to actual decisions in the real world	Limited to observed markets, estimates may be confounded by unobservable factors and fail to forecast out of sample	WTP and WTA for existing products such as foods or farm inputs
Market experiments	Uses bidding in auctions or choices among discrete options	Can be made to simulate actual choices, with high predictive value	Can be expensive to run when conducted with real-life choices in real-life settings	WTP for new or different products or services, often including environmental or health attributes
Hedonic valuation	Uses prices paid for things with different combinations of attributes	Can be used with either real-world market prices or experiments with new products and services	Limited to attributes of things with which buyers have enough experience and different options to reveal their needs and preferences	WTP or WTA for environmental or health attributes that affect the value of homes, vehicles, wages or other things
Travel cost and wait times	Uses data on time and travel cost to an amenity or to obtain a service, such as parks or health care	Corresponds to actual decisions in the real world	Difficult to isolate valuation for different attributes of the amenity or service, and many other factors also influence time use	WTP or WTA for recreational sites and amenities, or things that are rationed through wait times such as some health services

(continued)

Table 6.2 (continued)

Method	*Description*	*Benefits*	*Drawbacks*	*Typical use*
Stated preference methods				
Contingent valuation (CV)	Asks people about their choices under alternative conditions	Low cost, and can vary how questions are asked to reflect many scenarios of interest	Hypothetical answers without consequences often do not predict actual behavior	WTP or WTA for changes in water quality, outdoor recreation, wildlife preservation, biodiversity, climate and air quality
Choice experiments (hypothetical)	Asks people to state their preferences between described alternative scenarios or goods	Low cost, and can vary the options between which people are asked to choose	Hypothetical choices may not predict behavior, unless there are actual things at stake	WTP for new or different products or services, often including environmental or health attributes and label changes
Inferred valuation	Asks people to predict how much *others* would value a nonmarket good or service	Focus on another's utility rather than one's own may reduce bias in responses	Hypothetical choices may not predict behavior	WTP for new or different products or services, often including environmental or health attributes and label changes

A personal example of the difference between valuation for collective action and one's individual choices would be William's interest in gardening. He worked on farms and enjoyed home gardening earlier in his life, and in surveys or choice experiments, when asked about his willingness to pay for a new community garden, or his willingness to accept the loss of a community garden than exists, he would place a high value on those investments. But when actually faced with a choice to do some gardening, the opportunity cost of doing other things with that time is usually sufficient to keep him away. William's high valuation of gardening for others but not himself could be a form of hypocrisy due to social desirability bias (he wants others to think he likes gardening) or free ridership (he wants others to do the work, while he enjoys the result), but there are also option values involved (he genuinely wants gardens to exist in case he might use them in the future), as well as existence value and altruism (he genuinely believes others might benefit from having gardens, as he did in the past). Different kinds of real-stakes preference elicitation might be able to distinguish among those motivations, and similar analysis for other community members might help guide public investment in community gardens.

Comparing Costs to Benefits: Net Present Value and Cost-Effectiveness

To count the effects of a policy, analysts must compare costs to benefits. When analysts can count both in monetary terms, they can compute the two as ratios or a sum over time in a *cost-benefit analysis*. For other questions, analysts use monetary units only for costs and measure impacts in natural units for *cost-effectiveness analysis*. Analysts typically focus on the *incremental cost-effectiveness* of the decision, at a given level of everything else in society. For example, if we are studying the incremental cost-effectiveness for health of a voucher for fruits and vegetables, we should do that analysis in the context of the existing markets and other government programs that might exist for the population of interest. How analysts estimate the incremental cost of an initiative can drive the results, with important variables including the opportunity costs assigned to resources used for the initiative, based on what other things the people involved might be doing with those resources instead.

Once researchers have estimated the initiative's total costs and its total effects or benefits for the population of interest, analysts can present costs and effects in terms of absolute levels or relative ratios. The absolute level of gains for a population are often expressed in monetary terms, subtracting costs from benefits to obtain the *net present value* (NPV) of the change. For the NPV to accurately represent the net gains from a policy or program, all costs and benefits must be in comparable 'present value' terms representing all else that money can buy. This requires appropriate unit conversions and discount rates for each element of the initiative's costs and benefits. Similarly, a comparative effectiveness study might show net changes in the absolute level of various outcomes, such as total CO_2-equivalent gases in the atmosphere from different environmental policies or programs, or DALYs lost to various diseases from different health interventions.

When the effects of an intervention remain in natural units such as life years saved, then costs must be compared to effects in the form of an *incremental cost-effectiveness ratio* (ICER). The same kind of ratio can be used when effects are measured in monetary terms, which yields a *cost-benefit ratio* (CBR) for the change, and there is no difference in results when ratios are inverted, for example to show life years saved per dollar invested, or benefit–cost ratios. Benefits relative to costs can also be presented in percentage terms as the initiative's *internal rate of return* (IRR), which is the implied interest rate offered by the future benefits in return for investment of the costs.

Comparing policies and programs using the absolute level of their impacts (such as NPV or DALYs) versus relative ratios of cost-effectiveness (such as ICER or CBR) leads to different rankings whenever there are differences in the scale of the policy or program. For example, a school breakfast program that reaches only some children could have a higher cost-effectiveness ratio but smaller total impact than changes in school lunch that affect every child. In some cases, program scale is fixed by its demographic or geographic limits, but cost-effectiveness ratios are often used to guide decisions about which programs should be replicated or scaled up from initial trials to the entire population they could serve.

The difference in impact between small and large programs is important because some interventions have economies of scale, where the full program is more cost-effective than the smaller version. These increasing returns arise to the extent that the intervention has high fixed costs of setup and low marginal costs of delivery, or network effects where each additional participant makes the program more valuable for other participants. In practice, initial trials and pilot programs are sized to take advantage of most such scale economies, and expansion to reach the entire potential population is subject to the same diminishing returns that limit supply of other things.

Even when small trials of pilot programs aim to be done under representative conditions, the initial steps taken to implement a given policy or program are typically the most cost-effective actions, and scaling up requires additional steps that are often increasingly costly or less effective than what can be done on a smaller scale. For example, the cost-effectiveness ratio of adding fruits and vegetables to school meals might be high in a pilot program where the participating staff are interested in the idea, school facilities are suitable and local supplies of attractive products are available, but then expansion brings in staff with other interests, at schools with less favorable kitchen and classroom layouts, and less attractive local supplies of fruits and vegetables.

Amelia had the opportunity to work in school food service in 2021. One of the rules is that children participating in the National School Lunch Program (NSLP) are offered at least five components for lunch: grains, meat/meat alternatives, fruit, vegetable and fluid milk. While a student is offered five items, they are required to take three items, one of which must be a fruit or a vegetable. The school food service staff consistently worked at preparing fruit and vegetable servings that the children would enjoy, including by cutting fresh vegetables in nice ways and presenting them with contrasting bright colors and alternating available options as often as possible.

Part of the motivation for Amelia and the staff to prepare vegetables carefully was for the children to benefit directly from eating that day's meal, but they also saw the work as educational. They wanted the children to talk with their friends about what was on offer that day, to build understanding and expectations about what meals would be desirable for themselves later in life. The educational value of each meal extends beyond nutrition to community building with local farmers or the health teacher. Nonmarket effects like these are difficult to measure and call for close attention to the short- and long-term goals of each program.

Cost-effectiveness ratios are generally lower for scaled-up programs than for their initial pilot or trial versions, but even at the larger scale they may have higher value than other public investments at population scale. All programs are subject to some version of diminishing returns. Applying economic principles to cost-effectiveness analysis allows us to anticipate how the costs and effects of trial-sized programs might differ from full-scale results, and thereby guide public-sector decisions towards the set of all interventions that can help the entire population achieve their highest potential level of wellbeing.

6.2.3 Conclusion

Cost-effectiveness analysis can help guide government policies and programs, informing decision-makers about the best ways to address market failures and overcome previous policy failures through new collective actions. This section introduces the toolkit used to improve outcomes for both environmental sustainability and population health, in ways that address the distribution of gains and losses and impacts on equity of each change in policies or programs. Successful use of cost-effectiveness analysis to improve outcomes for each population calls for tailoring the economic principles seen in Chapters 1 through 5 to the specific needs of public-sector decision-makers.

A fundamental economic principle underlying cost-effectiveness is that each decision involves increments of change from the baseline alternative situation. The increments of change may be large, for example the national rollout of a new agricultural or food policy, but useful analyses focus on the difference between one scenario and another. We can then rank two or more options and help decision-makers choose based on their incremental cost-effectiveness ratios, or the total change in each outcome such as its net present value, relative to the alternative of no change in current policies and programs.

The practical work of cost-effectiveness analysis, like other applications of economic principles to agriculture and food systems, involves careful measurement of changes in the natural environment as well as human health, taking account of how people respond to intervention and how much the population values each change. Much of the work consists of careful accounting, ensuring that all units of measure consistently work as intended. Monetary values should measure real purchasing power for the average of all goods and services used by the population, and natural units should be converted to whatever measurement scale reflects the purpose of intervention.

Economic analysis of cost-effectiveness can help citizens, activists and decision-makers of all kinds understand why existing policies were chosen and help improve those choices in response to new challenges. This chapter focused primarily on improving average or total outcomes for entire populations, which depends critically on variation among people and over time as discussed in the next chapter.

CHAPTER 7

Poverty and Risk: Variation Among People and Over Time

7.1 Inequality, Inequity and Disparities in Agriculture and Nutrition

7.1.1 *Motivation and Guiding Questions*

So far, we have seen how each person's choice among their options leads to the societal outcomes we observe, in ways that depend on private transactions in markets and collective actions through policies and programs. We saw how market failures and policy failures can be understood and potentially overcome, allowing each population to reach higher levels of wellbeing. Our analytical diagrams helped explain outcomes at any one point in time, for each person and the population, showing the causal mechanisms needed to make qualitative predictions about the total or average outcome per person in the group. This chapter begins the second half of this book, turning from qualitative models to empirical measurement: how do economic principles play out in practice? How well have individuals and populations succeeded in meeting their needs?

To describe observed patterns, we use scatterplots, bar charts and line graphs that show differences between groups and also changes over time. The economic principles introduced in Chapters 1–6 were shown in stylized models, and now we shift from theory to observation of stylized facts. Each metric or indicator results from primary observations, such as surveys of people or an organization's administrative records, transformed into a variable designed to track an important aspect of wellbeing such as food insecurity. The stylized facts we observe include both the total or average for entire groups, and also the degree of variation among individuals within groups.

W. A. Masters and A. B. Finaret, *Food Economics*,
Palgrave Studies in Agricultural Economics and Food Policy,
https://doi.org/10.1007/978-3-031-53840-7_7

This section begins our exploration of the data with the fundamental question underlying all economic measurement: do people have enough things to reach a socially acceptable level of wellbeing? Is the distribution of resources and outcomes among individuals and between groups improving or worsening?

By the end of this section, you will be able to:

1. Describe how economists measure deprivation, inequality and inequity using poverty lines, Lorenz curves and the Gini index;
2. Describe how poverty lines have been and are determined in the U.S. and around the world;
3. Summarize the findings of recent household surveys and other data on poverty, inequality and inequity in the U.S. and worldwide; and
4. Summarize the differences between measured poverty, inequality and inequity in market incomes before and after accounting for taxes, transfers and government programs.

7.1.2 Analytical Tools

The data we have are empirical observations, made by people to answer practical questions. To guide decisions, we need observations that correspond to the concepts we care about. This book begins our exploration of observed data with measurement of how well individuals and groups have achieved a standard of living that meets human needs and is socially acceptable.

The toolkit of economics starts with the causal diagrams introduced in the first half of this book, used to guide creation and interpretation of the measurement tools introduced now. Those models showed how production of food and other things is linked to consumption and each person's standard of living, with an important role for both individual choices and collective action in helping each person reach their goals. Each outcome is the result of multiple factors interacting in each ways that depend on market structure and public-sector intervention. Now that we turn to measurement, each data point we observe could potentially be explained using our analytical diagrams, and we will occasionally redraw those diagrams in this second half of the book, but our goal is to describe the most important outcomes for groups and individuals.

Understanding Deprivation: The Lived Experience of People in Poverty

Poverty is the state of not having sufficient resources to attain a population's minimum standard of living, typically defined in terms of the basic necessities required to participate in the economic and social life of that society. Some of these needs are universal human requirements, such as food and clothing, but the level and nature of basic needs such as housing, transport and communication vary over time and place. The criteria and methods used to measure whether people can meet their basic needs also vary, but generally involve survey data on household income, expenditure or assets relative to a *poverty line* or other criteria. Almost all governments and several international agencies track the 'headcount' number of people below various poverty lines to target social programs and evaluate economic policies, as well as the *poverty rate* defined as the percentage of each population living below a given poverty line.

Beyond material deprivation, many people experience social exclusion based on their appearance, ancestry or religious beliefs, legal status or other aspects of identity. The term 'marginalization' refers to exclusion from cultural or political influence, which can be both a cause and a consequence of poverty. Economic analysis shows how decisions at the margin of production and consumption drive the prices and quantities we see, and understanding the lives of people at the margins of society is similarly helpful to see the degree to which a population's goals are being met.

Economic analysis of poverty begins with the material requisites of wellbeing for individuals and households and adds up outcomes for social groups who have experienced varying degrees of social exclusion due to their group identity. Measurement starts with purchasing power over all goods and services, which is closely linked to a wide range of measurable outcomes such as the heights of children. Household incomes are closely linked to individual outcomes partly due to each person's own spending, and partly due to social and environmental factors that are correlated with both incomes and outcomes. For example, changes in child height are influenced by things each family buys or makes for themselves such as food and housing, as well as things that higher-income communities obtain through collective action such as clean water, and things that help drive the higher income such as the community's level of education. The data in this book focus on change in agriculture, food and nutrition, which is closely related to other aspects of life that would be measured in different ways. Other fields of economics focus on data relating to education and cognitive development, physical health and disability, mental health and distress, employment and livelihoods, housing and transportation or many other aspects of poverty beyond the focus of this book.

Measuring poverty is difficult due to limited data, especially about people and aspects of life that were not historical priorities for data collection and analysis. Data availability is itself an important aspect of economic and social development, steered by the willingness and ability of people to devote their time and resources towards obtaining more detailed and accurate information. The first major agricultural census of the English-speaking world was the Domesday Book done over 900 years ago by the King of England to guide tax collection. In recent decades many countries have attempted to collect nearly complete census data of all agricultural enterprises, and many more conduct nationally representative sample surveys every few years. In addition to those large and costly household consumption surveys, a wide range of other data is commonly used about specific aspects of household wellbeing.

The definition of poverty usually focuses on households because many aspects of each person's living standards are pooled among people living together, especially regarding the wellbeing of children. Measurement also usually focuses on income and expenditure over an entire year to smooth out short-term fluctuations in what people can acquire, and measurement of poverty often also aims to take account of assets and wealth, which provide useful additional information about people's ability to meet their needs over a longer time horizon.

Poverty can be defined and measured using either income or expenditure. Measuring income is preferred in populations where most work is in the formal sector, so labor earnings, profits from a business, or rent and interest payments from other assets are all recorded and can readily be reported as the individual or household's total income for the year. The resulting data may include only 'market income' or may be defined more broadly as after-tax income that includes all payments to the government and receipt of social assistance. Both distributions are important for equity. In places where a large fraction of households are self-employed family farmers or workers in the informal sector, most income is not recorded, and it is preferable to ask people about their consumption and expenditure over the past month or year. Those household surveys typically aim to ask about consumption from all sources, including food produced by the household themselves.

All poverty is inherently multidimensional, starting with the definition of income and expenditure as the household or individual's purchasing power for all goods and services. Some metrics also count education and health as separate dimensions of wellbeing, as in the Human Development Index used since 2010 by the United Nations Development Program (UNDP), which adds up progress in three directions: health (measured by height, weight and child mortality), education (measured by school attendance) and living standards (measured by a set of physical assets such as electricity and housing). Other organizations have proposed different multidimensional indexes as a summary metric for advocacy purposes, but researchers typically prefer to use separate indicators for health, educational attainment or other nonmarket aspects of wellbeing, for comparison to poverty in terms of market goods and services that could be obtained through the household's own income and expenditure.

Defining Poverty: Mollie Orshansky and the U.S. Poverty Line

One of the oldest poverty lines in continuous use by a national government was introduced in 1964 to guide U.S. President Lyndon Johnson's *War on Poverty* programs, using methods developed by an economist in the Social Security Administration named Mollie Orshansky. Orshansky's poverty line used market income relative to food spending and has remained the U.S. government's official definition of poverty with only modest adjustments over past sixty years. We will describe the U.S. poverty measurement methods and results in some detail, first because the U.S. experience demonstrates the close link between poverty measurement, household food spending and nutrition assistance, and because the resulting data offer an unusually long period of continuous measurement using a transparent and comparable method.

When Mollie Orshansky set out to develop a politically and socially acceptable poverty line for the U.S., the USDA had just published a revised set of low-cost food plans that would meet nutrient requirements using a variety of foods widely consumed by Americans. Orshansky had previously worked in the nutrition department at USDA, and she was able to use the most recent diet plan for 1961 to identify the cost of a minimally acceptable diet for households of varying size and composition. Orshansky had also worked with the USDA's nationally representative household food consumption survey of 1955, which showed Engel's law at work, driving lower-income households to devote a larger fraction of their expenditure on food. Orshansky found that the average U.S. household was spending one-third of their income on food, and successfully argued that having to spend more than that to buy a minimally acceptable diet was a clear sign of being poor in America.

The U.S. poverty line introduced in 1964 was defined as three times the cost of minimally acceptable USDA food plans for each member of the household, with small adjustments for households of one or two people. That procedure turned out to be consistent with many people's intuition about living standards in America at that time, yielding a threshold just over $3000 for a family of four. Having gained sufficient consensus for adoption of that standard, the next challenge was how to adjust the line for inflation over time. Until 1968 the Social Security Administration recalculated diet costs each year using new food prices, but in 1969 the U.S. Census Bureau and other Federal agencies introduced a simpler method that has been used ever since. They reverted to the 1963 diet costs for each size household and adjusted the resulting income level by the country's overall consumer price index (CPI) each year.

For calendar year 2023, the updated U.S. poverty level is around $30,000 per year for a family of four. Raising poverty lines by only the CPI, when other Americans' incomes have risen by more than CPI, has let the U.S. poverty line fall relative to the income of most Americans. When Mollie Orshansky set her threshold, it was 44% of the median income for a family of four, and as of 2023 the official poverty line is only 28% of the median income for a family of four. The USDA has also continued to update its low-cost food plans, which now add up to about $11,500 per year for a family of four which is 38% of the poverty line, instead of the 33% share used by Orshansky. The official U.S. poverty line has fallen relative to other incomes, but most U.S. anti-poverty programs set their threshold at a higher level. For example, the Supplemental Nutrition Assistance Program (SNAP) is open to households with gross incomes up to 130% of the poverty line, while eligibility for the supplemental nutrition program for Women, Infants and Children (WIC) allows up to 180% of the poverty line.

Beyond household income, measurement of person's wellbeing can include wealth and assets as well as age and disability status, all of which are counted in addition to income as factors in eligibility for many anti-poverty programs in the U.S. and elsewhere. A further question is how to account for differences in the purchasing power of household income and program benefits at each place and time. The U.S. national poverty line uses a single CPI reflecting the average expenditure pattern of consumers in all urban areas of the country, with a higher poverty line reflecting higher cost of living only for Alaska and Hawaii, but some anti-poverty programs recognize the role of regional price differences. The U.S. has especially large variation in housing costs, due in part to local government regulations that limit the placement and size of new buildings. Without those limits, housing supply would respond more quickly to demand, with prices set by the marginal cost of construction and utilities. Rules that limit the height and density of construction make supply inelastic, so rental costs vary with demand which is higher in places with higher incomes, due to both earning opportunities from local employment and local amenities that attract high-income residents. Variation in rental prices is one reason why eligibility for the U.S. housing assistance program known as section 8 is one half of each area's median income, and the SNAP formula also takes account of housing costs to some degree, by raising the assistance provided to most recipients for whom housing costs would otherwise exceed half of their net income.

Poverty thresholds are used not only to count the number or fraction of people in poverty and to determine eligibility for anti-poverty programs, but also to determine each household's *depth of poverty* below the threshold which can be used in anti-poverty programs to determine the level of assistance provided. In the U.S., for example, SNAP provides a variable level of cash-like assistance designed to ensure that households can afford the USDA's minimally acceptable diet, now known as the Thrifty Food Plan. The composition of that diet is adjusted periodically, most recently in 2021, and its cost is updated monthly based on national average food prices. The program's maximum benefit, provided to households with zero income, is the entire cost of the Thrifty Food Plan. Actual benefits are set by the SNAP formula, based on the longstanding expectation that food spending should not have to exceed 30% of the program participant's income, net of deductions such as the housing cost adjustment. Benefit levels are small for households near the threshold of eligibility, thereby linking the level of assistance to the population's depth of poverty.

Measuring Poverty: Trends and Disparities Among Groups in the U.S.

When the U.S. government adopted Mollie Orshansky's method in 1964, her formula was used retroactively to construct an estimate for 1959. The net result is more than sixty years of data to track changes in poverty rates and inequities between demographic groups as shown in the charts starting with Fig. 7.1.

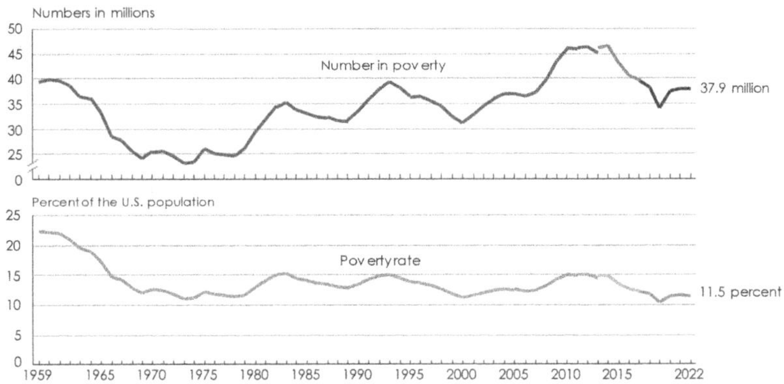

Fig. 7.1 Number and percent of people in poverty in the U.S., 1959 to 2022 *Source*: Reproduced from Emily A. Shrider and John Creamer, *Poverty in the United States 2022* [U.S. Census Bureau, Washington DC, September 2023]. Updated publications in this series are at https://www.census.gov/library/publications/time-series/p60.html

Figure 7.1 is the book's first descriptive chart, using line graphs to illustrate change over time. Later figures will use bar charts to compare magnitudes of discrete categories, or scatterplots to show a larger number of individual observations. As with the analytical diagrams in Chapters 1–6, the first element of each chart is its title and axis labels, identifying what's being shown. In Fig. 7.1, the lower panel shows a range from 0 to 25% of the U.S. population, and the top panel shows a range from 25 to 50 million people, with a break denoted // to show that the vertical axis does not start at zero. Along the horizontal axis, both lines are shown to have breaks in 2013 when survey questions about income changed slightly, and in 2017 when U.S. data-processing systems changed slightly. The note below the chart indicates its source. In this case we reproduce the actual chart published by the U.S. government, in part because their graphics are of very high quality, but also because comparable charts are published each year so that updated versions can readily be obtained from the U.S. Census Bureau website.

The changing prevalence of poverty shown in Fig. 7.1 provides a valuable introduction to data visualization. Here we focus on change over time, and later charts will show differences by income level. Incomes often (but not always) grow over time, so both kinds of chart trace out patterns associated with the process of economic development, similarly to the way we might trace out a child's height relative to other aspects of child growth. In Fig. 7.1 and other time series, we can see some *fluctuations* that rise and fall repeatedly like waves, some sustained *trends* that persist from year to year or decade to decade and some *inflection points* where the trends change. We also notice *artifacts* created by the measurement method that do not reflect reality, in this case the apparent jump up in 2013 that was created by a change in how the survey asked people about their income.

Figure 7.1 shows that in 1959 about 40 million people or 22% of the U.S. population had market incomes below the poverty line. In other words, more than one in five Americans could not afford to buy the USDA's low-cost diet and still spend only a third of their income on food. By contrast for the world, a comparable kind of metric introduced by the FAO and the World Bank in 2022 showed that about 3 billion or 38% of the entire global population could not afford a benchmark low-cost diet. The global benchmark diet and income shares used for that global monitoring differ from those initially used to define the U.S. poverty line, but the same procedure was applied almost sixty years later.

As shown in Fig. 7.1, poverty rates in the U.S. dropped sharply for a decade from 1959 to 1969, followed by fluctuations in the poverty rate around a trend increase in the number of people in poverty, as the overall U.S. population grew. The absolute number of people in poverty peaked in 2010–2014, then both the rate and the number dropped sharply to a historic low rate in 2019 just before the COVID-19 pandemic, then rose and stabilized in 2021–2022 around the previous low points of 1973–1974 and 1999–2000 at a poverty rate around 11.5% of the U.S. population.

The rise in poverty from 2008 to 2010 drove a reassessment of how poverty should be measured, aiming to capture a household's ability to meet basic needs and counting their receipt of government benefits instead of only market income. This effort was led by Rebecca Blank, an academic economist who rose to leadership of the U.S. Department of Commerce in 2011. At that time the government began publishing a Supplemental Poverty Measure (SPM), drawing on decades of research and experimentation with different data sources. In 2019 the U.S. government decided to retain the simpler 'official' poverty line based on market income to determine program eligibility, while using frequently updated SPM procedures to track changes and disparities in poverty after receipt of program benefits.

The new methods introduced in 2011 aimed to improve measurement of change and differences among groups with as much similarity as possible on the initial baseline number and percent of all Americans living in poverty. Calibrating the supplemental measure so national totals would be like results using the official measure helped decision-makers focus on changes and differences, avoiding debates about whether the definition of 'poverty' was too high or too low a standard of living. Using the SPM for monitoring purposes instead of program eligibility is also helpful for decision-making, since it allows program benefits to be included in the new poverty measure, leading to the results shown in Fig. 7.2.

Results shown in Fig. 7.2 reveal little difference between the two poverty measures from 2009 to 2019, as the rise of poverty rates at the start of the period was followed by the same gradual decline found by both measurement methods. The big change came during the COVID-19 pandemic, when the

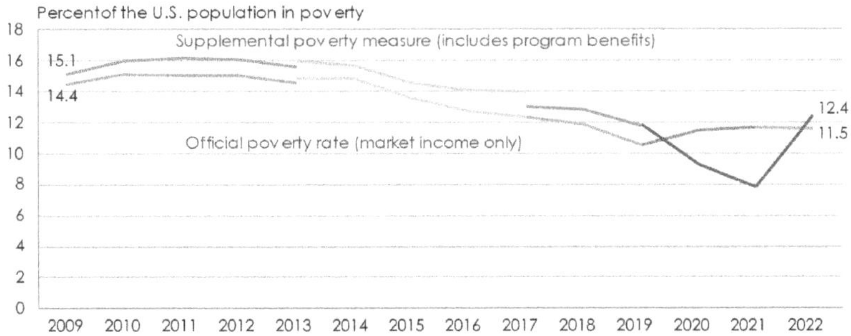

Fig. 7.2 U.S. poverty rates using official and supplemental measures, 2009 to 2022 *Source*: Reproduced from Emily A. Shrider and John Creamer, Poverty in the United States 2022 [U.S. Census Bureau, Washington DC, September 2023]. Note methods changed in 2013 and 2017, creating breaks in the series that are artifacts of measurement instead of actual changes in those years. Updated publications in this series are at https://www.census.gov/library/publications/time-series/p60.html

official poverty rate in terms of market incomes jumped up in 2020 due to job losses, and then stayed high due to increases in the CPI that raised the poverty line by about as much as incomes had risen. In contrast, the supplemental measure showed an accelerating downward trend in the poverty rate due to Federal spending on pandemic-response programs in 2020 and 2021, and a reversion to the pre-pandemic poverty rate when those programs ended in 2022.

The development and use of the supplemental poverty measure provides a much clearer picture of what payments and receipts move people into or out of poverty each year, revealing the important role of nutrition assistance and health spending. When the Census Bureau calculates the supplemental measure, they can incrementally remove each adjustment to market income and observe how many people would have been below the supplemental poverty line if that category of spending had not been present. The results are shown in Fig. 7.3.

The bar chart in Fig. 7.3 is designed to show both change over time through the COVID pandemic and comparison between spending categories. Each category refers to a particular type of payment tracked by the Federal government, ranked in order of impact on the number of people in 2022. Details of each payment type are specific to the U.S., but somewhat similar patterns could be observed elsewhere. Here the vertical axis shows the number of people raised out of poverty, so negative numbers mean fewer people in poverty, and lighter colors in more recent years, so that the category labels are visible.

From the left of the diagram, the categories are tax credits on earnings paid when people file income taxes, whose impact on poverty declined during the period of COVID-related unemployment in 2020, then the burst of COVID

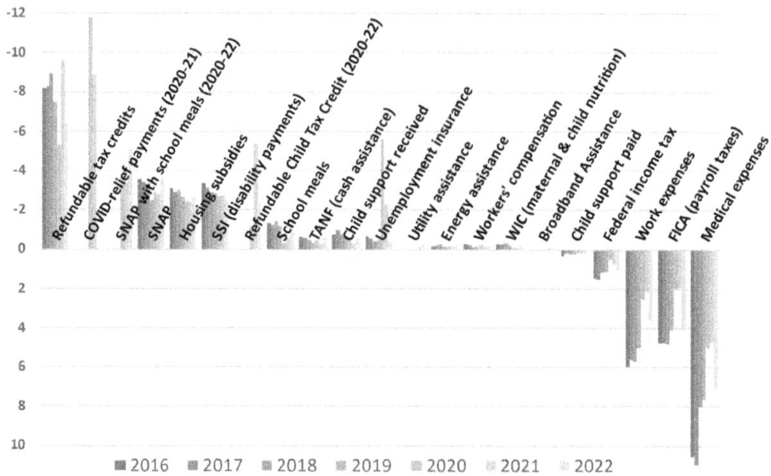

Fig. 7.3 Millions of people moved out of or into poverty by category of spending, 2016–2022 *Source*: Authors' chart, using data for 2016–2019 extracted from Table A7 of Liana Fox [2020], the Supplemental Poverty Measure 2017 and 2019, and then Table B8 of Poverty in the United States 2021 and 2022 [various authors], all from U.S. Census Bureau, Washington DC. Data shown omit Social Security payments, which moved 26 to 29 million people out of poverty each year over this period, primarily Americans over 65 years of age. Updated publications in this series are at https://www.census.gov/library/publications/time-series/p60.html

relief payments in 2020 and 2021, as well as the use of SNAP to provide additional meals for children despite school closures in 2020–2022, then SNAP itself, followed by housing assistance through section 8 and other programs, the U.S. Supplemental Security Income (SSI) program for people with disabilities, the temporary tax credit per child in 2020 and 2021 that was allowed to expire in 2022, then school meals, the small remaining U.S. program of cash assistance known as Temporary Assistance to Needy Families (TANF, formerly known as 'welfare' payments), private child support received (typically from a non-custodial parent), unemployment insurance (which spiked up in 2020), programs to help with household utilities, energy for heating in winter, and worker's compensation for injuries on the job, the special nutrition program for Women, Infants and Children (WIC), and a small new broadband assistance program.

On the right side of the diagram are payments made by people that might push them below the poverty line, notably the payment of child support, Federal income tax paid, work-related expenses such as uniforms and travel costs, payroll taxes to pay for social security and other programs under the Federal Insurance Contributions Act (FICA), and then medical expenses. These payments differ and fluctuate in ways that are extremely revealing about the nature of deprivation and poverty in the U.S. and potentially elsewhere. For example, by far the most important cause of falling into poverty before the pandemic was uninsured medical expenses on the right of the chart. That kind of expense became less burdensome due to the expansion of Federal health insurance and was particularly low during the pandemic when COVID displaced a large fraction of other health care services.

For this book the most important insight from Fig. 7.3 is the relatively large role of Federal food assistance. Adding up the effects of SNAP, school meals and WIC, those three programs accounted for 22% of the impact on number of people in poverty shown in the pre-pandemic period (2016–2019), then 18% during the period of peak pandemic aid (2020–2021), and over twice that fraction at 39% after most COVID aid was ended but food assistance rose in the most recent year (2022). The precise number affected by a combination of programs differs from the sum of their individual effects because some people participate in multiple programs, but food assistance clearly plays a very large role in anti-poverty programs in the U.S. as it does elsewhere. In 2021 the Thrifty Food Plan aspect of the SNAP benefits formula was adjusted upwards to ensure that recipients could afford to meet Federal dietary guidelines and other criteria, and the expansion of SNAP around school meals was continued while other pandemic aid was cut, which explains why the combined food assistance programs accounted for almost 40% of the numbers lifted out of poverty shown for 2022 in Fig. 7.3.

The supplemental poverty measure is particularly helpful to address disparities between groups. In the U.S. census and other surveys, respondents are invited to self-identify themselves in terms of several non-exclusive categories. These can then be used to compare groups such as the six categories shown in Fig. 7.4.

Fig. 7.4 Poverty rates using the supplemental measure by census category, 2009–2022 *Source*: Authors' chart of data from appendix Table B-2, Number and Percentage of People in Poverty Using the Supplemental Poverty Measure by Age, Race, and Hispanic Origin: 2009 to 2022, in Emily A. Shrider and John Creamer, Poverty in the United States 2022 [U.S. Census Bureau, Washington DC, September 2023]. Note methods changed in 2013 and 2017, so changes at that year may be artifacts of measurement. Updated data and details are available at www.census.gov

Labels for each line in Fig. 7.4 are aligned in sequence of each group's poverty rate in 2022. Results for the American Indian and Alaska Native category are highly variable due to the relatively small number of survey respondents, and the Census Bureau reports a margin of error of ±4% around the reported level of 23.2% in 2022. In contrast, among people who report themselves to be Hispanic of any race, 19.3% were in poverty in 2022, and among respondents who classify themselves as only Black and not also any other race or Hispanic ancestry, 17.2% were in poverty in 2022, both with an estimated margin of error around 1%. Below that is the combined total of all people in the U.S., whose poverty rate is almost identical to that of respondents who classify themselves as only Asian and not also any other race, or the group of people who report multiple racial categories, and above the group who classify themselves as only white and not any other race or Hispanic ancestry.

The large drop and then rebound in poverty rates shown in Fig. 7.4, and the reduced disparity in poverty rates between groups to 2021 followed by an increase to 2022, clearly illustrates the value of tracking poverty in ways that closely follow the actual lived experience of every survey respondent in each group. Numbers capture only some aspects of life, but they allow us to compare groups in ways that count each person in the group equally, in contrast to the images or stories that are shared through commercial news or social media. The images and stories that we all see and remember were deliberately selected to attract and retain our attention. Every reader of this book will have different personal experiences, a different group of friends and acquaintances, and different news sources, all of which are important sources of information about individual lives. For questions such as disparities in U.S. poverty rates, totals and averages such as those shown in Fig. 7.4 are helpful because they add up everything that survey respondents themselves said when each person was asked the same questions. Thanks to the supplemental poverty measure championed by Rebecca Blank in the mid-2000s, we can track trends and disparities in the U.S. much more clearly than would otherwise be possible, as illustrated in Fig. 7.4.

The poverty data shown in this section are specific to the U.S., but their basic principles are useful for understanding how policies and programs affect whether a given person and their household fall below or above a country's poverty line. Most importantly, sixty years of data using the official U.S. measure reveal how millions of children and adults are pushed into poverty during periods of economic downturn, while millions of others remain in poverty even after decades of economic growth. These data show how the number and percentage of people in poverty can be cut dramatically, as occurred in the 1960s and again in the 2010s, then most sharply through the one-time emergency programs in response to the pandemic during 2020 and 2021. The disaggregated data revealed by the U.S. Supplemental Poverty Measure are particularly helpful in revealing the importance of different government programs and policies, including especially the large role played by U.S. nutrition programs (SNAP, WIC and school meals) in lifting people out of poverty, and changes in disparities among groups that account for a wider range of entitlements and purchasing power than just market income counted in earlier poverty lines.

Global Poverty: International Comparisons and Trends for Africa and Asia

Looking across countries, each government sets its own national poverty line, and international organizations use data from each country for global statistics. The organization primarily responsible for measuring poverty is the World Bank, which hosts the global office of the International Comparison Program (ICP) that works with national governments to obtain local prices in each country for a standardized set of goods and services representing commonly purchased items in each region of the world. Comparing price levels for the same product in different places allows the ICP to compute purchasing power parity (PPP) exchange rates for every country, converting local currency into U.S. dollars of a given year. The validity of these calculations is limited by data quality and methodological concerns, but in principle each PPP dollar can buy the same quantity of goods and services in every country of the world. The World Bank and many others use PPP exchange rates to convert local prices to those international dollars and thereby compare total production of goods and services in each country. The sum of each country's output is known as Gross Domestic Product (GDP). Once a country begins to experience economic development its GDP can grow exponentially for many decades, leading to extremely wide differences between countries in total production per year as shown on the horizontal axis of Fig. 7.5.

The vertical axis of Fig. 7.5 shows the national poverty lines used by country governments at each level of total output per person. Not all governments have an official poverty line, and many do not update them every year, so the chart shows the most recently published poverty line for each country at the country's level of output in that year. Among the lowest levels shown is for Niger, whose national poverty line was set in 2014 at the local currency equivalent of \$1.87 per day. Ethiopia and Benin have higher incomes but similar poverty lines in terms of real purchasing power, at \$2.04 and \$1.77, respectively. China has a much higher level of total output per person but maintains a low poverty line at \$3.07, and countries above that level of total output tend to have much higher poverty lines, up to the level of the U.S. and other high-income countries.

The central insight from the data in Fig. 7.5 is that poverty lines set by national governments start at a floor around \$2.15 per day in real purchasing power and are higher in countries with more output per person, especially where output exceeds about \$10,000 per year. When the World Bank introduced its modern global poverty metric in 1990, they used the average of eight low-income countries' national lines which happened to be almost exactly

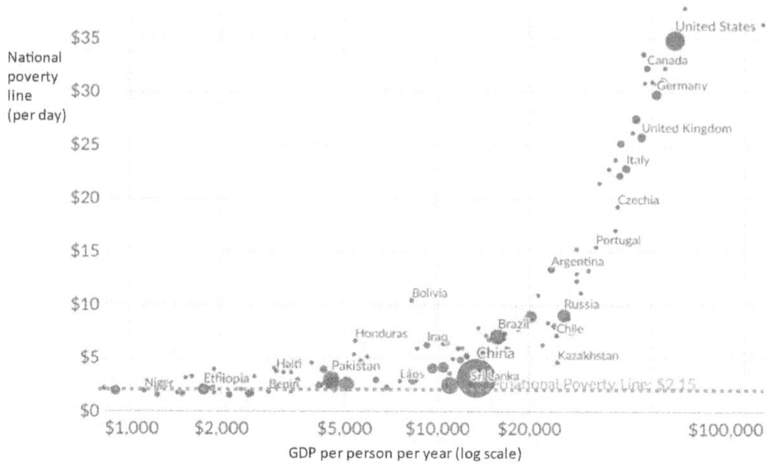

Fig. 7.5 National poverty lines at each level of national income per person, 2001–2018 *Source*: Reproduced from Joe Hasell, Max Roser, Esteban Ortiz-Ospina and Pablo Arriagada [2022], Our World in Data: Poverty [https://ourworldindata.org/poverty], using updated data based on Dean Jolliffe and Espern B. Prydz [2016]. Estimating international poverty lines from comparable national thresholds. *The Journal of Economic Inequality*, 14(2), 185–198. Data shown are national poverty lines per person per day for a total of 152 countries, at the country's level of income as measured by Gross Domestic Product [GDP] per person per year, all converted from local currencies using PPP exchange rates into 2017 U.S. dollars. Observations are for the latest available year and range from 2001 to 2018. Countries are shown proportional to population with larger countries labeled for convenience. Shading refers to World Bank country groupings, which are [from left to right] lower, lower-middle, upper-middle and upper income. The horizontal axis is shown using a log scale, so that gaps from one to ten to a hundred thousand appear of equal width, due to exponential income growth over time that creates the large gaps shown

$1.00 per day in 1985 U.S. dollars. That same method has been updated with each successive round of PPP revisions, to $1.08 in 1993 U.S. dollars and then $1.25 in 2005 U.S. dollars, $1.90 in 2011 U.S. dollars and most recently the $2.15 line shown in Fig. 7.5, which is based on the average poverty line used by the 15 lowest-income countries of the world.

The existence of an *extreme poverty* threshold below which any person would be considered poor, originally set at $1/day in 1985 prices and now at $2.15 in 2017 prices, is closely related to the cost of food required for day-to-day survival, with some allowance for other expenses such as clothing, housing and transport. In 2020, a team of Tufts University researchers working with the World Bank and the Food and Agriculture Organization (FAO) used ICP price data from 170 countries in the year 2017 to compute the lowest possible cost of reaching nutritional goals using locally available foods. They found that, on average over all countries, meeting daily energy needs from the lowest-cost starchy staple would cost at least $0.79, or about half of the World Bank's $1.90 extreme poverty line at that time. In actual practice, people living in extreme poverty typically spend 60–80% of their income on food, because they may not have access to the absolute lowest-cost items and usually combine their starchy staple such as rice or cassava with at least one type of more expensive food such as beans or a vegetable. A sufficiently diverse diet to meet all essential nutrient needs, however, is often prohibitively expensive even with the least costly of all locally available foods. At 2017 prices, a minimally supportive diet was found to cost a global average of $2.33 for a healthy adult woman's estimated average requirements (EARs), $2.71 to reach her recommended dietary allowances (RDAs) and $3.75 for an overall high-quality diet as recommended in national dietary guidelines.

The World Bank's international poverty line of $2.15 is clearly inadequate for meeting needs that people in higher-income countries have long considered essential such as a high-quality diet but counting the number and proportion of people below that extreme poverty threshold is still helpful to target services and track outcomes for the world's most vulnerable people. In 1990, governments around the world signed on to the *Millennium Development Goals* (MDGs), aiming to halve the proportion of people in extreme poverty. That goal was achieved by 2015, at which point governments endorsed the *Sustainable Development Goals* (SDGs) that aimed to end extreme poverty by 2030. Progress towards that more ambitious goal has been interrupted by the COVID pandemic and associated economic downturn, but poverty reduction efforts have succeeded in the past and could do so in the future.

Data about poverty are itself a major constraint on the world's ability to understand and address it. People in poverty are often geographically isolated, living in rural areas with few services of any kind. The most basic facts about their lives may not be recorded or remembered unless it is of direct use to them. For example, many people in very low-income places grow up without knowing their birthday: they never received a birth certificate and were not asked to provide the exact date until it was too late to remember. Communities in poverty are deprived of many things, including information about themselves and others to guide social services and political representation. This dimension of deprivation is known as *data poverty*, capturing the role of information in shaping our understanding of living standards and our ability to compare ourselves to other people.

For global poverty in terms of market incomes, comparable data are available from 1990 onwards, based on household surveys with local currency values converted into PPP terms. Earlier surveys used paper-and-pencil questionnaires, laboriously processed by hand using calculators and spreadsheets. Now interviewers often record peoples' responses electronically and upload the results for automated analysis in near real time. Much of what is known about poverty still comes from face-to-face visits, but phone surveys and remote data collection are increasingly used, such as satellite imagery about lights at night. Geocoding allows analysts to link survey data about individuals with information about their environment such as local public services, market infrastructure and agroecological conditions. These changes have greatly enhanced our understanding of living standards and ability to improve them, raising a wide range of new questions. Ethical review prior to contacting individuals for data collection has become a high priority for scientific researchers, so survey designs are typically submitted to the Institutional Review Boards (IRBs) of both the organization carrying out the research and a governing body in the place where the survey will take place.

Figures 7.6 and 7.7 track results compiled by the World Bank's global poverty researchers, using over 1900 surveys from 183 countries assembled in an online database known as the Poverty and Inequality Platform (PIP). Many of the underlying surveys ask respondents about their income, typically including taxes paid and benefits received as in the U.S. supplemental poverty measure, but for people in very low-income settings it is often more practical to ask about total spending over the previous month or year. The PIP database uses both income and expenditure surveys to estimate the number and proportion of people in each country below any given poverty line. Results shown here are for the currently applicable World Bank standard of $2.15 per person per day at 2017 PPP prices, starting with the number of people in Fig. 7.6.

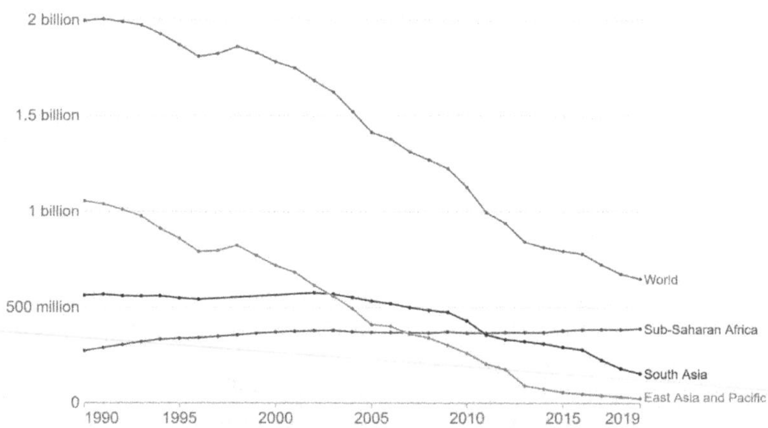

Fig. 7.6 Number of people living on less than $2.15 per day in selected regions, 1990–2019 *Source*: Reproduced from Joe Hasell, Max Roser, Esteban Ortiz-Ospina and Pablo Arriagada [2022], Our World in Data: Poverty [https://ourworldindata.org/poverty], using data from the World Bank Poverty and Inequality Platform [2022]. Data shown are estimated by World Bank researchers, based on income or expenditure reported by people in a total of 1939 surveys from 183 countries, with values in local currency in each year converted to 2017 U.S. dollars using purchasing power parity [PPP] exchange rates for comparison to the extreme poverty line of $2.15 per day

As shown in Fig. 7.6, in the early 1990s there were about 2 billion people in extreme poverty worldwide, of whom about half were in East Asia and the Pacific, largely in China, and a fourth were in South Asia, largely in India. By 2019, the worldwide total had been cut to under 0.7 billion, most of whom are in Africa. The near elimination of extreme poverty in East Asia took about 30 years, interrupted by two years of worsening poverty in 1997–1998. South Asia had a roughly constant number of people in poverty from 1990 to the early 2000s, after which its reduction parallels the trends elsewhere, whereas in Africa the number of people in extreme poverty continues to rise. The limited available data for later years suggest that the number in poverty rose during the pandemic years of 2020–2021 but could decline again afterward if national governments take appropriate action to control disease and reduce poverty.

Much of the change in numbers of people in poverty is due to differences in population growth, which varies widely by country and income level, so it is helpful to see the same data in percentage terms as shown in Fig. 7.7.

The poverty rate data in Fig. 7.7 reveal that, as recently as 1990, about 38% of the whole world's population and 66% of people in East Asia and the Pacific were living in extreme poverty. By 2019, the global rate had been cut to below 8.5%. In South Asia, the percentage of people in extreme poverty was cut from 50% in 1990 to about the global average in 2019. In Africa, the extreme poverty rate peaked in 1994 at 59%. During the 1994–2010 period

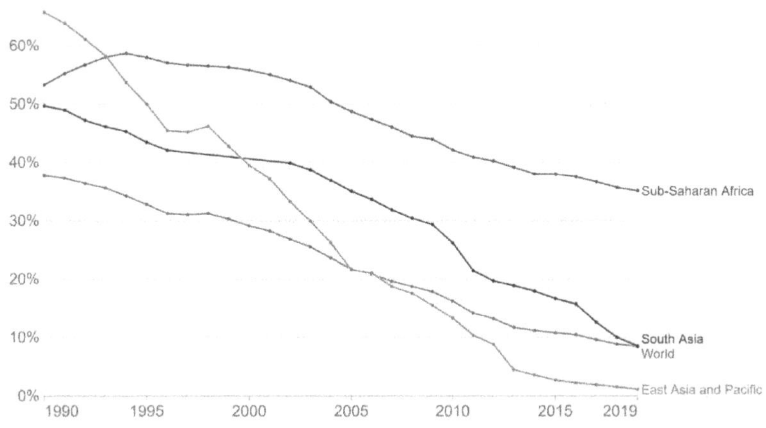

Fig. 7.7 Percent of people living on less than $2.15 per day in selected regions, 1990–2019 *Source*: Reproduced from Joe Hasell, Max Roser, Esteban Ortiz-Ospina and Pablo Arriagada [2022], Our World in Data: Poverty [https://ourworldindata.org/poverty], using data from the World Bank Poverty and Inequality Platform [2022]. Data shown are estimated by World Bank researchers, based on income or expenditure reported by people in a total of 1939 surveys from 183 countries, with values in local currency in each year converted to 2017 U.S. dollars using purchasing power parity [PPP] exchange rates for comparison to the extreme poverty line of $2.15 per day

Africa's poverty rate declined in parallel to declines in South Asia and East Asia and the Pacific, then continued at about the same rate and did not experience the accelerated declines that occurred in Asia shown in the late 2000s and early 2010s. The terrible setback due to COVID in 2020–2021 and the difficult recovery since then is not shown in Fig. 7.7 but can be monitored using the survey data assembled by the World Bank and other researchers.

Inequality, Lorenz Curves and the Gini Index

Many aspects of economic and social life are shaped by inequality, below and above any poverty line. The degree to which incomes are concentrated among a few people within any population can conveniently be measured using *Lorenz curves* defined in Fig. 7.8. The curves, first drawn by Max Lorenz and published in 1905 while he was still a student at the University of Wisconsin, allow all kinds of distributions to be visualized and compared in a standardized manner. His insight was to transform the data into cumulative proportions of all people and their total income, so that the number of people and units of measure would not influence the results. A perfectly uniform distribution with complete equality would be drawn as a diagonal line, along which each additional person accounts for the same proportion of income. Soon after Lorenz showed how distributions could be drawn using standardized curves, in 1914 the Italian statistician Corrado Gini published the idea that inequality could be summarized by the area between a Lorenz curve and that line of equality, as shown with real data for the U.S. in Fig. 7.8.

The Lorenz curves shown in Fig. 7.8 are drawn for money income in the U.S., pooled within households and counted for individuals using the same adjustments for household size and composition that were developed for the supplemental poverty measure. The chart contrasts Lorenz curves for income before and after taxes, which for this calculation counts Federal and state income taxes and credits or rebates, as well as U.S. payroll taxes (FICA). The Gini index is calculated as the population's cumulative gap between equality and their Lorenz curve (area A), as a fraction of complete equality (area A + B). That index ranges from zero, if there were perfect equality, to one if there was complete inequality where only a single person earns any income.

The Gini index, also known as the Gini coefficient, is a very convenient summary statistic, but like any summary it omits potentially important information. For example, the Gini coefficient does not distinguish between inequality at the top or at the the bottom of the income distribution, so the U.S. Census Bureau and others typically complement it with a variety of other data to answer more specific questions. As a person, Corrado Gini himself has been harshly judged by history due to his support for fascism and eugenics, but by coincidence the name of his index can also be read as the acronym for a *G*eneral *in*dex of *i*nequality.

The simplicity and clarity of Lorenz curves make the resulting Gini coefficients the most widely used measure of inequality across countries and over

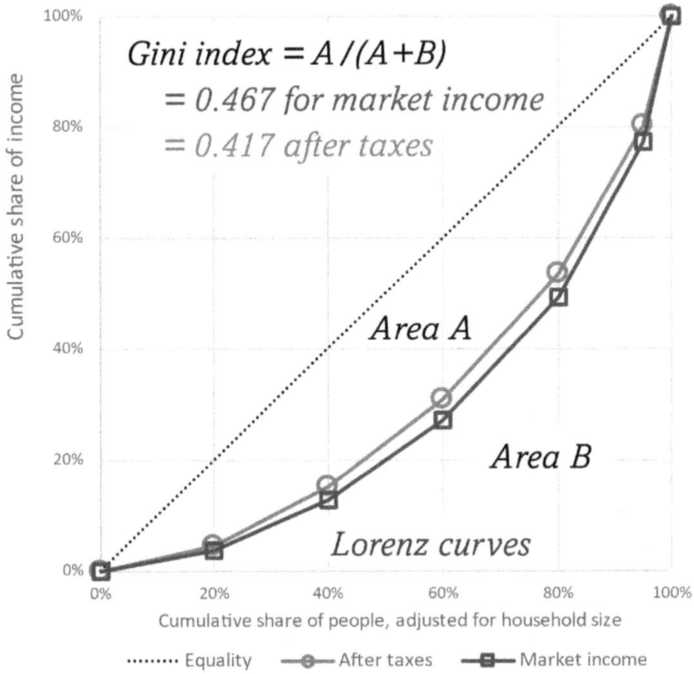

Fig. 7.8 Lorenz curve and Gini index for income before and after taxes in the U.S., 2022 *Source*: Authors' chart of data from Table B-4 in Gloria Guzman and Melissa Kollar, Income in the United States 2022 [U.S. Census Bureau, Washington DC, September 2023]. Updated publications in this series are at https://www.census.gov/library/publications/time-series/p60.html

time. Figure 7.9 uses a large collection of these ratios estimated using comparable methods in a wide range of countries over many years, plotted against the country's national income per person. Here, the horizontal axis differs slightly from the measure of each country's total production (GDP) shown earlier, because here we focus on gross national income (GNI) which includes not just production within the country, but also remittances and other income from abroad, net of payments to foreigners, again on a log scale in the horizontal axis of Fig. 7.9.

Showing a very wide range of Gini coefficients values on single chart is helpful to address a common hypothesis about inequality that was first formulated by Simon Kuznets, whose early observations of economic development led to a paper in 1955 suggesting the possibility of an inverted-U relationship between a country's inequality level and its average national income per capita. The Kuznets hypothesis is based on the idea that in very low-income countries almost everyone might be near the floor level of subsistence, so there would be little inequality because everyone is poor. Then as some people in that country get rich inequality might increase, until others catch up and the

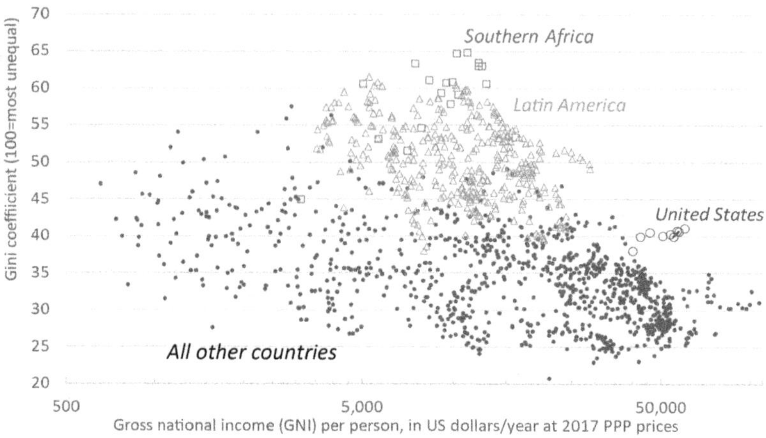

Fig. 7.9 Income inequality at each level of national income per person, 1967–2018
Source: Authors' chart of data from World Bank estimates, from https://databank.worldbank.org. Data shown are a total of 1353 observations from 137 countries in each year for which both Gini coefficients and GNI are available. Gini coefficients are estimated from household survey data by World Bank researchers and denoted SI.POV.GINI. Gross national income per person at PPP prices is estimated from national accounts and denoted NY.GNP.PCAP.PP.KD

distribution becomes more equal at a higher level of income. Kuznets himself saw the hypothesis as a conjecture, to be tested over time as better data became available.

What Fig. 7.9 reveals is that, at least for the modern era since 1967, there is no general inverted-U relationship when looking across the world as a whole. Instead, there is a wide range of Gini coefficients at each level of income and strong regional clustering. At the top, the highest levels of inequality are observed in the five countries of Southern Africa, Botswana, Eswatini (formerly Swaziland), Lesotho, Namibia and South Africa. These are countries dominated by the history of apartheid, by which European settlers seized land and severely limited all economic opportunities for indigenous Africans until the 1990s. The next highest group are the 18 countries in this dataset from Latin America, namely Argentina, Belize, Bolivia, Brazil, Chile, Colombia, Costa Rica, Dominican Republic, Ecuador, El Salvador, Guatemala, Honduras, Mexico, Nicaragua, Panama, Paraguay, Peru and Uruguay. The history of those countries was also dominated by European settlers who seized land and limited opportunities for indigenous people. A third outlier is the U.S., which has much more inequality than other countries at the same level of income.

The pattern shown in Fig. 7.9 reveals how countries other than the settler societies of Southern Africa, Latin America and the U.S. have a downward sloping pattern from values between 30 and 50 among the poorest countries, to values between 20 and 40 among richer countries. Kuznets was right to be skeptical: there turned out to be no inverted-U in the modern era, just a wide range of variation around the world and over time and a modest tendency for higher-income countries to have less inequality. The cross-sectional pattern has an apparent inverted-U only because the Southern African and Latin American countries that were conquered and settled by colonialists are now in the middle-income range today.

Inequity and Disparities by Gender, Ethnicity, Nationality and Race
So far, we have seen how data from individuals and households can be added up and compared over time and among countries and regions, including the example of disparities between racial and ethnic groups in the U.S. shown in Fig. 7.4. Inequity between demographic groups, sometimes called *horizontal inequality,* played a major role in agricultural history and remains a central concern in modern agriculture and food systems.

In Southern Africa and the Americas, the colonial conquest and slavery that gave rise to the inequality shown in Fig. 7.9 were often practiced explicitly for the purpose of controlling agricultural land and labor, preventing enslaved people and colonized lands from being used for self-employed family farms. Control of agriculture took different forms in other regions, for example through concentration of land ownership by inheritance so that others had no choice but to work as tenant farmers, giving up a large share of each year's harvest to landlords. Those systems were sometimes overthrown in violent revolutions, with land reforms and other efforts to equalize access to land and allow people to work for themselves, but social relations remain marked by ancient agricultural practices all around the world.

The term *inequality* generally refers to differences among individuals or households, while *inequity* and *disparities* generally refer to differences between groups that are unjust and undesirable. Historically, a very wide range of criteria have been used to segregate and discriminate around the world, creating barriers to social inclusion that persist in each region. The categories used in the U.S. census shown in Fig. 7.4 illustrate some of the ways that groups are formed. In the U.S., the main categories offered to respondents in the 2020 census were American Indian and Alaska Native (ancestry present before colonial settlement), white (ancestry from all parts of Europe and the Mediterranean or Middle East), Black (everyone of African ancestry, both descendants of enslaved people and also immigrants), Asian (often but not always more recent immigrants from East, Southeast or South Asia) or Hispanic (a designation typically selected by people of Spanish-speaking ancestry from the Americas). All these categories have vague boundaries today and are self-declared by the survey respondent, but they trace their origins to sharp divisions involving violent conquest and legally enforced limits on what people in marginalized groups could do.

The legacy of past and ongoing discrimination between groups is clearly visible in agriculture and nutrition worldwide, as advantages or disadvantages are transmitted and shared leaving some groups with fewer resources of all kinds, while others accumulate high levels of wealth, education, social and political connections as well as physical health. Resources of one kind are commonly used to build other strengths, and deprivation in one dimension has costs in other realms as well. Various kinds of social inclusion or exclusion may overlap, creating new kinds of privilege and injustice at the intersection of multiple social identities.

Boundaries of social groups and barriers to inclusion that people face differ greatly by country and region of the world, and may be based on distinctions of ancestry, religion or other factors that exist only in that place. Racial and ethnic categories are also periodically redefined, for example through the different questions asked in each successive U.S. census. In some countries like the U.S. there are explicit nondiscrimination rules, or countries like India have reservations or quotas in favor of previously excluded groups, and there are also countries like France or Germany and Rwanda where information about ancestry was so violently abused to commit genocide in recent memory that asking about ancestry is now illegal or strongly discouraged.

One of the few inequities that can be traced using internationally comparable data over long periods of time is the gender gap in earnings. People usually live together in households and pool resources to some degree, but the autonomy and power of each person within a household depends in part on what they can earn through outside employment, and throughout history almost all societies have been organized to offer higher wage employment for men than for women. Data on that gender gap in earnings are shown in Fig. 7.10.

As shown on the vertical axis of Fig. 7.10, the male–female gap in earnings of full-time employees ranges from under 5% to almost 50% of male wages. The gray background lines show trajectories for the 40 countries with available data, in addition to the 4 countries highlighted. Many countries have noisy data with sharp rises and falls that are likely to reflect measurement error, but the four highlighted examples illustrate provide a clear indication of how countries differ in the level and trends of the gender wage gap. All four countries highlighted in Fig. 7.10 have greatly narrowed the gap, with notable differences in the speed at which opportunities for men and women have converged. Summary statistics like Fig. 7.10 do not tell us anything about the causal mechanisms behind social change, but observing these patterns demonstrates that societies differ in many important ways, and that large disparities such as the gender gap in wages can be reduced over time.

7.1.3 Conclusion

This section describes the economic toolkit used to measure poverty, inequality and inequity, starting the second half of the book with example data from the U.S. and worldwide. In each case, we focus on data visualization, using line graphs or bar charts and scatterplots to put all available

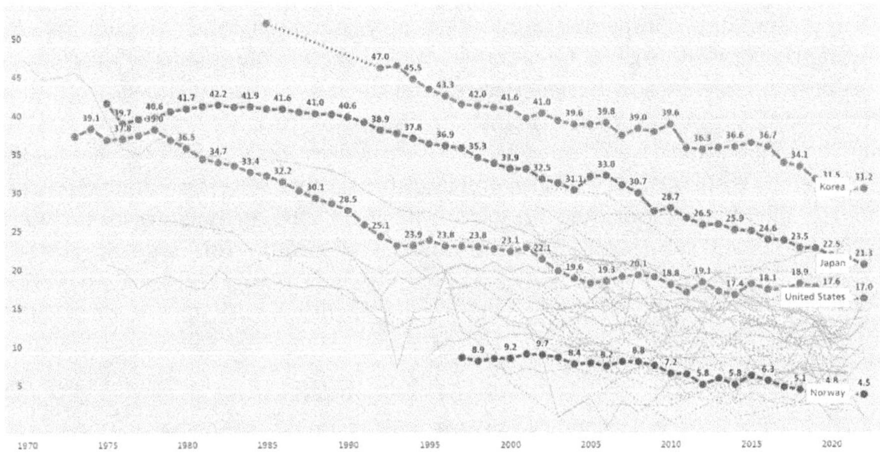

Fig. 7.10 Gender earnings gap among full-time employees in selected countries, 1970–2022 *Source*: Reproduced from OECD, Gender wage gap indicator [https://doi.org/10.1787/7cee77aa-en]. Data shown are male minus female, as a percent of male, using median earnings of all full-time employees. Updated versions of this chart are at https://data.oecd.org/chart/7bUQ

observations of that thing on one figure. The charts of data presented in this section summarize what millions of survey respondents had to say about their lives, counting each one equally to provide an overall picture of trends over time and differences between countries, regions or groups.

Some of the charts shown in this section are images reproduced directly from the source, while others are original data visualizations created for this book to show standard data in a new way. In all cases, readers can go to the source mentioned in the note below each figure to learn more about how each variable was constructed and obtain updated information if available. Data about variation within individual countries like the U.S. are usually best obtained directly from their national statistical agencies such as the Census Bureau, while cross-country comparisons often come from international organizations that work with data from their member countries, such as the World Bank for poverty measurement and the OECD for monitoring gender gaps.

The charts made or chosen for this book aim to provide the broadest, most meaningful and accurate possible picture of the concept to be illustrated. Online access to data is now such that observers can understand the world by combining all the available data to see a bigger picture than was previously possible. In the past people had to zoom in, choosing specific examples in hopes that those would represent a larger truth. Now we can zoom out, showing differences between whole countries or continents over time, using all available data to limit the problem of selection bias in what we would otherwise be able to see from our own individual perspective.

Measuring and comparing levels of poverty, inequality and inequity is challenging but not impossible. Great progress has been made thanks to innovators who developed new and better measurement tools, and then the vast number of data collectors, respondents and analysts who provided the information that was then transformed into the final data we see. Compiling these data accurately is difficult and expensive. The information is in the public domain, and the agencies responsible for data collection and analysis are not always sufficiently well supported, but the sources shared in this section provide a remarkable picture of the partially completed task of eliminating poverty, inequality and inequity in the U.S. and around the world.

7.2 Vulnerability, Resilience and Safety Nets in the Food System

7.2.1 Motivation and Guiding Questions

The previous section focused on differences among people, and the resulting inequality and inequity in the food system and the economy as a whole. For any one person or household, how can we understand variation over time? How do we all protect ourselves against random events like illness or the weather?

Vulnerability to risk plays a major role in agriculture and food systems, worsening poverty and malnutrition. For any one event it is usually impossible to distinguish luck from other factors, but farmers and others can learn from experience how to protect themselves from adverse events. Can interventions help people manage risks and thereby improve outcomes?

Farmers and other people protect themselves to some degree by diversifying activities among different risks and by holding stocks of food to protect against shortfalls. With certain kinds of risk, people might be able to pay in advance for private insurance or obtain help through informal social insurance among members of an extended family and other mutual aid groups. Many people are also helped by public-sector insurance and safety nets, commonly known as social assistance. Most importantly, people can sometimes save and invest in productive activities that provide increasing wealth over time, which they use to avoid or protect themselves from every kind of risk. This section explores how each path can help people escape from poverty and deprivation described in the previous section of this chapter.

Food economics focuses on risk management in part because each person needs roughly constant amounts of food every day, whereas agricultural production is seasonal and fluctuates randomly. Farm households must manage production risks and meet their own consumption needs, while many nonfarm enterprises engage in food storage and transport to bridge times and places when food is more scarce or less scarce. Nonfarm consumers also face food insecurity, usually because of variation in their individual earnings or nonfood expenses, but also when their entire community faces food scarcity and price spikes. Managing every one of these risks involves some combination of individual resilience, insurance of various kinds and ultimately some kind of social assistance.

By the end of this section, you will be able to:

1. Define and compare risk and uncertainty, risk aversion, vulnerability and resilience;
2. Describe how diversification, savings and insurance are used to protect against risk;
3. Explain why insurance is available for some risks but not others, using the concept of asymmetric information and possibility of adverse selection or moral hazard; and
4. Describe and summarize results of how food insecurity and other aspects of vulnerability and resilience are measured in the U.S. and around the world.

7.2.2 *Analytical Tools*

This section addresses the role of *uncertainty* and *risk* for farmers and food consumers. These terms are sometimes used interchangeably, but they can also be given more precise meaning. Most often *uncertainty* refers to lack of knowledge in general, whereas *risk* refers to situations where people have learned something about the probabilities and magnitudes of each possible outcome, such as a short-term weather forecast where people know the risk of rain later than same day.

In situations of extreme uncertainty, people have no evidence at all about probabilities or magnitudes, so people's choices are purely a matter of faith. Economic analysis of risk begins when we have some evidence about the likelihood of dangers and opportunities ahead. The probabilities and magnitudes of each outcome are always uncertain and likely to change over time, but people can learn from experience and make choices based on the possible outcomes they anticipate. Analysis of risk often focuses on the probability and severity of possible harms, balanced by interest in the probabilities and potential gains from favorable events.

The degree to which a given adverse event causes harm is a person's *vulnerability* to that danger, and the opposite of vulnerability is *resilience*. Like other terms, vulnerability and resilience are sometimes defined narrowly. Vulnerability can be used to mean that the risk itself is higher, for example that droughts or floods become more frequent, and resilience can be used to mean only recovery after outcomes have worsened, for example replanting a field after it was destroyed.

One aspect of poverty is high vulnerability to risk, and those vulnerabilities may be so extreme as to create *poverty traps* that push people back into poverty even after favorable events have occurred. More generally, even at higher-income levels most people are *risk averse* to some degree, meaning that people prefer greater certainty around whatever average outcome they may face. All these concepts play an important role in agriculture and food systems as described in this section.

Example Time Paths of Wellbeing for Low-Income Farm Families

To visualize the role of all kinds of risk in relation to poverty status, it is helpful to use a chart of possible trajectories drawn in Fig. 7.11.

Trajectories over time are rarely observed with sufficient frequency to see month-to-month changes in total income, consumption or expenditure, so the examples in Fig. 7.11 are purely hypothetical for the purpose of visualizing the basic terminology of risk. The scenarios shown tell the story of seasonal fluctuations experienced by very low-income farmers with a single harvest each year, but the same concepts would apply to other people facing other kinds of risk.

On the vertical axis of the three panels we have an index of consumption or wellbeing that starts at 100 in June of some year. Each panel then traces a sequence of harvest seasons that occur in the last few months of each calendar year, followed by a 'lean season' when wellbeing is typically lowest when stocks from the previous harvest are running out. The stylized scenarios in Fig. 7.11 are examples to illustrate some of the terminology needed to discuss risk management. In each case there is a contrast between two trajectories, with the lighter shaded line having a more advantageous outcome, and in each panel the second harvest is better than the first or third harvests.

The top panel of Fig. 7.11 shows a situation of *chronic poverty,* where seasonal fluctuations affect only the depth and duration of lean seasons before

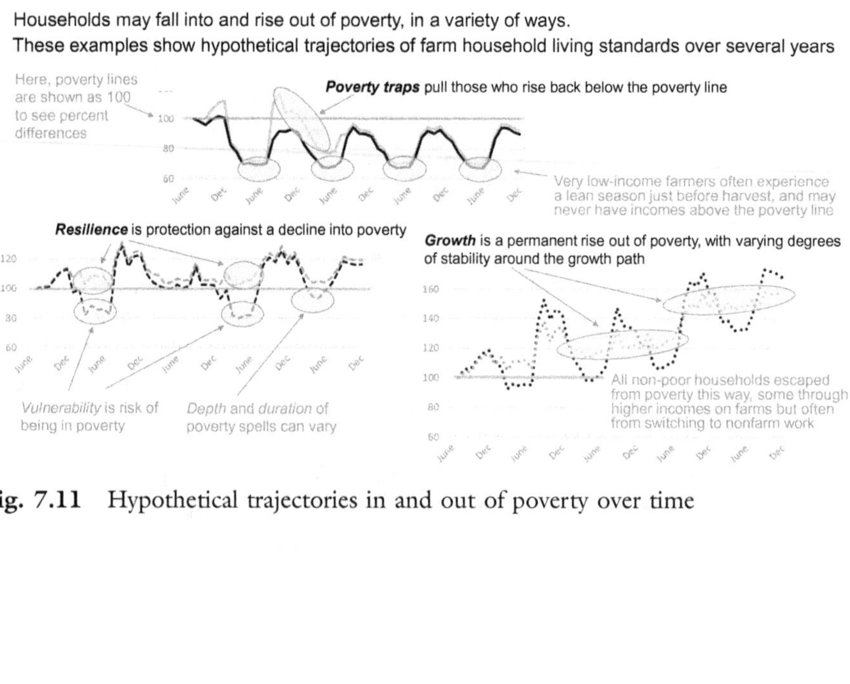

Fig. 7.11 Hypothetical trajectories in and out of poverty over time

each harvest. The person's wellbeing is traced by the dark solid line, and even a successful harvest in the second year lifts the person out of poverty only temporarily along the light-colored line. Persistent poverty can take many forms, but a common situation might be that the person has no secure and rewarding way to save and invest the proceeds from a good harvest. Economists use the term *poverty trap* to investigate possible causes of persistent poverty and ways to escape it, such as offering sufficiently rewarding opportunities for successful harvests to generate long-term gains over time.

The lower left scenario in Fig. 7.11 contrasts a situation of high vulnerability to *recurring poverty* in the dark dashed line with resilience in the lighter dashed line. Here the term resilience is used in a very general sense to mean protection against falling into poverty, without necessarily any gains in good years or improvement over time. In the lower left panel, resilience in the lighter dashed line takes the form of avoiding a decline into poverty during the lean seasons, for example thanks to improved crop storage.

The right scenario of Fig. 7.11 shows the possibility of a *growth trajectory* in which the proceeds of each harvest are reinvested to improve outcomes over time and lift the person permanently out of poverty. In this case the lighter dotted line shows a more stable trajectory within each year which would be desirable, but both paths have a similar growth rate from year to year and similar endpoints in the long run. All high-income communities emerged from poverty this way at some point in their history, and some can have sustained exponential growth for many decades. For farm families and agricultural communities that become wealthy, part of the story is increasing productivity per acre or hectare of land, but since total land area in each place is limited the growth path requires having many farmers switch into nonfarm work so that the remaining farmers can take over their land.

Risk Management Strategies: Diversification, Precautionary Savings and Insurance

A first strategy to manage risk is *diversification*, for example by farmers who plant a variety of different seed types in different ways, and have livestock and nonfarm activities. Diversification is a form of self-insurance, by which people avoid betting too much on any one proposition, even if people know it would have higher payoffs on average in the long run. For example, a farmer may know that keeping cows for dairy is more profitable on average than anything else they could do with their land and labor, but an episode of illness or other problems would be devastating, so farmers usually cannot start dairying unless they have enough wealth or other income sources to offset the risk of a bad outcome.

When diversification takes a producer away from their higher-growth options, putting resources into additional activities to spread risk provides resilience at the cost of lower growth. In some cases, however, diversification also supports growth through complementarity among activities. For example, farmers growing a cereal grain that uses nitrogen often rotate or combine it with a nitrogen-fixing legume like cowpeas or soybeans, because the agronomy of soil nitrogen favors rotation or intercropping of both crops on the same fields. Crop-livestock integration can be another source of complementarity, using crop residues as feed and returning the manure to fields.

Diversification to limit risks and complementarity to increase total output are both helpful only to a limited degree. Most farmers choose to focus on a just a few different crops or animal products, perhaps two to five different species, although some farms that serve consumers directly or grow food for themselves might produce a dozen or more different kinds of vegetables and other crops, and keep different kinds of animals. For livestock and crop enterprises with scale economies, increasing returns can lead farmers to focus on just one species as in specialized dairy or cattle operations and sugar or tea plantations, but those returns may be more variable making specialization affordable only to farmers with relatively high wealth or other ability to absorb risk.

At each level of diversification or specialization, an important strategy to manage risk is precautionary savings or storage, simply to hold over some output from good times into bad. In very low-income settings, there may be few ways to store grain or save money securely, so improvements in storage and savings can be very helpful to limit downside risk even if they do not result in long-term growth. If productive investment opportunities are available, however, then even a person's seasonal or precautionary savings can be used to fuel growth.

For some kinds of risk people can acquire insurance, paying in advance to fund a pool of resources from which each person is paid when a bad outcome has occurred. Informal kinds of *social insurance* are an important feature of all societies, as people in extended families and other groups provide mutual aid to each other in times of need. In those settings, even the lowest-income members of the group often share some of what they have, and those who are more fortunate are expected to provide for others.

Social insurance can be formalized to some degree, for example in rotating schemes among neighbors or friends where each member agrees to contribute something each week or month. That creates a pool from which one member draws, either in times of need or on a regular basis. When withdrawals are on fixed schedule, for example a group of twelve people who contribute \$10 monthly until their designated month when they receive \$110, the pool serves as a rotating savings and loan society. When withdrawals are based on need, for example burial societies to which people pay each month and receive help for funerals, the pool serves as both savings and insurance.

Formal insurance schemes can operate as nonprofit social enterprises or as for-profit businesses, sometimes organized as a 'mutual company' owned by its customers. All insurance providers ask people to pay a lump sum in advance or a regular premium in exchange for a given level of coverage. Insurance of that type can be provided for only certain kinds of risk. The fact that people can buy insurance for some risks but not others is a familiar fact that we all may take for granted, simply assuming that some risks are insurable while others are not, but insurance provision differs across countries and can change rapidly when new technology or other innovations alter the kind of risk that can be insured.

For some risks, formal insurance is optional and people can choose to buy it, such as insuring against breakage or theft of property. In agriculture, the oldest and most universal example is insuring a field of crops against damage from hail, which was among the earliest formal insurance plans introduced in Europe in the late eighteenth and nineteenth centuries. For other risks, insurance is provided by private enterprises but required by law, such as automobile insurance in most countries, and a few kinds of risk are typically insured directly by governments, such as unemployment insurance. All three kinds of insurance are commonly observed to help pay for health care services. Some health insurance is provided directly by governments, some is provided by private enterprises to everyone under a government mandate, and some is provided privately if people choose to pay for it. The role of government mandates and public insurance alongside private insurers is crucial aspect of risk management in agriculture and other domains.

Market Failures in Insurance: Adverse Selection and Moral Hazard

Economists explain the market for insurance as a problem of limited *information* about the risks faced by each person. If the insurance provider could easily assess the probabilities of each outcome, they could calculate the *expected value* of payouts over time. Expected value is the probability of each outcome multiplied by its value. For example, in nineteenth-century France if a field's risk of being destroyed by a hailstorm each year were one in a thousand, and the payout to cover the crop's value were ten thousand francs, then an annual premium of ten francs would exactly cover the expected value of that risk. An insurer with a thousand such customers would pay out once each year on average and exactly break even in a normal year. To be more confident of breaking even each year they would need a larger number of customers, and to cover a few bad years in a row they would need financial reserves. Such an insurance plan would be *actuarially fair*, meaning that a nonprofit or mutual insurance company could arise and persist indefinitely, and a for-profit insurance provider might be able to charge even higher premiums but still find customers whose risk aversion makes them willing to pay more than the expected value of the risk they face.

The fundamental market failure that causes insurance to be provided for some risks but not others is *asymmetric information* between each customer and the insurer. One kind of information asymmetry is hidden attributes affecting risk that only the customer knows, for example if a farmer knew that certain fields were more vulnerable to hailstorms than other fields. Another aspect is hidden actions by the customer, for example if a farmer who had bought insurance then chose to plant riskier crops in ways that the insurer cannot observe. Insuring a standing crop against damage from hailstorms emerged early and persists everywhere in part because there is almost no asymmetric information about that kind of risk. There is little that farmers can know or do that would alter the odds of being hit by a hailstorm, which then destroys all standing crops in the place where it hits. An insurer who has observed hail damage for a many years can guess the odds and issue the plan, receive premiums, verify claims by visiting each field after a storm to see that the crop was in fact destroyed, pay compensation and continue to operate for many years. If the insurer is a relatively small company serving a limited area, covariance among their customers' risks creates the possibility of many claims in a single year. Each local insurer's risks can then be pooled in a market for 'reinsurance' whereby they are compensated by a larger, different insurance company in the event of extreme losses. The market for reinsurance is also limited by asymmetric information and works only when the reinsurer is confident that the local insurer does not know more about their risks than its reinsurer, or takes on more risk after they are reinsured.

Insurance plans for farm risks beyond hailstorms are often offered and can succeed to the degree that they overcome the market failures caused by asymmetric information. When there is hidden information about their risks that customers know but insurers cannot see, the cause of market failure is ***adverse selection***. As that term implies, the problem is that customers with higher risks will be able to self-select into buying insurance. When there are hidden actions that customers might take that increase risk once they have insurance, the cause of market failure is known as ***moral hazard***. That term arose in the nineteenth century when insurance providers argued that riskier behavior was immoral. The language used to explain how asymmetric information causes market failure is similarly colorful, as both adverse selection and moral hazard routinely cause insurance markets to 'unravel' in a 'death spiral' towards bankruptcy unless governments intervene.

Information asymmetries that cause the unraveling of insurance markets can be illustrated by the many attempts to create agricultural insurance for fire damage, crop yields or livestock survival. The oldest of these is fire insurance. Returning to our example of nineteenth-century France, if an insurer's survey of past fires shows that one in a thousand farm buildings burn down every year, each causing more than ten thousand francs of damage, to cover their costs they might need to charge an annual premium of eleven francs for a payout of ten thousand francs in the event of a fire. Farmers who know they have lower than average fire risks would not sign up so only higher risk customers enroll, which is adverse selection. Furthermore, those farmers who do enroll might take less care to avoid fire, which is moral hazard.

The effects of adverse selection in enrollment, and of moral hazard among those who have enrolled, are a predictable unravelling of the market over time. After launching what appears to be an actuarially sound insurance plan, adverse selection leads to only those with high fire risk to sign up, and moral hazard might lead some of them to incur even higher risks because they have insurance. The result is a higher probability of fires among the insured population, for example on average two in a thousand buildings might burn, so the plan is no longer actuarially sound. The insurer loses money on average but might stay in business and raise their premium above twenty francs. That does not solve the underlying problem, however, because now only those whose risks are higher than two in a thousand would sign up and once insured, they might do riskier things, so the insurer might then find that three in a thousand insured buildings are burning. Raising their premium again to above thirty francs would just worsen the problem.

Experienced insurers anticipate the problem and avoid introducing plans that face asymmetric information, but it is not always possible to predict whether adverse selection or moral hazard will occur. It may also be possible to fix the information asymmetry. In the case of fire insurance, the losses are so devastating that people have a very strong incentive to make insurance work. Early fire insurers in nineteenth-century Europe discovered that they could make plans sustainable by employing fire inspectors to verify that customers have precautions in place before the plan is issued and by employing fire investigators who authorize payouts only if they can determine that the cause was not negligence or another moral hazard. Private enforcement of these rules by insurance companies is only partially effective, so in the twentieth century governments increasingly intervened with building inspectors who enforce fire safety codes and fire investigators who determine the cause of every fire. Those public services, along with firefighters who limit the damage when fires occur, then allow more diverse private companies to compete and offer lower-cost fire insurance to everyone in the areas covered by the government's fire prevention programs.

Crop and livestock risks are extremely important for farmers, but insurance providers have rarely been able to overcome asymmetric information enough to make plans sustainable. Instead, the importance of those risks for farmers has sometimes led governments to intervene by introducing subsidized plans, expecting to cover only some of the plan's losses. If the underlying market failure is not addressed, however, then the death spiral runs in reverse as the government payout grows over time as increasingly high-risk, low-return activities are enrolled in the plan. For example, from the 1930s until the 1980s, the U.S. government offered only very limited crop yield insurance for which only some U.S. acres were eligible and were enrolled. In 1994 and then in 1996, new policies authorized payment to support insurance plans covering a wider range of losses, including not just yield but also total revenue. Farmers responded by enrolling a larger fraction of riskier acreage. Each successive round of policy change has allowed payouts to grow, feeding an upward spiral towards enrollment of almost all eligible acres and government absorbing a larger fraction of program payouts. The program still uses the terminology of insurance, but payouts became so frequent and predictable that farms came to rely on these plans for regular revenue, not just in exceptional years.

Technological innovations can sometimes overcome asymmetric information and solve the underlying market failure, allowing new insurance markets to emerge. For example, remote sensing of weather conditions has led to many experiments with 'parametric' insurance, where payouts are triggered by an index of specific conditions such as prolonged drought. Payouts can even be triggered by forecasts, leading to 'anticipatory' payments to farmers that might help them escape the harms caused by extreme weather. Whether this kind of payment can be sustained depends in part on whether the plan is actuarially sound from the start, meaning that its expected payout is covered by its revenues, but also that the plan avoids both adverse selection and moral hazard over time.

Government intervention can help solve insurance market failures in several ways. One approach is to address the adverse selection and moral hazard problem directly, as in the example of fire codes, fire inspectors, fire investigators and fire fighters, all of whom work together to limit fire risk and make it insurable for everyone. Another approach is an insurance mandate, overcoming adverse selection by ensuring that people at all risk levels pay for coverage. The mandate can be universal, as in automobile accident insurance, or based on any criterion other than the person's health risks, such as all employees of a company as in the U.S. system of employer mandates. In each case, insurance mandates are usually accompanied by efforts to reduce the risk itself and limit risky behavior through policing, for example regarding auto safety and traffic laws, which can itself improve lives and makes the remaining risk insurable at lower cost to consumers.

Extending insurance to a wider range of dangers can reduce the role of randomness in life but ultimately covers only a fraction of the risk that people face, making risk management a central problem for all enterprises and every household.

Risk Aversion and Risk-Reward Choices in Production

People differ in their attitudes to risk, based in part on their beliefs about probabilities and impacts, but also on their wealth and resilience. One way of picturing a person's attitude to risk is by imagining a utility function, capturing the usefulness of income and consumption expenditure to reach higher levels of subjective wellbeing. The utility of income includes purchase of goods and services such as housing, food and so forth that help a person achieve all of their goals including health and longevity, education and knowledge, care for one's family and gifts to others. An example utility function is shown in Fig. 7.12.

The solid curve in Fig. 7.12 shows a utility function whose bowed-up shape captures the risk aversion that people often (but not always) reveal in their choices. As income increases from left to right the curve is steeper at first, indicating how increments of income are spent on higher priority needs, and the curve eventually becomes flatter indicating diminishing marginal utility of income. Additional income remains useful as shown by the positive slope throughout the range.

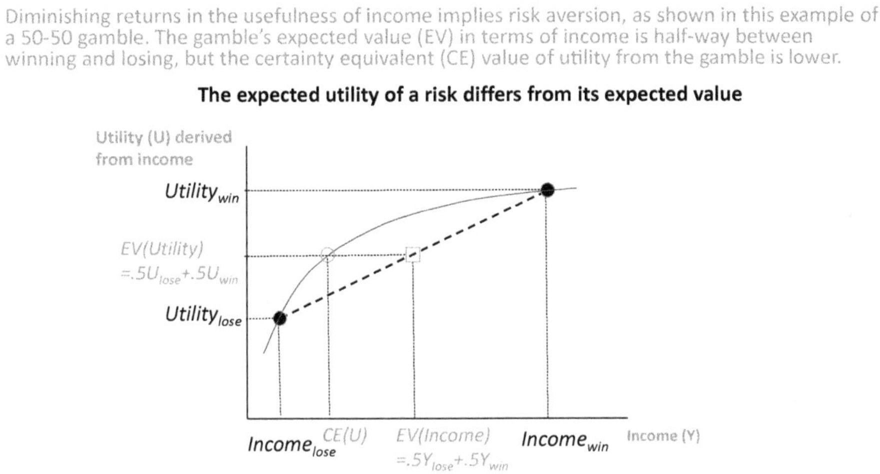

Fig. 7.12 Risk aversion reflects higher priority needs at lower levels of income

In the situation shown, a person is considering a 50–50 gamble whose payoffs are shown by the two dots. The dashed line connects those two dots, showing the location of the hollow square and hollow circle used to show the effect of risk aversion on behavior.

The horizontal axis shows income from the gamble if they lose or win, the expected value of which is half-way between the two levels of income. For example, a coin toss for $100 or nothing has an expected value of $50. If a person did this many times, on average they would earn $50 in addition to the base level of income when they lose, denoted along the horizontal axis as *EV(Income)*.

The vertical axis shows the usefulness of income for wellbeing, which is bowed up to show how a person would meet their highest priority needs with their first increments of income, and each additional unit of income after that would be spent on things with diminishing marginal utility for their wellbeing. The curve shows this person's level of wellbeing at each level of income if they lose or if they win. With 50–50 odds, the expected value of utility is half-way between the two levels along the vertical axis as shown by the dashed line, denoted *EV(Utility)*.

The hollow circle along the utility curve shows both the subjective usefulness of the gamble for this person along the vertical axis and the amount of income that would be equally useful to them if obtained with certainty. This value along the horizontal line is known as the *certainty equivalent* (CE) value of the gamble. If the person could be guaranteed that certainty-equivalent value, it would have the same expected utility for them as the expected utility of the gamble. In monetary terms the CE of utility from the gamble, denoted *CE(U)*, is lower than the expected income, *EV(Income)*, because this person has higher priority needs for small increments of income than for further increments at higher-income levels.

Risk aversion has enormous practical importance for agriculture. For example, if the gamble in Fig. 7.12 were adoption of a risky new farm technology, the farmer's utility from it would be lower than the expected value of the payoff. Farmers in this situation might miss out on a growth opportunity due to the consequences of experiencing a bad year. Many people routinely make choices that reveal risk aversion of this type, showing a preference for greater certainty even if the average payoff is lower, whenever they have high priority needs for additional income over the relevant range.

When many people in a society show risk aversion towards certain kinds of activity such as new technology adoption, we observe a risk-reward tradeoff where higher risk activities offer higher payoffs on average. But people do not always show risk aversion, especially for risks that are harder to assess and in situations where short-term emotions rather than long-term wellbeing drive decision-making. For example, it is very difficult to assess risks when comparing outcomes with very small probabilities, such as the odds of winning a lottery. It is also difficult to assess risks when emotions cloud judgment, as in sports and other competitions. In those situations, people routinely show *risk-loving* behavior, where their certainty equivalent willingness to pay for a lottery ticket or a bet on sporting events exceeds the expected returns from that gamble. In those situations, people are taking on risk that also leaves them with even lower income on average.

People who assess risks accurately and can afford to make more risk-neutral decisions will have higher incomes in the long run. In situations illustrated in Fig. 7.12, risk aversion can be driven by high priority needs for small increments of income. Interventions can help people take advantage of high return but potentially risky opportunities not only by helping them assess those risks accurately, but also by ensuring that basic needs are met so they can focus on average outcomes over the longer term.

Low-income people with high priority needs, like others throughout the income range, do not actually show consistent levels of risk aversion across distinct kinds of gambles. For example, many people show risk-loving behavior by buying lottery tickets on the same day that they show risk-averse behavior towards other kinds of risk. That kind of inconsistency could be due to the genuine usefulness of dreaming about winning the lottery but could also be caused by misjudging the odds of winning. Another kind of inconsistency arises when people show extreme risk aversion in some decisions, for example buying insurance whose cost of premiums far exceeds the expected utility of payouts such as extended warranties for small kitchen appliances.

Inconsistent attitudes to risk, whether extreme risk-aversion to some dangers or risk-loving willingness to gamble on some opportunities, leave people with lower total income and wealth over time. If people were better informed and felt more secure, they might regret those choices. These observations help explain the outcomes we see, including government regulations about gambling and insurance, because both kinds of products allow sellers to create a false impression about the likelihood and value of winning (in the case of gambling) and a false impression about the likelihood and value of payouts (in the case of low-value insurance).

The general case illustrated in Fig. 7.12 underlies the typical situation in which farmers and other producers show risk aversion, thereby missing opportunities for high-return activities. For people in or near poverty, where a bad outcome could lead to destitution from which they might never recover, risk aversion is a necessary and unavoidable consequence of their low incomes. If people in that situation tried the high-return activity, some might be lucky but on average the investment would lead to regret. There are many other situations in which producers are well advised to show a high degree of risk aversion, for example when bad outcomes would lead to bankruptcy and a permanent loss of the family farm or other enterprise.

In agriculture and other activities, the widespread need for risk aversion to protect lives and livelihoods often creates a risk-reward tradeoff, leaving higher return activities available for people with less risk aversion. Accurately perceiving each set of probabilities and payoffs is difficult, and some high-risk activities actually offer low rewards on average. People reach their highest available level of income in the long run when they perceive risks accurately and can afford to act in a risk-neutral manner. Escaping from poverty therefore requires not only having high return activities available, but also having sufficiently accurate information and sources of resilience such as social insurance and safety nets for low-income people to adopt those innovations. Interventions that provide high-return options, help people assess those options and ensure enough resilience for them to act in a risk-neutral manner have helped many millions of people move onto the growth trajectory illustrated at the start of this section in Fig. 7.11.

Consumer Prices and Food Crises

Risk and risk management is important not only for farmers but also consumers. Both groups face risk in their own production and income, and risk in market prices for what they buy and sell. The prices received by producers and those paid by consumers differ widely because of value added after harvest, which includes all kinds of food processing and packaging, handling, distribution and retailing at the point of sale. An important part of those value-added services is storage and transport designed to smooth availability over space and time.

Food availability for consumers at each location provides a greater diversity of items whose prices are more stable than what is produced at any one location. Those marketing services, which include the food manufacturing industry that transforms agricultural products into packaged and processed items, account for about 85% of the cost paid by consumers for food purchased at grocery stores in the U.S. About 15% of consumer spending is the farmgate cost of raw products purchased from farmers, about 30% is the cost of food processing and packaging, and the remaining 55% is the cost of distribution and retailing.

The data on cost shares for retail products in the U.S. come the USDA's 'food dollar' calculations, which are based on the physical flow of goods and recorded transactions discussed in Chapter 9 and reported in Fig. 9.4. The FAO provides similar estimates for a few other countries. The fraction of consumer food spending that goes to farmers is somewhat larger in lower-income countries, and larger for some types of food, but even for raw products in almost all places the demand and supply of distribution and retailing to consumers leads to more spending on marketing services than for production on farms, or for transportation and storage from farms to consumers. In the U.S. and other high-income countries, retail food prices are mostly driven by the cost of processing, packaging, branding and retailing, including advertising which is estimated by the USDA to account for 2.6% of grocery costs.

In the U.S. and many other countries, processing and retailing services drive retail prices and determine the composition and healthiness of each item sold. Transportation and storage play a different role in the food system, allowing each community's food consumption to be more diverse and stable than its food production. Transport and storage to smooth and diversify consumption turn out to be a low fraction of all food costs in the U.S. and other high-income countries but can be expensive in low-income settings.

The cost of transportation to consumers depends primarily on infrastructure and volumes shipped and can be extremely low when products are moved on large vehicles. Once products are loaded on a truck, train or boat, the amount of energy, equipment, personnel or other resources per mile for each unit transported is much lower on larger and slower vehicles like trains and ships that carry many times their own weight and do so more efficiently with less friction and fewer stops and starts than smaller vehicles.

For storage, the cost of stockholding to smooth prices over time is influenced by infrastructure, but also by the urgency with which people need money for other things. Once items are loaded inside a warehouse, the cost of stockholding involves some use of energy, equipment and personnel but varies mostly with the opportunity cost of keeping the products instead of selling them and using the funds for other things.

Low-income countries and places with poor infrastructure for transport and storage have greater consumer price variation, but the basic pattern of price dynamics is somewhat like the story observed in the U.S. as shown in Fig. 7.13.

The data shown in Fig. 7.13 are indexes set to 100 for the month of January 1990, to observe percentage changes since then for each category of food prices. Each index is a weighted average of representative items sold in each category, where item weights are proportional to sales. For example, if wheat accounts for 5% of all unprocessed food sold by farmers, its price changes would account for 5% of changes in the index. All four food price indexes are shown relative to the consumer price index for all goods and services, so the

Fig. 7.13 U.S. price indexes for consumer and producer prices, January 1990–August 2023 *Source*: Reproduced from Federal Reserve Economic Data [FRED], using price indexes from the U.S. Bureau of Labor Statistics as the average for each category relative to the overall U.S. consumer price index for all goods and services. Updated versions at https://fred.stlouisfed.org/graph/?g=12MMl

lines track the real value of each type of food in terms of all other things sold in the U.S.

The lowest line shows prices paid for unprocessed foods to farmers and traders. Figure 7.13 shows that the aggregate of all food sold by farmers has brief spikes and long valleys. The peak of those spikes occurred in August 1996, May 2004, July 2008, April 2014 and April 2022. Prices drop sharply after each peak, and then often trend downward for several years before hitting bottom, and sometimes staying low before beginning a gradual climb up to the next peak. Each individual item would have different price trajectories, but this general pattern reflects how each year's supply-demand balance affects stockholding for raw materials. In years of declining prices when supply growth exceeds demand increases, storage bins for grain and other crops fill up. People respond with less investment in supply and more demand, so prices rise and stocks are used up.

The peak prices for farm commodities in the lowest line happen when stocks approach zero, just before buyers expect replenishment from the next harvest. Stockholding is not precisely measured, in part because much of it is 'pipeline stocks' held temporarily at each stage of the value chain, but the fact that participants in food markets hold a variable level of stocks in anticipation of future harvests plays a central role in food price risks. *Food price crises* occur when some buyers fear not being able to acquire enough of the materials they need to keep operating, so they are willing to pay very high prices until their pipeline stocks are replenished, and everyone else responds similarly leading to a runup in price to a peak just before the next harvest arrives.

The light-colored central line in Fig. 7.13 shows producer prices for processed foods, as sold by food manufacturers to grocery outlets and food service providers. Their price trajectory is like an attenuated echo of the prices of raw materials, with a lengthy period of declining real prices received by food manufacturers from 1990 to a low in mid-2006, after which prices rose to a peak in late 2014 before falling again to 2019 just before the pandemic. The onset of COVID drove a sudden wedge between prices paid to farmers that plummeted from January through April 2020 and prices paid to food manufacturers that shot up in April and May 2020, before recovery drove both up faster than general inflation to their peak in May 2022.

The dark, heavier line shows consumer prices for food at home, which have smaller fluctuations around general inflation, which would be a horizontal line on this chart. There are noticeable peaks in grocery prices soon after the peaks in farm and processed goods prices, and an almost 10% fall in real grocery prices from 2015 through 2019, but the overall average of cost items sold at grocery stores mostly tracks general inflation, unlike the top line showing prices for food away from home at restaurants and food service establishments.

The top line shows how prices for food away from home tracked grocery costs until the 2009–2014 period when they did not fall as grocery prices did, and especially the period since 2014 when restaurant prices kept rising as grocery prices fluctuated. The difference is that wages and rents play a larger role in restaurant and cafeteria costs than in groceries or general inflation. Like other price indexes, the data shown in Fig. 7.13 do not fully take account of changes in product quality within each category, and some of the rising average cost of restaurant meals since 2014 could potentially be attributable to higher average quality, in addition to higher real wages for workers and higher real rents and other costs paid by restaurant owners.

The food price crises and periodic spikes in costs of raw agricultural products are extremely important sources of risk for farm families and food market participants. For consumers buying retail products the resulting percentage price changes they experience are much smaller in magnitude as shown in Fig. 7.13, but still important for both the U.S. and a global average as shown in Fig. 7.14.

The food price data in Fig. 7.14 are average food price inflation in real terms, relative to the overall consumer price index for all goods and services, over the previous 12 months starting in January 1998 for the U.S. and January 2000 for the global average. The global average has some change in composition as an increasing number of countries reported data over time, but the overall picture reveals some degree of synchronization in food price spikes around the world.

Periodic food price crises as shown in Fig. 7.14 represent entire years of sustained monthly rises in the real cost of food relative to all other goods and services, followed by sharp falls in the relative cost of food. These price crises are of enormous importance to consumers and political leaders, often attracting intense media attention.

When food prices spike up many households have great difficulty meeting basic needs. By Engel's law we know that lower-income people spend a larger fraction of their total income on food. For example, a low-income household spending 50% of their available resources on food and facing 4% higher food

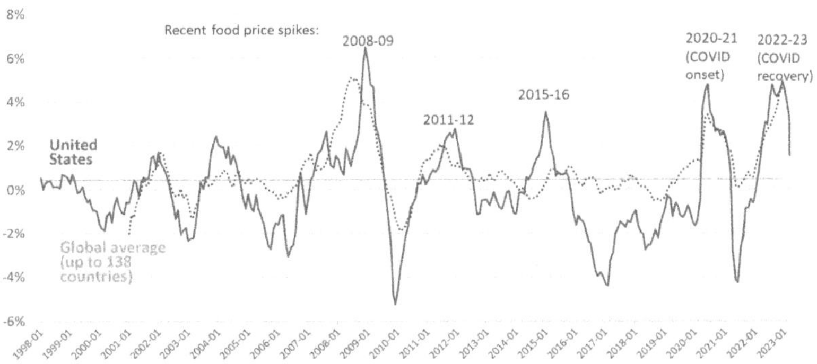

Fig. 7.14 Average rise in real food prices over the previous 12 months, January 1998–June 2023 *Source*: Authors' chart of own calculations. U.S. data are calculated from the Bureau of Labor Statistics, and global data are from the IMF, averaging over all countries reporting monthly consumer price indexes [CPI] for food and for all goods and services, January 2000–December 2022. Each observation is the average monthly rise over the previous 12 months, times twelve for an annualized value. Number of countries rises from 51 in January 2000 to 95 in 2005 and then 138 from 2015 onwards. Raw data for all countries are at https://data.imf.org and an updated chart for the U.S. is at https://fred.stlouisfed.org/graph/?g=12Myr

prices would have 2% lower real income overall. By Bennett's law we also know that lower-income people will already be reliant on the lowest cost sources of dietary energy before the food price rise, so they cannot switch to lower-cost foods. What we actually observe in these cases is cuts in spending on other things such as education and health care. Middle-income people spending 20% of income on food face a smaller cut in overall real income and have a choice between downgrading their diet quality to what lower-income people normally consume and cutting back on other things as lower-income people do.

For many consumers, food price crises are poverty crises. But high costs for consumers coincide with high prices paid to producers, and the lowest-income people in low-income countries are farmers who produce food. Most of those farmers sell some or most of their production every year to pay for other things, including foods that they buy because their own farms are suitable only for certain kinds of production. On balance, most such farmers benefit from periods of high prices and suffer during the long periods of low prices before the runup and brief peak in prices seen during food crises. For farmers with larger quantities available to sell, the brief periods of high prices are among the few high-income years they ever experience, while for other farmers their own production and sales simply offset the higher prices of purchased foods, insulating them from the crisis.

Hunger, Energy Balance and the Prevalence of Undernourishment

Price spikes and food crises are important, but access to sufficient food can be an everyday challenge even when prices are low. Throughout human history people have devoted enormous efforts to ensure that we all have enough food to power each day's work and maintain our own health. Despite those efforts, many people experience hunger and food insecurity, and the economics of that problem begins with an understanding of energy balance over time.

When people eat less than their body needs, hunger drives us to seek more food in ways that nutritionists now know is caused by a variety of unconscious mechanisms. Those drivers include feeling hungry and related physiological responses such as fatigue and other symptoms that cause us to seek more food, in ways that are mediated by hormones and other physiological responses. Hunger also results in emotional responses and increases irritability and stress. Some of these mechanisms can be altered by appetite-suppressing medications such as semaglutide that mimics GLP-1 hormones, but for almost all people energy balance is achieved through conscious effort or unconscious regulation in ways that may be easier or harder to sustain from day to day.

The amount of food each person needs to maintain health will grow with body size starting in utero through childhood and adolescence, rising temporarily for pregnancy and breastfeeding, and vary with physical activity, recovery from injury and disease. Some people can meet these needs with ease, while many others must overcome great challenges to sustain intake in balance with energy expenditure. A schematic view of the mechanisms involved in maintaining energy balance is shown in Fig. 7.15.

The sketch in Fig. 7.15 shows how economic and psychosocial factors interact with biological or physiological processes to determine dietary intake. These mechanisms and their interactions remain poorly understood, but evidence from around the world in very diverse settings clearly demonstrates the importance of autonomous processes underlying food consumption.

Through most of human history and continuing today, most people meet their energy needs with no knowledge at all about how much energy is in their food. The energy contained in food and its use for metabolism was not measured or even known to exist until the 1780s, when French chemist Antoine Lavoisier invented a device using melted ice to measure the heat present in food and released by animals who ate that food. Lavoisier called that heat 'caloric', after the Latin word *calor* (also Spanish, or *chaleur* in French). In the 1840s English physicist James Joule showed that calories of heat were linked to physical motion, showing the relationship between each kind of energy.

Researchers now use kilocalories (kcal) and kilojoules (kJ) interchangeably to measure the energy in each item, but consumers usually have no idea how many calories or joules they have eaten each day. Many countries require food manufacturers and restaurants to post that information for individual items,

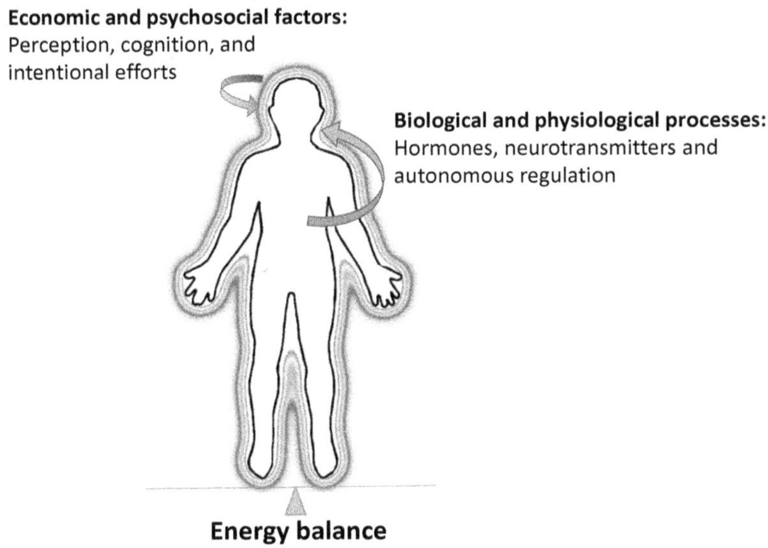

Fig. 7.15 Interaction of conscious and unconscious mechanisms for energy balance
Source: Authors' infographic, using human body outline sketch in the public domain from www.seekpng.com as image number u2q8r5w7t4a9i1i1

and a person's energy intake can be estimated using a food diary or nutrition assessment. Although the scientific discovery and disclosure of energy in food is important for food policy, abundant evidence demonstrates that energy balance is not a conscious choice. Food choice plays a role in diet composition which influences a person's future health, but total energy consumed over the course of a week or a month is driven by dietary practices in response to the biological and physiological processes as shown in Fig. 7.15.

The degree to which societal factors such as poverty and food scarcity prevent people from meeting their biological needs has been debated since antiquity. As soon as human energy requirements were first measured, they were found to be closely linked to body size and composition, and as soon as calories in food could be counted people began to compare the two. In 1961, an Indian statistician named P.V. Sukhatme devised a method to compare each country's total food consumption to a standardized distribution of likely dietary intake relative to various body sizes for its population, and thereby track what the FAO still computes each year as the country's *Prevalence of Undernourishment* (PoU).

The FAO began reporting their PoU estimate in 1974, at which time they calculated that 462 million of the world's 4 billion people lived in countries where the distribution of intake was unlikely to meet their needs. FAO continues to report that number every year, finding for example that in 2022 a total of around 735 million of the world's 8 billion people were undernourished in this sense. Observers sometimes interpret this as the number of hungry people in the world, but the estimate does not actually derive from comparing individual intake to individuals' energy requirements. It is only a rough estimate of likely intake relative to what people would need if intake followed a standardized lognormal distribution, and if each person had a body size indicating a balance between calorie intake and expenditure, which are not actually the case. What the FAO's undernourishment data show is each year's change in a country's total food consumption relative to its total population and demographic composition. That is an extremely useful number so the FAO continues to publish it, even as they adopt more granular measures such as their food insecurity scale introduced in 2014, and the cost and affordability of healthy diets indicator introduced in 2022, which we discuss in turn below.

Food Insecurity in the U.S. and Worldwide

In the early 1980s, a graduate student in nutrition at Cornell University named Kathy Radimer had recently returned from Peace Corps service in West Africa and found herself in the U.S. at a time when many people were struggling with an economic downturn caused by high unemployment. Community leaders and researchers had long spoken of widespread hunger in America, but clearly conditions in the U.S. were quite different from what Radimer had seen in Africa.

Radimer's Peace Corps work had been in Burkina Faso and Cameroon, where more than half of the population lived on incomes below a dollar a day. Even the lowest-income people in America seemed wealthy in comparison. The U.S. clearly had an abundant diversity of food year-round, the FAO's official PoU measure showed almost no undernourishment, and even low-income Americans did not show obvious signs of undernutrition. Despite the arguments of community leaders and researchers who worked closely with low-income peoples, the U.S. government at that time openly dismissed the idea that Americans were going hungry.

In part because of her varied experiences, Radimer approached the measurement of deprivation in a new way. Her dissertation, entitled *Understanding hunger and developing indicators to assess it*, did just that. Radimer conducted long, open-ended interviews with dozens of low-income caregivers about how they met their family's food needs, and then experimented with many kinds of questions about food choice and meal preparation. Radimer's research discovered that the clearest way to ask people about hunger was to ask a series of questions such as whether they had recently skipped meals, eaten less or different foods, eaten fewer foods, felt hungry and not eaten, run out of food, worried about whether there would be enough food, not eaten balanced meals, or similar experiences of food-related deprivation, with every such question framed as whether the respondent had that experienced that episode of deprivation because they couldn't afford or didn't have enough money to buy the foods they usually consumed.

The novelty in Radimer's approach was to ask each question in the same terms that respondents had themselves used. Radimer learned that people with a wide range of dietary practices reported a similar set of responses to being unable to obtain their usual foods. She found that people remembered those experiences vividly even after several months, and that people facing more severe deprivation reported having done a larger number of different things. Most importantly, Radimer discovered that people said the reason they could not obtain their usual diet is that they had run out of money to buy food. Respondents said they ran out of money to buy their usual diet due to both loss of income and increased expenses, and almost always reported that they ran out of money for food because a sequence of shocks had depleted their savings.

Kathy Radimer's dissertation was published in 1990, and the basic idea was quickly adopted by other researchers as a ten-item Radimer/Cornell Hunger and Food Insecurity Scale. By 1995 the USDA had adopted a version of her approach as an 18-item Household Food Security Survey, and in 2014 the FAO adopted a shorter version for global use as an 8-item Food Insecurity Experience Scale. Both ask generally similar questions about whether the respondent had experienced each kind of deprivation at any time in the past 12 months. The results have been of extraordinary value in helping governments and researchers measure deprivation in many different contexts, identifying when and why so many people around the world experience episodes of hunger and deprivation even when prices are low, and food is abundant for other people in their community.

The USDA and FAO versions differ slightly, in revealing ways. For example, the USDA survey asks one short question first to screen out respondents who say that over the past 12 months their household always had 'enough of the kinds of food we want to eat', then if needed continues with the remaining questions. Also, the USDA counts people as food insecure if they answer yes to three or more questions, whereas the FAO procedure gives each question different weights based on the probability that a yes on one of them predicts other yes responses. The FAO technique is designed around the idea that each question is a different aspect of the same underlying thing, so questions that predict other yes responses are strong indicators of that thing, whereas in the USDA method all questions have equal weight.

The measurement of food insecurity continues to evolve, in ways that provide important insights into the stresses and difficulties that caregivers experience when providing food to their families. Researchers are experimenting with more frequent surveys and shorter recall periods, asking different people in each household or asking similar questions in different ways, but Kathy Radimer's discovery provided a feasible way to quantify an aspect of human wellbeing that had previously not been measured, revealing trends and disparities like those shown in Fig. 7.16.

Data in Fig. 7.6 show how a population's responses to the food insecurity questionnaire are extremely revealing about trends and patterns of deprivation.

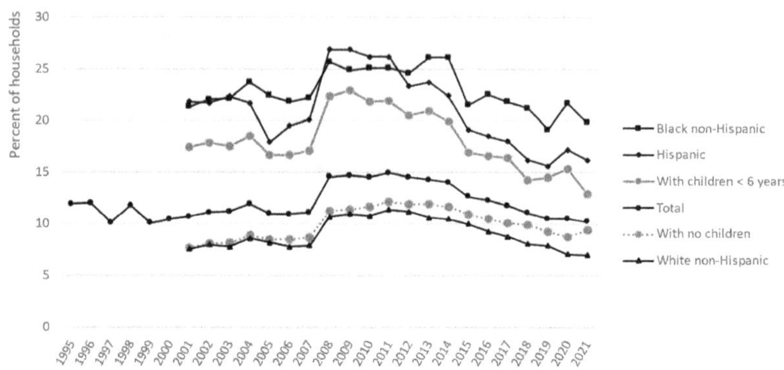

Fig. 7.16 Experience of food insecurity in the U.S., 1995–2021 *Source*: Authors' chart of data from USDA, Economic Research Service, based on the Current Population Survey supplement of Household Food Security Survey questions. Updates available at https://www.ers.usda.gov/topics/food-nutrition-assistance/food-security-in-the-u-s

Results for the U.S. begin in 1995 and changed little for more than a decade from 1995 until the sharp rise in 2008.

The sudden increase in food insecurity during 2008 reflected loss of jobs and lack of credit from banks that was in some ways like the conditions that had sparked Kathy Radimer's original research in the early 1980s. Both periods saw a sharp rise in poverty rates as shown in Fig. 7.1. We will address these spikes in poverty and unemployment when we turn the macroeconomy in Chapter 9. Downturns in activity can originate anywhere in the economy and then spread to other sectors, with the 2008 caused by a wave of housing mortgage defaults, bank failures and inability to make new loans to all kinds of businesses, leading to high unemployment and low incomes across the U.S.

Just before the unemployment and credit crisis of 2008 there had been a worldwide spike in agricultural product and food prices peaking in 2007, as shown by U.S. producer prices in Fig. 7.13 and global consumer prices in the dotted line of Fig. 7.14. Consumer prices for food relative to all other things in the U.S. peaked in December 2008 and fell back sharply to a historic low in December 2009, while the wave of unemployment kept rising and the number of unemployed Americans did not peak until 2010 and poverty rates stayed high for several years as shown in Fig. 7.1. Despite a return to low food prices, food insecurity rates remained elevated and fell only gradually after the crisis, as it took several years for households to recover and accumulate sufficient savings to reliably obtain their usual diets and report experiencing no food insecurity over the previous 12 months.

A particularly important feature of the food insecurity measure is its use to identify disparities between groups, for which the data in Fig. 7.16 begin in 2001. The levels and changes in those disparities generally follow the patterns found by other measures of poverty and deprivation, with added detail relating to the challenge of meeting regular food expenditures for households with preschool children. As shown in Fig. 7.16, food insecurity among households with children under six years of age rose above 20% for several years after the 2008 crisis and then fell sharply to below 15% just before the pandemic. The gap between households with preschoolers and households without any children fell from a difference of more than 10% to under 5% in 2018. The gap widened again in 2020 with the onset of COVID and was cut to a historically small gap in 2021 which was the year of the U.S. child tax credit shown in the previous section's Fig. 7.3.

Food Access and Affordability of Healthful Diets

The introduction of food insecurity measurement in 1995 occurred during a period of relatively low and stable U.S. food prices shown in Fig. 7.13, more than a decade before the food price spike and the high rates of food insecurity observed for several years thereafter in Fig. 7.16. From the 1990s until the late 2010s there was an increasing abundance of agricultural products globally, especially cereal grains, vegetable oil and other low-cost sources of dietary energy, and steady declines in the share of people experiencing extreme poverty worldwide as shown in Fig. 7.7.

During the period of relative food abundance from the 1990s to the late 2010s, the focus of food policy shifted from quantity to quality, with increasing evidence about how a person's usual diet influences their future health. The U.S. National Health and Nutrition Examination Survey (NHANES) and other data sources worldwide revealed increases in the prevalence of overweight and obesity as well as a growing burden of diabetes, hypertension and other diseases, all of which were closely correlated with changes in the composition of foods available and their share of food consumption. The lowest-income countries were also seeing increases in total food consumption, with increases in children's heights as well as weight throughout the life course. All countries continued to experience undernutrition in some dimensions such as iron-deficiency anemia, and those were increasingly understood in terms of dietary patterns and the types of foods consumed, affecting the balance among food groups and displacement of more healthful foods with less healthful foods when meeting daily energy needs.

The worldwide shift in attention from food quantity to diet quality that began in the mid-1990s took many forms, and coincided with improvements in data availability and research on the types of food being produced and consumed in the U.S. and globally. For food economists, an important consequence of this nutrition research has been to show the difference between foods that would be chosen if consumers wanted only to improve their future health, in contrast to foods chosen based on revealed preferences and effective demand. The gap between foods for health and foods actually chosen could be due to the fact that consumers cannot know and may be misled about the impact of each item on their future health, and even if consumers did know the true healthiness of each food, they would have many other priorities beyond health such as taste, convenience and aspirations.

New evidence on diet-health relationships since the 1990s has allowed food economists to measure access and affordability of high-quality diets, thereby indicating whether consumption of certain foods is due to being at a place and time without access to higher-quality options (measured by unavailability or high prices for more healthful foods), or unaffordability of those options (measured by diet costs relative to household income), or displacement of more healthful foods by less healthful foods (despite the affordability of more healthful options). Ability to measure food access and affordability of high-quality, supportive diets result from a set of simultaneous shifts in the U.S. and worldwide.

One shift occurred in the U.S., as nutrition researchers increasingly emphasized balance among food groups for example in the official national Dietary Guidelines for Americans (DGAs). The U.S. government first produced its DGAs in 1980, based in part on evidence from the first round of NHANES data collected in the early 1970s when the most important concerns involved deficiencies in several vitamins and minerals. Government funding for the DGAs specified a revision every five years, and by the late 1980s there had been such large increases in consumption of animal fats and vegetable oil which was strongly correlated with increased cardiovascular disease that the 1990 edition called for limiting all kinds of fats and oils.

The 1990 edition of the U.S. DGAs introduced the idea that balance among food groups could be illustrated using a 'food pyramid' with basic starchy staples at the bottom, showing the relative importance of different food categories. That visual food guide was soon found to be unhelpful as evidence emerged that rapid increase in U.S. consumption of refined flour and added sugar from the late 1980s through the 1990s was linked to high rates of diabetes and obesity. Based on new data from the 1990s, the 2000 edition of the DGAs introduced a recommended level of vegetable and fruit consumption, the 2005 edition shifted the pyramid to reduce the visibility of starchy staples, and the 2010 edition switched visual metaphors to shares of a meal with a fork, a dish and a glass of milk known as MyPlate. Each generation of American children grew up with these pyramids and then the MyPlate guidance on school walls, in pamphlets and online, and the DGAs also influenced the composition of meals at school and other government facilities.

The 1990s shift in focus to diet quality defined in terms of food groups occurred globally, not just in the U.S., as other countries introduced their own dietary guidelines in response to the growing gap between actual consumption and evidence about which foods would best improve consumers' future health. One significant step occurred in November 1996, when the United Nations brought government leaders to a World Food Summit at the FAO headquarters in Rome. The official summit declaration, signed by representatives of 186 countries, defined food security as **'when all people, at all times, have physical and economic access to sufficient, safe and nutritious food to meet**

their dietary needs and food preferences for an active and healthy life'. This phrasing had evolved from earlier government declarations, extending the goals of government intervention from simply having enough food in each country each year to year-round access to healthful diets.

The rising importance of diet quality in policy documents was accompanied by an explosion of new data about the nutritional composition of foods purchased and consumed, due in part to the U.S. Nutrition Labeling and Education Act of 1990 and similar legislation adopted elsewhere. Implementation of that law, which was based on concerns from the 1970s and 1980s about vitamins, minerals, fats and other specific nutrients, led to the nutrition facts panel on packaged foods, and USDA publication of those data for all foods consumed in the U.S. as recorded in the U.S. flagship National Health and Nutrition Examination Survey (NHANES). Other countries made similar investments in food composition data and dietary recall surveys, leading to stronger evidence about diet-disease relationships.

As incomes rose and people shifted towards more packaged and processed foods, fortification and supplementation programs came to fill gaps in requirements for individual vitamins and minerals. But packaged and processed foods are highly palatable and easy to consume, especially for people looking to save time on food preparation, so intakes of refined carbohydrates and added sugar, animal fats and vegetable oil, added salt and other ingredients often increased to harmful levels. Those excesses, driven in part by increased use of food away from home, displaced more healthful foods needed for balanced diets, especially vegetables and fruits, animal source foods like fish or eggs and dairy as well as meat, and sources of plant protein such as legumes, nuts and seeds. All these nutrient-rich food groups are more expensive than the starchy staples especially refined grains, vegetable oil and sugar, per unit of dietary energy, due to greater difficulty of production and distribution.

In high-income countries, increasing awareness of the difference between a high-quality diet and what people were consuming led to focus on access to more healthful items as a possible cause of disparities in diet quality and health. For example, in 1995, a Department of Health report from the government of Scotland described low-income urban neighborhoods as *food deserts*, referring to the relative lack of larger grocery outlets selling a variety of fruits, vegetables and other foods increasingly known to be protective against diet-related diseases. That term became widely used in the late 1990s and early 2000s, fueling an explosion of research using newly available geocoded data and mapping tools to describe the distances that households would have to travel to reach larger markets with a greater variety of healthful offerings.

Many ways of measuring food deserts and access to healthful items were tried during the 1990s and 2000s. The U.S. Congress directed USDA to conduct an official study of food deserts in 2008, leading even more research and development in the 2010s of rich geocoded data on each location's food environment, typically defined in terms of the type and number of retail outlets at each place. Those data included a pioneering U.S. National

Household Food Acquisition and Purchase Survey (FoodAPS) implemented in 2012–13 asking individuals where they had obtained each type of food they consumed, and increasing use of 'scanner' data showing the exact price and item purchased from specific transactions. Almost all scanner data are initially proprietary, used by retailers and manufacturers for internal decision-making, but in the 2010s the USDA and others increasingly purchased these data for public-sector use in policy analysis.

During the 2000s, new data about the nutritional attributes of foods allowed health scientists, initially led by Nicole Darmon in France and Adam Drewnowski in the U.S., to begin matching purchased items to their sales price. They found that foods with the lowest cost per calorie tend to have the most calories per unit of weight or volume, and the highest ratio of calories to the full set of nutrients needed for health. The ingredients providing the energy in these low-cost, calorie-dense foods tend to be the least expensive agricultural products per calorie, which are not only starchy staples, but also vegetable oil and sugar. Food processing often uses those raw ingredients in combination with other foods, transformed in ways that often remove moisture and fiber which raises calories per gram of solid foods, and adds sugar to beverages leading to high calories per liter.

The health scientists' findings of high calorie content in low-cost foods, especially highly processed and packaged food, led to the idea that 'food deserts' with few healthful options were more accurately seen as 'food swamps' where the lowest cost options meet energy needs without attributes required for health. These same patterns led to the observation by health scientists that ultraprocessed foods (items with the most processing, including added ingredients as well as removal of naturally occurring food attributes) were particularly harmful to health. That view arose not only because these items contained inexpensive refined flour, oil and sugar that delivered palatable calories without other needed nutritional attributes, but also because their other ingredients, processing and packaging as well as advertising and marketing efforts had made those products tastier and more attractive than other foods.

By the 2010s, health scientists increasingly found that highly processed foods and meals away from home were contributing to diet-related diseases by displacing foods with attributes needed for future health such as vegetables and fruits, animal source foods like fish, eggs, dairy, and meat, and sources of plant protein such as legumes, nuts and seeds. Those food groups were clearly more expensive ways of meeting daily energy needs than plain carbohydrates and vegetable oil. Health scientists also found that the nutrient dense food groups consumed by higher-income people worldwide were primarily meat and some types of fish or seafood that delivered only certain nutrients and not others. The gap between effective demand at higher incomes and foods needed for health was increasingly seen to consist of high consumption of highly processed foods, meals away from home, and meat or other foods that displace the mix of vegetables, fruits, legumes, nuts and seeds, and fish or eggs or dairy that is associated with long-term health and communicated in dietary guidelines.

To measure access and affordability of healthful diets using the toolkit of economics, from the mid-2010s a series of projects began assembling retail prices, matching items to their food composition and automating the selection of the lowest cost items that would meet health needs. Using the least expensive items for health isolates the cost of healthiness from the cost of other attributes such as taste, convenience and aspirations, distinguishing the cost and affordability of healthful diets from other drivers of food choice. This method was adopted in 2022 by the FAO and the World Bank as a new metric of food access, producing the cost data shown in Fig. 7.17.

The data shown in Fig. 7.17 contrast the cost of the least expensive items for health with national average food expenditures, per person per day, in countries at each level of national income. A first discovery is that the lowest-cost locally available foods, when added up in proportions needed for health, are not less expensive in low-income countries. To meet the daily needs of a representative adult they would cost in the range of two to four dollars per day in purchasing power parity terms. This is surprising because travelers from high- to low-income countries typically find food to be inexpensive, but those impressions come from converting currencies at market exchange rates. In terms of the local population's purchasing power, costs are similar across

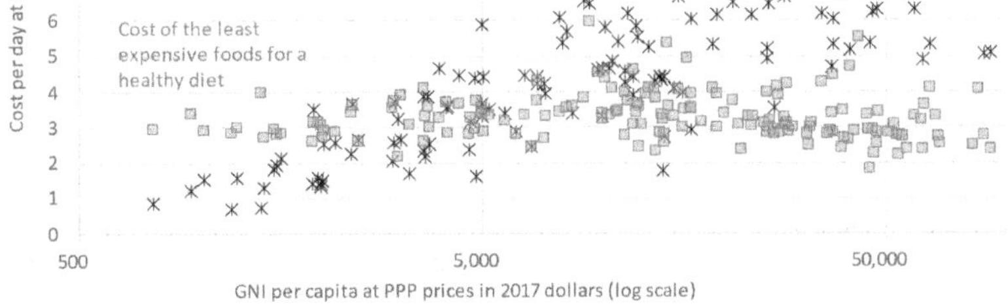

Fig. 7.17 Cost of the least expensive foods for a healthy diet and actual food spending in 2017 *Source*: Authors' chart of diet cost data from FAO, World Bank and the Food Prices for Nutrition project, using item prices reported by national statistical organizations through the International Comparison Program [ICP] downloaded from https://databank.worldbank.org/source/food-prices-for-nutrition. Food expenditures are derived from those data, and national income [GNI] is from the World Development Indicators https://databank.worldbank.org/source/world-development-indicators

countries for the same reason that grocery prices follow general inflation over time in the U.S., which is that the cost structure of retail food items includes a mix of labor and facilities, energy and other resources that is broadly aligned with costs for all goods and services.

The cost of sufficient foods for a healthful diet does not differ by income level, but actual spending per day on food does rise with income as shown in Fig. 7.17. This result follows Engel's law and Bennett's law, as people in higher-income countries have average spending on food that is more than twice the cost of the least expensive items for health because people have money to spend and choose foods for reasons other than health such as taste and aspirations, convenience and sociability. In lower-income countries, however, on average people spend about half as much as the cost of a healthful diet, because they lack the income needed to acquire sufficient quantities of more expensive food groups such as vegetables, fruits and animal source foods. These disparities between national averages reflect similar disparities within countries and drive a big gap in affordability that differs from the older measure of food insecurity as shown in Fig. 7.18.

The unaffordability data in Fig. 7.18 are designed to provide the most useful available estimate of how many people globally do not have enough available income to obtain a least-cost healthful diet in their country. For this measure, available resources are defined as just over half (52%) of each person's income, while each country's income distribution is estimated by the World Bank using the same set of household surveys from the poverty data in Figures 7.6 and 7.7. Combining those income data with diet costs shown in Fig. 7.17 reveals that over 90% of the population in the lowest-income countries but fewer than 5% of people in high-income countries cannot afford a high-quality diet. This result is partly due to fact that diet costs are not lower for low-income people, and partly due to the definition of affordability used by the FAO and the World Bank for this way of measuring food access.

The threshold of affordability for the purpose of global monitoring was defined by the FAO and the World Bank as the average fraction of total household expenditure that is spent on food in low-income countries, which happened to be 52% in 2017. This definition of affordability was proposed and retained by the FAO and the World Bank as the most useful of the available options, first because that definition sets the threshold of income needed for nonfood expenditure at the average observed in the low-income reference population that is most relevant to global food security, and second because that threshold is computed from the same data as diet costs and would be updated at the same time for monitoring change in the future.

The procedure used for calculating the unaffordability of healthy diets shown in Fig. 7.18 is closely related to the methods used for calculating poverty rates and deprivation in general but adapted to the needs of monitoring global access to sufficient quantities of the lowest cost local items in each food group. For example, the U.S. poverty line was originally computed by Mollie Orshansky in 1963–64 as three times the cost per day of the USDA's

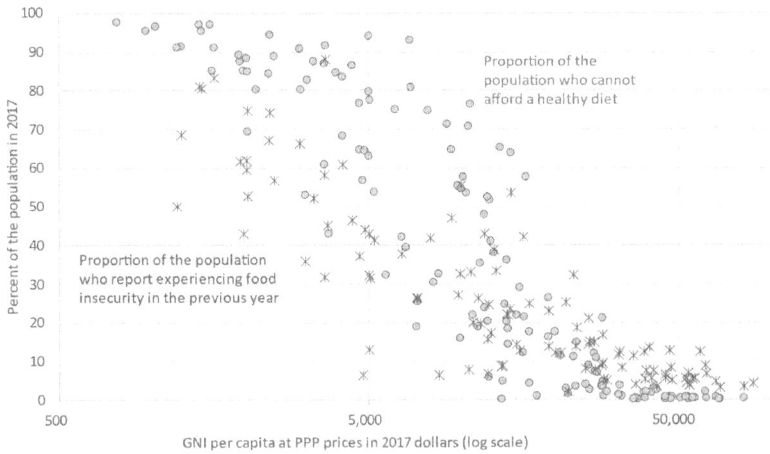

Fig. 7.18 Unaffordability of healthy diets and prevalence of food insecurity in 2017 *Source*: Authors' chart of data showing the prevalence of moderate or severe food insecurity in the previous year based on the FAO's Food Insecurity Experience Scale [FIES], and unaffordability of healthy diets from FAO, World Bank and the Food Prices for Nutrition project, using item prices reported by national statistical organizations through the International Comparison Program [ICP] and each country's income distribution estimated from household surveys by the World Bank. Unaffordability is defined as the fraction of people whose income available for food is below their country's cost of a healthy diet, based on World Bank estimates of income distribution and allowing 52% of income to be spent on food, from https://databank.worldbank.org/source/food-prices-for-nutrition. Experience of food insecurity and national income [GNI] is from https://databank.worldbank.org/source/world-development-indicators

low-cost food plan. That diet plan included a wider range of more expensive foods than the least-cost healthful diets used for global monitoring today, and the income share for food was based on the U.S. national average which was 33% in 1955, lower than the share in low-income countries which was 52% in 2017.

The FAO and the World Bank introduced the unaffordability metric for global monitoring in 2022, with locally adapted versions rolled out for use within countries at the same time. These methods capture access to foods that would just meet health needs. For use in measuring deprivation more generally, costs would be higher to reflect food preferences and time use in meal preparation, and income shares available for food would be lower to reflect nonfood needs above actual average spending in low-income countries. The primary purpose of capturing food access using affordability of least-cost items is to distinguish among three possible causes of unbalanced diets: (1) in some places, even the most affordable items in the more expensive food groups such as vegetables or fruits have unusually high prices, and could be made more accessible by reducing costs to international standards through improved production and distribution; (2) for some households at each place, available incomes could be below the cost of a healthy diet, so affordability would require higher incomes or safety nets; or (3) some populations might have access and be able to afford a healthy diet, and yet consume other foods instead for a variety of reasons such as meal preparation costs, tastes and aspirations.

The food insecurity data in Fig. 7.18 are the FAO's global counterpart to the U.S. data in Fig. 7.16, based on an eight-question FIES scale of whether the person skipped meals, ate less or differently than usual, went hungry or had other similar experiences for lack of money to buy food. In low-income countries, the fraction of people with food insecurity is much smaller than those who cannot afford a healthful diet because the FIES questions refer to a person's usual diet which is much less expensive because it contains much more starchy staples than a healthful diet. In high-income countries, many more people report being food insecure than cannot afford a healthful diet, as their usual foods are much more expensive than the very basic items included in the least-cost healthful diet.

Comparing the two kinds of data reveals how food insecurity prevalence, which refers to people having run out of money to buy their usual diets, successfully captures the financial vulnerability of people with low savings. But it does not capture nutrition security, which would require access to high-quality diet items that the world's lowest-income people cannot afford, and that higher-income people might not want to use because they are too time consuming to prepare and not sufficiently preferred for other reasons. The actual items included in these least-cost diets are foods that could be eaten and would be healthful, but they are not the most delicious or attractive meal options. Food access measurement can guide agricultural production and distribution to make low-cost options available and can guide social assistance and safety nets to ensure affordability of those options, but actual food choice depends on other aspects of deprivation as well as revealed by experiences of food insecurity and by poverty measurement discussed in this chapter.

7.2.3 *Conclusion*

The measurement methods discussed in this chapter extend the economics toolkit to deprivation over time and among people worldwide. An important aspect of these metrics is to look beyond effective demand and consumer surplus to the foods and other things that people are not buying due to lack of purchasing power, both episodically due to running out of money as in experiences of food insecurity and chronically due to high cost and low average incomes as in unaffordability of high-quality, supportive diets.

Economic analysis of deprivation reveals a close relationship between risk and poverty, and close links between risk management and poverty alleviation. One reason is that poverty itself may be transient, so that reducing risk limits the number of people who ever experience poverty. Another reason is that risk aversion in consumption and other observations imply diminishing marginal utility of additional income, as people devote their initial spending to their highest priority needs. To the extent that people know that about themselves, they can understand it to be true of others as well, leading to the social insurance and mutual aid we observe.

The measurement and analysis of poverty, risk,and the relationship between them helps explain how and why people engage in collective action to pool resources, for example using premiums paid for insurance. Pooling to manage risks and limit deprivation is done through private enterprises such as insurance companies, through the voluntary nonprofit sector such as community food pantries and mutual aid groups, and through national governments such as the USDA and international organizations such as the World Food Program (WFP).

Each population's efforts to smooth risk and protect against poverty often focus on food. One domain of intervention is in agriculture, where high variability in both production and prices makes it important to smooth risks for farmers, helping them gain resilience and achieve income growth. Market failures limit the role of private insurance in protecting farmers against risk, driving a shift towards other kinds of assistance. Another domain is for consumers, to smooth and support wellbeing by addressing how high food prices and low incomes cause deprivation. Meeting daily food requirements is a universal human need that occupies a large fraction of resources for low-income people, leading many societies to focus on ensuring that all people can always access sufficient food for an active and healthy life.

In recent decades, health scientists have identified differences between the foods that would be used if people sought only to improve their long-term health, and the foods that are actually demanded and supplied as income rise. In higher-income settings that distinction creates a difference between the use of food assistance to absorb risks and alleviate poverty generally, and the use of food assistance to reach nutrition and health goals. The following chapter addresses that difference, as for example in the question of whether assistance is provided in kind, as in the U.S. WIC program that gives people fixed quantities of specific foods, or provided using more cash-like transfers, as in the U.S. SNAP benefits that can be used to pay for all kinds of food at local grocery stores.

This chapter's exploration of the economics toolkit to address poverty and risk reveals how designing successful risk management and social assistance programs is a work in progress. People have strong motivations to overcome deprivation in our own lives and for others, but doing so requires overcoming a variety of market failures, policy failures and practical obstacles. As shown in this chapter, the risk management and social assistance toolkit has allowed sharp reductions in many kinds of extreme deprivation and disparities between groups, with very large remaining needs to be addressed in the future.

CHAPTER 8

Food and Health: Behavioral Economics and Response to Intervention

8.1 Behavioral Economics of Food Choices for Future Health

8.1.1 Motivation and Guiding Questions

Each person's food preferences and habits are formed by trial-and-error experiences, modifying traditional culinary practices under new circumstances. Given what nutrition researchers have discovered about how foods affect our own future health, can we all alter our choices to improve health outcomes? And can we all do so in a way that also helps us achieve our other goals, such as the pleasures of eating, our social aspirations and need to save time for other activities?

Some of the obstacles to food choice for future health are familiar problems faced by any ongoing behavior that affects our future wellbeing. Psychological and cognitive constraints on decision-making create well-known patterns of behavior with preference reversals, for example eating a lot of salty chips or sweet biscuits for a snack and later wishing we had chosen an apple or banana instead. These self-contractions prevent us from reaching the highest attainable level of wellbeing in the long run for our future self. This section introduces some aspects of each person's own individual psychology in decision-making, such as present bias and loss aversion, while the next section focuses on social psychology and the effect of other people on our decision-making.

Some psychological and cognitive influences on decisions can be addressed by the toolkit of *behavioral economics*. Like other fields of economics, we start with the idea that people have learned from experience and done the best they can, but then add constraints related to the difference between immediate choices for our present self and the interests of our potential future selves. For

W. A. Masters and A. B. Finaret, *Food Economics*,
Palgrave Studies in Agricultural Economics and Food Policy,
https://doi.org/10.1007/978-3-031-53840-7_8

food economics, choices are influenced not only by the psychology of decision-making, but also by biological and physiological influences on appetite and food choice, mediated by hormones and other involuntary mechanisms. This section briefly introduces a few important influences on food choice, focusing on how taking account of both psychology and physiology factors in decision-making can be considered when planning how to meet our own food needs or designing interventions to help others improve their long-term health while also meeting other objectives.

By the end of this section, you will be able to:

1. Define preference reversals and explain their consequences for how a person's wellbeing can be understood by themselves or others;
2. Define loss aversion and status-quo bias, and describe its consequences for decision-making;
3. Define discounting and present bias, and describe its consequences for decision-making;
4. Describe how individuals and decision-makers in communities and the government can take account of behavioral factors to improve wellbeing over time.

8.1.2 Analytical Tools

This section introduces some insights from research in health behavior and psychology that can be incorporated into food economics, for the purpose of improving economic analysis and interventions in the food system.

Like other aspects of economics, our purpose in this section is to help explain, predict and assess everyday experiences, which Alfred Marshall described in 1890 as 'the ordinary business of life'. We do this on the premise that each person can learn from experience and has chosen what we observe in pursuit of their wellbeing. Behavioral economics aims to take account of ordinary behavioral and psychological biases observed repeatedly in many populations, anticipating their effects to improve average outcomes in each community. Our goal is to identify patterns that can be addressed with the toolkit of economics such as taxes and regulation, in contrast to disorders that would be addressed with health services and medical intervention.

An important preface to this topic is that many readers will themselves have experienced disordered eating that can be life-threatening and calls for medical attention. Readers who have experience with any eating disorder will know that specialist care is often needed, may be available and should be sought as soon as possible. For some readers, it may be unhelpful to read this chapter of the book, because eating disorders or difficult relationships with food could potentially be worsened by discussing the psychology of food choice outside the context of specialist care. For others, it may be helpful to see how everyday influences on food choice can be understood and addressed using economic principles.

Cognition and Psychological Constraints on Decision-Making

The term *cognition* refers to mental processes by which people receive information, for example about the healthiness of foods, and translate that information into understanding, knowledge and actions. Cognition is closely linked to memory and emotions and interacts with autonomous biological factors such as hormonal responses to digestive processes and blood sugar, or involuntary responses to seeing or smelling different foods that can range from mouth-watering triggers of salivation to gag reflexes and impossibility of eating. Using cognition to guide food choice is difficult and requires anticipating many aspects of how the mind and body are likely to react in each future situation.

A *cognitive bias* is a systematic pattern that causes someone to seek out or process information in a way that does not accurately reflect conditions around us. One important pattern is *confirmation bias,* by which people seek and retain information that is consistent with our prior beliefs. Confirmation bias can sometimes be helpful, by giving us a heightened ability to find things we all care about. For example, if a farmer is scouting for insect damage in their fields, they may be well served by believing insects could be anywhere and looking only for them, even if that means not seeing other things.

A related concept is *motivated reasoning*, in which people seek logical explanations that serve our purpose. Again, this kind of cognitive bias can be useful, for example to avoid dangers, people would want to be skilled at thinking of worst-case scenarios, and to get along with other people it can be helpful to think of charitable explanations for their actions. Cognitive biases become harmful when they become excessive, leading to tunnel vision and believing only what people want to believe, and can readily influence food choice. False beliefs about nutrition and health can easily arise by coincidence, for example due to the longevity of a person or group with a specific dietary practice, and then persist for many decades due in part to confirmation bias and motivated reasoning.

An important kind of cognitive bias that can affect food choice and health behavior is *overconfidence* in one's own ability to control events. In surveys around the world, many people routinely report that they are more skilled than others at everyday tasks and understate the probability that their own mistakes could cause them harm. We can readily see how having some people with that bias could be helpful, for example as the overconfident people are willing to take risks at their own expense to do things that could potentially help others.

A different aspect of nutrition and cognition concerns *cognitive function,* and a person's ability to assimilate new information and draw conclusions of any kind. The brain itself runs on nutrients and uses more total energy in proportion to its size than other organs in the body. Our cognitive ability is lower when hungry, and many other kinds of stress may limit cognitive function. One of the most frequent sentiments that Amelia hears from patients who are working on intentional weight loss is how surprised they are when eating more frequently, such as three meals and two snacks per day, helps them lose weight. One of the reasons for this is that eating frequently provides our body's cells with the nutrients they need to function well, and it is much easier for the body to manage the use of these nutrients if they are provided frequently and regularly in a predictable manner as opposed to between episodes of voluntary dietary restriction.

Deficiencies of specific micronutrients like iodine during fetal development have well documented links to cognitive development, and entire food groups could also play a role, for example due to the diverse phytochemicals in many fruits and vegetables, and polyunsaturated fatty acids in certain nuts and seeds, oils and seafood. When the impact of individual nutrients is isolated, supplementation or fortification such as use of iodized salt can lead to improved outcomes in the long run, but in most cases the role of nutrition in cognitive function has been associated with the same overall diet quality that is tied to immune function and cardiometabolic health generally.

Beyond cognition as such, a *psychological* or *behavioral bias* is a systematic pattern that causes someone to act in a way that is not consistent with their own future preferences. The two most fundamental patterns addressed in this section are loss aversion and the resulting *status-quo bias*, and time inconsistency in discounting also known as *present bias*. Status quo bias leads people to stay with what they already have instead of an alternative, even if cognition tells us that the alternative is likely to be better. Present bias operates over time and leads us to be more concerned with the immediate future (e.g., a one-day delay from today to tomorrow) than the more distant future (a one-day delay for an event or deadline next week or next month), even if cognition tells us that the two delays would be equally valuable.

Both status quo bias and present bias are related to risk aversion in ways that are potentially useful, especially to offset limitations to one's own cognition such as confirmation bias and motivated reasoning. Status quo bias could be useful to avoid overly optimistic assessments of alternatives to what one already has, while present bias could reflect greater uncertainty about the more distant future. Both aspects of behavior relate to cognition through the challenges of risk perception, and the difficulty of assessing risks especially when small probabilities are involved. We will return to both biases after spelling out the basic challenge of using cognition and planned behavior to improve diets for health.

The evolving scientific evidence about dietary practices that would most improve long-term health for people in the U.S. is described in the scientific report of the advisory committee convened every five years to make recommendations in the Dietary Guidelines for Americans (DGAs). Similar reviews are conducted in other countries and done for a variety of specific topics. The public version of dietary guidelines then simplifies the key messages, with a larger role for political influence, but on the major aspects of food for health all these documents deliver consistent advice based on strong scientific evidence. The central question regarding behavioral biases is why people who learn about those guidelines and seek foods that would improve their future health might not act on that knowledge.

One reason for the difficulty of following dietary guidelines could be that the high-quality scientific consensus they embody is drowned out by other messages. Interest in food and nutrition leads to exaggerated media coverage of individual studies with low validity, and frequent sharing of false beliefs that appear attractive despite having been ruled out as inconsistent with the evidence. But even if people had sufficient cognitive ability to identify accurate guidance, it would still be a challenge to ensure that people's everyday decisions about what to eat meets their long-term goals.

To some degree, the interests of our future self are already embodied in our present self's autonomous impulses. Human physiology evolved and arose long before cognitive skills or language, driving even a newborn infant to eat in ways that promote their future health. One such imperative is energy balance, with autonomous signals such as GLP-1 or other hormones in the brain and body triggering efforts to maintain body mass through adequate intake to replenish energy expended through metabolism and physical activity. These mechanisms evolved in the past under different conditions and create difficult challenges for nutrition behavior today, with an important biological constraint being that weight gain can occur more readily than weight loss. Episodes of weight gain can be triggered by a wide range of causes, and the body then defends its new size. Evidence from GLP-1 agonists such as semaglutide clearly demonstrates the role of autonomous, involuntary processes regulating appetite and dietary intake, and the difficulty of achieving similar results through intention alone. Obesity can therefore be seen as a change in physiology for which interventions could focus on prevention and harm reduction, requiring intentional efforts in shaping the food environment, culture and technology to help align revealed preferences and effective demand with the needs of our future selves.

A useful way to address the alignment between our present and future selves is to consider aspects of food that we all can taste and feel soon after eating, in contrast to aspects of food whose consequences are felt much later in time. In this framework, the immediate aspects of food are its *hedonic* attributes, derived from the Greek word for pleasure. A *hedonist* is a person for whom only those immediate pleasures have any meaning. Behavioral economics enters the picture because people are not purely hedonistic, but also understand that food can serve an *instrumental* purpose leading to better or worse outcomes for us in the future, as shown in Fig. 8.1.

The classification in Fig. 8.1 shows how each kind of food or health behavior might have different hedonic values from most enjoyable to most unpleasant, and have different instrumental values for one's future self from most harmful to most beneficial. In the top-left quadrant are items that are

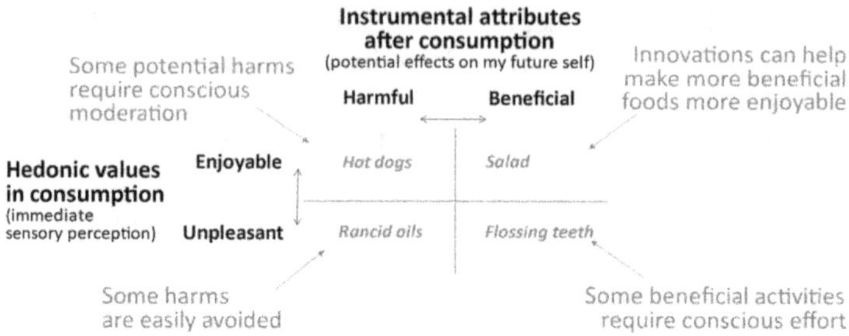

Fig. 8.1 Instrumental attributes versus hedonic values in consumption

immediately enjoyable but potentially harmful in some ways. An example is hot dogs or other cured meats and salty snacks, as well as sweets and candy, alcohol and so forth. In the top-right quadrant are items that are immediately enjoyable and beneficial in the long run, such as salad and other vegetables or fruits. The bottom row is items that have negative hedonic value. Some unpleasant things are harmful, such as rancid oil, but some things that most people consider unpleasant can be beneficial. The example given here is using dental floss for oral health, which is related to dietary intake and nutritional status.

Thinking about food and nutrition in this framework can help us identify the different kinds of actions to improve different aspects of food choice and nutrition. For items in the top-left quadrant, people need guardrails and other constraints, such as eating sweets only as dessert after an otherwise supportive meal. For the top right, people need steps that make beneficial foods even more enjoyable, such as more delicious and convenient ways of eating vegetables. The bottom left usually takes care of itself, and the greatest challenges are often in the bottom right. In some cases, a technological innovation can turn a chore into a pleasure, such as the development of better-tasting toothpaste, but the long history of dental floss suggests that some desirable things are not much fun for anyone. For those needs, each person may need to use conscious effort and slow thinking to set themselves up for success each day, creating the conditions for a daily routine that builds new habits.

Indifference Curves for More Healthful vs Less Healthful Foods

We can bring both physiology and psychology into our economic analysis of food choice using indifference curves. Each person's preferences, drawn as a set of indifference curves that trace levels of wellbeing, can shift over time due to a person's circumstances as shown in Fig. 8.2.

The sequence of indifference curves shown from left to right in Fig. 8.2 traces William's food preferences over time. His food choices in the 1970s and 1980s involved a delightful range of after-school snacks. Some were already known to be less healthful such as grape soda, while for other foods the difficult news came later like the nitrates in beef jerky and trans fat in the packaged

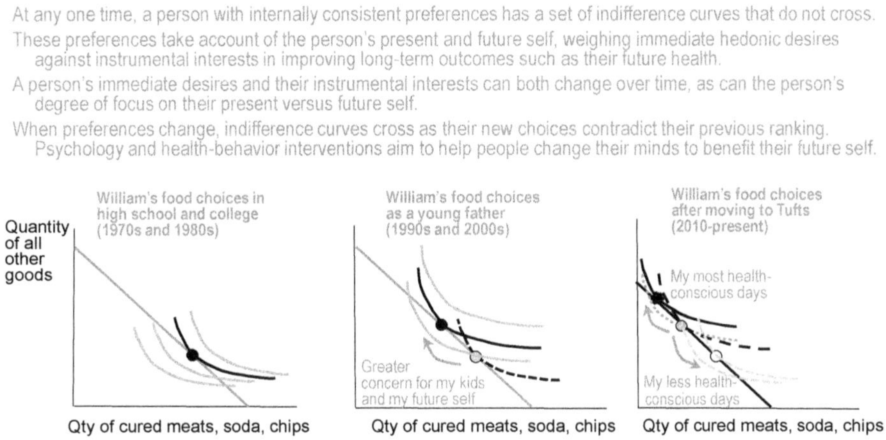

Fig. 8.2 Preferences can change, and turn towards more healthful or less healthful items

pastry that William would buy from vending machines. Most of these treats were guilty pleasures kept out of his parents' sight, and they disappeared from William's diet once his own children were born in the 1990s. Then after 2010, when William moved to teach in the School of Nutrition at Tufts, his diet shifted even further towards the dietary guidelines that his colleagues had helped write. Some of the shift involves greater awareness about epidemiological evidence, but much is due to peer pressure and daily reinforcement. Even in that new environment, however, preferences can shift and contradict themselves, with occasional eating days that feel just like high school.

An important insight from William's own history is that having children changed his preferences in the 1990s, making him more concerned about his own future health. At any one point in time, each person's own long-term wellbeing may be more influential or less influential on their decision-making. One way to understand this problem is to draw the different long-term preferences that a person might have instead of their actual choices, as illustrated in Fig. 8.3.

The two panels in Fig. 8.3 show choices for less healthful foods on the left, and more healthful foods on the right. In each case the person's revealed preferences and actual choice are shown in a solid dark curve and observed point. Each person typically knows more than any observer about what they need, so economists typically use the preferences revealed by actual choices to infer their wellbeing. For food choice, however, researchers have discovered effects on a person's long-term wellbeing that differ systematically from revealed preferences and observed choices. For a person's long-term health, they would consume less of the foods with less healthful attributes on the left panel, and more foods with more health-promoting attributes on the right panel.

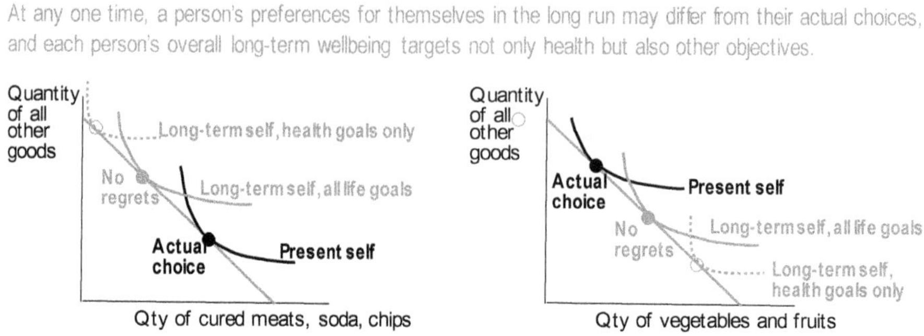

Fig. 8.3 Differences between long-term goals and actual behavior

The analytical diagrams in Fig. 8.3 can be called a dual-self model of decision-making, comparing each person's present self at each moment in time to their own future self some years later. In fact, each person may have multiple future selves, each consistent with different long-term goals. The dotted gray curve shows a hypothetical set of preferences that targets only health, but that is unlikely to be a real set of preferences because people also want to enjoy life and pursue a variety of other goals in addition to health. The solid gray curve shows preferences consistent with overall long-term wellbeing, with a gray dot at the point of consumption where they have no regrets and would not change their past choices.

Many foods are neutral for health so there is little or no difference between the black and gray curves, but some foods have large gaps between what people consume and what they would prefer if they took their own long-term needs into account. Actual choices are always made by the present self so the gray dot cannot be observed directly, but Section 6.2 of this book introduced how choice experiments can be used to elicit preferences between hypothetical situations. For cost-effectiveness analysis of health interventions, choice experiments involving a series of disease scenarios are used to obtain weights on different conditions when counting quality-adjusted life years (QALYs), and similar rankings are elicited from external assessments of severity for disability-adjusted life years (DALYs). Similar methods could potentially be used to elicit a person's long-term preferences regarding the long-term health consequences of different food choices, but behavioral biases can make it difficult for people to achieve those objectives.

Predictability, Preference Reversals and Behavioral Biases

The toolkit of behavioral economics concerns systematic inconsistencies in the preferences revealed by observed choices. These inconsistences would be illustrated by indifference curves that cross each other, such as the variation in William's preferences for less healthful versus more healthful foods shown in Fig. 8.2. Often that variation is simply random, as in the panel on the right of that figure. Other variation is systematically associated with age or other demographic characteristics, as in the way that William's preferences changed when he had children as shown on the left of that figure. Preference reversals can also be illustrated by any set of at least three choices, for example between a piece of fruit, a glass of fruit juice or a fruit-flavored soda. Given all three options, when William was a child, he often drank juice, then as a teenager he drank a lot of fruit soda, and as an adult he almost always eats whole fruit at home but sometimes gets soda as a treat when traveling.

The preference reversals addressed in behavioral economics are not the systematic changes associated with demographic characteristics, or random and unpredictable changes, but only the preference reversals that are stable and similar enough among diverse people to be characteristic of entire populations. Populations will differ in the extent to which they experience these preference reversals, and many different variants have been identified regarding preference reversals in specific situations. These situation-specific preference reversals are often discussed in terms of a particular aspect of the circumstances in which people make each decision, generally known as framing effects or *choice architecture*. Then within each context, the two most common types of systematic reversals are loss aversion and *status-quo bias*, or myopic discounting and *present bias*.

Staying with the example of choosing between a piece of fruit, fruit juice and fruit-flavored soda, the impact of framing effects would be that a shop or vending machine pictures of smiling people might lead William to choose fruit, a picture of happy athletes drinking soda after exercise might lead him to choose soda, and pictures of a tropical beach holiday might lead him to choose juice. Status quo bias would be that after William has been drinking juice for a while he is unwilling to switch to whole fruit and vice versa. Present bias would be if William knows that switching to whole fruit would be more health promoting for him, but prefers to switch tomorrow instead of today, and similarly again on future days he prefers to switch tomorrow and might not actually do it for a long time. In all these cases there is a preference reversal that could lead him to regret his past choices, making it difficult to achieve long-term goals. Each specific effect is discussed below in turn.

Framing, Labeling and Choice Architecture

The circumstances under which a choice is made often influence people's preferences in systematic ways. For example, grocery stores typically put candy and other treats near the checkout lanes, in part to increase the likelihood that customers who would not otherwise buy those items will add them to their basket after meeting their planned food needs. That is an example of choice architecture, meaning that someone (in this case the store manager) has deliberately structured the customer's options in a way that is designed to influence their choice. Other circumstances that can influence choices include how products are labeled and the framing around them using words or visual prompts.

When stores put candy by the checkout, many of the resulting sales are due to convenience rather than preference reversals. For example, some people may want to buy candy when planned purchases turn out to have been available at low prices, so it is convenient to make that choice at the end. Other shoppers might regularly plan to buy candy even before entering the store but prefer to pick it up at the end so they can eat it on their way home. Sales involve preference reversals when customers make impulse purchases that are later regretted, or the sales involve children who demand the candy only when they see it and parents have no other way to exit the store.

If candy near the checkout causes purchases that customers later regret, we can expect that those customers would prefer to shop at a store where candy is available only on a regular shelf inside the store, perhaps on a high shelf so children are not prompted to ask for it. Such a store might attract mindful shoppers who are aware of their vulnerability, but it would consistently have lower profits than a store that exploited the opportunity to prompt impulse sales and child-driven sales by placing candy at the checkout. For that reason, the policy remedy to limit consumers' regret is government regulation or other initiatives that help consumers buy only the things that they want.

Governments routinely regulate choice architecture for many products, allowing them to be sold but only in certain ways. The example of candy at the grocery checkout is a convenient example because it is widely observed and easily understood, but the stakes are relatively low. Impulse sales of candy are not seen as a major cause of diet-related disease, and while this aspect of store layouts is challenging for many parents it is rarely among their greatest concerns. The most important longstanding regulation of choice architecture concerns when, how and where stores can sell alcohol, tobacco and other products with large negative externalities. For food sales, the main regulations involve what can be sold in or around schools, and only recently have government policies and other interventions come to address choice architecture for everyday nutrition of adults.

Interventions in choice architecture to nudge people towards buying more healthful food sometimes concern the sequence of decisions, for example using voluntary efforts to help people plan ahead of time and buy only what they actually want. Many people still use simple shopping lists to plan their purchases, but others adopt even more structured approaches such as meal planning and food logging to track what is eaten, increase awareness and avoid purchases that they would later regret. Amelia works on this by making grocery lists, eating a satisfying meal before doing grocery shopping and taking basically the same pathway through the grocery store every visit, but she finds these behaviors are often difficult to implement depending on the week. Advance planning can sometimes be encouraged within interventions, for example when nutrition assistance uses electronic benefit transfers that can be redeemed through online purchases in a phone app or website that encourages or requires making shopping lists in advance.

Regulations of the public food environment to improve food choice have long focused on information provision, such as the nutrition facts panel on the side or back of packaged foods, or calorie counts to indicate portion sizes on restaurant menus. In recent years, regulation of packaged and restaurant food marketing has generally shifted from that kind of numerical information to warning labels and other visual indicators, as well as updates to longstanding regulation of what words can be used to describe the contents of packaged foods, with quality standards for what can be sold under each product name.

Interventions in packaged food labeling include front-of-pack and front-of-shelf symbols such as the black stop signs required by law for potentially harmful foods in Latin America, or the traffic light symbols used in Europe and elsewhere. Traffic light symbols use the visual metaphor of red for foods to stop or limit, orange for foods to consume cautiously and green for foods to consume more often. Grocery retailers may also introduce their own ratings to position themselves as a customer-friendly enterprise, for example using a system of three to five stars to signal increasing levels of healthfulness.

Rules about the marketing of packaged food have addressed the words used in marketing for centuries. The oldest laws focused on basic foods, such as Britain's Assize of Bread to regulate its content, weight and prices introduced by King John in 1202, and Germany's beer purity laws introduced in 1516. Modern regulations about ingredients were introduced for all U.S. packaged foods in 1906 and has been repeatedly extended to cover a wider range of potentially misleading claims. For example, in 2022 the U.S. regulators proposed an update to what foods can be sold with the term 'healthy' on their labels, based on more recent evidence than the criteria used when the rule was first introduced in 1994.

The adoption of both mandatory rules and voluntary approaches to signaling the healthiness of foods relies on translating nutritional information into a discrete yes/no classification, a three- or five-point scale, or similar food ratings, as well as improved clarity about words like 'healthy'. Economists can expect that changes in dietary patterns, along with new evidence about how each food affects consumers' future health, will continue to drive demand for policies and programs that alter food marketing and choice architecture. Those efforts aim to help consumers get what they want and intend to buy. Limiting the degree of false advertising, deceptive claims and exploitative marketing can help reduce the frequency with which consumers regret their choices, but even when people know everything about their options economists have found at least two systematic sources of preference reversals: status quo bias and present bias, explained in turn below.

Loss Aversion and Status-quo Bias

One of the most consistent patterns of preference reversal for people everywhere is the asymmetry in valuation between things we already have and alternatives we might have instead. The psychologist Daniel Kahneman was awarded the economics Nobel Prize in 2002 for his work on this kind of behavioral bias, which was called ***prospect theory*** because it refers to the systematic undervaluation of prospective gains relative to the known losses of something a person already has. The central finding of prospect theory is known as ***loss aversion*** in settings where the choice is framed as loss versus gain, and known as ***status quo bias*** in settings where the choice is framed as what is versus what could be.

Status quo bias could be an important cause of inertia in food choice and the persistence of dietary habits and has a major effect on consumers' willingness to pay for familiar versus new products. Some people are curious and interested in experimenting, but on average people have a persistent preference for things they already have (their 'endowments') instead of the prospect of something else as shown in Fig. 8.4.

The diagram in Fig. 8.4 is designed to illustrate how information about alternatives things can influence a person's status quo bias. The vertical axis shows the price that would be paid for two equivalent items, for example a restaurant for pizza or other things shown by icons on the right side of the diagram.

Along the horizontal axis is the person's factual knowledge that the pizza they know is actually the same as the alternative pizza, ranging from complete uncertainty about their equivalence to near certainty that they are equally valuable at the right extreme of the horizontal axis. The two curves trace prices they are willing to pay to acquire the thing, or to accept in exchange for the thing they already have.

The solid curve traces a typical person's willingness to pay (WTP) for the thing, rising in factual knowledge about how good it is. In the case of a

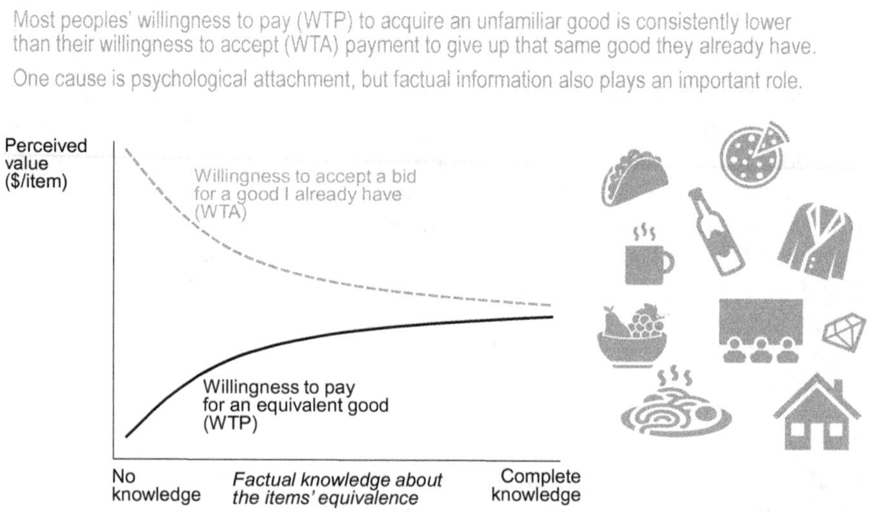

Fig. 8.4 Endowment effect and status-quo bias: it is hard to give up what we know

restaurant meal, a person's willingness to visit a new place might depend on whether that restaurant appears crowded or has been favorably reviewed by other people. Then after visiting the place oneself, its value depends on how reliably successful that restaurant has been in meeting the person's needs.

The dashed curve traces a person's willingness to accept (WTA) an alternative version of the thing, in place of the one they already have. For example, if a person lives in an environment with a certain mix of amenities including its existing pizza restaurants, the dashed line shows the compensation they would need to accept a change in that environment or a move elsewhere. A high WTA means a lot of compensation would be needed.

As knowledge increases about the actual equivalence between what a person already has and the alternative they would have instead, we can imagine how the gap between WTP and WTA shrinks. In other words, efforts at quality assurance or certification and guarantees can help people be more willing to make a switch. People are attached to the things they already have, but one reason for that is that they do not have personal experience with the alternative. Free or discounted trial periods and money-back guarantees are widely used in private-sector marketing, and other kinds of quality assurance to build trust are often needed to help people gain the confidence to try new things.

The gap between WTP and WTA is a form of asymmetric information between potential buyers and sellers, introduced in Section 7.2 to help explain why insurance is available for only certain kinds of risk. As shown there, insurance provision is sustainable only when sellers can overcome both adverse selection from hidden information (whereby only the highest-risk customers would buy insurance) and also moral hazard from hidden actions (whereby people who buy insurance then engage in riskier behavior). For physical products like food, asymmetric information limits transactions in ways known as the *market for lemons,* after a study by George Akerlof published in 1970. His lemons were not fruit, but the name given to automobiles whose manufacturing defects were discovered by the car's owner only after purchase. Akerlof showed how used cars could not be sold for prices above the low value of those lemons unless the sellers could somehow prove that their car is of higher quality than the worst lemon. A similar problem arises for food products and restaurant meals, where high-quality products can be sold at a sufficient premium to cover their cost of supply only if they are able to credibly signal their actual quality.

Later studies explored the various ways that sellers can provide signals that their product is of high quality, including setting a high price accompanied by visible commitments to brand reputation such as advertising, costly packaging and expensive retail environments. Potential buyers who observe that other people are repeat customers might then trust that the product is indeed worth its high price. The high cost for any seller to signal their own quality leads to demand for trusted intermediaries who set standards and do product testing for quality assurance, either privately for a fee or in the public sector. The importance of these quality signals for all kinds of markets led to the Nobel

Prize in economics being awarded to George Akerlof, Michael Spence and Joseph Stiglitz in 2001. Subsequent studies building on their work have shown how interventions can facilitate transactions that would otherwise not occur, overcoming status-quo bias through lower cost ways to trust that products we have not yet tried are in fact of high quality.

Myopic Discounting and Present Bias

Everyone has some degree of time preference, preferring that good things occur sooner and that costs are paid farther out in the future. Each person's choices between things now and things later reveal a *discount rate,* which is the percentage reduction in willingness to pay for a given delay. The role of discounting was introduced in Section 6.2 for the purpose of cost-effectiveness analysis from a public-sector perspective, and it also matters for individual choices.

For example, a typical discount rate for consumption might be 5% per year, implying that the person would require 105 units of something after one year in exchange for 100 of that thing now. Higher discount rates imply greater impatience, and a willingness to accept that requires more compensation in the future for giving up something today. Lower discount rates imply less time preference, and a discount rate of zero would apply to those rare choices in which a person might be indifferent between now and later.

Discount rates are positive in part because productive activities usually offer a positive return to savings and investment. Each individual and every community has some opportunities to put resources into production and earn some return on that activity. Positive returns to investment need not be financial. For example, a farmer might be able to set aside 100 units of grain as animal feed on their own farm, and thereby obtain products worth 105 units of grain after one year. The available investments are the person's demand for savings, and their supply of savings is their willingness to give up consumption today for more in the future, leading to the discount rate we observe.

People may apply different discount rates to different decisions, for example due to differences in uncertainty about how much they will value each thing in the future. If a person is less certain about their valuation of something in the future, they will need larger average returns to offset our risk aversion. Different people will also differ in their discount rates, and that can be an important cause of differences in health behavior. A person who is more patient, with a lower discount rate, is more willing to give up something today in exchange for greater health and longevity in the future.

Differences in discount rates are an important factor in behavior. In some cases, higher discount rates for some people or some decisions are a kind of market failure that could be remedied by improved markets for savings and investments, or other measures to address risk and risk perception. For people whose high discount rates are due to lack of confidence that their sacrifices will be worthwhile, coaching and other ways to help people become more willing to invest in their future self can be a big step towards higher wellbeing over time.

The problem of myopic discounting and present bias is not simply that people are impatient and have high discount rates, it is that the percentage discount rate is larger for delays that occur sooner. In extreme cases, a person may be very high discount rates for goods now versus later, but not much difference between different degrees of delay. Those preferences are *time inconsistent*, because when the future comes it will be the present. For unpleasant things that would pay off later, a person might postpone it from now until tomorrow, and then do that repeatedly over time such that the thing is never done. Myopic discounting like this is called 'present bias' because the person lives in an eternal present, always regretting what they did yesterday.

The usual remedy for present bias is a *commitment device*, whereby people realize that they have present bias and commit to doing specific plans or programs in the future. Some commitment devices involve an individual's own actions for themselves, for example when people buy exercise equipment that they put in the living room as a way of making actual use of it more likely in the future. Both authors of this book tried that, and it worked pretty well. A more popular type of commitment device that works even better is mutual accountability in groups, where people commit to telling each other whether they accomplished their goals, thereby serving as a kind of future self for each other. The ultimate such commitment device is government laws, in which people vote to commit the whole group to some course of action.

Myopic discounting could take many mathematical forms. An extreme case of present bias would involve an infinitely high discount rate from today to tomorrow, and no further discounting thereafter. More commonly, myopia is modeled as *hyperbolic discounting*. This functional form has a discount rate that declines continuously with distance from now, as illustrated in Fig. 8.5.

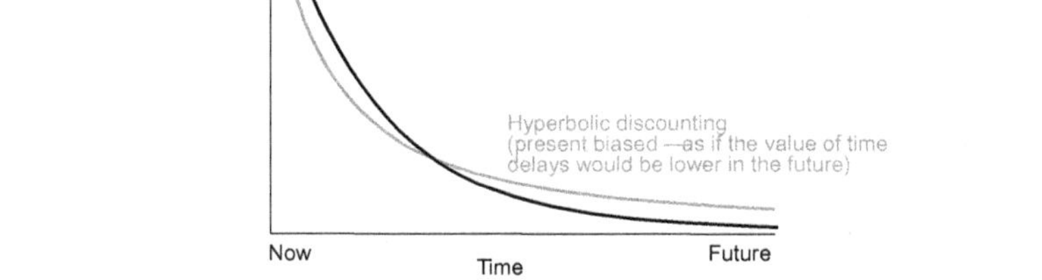

Fig. 8.5 Exponential and hyperbolic discounting

Along the vertical axis of Fig. 8.5 is the value of something received today, for example 100 units of something. Along the horizontal axis is the distance in time from now that this value might be received. The solid line is a time-consistent discount rate, for example 5% per year, such that after each year the next year's value is 5% lower. In contrast, the gray line is hyperbolic in functional form, discounting delays from now to next year by more than the discount from next year to the following year. Such preferences are *time inconsistent,* setting up the person's future self to regret their past decisions and again seek some kind of commitment device.

Social Preferences: Altruism and Behavior in Groups

Each individual's preferences are influenced not only by their own circumstances, but also by what they see or are told about the lives of other people. That aspect of decision-making is known as *social preferences*. The most fundamental of all social preferences is *altruism*, defined as concern for the wellbeing of others. Almost all people are observed to have a significant degree of altruism in their preferences, as elicited in a variety of experimental settings as well as analysis of observed behavior such as time, money and other resources donated or spent caring for others. Altruistic impulses differ among aspects of wellbeing, and some of humanity's most altruistic impulses include wanting others to have adequate access to food for health.

Altruistic behavior is influenced by many factors, starting with beliefs about whether each act of generosity will actually help the recipients. Ensuring access to sufficient food is an attractive way to help others in part because everyone needs to eat, and we are often able to observe whether food is needed and how aid related to food is being used. An important limit on altruism, however, is beliefs about how giving might affect the behavior of recipients, including concern that giving aid will lead to dependency. Some forms of assistance can be harmful, so an important role for economics has been to measure how people respond to aid in the short and long run.

Donor behavior is influenced not only by beliefs about how aid affects recipients, but also by its costs and benefits for the donor. Food is sometimes used as a vehicle for assistance when donors have more of it than they want, and even those who give food regularly will vary the amount based on its scarcity. Beyond the aid itself, an important aspect of social preferences related to altruism is *signaling*. Any visible action conveys information to other people, and providing assistance can be a valuable signal of friendly intent and mutual respect. In some cases, the signal is used to mask other actions, as when a person or organization accused of doing harmful things attempts to deflect the accusation through conspicuous acts of generosity. In other cases, the signal is a genuine effort at social coordination, as when people try to strengthen a community by sharing food. Recognizing that actions have mixed motives can help improved outcomes, first to avoid being misled by signaling, but also to help increase the extent to which charitable food assistance meets the real needs of recipients as well as donors.

Living in groups affects behavior and shape food systems in various ways beyond altruism. A first kind of effect is due to people taking cues from each other about how best to produce and consume food. The result can be a valuable *wisdom of crowds*, as when farmers share their experiences, so each imitates best practices, or a dysfunctional *madness of crowds*, as when people respond to news by hoarding food which itself creates scarcity. The economics of group behavior is introduced in Section 6.1 on social choice, but many other important patterns discovered in social psychology and sociology can be useful in food economics. These patterns include preferences for reciprocity and equity, often following moral principles to uphold rules of behavior that are valued in themselves, beyond the consequences of any one choice. This kind of group behavior often has deep roots identified by anthropologists regarding specific communities, providing the context-specific knowledge of local conditions needed for appropriate use of economic models.

8.1.3 Conclusion

People cannot see, taste or smell the degree to which a food is needed for our future health, so we all rely on past, personal trial and error and recent scientific research to provide guidance on what dietary patterns would best meet our long-term goals. Understanding what each of us should do is limited by a variety of cognitive limitations, including confirmation bias and motivated reasoning as well as overconfidence in our own abilities, all of which make it difficult to learn and retain accurate information about how each kind of food affects our future health.

Even those of us who know all about the latest scientific consensus on food and health may find it difficult to act on that knowledge, due to a variety of behavioral biases. Loss aversion leads many people to have a strong preference for the status quo over any changes, and myopic discounting leads us to be present-biased and unable to act in our own long-term interests. Behavioral economics shows how framing, labeling and choice architecture can be used to nudge our choices towards or away from those future interests and influence the degree to which people experience regret and achieve the population's full potential. All these factors help shape existing food systems and create opportunities for interventions to improve outcomes over time.

8.2 Interventions for Behavior Change

8.2.1 Motivation and Guiding Questions

The previous section introduced some of the many systematic factors driving food choice relating to a person's future health, based not only on direct costs and benefits for each individual, but also on a richer understanding of human decision-making informing the field of behavioral economics. Can interventions act on that understanding to help people reach a higher level of wellbeing? What are the effects of existing policies and programs, and could they be modified to improve food choice and diet quality?

This section includes discussion of policies that alter food prices, such as trade restrictions and taxes or subsidies on production and sales. Those are important determinants of behavior for society because they affect the entire market as discussed in Chapter 6. The focus in this section is on interventions serving specific groups, often based on their risk of food insecurity or diet-related diseases to address the disparities discussed in Chapter 7. Our focus is specifically on economic interventions that provide material benefits to the recipients, including monetary assistance as well as in-kind transfers of food or credits that can be redeemed for food in local markets.

Beyond economic interventions that alter prices or provide transfers, behavior-change interventions include a range of efforts at education and communication, from mass media and advertising to school and community-based programs, meal planning and self-monitoring with mobile phone apps and connected devices, group discussions and individual counseling. Government programs in health communication typically focus on promoting adherence to national dietary guidelines, while private initiatives often advocate for other goals. Total spending on all nutrition education is a small fraction of the advertising and marketing efforts of food companies themselves but can be effective when the information or advice is actionable and meets the user's needs.

By the end of this section, students will be able to:

1. Use indifference curve and budget lines to explain and predict how people might respond to nutrition assistance and other programs;
2. Explain how policies that aim to alter price or preferences differ from programs that transfer material assistance using cash, vouchers or in-kind aid;
3. Explain how the recipient's use of their own resources to obtain additional quantities of something affects how cash assistance differs from in-kind aid or vouchers for it; and
4. Explain how the impact of restricting use of a voucher for something depends on whether recipients also spend some of their own resources to obtain it in additional quantities.

8.2.2 Analytical Tools

The economics toolkit is built on predicting choices and assessing outcomes using a set of models like those drawn in Chapters 2–6. Analysts use formative research and prior knowledge to choose a model specification suited to the situation, then test the model's predictions and quantify its parameters to the extent that data are available. Some testing and parameter estimation can be done with choice experiments that reveal individual willingness to pay and marginal rates of substitution, while a whole population's preferences can sometimes be estimated statistically using a system of equations to obtain price and income elasticities of demand.

The analytical diagrams that help us explain and predict individual choice are particularly useful to analyze potential interventions, showing the three basic mechanisms through which a policy or program could alter diet quality, as shown in Fig. 8.6.

As in our other analytical diagrams for individual choice, Fig. 8.6 places the thing of interest along the horizontal axis, in this case more healthful food, and other things on the vertical axis. The first panel shows a transfer of the healthful food itself, through an in-kind gift or voucher. In this scenario the transfer cannot be used for other things, so the diagonal expenditure line shifts only to the tight. The horizontal segment at the top of the new expenditure line indicates that the transfer cannot be used for other goods and services.

The second panel of Fig. 8.6 shows an intervention that makes the healthful food easier to obtain, due to a lower market price for each unit or easier access and use of the thing once it is acquired. That can help people consume more of the healthful food by rotating the budget line outwards. This type of intervention does not increase the purchasing power for all other goods but might result in an increased consumption of other goods too besides healthful food as we saw in Chapter 2 on consumer behavior.

Finally, the third panel of Fig. 8.6 shows how behavior-change programs as well as advertising, education, and prevailing cultural narratives about food can change consumer behavior by shifting the indifference curves themselves. In practice, programs that provide vouchers or change price are often accompanied by messaging campaigns, thereby changing both purchasing power and preferences at the same time, but using these diagrams allows us to distinguish

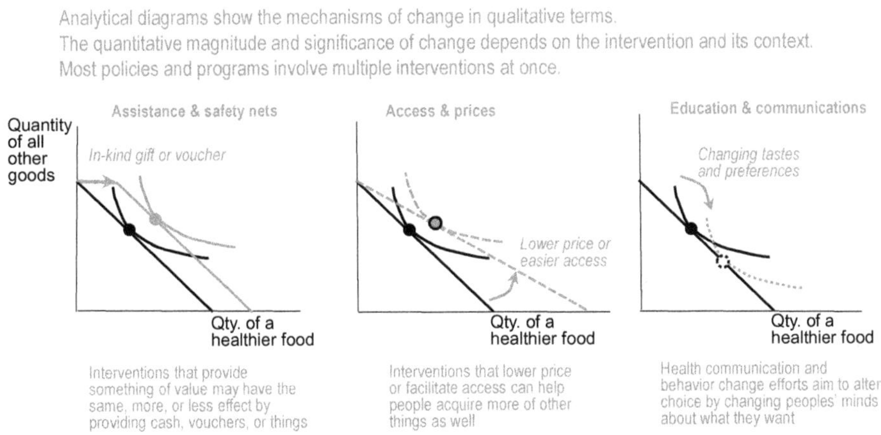

Fig. 8.6 Interventions can alter food choice towards more healthful items

between these mechanisms using different kinds of shifts and movements along indifference curves and expenditure lines.

Figure 8.6 shows three separate interventions, but actual policies and programs often combine multiple forms of intervention as discussed in Chapter 6. Many programs that provide transfers or alter prices to improve health also provide some behavior-change communication, and empirical studies often find that each is more effective when combined with the other. Combining vouchers and price changes with information is routinely done in the private sector when retailers or manufacturers provide coupons or discounts along with their advertising. The transfer or discount attracts the beneficiary's attention and helps them act on the information provided, while the health communication or marketing content provides a narrative that makes the desired behavior meaningful and attractive.

Impacts of Vouchers and In-kind Transfers

Programs that aim to help particular groups may transfer physical items, such as nutrition assistance through a food pantry or a school meal program, or they may use coupons or vouchers and electronic transfers to help people buy those items from market vendors. Vouchers can be pieces of paper, or electronic benefit transfers such as the debit cards used in the SNAP program today, or the mobile phone accounts used to transfer money in many low-income countries.

The way that transferring a particular thing affects peoples' use of it is illustrated in Fig. 8.7. The first panel of this figure shows the same scenario as the previous figure, but the second panel shows what might happen if the transfer were larger: at some point, sufficiently large transfers will provide all of what the recipient would want to consume of that item. And as shown in the third panel, in that situation the recipient might be able to reach an even higher level of indifference by trading away the transferred item for other things, as shown in Fig. 8.7.

The left-hand panel of Fig. 8.7 shows the usual situation for a program like SNAP in the U.S., which as the name implies is designed to be supplemental for most recipients. SNAP beneficiaries are given a debit card that is recharged monthly with their benefit allotment, for the purpose of buying eligible foods and beverages at any licensed grocery outlet. At each store visit the recipient might use the SNAP card to redeem their benefits or use their own cash to buy other groceries. When recipients of the transfer also use some of their own cash on the transferred items, economics jargon describes the transfer as *infra-marginal*, meaning that the transfer is less than the last or 'marginal' unit that the recipient decides to consume in that period, based on their income, preferences and the prices they face.

The middle panel of Fig. 8.7 shows the usual situation for a program like WIC in the U.S., which is designed for most recipients to provide the entire allotment of the transferred items that they should consume each month. A program of this type is designed to be *extra-marginal,* meaning that it

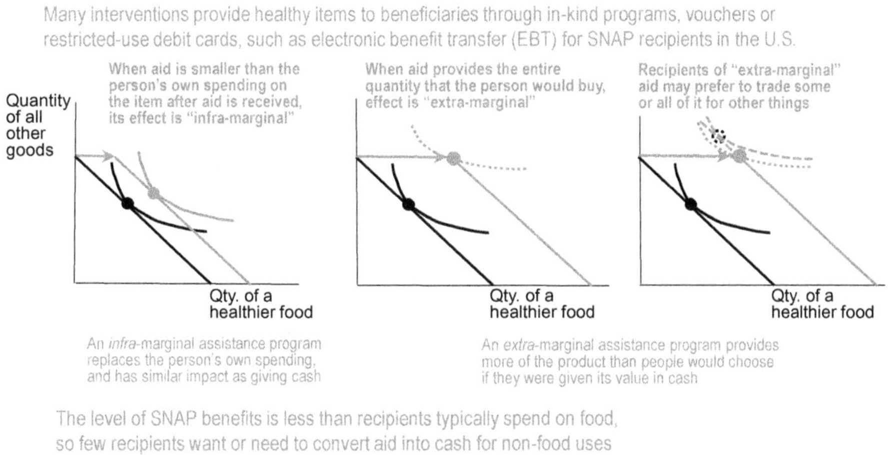

Fig. 8.7 Effect of a transfer depends on peoples' preferences

provides more of the product than people might choose if they were given its value in cash. Because the program provides more of those items than they would choose for themselves, recipients who had as much additional cash as the value of the transfer would consume more other things and less of the transferred item than intended by the program.

The difference between infra-marginal and extra-marginal transfers is readily observable based on how recipients use their own money once enrolled in the program. If they buy additional quantities of what is transferred, then even an in-kind transfer is like cash because its effect is to expand the total quantity of all things that the beneficiary can acquire. Consumption of the transferred good may not increase as much as the transfer, because it leads to a higher total income and expenditure and may lead to increased consumption of other things as well as what is transferred. Only in the case of extra-marginal programs will the quantity transferred determine what is consumed.

For many assistance programs, a central concern is whether recipients will attempt to trade away what is transferred or use it for other purposes. Figure 8.7 reveals that recipients have an incentive to do so only when the transfer is extra-marginal for them. In the WIC case, converting the transferred items into other things has so little value that very few beneficiaries even bother to try, but there are situations where a voucher or in-kind transfer so far exceeds the beneficiary's marginal choice that they would prefer cash instead. On the other hand, as shown in the left panel of Fig. 8.7, most SNAP recipients have no incentive at all to use their benefits for ineligible goods, since they want and need the groceries on which they already spend some of their own cash, so it is in their own interest to use the program as intended.

Impacts of Limiting Redemption Options

Restricting benefit redemption to discourage use of less healthful items is another widely debated aspect of nutrition programs. In the U.S., for example, SNAP benefits can be redeemed for any food and beverage item in a typical grocery store. The only prohibitions are against alcohol, dietary supplements, and hot or prepared foods for immediate consumption, although waivers to allow hot or prepared food purchases were granted to help people cope during the COVID pandemic. Public health advocates have often argued that less healthful items should be restricted as well, starting with sugar-sweetened beverages.

The effects of limiting which foods can be obtained with nutrition assistance can be shown in our food-choice diagrams by placing that food along the horizontal axis as shown in Fig. 8.8.

In Fig. 8.8, the vertical axis shows all other things on which program benefits can be spent, and the horizontal axis shows the items that might be prohibited such as sugar-sweetened beverages. As before, the black lines show a recipient's situation if they had only their own money to spend, and the gray lines show their situation with the program in place. The left side panel shows recipients with two different kinds of response to the program: the solid line indifference curve is an example of a recipient whose purchases of the less healthful items might rise a little, while the dashed indifference curves show a recipient whose purchases of it would rise a lot.

The central and right-side panels show the consequences of restricting redemption for each kind of person. Since the benefit can no longer be used to increase expenditure along the horizontal axis, the expenditure line cannot continue to the right of the person's own available funds, cutting off the gray expenditure line with a vertical segment. This is exactly analogous to

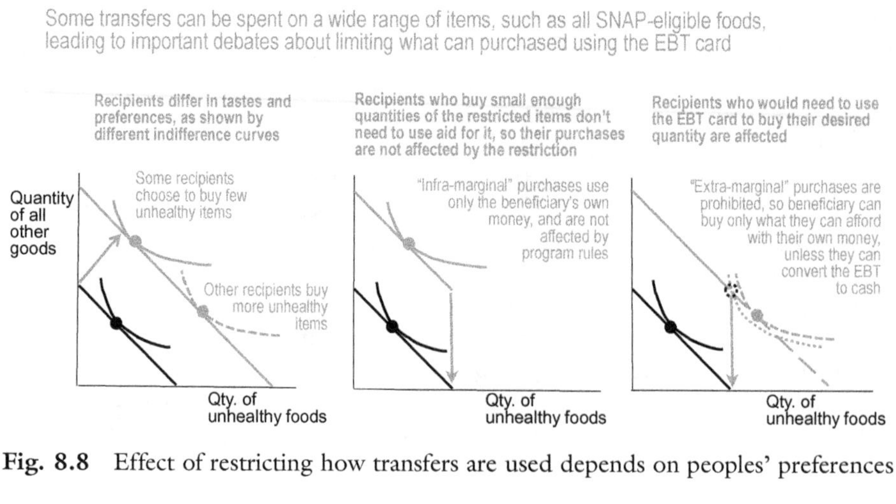

Fig. 8.8 Effect of restricting how transfers are used depends on peoples' preferences

the horizontal segment of the gray expenditure line shown in the previous Fig. 8.8.

The central panel shows a person who consumes sufficiently little of restricted item, with or without the restriction, that they can afford their desired quantity with only their own money. As shown in the diagram, restricting their use of the EBT has no effect on affordability. For them, the only impact of the restriction is that they must remember to use their own money for the restricted item and use the benefits for other things instead.

The panel on the right shows someone who wants to consume an 'extra-marginal' quantity of the restricted item. Once the restriction is imposed, they can consume only as much as they can afford using their own cash. And as before, they may be able to reach a higher indifference level by converting some of their benefits into cash to buy more of the prohibited item, whereas previously they had no incentive to do so.

The analysis of transfer programs in Figs. 8.7 and 8.8 focused only on affordability. In practice these programs attract news coverage, social media activity and behavior-change communication that could alter preferences, which would be drawn as a shift in the indifference curves. Using analytical diagrams to distinguish among kinds of effects is useful for a wide range of program design and management decisions, revealing the economic mechanisms behind many everyday behaviors in food and nutrition. The diagrams play out the consequences of human agency and choice under each scenario, allow us to describe, predict and assess the consequences of each intervention in terms of what would be in any person's best interests.

The diagrams presented here are qualitative, meaning that they show the direction and relative magnitudes of change even when no numbers are involved, and embody abstract principles applicable to all human behavior. A great deal of additional work is required to apply these principles in any case, and to translate the results back into communication with others about what each change might feel like, but using this framework reveals underlying similarities behind situations that might seem entirely different.

8.2.3 Conclusion

Interventions that act on new information about how foods affect health can be guided by economic models, using prior knowledge of the context to identify which model specifications are most appropriate, and what parameter values such as price or income elasticities would help predict the impact of each change. These models are particularly useful when considering interventions that provide vouchers or in-kind nutrition assistance, delivered by governments or private organizations. Using these methods, economists and health scientists can work together to address market and policy failures in ways that take account of cognitive and behavioral biases, leading to improved outcomes for populations currently facing high burdens of diet-related disease.

CHAPTER 9

Food in the Macroeconomy: The Whole is More Than the Sum of its Parts

9.1 National Income and the Circular Flow of Goods and Services

9.1.1 Motivation and Guiding Questions

This section introduces *macroeconomics*. Previous chapters were 'micro'-economics, not because they focused on small things but because the analysis in Chapters 2–8 concerns individual decision-making and its consequences. In contrast, 'macro'-economics is the study of an entire economy, with its given population in a fixed geographic area.

The toolkit in this chapter allows us to measure and compare economic activity in each country, revealing much greater disparities between countries than within them. Why are some societies so much richer than others? How does the role of agriculture and food systems evolve as countries grow and develop? And what can be done about the economy's occasional slowdowns, when waves of simultaneous job loss across the entire society cause a spike in unemployment and potentially several years of higher food insecurity?

Both macro- and microeconomics concern the flow of goods and services among people, produced using natural resources plus human inputs used to obtain the living standards we observe, including individual and public health. Microeconomics studies one activity at a time, while macroeconomics puts all activities together in a circular flow among all the people in a country, plus their trade and investment flows with the rest of the world. The sum of all activities is a closed system spanning the whole world, and each country is a subset of that global circular flow.

W. A. Masters and A. B. Finaret, *Food Economics*,
Palgrave Studies in Agricultural Economics and Food Policy,
https://doi.org/10.1007/978-3-031-53840-7_9

The diagrams in previous chapters used money only as a unit of measure, comparing the cost of each thing to all other goods and services. In microeconomics, many questions involve activity in which no money changes hands. For macroeconomics, however, money plays a central role. Money is a lubricant determining how easily goods and services circulate between buyers and sellers, and managing the supply of money allows a government's central bank to limit the downturns when people stop buying from each other.

Because macroeconomics is about the circular flow of goods and services, the field makes a clear distinction between 'the economy' and everything else in society. The economy in this sense is the sum of all transactions among households, businesses or the government. Activities that are not measured transactions, such as meal preparation within the home, could still be studied with economics but are not measured as part of the circular flow of goods and services studied in macroeconomics. The economy grows and fluctuates in relation to the money supply and other influences, and macroeconomists pay close attention to how that circular flow relates to both underlying natural resources and the nonmarket goals of people and their governments.

By the end of this section, you will be able to:

1. Show how a country's economy can be described using a circular flow diagram of transactions among people within the country plus their trade with others;
2. Define and explain national accounting for value added, national income and GDP, and describe some of the nonmarket activities not included in GDP;
3. Define and explain the money supply, inflation and the use of a CPI to measure real income over time;
4. Define and explain how government enters national accounts, and the potential influence of fiscal and monetary policy on the economic activities of a country's population.

9.1.2 Analytical Tools

Macroeconomics is about how each market affects other markets. While the models in Chapters 2–6 could be drawn using two-dimensional analytical diagrams, macroeconomics involves a wider range of simultaneous interactions. These relationships can best be shown using a circular flow diagram and the accounting principles that allow us to measure and describe the sum total of all activity in the economy.

The Economy Is a Circular Flow of Goods and Services

In macroeconomics, 'the economy' is defined and measured as the sum of all observed transactions between individuals, households and enterprises of all kinds, including government agencies. This definition allows us to understand how each part of the economy interacts with all other parts, how the economy as a whole interacts with the natural environment, and how governments can steer economic activity towards sustained improvements in human health and wellbeing.

To measure the economy and see how governments influence its growth and development, we can draw distinct kinds of economic activity interacting with each other in a circular flow diagram such as Fig. 9.1.

The elements of Fig. 9.1 refer to a specific country, showing transactions between their national government, households, firms and foreigners, each at the center of the diagram with different kinds of transactions flowing among them. For the world as a whole, the global economy is the sum of all countries' transactions, for which data collection and some degree of coordination is performed through the United Nations and other international organizations. There is no global government corresponding to the top row of Fig. 9.1, but the World Bank and its sister organization the International Monetary fund play some of the same roles for the world that each country's own central bank does for their national economy.

On the left side of Fig. 9.1 is the set of all goods and services exchanged between people each year. That element of the diagram is shown as a stack of two-dimensional sheets to illustrate that each thing is exchanged in a market like those drawn in Chapters 2–6.

One the right side of Fig. 9.1 is the set of all natural resources and other factors of production, and the financial assets that people hold from year to year, with arrows showing how each thing is used in the economy. Each of those is similarly shown as a stack of many different layers, one for each kind of wealth including land and other natural resources, human resources in terms

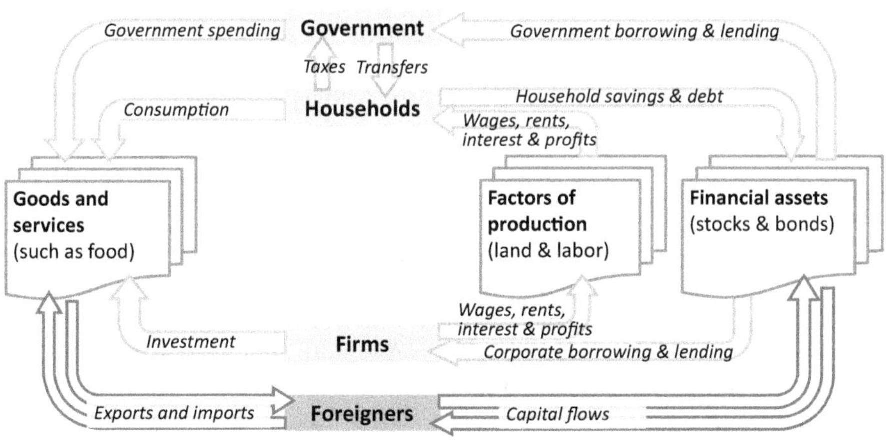

Fig. 9.1 The macroeconomy is a circular flow of income and expenditure

of public health and productive skills, the built environment with its infrastructure and facilities, and financial assets used by individuals, organizations and the government.

Arrows between elements show transactions. These are flows between people in different roles, drawn in the central column of the diagram around the households where people live, and the firms in which people work, as well as the country's own government agencies and the country's interactions with foreigners outside the country whose economy is shown in the diagram.

The organizations shown in the central column of Fig. 9.1 are defined in terms of what they do, not who they are. The distinction between 'households' and 'firms' concerns their activities: households use goods and services for consumption, while firms use goods and services for production. Family farms are both a household and a firm, and firms can be organized in many ways ranging from self-employed individuals to partnerships, businesses and nonprofit enterprises.

The economy consists of both stocks and flows. Stocks are the country's wealth, allowing its people to draw on land and natural resources as well as financial assets, while flows are income and expenditure each year. Arrows illustrate the flow of transactions using resources and assets to produce goods and services. Agricultural commodities and many other things can also be stored from one year to the next, and that kind of stockholding is closely linked to macroeconomics including food price spikes when stockholding nears zero, and longer periods of lower food prices when stocks are abundant.

Measurement of the circular flow in Fig. 9.1 focuses on things that are bought and sold with money. That focus allows economists to distinguish the market economy from nonmarket activities, and help governments manage the economy in pursuit of sustained improvements in wellbeing. Some people pursue money for its own sake, especially when financial data are compared and used in rankings. Some people like to compete for more money in the same way that many people like to compete in sports or other ways and harnessing that competitive spirit can be useful to achieve social goals, but for most people the purpose of money and competition is to deliver more of the real goods and services that people need for environmental sustainability, human health and wellbeing.

Macroeconomic Data Tracks the Level and Change in Economic Activity

The stocks of wealth and flows of income shown in Fig. 9.1 can be measured in various ways, none of which capture everything at once. Measurement methods discussed in this chapter advanced rapidly after World War II when the United Nations sought to standardize recordkeeping, and they continue to evolve in response to changes in what we want to measure and innovations in how economic data are collected and transformed into national accounts.

Data about the economy originate from individual market transactions, such as each person's grocery purchases. Those transactions are then added up

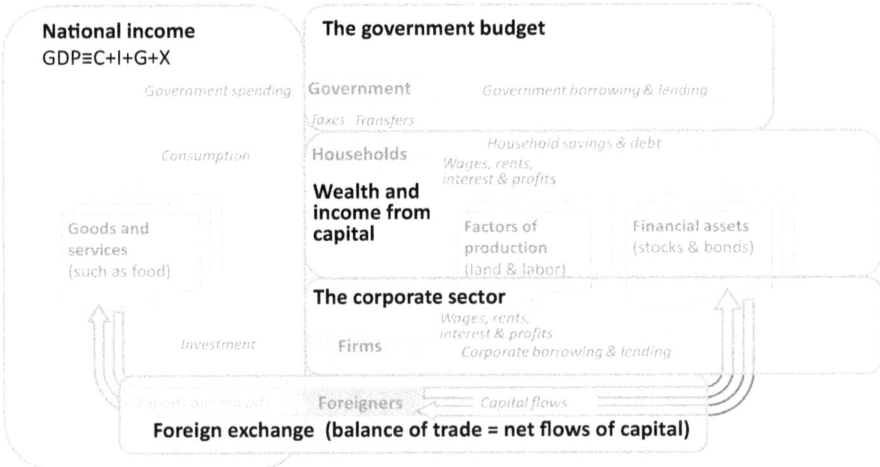

Fig. 9.2 The macroeconomy can be described and measured in multiple ways

and reported to national statistical agencies in a variety of ways and reported in summary statistics about each part of the macroeconomy shown in Fig. 9.2.

On the left of Fig. 9.2 is *national income*, capturing the sum of all goods and services flowing through the economy. This is the *real economy*, adding up all income and expenditure in monetary terms. In national income, each country's currency is used only as a unit of account. Goods and services are added up in proportion to their monetary value in part by necessity, because the quantity and quality of things often cannot be measured in any way other than its price. For example, health care and food services are recorded in economic data based not only on the number of things or hours spent, but also the skill and quality that helps determine its market price. Market failures such as monopolies and externalities create gaps between market prices and social opportunity costs, and where data on those values are available, they are used to augment the basic economic statistics shown in Fig. 9.2.

National income at market values is shown at the top left of Fig. 9.2 as using the accounting identity GDP≡C + I + G + X. In that equation, the triple equals sign indicates a definition, as the system of national accounts defines each country's gross domestic product (GDP) to be the sum of consumption spending by households (C), investment spending by firms (I), government expenditure and investment (G), plus net exports (X) of things sent or brought from abroad, counting all exports minus all imports. The sum of all economic activity in a country is called its 'gross domestic product', providing useful terminology to contrast how GDP is measured with the other things we all care about.

The G in GDP refers to measurement of 'gross' flows each year, in contrast to 'net' flows that might account for changes in a society's stock of natural or human resources. Many attempts to measure net flows have been introduced over the years, aiming primarily to count the depreciation of physical assets like infrastructure and buildings, and the degradation of natural resources like depletion of water supplies and mineral reserves. A measure of net flows would also include the costs of climate change, and changes in the health, education and skill level of the population. Due to uncertainty about how to value resource stocks and interest in each one, national statistics report data on each aspect of the environment and human capabilities separately.

Keeping GDP as gross flows then allows the stock of environmental resources, public health and human welfare to be measured as the objectives or purpose of economic activity. The most important such targets were the Millennium Development Goals (MDGs) adopted by 191 governments through the United Nations in 2000, followed by the Sustainable Development Goals (SDGs) adopted by 193 governments through the UN in 2015. These goals specified a variety of indicators to measure progress from 2000 to 2015 through the MDGs, and then 2015 to 2030 through the SDGs. Individual governments also specify their own short- or long-term goals beyond annual GDP and use international agreements to coordinate efforts such as the Paris Accord on climate change adopted in 2015.

The DP in GDP is for 'domestic production', aiming to count all economic activity within the country's borders. That definition is useful partly by necessity, in situations where national statistical agencies can obtain consistent data only about transactions that occurred among entities physically located in the country. But many populations conduct a significant fraction of their economic activity outside their home country, leading to the development of gross national product (GNP), more recently known as gross national income (GNI). These refer to the population's total income and expenditure in the country, including remittances and wages earned abroad as well as net returns on assets owned in other countries.

Both GDP and GNI are in current use for different purposes. GDP is still used for basic national income accounting as in Fig. 9.2, while GNI is a preferred but more complicated way to measure the income of populations available to be spent on goods and services. For most countries there is little difference between GDP and GNI, because their flows of labor earnings and asset returns offset each other, but when GNI is available it can be very useful for countries with large flows of remittances or other payments to and from other places.

The government budget, at the top right of Fig. 9.2, is of specific interest. That shows the government's 'fiscal' accounts, adding up its net budget deficit (revenues minus expenditures) which is always equal to net lending (lending minus borrowing). The fiscal role of government is important first because its expenditures enter GDP directly with the provision of public goods and services. In most countries a large part of GDP consists of public-sector activity, including health care provision and support for agriculture. Those expenditures are funded by taxation which is itself an important policy instrument, and by government borrowing and lending which can help stabilize (or destabilize) the banking system. A small fraction is also funded by expansion of the money supply. That kind of government revenue is known as 'seigniorage', and is managed by the central bank as part of the country's monetary policy.

The total wealth of society, in the middle right of Fig. 9.2, is not generally added up to a single total. Each form of 'capital' is counted separately, in part because of differences in accounting frameworks, ownership and valuation. The term capital in this context refers to any kind of valuable resource used for production and consumption, using that word to denote a stock that could be built up or drawn down. Natural capital is the stock of land, water, air and ecosystem services on which society relies. Human capital is the health and education or skill level of the population. Improving outcomes in both of those domains is often a goal for governments, to the extent that they can be measured and used in politically feasible ways. Land and facilities, including both public infrastructure and private real estate, are also important underpinnings of the economy, as are the financial instruments such as stocks, bonds and bank accounts used by people and enterprises to save for the future and invest in productive activities.

The corporate sector at the lower right of Fig. 9.2 includes private-sector organizations of all kinds, from small partnerships to nonprofit and for-profit enterprises. Each individual in society can belong to multiple organizations, and many organizations have complex legal structures with multiple entities, so data usually report the sum of all private-sector activity as a single total, often broken out by functional categories such as farm production, grocery retailing or health care services. Each of those subsectors would have a mix of organizations, sometimes including the work of a single person.

The foreign sector along the bottom of Fig. 9.2 shows net trade (exports minus imports) which always equals net capital flows (lending minus borrowing). These equal each other because anyone who wants to import or export actual goods and services must make a corresponding exchange through the banking system, for example exchanging dollars for pesos when trading between the U.S. and Mexico. All the individual transactions are pooled in banks, creating supply and demand for currency exchanges between every pair of currencies such as U.S. dollars to Mexican pesos, and also U.S. dollars to Canadian dollars, and also Mexican pesos to Canadian dollars. As each country's net trade balance evolves, demand and supply for lending and borrowing must keep up to provide that currency, which is done like any market equilibrium by bids and offers that lead to a different exchange rate between currencies or interest rate when holding that currency.

Macroeconomic Variables and the Definition of GDP

The different kinds of macroeconomic variables shown in Figs. 9.1 and 9.2 can be very confusing and are summarized in Table 9.1.

The columns of Table 9.1 indicate whether the data refer to a 'real' variable adding up the quantities of goods and services for which money is just the unit

Table 9.1 Types of macroeconomic variables

Type	*Real*	*Monetary*
Domestic	Private consumption, private investment, government expenditure (consumption and investment), private savings	Inflation, interest rates
International	Exports, imports, capital flows and remittances	Exchange rates

of account, or a 'monetary' variable which tracks the role of money in the economy. The rows track whether the data track a domestic variable affecting transactions within the country, or transactions that involve foreign exchange.

Every variable in the economy involves both a quantity and a price. The monetary variables are 'macro'-prices that are defined in terms of the macroeconomy itself. One set of macro-prices is the cost of things now versus later, measured as the rate of inflation in average prices from year to year, and the interest rate on savings held from year to year. Another set of macro-prices is the cost of things in this country's currency versus all other currencies. These currency exchange rates link the market for each country's exports and imports to the capital flows in or out of that country, which in turn relates to its inflation and interest rate.

For agriculture and food systems, we use macro-variables primarily to convert the cost of things in different countries and different years into real terms, by adjusting for inflation and purchasing power parity exchange rates. Monetary variables are also important influences on agricultural commodity and food markets, as traders hold on to commodities in storage when they expect inflation to rise, which can contribute to food price spikes. Most of the time, however, our focus is on the real variables used to calculate national income itself in the definition GDP≡C + I + G + X.

Consumption (the C in the definition of national income) typically accounts for more than half of GDP. It is measured as the total value of goods and services sold by businesses to households each year. This is relatively straightforward for many goods and services, but creates the apparent anomaly that GDP goes up when people switch to buying from a business instead of doing for themselves at home. Some of the growth and difference in GDP we observe is purely due to that transition from household work to paid employment for cooking, cleaning, caring for dependents and so forth. That aspect of national accounting is intentional because the goal of GDP is to monitor market activity. The only home-produced product that is counted in GDP is farmers' consumption of food, for which an estimate is included in countries where that is a significant part of economic activity each year.

Investment (the I in the definition) is the total value of businesses' purchase of equipment and facilities intended to last more than one year, plus their accumulation of inventories. This is a smaller fraction of GDP than consumption but plays a crucial role in growth and development because each year's investment can use new technologies to replace previous ways of doing business. The most important of these technology transitions is to replace fossil fuel use with electricity powered by renewables, but many other improvements are possible in terms of productivity and working conditions, as well as the quality of products sold.

Government activity (the G in the definition) is its actual provision of goods and services, which includes both physical infrastructure like road construction and also services such as education or health care. The government's transfer payments such as social safety nets or pension payments enter GDP when they are spent in the private sector, either by households for consumption or by businesses for investment.

Net exports (the X in the definition) are the total flow of goods and services from any given example country that is sent elsewhere in exchange for money. This is the sum of all exports minus all imports. Often the same thing is both exported and imported over a year, including many food products. Exports are added to GDP because they are income not counted elsewhere, and imports are subtracted to avoid double counting the thing when used for C, I or G.

The relative size of the four components in the U.S. economy is shown in Fig. 9.3.

Percentage shares of the U.S. economy are shown in Fig. 9.3 using a chart from the central bank's online source of Federal Reserve Economic

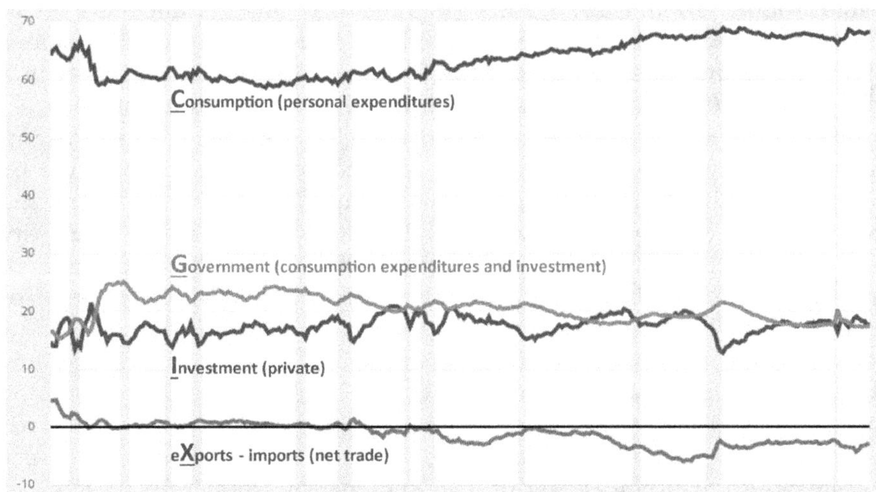

Fig. 9.3 Shares of GDP as C + I + G + X (consumption, investment, government and net exports) *Source*: Reproduced from Federal Reserve Economic Data [FRED] using quarterly data from the Bureau of Economic Analysis, not seasonally adjusted. An updated version of this chart is at https://fred.stlouisfed.org/graph/?g=19UU2

Data (FRED). This data-visualization service is designed to track and report economic activity to the public, with detailed explanations for each data series. Later in this section we will use FRED charts to see various aspects of the macroeconomy. Focusing first on percentage shares of the economy in Fig. 9.3 reveals fluctuations over time, before we turn to its size and growth.

The vertical gray lines in this and other charts show periods of downturn in private economic activity known as *recessions*. The start and end of each recession is determined by a committee of academic researchers convened by the National Bureau of Economic Research (NBER), an independent nonprofit organization, based on three criteria: the depth of downturn, its diffusion across multiple sectors of the economy and its duration over several months. The committee's judgments are subjective to some degree, but preferred to other possible definitions of recession in part because each slowdown is unique in some ways.

Starting from the top of Fig. 9.3, spending by households on personal consumption expenditures accounts for about two-thirds of economic activity in the U.S. That share was around 65% immediately after World War II and then dropped to 60% from 1951 through 1981, before rising to a peak of 69% in 2009. Personal consumption as a share of activity fell gradually over a decade to 67% in 2019, dropped to 66% in the COVID recession of 2020 and snapped back up to 68% from 2021 through 2023.

Government spending on consumption and investment shown in Fig. 9.3 rose sharply from a low of 15% in 1947 to 25% in 1952–1954 and then fluctuated around 24% until 1970. After 1970 the share of government activity in the economy fell gradually to 18% in the late 1990s, before rising just above 21% in 2010 and then falling back to 17% in the 2017–2023 period, with a brief spike to 20% in mid-2020 at the start of the COVID pandemic.

Private-sector investment is the category of GDP with the most short-term variation from year to year. Investment, defined here as real expenditure by businesses for inventories, equipment and facilities, drops sharply during the recessions marked by gray vertical bars and rises gradually as a share of activity during each period of recovery and growth. The pace and composition of investment differs as businesses pursue new opportunities in each period of growth.

Trade enters national accounts as exports minus imports, tracing the flow of spending on real goods and services. In 1947 exports exceeded imports by about 5% of GDP, leaving a smaller share of all goods and services available for domestic consumption, investment or government activity. Postwar recovery quickly closed that gap leading to a lengthy period from 1950 to 1982 in which exports roughly equaled imports, with some fluctuations around each period of recession. In the mid-1980s, and then again to an even greater extent after 1997, net trade fell to about −5% of GDP. Having negative net trade allowed the sum of domestic consumption, investment and government expenditure to reach 105% of GDP, as imports exceeded exports which raised the quantity of goods and services available inside the country. Net trade moved back towards zero in the recession of 2008–2009 and stayed around −3% from 2012 to 2020, before falling to −4% in 2022 and 2023.

The expenditure shares shown in Fig. 9.3 are a helpful starting point for macroeconomics, revealing how household consumption relates to business investment, government activity and international trade. We can then trace where those expenditures come from, in terms of income earned by workers and owners of resources used in production, as they transform and add value to the inputs they buy from other people in the economy.

The Equivalence of Expenditure, Income and Value Added in GDP

Each country's GDP is calculated by national statistical agencies using a variety of data sources, updating each variable monthly, quarterly or annually. Statistical agencies often provide forecasts that may depend on expectations about the size of upcoming harvests, and make revisions of past data when more accurate data become available. Various data sources can be used because GDP is a circular flow, so information can be obtained from any side of the transaction.

The definition of national income in expenditure terms as GDP≡G + C + I + X is the most convenient way of introducing analysis of the macroeconomy, by focusing on how money is spent. The circular flow can also be defined and measured as income earned and received, and as value added created when turning inputs into outputs. The three equivalent ways of seeing economic activity are shown in Table 9.2.

Our example economy in Table 9.2 consists only of the food system, with three kinds of enterprises: primary input suppliers such as energy and service providers, farm families that use some of those inputs to grow food and food businesses that use farm produce plus other inputs to make final products for sale to households. This could be an entire toy economy that only consumes food, or a subset of the whole economy, which would require additional

Table 9.2 Accounting for the circular flow of sales, value added and income

	Primary inputs	*Farm families*	*Food businesses*	*Totals*
Final sales (expenditure)	$200	$500	**$1000**	
− inputs to farms and businesses		$100	$100	
− farm produce used in food businesses			$500	
= **value added**	$200	$400	$400	**$1000**
Income (payments for labor and capital)				
wages to employees	$80	$50	$200	
+ rents for land	$20	$100	$50	
+ interest on loans	$70	$50	$100	
+ profits and net farm income	$30	$200	$50	
= **total income**	$200	$400	$400	**$1000**

columns and rows to show the government, nonfood businesses and foreign trade. To make the arithmetic clear, the total amount of market activity in this economy is $1000.

The size of the circular flow can be measured simply by total consumption, which in this case is final sales of food worth exactly $1000. That is the 'expenditure' approach to measuring the economy, with just the one consumer good in this case as the 'C' in GDP≡G + C + I + X. Additional columns and rows would be needed to show government services, business investments and net exports, and we would then add those to obtain everyone's total spending in the economy.

An alternative way of seeing the circular flow is through *value added*, often described as 'value chains' as goods and services flow from one enterprise to another. Here we see that the initial input suppliers have sold $200 worth of energy and services, half to farmers and half to food businesses. Farmers used that $100 of energy and services to make products that they sold for $500 to food businesses, which used that plus $100 of energy and services to make the food they sold. The value added by food businesses is $400 of their $1000 in sales, and the value added by farmers is also $400 of their $500 in sales. The input providers are called 'primary' producers because they use only labor and capital, so their output of $200 is entirely value added. The sum of value added is their $200 in primary production, $400 on the farm and $400 by food businesses, thereby accounting for all this economy's market activity.

The third way of describing the circular flow is through peoples' income. Individuals and households are shown in the accounting framework as either employees who earn wages, owners of land who are paid rent, lenders of money who are paid interest, the owners of businesses that earn profits and farm families that live on their net farm income. In this simple economy there is no separate real estate or banking sector, but just individual people who are landlords and lend money to others as was commonly done for much of human history.

The four kinds of income (wages, rent, interest and profits) are itemized separately in national accounts because they represent the returns to different kinds of capital or resources. Each kind of income represents payments for a 'factor' of production, using that term to emphasize that these resources are the underlying foundations of market activity. Wages can be seen as returns to human capital, meaning each family's investment in their own health, education and skills. Rent is returns to land and the natural resources on that land, as well as any investments to augment the value of land such as buildings. Interest is the return to financial capital, including each household's savings that are invested in other enterprises, and profits (or net farm income) are returns to the owners and managers of each enterprise.

Our imaginary economy has values that are round numbers, chosen to allow easy comparison of the labor, capital and other resources used in each kind of enterprise, but they represent useful orders of magnitude to see how elements of the macroeconomy all fit together. Starting with food consumers, in this example, the $1000 cost of food bought by consumers was spent on $200 in primary inputs such as energy, $400 in value added by farmers and $400 in value added by retailers. Focusing on farmers, their total sales of $500 were spent on $100 in primary inputs leaving $400 in value added, that came from $50 in wages to employees and $50 in interest paid to lenders, with the remaining $100 in land rents plus $200 in net farm income accruing to the farm families if they own their land.

Macroeconomic accounts are typically presented first using national totals per year, as in Table 9.2, and then compared with the number of people engaged in each activity to see flows per person. As we will see, in low-income countries with few off-farm employment opportunities the available agricultural land is divided among many farm families, so farmers' income per household is extremely low. The primary sector, including the provision of energy and water or other utilities, typically employs relatively few people at high wages. In contrast, food businesses often involve labor-intensive activities that require less training, experience and formal qualifications than other jobs, so it employs a larger number of lower wage workers than other sectors of the economy.

The nature of employment and resource ownership also differs by sector. In the stylized example of Table 9.2, farm families use hired workers and pay wages totaling $50 per year or 10% of their farm revenue. In a real food system that would typically consist of seasonal or part-time help as well as contract service providers, although some crops and many livestock operations are grown with full-time employees. Farm families in this example also pay a total of $100 or 20% of revenue to landlords. In the U.S. and many other countries, farmers typically inherited some of the land they farm, and rent land from other people who inherited or bought land as an investment. This stylized example also shows farm families paying interest of $50 or 10% of revenue, which might apply if they had borrowed money to buy land or large amounts of equipment or had accumulated debts for their own living expenses in years of low farm income. In addition to these factor payments, farm families also purchased inputs worth $100 or 20% of revenue. This example has those inputs coming only from the primary sector which sells only energy and services, and in real economies with a manufacturing sector there would be fertilizers and crop chemicals, equipment and machinery as well as farm buildings.

National accounts data are collected and reported for the purpose of macroeconomic management, but they can also be used to understand food systems. Agriculture and food businesses account for a large fraction of all activity, especially in lower-income countries and for lower-income workers and consumers within each country, so improving the collection and presentation of these data is an important priority. The United Nations has a Statistical Commission that aims to standardize reporting, with country efforts to improve measurement supported by the World Bank (which lends to governments for public expenditure) as well as the International Monetary

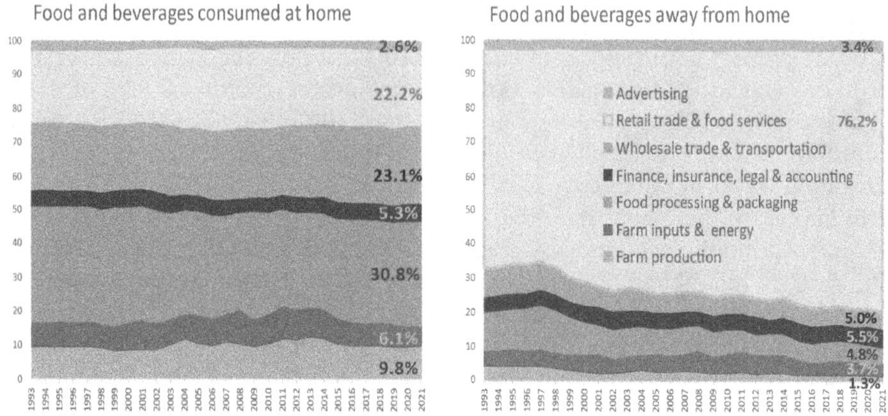

Fig. 9.4 Value added in the U.S. food system, 1993–2021 *Note* Authors' chart of data from the USDA Economic Research Service (2023), Food Dollar Series, available at https://www.ers.usda.gov/data-products/food-dollar-series

Fund (which lends to governments to help stabilize their money supplies, inflation and exchange rates). Within the UN system, the FAO's statistics division maintains macroeconomic data on agriculture, including efforts to produce global versions of the U.S. data presented in Fig. 9.4.

Value Added in the U.S. Food System
Actual data for the U.S. are used each year by the USDA to monitor the food system, including a real-life version of the value added row in Table 9.2. Their annual publication on this topic is known as the 'Food Dollar' series, providing consistent measurement of value added shares accounting for all consumer food expenditure as shown in Fig. 9.4.

Each panel of Fig. 9.4 traces shares of the food dollar in terms of value added since 1993, with the most recent available percentage shares for 2021 on the right. From the bottom up each share is stacked up to 100% of consumer spending. The left panel shows how farmers' share of the U.S. food dollar hovers around 10%, with primary inputs purchased by farmers adding another 6%. The sum of those two shares rose noticeably in the decade from 2004 to 2014, corresponding to the period of high producer prices for unprocessed foods at that time shown in Chapter 7, Fig. 7.13. Food processing and packaging now accounts for about 31% of retail prices, a slight decline from the 1990s. Interest paid to financial firms by food businesses, together with their insurance premiums paid, and legal or accounting fees adds up to around 5%. About 23% of food prices is the cost of transport and bulk handling of commodities and products, about the same as the 22% that is the cost of retail service provision at the point of sale.

The right panel shows similar data for food away from home. U.S. spending at restaurants and other food service establishments rose from about one-third of total food spending in the early 1990s to about half in 2019, plummeted during the pandemic in 2020 and recovered quickly to above half since 2021. As shown in the right panel, about 76% of that spending is on value added in the food service sector itself. That share had been as low as 63% in 1997, then expanded to its current level, and a relatively stable 5.5% share of consumer costs is the food service industry's payments for financial, legal, accounting and insurance services. The food service industry's spending on food and beverage ingredients as such averages 15% of total expenditure, adding up the share to farmers (1.3%), farm inputs and energy (3.7%), food processing and packaging (4.8%) and wholesale trade and transport (5.0%).

A notable feature of the Fig. 9.4 is the roughly constant share of spent on advertising, now around 2.6% for food at home and 3.4% for food away from home. Overall food spending in the U.S. is about $6200 per person, so total food advertising amounts to about $161 per food consumer each year. The combined total is roughly $60 billion per year, more than the U.S. government budgets for the National Institutes of Health (NIH) and Centers for Disease Control (CDC) combined. The data shown in Fig. 9.3 correspond to the 'value added' row of Table 9.2, and could also be broken out in other dimensions, for example to break out energy costs regarding contribution to climate change, or employment and wages to address equity in the food system.

Governing the Macroeconomy: Fiscal and Monetary Policy

Our circular flow diagram in Fig. 9.1 reveals a central role for government in shaping the macroeconomy, first through *fiscal policy* by the way it raises and spends tax revenues and borrowing for government operations, and through *monetary policy* by introducing and regulating the supply of money used by businesses.

Fiscal policy shapes the composition of the economy through the ways that government revenue is spent and the rates at which different kinds of wealth and income are taxed. Fiscal policy also drives the fraction of each year's government spending that is raised from taxpayers each year versus borrowed from investors to be paid back in the future. Unlike an individual or a private company, governments can print their own currency and can raise revenue by taxing the entire economy. In the U.S. and most other countries, lending to government offers investors the safest possible place to store savings, which is itself a valuable service, so government pays the lowest available interest rate on its borrowing. That safety arises in part because the overall economy grows over time, providing a larger tax base from which government revenue is raised.

The fact that governments repay loans by taxing their own citizens leads to a fundamental principle of fiscal policy, which is that governments can keep borrowing forever with no change in the tax rate as long as the interest rate it pays (commonly denoted r) is lower than the growth rate (g) of the tax base. For example, government spending might be 40% of total national income each year, financed by a taxing all that income at an average rate of 30%. They could sustain that indefinitely by borrowing the remaining 10% from investors, without ever raising tax rates as long as the tax base grows as fast or faster than the interest paid. In practice all these variables fluctuate, with variation in both the amount of borrowing and hence accumulated debt on which interest is paid, as well as interest rates and growth rates. An important function of fiscal policy is therefore to complement monetary policy in helping to stabilize the economy, as well as shaping its evolution and growth rate.

Monetary policy consists of issuing physical money (coins and bills) and regulating the banking and credit sector through which people borrow and lend money for future use. Issuing enough money and regulating financial firms in ways that facilitate transactions and maintain trust in the banking system is usually done through a central bank that operates as a politically independent but accountable part of each national government. In the U.S., central banking is done by the Federal Reserve, whose balance of political independence and accountability is maintained by having it be controlled by a seven-member Board of Governors appointed by the President for terms that last for 14 years. This means that a new board member is appointed at least every two years, and the fraction of board members appointed by each party is proportional to their time in office over the previous 14 years.

Like fiscal policy, monetary policy influences both the composition and stability of economic activity over time. The central challenge is to inject and withdraw money and regulate the banking system in ways that accommodate growth and offsets fluctuations in the real economy. If the central bank injects too much, the supply of money grows faster than the supply of goods and services, leading to inflation. If there is too little new money and credit from banks, firms cannot grow leading to less employment. The U.S. and other central banks typically have a 'dual mandate' to keep inflation and unemployment low, so that the real economy can grow to help people achieve their highest potential level of wellbeing over time.

The link between inflation and unemployment arises in part from the downward rigidity of nominal wages or salaries. When revenue declines, businesses typically cut the number of employees instead of reducing the wage or salary paid to each person, and when demand rises, they hire again if necessary, by offering higher wages and salaries. Other kinds of prices are also rarely reduced when demand falls, as sellers prefer to keep prices constant until sales recover, then raise prices when demand increases. Many but not all wages and many prices are sticky in this sense, like a ratchet that sometimes rises but rarely declines. Most importantly for the food system, when demand for farm commodities declines their prices can drop sharply. When that happens, farmers remain on the farm, whereas in nonfarm employment when demand declines people lose their jobs.

Another link between inflation and unemployment arises from the circular nature of each country's economy. Investment and growth opportunities can arise in any sector of the economy, and when enterprises in that sector then hire people and buy products from others, they in turn hire more people and buy other products which spreads growth to other sectors and regions. When the economy is running smoothly there are attractive opportunities for new value added in many sectors that expand supply and demand at about the same rate, so that gradual economic growth at a few percent per year can proceed with little change in the economy's average price level. Sometimes that growth accelerates into a boom period of even faster growth, during which a rising fraction of the workforce enters paid employment and credit expands to finance new enterprises. The economy's various enterprises are each other's customers, so when the circular flow of activity falters, the slowdown can happen suddenly with contagious job loss throughout the economy.

Economywide slowdowns, known as *recessions*, can occur at any time and originate in any sector. When demand slows for one set of businesses, those enterprises cut jobs and reduce purchases of inputs from others, which leads others to cut jobs and reduce their own purchases. The flywheel of economic growth then goes into reverse, reducing income and employment from month to month. Such downturns can be deep and long-lasting, potentially turning into depressions that last for years with low levels of different goods and services in the economy until growth resumes.

For much of economic history these downturns ran their course until people eventually found work again, sometimes after a period of profound impoverishment. The most recent very deep downturn began in late 1929 and lasted through the 1930s. That 'great depression' led a British economist, John Maynard Keynes, to show how fiscal policy could step in to fill the gap in private-sector demand by buying goods and services for the public sector, and central banks could do the same with monetary policy to provide cash and credit for individuals and businesses. These 'Keynesian' responses have since made recessions shorter and less severe, reducing the hardships they cause for employees who lose their jobs and farmers who face periods of low prices.

The connection between the real economy and monetary policy can be seen in accounting terms, through the 'velocity' at which transactions occur in the economy. Over the course of a given year, the price of each thing in the economy (denoted P) could be multiplied times the quantity (Q) of that thing, to show the total money value of everything in the economy. For prices to remain stable, total activity would need to equal the money supply (M) of cash or credit from banks times the number of times each dollar changes hands, knows as its velocity (V). Given those definitions, stable price implies that $P \times Q = M \times V$. When M or V declines at the start of a downturn, for example because banks are issuing fewer loans and people are increasing their savings instead of spending everything they earn, there must be a corresponding decline in $P \times Q$. For farmers it is P that falls, but in other parts of the economy prices are sticky so it is Q that falls, meaning a reduction in the real quantity of things produced and workers employed to do things.

Real Gross Domestic Product per Person

The flow of goods and services through an economy, measured using national accounts as in Table 9.1, allows comparison of total output per person in each population in real terms. The purpose of calculating real GDP per person is to track the total quantity of goods and services available in a country at each point in time, adding up all activity in the private and public sectors.

The value of activity is initially reported in nominal values using current prices and converted to real terms using constant values in a base year. For total output, adjusting for inflation is done using a GDP deflator, multiplying change in each price times its share of national output. That weighted average can use historical shares from a past year known as a Laspeyres index, or current-period weights known as a Paasche index, each named after the nineteenth-century statistician who argued for that approach. To keep up with changes in each item's share of output, including especially the introduction of entirely new items, since the 1990s the U.S. and other countries use chained indexes, for which weights are a continuously updated average of current and immediate past shares. The base year price level used for reporting is arbitrary, and by convention both U.S. and many global data now report real output in terms of prices from 2017.

Data on changes and levels in real output are available for the U.S. since January 1947, as shown in Fig. 9.5.

The left axis of Fig. 9.5 shows percent changes in each quarter relative to that period in the previous year, and the right axis shows the level of GDP each quarter in 2017 dollars. Data are reported quarterly and are seasonally adjusted, combining information from different sources to produce a complete table of national accounts like Table 9.1.

Percent changes in GDP reveal the episodic pattern of economic growth, commonly called the business cycle. From 1947 to 1961 there were four peaks where real GDP reached more than 5% above its level at that time the previous year, and four troughs where real GDP declined to around 2.5% below its level the previous year, all corresponding to recessions as indicated by the NBER. In the 1960s there was a long boom period of continuous growth, followed by four recessions between 1970 and 1983. The slowdown and declines from 1980 to 1983 were particularly important with just one brief quarter of growth above 2.5% and several quarters below −2.5%. That period was followed by two long booms in the 1980s and 1990s punctuated by shallow recessions in 1990 and 2001, before the smaller boom for the 2000s and the very deep and prolonged recession in 2008–2009, followed by sustained growth up to the pandemic recession of 2020 and recovery since then.

The level of GDP per person on the right axis of Fig. 9.5 shows how episodes of growth cumulate over time. The pattern of growth is like a family marking each child's height on a door or wall in their home, with growth spurts cumulating in transformational change and development over time. The total size of the U.S. economy shrinks back slightly after each period

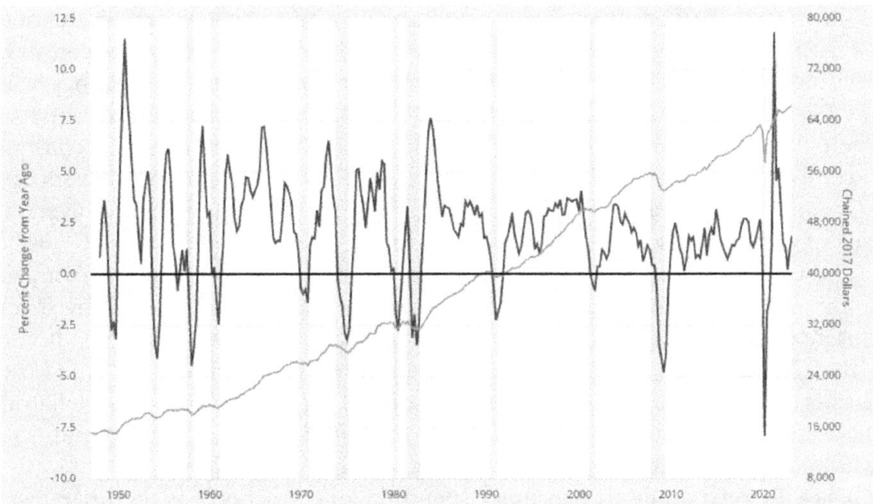

Fig. 9.5 Percentage changes and level of real GDP in the U.S., January 1947–April 2023 *Source*: Reproduced from Federal Reserve Economic Data [FRED] using quarterly, seasonally adjusted real U.S. gross domestic product [GDP] from the Bureau of Economic Analysis. The same data are shown as percent changes from one year earlier in the thin line against the left axis, and as the level of real GDP per person in 2017 U.S. dollars on the right axis. Updated versions of this chart are at https://fred.stlouisfed.org/graph/?g=19Q7r

of growth, but the accumulation of new activities has expanded total output per person by a factor of four over this period, from a level of around $16,000 per person in the late 1940s to over $64,000 since 1921. The total quantity of goods and services doubled over the 33 years from 1947 to 1980, and then doubled again over the 40 years from 1981 to 2021.

Total output per person is just that, tracking the total monetary value of all goods and services that people provide to each other in a country. In Chapter 10 we will address how growth in GDP and national income over time and differences across countries relate to wellbeing and the composition of activity, especially in the food system. Before that we need to address the purchasing power of income earned in GDP, using a consumer price index.

Inflation and the Purchasing Power of Money

In our discussion of risk and food crises in Chapter 7, Figs. 7.13 and 7.14 showed variation in the cost and price of food relative to the prices of all other goods and services in the U.S., while Fig. 7.17 compared the cost of a healthful diet across countries in purchasing power parity terms. That is consistent with a focus on the real economy, where the price of something is defined in relative terms as the quantity of all else that must be given up to acquire it.

Now in macroeconomics, we are concerned with overall *inflation*, defined as a rise in the average price level of all goods and services in the whole country, or equivalently a decline in quantity of things that a unit of currency can buy. For measuring a country's output in Fig. 9.4 we needed a GDP deflator, which counts all activity including the public sector. To measure purchasing power for households, each country's national statistical organization produces a *Consumer Price Index* (CPI), tracking percentage changes in the average price of goods and services sold to individuals.

The CPI is intended to capture the cost of living for an average person, so each item's weight in the average is its share of total consumer spending from household survey data. For example, in the U.S., the share of food at home in the CPI is 8.7%, and the share of food away from home is 4.8%. Those weights differ from each item's share of national income for the GDP deflator, where total expenditure on food away from home is larger than expenditure on food at home due to food at schools and other institutions.

The CPI refers only to consumer spending and is defined as the price level relative to 100 in a base period. The consumer price index can also be reported in terms of percentage changes from period to period, like GDP growth but for prices. Both the level and growth in CPI are shown in Fig. 9.6.

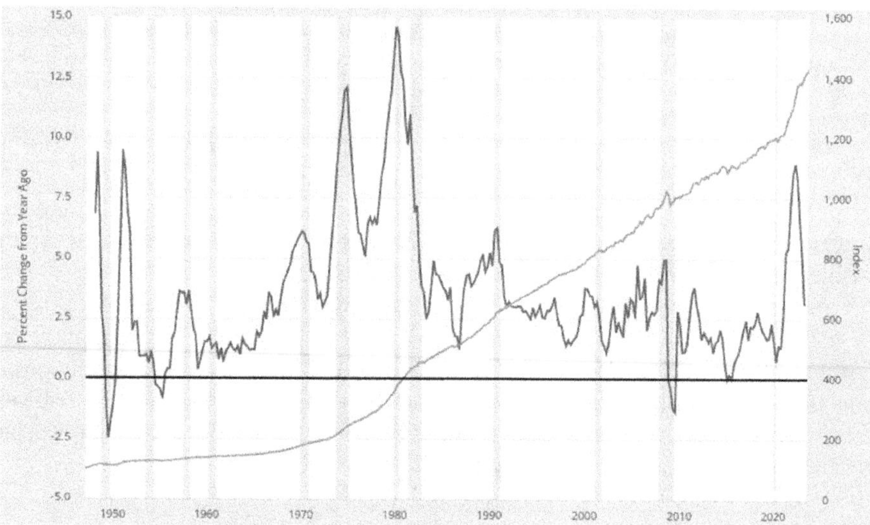

Fig. 9.6 Percentage changes and level of the U.S. consumer price index, January 1947–August 2023 *Source*: Reproduced from Federal Reserve Economic Data [FRED] using the monthly U.S. consumer price index [CPI] from the Bureau of Labor Statistics. The same data are shown as percent changes from one year earlier in the dark line against the left axis, and as the price level relative to a value of 100 in January 1947 on the right axis. The black horizontal line shows a percentage change of zero. Updated versions of this chart are at https://fred.stlouisfed.org/graph/?g=19P5E

The left axis of Fig. 9.6 shows each month's CPI as a percentage change since the same month one year earlier, and the right axis shows its level since a value of 100 in January 1947. When percentage change is above the dark horizontal line at a percent change of zero, the price level has risen over the past year. Monthly fluctuations reveal the volatility of inflation. Commodity prices like food or oil and gas often drop suddenly, while other prices like apartment rents are sticky and rarely decline but may rise sharply during periods of sustained inflation. The chart shows that, after a few short bursts of inflation in 1948, 1951 and 1956–1958, year-to-year changes in the CPI stayed low in the early 1960s and then rose to dramatic peaks in 1974 and 1980. The Federal Reserve then took action to reduce inflation by reducing the money supply, which combined with fiscal policy kept U.S. inflation fluctuating around 2.5% and trending downward from 1983 to the start of the COVID pandemic in 2020, after which inflation spiked in 2021–2022.

The vertical bars indicating periods of recession reveal how inflation typically (but not always) rises during the boom period in the runup to a recession, then falls during and after the recession. Each recession differs in terms of causes and responses to the slowdown, leading to a different time path of prices. Also, inflation here is shown as each month's price level relative to that month in the previous year which helps account for the zig-zag pattern we see, for example in the path of year-on-year inflation during and after the COVID recession of 2020. News of the pandemic starting in January 2020 led people to stay home and cut back on spending, with a massive job losses and decline in GDP shown in Fig. 9.5, but prices did not fall as they had in the previous recession in part because the U.S. government responded with much more generous unemployment insurance and safety net programs, keeping demand up for whatever could be supplied despite people being sick with COVID. Fiscal and monetary policy was much more responsive to the 2020 recession than it had been to the 2008–2009 recession, or the 1981–1983 recession before that, leading economic activity to snap back in 2021 as shown for GDP in Fig. 9.5. In 2021–2022 the sudden return to spending raised demand for goods faster than supply could respond, leading to the spike of inflation that peaked in mid-2022 as shown in Fig. 9.6.

In summary, the rise and fall of inflation traces the degree to which fiscal and monetary policy successfully expands the country's money supply just fast enough to accommodate real growth in economic activity. Governments and central banks around the world differ in their willingness and ability to manage economic development in this way, contributing to the differences in economic development discussed in the next chapter.

9.1.3 Conclusion

This section showed how the whole economy, as measured using the toolkit of macroeconomics, differs from analysis of individual activities using microeconomics. The economy as a whole is a circular flow within each country involving households, businesses and the government. Because each person's spending is another person's income, the circular flow can accelerate in periods of growth spurred by supply and demand for new things, and then slow or stop during periods of recession when people slow their purchases from each other.

The government plays a distinctive role in the macroeconomy, different from the public sector's role in governing individual markets, due to the need and opportunity for monetary policy to stabilize and support the pace of economic growth by managing the supply of money and credit, and for fiscal policy to offset fluctuations in private demand by managing public-sector activity. As shown in the next section, downturns have severe impacts on households and the food system, while growth drives changes that lead to the next chapter on long-term economic development in agriculture, food systems, nutrition and health.

9.2 Recessions and Unemployment, with Links to Food Jobs and the Social Safety Net

9.2.1 Motivation and Guiding Questions

So far, we have seen how understanding macroeconomic growth and development requires a different kind of analysis than our analytical diagrams for individual markets. In this section we focus on fluctuations, and the following chapter focuses on long-term growth and differences across countries. Fluctuations are marked especially by the onset of recessions with simultaneous job loss across multiple sectors and regions of the country. How do those waves of unemployment hit different groups in society, and relate to demographic trends in employment outside the home?

Food system jobs and livelihoods play a distinctive role in the economy and are affected differently by fluctuations and growth in market activity. Farm production is done mostly by self-employed family members whose earnings fluctuate, while employees in businesses lose their jobs when demand for their product declines. Also, historically and today at low-income levels most food preparation is done by family members within the home, but economic growth involves a larger fraction of time spent in paid employment including food transformation and marketing after harvest, and food service for meals away from home. This section includes coverage of how the composition of employment varies over time, in society as a whole and in the food system, and how social assistance and safety nets, including food assistance, can respond to limit the impacts of income loss.

By the end of this section, you will be able to:

1. Describe how and why periods of economic growth are interrupted by recessions, with downturns in spending and periods of high unemployment;

2. Explain how the circular flow of transactions within a country transmits a downturn in demand from one sector or region to other parts of the country;
3. Describe the available data on how growth and recessions relate to nutrition assistance programs, farm employment and food system jobs; and
4. Describe the available data on changes over time in labor force participation and disparities among groups in employment and earnings.

9.2.2 *Analytical Tools*

This chapter concerns the macroeconomics of employment, in terms of supply and demand for labor of all kinds. The tools needed begin with measurement, but also return to analytical diagrams for the supply and demand of worker for each sector as shown in Fig. 9.7.

The analytical diagrams in Fig. 9.7 help explain the wages or salaries paid for a specific type of worker in a particular location, drawn with a relatively steep and inelastic supply of labor from people who need to find a job, and a somewhat flatter more elastic demand from employers. The left panel illustrates one way that people might mistakenly believe labor markets work, which would be a perfectly competitive market in which all workers and all jobs are identical, so employers adjust wages until supply just equals demand. In a perfectly competitive equilibrium, there would be no unemployment, with just one applicant for each opening and just one job offer for each candidate, so candidates would be indifferent between jobs. That is unrealistic for many reasons, including that each worker and each job is unique in some ways, so employers typically want multiple applicants from whom to select, and want to offer a sufficiently high wage that successful candidates will be motivated to stay in the job.

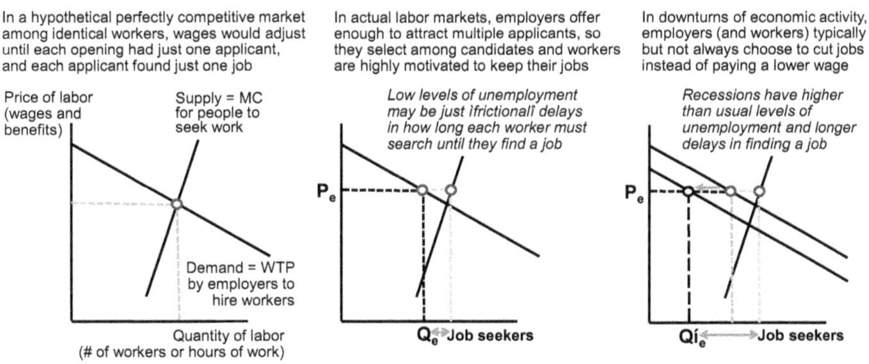

Fig. 9.7 Labor supply, labor demand and unemployment in good times and bad

Structural features of the labor market make the observed market equilibrium somewhat like the middle diagram, where competing employers all offer a wage sufficient to make their jobs attractive to multiple candidates, resulting in some degree of unemployment while workers and employers search for the best fit. When unemployment is low there are relatively few candidates for each position, and job searches as well as job vacancies are brief, but there is still 'frictional' unemployment as some workers spend several weeks or even months looking for their preferred position. In settings where workers are desperate for a job as soon as possible, and employers are willing to take the first candidate they find, frictional unemployment might fall to near zero. Other factors could increase frictions, such as a geographic distance between existing workers and newly available jobs, credential requirements that make it difficult for candidates to apply, or monopsony power when only one employer seeks a specific kind of worker in a particular place. Those kinds of market failures would lead to higher levels of unemployment at all times, but a kind of unemployment that can be of even greater concern is what happens when demand for all kinds of goods and services stops growing or begins to decline.

The right panel in Fig. 9.7 shows what typically happens during downturns. When a business experiences a cut in demand, for example 10% fewer customers, managers typically choose to reduce the number of workers instead of paying each worker lower wages for the same work or asking each worker to do fewer hours at the same wage. Exceptions to this are typically casual or gig labor and self-employment. In many jobs the employer prefers a fixed schedule so would not want to reduce number of hours for all workers proportionally, and managers also want workers who remain on the job to remain highly motivated. Both factors imply that instead of cutting the income of those who remain employed, there is widespread job loss and a higher unemployment rate during the downturn, and then workers are hired back as the economy recovers.

Unemployment and Real Wages

There is no single unified labor market for the entire country. Different workers and different jobs pay different wages, but macroeconomic fluctuations cause synchronized swings in demand for many types of labor, leading to economywide fluctuations in employment and earnings. The synchronized booms and busts in U.S. labor markets, and the much larger fluctuations in unemployment than in wages, are shown in Fig. 9.8.

The central fluctuating line in Fig. 9.8 is the official unemployment rate in the U.S., defined as the number of people actively looking for work over the past month who do not yet have a job, divided by that population plus those in either full-time or part-time employment. Other ways of defining unemployment generally move in parallel to this headline measure, which is easily described as the share of the country's workers who are actively looking for a job. Over each business cycle since 1947, this rate attains its lowest levels in the

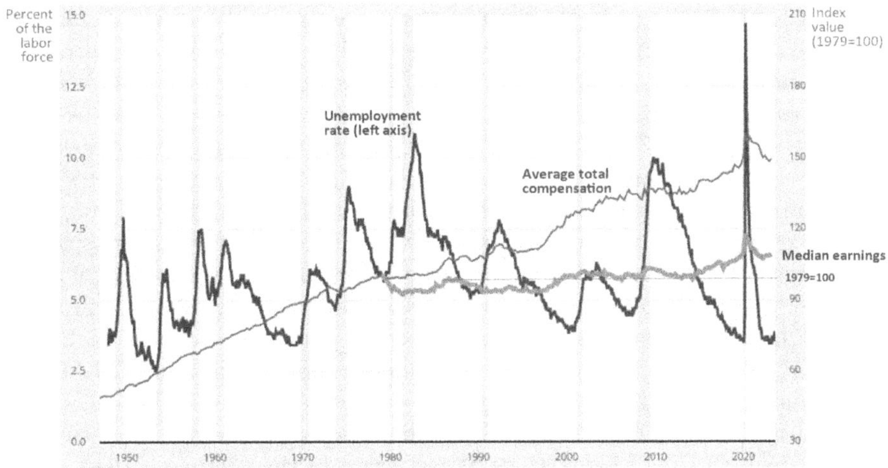

Fig. 9.8 Unemployment and real wages in the U.S., January 1947–September 2023
Source: Reproduced from Federal Reserve Economic Data (FRED) using the seasonally adjusted monthly data from the Bureau of Labor Statistics for unemployment on the left axis as a percentage of people actively looking for work, and two measures of workers' earnings relative to January 1979 = 100: the average total compensation all workers in the light line since 1947, and the median usual earnings of full-time workers in the thicker line that begins in January 1979. Updated versions of this chart are at https://fred.stlouisfed.org/graph/?g=19QMp

months just before a recession, when the lowest possible frictional unemployment rate falls to somewhere between 2.5% and 5%. The unemployment rate then spikes abruptly during the recession as businesses conduct simultaneous job cuts due to reduced output, and workers are later hired back. The unemployment spike during the COVID recession of 2020 was exceptionally high but also exceptionally short-lived. By December 2021 the unemployment rate had dropped back to its pre-recession lows below 4%, a level not seen since the late 1960s.

The lighter lines show workers' earnings in real terms, after adjusting for inflation. The wage rigidity illustrated in Fig. 9.7 applies most directly to nominal wages, but the wellbeing of workers depends on the real value of those wages which are shown here in index number terms, relative to a value of 100 in January 1979. The longest available time series is the thin line since 1947 showing average total compensation to full time workers. That compensation includes health insurance and other benefits and is shown to have risen steadily through the 1950s and 1960s, faltered in the 1970s and then been almost unchanged from 1980 to 1985 before rising in the 1990s, 2000s and especially after 2014.

The thicker line starting in January 1979 shows median usual wages paid to full-time workers. That differs from average total compensation per hour in three main ways: it shows the median which means less influence of high earners who raise the average, it refers only to wages and so excludes health insurance and other benefits, and it counts only full-time workers in contrast to the part-time workers included in total compensation per hour. The first two differences help explain the much smaller rise in median wages than average earnings between 1979 and 2010. Since January 2011, median wages and mean hourly compensation have moved in near lock step, staying flat to 2014 and then rising significantly over the five years just before the pandemic.

Wage changes during the pandemic are a valuable illustration of selection and composition effects, as the apparent spike in median wages and average compensation in 2020 occurred only because lower-wage workers were more likely to lose their jobs. Median and average earnings dropped as lower-wage workers were rehired and as post-pandemic inflation eroded their buying power, but as of early 2023, mean compensation was about 50% above its level at the start of these data in 1979, and median wages were about 8% above the level at which they had been in 1979 and again in the 2000s to 2014. That change implies growth in median real wages of about 1% per year during the 2014–2022 period. The absolute level of median wages in 2022 is not shown on the chart but amounts to about $27 per hour in 2022.

Recessions and the Safety Net: Unemployment Rates and SNAP Benefits in the U.S.

Government spending can help stabilize the economy to some degree, by spending public funds to fill the dip in household incomes caused by recessions. The government then recovers those funds later through taxation, in the same way that it pays for public investment in infrastructure or other activity. Making countercyclical payments effectively is administratively difficult because their effectiveness depends on being disbursed immediately throughout the affected population. Countercyclical expenditure can also be politically difficult because it requires the government to spend more at a time when the population is spending less, leading voters and taxpayers to feel as though the government is out of step and not experiencing their hardship.

Government programs that respond quickly to downturns are known as automatic stabilizers. These instruments of policy play some role in the economy even during periods of growth and are designed so that public spending can respond quickly as soon as jobs are lost. Unemployment insurance is an important kind of stabilizer, as are taxes that rise with income during periods of growth and then decline automatically in recessions. Those stabilizers are primarily sensitive to income variation for high earners, which limits their effectiveness in offsetting the effects of a recession among low-income people.

In the U.S., an increasingly important stabilizer is the use of SNAP benefits, which can respond quickly because eligibility is well defined, and many eligible people are able to access initial or expanded benefits soon after they experience income loss. The program is already in place and being used by those in need. People cannot know whether an individual case of hardship is due to an economywide recession or own local circumstances, and the program responds to them equally. No policy decisions are required because funding for the program is authorized as an entitlement, meaning that the Federal government will reimburse states for any level of spending that adheres to program rules. The entitlement is authorized every five years or so as part of a food and agriculture package known as the Farm Bill, assembling the interests of all food system participants including the anti-poverty community that supports SNAP.

As its name suggests, SNAP is authorized under the 'nutrition' title of its authorizing legislation, and its benefits can be redeemed only for food. SNAP benefits are designed to supplement the recipient's own spending, and the benefit formula generally ensures that recipients do indeed spend some of their own money on food in addition to the assistance received. The analytical diagrams in Section 8.2 show how this makes the program like a cash benefit, as recipients use their benefits card for groceries until its monthly balance runs out and then switch to their own money. That feature ensures that recipients use the card as intended and have no interest in converting SNAP benefits to any use other than buying food.

The advantages of giving low-income people a debit card with which to pay for groceries have made SNAP a popular program with program beneficiaries, government policy makers and businesses in the food sector. Since its introduction in the 1960s, the program grew to account for about 4% of all U.S. spending on food at home during the period from 1981 to 2007. The 2008–2009 recession led to a sharp increase in SNAP use to 9% of U.S. food spending in 2011 and 2012, falling back to 5% in 2019. The program was particularly attractive an instrument to help eligible people during and after the COVID recession, with total payments rising to 8% in 2020 and then 12% in 2021, partly due to emergency provisions for eligibility as well as an increase in the benefit level for 2021.

The increase in SNAP use and the program's responsiveness to need around recessions is shown in Fig. 9.9.

Figure 9.8 shows the same unemployment line as the previous chart but starts in 1965 to show the gradual expansion of SNAP since its beginnings in 1967. The program was introduced at a time of rising incomes and falling unemployment, when many Americans were becoming increasingly prosperous, but voters and government officials understood that not everyone could acquire a similarly high-quality diet. Pilot programs were launched in the form of 'food stamps' that recipients bought with their own cash, as a way of ensuring that the benefit supplemented their own spending, and the USDA used a set of low-cost food plans to show how the benefit level could ensure access to sufficient food to meet nutritional needs.

As shown in Fig. 9.8, the SNAP program grew quickly and became strongly countercyclical in the 1990s, shrinking when unemployment fell and rising soon after spikes in unemployment caused widespread loss of income and wealth. Program spending is shown on the right axis, in real purchasing power

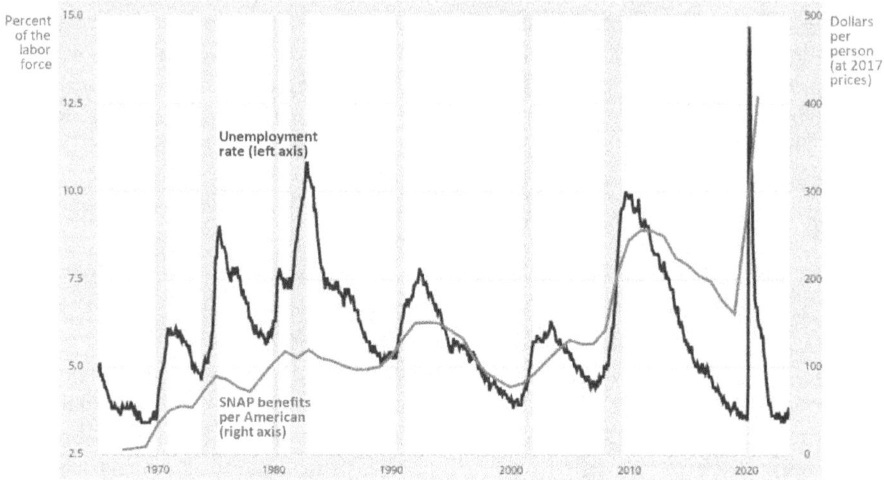

Fig. 9.9 Unemployment and SNAP benefits in the U.S., 1967–2021 *Note* Reproduced from FRED using the same unemployment data shown in Fig. 9.8, with the addition of benefits paid through the U.S. Supplemental Nutrition Assistance Program [SNAP]. Benefits are shown per person [not per beneficiary], counting the entire resident population plus armed forces overseas. The value of benefits is in real terms deflated by the consumer price index for food at home, in U.S. dollars at 2017 prices. Updated versions of this chart are at https://fred.stlouisfed.org/graph/?g=19VyB

for food in 2017 U.S. dollars, per person in the U.S. The initial rollout in the 1960s and 1970s occurred gradually, reaching an expenditure level of about $100 per person by 1980. The program was not initially designed to expand quickly in recessions; benefit levels did not rise in response to the 1983–1984 recession. SNAP spending then fell as unemployment declined, and a variety of program changes made it such that spending rose in response to the recessions of 1990 and then fell back to earlier levels in 2000, before rising in the recession of 2001. Most importantly for the current period, changes at that time positioned the program to expand quickly during the 2008–2009 recession, and again even faster in response to the pandemic in 2020 and 2021.

SNAP data in Fig. 9.8 are for the entire year which hides the speed of response but does reveal how hardship typically persists for some time after each spike in unemployment. Households continue to receive benefits only as long as they remain eligible. Many remain beneficiaries for less than a year while others stay on but at varying levels of benefit. Total SNAP spending is not an ideal measure of hardship, but it is extremely useful, capturing some aspects of the extent and depth of the deprivation people would face if they had only their market income. Eligibility is determined based on a fixed formula that takes account of earnings and assets, and payments depend on how far the household's income is below the cost of foods itemized in the USDA's Thrifty Food Plan. Program rules change over time, with for example a revision of the

Thrifty Food Plan in 2021 that led to higher payments per beneficiary, and use of the program to deliver cash-like benefits in place of school meals during the pandemic as shown in Fig. 7.3 in the section on poverty measurement. The program's core features include that kind of flexibility, making its basic design helpful for policy makers, attractive for beneficiaries, and highly informative about the way that governments can respond to both chronic and temporary hardship in the economy.

Employment, Minimum Wages and Low-Wage Jobs in the Food Sector
One frequently discussed aspect of wages and unemployment is the role of government-mandated minimum wages for certain kinds of workers. In the U.S., the federally mandated floor on wages that can be paid to most workers has been unchanged at $7.25 per hour since 2009. As of 2023 that rate still applies in 20 states, while 30 states and several cities have mandated higher minimum wages, reaching up to $17 for the city of Washington DC.

Minimum wages could be especially relevant for the food sector, which includes a large fraction of all work that can be done with limited on-the-job training and few formal qualifications. These jobs are open to the widest range of potential candidates, so employers can offer some of the economy's lowest wages and still attract applicants. A complicating factor is that U.S. food service and restaurant workers receive some of their compensation as tips. Tipped jobs are subject to a lower Federal minimum for their base wages, but there are little data about actual tips received.

Setting and enforcing a minimum wage could affect the unemployment rate if its level were set above the equilibrium wage shown in the middle panel of Fig. 9.7. To show its effect we would draw a horizontal minimum above the equilibrium level and observe that offering that higher wage elicits a few more job applicants along workers' labor supply curve but leads employers for that kind of job to cut back on offers along their labor demand curve, potentially increasing unemployment above its frictional rate. The number of additional lower-wage jobs employers might have offered, if any, is extremely difficult to estimate. Each type of job has its unique supply and demand curves, and variation in the degree to which employers want to pay a wage sufficient to attract multiple applicants and keep employees highly motivated, which is why equilibrium wages are typically above the intersection of supply and demand in Fig. 9.7.

Whether and how minimum wages influence the number of jobs in an entire economy extends beyond impacts shown in supply-demand diagrams for a single type of job. Those diagrams hold all else constant, and if the minimum is set above the equilibrium, it would affect the local economy, shifting each supply and demand curve and potentially even raising the number of jobs. In 2021 the Nobel Prize for economics was awarded to David Card for research with Alan Krueger and others on this topic, showing that different effects offset each other leading to no significant change in the number of jobs.

The topic's importance is such that surveys of academic economists include questions on whether U.S. minimum wages raise the unemployment rate. Prior to Card and Krueger's research, most economists consistently said that minimum wages do raise the unemployment rate, but Card and Krueger's findings were so convincing that most economists switched to say that the U.S. the minimum wage is too low to have a significant effect on the number of jobs.

Minimum wages could have a significant impact on workers regardless of whether they affect the number of jobs. One clue as to whether a worker's job is affected would be whether they are paid exactly the minimum. That could be a coincidence, but jobs paying exactly the minimum wage provide a rough indication of the extent to which the law alters employment conditions. There are no data directly counting the number of such jobs, but the U.S. Bureau of Labor Statistics uses the same survey as the median earnings reported in Fig. 9.8 to produce an annual report on the number and characteristics of minimum wage workers. That survey asks workers to self-report their usual wages along with other data about themselves, leading to the results shown in Fig. 9.10.

The Bureau of Labor Statistics cautions that survey respondents may report wages at exactly the minimum even if their actual wage is different, just because that number is easily remembered. Misreporting of that type would shift the levels shown in Fig. 9.10, but the trends reveal a clear pattern over

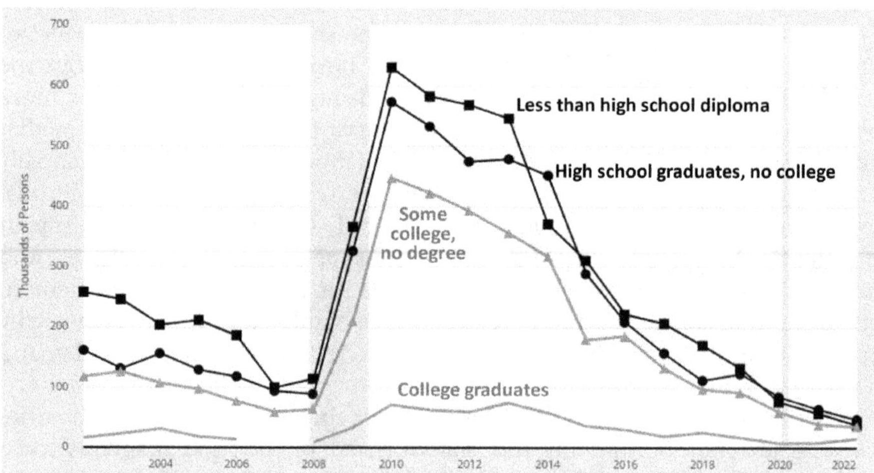

Fig. 9.10 Number of workers paid hourly at the Federal minimum wage in the U.S., 2002–2022 *Source*: Reproduced from Federal Reserve Economic Data [FRED] using Bureau of Labor Statistics, Characteristics of Minimum Wage Workers. Data are national totals estimated from self-reported wages for Current Population Survey respondents over 16 years of age. Updated versions of this chart are at https://fred.stlouisfed.org/graph/?g=19RsF

the business cycle. The number of minimum-wage earners was falling during the growth period before the 2008–2009 recession, which drove the number up sharply even among college graduates. For workers with less education, the number in minimum-wage jobs fell sharply from 2011 onwards, converging to similarly low levels in each category by 2022.

Food system jobs are disproportionately at and around the minimum wage, partly because there are fewer barriers to moving in and out of these jobs. The relative importance of each sector can be seen in the Bureau of Labor Statistics' annual report on characteristics of minimum wage workers. In 2022 they estimate that 79 million workers were paid hourly. Of those, about 7 million listed their occupation as food preparation and food services, and 0.7 million were in farming, fishing or forestry. The number of workers who reported being paid exactly the minimum wage was 141,000 or about 0.2% of the national total, and of those paid the minimum wage about 48,000 (34%) reported their occupation as food preparation and food service, and only 4000 (0.3%) were in farming, fishing or forestry. A decade of rapid growth in wages and national income, only 0.7% of the country's food service workers report being paid exactly the Federal minimum wage in 2022. The same report for previous years shows that share had been ten times higher at 7.0% in 2010, up from 2.8% in 2002.

Food system jobs include a large fraction of all tipped workers, many of whom have low total earnings. There is no authoritative measurement of income from tips, but the Bureau of Labor Statistics' annual report on minimum wage workers also reports on those who report being paid less than the Federal minimum. The data for 2022 and 2010, together with those reporting being paid exactly the minimum, are shown in Table 9.3.

In 2022, of the 7 million workers who reported their occupation as food preparation and services, 8% reported being paid less than the Federal minimum, which typically means they also earn tips—although many tipped workers actually earn more than that and might report doing so on the Current Population Survey used for these data. Back in 2010, a much larger fraction of workers reported being paid exactly the minimum and below the minimum, reflecting the large increase in demand for labor in the U.S. over the years from 2011 to 2022.

Food and Farm Employment in the U.S.

Employment opportunities relating to food are closely tied to macroeconomic conditions. Long-term changes and differences among countries in agriculture and food systems are addressed in Chapter 10, including how demographic changes and off-farm opportunities alter the number of owner-operator farm families. Here we focus only the number of hired workers and employees, for which the most reliable data in the U.S. come from surveys of business establishments conducted by the Bureau of Labor Statistics to count nonfarm employees and surveys of farm operators conducted by the National Agricultural Statistics Services to count hired farmworkers, both available since

Table 9.3 Number of U.S. workers at or below the Federal minimum wage in 2022 and 2010

	2022			*2010*		
	Hourly workers (thousands)	*At minimum (percent)*	*Below minimum (percent)*	*Hourly workers (thousands)*	*At minimum (percent)*	*Below minimum (percent)*
Total	78,729	0.2	1.1	72,902	2.5	3.5
By occupation						
Food preparation and serving	6961	0.7	8.0	6604	6.8	18.9
Farming, fishing, and forestry	656	0.0	0.6	621	2.3	3.2
All other occupations	71,112	0.1	0.5	65,677	2.1	1.9
By industry						
Leisure and hospitality	9558	0.7	6.0	8751	7.0	16.0
Agriculture	802	0.0	1.0	726	2.1	2.2
All other industries	68,369	0.1	0.4	63,425	1.9	1.8

Source: Authors' summary of data extracted from U.S. Bureau of Labor Statistics, Characteristics of Minimum Wage Workers for 2022 and 2010. All variables refer to workers paid hourly who are at or over 16 years of age. Updates are at https://www.bls.gov/opub/reports/minimum-wage, with additional data at https://www.bls.gov/cps/tables.htm

January 1990. Trends and fluctuations in the two kinds of food system employment are shown in Fig. 9.11.

The data shown in Fig. 9.11 omit self-employed farm family members which the USDA counts separately. By the USDA's definition there are roughly two million farm operations in the U.S., with roughly three million self-employed family members. What Fig. 9.11 shows is that the number of postharvest food system workers, those employed off the farm to transform agricultural output into retail products, has risen very rapidly since 1990 for food away from home from 6.4 to 12.4 million food service workers, and risen slightly for the grocery and packaged food sector from about 2.8 to 3.2 million food and beverage retail workers, and 1.5 to 1.7 million food manufacturing workers. The number of hired farm workers fluctuates seasonally, like food service workers, but has trended downward from over one million to about 0.8 million hired farm workers and employees.

Macroeconomic fluctuations that affect overall employment have a minor impact on farm, food manufacturing and grocery store jobs, which are affected primarily by other factors such as mechanization of farm work, and trends such as the reduction in retail grocery jobs in the 2000s and then its recovery after

Fig. 9.11 Farm and food system employment in the U.S., January 1990–September 2023 *Source*: Authors' chart of USDA and BLS data, shown as millions of workers by month for food sector employment and seasonally in January, April, July and October for hired farm workers. Food employment is from U.S. Bureau of Labor Statistics, Current Employment Statistics survey, not seasonally adjusted. Updated data are at https://www.bls.gov/ces/data/employment-situation-table-download.htm. Farm data are from USDA National Agricultural Statistics Service, Farm Labor Survey and includes only hired workers [not self-employed or unpaid]. Data for July 2007 are missing. Updated values are at https://www.nass.usda.gov/Surveys/Guide_to_NASS_Surveys/Farm_Labor

2012. Most importantly we see almost continuous increase from year to year for the number of jobs in bars and restaurants as well as other food service establishments, except for decline during the 2008–2009 slowdown, and the sudden collapse followed by quick recovery during the COVID pandemic.

Seasonality in both farm and restaurant work has an important influence on the kind of jobs that are offered. So does the fact that farm work is dispersed across rural areas, and that many restaurant and food service jobs can be done by people with few other options. Both categories offer relatively low-wage work, with no growth in hired farm opportunities and rapid growth in food service employment. Food manufacturing and retailing have more higher wage opportunities but grow slowly.

Labor Force Participation and Disparities in Employment

Trends in food system jobs and evolution of the macroeconomy have a major impact on labor force participation, meaning the shift from unpaid work within the household to working for others outside the home. Other factors also influence that shift, including the demographic composition of households, duration of schooling and the physical and mental health of household members. To adjust for changes in population age and years in school, it is helpful to focus on labor force participation during the years of peak employment in the 25–54 age range. Those data are compared between men and women and to the whole population in Fig. 9.12.

As shown in Fig. 9.12, the fraction of all people who have a job rises during periods of economic growth and drops during recessions, with major differences by age group and between men and women. For the overall U.S. population, there was little or no trend in the 1950s and 1960s while employment rates rose for those aged 25–54, because of the baby boom in children born after World War II and increased schooling that raised the share of people under 25 who were not working. Similarly, the overall U.S. employment to population ratio has declined since the late 1990s while employment rates have fluctuated without a trend for those aged 25–54, now due to the rising fraction of people who are older and no longer working.

The data for female labor force participation in the 25–54 age range begin only in the late 1970s, showing a sharp rise to the late 1990s, followed by decline and recovery after 2011, while male participation has trended downwards since the late 1960s. That downward trend in male participation

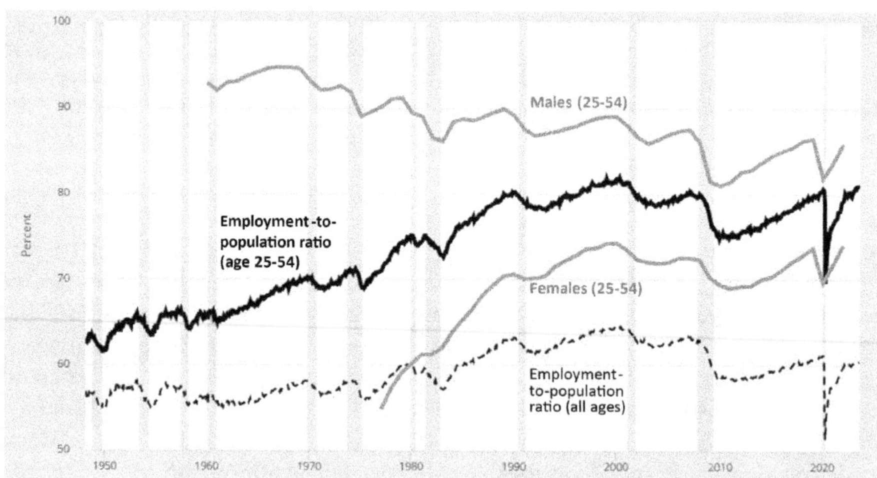

Fig. 9.12 Percent of the U.S. population in paid employment by group, January 1947–September 2023 *Source*: Reproduced from Federal Reserve Economic Data [FRED] showing the entire U.S. population's employment-population ratio [dashed at bottom], the corresponding ratio for those aged 25–54 [in solid black], and the ratios for males [upper gray line] and females [lower gray line] also aged 25–54. Data are from U.S. Bureau of Labor Statistics and the OECD, using household responses from the Current Population Survey. Updated versions are at https://fred.stlouisfed.org/graph/?g=19Ts1

involves both larger drops during recessions and less increase during periods of growth. These trends are among the most fundamental and hotly debated aspects of economic development in the U.S., particularly regarding the causes of declining male participation, and why female participation stopped increasing in the late 1990s.

The overall rise in employment rates through the 1990s for adults aged 25–54 had profound effects on the food system, contributing to higher incomes and greater interest in reducing household on many tasks including meal preparation. Analysis of those trends is the focus of Section 10.2 in the following chapter.

Beyond the male–female disparities in whether people are employed for pay, there are large disparities in earnings from those jobs. The black line below is median weekly earnings first introduced in Fig. 9.8, now accompanied by levels by demographic group in Fig. 9.13.

The gaps in median earnings shown in Fig. 9.13 are driven by structural factors in U.S. society, especially the legacy of slavery, dispossession and violence against Black Americans, and challenges facing recent immigrants and others of Hispanic or Latino descent in addition to the many factors limiting women's earnings. The trajectories of each group move roughly in parallel as macroeconomic shocks spread throughout the economy. During recessions, median earnings of those who remain employed tend to rise as lower-wage

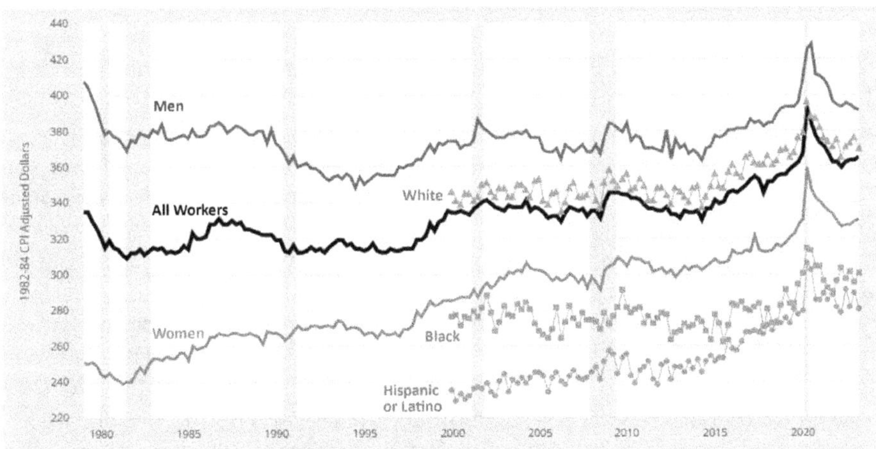

Fig. 9.13 Median weekly earnings by sex and racial category, January 1979–June 2023 *Source*: Reproduced from Federal Reserve Economic Data [FRED] showing real median weekly earnings for full time workers aged 16 and over, in U.S. dollars at 1982–1984 prices, from U.S. Bureau of Labor Statistics. The price level in 2023 happens to be about 300% of the price level in 1982–1984, so the average weekly earnings shown of around $360 in 2023 have a value in current dollars around $1080 per week or roughly $27 per hour. Updated versions are at https://fred.stlouisfed.org/graph/?g=19TsL

workers lose their jobs, and then median real earnings often fall in the recovery period after recessions partly because those lower-wage jobs return and reduce the median, but also because inflation erodes the real purchasing power of those wages. Many factors led to stagnation of median real wages, especially for men, until the 2010s, and contributed to the rapid rise in median real wages over the past decade through the pandemic and afterward.

Relative earnings, expressed as female-to-male ratio and similar gaps by racial category, can be calculated from the data in Fig. 9.13 and reveal when there have been periods of convergence between groups, divergence or parallel movements with no change in disparities. Median earnings for women were 62% of male earnings at the start these data in 1979, and that ratio rose almost continuously to 78% in 1994. There was no further convergence during the 1990s, then a small rise to 82% in 2005 and a further very small increase to 84% of median male earnings by mid-2023. That trajectory contrasts with the Black-white ratio that has stayed close to 80% throughout this period, dropping briefly to fluctuate between 75% and 80% in the period from late 2014 to 2018, before rising to 83% in mid-2022. The Hispanic-white ratio was around 68% in the early 2000s, and rose steadily to around 75% since 2020.

Each worker's pay is often a function of their seniority and experience in their line of work, contributing to the persistence of any initial disparities in employment opportunities. To complete this section on how macroeconomics affects job opportunities we return to the unemployment rate first introduced in Fig. 9.8 and show disparities around that in Fig. 9.14.

The disparities in unemployment rates shown in Fig. 9.14 differ from earnings disparities shown in Fig. 9.12 and have much greater variation over time. This variation drives change in the food system in part because job loss causes food insecurity as discussed in Section 7.2, especially when combined with low family wealth leading households to exhaust their savings and run out of money to buy food. The spike in unemployment around each recession is particularly steep for Black workers (top line) and Hispanic or Latino workers (second from top), reflecting the financial precarity that underlies the food insecurity rates shown in Fig. 7.16.

During the recent period of economic growth since 2011, unemployment rates have converged to historically low levels for all groups. The recession of 1982–1983 had raised Black unemployment from under 12% to over 20% while white unemployment rose from under 5% to 9%. The Black-white difference reached over 10% in 1984 and then fell to around 5% in the 2000s, before the 2008–2009 recession raised it again to just above 7.5% in 2011. Since then, the gap has narrowed sharply to around 2% in 2019 before the COVID recession, then back down again to 2% in late 2022 and 2023.

9.2.3 Conclusion

This section traces the short-term fluctuations around longer-term economic growth that drive change in employment, earnings and the living standards of

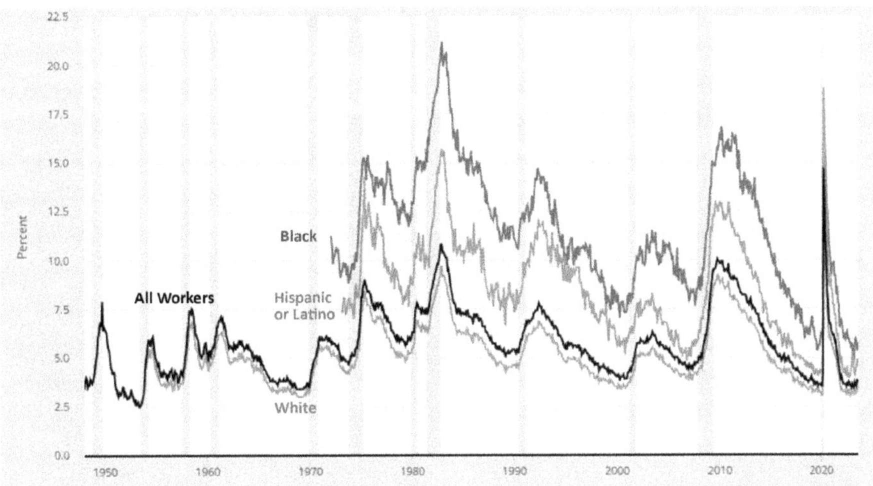

Fig. 9.14 Unemployment rates by racial category, January 1949–September 2023
Source: Reproduced from Federal Reserve Economic Data [FRED] showing the fraction of workers 16 and over without a job who were actively looking for employment, as a fraction of that group plus those employed, from the Bureau of Labor Statistics. Updated versions of this chart are at https://fred.stlouisfed.org/graph/?g=19TI1

each group in society. The circular flow of activity in each country leads to new job openings and higher wages when innovation and investment opens new opportunities, triggering a period of development and growth. When growth falters, a wave of cutbacks in spending causes simultaneous job loss across sectors and regions of the country.

Recessions and unemployment are particularly harmful for households with low wealth who may run out of money for groceries and therefore experience food insecurity unless governments intervene with monetary and fiscal policy to stabilize incomes. Periods of growth also favor some activities more than others, sometimes widening and sometimes narrowing the disparities between groups. In the U.S., after the very deep and long recession of 2008–2009 and its aftermath of high unemployment, workers experienced more than a decade of rapid increases in real income and reduction in some but not all the country's longstanding extreme disparities.

The ability of government to manage macroeconomic crises was severely tested by the COVID pandemic, whose direct impact on those affected was worsened by sudden loss of employment and income in 2020–2021. A variety of policy responses helped speed economic recovery in the U.S. and elsewhere, such as increased use of food assistance through SNAP and similar programs in other countries. Private enterprises in the food system can also be important sources of macroeconomic resilience, including the role of food retailing and food service businesses in job creation for people who might not otherwise find employment.

CHAPTER 10

International Development: Systemic Change Over Time

10.1 Agricultural Transformation: Demography, Urbanization and Farm Size

10.1.1 Motivation and Guiding Questions

Where does economic growth come from? Why do some countries have so much more stuff—a larger quantity of more diverse goods and services—than other populations? And how does change in the country's entire economy relate to its agriculture, food systems, nutrition and health?

In the previous chapter we introduced how economists measure and understand each country's economy, and now we turn to the factors that drive expansion of economic activity over time, using natural and human resources to supply goods and services. Environmental sustainability, social inclusion and living conditions all depend on both the total size of each population and activity per person. What drives change in the number of people, and how does that demographic change relate to economic activities, dietary patterns and disease?

The dynamics of population size and age structure, together with resource constraints and demand for different types of goods and services, cause economic growth to trace out somewhat consistent patterns of change over time and differences across countries. These patterns involve the rise and fall of variables such as the number of children per adult, or the number and size of family farms. Other variables keep rising but their composition changes, for example as national incomes grow but shift from resource-using to resource-saving activities. Similarity in the rise-and-fall dynamics of some variables, and the way that activities change as they grow, results from aspects of economic

W. A. Masters and A. B. Finaret, *Food Economics*,
Palgrave Studies in Agricultural Economics and Food Policy,
https://doi.org/10.1007/978-3-031-53840-7_10

life that remain mostly unchanged, such as the fact that most farms remain family enterprises.

Taken together, the changes in society we observe to be associated with economic growth are developments in some ways like human development more generally. Like the development of each person, change occurs gradually in unique ways and is not predetermined but is shaped by the environment in ways that allow us to steer growth towards more desirable outcomes.

By the end of this section, you will be able to:

1. Describe how accumulation of capital from investment in physical and human resources enables growth of income and expenditure over time;
2. Describe Preston curves, and explain how innovation enables people to obtain more longevity or other nonmarket goals at each level of national income;
3. Use the available data on demographic transition to explain and describe the rise then fall in population growth rates, size and age structure of the population; and
4. Use the available data on structural transformation and urbanization to explain and compare the rise then fall in rural populations in countries and regions around the world.

10.1.2 Analytical Tools

This chapter concerns the process of economic growth and change over time. Because growth occurs gradually, from different starting points at different speeds, many aspects of growth over time are also visible in comparisons across countries. The patterns of development traced out in one country over time are not quite the same as cross-country differences associated with higher incomes, but observing both changes and differences helps us understand underlying causes and make the choices needed for more sustainable and inclusive economic development.

The patterns we observe in changes over time and differences between countries are caused by underlying similarities, with unique features and obstacles in each case. Centuries of observation and decades of modern research on economic development have characterized stylized trajectories of change. These patterns often involve a shift from one condition to another, or a rise and then fall in some variable, explained to some degree by structural models of underlying interactions.

Our focus in this half of the book is data visualization. Each chart or table aims to include all available observations for the variables shown, to limit selection effects from choosing only some countries or time periods. The notes and text around each chart or table introduce what was observed, and how the many underlying observations were transformed into a meaningful variable. We aim to draw each kind of data from the most authoritative organization responsible for monitoring that aspect of economic development, reproducing their own charts where possible. Each chart typically has either years or income along the horizontal axis. Outcomes on the vertical axis often trace out trajectories for individual countries that cover some of the range seen across countries, allowing to see both similarities and differences.

For income and economic activity, the underlying driver of change identified by economics research is *capital accumulation*. This refers to capital in all its forms, also known as *factors of production*, starting with natural resources especially land, water and air, complemented by physical capital such as public infrastructure or buildings and equipment, and human resources including health and education. The productivity of all those factors, in terms of goods and services produced with the limited quantity of resources available, is determined by how resources are used to make things. Each population's income and economic activities, including its sustainability given planetary boundaries, is therefore driven by both the accumulation of capital and innovation in how resources are used.

Each country's limited land and other natural resources, the dynamics of population growth as each person ages from one life stage to another, and similarities among people in our needs and demand for food, all combine to make capital accumulation and innovation trace out common paths of development followed by many but not all societies around the world. These patterns include a *demographic transition* in population size and age structure, a *structural transformation* in and between sectors of the economy, a *food system transformation* in how food is made and delivered and a *nutrition transition* in diet quality and health outcomes associated with what we all eat.

Capital Accumulation: Innovation and Investment in Physical and Human Resources

The foundation of every country's economy is its land and natural resources. For most of human history that's almost all there was, as people hunted and gathered and then grew the foods they needed. Population growth was slow, and most people had very few things, but migration gradually led to settlement of almost all places around the world, and civilizations emerged under a wide variety of circumstances.

The process of economic development is most simply described as accumulation or buildup of capital in all its forms, complementing a country's natural resources with public and private investment in both physical and human resources. Those investments are closely tied to innovations, meaning the invention or development of a new technology or institutional arrangement. Innovations lead people to invest in new ways of doing things, using the available land and natural resources in a new way that produces more goods and services, some of which is saved and reinvested in additional capital.

Economic models of capital formation and growth begin with a formulation devised by Robert Solow in the 1950s, for which he was awarded a Nobel prize in 1987. Solow's approach was simultaneously also developed by an Australian economist, Trevor Swan, and Solow was awarded the prize in large part for how he and others used the Solow-Swan model to guide research and public investment in education and new technologies, in ways that help raise long-run incomes given fixed natural resources.

The Solow-Swan model itself has no role for innovation. In its simplest form, the model specifies that capital investments offer a rate of return which depends on how much capital has been accumulated, so people save and invest until additional investments are no longer worthwhile. At that point the economy has reached its highest attainable level of income per person. It might take many decades to reach that steady state outcome, but in the simplest Solow-Swan model each person would eventually have all the education and health care as well as tools and equipment known to exist. They would then save and invest just enough each year to replace the capital that depreciates or is lost over time, and thereby use the available land and natural resources in a sustainable manner.

The Solow-Swan approach captured many observed facts about the world and accurately predicted some aspects of global economic development in later decades, but it was most important for what was left out of the model and came to be a later focus of additional research. The main prediction that proved correct is how low-income countries with little capital per person could potentially grow very fast with high returns on new investment, catching up to high-income countries who would typically experience a growth slowdown as their capital stock grew towards its steady-state maximum.

The puzzling aspects of economic growth that could not be explained from within the Solow-Swan model included why some countries started their growth process earlier or later than others, and what determined their pace of growth and ultimate level of income per person. Those factors were the real subject of Robert Solow's research. In statistical tests of the model, each population's income could be explained by their accumulated education as well as physical capital and natural resources available to them, plus or minus variation in the productivity with which those factors of production are turned into income. That overall factor productivity differs by country and varies over time and is actually measured as the residual between observed income and what would be predicted based only on observed capital and natural resources. Robert Solow memorably referred to this residual as 'a measure of our ignorance' about what determines the technologies and institutions in each country, and hence the productivity of new investments that would influence their growth path.

In the decades after publication and use of the Solow-Swan model, economists focused their attention on what factors influenced the productivity of available technologies, and what institutional arrangements facilitate investment in the most productive technologies to achieve sustainable economic growth. A wide range of influences were discovered, including important roles for geography and proximity to places with complementary resources, as well as politics and incentives for governments to invest in public goods and services that complement what the private sector can provide.

A major step forward in the study of economic development has been the large-scale use of field trials, with randomized assignment of interventions in real-world settings around the world. Theoretical predictions can then be compared to observed outcomes, yielding a much richer set of data than could be obtained from naturally occurring variation in human circumstances. The use of randomized trials to test interventions in low-income settings was pioneered in the 1990s by a group of economists led by Abhijit Banerjee, Esther Duflo and Michael Kremer, for which they were awarded the Nobel prize in 2019.

Modern growth theory, and its real-world use to guide public and private investments in both low- and high-income settings, is designed around two sides of the same question: how to help low-income people escape poverty, and how to help high-income people use resources sustainably. The two questions are intertwined because the frontier of available technologies in the world, ranging from crop seeds to solar panels and everything else, drives the ability of both low- and high-income people to use the world's natural resources in more efficient and productive ways. For most of the twentieth century, technologies made increasing use of fossil fuels, and now the twenty-first century innovation is focused on electrification powered by renewables. Within agriculture and food systems, twentieth century innovation focused on increasing quantities of dietary energy and whatever kinds of food people wanted to buy, while twenty-first-century innovation is focused on improving diet quality for health and longevity. The many twists and turns of history can be studied in infinite detail but can also be seen in stylized form as patterns of transition in a few summary variables over time.

Patterns in Development: Four Transitions Associated with Economic Growth

Research on changes during economic growth has identified many different trends and transitions, each described in slightly different terms for different audiences. The most important of these for the food sector are summarized in Table 10.1.

The four transitions listed in Table 10.1 are discussed in turn throughout the remainder of this book. Each has been documented and described in different ways by different researchers, for different purposes. The table itself mentions only some aspects of each transition and is not intended to be a complete list of all changes associated with economic growth.

Here we summarize the four transitions very broadly, in ways that are most useful for food economics. Our focus is on how these transitions relate to economic growth, which itself occurs with very different timing and speed in different countries. Some populations experience rapid economic growth and capital accumulation, while others experience no income growth at all for decades or even centuries, and some have negative growth and destruction of

Table 10.1 Four transitions associated with economic growth and capital accumulation

Domains of change	Typical shifts, with varied speed and timing across countries
Demographic transition	*Rise then fall in population growth rates*
mortality & epidemiology	improved child health, shift to chronic and acute disease at older ages
dependency & ages	rise then fall in child population, rise in older population
fertility & birth timing	fewer births per woman, later first birth and wider spacing
Structural transformation	*Urbanization, shifts in location and composition of economic activity*
Employment	rise in manufacturing and services, greater specialization
agriculture & farm size	fall in farm share of population and income; rise then fall in number of farmers
Education	rise in primary, secondary, higher education and preschool enrollment
Food system transformation	*Diversification of diets, specialization and intensification in production*
crop and livestock systems	more intensive use of inputs, more (then less?) animal source foods
dietary transition	more packaged and processed foods, more meals away from home
nonfood use, loss & waste	more feed and industrial uses, less supply chain loss, more consumer waste
Nutrition transition	*From undernutrition to higher and lower-quality diets*
anthropometric status	taller children and adults, more overweight and obesity
micronutrient deficiencies	more needs met by new dietary patterns, some supplementation & fortification
diet-related disease	more burden of diabetes, hypertension, some cancers; less frequent infection

their existing capital stock. Also, for a given speed of economic growth, the pace and nature of changes in the four dimensions listed in Table 10.1 can vary greatly around the global average pattern of transition, revealing the important role for policy choice in determining the trajectory of each population and the world.

The first change in Table 10.1 is the *demographic transition*, regarding the composition and size of a country's population. Our ancestors emerged several million years ago in Africa, and populations then spread around the world with very slow, gradual increases in the total number of people. For most of human history, population growth was well below 0.1% per year, meaning that it took several years for a community of 1000 to add one more surviving child. The demographic transition began just a few hundred years ago, at different times for different populations, when the number of surviving children began to grow, and they had children of their own.

The start of demographic transition is triggered by improvements in child health, whose survival to have children of their own leads to a rise in the number of children per adult, and an accelerating rate of growth in the total population over time. During this phase, a community's population growth rate could rise to as fast as 4% per year, and for the world, that rate peaked at around 2% in the 1960s. By the time that peak is reached, many communities have already delayed and reduced the number of births per woman, which after the 1960s was facilitated by use of modern contraception. As the birth rate declines, the average age of the population rises and the burden of disease shifts to illnesses experienced primarily by older people, and the total size of the population eventually peaks and then declines if deaths outnumber births. For the world, the UN projects that peak population will occur in the 2080s, which is within lifetime of some people reading this book.

The second change in Table 10.1 is the *structural transformation* of each economy, consisting of urbanization and shifts in the composition of economic activity from primarily food to a wider variety of goods and services. Agriculture's share of employment and income declines, but the rising number of young adults caused by demographic transition typically outpaces the number of new nonfarm opportunities for many decades. For example, if a population with 3% annual growth in the number of adult workers has very rapid capital accumulation (including education) leading to an 6% annual growth in the number of nonfarm jobs, it experiences a rapid shift into nonfarm employment, but the number of farmers continues to grow until the share of workers already in nonfarm jobs reaches more than 50% of the workforces. The natural resource base for each population is limited, so any increase in the number of farmers implies a reduction in land area and natural resources per farmer. That population growth and shrinking land per person causes impoverishment, unless productivity per farm rises, or growth of nonfarm employment allows a decline in the number of farms and a corresponding increase in land area and water or other resources per farm.

The process of structural transformation into activities that use less land per person is driven by the speed of economic growth per person, interacting with the demographic transition and the size of the nonfarm employment at each point in time. Historically, the U.S. reached its peak number of farmers and smallest average farm size around 1914, then experienced accelerating change to a peak annual rate of decline in the number and rise in size of farms in the 1950s, followed by a slowing rate of change to almost no further decline in the national total number and average size of farms since the 1990s. Other countries have experienced similar transition with very different speeds and timing. The world has probably already reached its peak number of farmers, with declining numbers in many regions and continued increases only in Africa, where the peak number of farmers is unlikely to be reached until well past the 2050s.

The third change in Table 10.1 is a *food system transformation*, defining the 'food system' as all activities relating to food, including the supply of farm inputs and availability of land or other natural resources for farmers as well as postharvest transformation, distribution and marketing of food to consumers. As societies accumulate capital and earn more income from a greater variety of things, the food system uses those as inputs to food production both on and off the farm. For agriculture itself, the process of intensification complements the natural resource base of land, water and biodiversity with increasingly capital- and knowledge-intensive methods, initially to raise yields (total food output per acre or hectare), especially when available area per farmer is falling so the labor to land ratio is rising, and then to focus on mechanization when the number of farmers begins to decline so each can operate over land previously farmed by their neighbors. Innovation also gradually shifts towards more of the outputs that higher-income consumers seek, produced in ways that cause less environment harm and provide other benefits sought by higher-income communities.

Each country's food system transformation changes not only how agricultural products are made, but also a *dietary transition* in what is consumed. This transition in dietary patterns involves both the share of dietary energy from each major food group such as starchy staples or dairy, and food attributes such as whole versus refined grains and fermenting or adding sugar to dairy. At the lowest observed levels of income, people get almost all their dietary energy from the very least expensive foods per calorie. For most of history that was starchy staples, but in the twentieth century the cost per calorie of vegetable oil and sugar fell to be about the same as starchy staples. For survival people also need additional protein and micronutrients, for which the least cost sources are beans and lentils or other legumes and pulses, and very low-income people also consume small amounts of vegetables and fruits when they are in season. As incomes rise from the lowest levels we observe, most populations have a high-income elasticity of demand for meat and other animal source foods (dairy, eggs and fish), and especially for fried foods and items with added sugar and salt, as well as refined grains and other processed or packaged foods, and meals away from home.

The food system transition and dietary transition are two sides of the same phenomenon, involving supply and demand for each food attribute. For each type of food, the quantity sold equals the quantity purchased, but not all food produced is eaten by people. During the transition, nonfood uses of farm products are of growing importance. An increasing share of land and other natural resources is used to sustain livestock, and some crops are used for fuel and other industrial uses. Of the food that is intended for people, losses due to spoilage and breakage on the farm or in supply chains decline due to increasing speed and precision of handling, while kitchen and plate waste by consumers increases due to the cost of food ingredients being a smaller fraction of total meal costs, even for meals prepared at home. There is also a rise in the quantity of food consumed by household pets, especially in societies with large numbers of relatively large dogs. In addition, most people are concerned about the welfare of livestock and wild animals and have a variety of health and environmental concerns about their food as well as different preferences and aspirations. All these factors lead to a variety of dietary patterns in the population, supplied by a continuous flow of new food items in retail shops and new kinds of restaurants and food delivery services.

A fourth category of change in Table 10.1 is known as the *nutrition transition* in diet-related health outcomes. This transition in a population's nutritional status is both cause and consequence of the demographic and epidemiological transition described in the first row of the table. Nutritional variables are commonly categorized using an ABCD list to aid memory, starting with *A*nthropometry such as measured heights and weights, then *B*iomarkers which include blood and urine samples tested for micronutrient levels, *C*linical signs and symptoms of disease, and *D*ietary assessment of individual intake relating to those diseases. During the nutrition transition, children born in each successive generation can gain height very quickly relative to their parents, converging over several generations to the heights of healthful people from almost anywhere in the world. Attained heights are mostly determined in the first thousand days after conception, in utero and infancy up to two years of age and driven by exposure to disease as well as dietary intake. The nutrition transition also involves children and adults gaining weight relative to height, sometimes during relatively brief episodes of weight gain over a few months or years of stress and other contributing factors, causing a change in body composition that is difficult to reverse.

The nutrition transition in terms of biomarkers or clinical signs and symptoms typically involves gradual elimination of specific micronutrient deficiencies, such as vitamin A deficiency that can cause night blindness, or iron deficiency that can cause anemia. The micronutrient deficiencies observed at lower incomes can potentially be eliminated by dietary diversification to the extent that people move towards a balanced diet with higher levels of vegetables, fruits, dairy, fish and other nutrient-rich foods, but even in high-income countries many populations have some remaining deficiencies that are most cost-effectively filled by supplementation or fortification with individual nutrients. Fortification refers to adding nutrients to a food for the general population, such as folate (vitamin B9) that has been added to U.S. flour supplies as folic acid since 1998 to prevent neural tube defects in pregnancy, following an earlier U.S. program advocating that pregnant women take folate supplements. The switch from a supplements-only policy to fortification for everyone was done to reach more women before they know they are pregnant, on the grounds that other people might not need the additional folate but are not harmed by it. Gradually eliminating all major deficiencies in specific nutrients then shifts the burden of diet-related disease to cardiometabolic conditions such as diabetes, hypertension and some cancers, as well as food safety concerns from contaminants and water- or airborne diseases. That epidemiological transition in the timing and composition of disease burdens is partly due to rising exposure to some risk factors, and partly due to reductions in competing risks that were previously a more likely cause of death.

Preston Curves: Changes Associated with Income Can Shift Over Time

The summary Table 10.1 listing four major transitions associated with economic growth describes a global average trajectory over time and pattern across countries. As we will see there is substantial variation around that global average, and systematic shifts in how the transition takes place due to new technologies and policy changes. These shifts are known as Preston curves, after the demographer Samuel Preston who first observed the relationships illustrated in Fig. 10.1.

The type of curve shown in Fig. 10.1 was first published by Samuel Preston in 1975, and the version here was first created by economist Max Roser in 2013 as one of the initial charts in an online data-visualization project called Our World in Data. The pictures shown in this chapter begin here because Preston curves are a natural starting point for understanding international development, and because the specific chart reproduced in Fig. 10.1 is due to a Swedish physician named Hans Rosling who championed the use of data

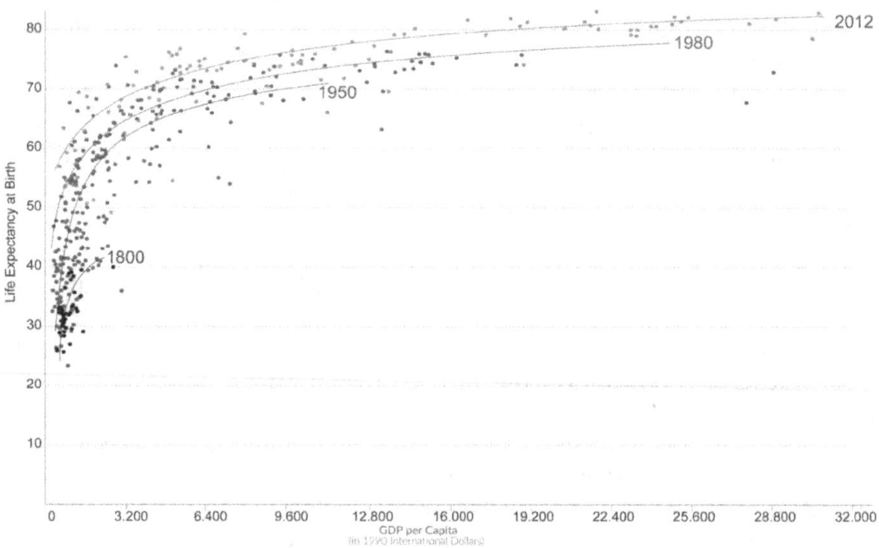

Fig. 10.1 Preston curves of life expectancy at each level of GDP, 1800–2012 *Source*: Reproduced from Max Roser, Esteban Ortiz-Ospina and Hannah Ritchie [2019], Our World in Data: Life Expectancy [https://ourworldindata.org/life-expectancy], using life expectancy data compiled from various sources by Gapminder [https://www.gapminder.org/data] and GDP estimates from the Maddison project at University of Groningen [https://www.rug.nl/ggdc/historicaldevelopment]

visualization to build intuition about large-scale changes we would otherwise not be able to see. Most data visualizations in this chapter are from national governments and international organizations because those are the most authoritative sources of the original observations, but in some cases like these Preston curves we use images compiled from multiple sources such as the work of Our World in Data.

Preston curves have real national income on the horizontal axis. In Fig. 10.1 and most other visualizations, income is shown in logarithmic terms to capture the exponential nature of growth and change. Values are shown at 1990 prices. Conversion to more recent terms would require multiplying by about 1.9 to convert obtain purchasing power parity dollars at 2017 prices, meaning that the horizontal axis labels range from about $6000 to $60,000 per person in each year.

Life expectancy shown on the vertical axis of Fig. 10.1 is the starting point for this chapter in part because survival is the most fundamental of human development goals, and the epidemiological transition towards longer lifespans relates to income in ways that also characterizes other transitions. Increases in life expectancy begin with improved child survival, which is the first step of all growth processes listed in Table 10.1.

Preston curves combine a scatterplot of individual country observations with a best-fit line through those points collected for four specific years. In 1800 all countries for which data was available were poor by modern standards, with incomes per person below $3200 in 1990 dollars, and less than 40 years of life expectancy due primarily to high infant and child mortality. By 2012 there were still some countries with incomes like those observed in 1800, but most of those had more than 60 years of life expectancy due mainly to improved child health. Also, by 2012 some countries had experienced over two hundred years of economic growth leading to ten times more goods and services per person, with the highest income countries reaching above 80 years of life expectancy.

The upward shift in the Preston curves for 1800 and then 1950 primarily involved cleaner water and sanitation, plus improved nutrition. There were very few modern medicines before 1950. The first globally successful antibiotic, penicillin, was discovered in 1928 and not deployed worldwide until the late 1940s, and the first globally effective vaccines were developed in the 1930s, first against airborne viruses that cause influenza, and then against the mosquito-borne virus that causes yellow fever. As those and other interventions were rolled out, from 1950 to 1980 the worldwide Preston Curve rose by over 10 years in the poorest countries, and by about 5 years in the richest countries. A similar and even larger shift occurred from 1980 to 2012.

Successive upward shifts in the Preston curve over the late 20th and early twenty-first centuries were caused by many different new technologies for both prevention and treatment, such as the use of oral rehydration therapy for recovery from cholera and other diarrheal diseases that was disseminated worldwide starting in the late 1970s. Some techniques spread faster than others depending on their ease of adoption and the pace of institutional innovation as well as political willingness to invest in public health services. Adoption often involves non-governmental organizations founded for specific purposes, such as Helen Keller International which initially aimed to assist blind people, then led global vitamin A supplementation campaigns starting in the 1970s to prevent blindness that also reduced child mortality, working together with government services led by the World Health Organization of the United Nations.

The Preston curves shown in Fig. 10.1 are all steepest at the lowest incomes, with a flatter slope at higher incomes and nearly horizontal line among the highest income countries today. That pattern of diminishing returns to income reflects how with some investments offer high impacts at low cost per person that can readily be adopted in low-income countries. These include many things that households do for themselves without scientific knowledge or intervention, such as seeking cleaner air and water, often with the help of collective action and government programs such as local water and sanitation improvements. Other interventions require more administrative effort based on scientific guidance, such as vaccination or supplementation campaigns.

Scatterplots around each year's Preston curve typically show more variation at lower incomes than at higher incomes. This reflects how countries can have low average incomes per person for different reasons under a wide range of environmental or other circumstances that influence life expectancy, while almost all countries with high national income invest in the technologies needed to approach the global frontier of survival and longevity. That pattern of convergence towards more similar outcomes at higher income levels applies primarily to goals that all societies have in common, such as life expectancy, but even for such a universal human objective each country has its own unique history and trajectory of life expectancy over time.

Country Trajectories: Life Expectancy and National Income in Four Example Countries

The data compilations and visualizations created for Our World in Data provide new and informative ways of seeing how transitions occur. Some of the variation we observe is measurement error, but the very wide range of experiences shown in the available data reveal both similarities and differences in how different populations have experienced economic development as shown in Fig. 10.2.

The background of Fig. 10.2 has trajectories in gray for 178 countries and territories, of which the highlighted examples are Ethiopia and Nigeria (the two largest countries in Africa), China and India (the two largest in Asia) and the U.S. Many other examples would be similarly revealing. The data for Ethiopia and Nigeria begin in 1950, partly because systematic data collection for many countries did not begin until formation of the UN in 1945, while

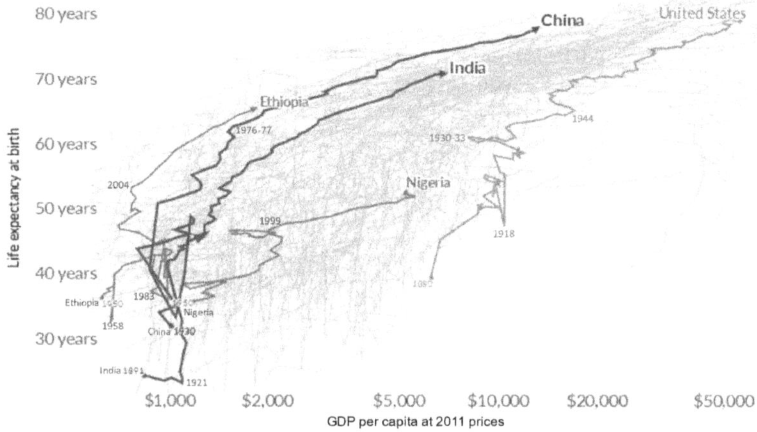

Fig. 10.2 Examples of growth and change in national income and life expectancy, 1880–2018 *Source*: Reproduced from Max Roser, Esteban Ortiz-Ospina and Hannah Ritchie [2019], Our World in Data: Life Expectancy, using data from diverse sources. Other countries can be shown by modifying https://ourworldindata.org/grapher/life-expectancy-vs-gdp-per-capita

the data for India and the U.S. begin in 1891 and 1880 respectively, and data for China begins in 1930.

Ethiopian data for 1950 shows a life expectancy around 36 years and average income of $622. Their trajectory was initially diagonal, upwards and to the right following the global pattern, but was interrupted by a severe famine in 1958, another in 1973, and an even more extreme famine in 1983–1985 followed by an income decline which lasted for a decade after 1993. When economic growth resumed in 2004, within four years the country had returned to the income levels of the 1970s and proceeded diagonally from there to a life expectancy in 2018 around 65 years at an income of $1838.

Nigeria data begin in 1950 with a similar life expectancy as Ethiopia at 36 years, but twice its national income level at $1200 per person. The country proceeded diagonally until a civil war caused famine in the province of Biafra during 1968–1970 marked an end to those improvements, with a decade of income decline starting in the late 1970s followed by a decade of no further change until income grow resumed in the late 1990s. Nigeria then returned to a diagonal path but at a much flatter slope than most other countries, with less gain of life expectancy than other countries achieved, to a life expectancy in 2018 around 53 years at an income of $5238.

The differences between Ethiopia and Nigeria are stunning, and clearly demonstrate how national income is not the sole determinant of life expectancy or any other aspect of economic development. In the 1950s, Ethiopia had one of the lowest levels of average income ever recorded, and it experienced some periods of improvement from there but did not begin its trajectory of consistent economic growth until 2004. In contrast, Nigeria entered the 1950s with higher income and began modern growth around 1999 but has not ever experienced the sharp rise in life expectancy achieved by Ethiopia.

The development trajectories of individual countries defy easy explanation. Entire books have been written about the development of even a single village, and whole libraries are devoted to the history of Africa. One of William's favorite expressions about international development is that we can learn so much from actually visiting each place: from a week of interviews, we could write a whole article, and from a year of study we could write a book, but if we stay long enough we usually learn that those partial truths can be misleading and much of what we see remains surprising. Both William and Amelia were able to live in various countries for multiple years, and William was able to return in the 2010s to places he'd lived in Zimbabwe, Haiti and Colombia more than 25 years earlier. With deeper immersion and a longer time frame, we find more unexpected aspects of how each place develops, just as we might from returning to our own childhood homes. Deep scholarship about individual people, places and communities is therefore essential to understanding their specific circumstances, while zooming out to longer time frames and large sample sizes is essential to understanding broad patterns of development for entire populations and the world as a whole.

India data in Fig. 10.2 begin with 1891, when India had a life expectancy of 24 years at an income level of $843 per year. India then had 20 years of unchanged or declining life expectancy and slightly rising income to one of the world's lowest recorded life expectancies at 23 years and an income of $1100 in 1911, at which point the country's life expectancy began a gradual rise. That rise occurred much more steadily than Ethiopia and Nigeria, despite famines in some regions of India during 1943 and 1972–1973. For the first 30 years of rising life expectancy, however, India was still under British rule and experienced no increase in national income at all. Independence came in 1948, when the country's national income was about the same level as 50 years earlier. India's income growth did not begin until 1951 and accelerated gradually, to reaching a life expectancy in 2018 of 71 years at an income of $6800 per year.

China data beginning in 1930 starts at a point very similar to where India was at that time, with a life expectancy of 32 years and an income of $1012 per year. Life expectancy then improved greatly to 49 years in 1958 but plummeted during a massive famine in 1959–1961 before recovering and continuing its rise. From 1930 to the mid-1960s China had no income growth at all, and income only gradually began to increase in the late 1960s and 1970s, accelerating particularly after a brief reversal in 1976–1977. At the start of China's modern period of growth in 1978, the country had slightly higher income than India ($1744 vs. $1540) and much high life expectancy (63.2 vs. 52.5). By the end of the period in 2018, China had much higher income ($13,100 vs. $6800) and only somewhat higher life expectancy (78 vs. 71 years).

U.S. data in this chart begin in 1880, with a life expectancy of 39 years at an income of $6256. Life expectancy then grew gradually except for a sharp drop during the flu epidemic of 1918, and income also grew gradually except for the large reversal in the great depression of 1930–1933, and the anomalously large expansion of GDP for World War II military spending that peaked in 1944. The relatively long and sustained period of economic growth led the U.S. to a life expectancy in 2018 of 79 years at an income of $55,300 per year.

The cloud of all countries' data in Fig. 10.2 allows us to see each country's trajectory in the global context. Ethiopia started and still remains at the left edge and upper edge of the cloud, meaning that it has unusually high life expectancy for its level of income. Ethiopia, Nigeria, India and China all had multiple large setbacks prior to their modern era of economic development, but then grew quickly along a diagonal path. China has consistently had greater life expectancy than India at each level of income. Nigeria has followed a development path with much less increase in life expectancy as its income rose, moving it from the center towards the right of the data cloud, towards the United States which is consistently on the right and lower edge of the cloud with low life expectancy for its level of income.

The purpose of showing five trajectories in detail is to demonstrate that the systematic patterns of development described in Table 10.1 are the result of broad social forces only when development advances. Economic growth can easily stall or go into reverse. It is only when growth occurs at all that additional income can be spent on child survival as shown in Figs. 10.1 and 10.2, with innovations that systematically improve outcomes at each level of income in the Preston Curves, as well as differences in the speed and direction of change in each development trajectory. In the following sections we examine the four major transitions of Table 10.1 in turn, using a variety of data sources and visualization techniques.

Demographic Transition, Population Size and Age Structure

The first major shift associated with economic development is the demographic transition, triggered by improvements in child survival and reduced mortality that are measured by overall life expectancy in the previous two figures, followed by lower fertility and a smaller number of children per woman. The speed and timing of these trends can best be seen in terms of a population's overall rate of births and deaths per thousand people, as shown with actual historical data for two example countries in Fig. 10.3.

The data in Fig. 10.3 show Sweden because it has recordkeeping available to us of births and deaths from the mid-1700s, and Mauritius because it is the only African country with similar recordkeeping from the late 1800s. These are each country's 'crude' rates in the sense of aggregate totals, shown per thousand people to avoid the decimals needed to show each as a percentage

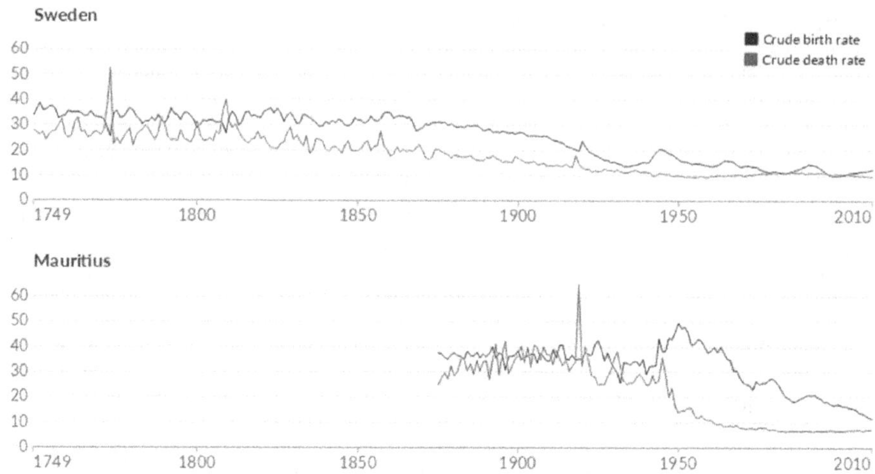

Fig. 10.3 The demographic transition in Sweden and Mauritius *Source*: Reproduced from Hannah Ritchie et al. [2023], Our World in Data: Population Growth, using data compiled by Brian Mitchell for the International Historical Statistics project at https://www.eui.eu/Research/Library/ResearchGuides/Economics/Statistics/DataPortal/IHS. Other countries can be chosen at https://ourworldindata.org/grapher/demographic-transition-sweden

of the population. One feature of these charts is that the country's population growth rate in each year is the gap between deaths and births, seen by counting the dotted horizontal lines between the two curves that trace intervals of 10 per thousand, or 1% annual growth in the population when births outnumber deaths.

These data show how Sweden's death rate was highly variable with no trend from 1749 to the 1820s, then began to decline and have smaller fluctuations until about 1880 when it declined faster and had very few fluctuations until the spike from the 1918 flu epidemic. The timing reveals how death rates fell long before any modern medicines were known, with very large year-to-year variation in population health that were also reflected in birth rates. During the early period from 1749 through the 1820s, the birth rate rose when deaths fell, and fell when deaths rose, as waves of infectious disease both raised mortality and limited fertility, followed a 'baby boom' of births when health conditions improved. After 1820 the birth rate generally stayed above 30 and declined only after 1870, opening a gap of around 10 more births than deaths per thousand people. Decline in birth rates happened long before any modern contraceptives were available, due only to social changes such as delaying marriage. That decline in fertility happened at about the same pace as the decline in mortality, leading to population growth of about 1% per year for over a century. It was only in the 1920s that birth rates started to fall faster than death rates, ultimately catching up to reach near zero population growth in the early 2000s.

The data for Mauritius show a very different story, with deaths fluctuating along a rising trend from 1875 to the 1910s, so the country had no population growth at all. There were then even larger fluctuations in both births and deaths, followed by a period after World War II when death rates plummeted, and birth rates spiked. In Mauritius from 1945 to 1950 birth rates rose in response to better health, as births had in Sweden during the 1749–1820 period, before people reduced their birth rates from 1950 onwards. Birth rates fell must faster than they had in Sweden, but death rates had dropped even faster, opening a population growth rate of over 3% per year until death rates stopped falling in the 1980s while birth rates continued to decline.

Each country's population growth begins with child survival, and in some cases a brief baby boom period of replacement fertility after periods of hardship and high mortality, followed by a sustained decline in birth rates. The timing and speed of change depends on the circumstances for each country. Countries like Mauritius that had increasing child survival in the mid to late twentieth century created a broad base of children who then grew up to form families of their own. That creates population 'momentum' from a larger size of each successive generation, and then population aging after the fertility rates of each generation have fallen.

The absolute number of people and age distribution of each country's population follows from their unique speed and timing of change in birth and death rates, but the synchronized rapid worldwide improvements in child survival and life expectancy after 1950 created a distinctive global demographic transition illustrated by Fig. 10.4.

The population pyramids shown in Fig. 10.4 are compiled by statisticians at the United Nations from country census data, using demographic models to infer the number of people at each age in each year for places with few observations in the top row for 1950, 1975 and 2000, and then to project forward for 2025, 2050 and 2075. These UN population projections continue to 2100, with variants shown in degrees of shading at the bottom of each pyramid in the second row. The lightest and widest shading shows the UN's 95% prediction interval, implying that only 5% of demographic scenarios would exceed that range, and the intermediate shading shows an 80% prediction interval. The primary estimate shown is the UN's median projection.

Population pyramids are constructed using the same data and techniques as life expectancy for each cohort of infants, based on demographic models known as life tables. A population's life table for a given year is based on mortality rates for people of each age and sex observed in the previous year, which provides the probability that a person of each age and sex will survive into the following year. Demographers then use the previous year's fertility rates for women at each age to calculate the number of infants likely to be born in the following year. The number of births each year depends not only on the average number of births per woman over their lifetime, known as the

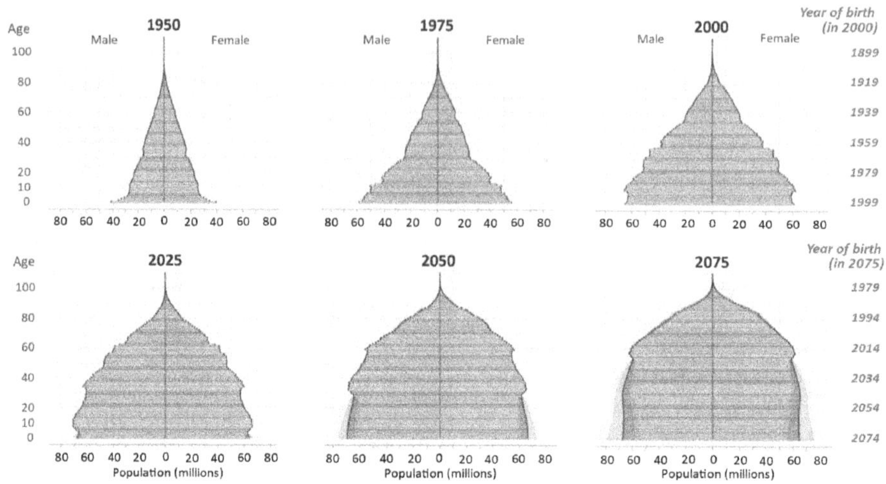

Fig. 10.4 The demographic transition worldwide: population pyramids from 1950 to 2075 *Source*: Authors' composite image of population pyramids reproduced from the UN Department of Economic and Social Affairs, Population Division [2022], World Population Prospects 2022 [https://population.un.org]. Population pyramids, growth rates and other data for individual countries and regions can be drawn at https://population.un.org/wpp/Graphs/DemographicProfiles/Pyramid

total fertility rate, but also the size of each cohort of women at each age and their birth timing. Delayed first births and spacing between births can greatly slow the rate of population growth, even if there is no change in the total number of children per woman.

The global demographic transition shown in Fig. 10.4 drives many of the changes in agriculture, food systems and nutrition described in Table 10.1. The global total is the sum of all countries, driving change worldwide based on each country starting the transition when their child mortality begins to fall, proceeding at different speeds with occasionally reversals. Some countries such as Sweden already experienced most of their historical transition prior to 1950, but most of the world population is experiencing a transition whose timing is more like Mauritius, with most of their decline in child mortality occurring after 1950.

Demographic transition can be described as a shift from population pyramids to columns with similar numbers of people in each age group. In the pyramid stage, the population at each age has a larger cohort of people younger than them. Each community has many newborns and young children per young adult, parents are caring for children throughout their adult lives, and older adults form a small share of the total population. Such pyramids can persist for decades or centuries with little or no and even negative population growth. When a larger fraction of children survives, as they did after 1950, the result is population growth and transition as shown in Fig. 10.1. The worldwide pyramid grew larger from 1950 to 1975 and 2000, with fewer newborns per adult but a growing share of the population who are school-aged children and young adults.

The age structure of the population can be as important as its total size, as shown in Table 10.2.

The magnitudes of change and growth provided in Table 10.2 summarize the global population pyramids in age groups that are especially relevant for economic development, growth and equity. Children aged 0–4 constituted 14% of the entire world population in 1950, dropping slightly to 13% in 1975. In most contexts those infants and preschoolers are cared for primarily by older girls and women, both in the home and as care providers in the community, severely limiting the ability of women to do any other kinds of work.

Table 10.2 Distribution and growth of the global population by age group, 1950–2100

	1950 (in %)	*1975 (in %)*	*2000 (in %)*	*2025 (in %)*	*2050 (in %)*	*2075 (in %)*	*2100 (in %)*
Dependency rates and size of the workforce							
Age 0–4 (infancy and preschool)	14	13	10	8	7	6	5
Age 5–14 (school-aged children)	21	24	20	17	14	12	11
Age 15–64 (youth and midlife, or working age)	60	57	63	65	63	61	59
Age 65 + (older adults)	5	6	7	10	17	21	24
Age 80 + (octogenarian and older)	*0.6*	*0.7*	*1.2*	*2.1*	*4.7*	*7.2*	*9.3*
Cohort growth or shrinkage over 25 years							
Age 0–4 (infancy and preschool)		+60	+13	+5	+3	−7	−11
Age 5–14 (school-aged children)		+83	+29	+9	−1	−6	−9
Age 15–64 (youth and midlife, or working age)		+70	+41	+10	−2	−4	−8
Age 65 + (older adults)		+55	+66	+38	+14	+4	−3
Age 80 + (octogenarian and older)		+77	+87	+103	+87	+35	+15

Source: Authors' summary of data from United Nations, Department of Economic and Social Affairs, Population Division (2022). *World Population Prospects: The 2022 Revision*. Updates and other variables are available at https://population.un.org/wpp. Data on family planning and contraceptive use are at https://www.un.org/development/desa/pd/data/family-planning-indicators

When the child dependency rate declines as shown in the top row of Table 10.2, women's time is freed to do many other things thereby contributing to growth of the economy. Claudia Goldin was awarded the Nobel prize in 2023 for pioneering work on this topic. Goldin's findings included how delayed births played a causal role in decision-making about women's education and careers, including the sharp rise in women's schooling and paid employment in the U.S. from the 1970s through the 1990s seen in Fig. 9.11 of the previous chapter. Goldin's work shows how delayed and declining birth rates allowed women to reach higher levels of schooling, often beyond that of men, even as their remaining childcare obligations then limit their professional advancement. This work helps explain how women's wages rose towards convergence with men's earnings into the 1990s as shown in Fig. 9.12 of the previous chapter, and identifies the need for assistance with childcare to permit continued convergence as shown for some other countries in Fig. 7.10 of our chapter on inequity.

The share of the world's population aged 15–64 plays an important role in economic development, as people in that age range are often increasingly experienced and productive at their work. From 1950 to 1975 that group declined from 60 to 57% of the world's population, limiting the world's ability to have a rising share of all people participating in the workforce. Then from 1975 to 2000 and 2025 the world population's share in that age range rose rapidly from 57 to 63 and 65%, contributing a 'demographic dividend' through greater labor force participation. From 2025 onwards the world will return to the 'demographic drag' experienced earlier as the share of working age declines.

The share of the population that is 65 or older, and even 80 or older, will continue to grow at an increasing rate. As shown by Table 10.2, the fraction of people who are 65+ grew from 5 to 7% in the half-century from 1950 to 2000 but will more than double from 7 to 17% from 2000 to 2050. As dependency shifts from children to older adults, including especially those 80 or older, the cost shifts from childcare to elder care, and from schooling to medical services. A disproportionate fraction of both childcare and elder care is done by women, but the time burden and cost of care arises somewhat later in each person's adult life and might be less likely to interrupt their initial work experience.

Cohort growth and shrinkage over 25 years, from one generation to the next, drive change in employment prospects especially in the food system. For the world as a whole the number of school-age children from 5 to 14 grew by 9% from 2000 to 2025 but is projected to decline by about 1% over the next 25 years to 2050. The number of young and working adults will also fall, even as the older population grows.

The demographic transition affects food and nutrition not only through the number of people, but also epidemiological shifts in the burden of disease, and changes in gendered time use as shown in Table 10.3.

Table 10.3 Vital statistics for the global population, 1950–2100

	1950	*1975*	*2000*	*2025*	*2050*	*2075*	*2100*
Population size and growth							
Total population (billions)	2.50	4.07	6.15	8.19	9.71	10.37	10.35
Growth rate (percent per year)	1.7%	1.8%	1.3%	0.9%	0.5%	0.1%	−0.1%
Crude birth rate (births per thousand people)	37	30	22	16	14	12	11
Crude death rate (deaths per thousand people)	20	12	8	8	9	11	12
Life expectancy and age-specific mortality							
Life expectancy at birth (years)	46.5	58.3	66.5	73.8	77.2	79.8	82.1
Infant mortality rate (deaths per thousand, age 0–1)	143	91	53	26	17	12	9
Under-five mortality rate (deaths per thousand aged 0–5)	224	133	76	36	24	17	13
Youth and midlife mortality (deaths per thousand aged 15–60)	379	251	183	130	109	93	75
Fertility and family planning							
Total fertility rate (births per woman)	4.9	4.1	2.7	2.3	2.1	2.0	1.8
Mean age of childbearing (all births)	29	28	27	28	29	30	30
Estimated demand for family planning (pct of women aged 15–49)		58.9	73.9	75.9			
Contraceptive use, any modern method (percent of women aged 15–49)		28.0	55.0	59.1			
Contraceptive use, any traditional method (pct of women aged 15–49)		10.5	6.8	6.2			
Sex-specific mortality and gender bias							
Sex ratio at birth (males per thousand females)	1054	1056	1075	1054	1047	1046	1045
Sex ratio of the total population (males per thousand females)	993	1004	1011	1009	1000	994	987

Source: Authors' summary of data from United Nations, Department of Economic and Social Affairs, Population Division (2022). *World Population Prospects: The 2022 Revision*. Updates and other variables are available at https://population.un.org/wpp. Data on family planning and contraceptive use are at https://www.un.org/development/desa/pd/data/family-planning-indicators

The demographic transition caused the world population to double over the 50 years from 1975 to 2025, from 4.07 to 8.19 billion as shown in the first line of Table 10.3. In so doing the percentage rate of growth from year to year has been cut in half, from 1.8 to 0.9% as shown in the second line. African countries such as Mauritius have experienced this change much faster and later in time than the world, but the pattern in terms of life expectancy and the epidemiological transition, fertility and birth timing mentioned in Table 10.1 occurs along similar lines.

The epidemiological aspect of demographic transition can be seen in the sharp fall in infant, child and youth or midlife mortality, shifting the burden of disease to chronic and noncommunicable diseases caused by risk factors whose impact is cumulative over time. The onset of cardio-metabolic diseases such as diabetes and hypertension most often occur in adulthood and is closely related to diet and other modifiable risks that are themselves associated with economic growth and development, as discussed in the next section of this chapter.

The timing of births as shown in the middle sector of Table 10.3 is a central aspect of social and economic development, greatly influencing women's participation in the economy. From 1950 to 2000 the total fertility rate fell from 4.9 to 2.7 births per woman, but much of that came from wider spacing and an earlier end of childbearing in the mother's adult life, so the average age at which mothers gave birth went down from 29 to 27 years of age. As fertility continues to fall to below replacement levels, postponing that first and second child is driving the average age of childbearing back up to 29 and then 30 in the decades ahead. Control over the timing of births is closely related to demand for and use of contraception. The fraction of women survey respondents worldwide who say they want to use family planning is estimated to have risen from about 60 to 76% from 1975 to 2025, with a doubling of the fraction of all women who use any modern method from 28 to 60%, and a decline from 11 to 6% in the fraction who use a traditional method.

Sex-specific behavior and gender roles underlie many aspects of the demographic transition, with two of the most important kinds of variation shown in Table 10.3. For humans and most other mammals, under normal conditions biological factors lead to a slightly larger number of males than females at births, and higher mortality for males in infancy, childhood and as adults. That gap is reflected in the sex ratios observed in 1950, when there were 1054 male births for every thousand female births, and the surviving population had only 993 males per thousand females. The UN projects that the world will eventually return to those same ratios in the future, but in the meantime, there has been a large swing towards more male births and more male survival.

The sex ratio changes shown in the last two rows of Table 10.3 reveal that from 1950 to 1975 there was almost no change in the sex ratio at birth, but a greater increase in male than female survival so the sex ratio of the population rose to 1004 males per thousand females. Over the next 25 years to 2000, the sex ratio at birth rose from 1056 to 1075 males per thousand females, and survival also continued to grow faster for males than females leading to the sex ratio of the whole population rising from 1004 to 1011. The mechanisms behind these changes include both gender bias and sex-specific mortality. There is evidence that a preference for sons contributes to neglect and even infanticide of girls in many settings, leading to millions of 'missing women' highlighted in the early 1990s by the economic philosopher Amartya Sen, whose many contributions led to his being awarded the economics Nobel prize in 1998. At the same time, biological factors leading to high child mortality affect boys more than girls, so reducing those harms has the opposite effect.

The changes in gender roles and other aspects of human development shown in Table 10.3 have profound consequences for agriculture and food systems. Economic principles can help us understand those changes and improve outcomes, for example by recognizing how decisions to change time use and household activities are often made in response to changes in opportunity costs. When differences between groups in access to schooling and earning opportunities are reduced or removed, people will reallocate their time to take advantage of those opportunities. Lifting barriers to participation reduces inequity and drives growth of the economy, creating a further round of new opportunities from economic expansion especially in agriculture and the food system.

Agricultural Transformation, Urbanization and the Food System

Economic growth is driven by accumulation of physical capital and human resources, interacting with demographic transition, allowing a country's people to use its land and natural resources in new and different ways. Many activities deplete or degrade natural resources at first, until the increasing scarcity and value of ecosystem services and other environmental attributes drives individual and collective action towards land-saving, nature-enhancing innovations. The most fundamental of these shifts is the transition from extraction and cultivation or production of physical goods in general towards more knowledge-intensive services.

The *structural transformation* of economic activity is generally defined as the switch from agriculture to manufacturing and services, as illustrated for the U.S. in Fig. 10.5.

The left panel of Fig. 10.5 shows how economic development in the U.S. drew workers first into manufacturing, which rose from 15 to 20 and then 26% of jobs from 1840 to 1860 and then the 1880s. Manufacturing employment fluctuated between 28 and 34% of jobs from 1900 to 1980, then fell to 15% by 2015. Employment in services fluctuated between 21 and 27% of employment from 1840 through the 1890s, but then grew continuously to 84% where it remained during the 2011–2015 period. Service employment fluctuated briefly during World War II, but otherwise grew consistently from year to year to the entire twentieth century, from 1900 to 2011.

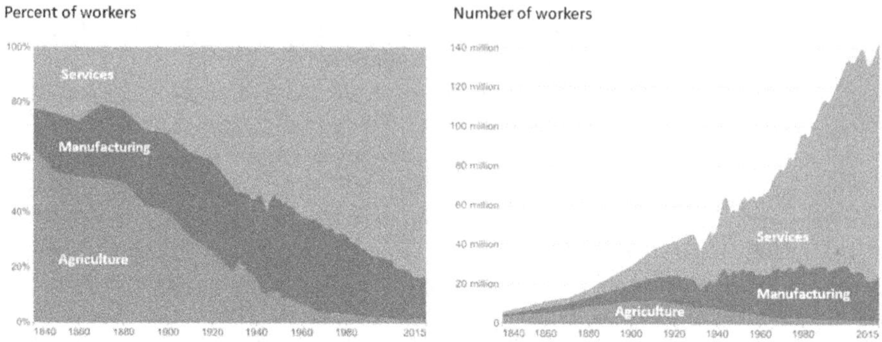

Fig. 10.5 The structural transformation of the United States, 1840–2015 *Source*: Reproduced from Our World in Data, updating data described in B. Herrendorf, R. Rogerson and A. Valentinyi [2014], 'Growth and Structural Transformation' in Handbook of Economic Growth Vol. 2B [Elsevier]. Data for other countries are at https://ourworldindata.org/structural-transformation-and-deindustrialization-evidence-from-todays-rich-countries

As shown at the left of the chart, farming was the principal occupation for 60% of Americans in 1840. The structural transformation then reduced the share of workers who are farmers almost continuously, except for a rise during the great depression (1930–1933) and during World War II. The pace of decline slowed in the 1990s when the share fell below 3%. Since 1996, the share of workers who are farmers has fluctuated between 1.5 and 2%.

A surprising aspect of structural transformation is how agriculture's declining share of employment interacts with demographic transition and changes in the total number of people entering the workforce each year, as shown in the right panel of the chart. The total number of U.S. workers in 1840 was 5.7 million, of whom 3.6 million were farmers. Because the total number of workers was rising quickly, in part due to immigration, the number of farmers kept rising for the next 70 years, to a peak around 12 million in 1910–1915. From the end of World War I in 1918 the number of farmers then fell steadily, with the fastest pace of decline between 1950 and 1970, before flattening in the 1990s. Since 1996, the number of farmers has fluctuated between 2 and 2.5 million.

The pattern seen in the U.S. is unusual primarily due to expansion of the country's geographic borders, primarily through conquest and displacement of native people as well as treaties to buy land from France, Spain and other colonial powers. The U.S. also had unusually high levels of immigration, and a long well documented experience of almost uninterrupted economic growth. To compare the 175-year history of the U.S. shown in Fig. 10.5 with structural transformation elsewhere, we can use the more recent and very rapid transformation of the economy in South Korea shown in Fig. 10.6.

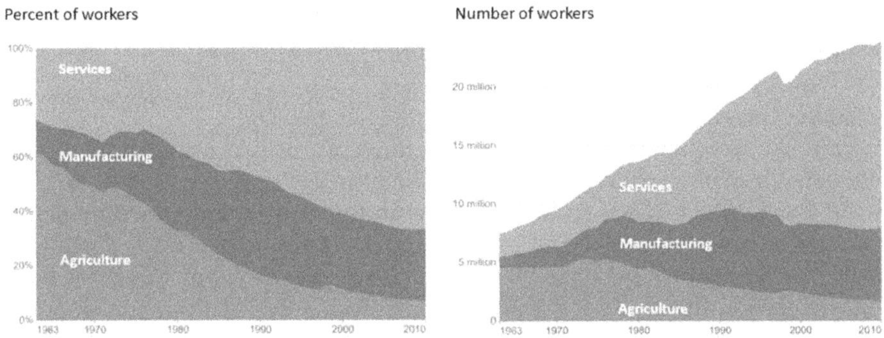

Fig. 10.6 The structural transformation of South Korea, 1963–2010 *Source*: Reproduced from Our World in Data, updating data described in B. Herrendorf, R. Rogerson and A. Valentinyi [2014], 'Growth and Structural Transformation' in Handbook of Economic Growth Vol. 2B [Elsevier]. Data for other countries are at https://ourworldindata.org/structural-transformation-and-deindustrialization-evidence-from-todays-rich-countries

The structural transformation of South Korea shown in Fig. 10.6 is like patterns observed in the U.S. and almost any other country experiencing economic growth, except that South Korea's transformation was unusually rapid. The growth trajectory of South Korea, when drawn in terms of national income and life expectancy, is like that of China in Fig. 10.2. The first available data for those variables in South Korea is around 1913, when the country had among the lowest incomes and shortest life expectancy ever recorded for any country.

Korea was ruled by Japan as a colony from 1910 to 1945 and entered the 1950s with the same very low level of income (around \$3 per person per day in 2017 dollars) and very low life expectancy (under 25 years) as it had in 1910. By 1963, at the start of Fig. 10.6, South Korea's national income and health had begun to rise, leading into one of the world's fastest periods of sustained economic growth ever recorded. Over the 47 years from 1963 to 2010, South Korea's income rose from \$5 to over \$90 per person per day at purchasing power parity prices of 2017, and life expectancy rose from 56 to 81 years.

South Korea's structural transformation from agriculture to manufacturing and services was unique primarily in terms of its speed. From 1963 to 1976 the fraction of workers who were farmers dropped from 62 to 43%, and the fraction in manufacturing more than doubled from 12 to 27%. The country's demographic transition led to such rapid growth of the entire workforce that the number of farmers kept rising throughout this period, growing from 4.6 to a peak of 5.3 million farmers, before the absolute number of farmers began its sustained decline since 1976. The share of workers in manufacturing peaked at 36% in 1991, and by 2010 the country's workforce was 67% in services, 26% in manufacturing and 7% in agriculture.

Economic Growth and Transformation in Sources of GDP

To compare development trajectories for the world it is helpful to use aggregate data for major geographic regions. The primary source of such data is the World Bank, which lends to governments in low- and middle-income countries and tracks a wide range of economic development indicators. Countries differ in whether and how they collect each type of data, but the most basic national accounting of GDP is available for almost all populations and is shown for selected global regions in Fig. 10.7.

The national income data underlying Fig. 10.7 were collected in each country's local currency, then converted to U.S. dollars at market exchange rates in each year and adjusted for inflation in the United States to show values in 2015 dollars. This provides the longest time frame over which consistent data are available for all low- and middle-income countries, revealing the main stylized facts of their economic growth and development since 1960.

The top line shows GDP per person for the world, rising steadily except for brief global downturns in 1974–1975, 1981–1982, 2008–2009 and then 2020. These synchronized downturns reflect the many linkages between countries through international markets and other conditions such as the global

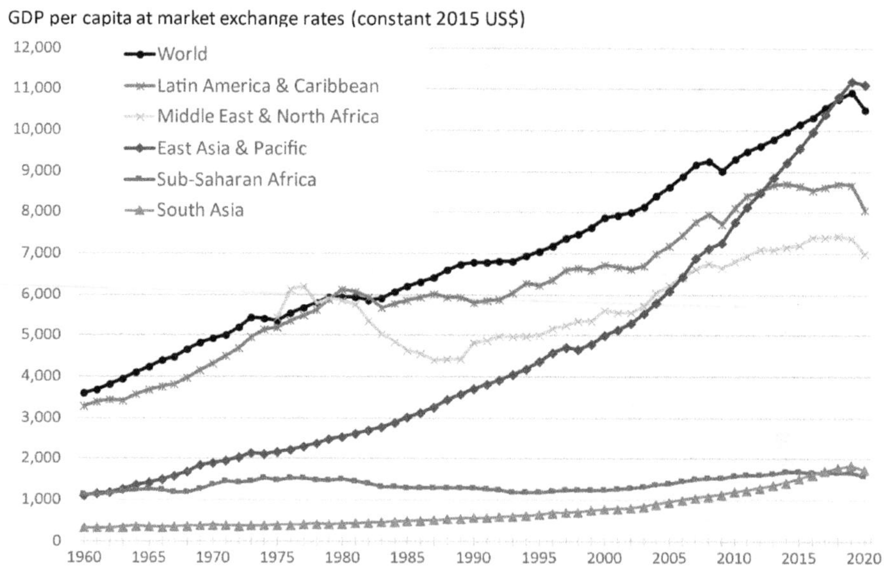

Fig. 10.7 Economic growth in selected regions and worldwide, 1960–2020 *Source*: Authors' chart of data from the World Bank, World Development Indicators. Updated values of these and related indicators are available from https://databank.worldbank.org/MacroDataBySector-AgTransformation/id/eb58207

COVID pandemic in 2020. Latin America and the Caribbean was close to the global average through 1980 but experienced three years of decline then no growth until expansion resumed from the early 1990s to 2014 when growth again stopped, ahead of the 2020 recession. The Middle East and North Africa experienced an even greater decline in the 1980s but resumed growth after 1990.

The three regions with low incomes in 1960 experienced very different trajectories. East Asia and the Pacific and Sub-Saharan Africa had similar incomes at first, but Africa grew only slowly through the 1960s and 1970s and experienced a lengthy period of decline from 1980 to the mid-1990s, before experiencing growth from 1999 to around 2015. In contrast, East Asia and the Pacific converged to surpass the world average income.

To measure a population's experience of economic development it is helpful to recognize that their income is used to buy goods and services locally, and international comparisons at market exchange rates may not reflect the quantity of things they can buy within their own country. For that kind of comparison, we would need prices for the same things in multiple countries, averaged over all items to construct purchasing power parity (PPP) exchange rates that account for differences in the price level between countries, just like a country's own consumer price index (CPI) accounts for changes over time. These PPP exchange rates were introduced in Chapter 7 to compute global poverty rates in Figs. 7.6 and 7.7, and are used here to compare national income in Fig. 10.8.

The PPP conversion factors that account for the difference between Figs. 10.7 and 10.8 are available only since 1990 and are shown here on the same axes for ease of comparison. Using local prices to compare real incomes reveals how populations in the Middle East and North Africa as well as Latin America and the Caribbean had purchasing power in their countries that are above the global average, instead of below it as suggested when using market exchange rates, but trends for them and for East Asia and the Pacific are unaffected by the difference.

Where currency conversions make a bigger difference to understanding economic growth is when comparing Sub-Saharan Africa and South Asia. Local prices for similar things turn out to be much higher in Africa, so a dollar at market exchange rates can buy larger quantities of goods and services in South Asia than in Africa. Comparing countries in terms of purchasing power reveals that total real income of South Asians caught up to that of Africans in 2005 and has since grown to average incomes per person that are about one-third higher in South Asia than in Africa, at $6000 in contrast to $4000 per person in 2017 U.S. dollars.

Structural transformation from agriculture to manufacturing and services is more difficult to measure than total GDP, but the World Bank's compilation of national accounts shows the share of value added produced in agriculture in Fig. 10.9.

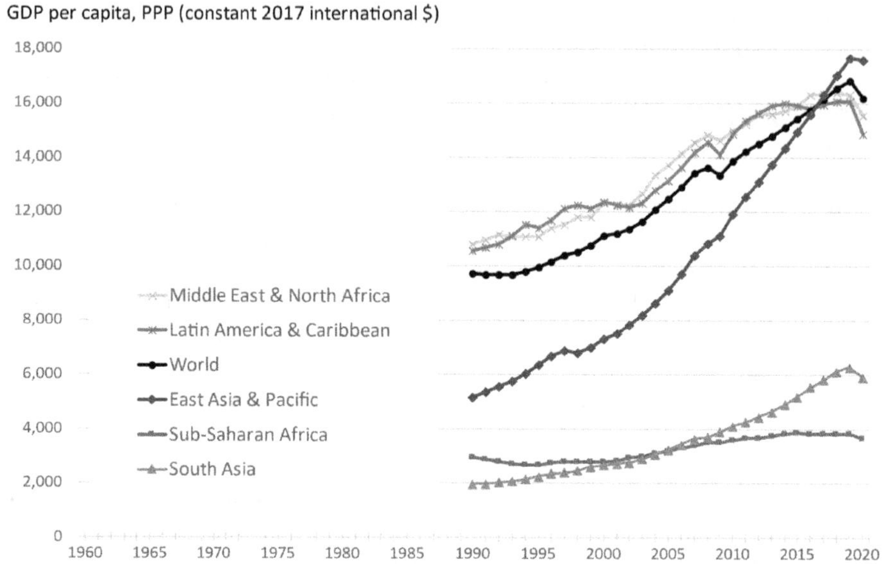

Fig. 10.8 Economic growth by region at purchasing power parity prices, 1990–2020 *Source*: Authors' chart of data from the World Bank, World Development Indicators. Updated values of these and related indicators are available from https://databank.worldbank.org/MacroDataBySector-AgTransformation/id/eb58207

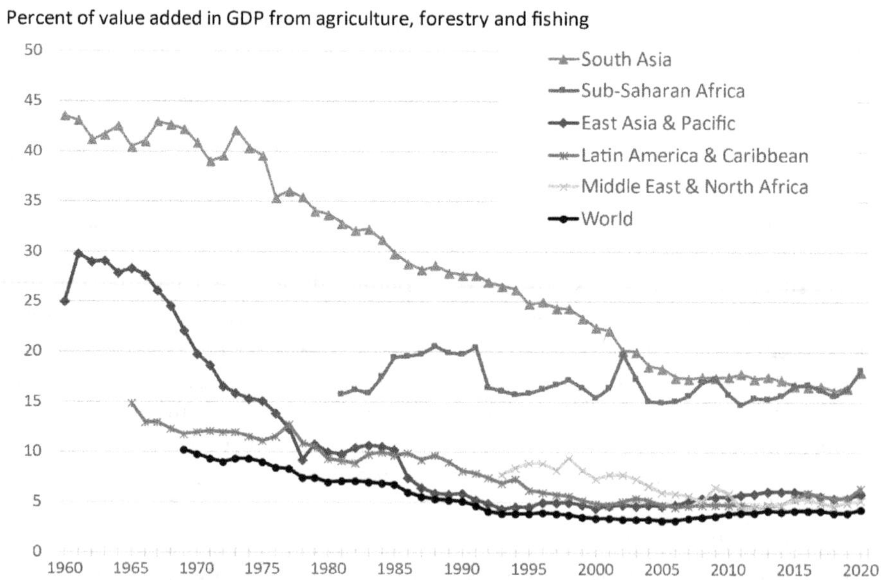

Fig. 10.9 Structural transformation in sources of income by region, 1960–2020 *Source*: Authors' chart of data from the World Bank, World Development Indicators. Updated values of these and related indicators are available from https://databank.worldbank.org/MacroDataBySector-AgTransformation/id/eb58207

These charts show structural transformation of the economy in terms of income sources before we turn to changes in employment. The data in Fig. 10.9 reveal how South Asia had been much more dependent on agriculture for its income than Africa or other regions, consistent with its lower level of resources and income per person but was able to increase its share of earnings from other sectors. In contrast Africa had much more mineral wealth, including oil and gas, so its share of earnings from agriculture was lower and has changed little since 1980, while the other regions converged to around 5% of GDP from agriculture.

The earlier comparison of structural transformation the U.S. and South Korea was in employment terms, and it is useful here to consider how Korean agriculture changed as a share of GDP, compared to several other countries in Asia and Sub-Saharan Africa using Fig. 10.10.

The trajectories shown in Fig. 10.10 reveal how individual countries can experience sustained reversals in their structural transformation out of agriculture, but also remarkably fast transition once they begin to accumulate the physical capital and human resources needed to expand nonfarm activity. Starting from the top left we see that the population of Bangladesh was dependent on agriculture for more than 50% of total national income through the 1960s to its independence from Pakistan in 1971. A series of crises led to a massive famine in 1974, after which policy reforms drove the sustained transition to only 12% of GDP from agriculture in 2020. Bangladesh's transformation after 1975 is similar and parallel to that of China, South Korea.

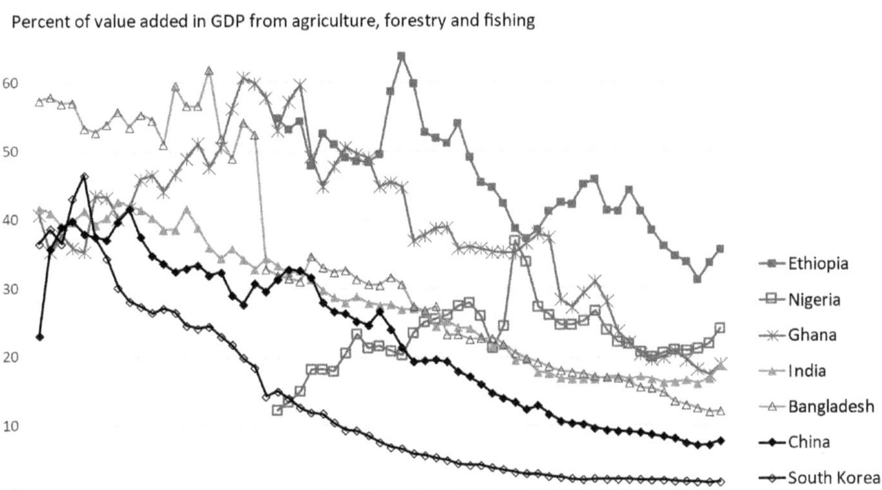

Fig. 10.10 Structural transformation in sources of income for selected countries, 1960–2020 *Source*: Authors' chart of data from the World Bank, World Development Indicators. Updated values of these and related indicators are available from https://databank.worldbank.org/MacroDataBySector-AgTransformation/id/eb58207

India also followed a similar path up to 2005 when further transformation stalled, and India also had a significant reversal back towards agriculture in 2019 and 2020.

Ghana, Nigeria and Ethiopia all had periods of reversed or paused structural transformation, in addition to the high variability in their agricultural shares of GDP due to both climatic variation and political instability in the decades since 1960. Starting at the left of the chart, Ghana was the first African nation to win independence from colonial rule, gaining control of its own government in 1957. From the 1960s to the early 1980s agriculture's share of Ghanaian income rose from around 40 to 60%, until a series of political and economic crises led to a change of direction in 1983 that brought rapid transition to below 20% in 2020. The data for Nigeria start in 1981, after which it also experienced a long period of reverse transformation until 2002. From 1981 to 2002, agriculture's share of Nigeria's national income rose from 12% to a peak of 37%, before falling back to around 20% in the 2010s. Ethiopian data on income shares begin with its period of famine in 1983–1985 and continued crisis until a new government took power in 1991, a year of peak reliance on agriculture at over 60% of GDP. Policy changes then put structural transformation in motion, driving down agriculture's share of GDP at about the same average rate as Ghana, to a low of just over 30% in 2018.

The structural transformation of income shares out of agriculture is closely related to growth of the economy, with some notable variation as shown in Fig. 10.11.

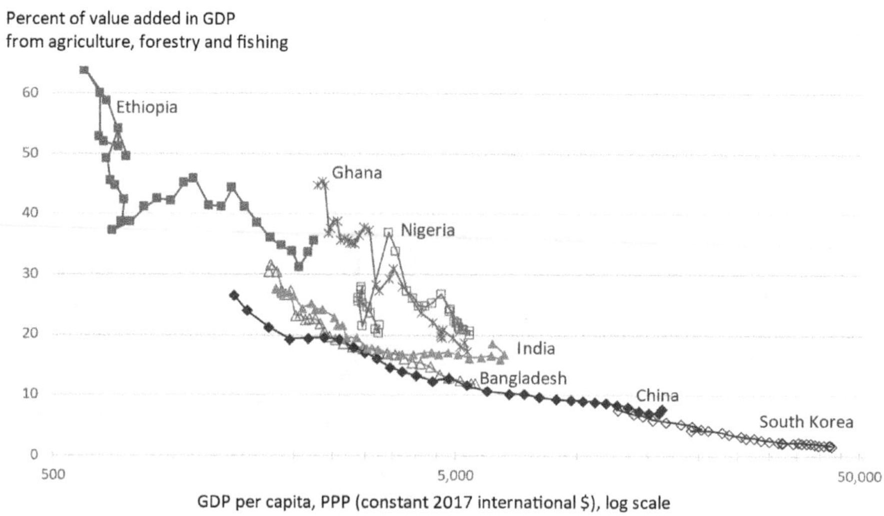

Fig. 10.11 Selected trajectories of growth and structural transformation, 1990–2020
Source: Authors' chart of data from the World Bank, World Development Indicators. Updated values of these and related indicators are available from https://databank.worldbank.org/MacroDataBySector-AgTransformation/id/eb58207

The vertical axis of Fig. 10.11 shows the same data as the previous chart, but instead of time along the horizontal axis we show GDP per person at purchasing power parity prices, in US dollars of 2017. The very wide range of incomes and the exponential nature of economic growth leads us to show that variable on a logarithmic scale, as we did for Fig. 7.9 showing inequality across countries in Chapter 7 on poverty and inequity.

Scatterplots with income on the horizontal axis are used for many aspects of economic development, and with the small number of countries in Fig. 10.11 we can connect the dots to show country trajectories over time as in Fig. 10.10. The trajectories reveal occasional reversals as in Ethiopia and Nigeria, and the distance between years reveals the speed of growth and transition, shown for example as the slowdown in China and South Korea's progression towards the bottom right of the chart. Comparing countries in a chart like Fig. 10.11 reveals both similarities and differences in paths of growth and transformation. As countries experience growth, they typically expand nonfarm activities faster than agricultural output at about the same rate, moving in parallel to lower share of income from agriculture as national income grows to the right.

One difference in development paths shown in Fig. 10.11 is that the African countries have notably higher agricultural shares of GDP at each income level than the Asian countries. That greater reliance on agriculture in Africa than in Asia could reflect Africa's relative abundance of agricultural land, with lower population densities and other factors that raise the relative cost and reduces the quantity of manufacturing and services at each level of income. Even so, to the extent that African countries have overcome these barriers to expand their economies, they have shifted resources into other sectors at about the same rate as other countries.

The seven countries shown on Fig. 10.11 are extremely different from each other in physical geography as well as social, cultural and political structures, and yet their growth follows a parallel path towards more non-agricultural activity. What forces drive investment and activity to expand other activities faster than agriculture expands?

Explaining Change in the Sources of Income: Inelastic Demand and a Fixed Land Area

Structural transformation of income sources away from agriculture when societies become wealthier could be caused by multiple factors, each operating differently at each place and time. The shifts revealed by agriculture's share of income shown in our charts occur gradually and are visible only when economic statistics are collected and compared, revealing deep commonalities in the underlying structure of agriculture and the food system.

One factor that contributes to structural shifts away from agriculture is Engel's Law, as consumer preferences lead to a low-income elasticity of demand. Engel's Law says that at higher incomes, demand for non-food items grows faster than demand for food. Among foods, Bennett's Law tells us that demand shifts to more expensive sources of dietary energy, including animal source foods and other products with high value added on the farm. That can help increase farm value added as national income rises, but much of the increased spending involves work after harvest that is not counted in the agricultural sector.

Another factor that contributes to structural shifts is low price elasticity of demand. Total dietary intake of all foods is almost completely inelastic with respect to both price and income when measured in energy terms. When food prices fall or rise there is substitution among foods towards more or less expensive sources of dietary energy, and changes in the nonfood use or loss and waste of farm products, but total calories consumed is driven by metabolic needs and other factors with little effect of price or income. Quantity in terms of weight or volume can grow as people buy more beverages and fresh foods with more water weight, but even non-caloric beverages have price-inelastic demand at quantities determined by preferences, convenience and aspirations.

Consumers' inelasticity of demand with respect to price could potentially imply that, when farmers adopt innovations and invest in increased production, the resulting outward shift in supply leads to more price reduction than quantity increase. That relationship holds for the entire aggregate supply and demand of all food in the world as a whole, and holds for the entire supply of foods that are too perishable and bulky to be traded internationally. In those markets, increased supply causes price to fall, so consumers can shift their spending to other things. But when foods are traded internationally, prices received by farmers are determined by the whole world's supply and demand, and by their own transport costs to and from their trading partners.

For foods that are traded with a large rest of the world, production at each place is determined by supply conditions, even if local consumers have inelastic demand. That separability of production from consumption makes Engel's Law relevant to structural transformation only for bulky, perishable products or for all products in the world as a whole. For products that can be stored and traded, a country that produces only a small fraction of the whole world's consumption can expand its production with very little impact on prices. In that case production is not limited by demand, but by the country's underlying land and resource constraints.

Explanations for structural transformation based on price effects are often known as Cochrane's technology treadmill. In the 1950s, an agricultural economist named Willard Cochrane noted how use of output-increasing innovations might be profitable only for the early adopters, whose increase in quantity sold drove price reductions that forced other producers to adopt the same technology but only for cost reduction. For example, a new seed that raises yield per acre would be used by early adopters on unchanged or even expanded area in ways that increase their farm income, but as that technology spreads to other farmers the price received by all growers of that product would fall, reducing their income unless they also adopt the new seed or cut back on resources used in farming.

Cochrane used the term 'treadmill' as part of an argument on behalf of farmers that government policies should restrict supply or at least slow its expansion to keep prices high. His book popularizing the treadmill idea appeared in 1958, at a time of rapid economic growth and unprecedented decline in the number of U.S. farmers shown in Fig. 10.5. Farm exits are painful, as the families that experienced the most financial hardship are often those most likely to stop farming. Cochrane argued that the declining number of farmers was due to insufficiently high prices for farm output, but subsequent evidence shows that prices mostly affect the value of farmland and have little influence on the number of farmers. Change in the number of farmers is mostly driven by changes in total rural population relative to the number of attractive new nonfarm jobs.

Experience with structural transformation since the 1960s shows that Cochrane's view of farmers on a treadmill, running to adopt new techniques just so they could stay in business, could more helpfully be reframed as Cochrane's flywheel. A flywheel is a mechanism which, once put in motion, sustains and distributes that energy to other parts of an interconnected system. In the U.S. and internationally, evidence since Cochrane's book shows how public and private investment in agricultural innovation accelerates the circular flow of economic activity, helping farmers make the most of limited farmland and driving growth in nonfarm activity. Places with lower farm production growth keep more farmers on the land only to the extent that they create fewer nonfarm jobs, and their lower farm productivity also raises the total land area and other resources used for food.

Cochrane's treadmill—reframed as a flywheel—explains how the spread of cost-reducing, output-enhancing innovations in agriculture helps drive economic development and environmental sustainability. For internationally traded products, higher productivity raises national income through net exports, and for nontraded goods higher productivity raises income through lower prices and less need to use natural resources and other inputs in farm production.

The decline in the number of farmers observed by Willard Cochrane in the 1950s turned out to be halfway through the eighty-year U.S. transition shown in Fig. 10.5. In the U.S. after the 1910s, as in South Korea after 1976, the declining number of farmers allows those who remain to adopt larger, faster machines and equipment with which to plant and harvest more area, including land rented or sold to them by neighbors who left farming. Mechanization generally does not increase total output, because its principal function is to cover more area in each day of work. Output of the farm sector depends mainly on yield increases and intensification of input use per acre. In the U.S. most crop yields had little increase until the 1940s, when new seeds raised returns to more intensive crop management that triggered an upward trend that continues into the 2020s. In contrast South Korea had experienced yield increases much earlier in time, including through labor-intensive investments in irrigated rice production.

In summary, the changing number of farmers is mostly caused by demographic factors and changes in the nonfarm sector. Mechanization to cover more land with less labor is often a response to that, while intensification to raise yields is driven by public and private investment in innovative ways to do more with less. The flywheel of economic growth can be accelerated and sustained by innovation and investments in new techniques anywhere in the circular flow of goods and services. In low-income settings, innovation in agriculture is especially important for economywide growth and sustainability because of its large size at the start of structural transformation, and its large environmental footprint that can be reduced by more efficient use of land and other natural resources. Agricultural productivity also matters greatly for equity and inclusion, because lowering the real cost of food allows low-income people to buy other things instead, and because farmers in low-income countries have incomes below their national average. All of these factors drive structural transformation and interact with the demographic transition to cause each year's change in the total number of farmers.

The Farm–Nonfarm Employment Transition: Why the Number of Farmers Rises and Then Falls

The number of farmers in each country is the country's workforce, minus those with solely nonfarm employment. Similarly, each year's change in the number of farmers is the change in the country's total workforce, minus the change in the number with nonfarm employment. Those facts by themselves are accounting definitions with no predictive power, but in low- and middle-income countries there are many young people entering the workforce each year, and few nonfarm job openings. Those nonfarm jobs typically offer higher incomes than a life of farming, but many young people who seek a nonfarm jobs cannot get one and become farmers out of necessity.

The gap in earnings and living standards between farmers and otherwise similar nonfarmers is largest in the lowest income countries. Farm incomes can catch up to nonfarm earnings but typically remain below the national average in most countries of the world. In the U.S., average farm incomes were less than half of average nonfarm incomes in the 1930s, then caught up and have exceeded nonfarm incomes since the mid-1990s. Convergence was possible in part because enough farmers left agriculture each year from the 1940s through the 1980s that the remaining farmers could often rent or buy land to expand their own operations. Those remaining farmers could both mechanize to cover the larger area per farm, and use more inputs to increase revenue per acre, thereby raising their income and wealth very quickly from year to year. By the late 1990s, most U.S. farmers had incomes above the national median and the pace of exits slowed to almost zero, as shown in the right panel of Fig. 10.5.

Countries often have a wide distribution of farm sizes and farmer incomes. Even in a country where most farmers have very low-incomes, some might control a lot of land or livestock and consequently have high-incomes. Survey data usually confirms that some farmers have incomes above many non-farmers, but that is complicated by the fact that the few higher-income farmers also often have non-farm income. The total income available per farmer in contrast to workers in other sectors is more easily seen with national income data, as shown in Fig. 10.12.

The data in Fig. 10.12 are the same shares of national income as Fig. 10.8 in the four lower lines, contrasted with the four upper lines for each region's estimated share of the workforce who are farmers. The shares of income are in terms of value added, which is defined in Chapter 9 with a numerical example in Table 9.2. Income from value added includes not just compensation for labor, but also the value of land and water or other natural resources used in farming, as well as the value of all buildings, equipment and livestock on the farm. Differentiating between a farmer's labor earnings and the returns to their land and other assets is often impossible because the farm family's efforts are embodied in the farm itself. The value added shares shown here are the best available estimate for each region or country as a whole.

To see how value added is distributed in the population we would need household surveys, but those are scarce and have limited coverage. Most countries rarely if ever conduct a complete census of agricultural enterprises, and they only occasionally conduct nationally representative household surveys. Household surveys are designed to represent the population in general, so they may miss important categories of farms, livestock operations and fisheries. The limited available data on farm operations globally is introduced in

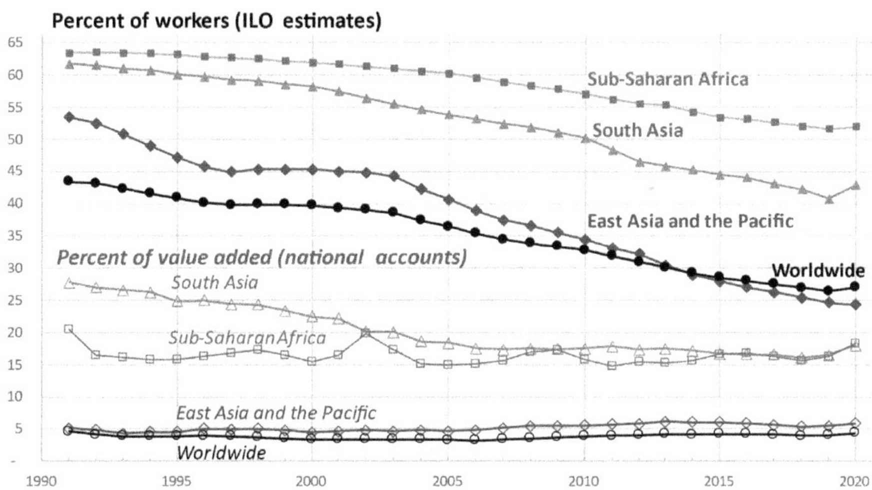

Fig. 10.12 Agriculture's share of employment and earnings in selected regions, 1991–2020 *Source*: Authors' visualization of data from the World Bank, World Development Indicators. Updated values of these and related indicators are available from https://databank.worldbank.org/MacroDataBySector-AgTransformation/id/eb58207

the next chapter. Historical data on farming as a share of the workforce is also scarce, which is why the data on employment changes shown earlier are just for the U.S. in Fig. 10.5 and for South Korea in Fig. 10.6. The estimates shown in Fig. 10.12 are produced by the International Labor Organization (ILO) of the United Nations by combining occasional surveys of principal occupation from 189 different countries, matched to the UN population projections by age and sex reported in Fig. 10.4 and Table 10.2, and then smoothed to infer values for missing countries and years.

The top line shows that Sub-Saharan Africa's workforce in the early 1990s was around 63% farmers, declining gradually to around 52% in 2019, rising slightly due to the loss of nonfarm jobs during COVID in 2020. The lower line shows that together those workers earned around 20% of total available income in 1990, which declined to just above 15% of all income in most years since then. South Asia and East Asia had somewhat faster shifts of the labor force out of agriculture, but in all cases including the world as a whole, farmers' share of income is much smaller than their share of employment, implying a much smaller pool of income per worker in agriculture than in services or manufacturing.

In Africa during the 1990s, having over 60% of workers who are farmers earn under 20% of total available income implies that average farm income was less than one-third of the national average. The value added produced per farmer in Africa was less than one-sixth that of non-farm workers. This enormous gap shrunk only slowly, so that by 2020 the 52% of workers earning 18% of income in 2020 had average farm incomes that were 35% of the national average, and one-fifth the value added produced per nonfarm worker. Like any average, these regional totals hide all the variation between and within countries, but they do mean that in any place where some farmers have above-average incomes, typically from controlling above-average land area, the remaining farmers must have even less than the national average earnings from agriculture.

The gap between farm and nonfarm incomes shown in Fig. 10.12, which is largest for Africa but also big in Asia and worldwide, implies that many people who are farmers would prefer to have a nonfarm job. Indeed, there is a continuous flow of people moving between farm and nonfarm employment, often within rural areas and small towns as well as migration to cities. Much of the flow from farm to nonfarm work is part-time activity or seasonal employment and circular migration, by which members of farm families try to gain nonfarm income while still living on and maintaining the family farm. Migration is also often exploratory, in which young people leave the farm to seek a nonfarm job and may return to the family farm out of necessity if they do not succeed. Migration routes of that type can be internal or international, linking a low-income farming community to far away destinations, as each wave of migrants help the next wave make the move if they can.

The flow of migrants from farm to nonfarm work takes many different forms in different places. In some countries, especially in Asia, rural households doing agricultural work may not actually own the land they farm. When the rural poor are landless in that sense, they may be tenant farmers who rent fields from a landlord, for either fixed price per year or a share of the output. Sharecropping and cash rents are used throughout the world, even by operators of large farms in the U.S. who rent parcels of land from neighbors. When tenants or even owners of small plots have low wealth, however, a series of bad years can push them into bankruptcy and drive them out of farming entirely, at which point they may go into nonfarm employment as low-wage workers. In other settings, including much of Africa, access to land is more egalitarian. In African history, many farm communities could simply expand into nearby areas formerly used for grazing and forests, and newly formed households would be granted land to start their own farms. That kind of area expansion has now ended in much of Africa, and in some countries, there are wealthy landowners attempting to control very large areas, thereby forcing other farmers onto smaller plots or out of agriculture as low-wage workers. Even so, the children of farmers who go into nonfarm work are often not the poorest. Migration itself can be costly, so those who migrate are those who can afford to search for a nonfarm job, and higher-wage positions often require formal education that the lowest-income youth may not have.

Rural education is an important aspect of economic transformation and agricultural development not only because it facilitates migration to higher earnings, but also because it facilitates innovation and adoption of new methods within agriculture, as well as growth of rural nonfarm activities that complement farming. Countries can often reach nearly universal literacy, numeracy and completion of primary education even at quite low incomes, but universal secondary schooling is much more difficult especially for farm families whose children at those ages are often needed on the farm. The growth of higher education and higher preschool enrollments is also important for agriculture and the food system and is increasingly widespread at higher levels of national income when more people have completed secondary school, and more people work outside the home.

The various kinds of farm to nonfarm migration make it difficult to quantify the magnitude movement in terms of labor hours or individual workers. For international comparisons, the best available measure is comparing the entire population living in areas of each country that are classified as either rural or urban. These classifications differ by country, so areas with a similar density of population might be classified as rural in one place and urban in another. Towns and cities also expand geographically, so a given home might be classified as rural for decades until it is reclassified as urban.

The rural–urban distinction corresponds only roughly to employment and earnings. Some people living in rural areas have no agricultural earnings at all, and those who are farming typically also earn income from nonfarm sources, including remittances from migration. Surveys of urban households also reveal significant levels of farming activity, sometimes on small plots within the urban area, and sometimes from land held elsewhere. Production and earnings from urban agriculture is visible and important, but small in magnitude relative to farming activity on the vast expanse of rural land. Within those rural areas, nonfarm activity is a necessary complement to agriculture for almost all farm families. Counting rural and urban people is not the same as the farm–nonfarm distinction, but for global monitoring it is the only kind of data available. The rural–urban distinction is also useful beyond just agriculture: each country's rural population provides a rough upper bound on the number of people using large areas of land for their lives and livelihoods, while urban people have a smaller geographic footprint per person.

Tracking the interaction between urbanization and population size can be done using the same demographic data that underlies population pyramids and projections based on life tables, adding data on the probability of migration at each age. Historical data and projections for the world as a whole are computed by the United Nations Population Division, as shown in Fig. 10.13.

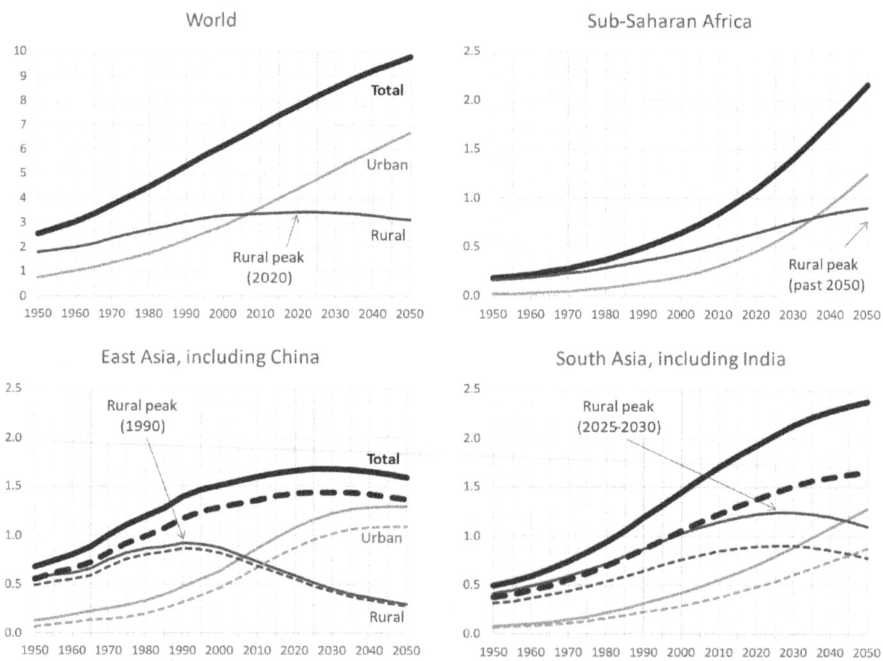

Fig. 10.13 Rural and urban population in selected regions and countries, 1950–2050 *Source*: Authors' chart of data from the United Nations, Department of Economic and Social Affairs, Population Division [2018]. *World Urbanization Prospects: The 2018 Revision*. Data shown are at five year intervals. Updated estimates will be available at https://population.un.org/wup/DataQuery

The top left panel of Fig. 10.13 shows the same world total as the population pyramids in Fig. 10.4, growing through the 1950s and 1960s at an accelerating annual rate that peaked in the 1970s then slowed. By these counts the world as a whole reached 50% urban around 2008 and is projected to reach 68% urban by 2050. Despite towns and cities growing much faster than population, urbanization was not fast enough to absorb all rural population growth until around 2020. The 2020s are in the middle of a long period of roughly constant rural population in the world total, so all the world as whole's population growth is in towns and cities.

The top right panel shows a similar dynamic at work in Africa, but with very different timing. Africa entered the 1950s with only 11% of its population classified as urban. Africa's urban population grew at around 5% per year in the 1950s, more than twice as fast as its total population growth of around 2%, but the urban share was so small that Africa's rural population grew at around 1.7%, almost as fast as its total population. Africa's total population growth rate then accelerated into the demographic transition, peaking at 2.8% in the 1980s, by which point about 25% of the population was urban. African cities were expanding at among the world's fastest rates, growing at around 4.8%, but they were still too small to absorb all of the continent's population growth so Africa's rural population expanded at over 2% per year. Africa is projected to reach 50% urban in the 2030s, and not reach its peak rural population until well past the 2050s.

Africa's low level of initial urbanization and the delayed start to its demographic transition have deep historical origins and powerful, long-lasting effects through the coming decades. Focusing just on the 2020s, Africa's urban areas are growing at twice the global average, and faster than cities in any other major world region. But Africa's rural areas are still growing at around 1.5% per year, while the rest of the world's rural population is already shrinking. That rural population growth rate means that a village of 1000 people must accommodate an average of 15 more people, for example because of 20 more births than deaths, and net out-migration of only 5 people. Their neighboring villages are also growing, and the total available land, water and other natural resources remains fixed or is worsening due to climate change, deforestation and water depletion.

Within Africa's rural areas, nonfarm activities can grow rapidly, perhaps even grow at some of the world's fastest rates like African cities do. But even so, the area of land and other natural resources available for each rural family across Africa is shrinking by about 1.5% per year in the 2020s. Productivity per acre or hectare must rise by at least 1.5% per year just to keep up.

In contrast to Africa's experience, East Asia's rural population (in the solid line of the bottom left) China peaked around 1990, and South Asia's rural population (in the solid line at the bottom right) is projected to peak in the late 2020s. The population of those regions is dominated by China and India, shown in the dashed lines. Throughout this period Africa's cities have grown faster than China's cities, and much faster than India's cities, but

Africa's total population growth is faster, and its initial urbanization is lower. In other words, despite Africa's world-record speed of urbanization, Africa's rural population will continue to grow for many decades, shrinking the land available per rural household, even as the rest of the world moves into an era of falling rural populations and increasing area per rural household.

10.1.3 Conclusion

This section on how agriculture changes during economic growth builds on our introduction to macroeconomics in the previous chapter, showing how all parts of a country are interconnected. Once we see economic activity as a circular flow of goods and services within the country, with international trade and capital flows to and from other countries, we can see how the linkages between agriculture and other sectors influence the evolution of agriculture over time and differences across countries.

One central finding concerns the role of innovation and investment in new ways of doing more with less, within agriculture and in other sectors. Economic growth can be sparked by innovation and investment in any sector, but in low-income countries the agricultural sector is especially important because it is large, employs relatively low-income people, and uses a disproportionate share of land and other natural resources.

A second core finding concerns the farm-to-nonfarm transition, and the demographic factors that drive an increase in the number of rural people and hence the number of farm families, shrinking the land available per rural household, for many decades until cities and the nonfarm sector are large enough to absorb all the region's rural population growth. All kinds of innovation are helpful, but during the period of rising rural populations, agricultural intensification for higher yields is the priority due to falling land area per worker, whereas after the rural population begins to fall yield improvement is less urgent for rural incomes, and the remaining farmers can take over their neighbors' land and mechanization becomes a higher priority.

The chapter began with Table 10.1 listing a set of four major transitions associated with economic growth. This first section addressed the demographic and structural changes affecting farm production, and the following section turns to transitions in the food system and nutrition.

10.2 Food Systems and Dietary Transition: From Inadequacy to Excess and Health

10.2.1 Motivation and Guiding Questions

What people eat is changing fast. This section continues our exploration of global and U.S. data by focusing on food system transformation and the nutrition transition, as summarized at the start of the chapter in Table 10.1. How are dietary patterns changing, and how do these choices relate to nutritional status and health?

The *food system* refers to all activities involved in the production, processing, packaging, transportation, storage, and marketing of food to end-users. In this section we focus on systemic changes in diet composition, and the following chapters return to the supply of food regarding international trade and policy in Chapter 11, and the institutional arrangements around agriculture and value chains in Chapter 12.

The *food system transformation* associated with economic growth involves a changing mix of foods produced by increasingly specialized suppliers who make more intensive use of physical capital and human resources. Innovation and investment allow producers to do more with less, giving each consumer access to more diverse foods from a wider variety of sources. Higher incomes allow consumers to acquire more expensive foods, but each item's nutritional impact on our future health is often unknown and sometimes misunderstood, making food one of the few expenditure categories for which increased spending can actually worsen health outcomes.

Changes in the health-related attributes of dietary patterns are known as the *nutrition transition*. With increased spending some aspects of dietary intake become more health promoting over time, reaching towards nutritional adequacy of attributes that are known to be desirable, while other aspects of newly consumed foods turn out to be harmful. Those harms may eventually be discovered and addressed, potentially leading consumers to converge on balanced diets that achieve adequacy without excess.

By the end of this section, you will be able to:

1. Use the available data on global consumption by food group to describe how income elasticities and other changes have altered the mix of foods consumed worldwide;
2. Use the available data on packaged foods and meals away from home to describe the dietary transition in how farm products are transformed for final consumption;
3. Describe how health researchers use anthropometric, biological, clinical and dietary data to measure nutritional status; and
4. Describe the nutritional and epidemiological transitions in risk factors associated with disease and premature mortality around the world.

10.2.2 Analytical Tools

Changes in global food systems, dietary intake and nutritional status pose enormous challenges for human health. New ingredients and new ways of producing and processing foods are introduced and consumed on a massive scale, altering nutrition in ways that may go unnoticed or misunderstood for years. Impacts on health are often cumulative and depend on interaction with other aspects of dietary intake, so they appear slowly over time in any individual and vary widely across a population.

In this section we describe how the world's dietary and nutrition transitions are measured and understood in the health sciences. The most widely used metrics reflect a scientific consensus about the attributes of a benchmark diet that would minimize disease risk over time. Actual diets differ from that benchmark, sometimes because people can afford only the least expensive sources of dietary energy that lack the nutritional attributes needed for health, and because food choice is driven by many other goals in addition to health.

As economic growth proceeds, food choices trace out each population's income elasticities of demand introduced in Section 3.2, including the patterns described there as Engel's law and Bennett's law. With higher incomes, people are able to buy a wider range of foods. Dietary diversification often helps reduce or eliminate deficiencies of individual nutrients, but also often involves excess intake of some foods and ingredients. Preventing those excesses takes time, so observed changes often transition from inadequacy to excess and only later to just-right nutrition. The nutrition transition involves food system changes in both the mix of farm or fish products produced in agriculture, and the post-harvest transformation of those products into food items and meals for consumption. Some nutritional attributes of foods needed for health are intrinsic to the agricultural product, and classified into nutritional food groups that may differ from other classification schemes. For example, the 'vegetable' food group includes tomatoes which are botanically fruits and excludes white potatoes because white potatoes are a starchy staple. Other nutritional attributes depend on how the item is processed and used in meal preparation, for example by removing the germ from whole grains to make refined flour or adding other ingredients such as salt or sugar. To describe the nutrition transition, we begin with change in agricultural supply and consumption by food group, and then turn to postharvest transformation of those foods.

Dietary Transition in Consumption by Food Group

Nutrition researchers have proposed many different food classification schemes, often associated with diet quality metrics. For example, the U.S. Healthy Eating Index (HEI) measures how closely an observed diet adheres to the Dietary Guidelines for Americans. The most recent HEI scoring system published in 2023 rates diet quality in terms of 13 nutritional attributes per thousand calories of dietary energy. Some of those attributes reflect an entire food group, such as total quantity of all fruits, all vegetables, or any dairy product, but most are individual nutrients like total sodium, or an aspect of processing like whole versus refined grains. The 13 attributes scored in the HEI are the U.S. government's official definition of a healthy diet, developed jointly by the USDA and the Department of Health and Human Services.

For international comparisons, in July of 2022 the five UN agencies mandated to monitor food security and nutrition around the world adopted a new approach for measuring food access, using the least expensive locally available items balanced across six food groups. The results of that approach, known as the cost and affordability of healthy diets (CoAHD), were shown at the end of our chapter on poverty and risk in Fig. 7.17. The use of least-cost diets by food group had been piloted in the FAO, IFAD, UNICEF, WFP and WHO annual report on the State of Food Security and Nutrition in the World for 2020, then modified and adopted for annual monitoring in their 2022 report. Monitoring food access in this way is done by FAO jointly with the World Bank, based on healthy diet basket (HDB) targets of total energy from each of six mutually exclusive food groups shown in Table 10.4.

The HDB targets shown in Table 10.4 are designed to reflect commonalities in dietary guidelines adopted by governments around the world. The HDB's purpose is to help UN agencies and national governments monitor global and national food systems for access to a balanced diet. It is not itself a dietary recommendation, in part because actual guidelines also specify attributes related to food processing and meal preparation and may specify slightly different food groups. For example, the U.S. HEI scores designed to capture the Dietary Guidelines for Americans has a specific recommendation for dairy, and a specific recommendation for seafood or plant proteins, in addition to limits on specific kinds of fatty acids that are often present in animal foods. Most other countries accomplish similar goals by combining dairy with meat and eggs, and sometimes grouping that with fish. Since the HDB aims to provide a minimalist lower bound on requirements to meet national guidelines, it combines all the animal source food recommendations into a single category.

HDB targets are designed to measure costs per day for a representative person and are specified in terms of the number of items for diversity within food groups, and the total calories from each food group needed to meet energy requirements with a balanced diet. Dietary guidelines are aimed at communicating with the public, so they choose locally representative foods and recommend quantities in terms of weight, volume or number of servings per day. Diet quality scores like the HEI then convert those to grams, cups or servings per thousand calories, so that the score can scale up or down with the total energy needed by each person given their height, weight and physical activity. The HDB directly targets the calories of food from each group to allow for substitution between items with different water weight, for example to substitute between large tomatoes, small tomatoes, tomato concentrate, and tomato paste and obtain the same quantity of tomato solids, and similarly to substitute between liquid milk, yogurt, soft cheese or hard cheese and obtain the same quantity of milk solids.

As shown in Table 10.4, high-moisture food groups like vegetables and fruits provide a small share of energy but a large and variable share of total weight in the HBD targets. These data focus on calories and weights for use in comparing healthy diet targets to quantities bought and sold. Dietary guidelines often also use areas on a plate for the prepared forms of each

Table 10.4 Healthy diet basket targets used for monitoring food access worldwide

Food group	*Dietary diversity (items)*	*Dietary energy targets (kcal)*	*Energy shares (pct of total) (in %)*	*Weight shares of example foods (as dry products) (in %)*	*Example foods and typical weights*
Starchy staples	2	1160	50	24–28	322 g of dry rice, or other cereals and root crops
Vegetables	3	110	5	23–30	270–400 g of carrots, onions, tomatoes, leafy greens etc.
Fruits	2	160	7	20–22	230–300 g of bananas, apples, oranges etc
Animal source foods	2	300	13	16–18	210 g of egg, or equivalent weight of dairy, meat or fish
Legumes, nuts and seeds	1	300	13	6–7	85 g of dry beans, or other legumes, nuts or seeds
Oils and fats	1	300	13	3	34 g of vegetable oil, or other oil or fat
Total	11	2330	100	100	1151–1351 g

Source: Food Prices for Nutrition project, for the World Bank DataHub on Food Prices for Nutrition (https://worldbank.org/foodpricesfornutrition) and the FAOSTAT domain on Cost and Affordability of Healthy Diets (https://www.fao.org/faostat/en/#data/CAHD). Methods used to obtain these data are detailed in journal articles and background papers by Anna Herforth and others at https://sites.tufts.edu/foodpricesfornutrition

food, typically calling for something like half the plate to be high-moisture, high-fiber fruits and vegetables, while a quarter or more of the plate is high-moisture, high-fiber starchy staples, and a quarter or less of the plate to be high-protein items which are either animal source foods or legumes, nuts and seeds.

Dietary transition in terms of food groups can be tracked relative to HDB targets, revealing whether supply-demand balances in national, regional and global systems are approaching or exceeding the minimal quantities per person that would be needed to support human health. The total quantity of each agricultural product available for consumption is estimated by the FAO using food balance sheets (FBS) for every country in the world, adding up total production plus imports minus exports, nonfood uses and losses along the supply chain to final sale. That estimate of quantity available for consumption is an upper bound on dietary intake because some of it would be kitchen and plate waste or destined for nonfood uses within the home.

Food Balance Sheet quantities per person are national averages, and to track its distribution in the population we would need household consumption and expenditure surveys (HCES) that typically ask about foods consumed over the previous 30 days or an entire year. Then to identify intake by individuals, we would need dietary recall surveys that typically as about foods eaten over the previous 24 hours. HCES are typically done only every five or so years, and 24HR dietary recall surveys are even more expensive and less frequently done. In contrast, FBS estimates of total consumption are available for every country in all years, from 1961 to the present.

Results comparing quantities available for consumption to the HDB targets for each food group, plus a seventh discretionary food group of caloric sweeteners, are in Fig. 10.14.

Figure 10.14 provides a unified picture of global dietary transition in terms of food groups, with the entire world average in dark black, and data for each of the major world regions above and below that global average. Panels for each food group are aligned and scaled so that total supply-demand balances range from zero up to the healthy diet basket target at the same point on each vertical axis. The HDB targets themselves are requirements for a healthy diet, and while the horizontal dashed line for sugar is the World Health Organization guideline that sugar intake be limited to 10% or less of total daily energy.

The pattern of dietary transition over time and between regions reveals how some food groups, especially legumes, nuts and seeds and to a lesser extent fruits, remain far below HDB targets even in high-income regions in recent years, while vegetables reach and surpass HDB targets only in East Asia. From the top left, the only region with below-target levels of starchy staples is North America, which the other panels reveal is due to displacement by high levels of animal source foods, oils and fats, and sugars. The next highest level of animal source foods and oils and fats is Europe and Central Asia, followed by Latin America and the Caribbean which has an even higher level of sugar than Europe and Central Asia.

The fastest changes shown in Fig. 10.14 are in East Asia and the Pacific, where animal source foods rose from lowest in the world in 1961 to just below Latin America and the Caribbean in the 2010s, and vegetables for which East Asia and the Pacific has had a uniquely rapid increase in quantities available for consumption since 1980. The food group with greatest uniformity in trends across regions is oils and fats, which has increased at roughly

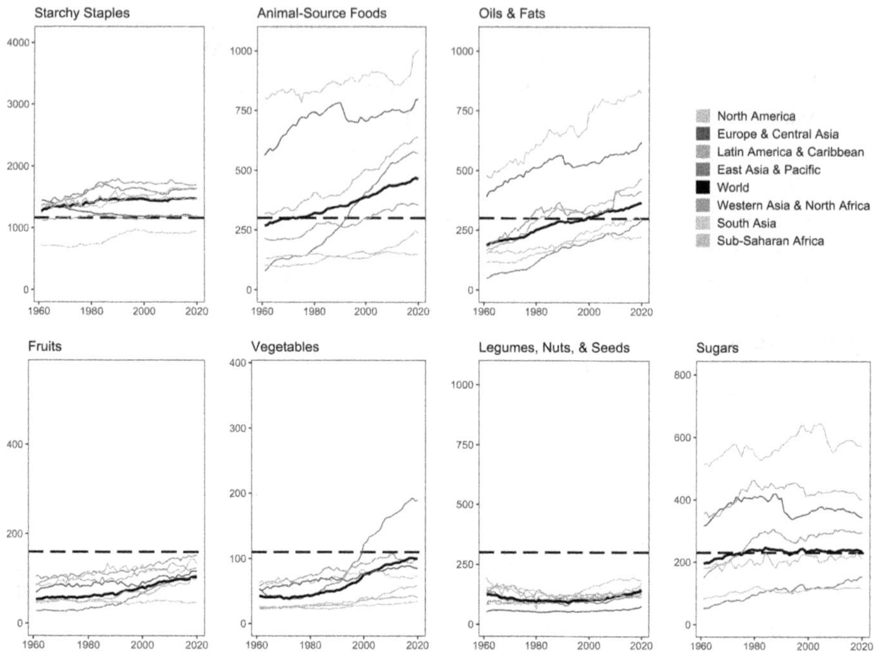

Fig. 10.14 The food system transition by food group in major world regions, 1961–2020 *Source*: Data visualization by Leah Costlow, showing kilocalories per person per day available for food consumption in each region using historical and current estimates from FAO Food Balance Sheets at https://www.fao.org/faostat. Panels are aligned with horizontal guidelines showing energy balance from each food group in the Healthy Diet Basket reference targets used by FAO to measure the cost and affordability of healthy diets, https://www.fao.org/faostat/en/#data/CAHD

similar rates everywhere over the entire period from 1961 to 2020. In contrast, sugar consumption has fallen or stayed constant in most regions, with the only exception being East Asia and the Pacific where it has risen steadily from the world's lowest level below Sub-Saharan Africa to slightly above Africa.

Returning to our description of food system transitions in Table 10.1, the central difference among regions and changes over time involve the very high level of animal source food consumption in North America and in Europe and Central Asia, and the sharp rise in Asia including South Asia that rose from below to well above the total for Sub-Saharan Africa which has barely risen since 1961. The future demand for animal source products is a central concern regarding the environmental footprint of the food system and for animal welfare. For health, having animal source foods as well as oils and fats above the HDB targets is not itself strongly associated with severe harms, unless the specific items consumed have high levels of saturated fats which is associated with cardiovascular disease. Having above-target levels of those food groups is harmful to health mostly by displacing other food groups whose attributes are needed, including especially the potential for future substitution into plant-based high protein foods from the legume, nuts and seeds group that is consistently under-consumed in all regions.

The fact that dietary guidelines and hence the HDB call for quantities of fruits, vegetables and legumes, nuts or seeds that are so consistently above what is actually consumed by most people is a puzzle for economists, because it implies that nutritional standards for health are beyond the range of variation typically observed. In fact, there is significant cross-sectional variation within societies in these food groups, and epidemiological evidence suggests that those who consume those higher levels do in fact have lower disease risk and greater longevity. Part of that could be a displacement effect from consuming less of the other foods that might be harmful, especially foods that are processed or prepared with high levels of salt, added sugar and other ingredients beyond the basic agricultural products shown in food balance sheets.

Some aspects of global dietary transition involve shifts among products within each food group, which is shown in Fig. 10.15.

Seeing global dietary transformation by food group in Fig. 10.15 yields an unusually clear picture of changing supply-demand balances for each type of agricultural product. Starting at the top left of, a first observation is the dominance of wheat and rice in total starchy staples consumption and reaching peak levels and then stabilizing since the 1990s. All other food groups are more diverse. Three agricultural products account for more than half of animal source foods (pig meat, poultry meat, and milk), and four account for more than half of all fruits (bananas, oranges, apples and coconuts).

Among the animal source foods, it is notable that bovine meat plays a modest and almost unchanged role in total dietary energy supply since 1961. Almost all the global increase in animal source food consumption consists of pig and poultry meat, plus dairy. Those three foods come from predominantly grain-fed animals often raised in confinement, and the genetic potential for rapid growth of pigs and poultry, and large volumes of milk per day from dairy cows, has been transformed by selective breeding. A visitor from 1961 would be astonished to see how pigs, poultry and dairy are produced in 2020, whereas beef production methods has changed much less.

The expansion of bananas among fruits, tomatoes and onions among vegetables, and groundnuts among legumes, nuts and seeds each derives from different aspects of agricultural and food system transformation. Bananas are unusual due to their genetic uniformity, as about half of global consumption and almost all the expansion since 1961 consists of the Cavendish variety, widely adopted to replace the Gros Michel and other varieties that were more vulnerable to fungal disease. The evolution and spread of new diseases inevitably threaten each production system, and the Cavendish may soon need to be replaced with other banana varieties or different fruits.

Almost all the growth in global consumption comes from species that were widely used in global diets prior to 1960. The exception is for vegetable oils,

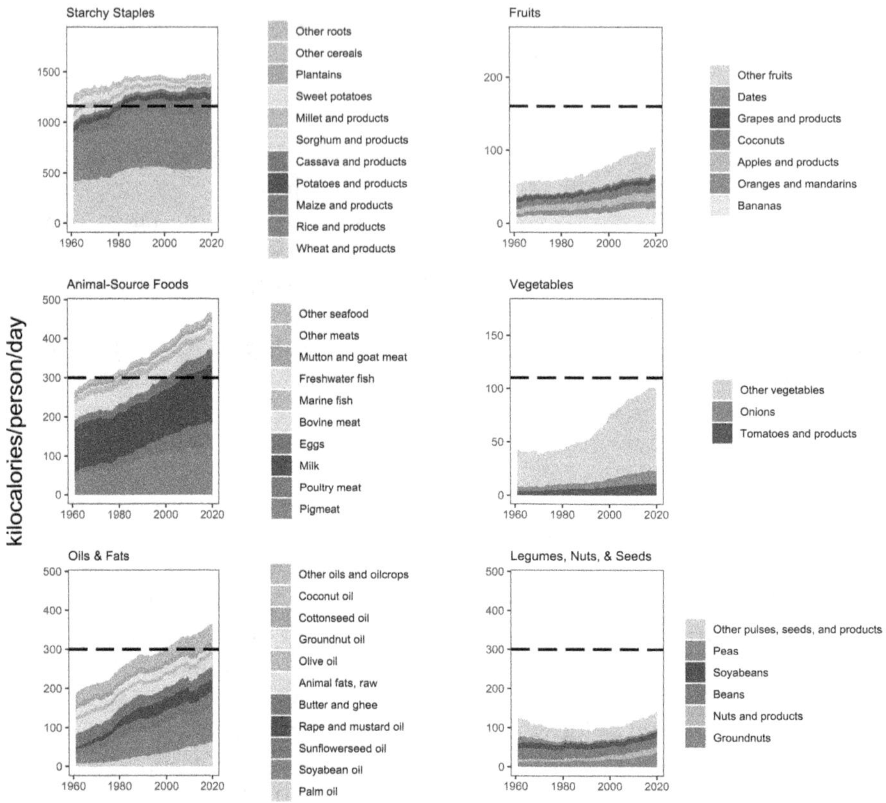

Fig. 10.15 Composition of the global food supply by food group, 1961–2020 *Source*: Data visualization by Leah Costlow, showing kilocalories per person per day available for food consumption in each region, merging historical and current estimates from FAO Food Balance Sheets at https://www.fao.org/faostat. Panels are aligned with horizontal guidelines showing energy balance from each food group in the Healthy Diet Basket reference targets used by FAO to measure the cost and affordability of healthy diets, https://www.fao.org/faostat/en/#data/CAHD

for which three large sources expanded rapidly in new ways: palm oil in tropical forest regions, soybeans initially in temperate areas and increasingly also tropical locations, and rapeseed expanded in temperate areas due to breeding of the canola varieties (so called due to being a Canadian oil with low erucic acid). Of these, soybeans and canola expanded with yield gains and cost reduction due to genetic improvement in yield potential combined with new forms of plant protection, while palm oil expanded primarily through area expansion. We will return to these questions of production-side changes in Chapters 11 and 12.

Dietary Transition Towards Packaged and Processed Foods

Changes in supply-demand balance for agricultural products by food group is just one step in dietary transition, much of which occurs through the ways that food is transformed after harvest for sale through processing or food preparation outside the home. These transformations turn the few hundred agricultural products shown in Figs. 10.14 and 10.15 into many thousands of distinct retail food items available at grocery stores anywhere in the world, many of which are newly introduced each year and may be available for only short periods of time.

Each retail product has its own distinct nutritional attributes, only some of which are disclosed publicly. Testing a food for all known aspects of nutritional composition would cost thousands of dollars per sample in a lab, so information disclosed to comply with regulatory requirements is typically based on recipes rather than testing, and composition data about those ingredients may be outdated or incorrect. Restaurant menu items have only recently been subject to any disclosure requirements at all.

Tracking dietary transition in the attributes of foods that are processed or prepared outside the home is difficult not only because those attributes are unknown, but more fundamentally because the total quantity of each item sold is usually private information, used by the suppliers themselves to guide their own marketing efforts. Some information is collected by private-sector firms that sell data and market intelligence reports to food businesses, and typically also use that data in consulting work for food businesses about market trends and opportunities.

For worldwide monitoring of the packaged food sector, one of the most useful kinds of data is collected by a marketing research firm named Euromonitor International. The origin of its name comes from the company's founding in London in 1972 when the UK joined the European Common Market, creating opportunities for statistical research to guide British firms for sales to Europe. The company's 'Passport' database later grew into a worldwide service, employing consultants who compile estimates of how much of each kind of branded product is sold every year in each of 40 countries. The company then uses food composition data to add up foods in terms of calories per person, which can be analyzed in many ways.

One particularly important dimension of dietary transition towards foods that are processed or prepared and consumed outside the home is the rise of caloric beverages, shown in Fig. 10.16.

The scatterplot in Fig. 10.16 shows total calories of all nonalcoholic beverages sold in each country from 2009 to 2020, converted to quantity per person per day for ease of comparison across countries. Along the horizontal axis is the total calories of all packaged foods or restaurant menu items tracked by Euromonitor. Based on other data, actual average intake per capita is usually 2000–3000 calories, around the healthy diet basket target of 2330. If the Passport data are accurate, the countries with less than 2000 calories in sales are consuming the rest from own production or other vendors not

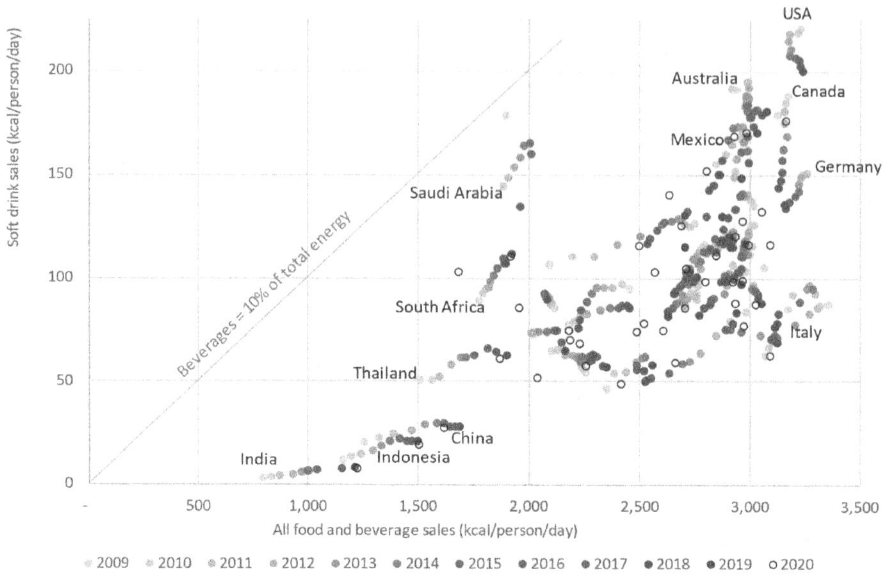

Fig. 10.16 Estimated dietary energy from non-alcoholic drinks in 40 countries, 2009–2020 *Source*: Authors' chart of data from Euromonitor International Limited ©2009–2020, all rights reserved and used here by permission. Each dot is the national average for one country, after converting annual sales data to total calories per person per day. Years are shown with darker shading to indicate the passage of time, with the pandemic year of 2020 as a circle. Details on the data source are available at https://www.euromonitor.com/our-expertise/passport

tracked by Euromonitor, while quantities above about 2500 calories involve kitchen and plate waste or nonfood uses.

The scatterplot uses darker shading for more recent years, with the pandemic year of 2020 highlighted as a circle. Most countries reveal an 11-year trajectory of dietary transformation in consumption of caloric beverages relative to all other foods recorded by Euromonitor, with 2020 as an outlier. The scatterplot shows an upward sloping pattern across all countries, with interesting variation in the speed and direction of change, including differences in how country data reflects pandemic response. Outliers above the international pattern include Saudi Arabia with high and rising sales but a sharp decline in 2020 for both soft drinks and all foods to the isolated dot just to the left of data for South Africa, whose data for 2020 continued the high and rising trajectory from 2009. From the bottom left we see countries such as India, Indonesia and Thailand experiencing what could be described as the early stages of a transition towards more foods that are packaged and processed or sold in restaurants of the type tracked by Euromonitor, with some upward slope. South Africa and Saudi Arabia are outliers above the pattern formed by other countries, while Italy is an outlier below the international pattern. Mexico is towards the far end of the global pattern, and Australia, the U.S., Canada and Germany are all countries where caloric beverage sales have declined noticeably since the start of these data in 2009.

One aspect of Fig. 10.16 is that scaling of the vertical axis is in units of 50 kcal and the horizontal axis is units of 500 kcal, so all points along the diagonal line shown on the chart would have 10% of all calories sold be from soft drinks. In fact, India and Indonesia have much less than that, but the trajectories for South Africa and Saudi Arabia are steeper than that line, so a rising fraction of all calories being sold in those countries are in beverage form.

Dietary Transition Towards Foods Away from Home

The pattern over time and across countries for restaurant and food service sales reveals a particularly notable aspect of dietary transition, as shown in Fig. 10.17.

The Euromonitor Passport data in Fig. 10.17 reveal the challenge of measuring the quantity sold of meals away from home, as several countries show linear change without the year-to-year fluctuations that would result from measurement error or variation in the actual trajectory. Each linear

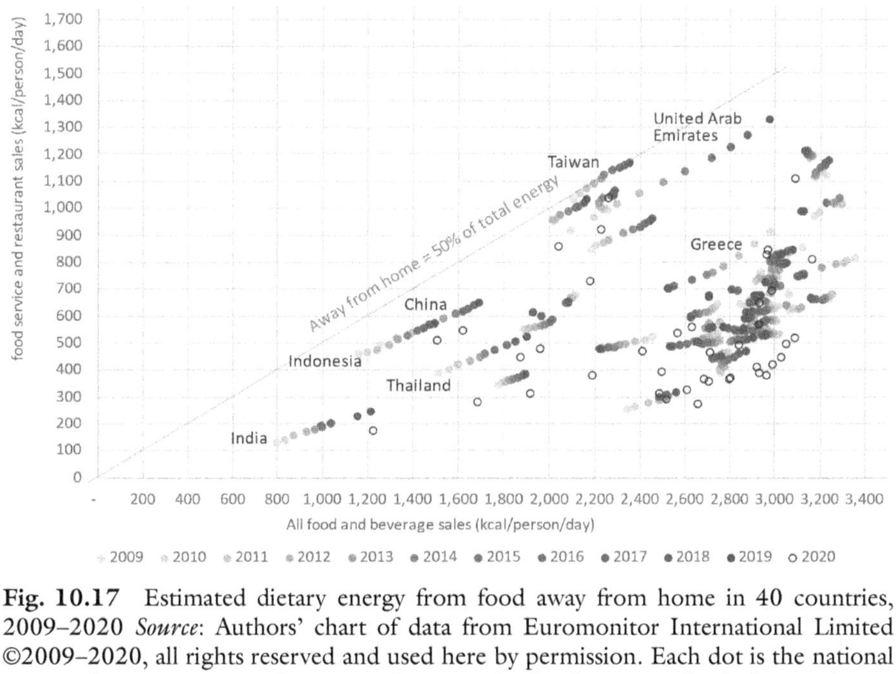

Fig. 10.17 Estimated dietary energy from food away from home in 40 countries, 2009–2020 *Source*: Authors' chart of data from Euromonitor International Limited ©2009–2020, all rights reserved and used here by permission. Each dot is the national average for one country, after converting annual sales data to total calories per person per day. Years are shown with darker shading to indicate the passage of time, with the pandemic year of 2020 as a circle. Details on the data source are available at https://www.euromonitor.com/our-expertise/passport

projection is nonetheless revealing of the information collected by Euromonitor consultants in each country, including especially the sharp declines in meals away from home during the pandemic year of 2020, and the challenge of undercounting food sold away from home.

Trends for each country can be compared to the diagonal line indicating 50% of total reported calories being sold by food service establishments and restaurants. Taiwan and some other countries are close to that line. It is possible that the share of calories obtained away from home declined over this period in countries such as India, Indonesia, Thailand and China, but it is also possible that those countries had growth in unmeasured food service activity such as street foods and prepared meals sold in open markets, as well as school meals and other institutional cafeterias.

Household surveys and dietary recall data often find that food away from home provides a growing fraction of total consumption. The quantity and composition of that food is typically unknown, due to the absence of nutritional composition data, and the limited ability of survey respondents to recall how much they ate of each item. To provide a more complete measure, we can turn to data collected for national accounts from the businesses themselves, regarding their total sales. These data do not track items sold so cannot be matched to food composition and nutritional attributes, but they can be adjusted for inflation and provide a much more precisely measure of the total value of foods served in restaurants and other establishments.

The U.S. trajectory for the total value of food served away from home spans almost a century, as shown in Fig. 10.18.

The two panels in Fig. 10.18 are designed to include all kinds of food and beverages consumed away from home, excluding alcohol. That total includes commercial sales reported by food service enterprises and administrative data on meals provided in schools and other public or private institutions. The data for food and beverages intended for consumption at home includes estimated values of food grown by the household, direct sales from farms to consumers, and food donated through the charitable sector. Our visualization combines the USDA food expenditure data with total spending by households on all goods and services, to provide the most complete possible picture of dietary transition from meals at home to foods served elsewhere from 1929 to 2020.

Starting from the top left of Panel A, the two years of observation in 1929 and 1932 show the decline in the share of spending on food during the great depression, when food prices fell even more than the cost of other things. By 1935 food prices and spending were at their historically high share of total personal consumption expenditure of around 22%, which then declined to stabilize around 6% of total spending in the 2000s. Meanwhile expenditure on food away from home was around 5% of the total in 1929 and through the 1930s before rising sharply during World War II, then returning to around 6% until the 2000s.

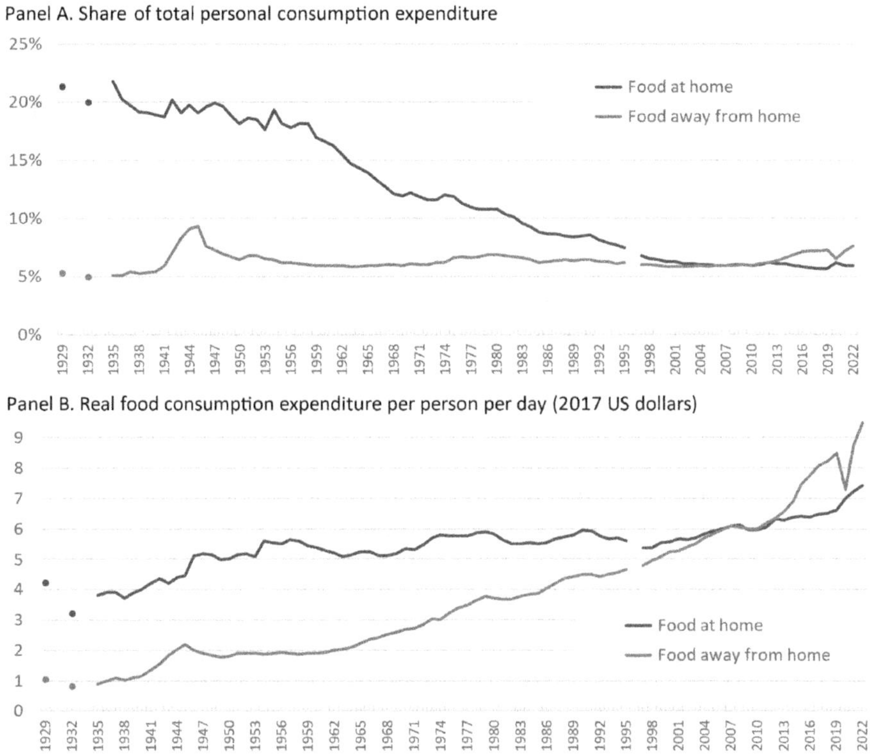

Fig. 10.18 Real spending on food at home and away from home in the U.S., 1929–2022 *Source*: Authors' chart of data on food expenditure from the USDA Economic Research Service [https://www.ers.usda.gov/data-products/food-expenditure-series], with total personal consumption expenditure from the U.S. Bureau of Economic Analysis [https://www.bea.gov/itable/national-gdp-and-personal-income]. Food expenditure data collection methods changed in 1997, so data for 1996 are omitted to show lack of comparability. Personal consumption expenditure [PCE] is personal income net of savings, interest payments and transfers paid to people abroad. Real values adjust for inflation using the Bureau of Economic Analysis PCE deflator

The roughly constant share of food away from home in total expenditure, over decades of rising incomes and increased total spending, implies a unit-elastic demand for food served away from home. Each 1% of additional total spending must have involved a roughly 1% increase in consumption of food and beverages away from home. In contrast, the top line for food at home follows Engel's Law, with increments of income spent primarily on other goods and services. The implications of that for the absolute level of spending is shown in Panel B, where expenditure is converted to daily values in 2017 dollars for convenience of comparison with other data about diet costs and food spending.

The top line in Panel B shows that the level of real spending for food at home rose significantly into the 1950s, from around \$4 per person per day in the late 1930s to around \$5.50 per day in the mid-1950s. That number stayed roughly constant in real terms until the early 2000s. The composition of that spending is not well documented, but one possible explanation is that upgrading of grocery spending to higher-value items was almost exactly offset by a reduction in the real cost of farm-to-market supply chains for those items, enabling real grocery spending to stay roughly constant for half a century.

The two panels of Fig. 10.18 show important changes in U.S. food spending since the 1990s. The USDA method for measuring food expenditure was revised in 1996, making the two data series not entirely comparable, but there is a sharp rise in spending for food at home from \$5.36/day in 1997 to \$6.60 in 2019. That rise then accelerated during the pandemic, reaching \$7.41 in 2020. Meanwhile spending on food away from home rose even faster. Using the new USDA data series real spending on food at and away from home had equalized by 2006, and after the decline in real spending around the great recession of 2008–2009, food spending away from home rose sharply after 2012 to \$8.48 per day in 2019 and snapped back after the COVID recession to \$8.74 in 2021 and \$9.51 in 2022. Those values are at 2017 prices, partly reflecting changes in the price of food and food service relative to all other goods and services, but also the sharply higher incomes and greater income equality experienced in the U.S. since 2012 as shown in Section 9.2 of the chapter on food in the macroeconomy.

The U.S. trajectory of expenditure for food and beverages at home and away from home is especially revealing when using monthly estimates of total sales before and during the COVID pandemic as shown in Fig. 10.19.

When describing events that took place during the period shown in Fig. 10.19, it can be difficult to recall the speed and magnitude of that disaster. Focusing just on the number of deaths, U.S. vital statistics maintained by the Centers for Disease Control (CDC) show that weekly mortality rates fluctuated normally and then spiked far above normal in mid-April 2020, spiked again even higher for three successive weeks in December-January 2021, and again for three successive weeks in January 2022. Between those peaks, U.S. mortality rates were well above average in most weeks, for a two-year cumulative total of more than 1.3 million excess deaths. About one fourth of those were due to other conditions whose mortality rates rose during the pandemic, with total mortality from COVID itself at more than one million deaths.

The data shown in Fig. 10.19 track how the U.S. food system responded to the pandemic with monthly sales reported by grocery outlets in the top line, and bars and restaurants in the lower line. These data differ from the USDA food expenditure series primarily in that they include alcohol in total spending on food away from home, but exclude food provided by institutions such as school meals. This shows how commercial spending on food away from home had surpassed commercial purchases at grocery stores starting in September 2019, and kept rising until the start of pandemic response in February 2020.

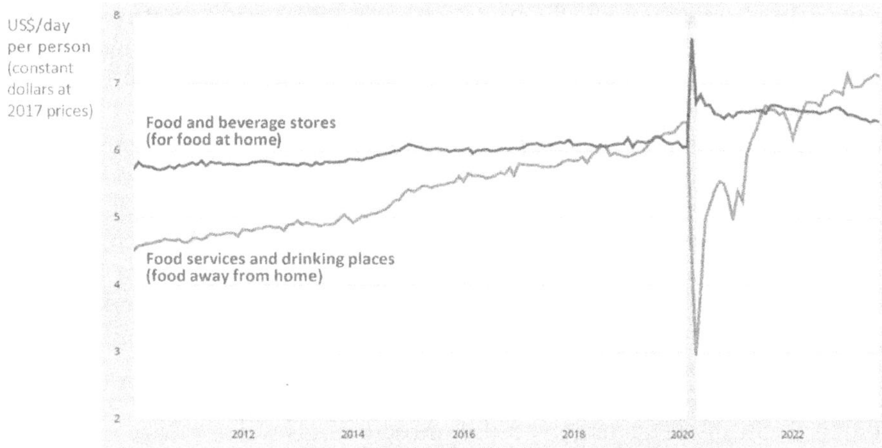

Fig. 10.19 Retail sales of food in the U.S. before and during the pandemic, January 2010–August 2023 *Source*: Reproduced from Federal Reserve Economic Data [FRED] showing data from the U.S. Census Bureau Monthly Retail Trade Survey, with preliminary advance estimates for August 2023. Values are deflated by the U.S. consumer price index. Data on food service and drinking places includes sales of alcohol, which are omitted from USDA food expenditure data. Updated versions of this chart are at https://fred.stlouisfed.org/graph/?g=1amTK

From February to April 2020, total sales of food away from home dropped from \$6.42 to \$2.95 per day. Food at home rose from \$6.06 in February to \$7.68 in March before falling back to \$6.71 in April and stabilizing around \$6.60 during 2021 and 2022.

Different communities experienced the COVID pandemic differently around the world, with varied levels of illness and mortality from the disease itself, and varied degrees and duration of isolation at home in response to news about the risk of infection. Some of stay-at-home behavior was a direct response to government policies, but U.S. cities and states did not begin to mandate lockdowns until mid-March, several weeks after restaurant traffic had already declined sharply. Communities also differed greatly in their ability and interest in returning to pre-pandemic trends. The national average experience of people in the United States, who quickly returned to high and rising levels of food spending away from home, indicates only what can happen when people return to high levels of employment and income growth as they have in the U.S., as shown at the end of Chapter 9.

Nutrition Transition in Physiology and Health: The ABCDs of Measuring Nutritional Status

Changes in food consumption affect nutritional status, altering lifelong health and disease risk in various ways summarized in Table 10.1 at the outset of this chapter as the ***nutrition transition***. That table summarized a few changes in nutritional status potentially caused by many different food attributes that affect metabolism and health. Modern knowledge of food composition began in the eighteenth and nineteenth centuries with measurement of energy in food, now described as coming from each of three macronutrients (protein, fats or carbohydrates). In the twentieth century biochemists then isolated and measured food composition in terms of over two dozen essential micronutrients that are needed for human metabolism, classified as either minerals (inorganic compounds, bringing elements known from chemistry in the periodic table) or vitamins (organic compounds produced by plants or animals). In the modern era of nutrition research, the nineteenth and twentieth century focus on essential nutrients has been complemented by measurement of many other bioactive compounds in food that also affect health.

All three kinds of nutritional attributes in food can have upper and lower bounds for health. Fluctuations within those bounds typically have no known consequences, in some cases due to known regulatory mechanisms that maintain homeostasis when dietary intake fluctuates within the normal range. Some example consequences of exceeding those bounds are listed in Table 10.5.

Specific compounds and attributes of food are sometimes associated with specific outcomes as shown in Table 10.5, but more often the attributes interact with each other to jointly determine nutritional status and health outcomes. This is particularly important for populations that have brought their intake of micro- and macronutrients to within the bounds beyond which they cause nutrient-specific diseases, so that remaining health risks are due

Table 10.5 Essential nutrients and other bioactive compounds needed for health

Type of compound	*Example effects of diet quality on human health*	
	Examples from excess intake	*Examples from insufficient intake*
Macronutrients (protein, fats and carbohydrates)	Diabetes from unbalanced diets; cardiovascular disease from excess of saturated fats	Low birthweight and stunted linear growth; underweight and wasting; insufficient weight gain in pregnancy and poor gestational health
Micronutrients (vitamins and minerals)	Hypertension from excess sodium; toxicity from excess of some vitamins in high doses	Blindness and poor immune function from Vitamin A deficiency; goiter and neurological impairment from iodine deficiency
Other compounds in food	Cancers caused by contaminants; malabsorption caused by anti-nutrients	Severity of illness worsened by low intake of phytochemicals from plants, whole grains and fermented foods that promote gut health

to interactions and other less easily detected aspects of food composition. Since the 1990s, nutrition guidance has increasing focused on overall dietary patterns, meaning the relative proportions of different food groups, first because that brings essential nutrients to within upper and lower bounds for most people, but also to ensure adequacy of other food attributes associated with health.

The measurement of nutritional status can be summarized using a convenient memory aid known as the ABCD approach, mentioned in the context of Table 10.1 at the start of this chapter. For convenience, the four categories are spelled out in somewhat more detail here before we turn to some of the observed data.

Anthropometry is the oldest category of data about nutritional status, measuring heights and weights or other dimensions of the body. The earliest datasets refer to heights of adult men in military service or other institutional settings. Later discoveries showed that almost all human populations converge to a similar distribution of adult heights when all nutritional and health needs are met, as each person reaches their genetic potential which has a similar distribution among people in all regions of the world. Other research showed that trajectories of attained heights were largely determined in early childhood, roughly the thousand days from gestation to the child's second birthday. That discovery was associated with the creation of standardized growth charts based on monthly measurement of a healthy reference population, ethnically diverse but given the highest standard of health care starting with prenatal nutrition, so that growth faltering or excess weight gain can be measured in terms of standard deviations around the median of that reference group. Weight gain or loss later in life is most commonly measured by adjusting for height using the body mass index (BMI), defined as weight divided by height squared. Conventional thresholds suggest that the lowest health risks are experienced by people with BMI between 18.5 and 25.0 kg/m^2, with higher risks associated with obesity which is defined as a BMI of 30 or above. Over time, improvements in anthropometry are refining these measures and diagnostic criteria for specific purposes, including the use of electronic imaging techniques and wearable sensors to measure physical and metabolic activity in more useful ways.

Biomarkers derived from physical samples have long been used to help diagnose nutritional status. The oldest measure is detection of sugar in urine to diagnose diabetes, dating from the seventeenth century. Since then, a wide range of innovations include faster and lower cost measurements at home or in field settings, such as photoelectric measurement of blood oxygen levels and pinprick samples to measure blood hemoglobin and diagnose anemia. The most used biomarkers for nutrition care in high-income countries are cholesterol and triglycerides to indicate cardiovascular health, fasting blood glucose to indicate problems with glucose metabolism, and blood urea nitrogen and creatinine to indicate kidney function. Frontier techniques include analysis of genetic material in stool samples to measure composition of the gut microbiome. All of these can potentially be used to diagnose imbalances and prescribe supplements or dietary changes for prevention as well as treatment after disease symptoms appear.

Clinical signs and symptoms of disease conditions sometimes relate to specific micronutrient deficiencies, such as discolored nails relating to zinc deficiency, neuropathy and fatigue associated with vitamin B12 deficiency, or impaired night vision linked to vitamin A deficiency. Like anthropometry and biochemical measures, these measures can be used in health services for early detection before nutrient-related diseases progress into severe illness and disability. More than one measure is typically needed, for example combining bone densitometry plus blood and urine tests to assess the role of calcium deficiency in osteoporosis. For research purposes, clinical techniques include isolating research subjects in metabolic chambers that account for all inflow and outflow of energy and nutrients. Metabolic chambers allow researchers to conduct trials that vary aspects of dietary intake or other factors and trace their consequences, with less of the background variation and measurement errors that limit research on diets in the population at large.

Dietary assessment is the toolkit used to overcome the difficulty of remembering and reporting what was eaten with sufficient accuracy to estimate nutrient intake. Early efforts include food diaries but those are invasive, difficult to sustain and likely to alter intake. Most often dietitians and survey staff use dietary recall after the fact, asking qualitative (yes/no) and sometimes quantitative (weight or volume) questions about broad food groups or specific items eaten over the previous day and night. Standard practices call for two 24-hr recalls on different days, followed by a set of data transformations to convert responses into estimated usual intakes, adjusting for infrequently consumed foods. Even with the most careful 24HR recall surveys, respondents typically report implausibly low total intake, so analysis of data is done on an energy-adjusted basis per thousand calories, or per 2000 calorie diet or some other benchmark such as 2330 kcal/day.

The ABCD classification used in nutrition textbooks can be extended to a longer memory aid, for example to add *E*nvironmental and social factors that interact with dietary intake such as bacteria, viruses and parasites linked to sanitation, airborne toxins and particulates from kitchen smoke or industrial pollution. In the health sciences, these are often described as social-ecological factors or social determinants of health. The ABCDE can be stretched further to add *F*ood system metrics, including farming methods, food safety and food processing, food waste and other variables that might affect diet quality, as well as *G*overnance factors that include labeling and disclosure of food composition, mandates for fortification like iodine in salt, bans on harmful ingredients like trans fats, or enforcement of food safety standards like hazard analysis and critical control point (HACCP) systems. Having this ABCDEFG classification in mind helps us remember the wide range of variables that could potentially be measured and used to characterize nutrition transition.

Nutrition Transition in Physiology and Health

Variation in attained height was reported by early travelers who noticed big differences in average stature of groups around the world. One of the first systemic records for large samples is the height of military recruits, especially in countries where conscription is broadly representative of the general population. Other samples include volunteer armies or prisoners who may be less representative of the population at large, but nonetheless reveal large differences and important similarities as illustrated in Fig. 10.20.

The countries shown in Fig. 10.20 are all success stories, in the sense of having significant increases in attained height over the twentieth century. The sample of successive cohorts is not globally representative of all countries, and by measuring only males enrolled in specific institutions they are not representative of all people within the countries shown, but they do show remarkable commonalities.

A first observation about these samples is that only Denmark and the Netherlands show sustained height increases in successive cohorts through the nineteenth century. The U.S. initially had very tall recruits in the early nineteenth century, with successively shorter cohorts until the twentieth century,

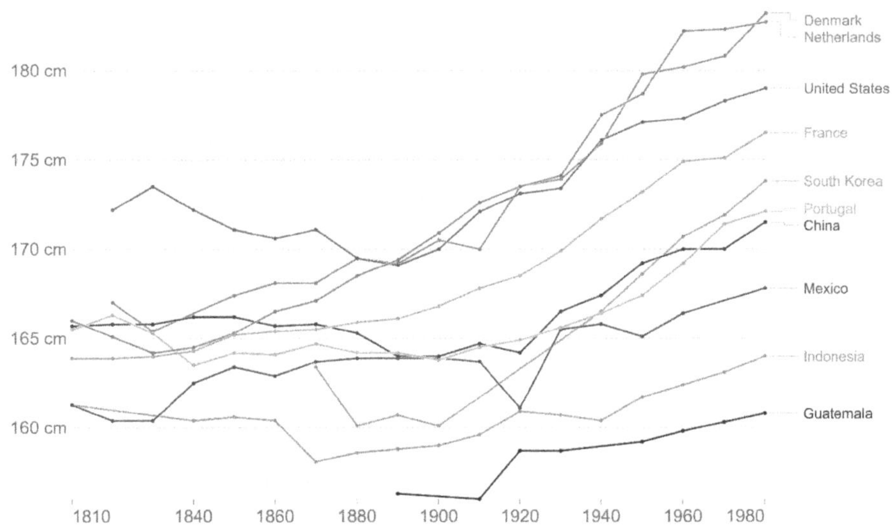

Fig. 10.20 Average heights of men by year of birth in selected countries, 1810 to 1980 *Source*: Reproduced from Max Roser, Esteban Ortiz-Ospina and Hannah Ritchie [2019], Our World in Data: Human Height [https://ourworldindata.org/human-height], based on Jorg Baten and Mattias Blum, 'Why are you tall while others are short? Agricultural production and other proximate determinants of global heights', *European Review of Economic History* 18 [2014], 144–165. Other countries can be selected at https://ourworldindata.org/grapher/average-height-of-men-for-selected-countries

most likely due to selection effects and enrollment of immigrants and others with more disadvantaged backgrounds.

A second observation is all successive cohorts grew taller over the twentieth century, even in the countries with least initial height. Early observers often believed that short stature of certain groups was an inherited trait associated with ethnicity, but it turns out that the mechanism of inheritance at a population level is environmental rather than genetic. Almost all populations now appear to have approximately the same distribution of genetic potential for attained height. Individuals differ in their genetic potential for height, for any sufficiently large population is likely to have sufficient variation within the group that their average potential height converges to the global average observed in well-nourished populations.

A third observation is that heights grew slowly and in parallel towards humanity's genetic potential height, without clear evidence of convergence to a frontier, at least in this set of example countries. Such a frontier must exist, but the data in this chart show that we still see the effects of gradually removing environmental and epigenetic constraints on each population's attainment. When large numbers of people are uprooted and move from low- to high-height locations, such as migrants from Asia to Europe or the U.S., they gain height from generation to generation much faster than successive cohorts within countries who experience less rapid change in environmental conditions.

Over time, nutrition researchers have identified just a few of the many mechanisms likely to be involved in determining whether a cohort achieves their genetic potential for height. Some of the most important findings involve timing, especially the fact that at least some height regulation occurs in utero and early infancy, influencing the child's trajectory long before the actual growth itself occurs throughout childhood and adolescence. Some of these effects work through the tempo of growth, delaying the onset and shortening the duration of growth spurts.

Concern about population growth in the late 1960s and 1970s led to surveys of women regarding fertility and family planning, and concerns about maternal and child health led to many surveys around the world focusing on women and children. For low- and middle-income countries, data from the Demographic and Health Surveys (DHS) funded by the U.S. government and run by local statistical agencies have now measured over 1.5 million mothers and their children under five around the world. Other data collection efforts such as the Multiple Indicator Cluster Surveys (MICS) led by UNICEF are also important for low-income settings, as well as national surveys run independently in each high-income country.

In the 1990s and 2000s, research efforts shifted towards understanding maternal and child health, but the frequency of surveys is still too low to permit annual monitoring in every country. Instead of that, the World Bank together with UNICEF and the World Health Organization (WHO) produce joint monitoring estimates by combining all available surveys for updates, resulting in the data shown in Fig. 10.21.

The top panel of Fig. 10.21 shows the prevalence of stunting in every region of the world for 2000, 2005, and then from 2010 to 2022. Stunting rates are a helpful indicator of a population's overall nutritional and health status affecting child development, capturing the sum total of all influences on whether the population is achieving their genetic potential for height. The metric is defined relative to the WHO's reference population of healthy children, a multiethnic cohort recruited in the late 1990s from households able to provide the highest standard of care throughout pregnancy and childhood in Brazil, Ghana, India, Norway, Oman and the United States. Stunting is defined as having a height-for-age under −2 standard deviations below the median of that healthy population. The same population also provides a distribution of child weights, and the same metric is used for child overweight as more than +2 standard deviations above the median. By definition, in a healthy population approximately 2.5% of children would meet these criteria,

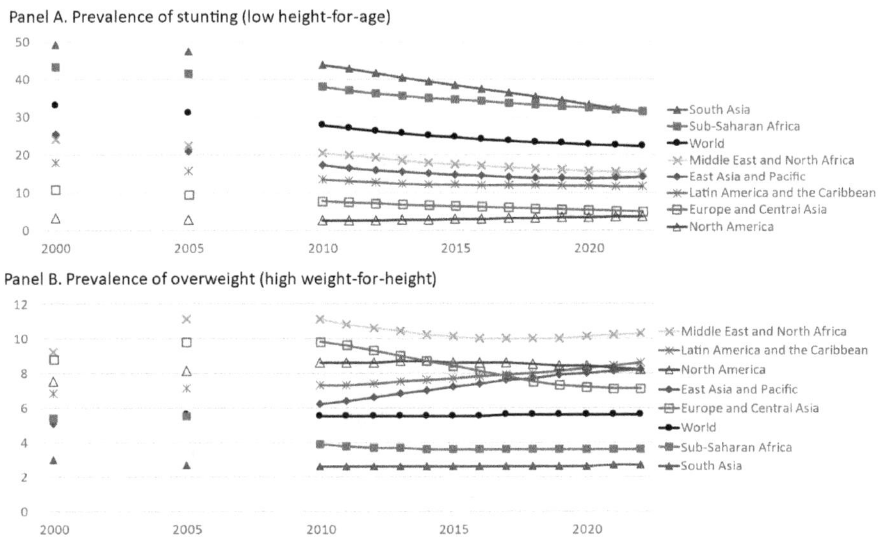

Fig. 10.21 Prevalence of stunting and overweight in children under five, 2000–2022 *Source*: Authors' chart of data from UNICEF, World Bank and World Health Organization Joint Child Malnutrition Estimates, published May 2023. Prevalence of stunting is the percentage of children aged 0–59 months who are below minus two standard deviations from median height-for-age of the WHO Child Growth Standards, and overweight is the percentage who are more than two standard deviations above the median weight-for-height of that healthy population. Methods are detailed at https://data.unicef.org/resources/jme-report-2023, with underlying survey data and results for individual countries at https://data.unicef.org/topic/nutrition/malnutrition

so the degree of stunting or overweight in a population is the extent to which their prevalence exceeds 2.5%.

The global estimates provided by merging all available surveys show that over 30% of all the world's children were stunted in 2000 and 2005, principally in South Asia and Sub-Saharan Africa where stunting rates were between 40 and 50%. Since then, child stunting in South Asia has dropped sharply, faster than the decline in Africa, leading to convergence at just above 30% in 2022. Stunting rates in all other regions have also fallen towards the benchmark level of 2.5% which is approximately characteristic of North America.

The bottom panel of Fig. 10.21 shows the prevalence of overweight, for which the world average was just above 5% in 2000 and remains near that level. Child overweight prevalence rose sharply from 2000 to 2005 in the Middle East and North Africa, Europe and Central Asia then declined in both those regions, and rose in North America. In Latin America and the Caribbean as well as East Asia and the Pacific, child overweight prevalence has continued to rise through 2022, and in North America it has declined since the late 2010s.

These data are far from definitive, due to limited survey frequency and sample sizes. Their focus on early childhood is also a limiting factor, and many efforts in recent years have expanded the window of measurement through adolescence. In higher income countries, monitoring also extends to adult men. What all these results show is continued variation in the experience of different populations living under different conditions, even at similar levels of real income and facing similar food costs. Nutrition transition clearly involves a variety of determinants beyond income and prices, some of which can be addressed by policy intervention.

Nutritional status in multi-dimensional, with multiple forms of malnutrition coinciding in each person and community, interacting to influence their susceptibility to disease over the life course. Children may have their linear growth be stunted in utero and infancy, and then experience a food environment that leads to rapid weight gain and a high level of weight-for-height, as well as deficiencies in a variety of micronutrient deficiencies. Those three dimensions of harm can be seen as a 'triple burden' of malnutrition affecting many communities around the world, contributing to disease risks that cumulate over the life course and drive large changes in longevity around the world.

Epidemiological Transition in Disease Risks

The attribution of mortality to specific causes and underlying risk factors is a challenging statistical exercise. All aspects of health interact with each other and contribute the progression of any given disease that might ultimately be listed as the cause of death. In recent years, the world's leading effort to correlate causes of death with potentially modifiable risk factors is known as the Global Burden of Disease (GBD) study, whose most recent complete accounting was published in late 2020 and is known as GBD 2019.

The complete set of risk factors used for GBD 2019 is based on variables for which data are available on both the risk factor itself, for example whether a child is breastfed, and its relative risk for a health outcome, such as diarrheal disease, which itself has a known relationship to disability and eventual mortality. A selection of risk factors related to nutrition, together with others for context, is shown in Fig. 10.22.

The selection of thirteen risk factors in Fig. 10.22 is a subset of all potentially modifiable behaviors and health conditions that are linked to premature death. The vertical axis shows the number of deaths per 100,000 people that are associated with variance in that risk factor, relative to the base rate of deaths without it.

In 1990, child and maternal malnutrition was the most important of these thirteen risks for early death, defined here as sum of risks from child growth failure and stunting, plus also suboptimal breastfeeding, low birthweight and short gestation, and three specific micronutrient deficiencies for iron, zinc and vitamin A. These are commonly found together and are jointly targeted by nutrition and health interventions, using a combination of prenatal and obstetrical care plus support for exclusive breastfeeding to six months of age followed by nutrition assistance, all designed to reduce eventual mortality and intermediate indicators such as stunting.

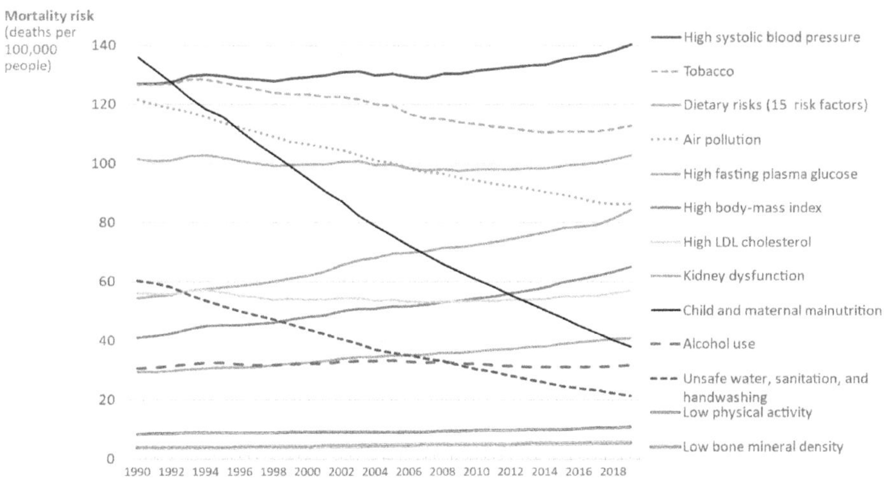

Fig. 10.22 Nutrition-related and selected other risk factors for mortality, 1990–2019 *Source*: Authors' chart of data from Institute for Health Metrics and Evaluation [IHME], Global Burden of Disease study [GBD 2019], ©2020 and used with permission. Data shown are estimated global number of deaths per 100,000 people associated with each risk factor or group of risk factors. Details on methods and the database query to reproduce a version of this chart with other related variables is: https://vizhub.healthdata.org/gbd-results?params=gbd-api-2019-permalink/9fd8c1a283a9a13959f2ee5dc69fe04c

The GBD 2019 data in this chart reveal how mortality associated child and maternal malnutrition has plummeted from 136 to 38 deaths per 100,000 people over the past three decades. That is a cumulative reduction of almost one death for every thousand people. The reduced burden of disease caused by child and maternal malnutrition is partly due to lower fertility and a smaller fraction of all people who are children, but also to improvement in conditions surrounding each birth as shown for example by lower stunting rates. A smaller but also dramatic decline has occurred in the number of deaths associated with unsafe water, sanitation and handwashing, and its associated transmission of water-borne diseases. Tobacco use and air pollution have also declined in importance but remain among the top four of these thirteen risks.

Those four risk factors shown in Fig. 10.22 to have declined in importance were the main targets of many public health interventions in the 1990s and 2000s. Those interventions generally have high levels of cost-effectiveness per life saved, and contributed to the higher level of life expectancy at each income level as shown in Preston curves of Fig. 10.1. Other factors such as tobacco and air pollution remain very important risk factors for early death, and there have been large increases in the burden of diet-related metabolic conditions.

In 1990, the next highest risk factor after child and maternal malnutrition was high systolic blood pressure, which can have various causes and for some people is worsened by high sodium intake. The importance of high blood pressure rose after the mid-2000s, and as of 2019 was associated with 140 deaths per 100,000 people, more than the 113 deaths now associated with tobacco use. After those two, the third most important risk factor is a combined set of 15 dietary risks including a diet low in five food groups (vegetables, legumes, whole grains, milk, or nuts and seeds) or high in three other food groups (red meat, processed meat, and sugar-sweetened beverages), or else low in four nutrients (fiber, calcium, omega-3 fatty acids, and polyunsaturated fatty acids) or high in two other nutrients (trans fatty acids or sodium). As of 2019, that overall metric of poor diet quality is associated with 103 deaths per 100,000 people.

The fastest-increasing risk factor is high fasting plasma glucose as an indicator for diabetes, rising from 54 to 84 deaths per 100,000 people between 1990 and 2019. High BMI also grew quickly in importance, rising from 41 to 65 deaths, and kidney dysfunction rose from 29 to 41 deaths per 100,000. These three are interconnected with each other and with high blood pressure as conditions that are closely tied to dietary patterns. An additional risk is posed by the 15 dietary factors that add almost as much additional mortality as tobacco.

The epidemiological transition towards increased importance of diet-related noncommunicable disease can be measured in many ways. The GBD 2019 results are the result of statistical modeling, not direct observation, but they clearly reveal how the interaction of economic growth, demographic transition and food system change have made diet quality a central concern for public health worldwide.

Causes of Difference Between Benchmark Healthy Diets and Actual Food Choice

As we saw in Fig. 7.17 at the end of our chapter on poverty and risk, many of the world's lowest-income people spend less on food than even a least-cost diet that meets minimal criteria for health, as specified in the healthy diet basket targets used at the start of this section to describe the dietary transition. As shown in Fig. 10.14, at higher incomes people typically meet their daily energy needs with larger quantities of animal source foods, oils and fats, and sugars than would be needed for a healthy diet, which displaces items from the other food groups that would be needed to deliver sufficient nutrients and other bioactive compounds for lifelong health.

The lack of convergence towards a balanced diet when incomes rise can most simply be attributed to the fact that the health attributes of food cannot generally be detected by the consumer and may often be misunderstood. Each person's beliefs about how eating a food would impact their future health reflects their own self-experimentation, remembering how their health changed after eating different things, and the centuries of trial and error behind humanity's varied culinary practices and food cultures passed down within families and communities. People also may have ideas about how their bodies have reacted to foods when previously tried, and they may be wary of trying again. People are also influenced by the news they read. That news influences food choice and is subject to strong selection effects, emphasizing certain things and not others based on the incentives that guide what is written, read and shared.

Amelia hears a lot of beliefs about food in her work as a clinical dietitian, with each person's different beliefs all deeply rooted in that person's background and experiences. Cultural and other differences drive wide variation in the composition of diets between individuals, communities and regions of the world. One of the very few constants is the need for sufficient total energy intake to maintain bodyweight, triggered by hormonal and other signals. The sources of that energy then vary in ways that are often culturally determined, like the clothes or shoes people wear. All humans need to maintain body temperature and protect our feet, but what people wear depends on social, historical and technological circumstances. The furniture in our houses has a similar mix of functional and cultural roles. Food differs from clothing, shoes or furniture in part due to its outsized impact on future health, influencing nutritional status and susceptibility to disease.

The dietary and nutrition transitions described in this chapter include the effects on food choice of popular or social media as well as professional guidance about food's effects on health. Past investments in nutrition research have generated rapid progress towards scientific consensus on some aspects of how food affects health, and information about that consensus is widely available through national dietary guidelines such as MyPlate in the U.S. or the Eatwell Guide in the UK. Those dietary guidelines are tailored to local circumstances but have many similarities because they draw on the same evidence about how food composition affects future health. They have some influence on food choice, but other information also matters including news about nutrition research.

The scientific consensus behind national dietary guidelines evolves with new evidence but is updated in ways that differ greatly from how news about nutrition research is shared in popular media. As with economics or other fields, consensus among full-time specialist researchers is formed by testing structural models and theories about causal mechanisms against multiple kinds of evidence. In nutrition, much of that knowledge comes from biochemistry and bench science, combined with experimentation on animals and clinical or epidemiological observation of people. There are few randomized trials in humans, for the same reason that there are few randomized trials of surgical techniques or the health impacts of smoking. Conducting double-blind, placebo-controlled trials would be impractical or unethical for many important research questions. Even when they are feasible, randomized trials in nutrition would need prohibitively large sample sizes and long duration of follow-up to avoid the false findings that often arise from small, short-duration trials.

Media reporting about nutrition research often focuses on individual studies that stand out and provide a compelling story. Simply repeating the scientific consensus as specified in dietary guidelines would not be interesting. Compelling stories aim to say something new, typically by identifying one specific food or nutrient that is unexpectedly helpful or harmful. Quite understandably, the positive stories about a helpful thing often refer to studies that turn out have been funded by food companies or industry groups producing that thing, and even when studies are conducted independently researchers themselves may be subject to confirmation bias and motivated reasoning. Researchers looking for evidence to prove a point or confirm their beliefs can readily find data to strengthen their arguments. Randomized trials with small sample sizes and short duration generate a wide range of results to choose from, as will the diverse methods and data sources used in observational studies. The most appealing results are then amplified in professional and social media, propelled by strong incentives that include the self-interest of industry groups and the prior beliefs and concerns of consumers.

Consumer beliefs about how food affects health are influenced to some degree by news about nutrition research and are also influenced by food marketing and package labels. Companies routinely use health benefits as a selling point, often for product differentiation in search of market share and price premiums that some consumers might be willing to pay for otherwise hidden attributes. Items with essentially the same nutritional composition are often sold under different brand identities at different prices to different groups of consumers. For example, a high-fiber whole grain breakfast cereal fortified with micronutrients with some sugar added might be marketed as a premium product emphasizing the whole grains and fiber to some buyers, a premium fun food when the added sugar is visibly sprinkled on top and showcased on the package, and as a low-cost food whose packaging emphasizes only the micronutrients. The same market segmentation applies to farm produce, for example the same vegetables could be sold as a premium product or as a low-cost generics, in fresh or frozen form.

The many drivers of dietary change and nutrition transition can be understood much more clearly in the light of two basic insights from health sciences addressed in this and previous chapters. A first insight is that a person's total food intake in terms of dietary energy per day is largely predetermined by their height, weight and physical activity level. Trajectories for attained height are heavily influenced by conditions in utero and infancy, long before the actual growth occurs. Weight gain can occur at any life stage and is rarely reversed, so higher weights observed in adulthood often reflect a physiological change that occurred in the past, perhaps many years earlier. A second insight is that diet-related conditions, including undesired weight gain, are driven by attributes of food that cannot readily be observed and may often be misunderstood. The food attributes that would support the future health of a given individual are a knowable fact available from scientific consensus, but there is no mechanism by which effective demand would align with health, and many reasons for people to consume foods other than those that would best support their future health. Those two insights create many opportunities for food economists to participate in the design and implementation of interventions to help people meet their health objectives, while also pursuing their many other goals in life.

Strengths and Limitations of Any 'Transitions' Framework

This chapter began with Table 10.1, listing four major transitions typically associated with economic growth: a demographic transition with rise and then fall in population growth rates, a structural transformation of the economy with urbanization and a rise then fall in the number of farmers, a food system transformation with diversification of diets made possible by specialization and intensification of production, and the resulting nutrition transition from deficiencies to excesses and perhaps ultimately balanced intake for longevity and health.

The economics of food aims to help explain transitions over time and differences among countries in terms of underlying mechanisms, each built up using the analytical diagrams in Chapters 2–6. Each analytical diagram is a structural model that aims to explain observations as the result of interactions which could potentially be improved through intervention. The diagrams sometimes include flow charts, such as the circular flow of economic activity in a population used to show the macroeconomy, using those as an accounting framework to ensure that all aspects of the system are considered.

Beginning in Chapter 7 we extend the toolkit to data visualization, observing trends or patterns over the longest time periods and the largest number of countries for which we can provide authoritative data. Many aspects of the observed data remain unexplained, perhaps due to measurement error, but seeing as much data as possible in scatterplots, line graphs, bar charts and numerical tables is helpful to ensure that we have not mistakenly focused on just a few examples or case studies that are not representative of the actual range of human experience.

Summarizing outcomes as stages in a transition can be helpful but is potentially misleading. For example, one might imagine the food system transformation as having a first stage when isolated family farmers produce food for themselves and their local neighbors, with little processing done outside the home. An archetype like that is easy to picture in one's imagination, and yet not widely observed in practice. Instead of stages, our description of transitions focuses on underlying mechanisms that cause systematic patterns of change over time, such as the rise and then fall in the number of farmers. These patterns do have turning points, such as the years when a country has its peak number of farmers, but as shown in our data visualizations the speed and timing of change depends on each country's policy choices and societal circumstances, and some countries experience periods of stagnation or even reversal when growth does not occur.

10.2.3 Conclusion

This chapter describes how the process of economic growth, meaning sustained increases in the value of goods and services provided by a country's people to each other, drives change over time and differences across countries in their agriculture and food systems, dietary patterns and nutritional status. The engine of growth is accumulation of capital, meaning valuable things made by people, including the health and education of people themselves. Capital accumulation allows people to rely less on just their land and natural resources, transitioning from having most people work as farmers to a manufacturing sector and ultimately the service economy in which most employment involves few physical inputs at all.

The food and health aspects of transition addressed in this section begin with dietary transition, as populations with higher incomes shift from diets based only on the least expensive foods, primarily starchy staples, to much higher quantities of animal source foods plus vegetable oil and sugar than would be needed for a balanced diet, leaving little room for the vegetables, fruits, and legumes, nuts and seeds that would be more health-promoting. The agricultural products in those food groups are also increasingly transformed into packaged and processed items and used in food service for meals away from home. That postharvest transformation may remove important aspects of important foods, such as removing the bran and germ from whole grains to produce refined flour with longer shelf life and may add ingredients such as sodium or added sugar which are often consumed in excess of individual needs. As societies discover how those foods affect health, and face changing environmental constraints on production, each country will have the opportunity and need for new kinds of policy intervention and private-sector food businesses.

CHAPTER 11

From Local to Global: International Trade and Value Chains

11.1 How Trade and Policies Link Local Markets to Global Food Systems

11.1.1 Motivation and Guiding Questions

This section expands our modeling toolkit to address interactions between markets in a global food system. In recent decades, a wave of globalization, driven by lower transport costs and openness to trade, has led to greater interconnection between countries. What explains the direction and quantity of trade flows that we observe, and the international prices at which trade occurs?

On average over time, countries can use their comparative advantage to earn gains from trade, but doing so alters income distribution and price volatility in systematic ways that can drive similar policy responses around the world. Losses drive more political engagement than gains, and concentrated impacts are especially important in driving the formation of politically active interest groups. How do governments respond to these pressures, taking account of both agricultural trade and domestic policies? Can we track how farm policies affect both producers and consumers?

International trade can help stabilize local markets by diversifying food sources, and also raise a country's vulnerability to world price spikes. In this section we address where, when and how trade can play a stabilizing role that improves a country's food security, and when do governments restrict trade in an effort to limit transmission of international price spikes to their own domestic consumers, in the context of trade regional and global agreements that governments use in response to political pressure and economic opportunities in their own agriculture and food markets.

By the end of this section, you will be able to:

W. A. Masters and A. B. Finaret, *Food Economics*,
Palgrave Studies in Agricultural Economics and Food Policy,
https://doi.org/10.1007/978-3-031-53840-7_11

1. Use supply, demand and trade diagrams to explain, predict and evaluate changes in quantities produced, consumed, imported and exported;
2. Use information about transport costs to quantify what people at one location would pay if they imported and would receive if they exported a product to or from the rest of the world, and describe how that price band limits the range of fluctuation at that location;
3. Use available data to describe changes in the volume of total merchandise trade, agricultural and food trade around the world; and
4. Use available data to describe changes in trade restrictions around the world, in terms of their effects on farm revenue and prices paid for food commodities within countries.

11.1.2 Analytical Tools

The analytical diagrams used so far in this book refer to either an individual person or a local market. Those diagrams revealed how individuals, communities and whole countries can take advantage of their differences to exchange things with each other, seizing their comparative advantage to earn gains from trade.

We first defined and used the concept of comparative advantage in Chapter 4 on social welfare, using Fig. 4.10 and other diagrams to show how a person or community is affected by trading with others. The level of each person or community's wellbeing depends on the absolute level of their productivity and resource endowments, but trade with others depends on differences in productivity. Each diagram until now focused on just one person or one market relative to a given price in trade. To see where that trade price comes from, we need to expand our diagram to see supply-demand balances in that market relative to the entire rest of the world.

Comparative Advantage, International Prices and Global Supply–Demand Balances

In all previous market diagrams, the possibility of trade with others was drawn as a horizontal line at the price offered for purchase or sale to people elsewhere. The quantities exported or imported did not affect the price in trade, on the grounds that the rest of the world is typically so large that changes in the one market of interest could not affect its supply-demand balance. Drawing each market as if it were an infinitely small share of the whole world, and therefore a 'price taker' with no influence on the rest of the world's prices, made the analysis simpler and clearer without affecting our results.

Previous chapters focused on just one community or country, and we could see the effects of their government policies on their population using a fixed international price. To see how each country's market connects to other countries, we need a more complicated diagram as drawn in Fig. 11.1.

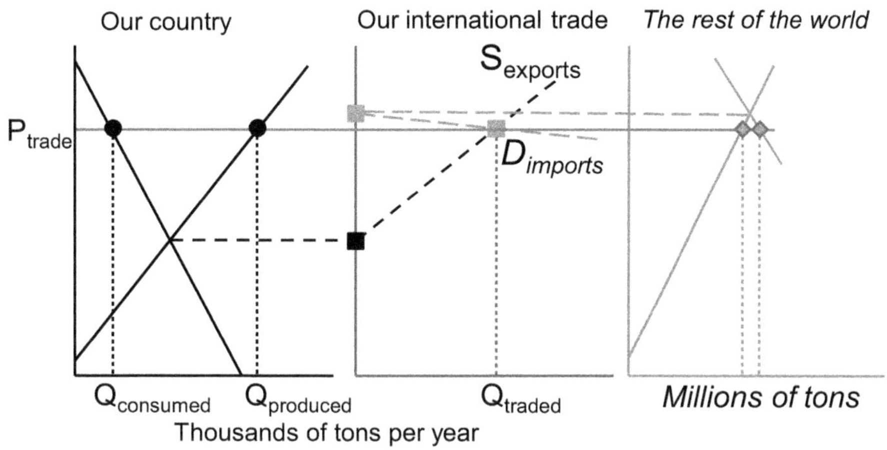

Fig. 11.1 Trade prices and comparative advantage in a three-panel diagram

The model of international in Fig. 11.1 is known as a three-panel diagram. It shows the entire world market for a particular product, such durum wheat or yellow corn, divided into producers and consumers in our country of interest on the left, and the entire rest of the world's producers and consumers on the right. The middle diagram shows the possibility of trade between our country and the rest of the world. The vertical axes of all three panels are aligned in the same currency, for example U.S. dollars per ton, but the horizontal axes differ. The rest of the world is likely to be a large place, with quantities measured for example in millions of tons, while our country of interest is likely to be smaller, for example with quantities measured in thousands of tons.

In our country on the left there would be a price in autarky at which we would trade nothing, corresponding to the lower square on the vertical axis of the international trade diagram. If others were willing to pay a price above that, our country would supply a quantity of exports that is equal to the gap between our country's production and consumption at that price. The dashed supply of exports line whose slope is flatter than our producers' supply curve, because it also takes account of our consumers' demand curve. Our country's elasticity of supply for exports is the sum of our own population's supply and demand elasticities.

Similarly for the rest of the world on the right there is a price at which it would not import anything, corresponding to the upper square on the vertical axis of the trade diagram. At any price below that, the rest of the world would import the gap between its production and consumption. Because the world is a big place, measured for example in millions of tons, that would be a large quantity of imports when measured in thousands of tons. That is why the whole world's demand for imports from our country is very elastic with respect to price, and could be drawn as an infinitely elastic horizontal line in earlier diagrams.

If we redrew this three-panel diagram by dividing the world into two equal-sized regions, each area's demand for imports from the other might have about the same price elasticity as the other region's supply of exports. Similarly we could redraw this diagram for our country when it is importing from a large rest of the world, and the price we pay in trade set by their highly elastic supply of exports.

Each country's comparative advantage for each product depends only on how its supply-demand balance compares to the rest of the world. A country whose domestic price is lower than prices elsewhere will have producers who can and would export, raising their country's price along their supply of exports curve until it meets the rest of the world's demand for imports at the international trade price. Similarly, a country whose price is higher than elsewhere will have consumers who would want to import, so allowing free trade would lead to imports and a decline in the domestic price to its level in international trade.

The three-panel diagram in Fig. 11.1 shows the market for just one product, but our country's comparative advantage in this market originates in our population's decisions about whether to produce this thing instead of other goods and services. The supply curve for this thing in our country is upward sloping because increased production draws resources that would otherwise be employed producing other things. A higher price in trade that leads to increased production for export in this market would cause supply curves for other things to shift left and down, reducing the country's comparative advantage in those markets and bringing in imports of those things. By definition, each country has a comparative advantage in exporting the things for which its supply and demand makes that product relatively abundant within the country, compared to other things which are relatively scarce so the country has a comparative disadvantage in production and an interest in importing.

Each country's overall trade balance, adding up all their imports and all their exports, is determined by the macroeconomic forces that alter the country's exchange rate as discussed in Chapter 9. For example if our country's currency is the peso, and foreigners start buying pesos for investments in our country, their use of dollars to purchase pesos will bid up the dollar-to-pesos exchange rate which lowers the price in pesos for all traded products, reducing exports of everything exported while increasing imports of everything imported. That change would need to be just sufficient to use the additional dollars that foreigners want exchange for pesos to pay for investments. Conversely, if foreigners pull their money out, the exchange rate would devalue and peso prices of traded products would rise, reflecting that the population of our country is now less wealthy and so imports less and ships more things to others.

As discussed in Section 9.1 of the chapter on macroeconomics, our country's monetary policy and the supply of pesos is managed by the central bank, while fiscal policies influence how many pesos or dollars the government wants to borrow or lend. All of those factors would influence the exchange rate, and hence the total volume of imports and imports, by attracting or discouraging a flow of foreign exchange into the country. When a country is attracting an inflow of foreign currency for capital investment, its balance of trade shifts towards more imports and less exports, but it is still the degree of comparative advantage for each product that determines which things are exported and which are imported.

The three-panel diagram in Fig. 11.1 is drawn for simplicity with a single price received by exporters and paid by exporters, for example in U.S. dollars. An important next consideration is the role of transaction costs, as shown in Fig. 11.2.

Business transactions often involve specialized jargon that is useful to learn. For international trade, as shown in Fig. 11.2, export prices are denoted as P_{fob}, meaning a free-on-board price which indicates that the good is available for shipment to any destination. The product is free of obligation to pay any taxes or other costs, and is on board a means of transport for outbound shipment. There would then be some transaction costs from that point onwards to the importer whose price is denoted P_{cif}, meaning that someone has paid the cost of the good itself, the insurance for loss in transit, and all freight costs for the transportation itself.

Every importer's P_{cif} is greater than every exporter's P_{fob}, by an amount equal or less than the transaction costs between them. If there were an importer-exporter pair for whom the P_{cif}–P_{fob} gap was larger than transactions costs, traders looking for opportunities would buy from the exporter and ship to the importer. There are many such traders around the world, looking for moments when the price at the origin of potential exports is low enough to justify transport, relative to the price at the destination of potential imports. These traders will then bid for space on transport vessels and all of the other services needed to complete the transaction.

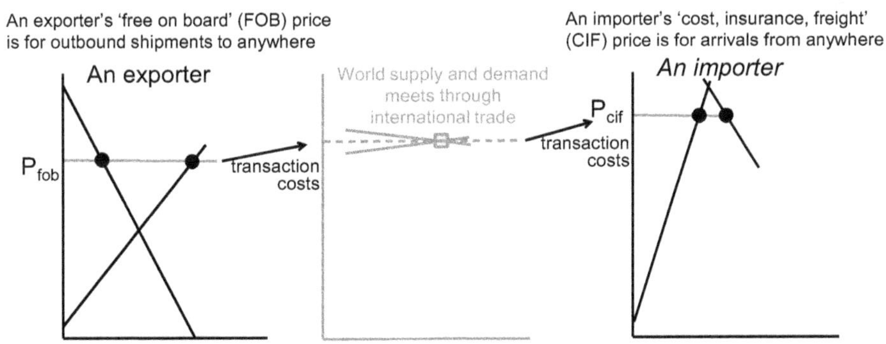

Fig. 11.2 Transactions costs make exporters' price received lower than importers' price paid

In world trade there are flows of everything to and from everywhere, with day-to-day adjustments in planned shipments based on news about changes in likely harvests or unexpected events in an origin or destination country. Most of the volume travels on a few routes, as traders look for the origins and destinations that would make the journey profitable. The lowest transport cost per mile is for ocean trade between deepwater ports on 'max'-size ships that carry over 50,000 tons of bulk grain. The vehicles move slowly but use little fuel per ton carried and each mile traveled. Loading or unloading between large ships and smaller boats, trains or trucks can be expensive and subject to congestion at port or other transit facilities. Each shipment may be loaded and unloaded multiple times, adding to its cost and delays.

The cost per mile of transporting each shipment is sharply lower on larger vehicles or vessels, so transaction costs depend on infrastructure and technology. For example, grain exported from inland farms in the U.S. is often shipped by truck to trains or barges that travel south down the Mississippi river to ports in the Gulf of Mexico. Grain may also be shipped by truck to trains to ports in the west and east. The USDA monitors and publishes transport costs on each route, partly to inform producers and end-users, but primarily to monitor conditions and address policy concerns about public investment and regulation of the transport sector that influences prices received by farmers and paid by end-users in each region of the U.S.

Illustrative examples of transportation costs for bulk grains shipped through the southern route to Latin America, Africa and Asia are in Table 11.1.

The U.S. data shown in Table 11.1 reveal how costs per unit of distance vary by a factor of 100, for similar products from U.S. farms to a deepwater port overseas. Local costs at either end of these journeys will differ, and are particularly high where conditions require smaller vehicles that use more fuel and labor or other resources per ton carried, including final shipments to end users. Handling loose bags or boxes can also be costly, leading to cost reductions when those are placed in standard-size containers for multimodal transfer from truck to rail to boat.

The specific time period for which these costs were observed is from January through March 2022, with forward quotes for ocean shipments a few months later. This was a period of high U.S. transport costs, due to congestion at transit points caused by rapid recovery of demand for traded goods after the COVID recession. Transport costs can also vary due to changes in the cost of fuel, labor, equipment and facilities at each location. Observing cost differentials within the U.S. for the same product at the same time to different destinations shows how the main differences are between roads, rail and water. Each step in efficiency of resource use can involve a 10× difference in cost, for up to a 100× difference in bulk grain transport costs.

Cost differentials among ocean routes are smaller than differentials between road, rail and water shipment, but the examples shown reveal systematic patterns that influence global food trade. Shipments to Central America via Honduras use smaller ships for a shorter distance and were about 7× more

Table 11.1 Transportation costs for bulk grain from the U.S. to overseas, January–March 2022

	Cost per shipment	*Distance*	*Cost per kilometer (ones or thousands)*	
	US$/mt	*km*	*US$/mt*	*'000s*
Road				
Short distance (25 miles)	$13.04	40	$0.33	$326
Middle distance (100 miles)	$39.19	161	$0.24	$243
Longer distance (200 miles)	$74.79	322	$0.23	$232
Rail				
Wichita, Kansas to U.S. Gulf (New Orleans)	$42.70	1090	$0.039	$39
River barge				
St. Louis, Missouri to U.S. Gulf (New Orleans)	$17.05	1207	$0.014	$14
Ocean shipping				
U.S. Gulf to Honduras, February 2022 (7820 mt)	$57.15	2104	$0.0272	$27
U.S. Gulf to Djibouti, March 2022 (10,000 mt)	$209.97	16,748	$0.0125	$13
U.S. Gulf to Sudan, March 2022 (35,700 mt)	$149.97	15,438	$0.0097	$10
U.S. Gulf to Sudan, February 2022 (35,780 mt)	$77.60	15,438	$0.0050	$5
U.S. Gulf to Japan, May 2022 (50,000 mt)	$78.90	20,000	$0.0039	$4

Source: Authors' calculations from USDA data. Trucking costs are from USDA Agricultural Marketing Service, Grain Truck and Ocean Rate Advisory (April 2022). Barge, rail and ocean shipping costs are from the USDA Agricultural Marketing Service, Grain Transportation Report (March 3, 2022). Trucking costs are averages for shipments of 25 mt (55,000 lbs) based on legal limit on U.S. highways, and rail and barge costs are averages, and ocean shipping costs are five of the 13 illustrative examples provided by the USDA in the Grain Transportation Report for March 3, 2022. More recent editions of these reports are at https://www.ams.usda.gov/services/transportation-analysis/GTOR and www.ams.usda.gov/GTR

costly per ton-kilometer than shipments to Japan, and twice as costly per ton-kilometer than the longer distance through the Suez Canal to the East African port of Djibouti which serves Ethiopia among other destinations. Using larger ships on that same route to Sudan is somewhat less expensive per ton, and two different shipments to Sudan of similar size differ in cost due to the Jones Act requirement that half of U.S. food aid be shipped on U.S. flag vessels. The Jones Act also requires that all commercial ocean shipments within the country be on U.S. flag vessels, which significantly raises the cost of food and all goods transported from the mainland to Puerto Rico and Hawaii among other destinations.

The data in Table 11.1 refer to outbound shipments from inland North America to Central America, Asia and Africa, and similar patterns would apply for onward transport inland within each continent, including Europe and South Asia. At each location there is a potential FOB price for outbound shipments and a potential CIF price for inbound deliveries. Where transport is feasible and free trade is allowed, this CIF-FOB band provides upper and lower bounds on prices at each inland location. Traders are looking for any potentially profitable price differences, bidding up prices where they are low and selling where prices are high, thereby ensuring that prices at each place are kept within bounds defined by transport costs. The result is a spatial *price surface* with higher prices at inland destinations towards which the product is flowing, leading up to spatial peaks at the places buying the product into which transport is most expensive. Conversely, the lowest prices are found at the most remote places from which the product is exported. The price surface is flattest between deepwater ports on the ocean, due to the relatively low cost per ton of shipping in large boats.

The Interaction of Storage and Trade

People respond to forecasts. Information suggesting that prices will rise in the future will lead people to buy or hold on to commodities, and traders will ship things towards the places where prices are expected to rise the most. Conversely, indications of a future price decline will lead people to sell before that happens, and prompt traders to ship grain out of that location. Some traders specialize only in transport, while others also own physical storage facilities so they can actively manage their own inventory. Stocks may also be held on farms after harvest and held by processors and distributors for varying periods of time before onward sale. A minimal level of 'pipeline' stocks is held by actors all along the value chain to maintain continuity of operations, and those enterprises will use operational facilities for storage if they believe prices will rise in the future, and then draw those down to the minimum needed for operational necessity if they believe prices will fall.

Many agricultural commodities are harvested almost simultaneously by different farmers in a given region, leading to a price decline over the few weeks or months after harvest. Even if physical storage could be done over more than one year, the anticipated arrival of each season's new crop typically leads actors in the value chain to draw down any stocks they might hold in advance of the price decline. They seek to avoid holding on to a product that could be bought later at a lower price, and therefore aim to have their storage facilities almost empty in time for the new harvest when prices will be lowest.

The month-to-month price rise after each harvest reflects the cost of storage, which differs greatly among actors in the food system. In low-income countries, farmers who grow basic commodities are often among the poorest people in society. They have urgent needs and high opportunity costs of holding on to whatever they have harvested, with limited access to any credit or insurance, so they typically sell immediately and use the proceeds to invest in school fees and health care, or to finance their seasonal migration and nonfarm activities for the offseason after harvest. If they did have access to loans in the past they may also have borrowed against the harvest and need to pay that back immediately. In contrast, many commodity growers in the U.S. and other high-income countries have access to credit at very low interest rates, and also have savings of their own, so they often invest in on-farm storage facilities that allow them to store their harvest for as long as they think will be profitable.

The actors along each value chain who hold the most stocks are those with the highest expected returns and lowest costs of storage, including both the operational expense of protecting commodities against damage or loss, and also the opportunity cost of keeping a valuable asset locked up in a bin or silo. Protecting commodities against insects and mold or other organisms is often more difficult in tropical places especially when there is high humidity in the postharvest months, and easier in temperate climates where temperatures and moisture levels usually fall after harvest. In high-income settings, where owners of stored products can borrow or lend funds as needed, the monthly cost of storage and hence expected price rise needed to justify holding stocks is mainly the prevailing interest rate on loans. In low-income countries, that monthly cost is often much higher, leading to a steeper expected price rise needed to justify holding on to stocks from one harvest to the next, and therefore a larger price decline immediately after harvest.

The actual trajectory of prices at any given location is subject to a continuous flow of news about likely future supply and demand, so prices bounce around randomly as people adjust their stockholding and trading behavior. To see the underlying pattern we must hold some things constant and conduct a highly simplified thought experiment, as in the stylized trajectory of prices shown in Fig. 11.3.

The model of price dynamics from which Fig. 11.3 is drawn reflects the market for a storable product like wheat at an inland location that sometimes has big harvests that exceed local demand and lead to exports, but more often has small harvests that lead to imports. Locations like this include many dryland regions of East, West and Southern Africa, so for example this could be the price of wheat in Addis Ababa, the capital of Ethiopia, where the wheat harvest usually starts in October. The diagram is intended to show the predictable equilibrium result of interaction between private storage and trade that would occur without government intervention. In reality, many governments (including Ethiopia's) buy and sell commodities or restrict trade in ways that make the picture less predictable.

The three harvests over the time period shown happen to be small, then big and then small again, leading to imports, exports and then imports, at prices indicated by the fluctuating dark line. The upper and lower light-colored lines are drawn based on actual historical price fluctuations of internationally traded wheat, for which Ethiopia's nearest ocean port is Djibouti. The upper line would be the cost of importing wheat from the world, and the lower line would be the price received when exporting wheat to the world, in both cases

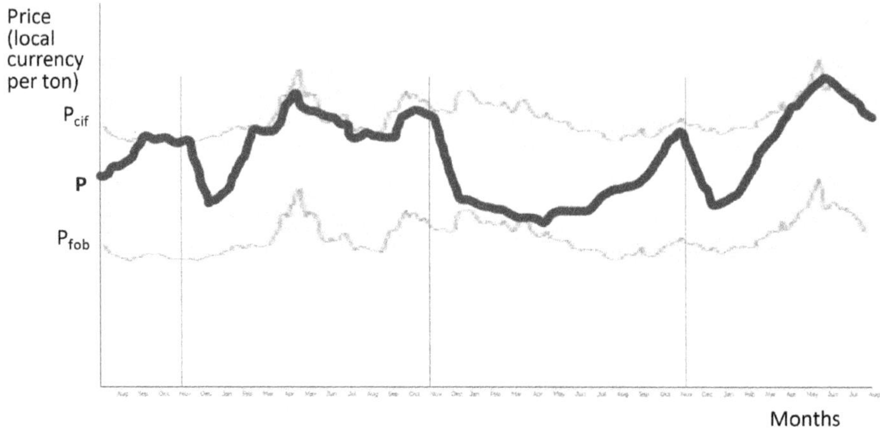

Fig. 11.3 Harvests and storage drive fluctuation in price within bounds set by trade prices *Source*: Authors' sketch of a hypothetical trajectory of prices over three years, with the arrival of harvests at the vertical guidelines. The light-colored upper line shows the hypothetical the landed cost of any imports [P_{cif}] and the lower line is the price that would be received for exports [P_{fob}], from ocean ports where the trajectory of prices is a three-year sample of the actual history of wheat prices available from the IMF. Actual prices for other commodities and time periods are at https://data.imf.org/?sk=90c0ef21-5c6f-4d2f-a99a-2dbcbfaca509&hide_uv=1

via Djibouti. For clarity in this scenario, we can imagine that transport costs to and from Djibouti remain constant throughout the period, although in reality they would vary with the cost of fuel and other inputs.

The dark line shows the actual price observed, which begins the period shown rising at the monthly cost of storage from the previous harvest. Traders have observed that price trajectory, and expect local stocks to run out around September so they would have ordered imports to arrive before that in sufficient quantities to last until the new harvest arrives in November. That harvest turns out to be small, so traders again place orders for imports. If they expect that the harvest will provide roughly four months of expected consumption, they will place sufficient orders for the eight months from March through the next harvest in November. That harvest turns out to be big, well larger than consumption needs, so prices fall to the cost of exporting. In this scenario the period of exporting lasts from January through April, because shipments cannot all occur simultaneously, but once traders have exported the difference between harvest and expected consumption for the year they will stop exporting, and prices will start to rise again at the cost of storage to their peak just before the next harvest. That harvest then turns out to be small, so traders again place orders for delivery by the time they expect imports will be needed, at which point the cost of importing dictates the price.

This stylized picture shows how a country that oscillates between exporting and importing might have prices that fluctuate within the CIF-FOB band.

That range of fluctuation would be wider in places with worse infrastructure or are farther from ocean ports, and widest of all if trade were completely impossible. In the absence of trade, prices would rise even higher after each small harvest, and would fall even lower after each big harvest. In countries that rely on uncertain rainfall such as wheat and other dryland grain producers, access to international markets not only yields gains from trade but also plays a stabilizing role. In these settings, the price-stabilizing role of trade can be seen as using the world market as a form of storage, selling into that market after large harvests when prices would otherwise have fallen even more, and buying from the market after small harvests when prices would otherwise have risen even more. Places where their own production is more consistent from year to year, or where their own storage cost is low, would benefit less from that stabilizing effect of being open to imports or exports. They would still have gains from trade in response to comparative advantage, but those would come at the cost of experiencing the instability of the whole world's supply-demand balance. Countries with very stable production of their own would not need or get the stabilizing effect of trade shown in Fig. 11.3.

Agricultural Trade and Globalization
Changes in the cost and benefits of international trade, relative to domestic activities, cause waves of globalization in the world economy. The most recent period of increased international trade occurred from the mid-1980s to the late 2000s. That boom in trade occurred mostly in the nonfood sector, but had important consequences for agriculture and food systems.

A major factor in the rise of trade was adoption of standardized shipping containers. These allowed cargo to be loaded and carried by truck, trains and ships without having to handle loose cargo, and could be locked and sealed or open the container in transit. Using multimodal containers of uniform size could sharply lower handling costs and reduce delays in transit, but depended on coordinated investment in new equipment and infrastructure. The sizes used today were agreed upon through the International Organization for Standardization (ISO) in 1968, after which new ships and port facilities as well as train and road transit were built around those standards, driving a sustained decline in transport costs for containerized freight.

Another big factor driving globalization was economic reform in China starting in 1981, enabling that vast country to rise from extreme poverty and industrialize quickly as the world's largest provider of manufactured goods. Other countries in East and Southeast Asia also experienced rapid economic growth and industrialization at that time. The previously industrialized, mostly service economies in North America, Europe and elsewhere generally welcomed the increased trade with China and other countries, despite the resulting displacement of their own manufacturing sector, and they undertook their own policy changes towards more openness to international trade.

A third driver of the 1980s–2000s globalization wave was the rise of computing and the internet, which fueled growth within each country, facilitated trade in physical goods, and also brought opportunities for trade in services. Services account for about two-thirds of the entire global economy, complementing the large agriculture and food sector in low-income countries, and also the industrial sector in middle- and higher-income countries. Some international trade in services involves people traveling, such as engineering firms whose staff live in one country but conduct site visits for projects elsewhere, and some occurs online such as customer service call centers.

The drivers and composition of increased trade in the 1980s–2000s mainly involved manufacturing and services, but globalization also affected agriculture and the food sector. The dietary transition to more animal foods and vegetable oils in Asia was made possible by rising imports, mostly bulk shipments of feed grains from North and South America, and also some containerized imports of food products including meat, dairy and some vegetables, facilitated by the rise of refrigerated containers known as reefers. International trade in services also contributed to worldwide food system transformation in branded foods, for both grocery stores and the restaurant sector. The creation of multinational brands typically involves some foreign direct investment, where a company operates its own facilities in multiple countries, but also licensing, franchise operations and joint ventures. Globalization of food services can spread even in the absence of physical trade, allowing the same brand names to appear in grocery stores and restaurant names all around the world even in very remote places.

Focusing on trade in physical merchandise and agricultural products, the total value of shipments from 1980 through 2022 is shown in Fig. 11.4.

Panel A of Fig. 11.4 shows trade volumes in value terms at 2017 prices, as dollars per person each year to adjust for global population growth. Values on the left axis show food and nonfood agricultural products, and on the right axis show all merchandise trade, both as the sum of all imports plus exports shipped between countries around the world. Levels and changes on the left axis are all exactly one-tenth those on the left axis.

In 1980 at the start of the period shown, total trade in food products (mostly bulk agricultural commodities) was worth around $150 per year per person on the planet, while nonfood agricultural products (mainly cotton and fiber, lumber and pulp, rubber and hides) accounted for another $50 per person, while the total for all merchandise trade was just under $1500. From 1980 to 1985 all of those values declined sharply, down to about $100 in food and $1000 in total merchandise trade. The early 1980s downturn was part of a deep recession in the U.S. and other countries, triggered by higher interest rates designed to stop rising inflation that had accelerated in the 1970s. From 1985 to 2022, total merchandise trade grew sharply in a stepwise manner, first a recovery from 1985 to 1990, then some growth from 1993 to 1995,

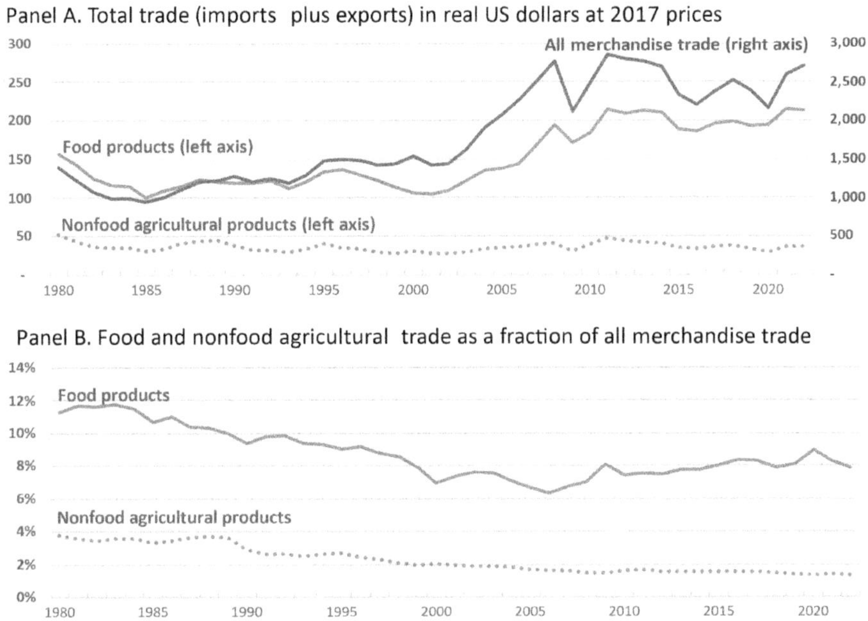

Fig. 11.4 Food and nonfood agricultural trade during the 1980s–2000s wave of globalization *Source*: Authors' chart of data from the World Trade Organization [WTO]. Original data are totals in current [nominal] US dollars, converted to trade per person using global population in terms of real U.S. dollars at 2017 prices using the CPI here: https://fred.stlouisfed.org/graph/?g=1axBm. These and related data on global trade are available from WTO Statistics here: https://stats.wto.org/?idSavedQuery=5601e036-62ef-423b-8735-981338215bf9

followed by rapid growth from 2002 to 2008. There was then another downturn in 2009, again part of a deep recession in the U.S. and recovery from that but no further growth in total trade up to the most recent data in 2022.

Panel B of Fig. 11.4 shows trade in food and other agricultural products as percentages of the total. From 1980 to 1983 those shares stayed roughly constant, but then for more than 20 years trade in nonfarm products grew faster than trade in food or other agricultural products. Food's share of global trade fell almost in half, from just under 12% in 1983 to just over 6% in 2006. The share of trade that was nonfood agricultural products fell even more, from 3.6% in 1984 to 1.6% in 2006. Since then food trade has grown faster than trade in other merchandise, so its share of the total has risen to 8%, briefly reaching 9% at the start of the pandemic in 2020. Returning to Panel A we see that the value of agricultural trade is actually more stable than all merchandise trade in this period, with smaller declines during downturns.

The wave of globalization, measured here as the real value of merchandise trade per person, consisted mostly of nonfood trade which almost tripled from $1000 in 1985 to $2800 in 2008. The quantity of food traded did not have sustained growth for the first 15 years of this period, as its value in 2000 was about the same as in 1985, but then from 2000 to 2008 the real value of global food trade doubled from \$107 to \$214 per person and remained at \$213 in 2022.

Agricultural Policy, Trade Agreements and the Political Economy of Protection

One reason for the later and smaller increase in food trade compared to other merchandise could be greater policy restrictions on trade in agriculture than in manufacturing. As we have seen, in any one country's markets, restricting imports generally imposes a small cost on each of the many consumers, while providing concentrated gains to a few producers. Each existing producer is well aware of what they gain from import tariffs or quotas, and will invest time and money in persuading the public and government officials that imports should be restricted. Those producers already have a working enterprise. They know what they would lose if more imports were allowed, and those potential losses are visible to everyone. In contrast, each consumer is unlikely to know that import restrictions raise retail prices, and even if they did, their potential gains from increased imports are in the form of lower prices and savings they would spend on many different things, so each person who would benefit has little at stake and is likely to remain inattentive to trade policy.

Political leaders in all kinds of countries face similar pressures. Many political leaders don't know or don't care that restricting imports harms their society as a whole, so they ally themselves with incumbent producers and agree to help them at the expense of others in their country. That dynamic leads governments to impose high barriers on their own populations, protecting whichever set of producers has the most political influence. But occasional reformers realize that coalitions of people in their country who would benefit from more open trade can be organized to pursue legislation that reduces those trade barriers and thereby improves the country's standard of living. When one country does that, other countries can export to them, creating the possibility of international agreements between reform-minded government leaders.

The world as a whole has no global government, but governments can sign treaties with each other and create jointly owned international organizations. Much of the modern landscape of international agreements was formed to manage recovery from World War II. The United Nations was created in 1945, and its various specialized agencies provide technical services and programs in collaboration with their counterparts in each country's government. Two of the biggest such agencies are the World Bank and the International Monetary Fund (IMF), created to provide some of the services that an individual country's central bank could do. In the 1940s, proposals to form a global 'International Trade Organization' alongside the IMF were rejected in favor of a simpler international treaty, ultimately signed in 1947 by just 23 countries as the General Agreement on Tariffs and Trade (GATT).

From 1947 to 1994, eight successive rounds of international negotiations through the GATT allowed governments interested in reducing trade barriers to agree on which tariffs and quotas would be reduced, by how much and over what time frame. A total of eight negotiating rounds each led to a revised treaty, that could then be signed by additional governments if they wished. Countries could always withdraw from the treaty, or raise tariffs and quotas in violation of the treaty, with the only enforcement mechanism being the GATT's own dispute resolution committees that allow member countries to impose their own retaliatory trade restrictions. Successive rounds created ever-greater incentives for more countries to join the treaty and follow its rules, deepening each other's commitments to keeping trade barriers as low as possible.

Agricultural trade was omitted entirely from the initial rounds of GATT negotiations, as too politically sensitive and unpredictable for governments to willingly be bound by a global treaty. Individual pairs or groups of countries would sign bilateral and regional treaties, of which the largest and oldest is the Common Agricultural Policy (CAP) among European countries launched in 1962. The CAP allows entirely free trade among the members, behind a common external tariff, with pooled funding for programs to assist farmers and shared regulations about environmental, food safety and nutritional aspects of the food system. Other regional agreements use varying degrees of integration and policy harmonization, such as the MERCOSUR agreement among South American countries launched in 1991, or the COMESA agreement among East and Southern African countries and NAFTA between the U.S., Canada and Mexico both signed in 1993.

The first global agreement on agricultural trade policy was reached in 1994, through the eighth round of GATT negotiations. Treaties are commonly named after the place where they are signed, in this case regarding the initial agreement on the scope and objectives of negotiations that were set at a meeting in Punta del Este, Uruguay in 1986. Previous global agreements had reduced non-agricultural tariffs and quotas so much that there was little further cutting to do, so the Uruguay Round focused on agriculture and cotton textiles as well as trade in services, foreign investment and intellectual property protection. Those topics proved to be so difficult that reaching agreement took almost a decade.

The conclusion of the Uruguay Round created a framework for trade policy that reflected and accelerated the push towards globalization of the late 1980s and 1990s. The secretariat in Geneva that implements the treaty was renamed the World Trade Organization (WTO), with an expanded mandate including the Uruguay Round Agreement on Agriculture. By design, the agricultural agreement specified only modest and gradual reductions to barriers already in place. Its primary goal was to establish categories of government intervention to be measured and compared, with limits on the degree to which new barriers could be introduced in the future. Those provisions, as well as farm trade aspects of regional agreements like MERCOSUR, COMESA and NAFTA, helped facilitate the increased trade observed through the 2000s.

In 2001, China joined the WTO and the organization launched its ninth round in Doha, the capital city of Qatar, with a mandate for negotiators to find areas of agreement that would be more favorable for low-income countries. As of late 2023 this Doha Development Round remains ongoing, with periodic meetings but little prospect of a new global treaty beyond what the GATT and WTO had already achieved. The largest benefits from trade agreements come from reducing the highest barriers, since those markets offer the most gains from additional trade, and the Doha round's development agenda called for negotiations on policy changes which economists estimate would generate much smaller and more uncertain gains than earlier rounds. Governments' willingness and ability to make agreements also depends on whether they expect each other to be increasingly valuable trading partners over time.

When global trade growth stalled after 2008, trade policy negotiations shifted from the pursuit of globalization to regional agreements and bilateral relations. The largest of the regional agreements was initiated in 2012, when the African Union launched negotiations among its 55 member countries towards an African Continental Free Trade Area (AfCFTA). Agreement on a treaty was reached in 2019, and implementation began in 2021 towards lower trade barriers among all African countries. Bilateral policies also became much more important, including a series of tariff increases between the U.S. and China in 2018–2020 that redirected trade to different partners.

Bilateral disputes, known as 'trade wars', involve a sequence of retaliatory tariffs or quotas on imports of specific products. In 2018, the U.S. government argued that China had violated the intellectual property rights of U.S. companies, and raised restrictions on a variety of manufactured goods imported from China in response. China immediately retaliated with restrictions on its agricultural imports from the U.S., leading to a sequence of similar retaliations on other products than ended in 2020.

Trade wars with individual partners are not aimed primarily at protecting domestic producers, and their effects on each country depend on how easily traders can switch to other partners. For generic commodities with global markets such as feed grains, bilateral restrictions mainly lead to higher global transport costs as traders are forced to use longer or slower and more expensive routes. Announcements of Chinese tariffs in 2018 led ships traveling from the U.S. to turn in mid-ocean towards other destinations, and ships from South America turned towards China. For more specialized products, finding alternative suppliers takes longer and is more expensive.

One important purpose of the GATT and WTO is to offer less costly paths to dispute resolution, by specifying the scope, extent and timing of retaliatory tariffs that would be allowed when a country is found to have violated the treaty. For example, in 2002, Brazil lodged a complaint with the WTO that some aspects of U.S. cotton policies lowered world prices and harmed their farmers, in violation of the Uruguay Round agreement. The WTO panel agreed, authorizing a specific set of retaliatory tariffs that Brazil could apply against imports from the U.S. Those would have disrupted supply chains for many influential companies, so the U.S. agreed to settle the case with a $300 million payment to fund the Brazilian Cotton Institute (IBA) and thereby assist the farmers who had been harmed.

The deeper and longer-term purpose of trade agreements is to counterbalance political forces that lead governments to protect favored industries within their countries, at the expense of their own people. The political economy of trade policy leads to systematic patterns of agricultural protection, as revealed by the data in Fig. 11.5.

The variables shown in Fig. 11.5 are compiled by the Organization for Economic Cooperation and Development (OECD), an agency funded by its 38 member countries to provide independent policy analysis on many topics including food and agriculture. This chart shows the percentage of farm revenue attributable to either trade policy or domestic programs, a metric developed in the 1970s to add up the value of different kinds of assistance to farmers across Europe. This producer support estimate was originally known as the producer subsidy equivalent (PSE), and is available from the OECD for 23 countries shown in gray, plus the five highlighted, shown here from 1986 to 2021.

From the top left, in Japan almost 60% of farmers' income was attributable to policy intervention in 1986, declining gradually to about 38% in 2021. Almost all of this comes from trade restriction at the expense of consumers. Occasional opinion polls show that Japanese consumers favor restricting food

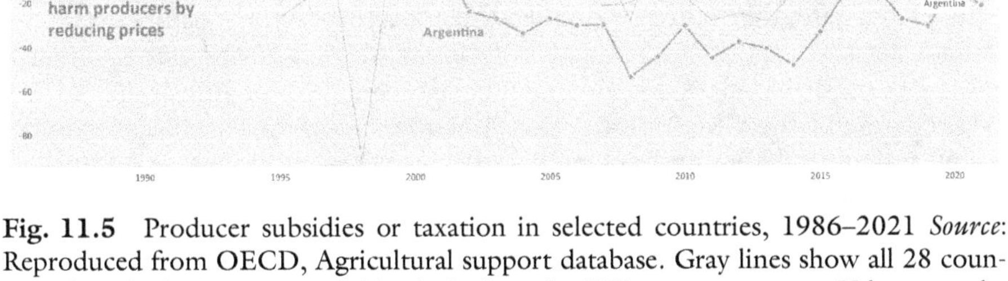

Fig. 11.5 Producer subsidies or taxation in selected countries, 1986–2021 *Source*: Reproduced from OECD, Agricultural support database. Gray lines show all 28 countries for which data are available, including the EU as one country. Values are the producer support estimate [PSE] sum of policy and program transfers to or from farmers, as a percentage of gross farm receipts. Details of methods and data sources are at https://data.oecd.org/agrpolicy/agricultural-support.htm, with updated versions of this chart showing other countries at https://data.oecd.org/chart/7dI9

imports even at their expense, which is understandable given the small cost to each consumer and their desire to maintain high farm incomes. The gray countries where an even larger fraction of farm income comes from farmers include South Korea and also Switzerland, Norway and Iceland, which are somewhat similar to Japan in terms of willingness and ability to pay high food prices in support of farmers. The OECD average of countries for which data are available was almost 40% in 1986, falling to 18% in 2020 and then rising to 23% in 2021 due to price fluctuations.

The U.S. level producer support was at 23% in 1986, declining to 10% of farm revenue in 2021. Unlike Japan, almost all of this comes from taxpayer support. The only major farm groups for whom higher revenue comes mainly from consumers are sugar growers due to import restrictions, and dairy due to domestic supply restrictions. For those commodities, the OECD estimates that the share of farm income due to policy in 2019–2021 was 45% for sugar growers of which almost all is due to higher prices, and 10% for dairy farmers of which about half is due to higher prices and the other half to government-funded programs. Wheat growers are also around the 10% while other crops such as corn at 7% and soy at 5% have that support entirely from program payments.

Producer support data in Fig. 11.5 shows how China had a near-zero level of assistance to farmers when their data begin in late 1990s through the early 2000s, rising to 16% in 2021. More dramatically, Argentina was also around zero in the late 1990s, but in the 2000s began imposing large taxes on exports of soybeans and quotas on export of wheat, maize (corn) and dairy, in an effort to collect government revenue and also keep domestic prices as low as possible during their recurring periods of economic crisis.

Each country's combination of policy instruments leads to a somewhat different set of impacts on consumers than on producers, as shown with the OECD's consumer support data in Fig. 11.6.

The data in Fig. 11.6 show the percentage of the value of raw farm commodities consumed within each country that is attributable to government policies. By analogy to the PSE, which is now known as the producer support estimate, this indicator is called the consumer support estimate (CSE). To indicate the level of assistance to consumers, the scale is reversed so that a positive number indicates consumer support through lower prices.

The name of the CSE indicator could be misleading in that the consumers of raw agricultural commodities are livestock growers, food manufacturers and industries such as biofuels, not final consumers of retail products for which ingredients may be a small fraction of the total price. In Argentina and the U.S., prices for most commodities are kept lower than they would otherwise be, by about 20% in 2021. China moved towards increasingly taxing its consumers to help its farmers and reached −14% in 2021, while the OECD average moved in the opposite direction from −30% in 1986 to −4% in 2021, and Japan's heavy taxation of consumers moved from −58% in 1986 to −33% in 2021.

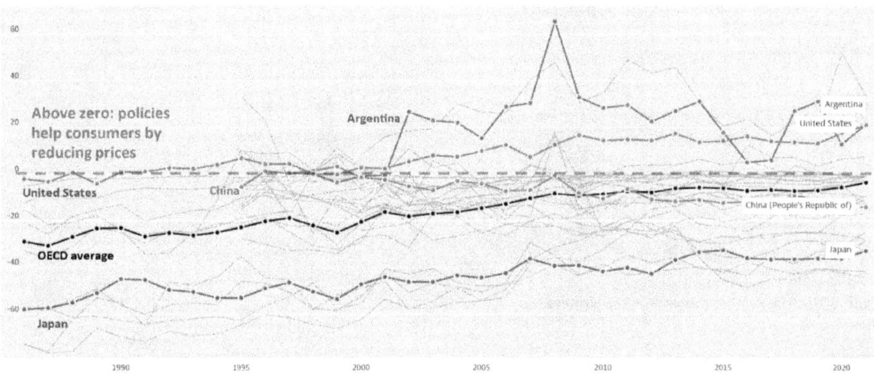

Fig. 11.6 Consumer support or taxation in selected countries, 1986–2021 *Source*: Reproduced from OECD, Agricultural support database. Gray lines show all 28 countries for which data are available, including the EU as one country. Data are consumer support estimate [CSE] totals of policy and program transfers to or from consumers, as a percent of agricultural product value consumed. Methods and sources are at https://data.oecd.org/agrpolicy/agricultural-support.htm, with updated versions of this chart showing other countries at https://data.oecd.org/chart/7dIk

For global monitoring over a larger number of countries, the available data have a shorter time period and less detail about each country than the OECD's agricultural policy monitoring reports. Also, in contrast to the PSE which was developed primarily to quantify government programs that help farmers and therefore expressed as a percentage of actual farm revenue with existing interventions, the global monitoring data are used mainly to monitor trade policy as is typically presented as a percentage of the product's opportunity cost without the policy. This percentage is the country's nominal rate of protection (NRP) to farmers when it adds up only the effect of trade restrictions at the country's borders, and the nominal rate of assistance (NRA) to farmers when it also includes the value of government programs and other measures to help farmers. For example, if farmers are growing a product that the country imports at a CIF price of $1 per unit with a tariff or quota that made the domestic prices $1.10, the tariff-equivalent NRP would be 10%. And if farmers grow 100 million units and the government also provides $5 million in subsidized inputs, that's another $0.05 per unit so the NRA would be 15%.

Data on tariff-equivalent effects of agricultural policies were first compiled in the late 2000s by the World Bank in a project on distortions to agricultural incentives. Updated versions of those data from the World Bank have been combined with OECD data and additional estimates from the FAO through a project with the International Food Policy Research Institute (IFPRI) known as the AgIncentives Consortium, which computed the regional averages shown in Fig. 11.7.

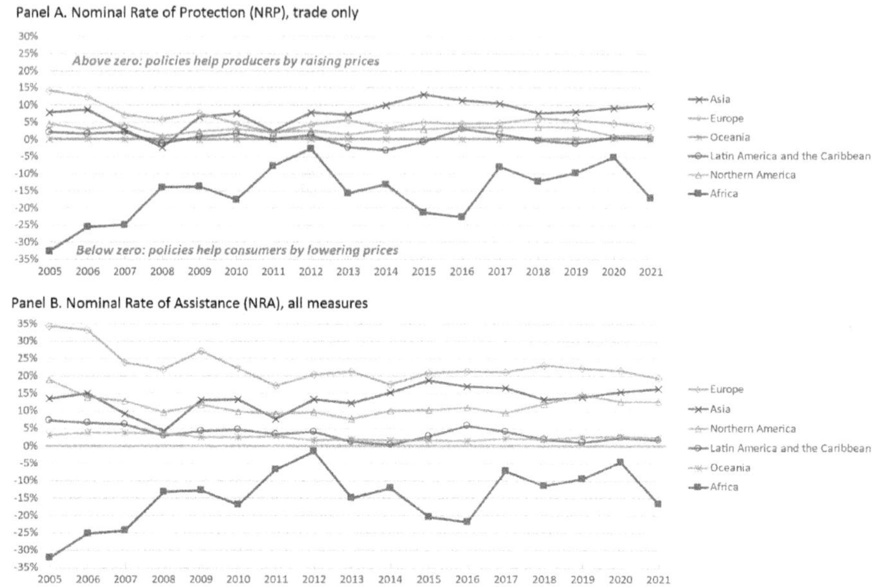

Fig. 11.7 Tariff-equivalent measures of agricultural policy support worldwide, 2005–2021 *Source*: Authors' chart of data from the AgIncentives Consortium [2023], using country observations from OECD, FAO, IDB and World Bank compiled for regional averages by the International Food Policy Research Institute [IFPRI]. Methods and more detailed data are available at https://www.agincentives.org

Starting at the top left of Panel A in Fig. 11.7, the overall average tariff-equivalent NRP for all of Europe was 14% in 2005, falling significantly due to reforms of the Common Agricultural Policy and other changes to 4% in 2021. Asia was around 8% in 2005, and fluctuated to end at 10% in 2021. North America had fluctuations around 2–5%, and Latin America had fluctuations around zero, while Oceania had an NRP very close to zero in all years. That region consists mostly of Australia and New Zealand which pursued their own 'unilateral' policy reforms towards freer trade in the 1990s, which helped spur economic growth in those countries but might not be politically feasible elsewhere.

The outlier region in Panel A is Africa, which had a large negative NRP throughout the period. Farmers received 33% less than what they would have been paid for their output in 2005, which fluctuated and ended at 17% less in 2021. Prices are reduced by trade policy when exports are taxed for the purpose of collecting government revenue, or restricted with quotas and other barriers to exports that keep prices low for urban consumers and industrial buyers inside the country. European colonial powers that ruled Africa from the nineteenth century into the 1960s imposed large export restrictions of this type, combined with policies designed to give farmers few options other than to continue growing the export crops that financed their colonial enterprises. After independence in the 1960s many African governments continued to restrict exports but used the funds for other things. In these contexts, where most workers are farmers and urban consumers are politically influential, continuing to limit agricultural exports was politically attractive even to independent governments. The benefits are highly visible and concentrated in cities, while the burden of taxation is spread through a small cost on each of many farm households who may not know that the low prices they receive are due to trade policy.

In Panel B of Fig. 11.7, the NRA includes not just the effects of trade policy in NRP, but also any domestic payments from government programs. That difference reveals how European payments raised total assistance to farmers above 33% in 2005, declining to 19% in 2021. Assistance in Asia fluctuated then rose to 19% in 2015 before ending at 16% in 2021, just above North America, while Latin America and the Caribbean as well as Oceania stayed much lower. In Africa there is very little program assistance to offset the large tax burden imposed by export restriction, so the NRA is similar to the NRP.

The high taxation of African farmers by their own governments shown here is sometimes done explicitly through export taxes, but more often it is done through government-owned enterprises in pursuit of direct control over the food supply. In some cases, there are export bans intended to help industrial food processors. An illustrative example is Senegal, where the French colonial government developed a large groundnut (peanut) sector for export, including the first local processing plant in 1920 to save transport costs by exporting oil instead of the whole grain. The government used state marketing agencies that set a single price for the entire country for the whole season, thereby excluding private traders who would otherwise buy from places and times with low prices to sell at other places and times, and they also blocked private exports to ensure that only colonial enterprises could handle the crop. After Independence in 1960, the new government eventually bought out the French processing and trading companies, but kept the processing plant operational in the belief that local industrial value added was preferable to exporting the raw grain. These processing plants have high operating costs, however, so their continued survival depended on restricting exports. As of late 2023, the government continues to restrict exports enough to keep those plants operational, despite the demands by farmer groups that they be allowed to export directly at the higher prices offered in trade.

11.1.3 Conclusion

The trends and patterns in farm support or taxation observed in recent years show how different political arrangements lead to different government policies, with large consequences for income distribution as well as economic growth in each country. The principle of comparative advantage shows how each population could gain by adjusting to trade prices, while also showing how openness to trade would disrupt existing businesses. Those distributional effects ensure that trade restrictions are often politically attractive despite missing out on potential gains from trade, and also reveal how governments can form treaties with other governments to maintain more open borders and thereby meet their political needs while also achieving their economic aspirations.

The era of globalization with rapid growth in trade volumes from the 1980s through the 2000s came from new technology that lowered the cost of transportation and communication, and also policy change that lowered government-imposed trade barriers. Some of that increasing political openness came from unilateral policy reforms, some of it came from bilateral and regional agreements and some from the global agreement to form the WTO in 1995. The swing towards global economic integration ended in the late 2000s, in favor of regional groupings such as the African Union's continental free trade area initiated in 2012 and signed in 2019. The future direction of trade policy is uncertain, but using economic principles and newly available data can potentially help civil society organizations and community leaders understand what is at stake and advocate for their interests.

11.2 Value Chains, Social Accounting and Institutions in the Food System

11.2.1 Motivation and Guiding Questions

The world food system is an interconnected web of national and local food systems, each with its unique characteristics. National food systems are shaped by country governments that control international trade, macroeconomic management and other decisions driving employment opportunities and income distribution, as well as national-level food and agricultural policies. Local food systems within countries are shaped by local governments. Within those systems, how do individual enterprises operate? How are individual food products grown, transformed and delivered to people, and what are the consequences of those activities for society?

The flow of an individual product from source to end-user is a *value chain*. In this section we introduce analytical methods used to understand value chains, and the societal *institutions* that shape how each value chain operates. By institutions we mean the organizational structures that govern the individuals and enterprises in a food system. These institutions may involve formal laws and organizational structures, or informal norms and practices. Each institution has its historical origins and is shaped by people's choices, for example the land tenure arrangements by which farm families might own, rent or otherwise gain access to resources for the farm they operate.

The value chain for each thing can be seen by tracing its physical flow downstream from origin to end-users, or the corresponding flow of purchases upstream back from end-users to the origins. Each item you ate yesterday typically had a mix of ingredients from different places, so tracing its origins would be like tracing the flow of water back upstream to its many sources. Each item produced on a farm last year could similarly be traced like the flow of water from a source out to its many destinations. Moving a food along the chain uses resources, measured in terms of value added as part of the circular flow of economic activity, which for environmental purposes can also be measured using life cycle analysis and social accounting for cost–benefit analysis.

The institutions that govern value chains, as well as the individuals and enterprises that actually handle each food along its value chain, almost all manage multiple foods at the same time. A few entities specialize in just one narrowly defined food such as coffee, but most individuals and enterprises diversify their operations to limit risks and benefit from economies of scope when the same facilities are used for different things. Each value chain is therefore part of a multiproduct web in which foods and resources flow to and from all parts of the food system.

By the end of this section, you will be able to:

1. Define and describe food value chains from farms to consumers, and the functions of enterprises along those value chains;
2. Define and describe horizontal and vertical integration by enterprises between and within value chains;
3. Describe the institutions and marketing arrangements along value chains used by farmers in origin regions, traders at and between terminal markets, and distributors to grocery outlets or food service providers; and
4. Describe how financial markets trading contracts for future delivery of farm commodities provide fluctuating forecasts of the product's cash price at the closing date of each contract.

11.2.2 Analytical Tools

Previous chapters have introduced the principal methods used in economics to explain, predict and evaluate each activity and their interconnections, using the individual choice diagrams for production and consumption, and the market diagrams for interaction of supply, demand and trade. In this chapter we provide some additional tools for visualizing each activity and describing the interconnections between them.

Value Chains and Institutions in the Food System

The circular flow of goods and services described in Chapter 9 on the economy is an interconnected web of many value chains. Each activity or enterprise uses the inputs it needs, and combines them to provide a value-added product as an input to other activities. From the perspective of each individual actor, what they use comes from an upstream source and flows on to a downstream destination. In some cases the product itself is unchanged, so value added is provided only through transport, storage and handling. In other cases the product is transformed by processing and packaging. Logistics of transport, storage and handling of a given product is generally described as its *supply chain*, while the term *value chain* refers to all aspects of a product's journey from origin to destination.

Value chain analysis in the food system allows us to distinguish between functions performed at different locations. These functions could all be performed by the same enterprise, for example by a farm that sells directly to consumers, but value chain analysis is most useful when functions are undertaken by separate enterprises with specialized structure and skills. Those enterprises then interact with each other through market transactions as illustrated in Table 11.2.

Vertical integration is when a single enterprise aims to directly control multiple functions along the chain from origin to destination. Horizontal integration is when a single enterprise expands to serve multiple value chains or a wider geographic area. The commercial success of vertically or horizontally integrated businesses depends on their ability to perform each function more cost-effectively than separate competing enterprises, each with their own structure and specialized skills adapted to their geographic location and other circumstances.

The alternative to vertical and horizontal integration is a sequence of markets along the value chain, in which specialist enterprises compete with

Table 11.2 Specialized functions, enterprises and transactions along food value chains

Specialized functions	*Enterprises and market transactions*
Dispersed in region of origin	
Farming and fishing	Producers sell to aggregators for onward shipment
Product aggregation	Aggregators sell to traders for onward shipment
At terminal markets and along transport networks	
Commodity trading and storage	Traders sell to each other, manufacturers or distributors
Food manufacturing	Manufacturers buy from traders or upstream sources
Food distribution	Distributors buy from manufacturers or upstream sources
Dispersed in destination regions	
Food service and retailing	Providers buy from distributors or upstream sources
Food consumption and nonfood uses	Consumers buy from retailers or upstream sources

each other to perform each function. The intermediate markets along a value chain could then be analyzed using the toolkit of supply, demand and trade models presented in previous chapters, revealing the potential for market failures that would affect the quality and price of products for every other stage of the chain. The institutions and policies governing the enterprises that perform each function, including the markets institutions for govern transactions between enterprises, determine the degree of quality assurance, price transparency and antitrust enforcement needed throughout the food system as a whole.

Individual enterprises in the food system often seek to analyze their own supply chains, looking for risks and opportunities to improve sourcing. Supply chain research looks upstream at where, how and from whom the enterprise's inputs are sourced, in contrast to marketing research that looks downstream at where, how and to whom the enterprise's products are sold. Supply chain analysis is sometimes focused only on private risks and opportunities affecting the enterprise itself, and many analysts are also concerned with the public health consequences or environmental, social and governance (ESG) impacts of how products are obtained and made.

Analysis of vertical integration in food supply chains can be traced back to the nineteenth-century French term *filière*, meaning a thread that can or should be followed. The *filière* approach to sourcing food ingredients was an important aspect of how France governed its colonies and overseas territories in the late nineteenth and twentieth centuries, identifying the most profitable and least risky places from which to source each product, and maintaining direct control over purchases from farmers, aggregation and transport to end-users in France or elsewhere. British and other colonial food systems were more likely to use markets with independent local traders, and the English term *value chain* emerged much later, regarding the need for large enterprises to make strategic decisions about where and how to source their inputs.

Each individual supply chain is embedded in a circular flow of economic activity at each location, drawing on natural resources in the environment and relying on infrastructure and other aspects of the macroeconomy. Those underlying resources are used by each value chain in ways that are governed by a set of institutional arrangements and organizational structures that regulate who can do what, where and when or with whom. Some institutions involve explicit legal rights and responsibilities, such as worker rights and titles for ownership of land that might or might not allow owners to subdivide and build or rent, while other institutions are informal arrangements that arise without needed to be codified into law, such as the practice of sharecropping by which tenants give landlords a fraction of the harvest each year.

All institutional arrangements are historical choices, made in response to geographic and other factors that influenced the costs and benefits of each approach. For example, in most of rural Africa until the late twentieth century, potential cropland was abundant relative to labor and the capital needed to use land productively, so there was little need or opportunity for people to buy or rent land. Plots for farming were allocated by community leaders in ways designed to maintain social cohesion and farming opportunities for each generation of new farm families. In contrast, by the early twentieth century East and South Asia was so densely populated from population growth and shrinking land area per farm that many farm families were too impoverished to own the land they farmed. Many were tenants who also borrowed money from landlords to repay at each harvest. In the Americas and Southern Africa as well as Australia and New Zealand, eighteenth- and nineteenth-century settlers from Britain and Europe had forcibly displaced native people and each settler farmer was granted a legal right to larger areas of land than they could plow. Land use depends on labor, including forced labor of enslaved people from Africa for plantation agriculture in the Americas, as well as the apartheid system used by settlers against the native population of Southern Africa, and the displacement and isolation of native people in the Americas. With sufficient political pressure these systems change over time, but they cast a long shadow over the land use and inequities we observe in each region today.

The individual enterprises that operate within each country's institutional framework vary greatly in size and scope, in ways illustrated by the food system diagram of Fig. 11.8.

The schematic diagram in Fig. 11.8 provides context for the functions listed in Table 12.1, and also for double-hourglass structure of the food system introduced at the start of our chapter on market power in Fig. 5.1. At the upstream end of each value chain are agricultural input and farm service suppliers, whose operations typically involve scale economies such that one or a few sellers provide inputs to many farmers at each location. Those farmers are drawn as a wider band to indicate the large and variable number

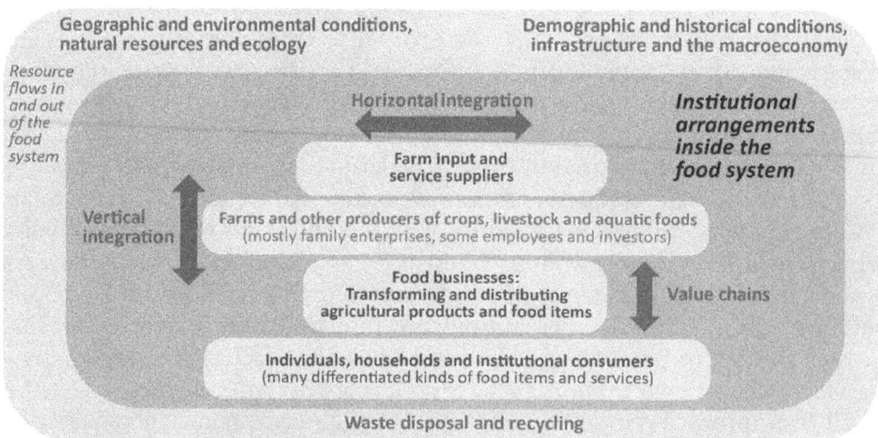

Fig. 11.8 Institutional arrangements and value chains in the food system *Source*: Authors' infographic, adapted from the nested framework of a social-ecological model showing each entity within its larger context

of individual enterprises in agriculture, most of which are self-employed families but sometimes include large-scale farms with a large number of workers per farm or fishing and livestock operation. Those producers typically then sell farm commodities and other products to business enterprises, whose scale economies are such that a few food businesses buy from many food producers and sell to many individuals and households or other end-users.

In the background of Fig. 11.8, behind all those individuals, households and enterprises, is a set of institutional arrangements in the food system, and around the food system there is a set of geographic and environmental conditions indicated at the top left, as well as a set of factors influenced by people listed in the top right. Environmental aspects of the food system include not only the natural resources used as inputs but also waste disposal and recycling of food loss and waste, shown at the bottom of the figure, with a note at the top left indicating the possibility of monitoring natural resource flows in and out of food systems, in addition to the value chains within each food system.

Value chains are shown at the right of the diagram, indicating the potential traceability of foods consumed back upstream to their origins on the farm. The double-hourglass part of this diagram was introduced as Fig. 5.1 to show how scale economies create the possibility of market power, and here we show that in the larger context of formal and informal institutions that help influence how enterprises operate inside the food system, and how they obtain and use natural resources.

Improving the social value of each food item calls for improvement at every stage of its value chain, involving different kinds of enterprises and transactions between them. Some items have only one link between initial producer and final consumer, for example at a farmer's market where growers sell directly to individuals. Opportunities for direct transactions of this type are a very attractive, high-value amenity for any community, but sales are typically season and farmers in each location can supply only some of the diverse foods that consumers want and need. More commonly there are multiple enterprises along the value chain, each undertaking different tasks and then selling onward to the next enterprise in the chain, calling for analysis and governance of how they operate and interact with the food system as a whole.

Horizontal Integration and Consolidation in Agribusiness and the Food Industry

Enterprises differ in how widely they operate across geographic locations and different kinds of goods and services. The commercial success of horizontally integrated operations depends on economies of scale and scope, referring to both the total size of the enterprise and the diversity of products that it sells. Horizontal integration can be cost-effective but leads to the risk that enterprises will be able to exercise market power, as explained in Chapter 5.

One source for scale economies not previously mentioned is the capacity and cost of facilities and equipment. The scale of any manufacturing or processing enterprise is influenced by the fact that expanding the size of a machine or the capacity of a facility generally reduces cost per unit of throughput. In chemical engineering and similar fields this is known as the six-tenths rule of cost reduction, whereby raising the capacity of a plant by 10% raises the total cost of its outputs by 6%. This rule of thumb arises because many costs rise with the surface area and hence the square of the diameter, length and height of things such as pipes and containers, while capacity rises with their volume and hence the cube of those dimensions. The six-tenths rule applies to expansion only up to the size limit beyond which the equipment might break, which is why innovations in metallurgy and equipment manufacturing have focused on stronger materials that increase the ratio of throughput to the quantity and cost of materials used.

The economies of scope that sometimes drive horizontal integration include the use of diversification to reduce enterprise risks, and the degree of complementarity between one activity and another. For example, meatpacking plants often combine a slaughterhouse with cutting and packaging a variety of products, from whole chickens and large cuts of beef or pork to final products in branded packaging for retail sale. Meatpacking enterprises may expand and diversify across locations and products for sale, but they almost never have their own tannery to sell hides and leather. The facilities and circumstances needed for a commercially successful tannery differ greatly from what is needed for meatpacking. That lack of complementarity implies that meatpackers either sell entire hides to a tannery, or dispose of them as waste if the cost of transport exceeds the product's value.

Economies of scale and scope are both important drivers of horizontal integration, and they may reinforce each other. For example, for much of agricultural history, selling crop seeds was an enterprise that offered only limited economies of scale. The six-tenths rule does not apply to most aspects of seed enterprises, which involves growing or contracting for others to grow the desired seeds, then ensuring that buyers can trust that the seeds being sold will germinate and grow to be the desired plant. In the U.S. and many other countries, seed houses were family enterprises that earned the trust of nearby farmers, and if successful they grew slowly to serve a wider area. In the 1980s the U.S. extended patent rights to plant biotechnology which led to greater concentration in the seed sector, and to horizontal integration with the large companies producing crop chemicals.

In the 1980s and 1990s when plant geneticists first used biotechnology in crop breeding they developed two main traits, insect resistance with genes from the *Bt* soil bacterium, and herbicide tolerance with genes from other soil bacteria. Those two genetically modified (GM) traits proved to be useful primarily in three main crops. The *Bt* trait was most valuable to control stem borers on cotton and soybeans in place of repeated pesticide sprays, and herbicide tolerance was useful mainly on soybeans and then cotton and corn, so that herbicide could be sprayed just once after the seed germinates to kill weeds without damaging the plant. That trait was engineered specifically to tolerate glyphosate, which had been sold under patent since the 1970s by a giant chemical company named Monsanto that had not previously been in the seed business, but they were able to acquire and invest in the development and sale of GM seeds in part to extend sales of glyphosate.

By the 2010s, the use of GM traits had created clear economies of scope between seeds and chemicals, driving even greater scale economies around complementarities between the two kinds of technology. By 2020, just two large seed-chemical companies sell more than half of all seeds for cotton, soybeans and corn, and together with two companies they dominate the global market for some other seeds. This very high level of concentration in seed supply results from horizontal integration with the chemical industry, and the interaction of scale and scope when producing and selling both kinds of inputs.

Many other examples of horizontal integration could be drawn from the agribusiness and food sectors of every country in the world. Some expansion occurs through innovation and investment in a successful new approach to each business, as in the example of Walmart's development of computerized and networked inventory control in the 1970s and 1980s, which allowed them to expand geographically at lower cost than other retail outlets. Expansion through mergers and acquisitions risks introducing more market power than cost reduction, leading to antitrust and competition policies designed to limit the degree of concentration in each market.

Vertical Integration and Control of Farm-to-Consumer Supply Chains

Many agricultural and food products have long value chains, flowing out from a few locations of geographically concentrated production to many destinations and geographically dispersed consumers. At the same time, there is an offsetting interest in short supply chains, including direct farm-to-consumer marketing, as well as vertical integration of long chains so that end-users have more control over the source of each product.

An extreme case is the market for lettuce in the U.S. In the 2022–2023 marketing year, about three-fourths of all U.S. lettuce in the cold winter months came from the irrigated low desert of Yuma County, Arizona, with the remainder coming from a similar environment in southern California and some also from Florida. During the spring and summer small-scale producers around the country serve their local markets. Seasonal production can be extended with greenhouses or hydroponic and aeroponic production inside climate-controlled buildings, but large-scale production for supermarkets and restaurants in the summer is mostly from central California.

Production is often geographically concentrated due to location-specific resources and infrastructure, and the resulting community of people with specialized knowledge and skills. Consumption tends to be geographically dispersed because consumers want greater dietary diversity and more stable supplies than farmers in their own location can produce. Economic growth leads some foods to have longer value chains, when investment in transportation infrastructure and production capacity allows some production locations to develop based on comparative advantage and specialized knowledge. At the same time, economic growth also creates opportunities for some short value chains, when consumers prefer products from their own community and local suppliers have sufficient capital to invest in producing near those consumers.

One concern about long value chains involves risk in production and transport. Concentrated sourcing makes it easier to trace outbreaks of foodborne illness or changes in supply back up the value chain, drawing attention and interest in all aspects of where and how the product is grown and distributed. To limit those risks, suppliers seek both diversification of origins and also greater control over each supply chain. Food consumers everywhere seek out products from their own community partly due to trust and accountability when buyers and sellers know each other, and partly due to the cultural and historical significance of food from their own region.

The structure of value chains involves not just distance but also the number and nature of transactions. Long value chains have existed since antiquity, for example ancient Rome used wheat and other products transported across the Mediterranean sea from North Africa and southern France. Transport over land is more difficult so ancient trade routes often depended on river systems, but high value spices and other products can readily be carried and herds of cattle have been moved through long trade corridors since long before the nineteenth-century rise of ocean shipping and railroads led to very long supply chains for many foods all around the world.

A typical supply chain structure involves farmers in a given area selling to a local aggregator who assembles the product for onward sale. In that initial stage, scale economies often lead to just one or a few buyers serving many farmers in a given location. Those farmers can sometimes form a cooperative to provide that service to themselves and limit the use of market power against them. Local aggregators may provide initial processing, storage and packing for pickup or delivery to long-distance traders, who specialize in transport from aggregators to a terminal market, for example in a major city, where the product may be sold to another long-distance trader serving a different terminal market. Each of these links in the chain may involve some degree of processing, storage and repacking to serve different end-users. Ultimately traders will sell in bulk to food manufacturers, or to distributors for onward sale in smaller volumes to food service providers and grocery outlets. Each link in the supply chain involves specialist providers of that particular kind of postharvest transportation and transformation.

Products sold along the chain from farmers to aggregators, traders, processors and end-users can be generic commodities when each shipment is sufficiently uniform to substitute for any other, or a differentiated product for which each shipment has its own unique quality and price. In some cases the exact same product can move as both a commodity and a differentiated item, for example when identical butter from the same dairy processor is sold in both generic and premium packaging. The product standards that define a commodity are based on a variety of attributes, including genetic traits and the product's condition. For example, in the U.S. there are six main classes of wheat, and each is priced based on protein content as well as moisture and other attributes.

Transactions between actors along the chain may be done privately, or in a market where prices and quantities are visible to the public. With private transactions, information about the sale may be a closely guarded secret that facilitates the exercise of market power, including price discrimination and cartel behavior. One prominent example in the U.S. involves the supply chain for poultry meat, much of which is sold under private contracts with a small number of poultry processors. Those processors had been voluntarily reporting the prices they were paying to a market newsletter published by the Georgia state department of agriculture, but in 2016 those prices were revealed to have been false. Subsequent lawsuits over secret monopoly pricing were settled in 2021, with one processor paying $75 million and another $221.5 million to its end-users. Price fixing cartels between two or more processors rely on them credibly revealing quantities and prices to each other, while keeping that information hidden from the public. In September of 2023 the U.S. government filed an antitrust suit accusing a private data provider of doing just that, serving as the intermediary for a cartel of meat processors to hold back supply and raise prices against end-users such as processed food manufacturers, grocery stores and restaurant chains.

The vulnerability of end-users to upstream problems along their supply chains can lead large buyers to seek control through vertical integration, buying out the intermediaries. This prevents market power being used against them, but raises the risk that they will have even more market power to use against farmers or consumers. Ultimately, the extent of vertical integration depends on the ability of the end-user to actually manage each activity along the chain, and the willingness of antitrust authorities to allow a large fraction of the market to be controlled by a single entity.

When separate enterprises control different links in the supply chain, growers and consumers both have a strong interest in price transparency and lower transaction costs among the intermediaries between them. Those goals are typically achieved by organizing a competitive market among traders at each terminal market or other location. Where those intermediary markets use auctions with bids and offers, the market operator is often itself a private enterprise, and there is competition among market operators. For example, in the U.S. there are over 2000 privately run cattle auction houses, each financed by fees on every transaction. Where markets host competing vendors selling side by side in a physical building or open space, the marketplace is more often built and managed by local government or a trade association which rents the space to vendors. Market spaces may also arise spontaneously when vendors cluster together in a neighborhood, as in the part of a city where fish traders might be located based on transportation or other advantages. How each market is managed can have a large impact on transaction costs, and the degree to which any individual or group of traders can exercise monopoly or monopsony power in that market.

Commodity Trading and Financial Markets

When sufficiently large volumes of a standardized commodity flow through a terminal market, it can be worthwhile to create a separate financial market in contracts for future delivery. The first well-documented futures market arose for rice in Osaka in the early eighteenth century, building on the earlier and still common practice of buyers writing forward contracts for purchase at a later date. A forward contract implies that the buyer will take possession of the product when that date arrives. In a market for futures, the contract itself is bought and sold, and only the final holder of the contract on its closing date actually takes possession of the physical commodity. The largest commodity futures markets in operation today are in Chicago, founded in the mid-nineteenth century.

Once people are trading commodity futures, derivative contracts based on future prices can readily be created. These include call options allowing the owner to buy or put options allowing the owner to sell, with each contract specifying an expiration date and the strike price at which the specified quantity could be bought or sold if the owner chooses to exercise their option. In financial markets, participants with 'long' positions are holding rights to sell and benefit if prices rise, while participants with 'short' positions need to buy and benefit if prices fall. The availability of derivative contracts allows producers and commercial buyers of each commodity to hedge the price risks imposed by their physical position in the market. For example, a grain processor or bakery that needs a large quantity of wheat every month starts with a short position in the physical market. That exposes them to the risk of price rises, so they can pre-purchase the product with forward contracts or buy futures to lock in the price they pay, giving them a long position in financial markets. Grain farmers can take the opposite side of that transaction, agreeing to a forward contract or selling futures and buying put options to set a lower limit on the price at which they will eventually sell, to offset the long position they hold prior to harvest. Hedging decisions involve an implicit prediction about price, and market participants as well as outside observers can use the same contracts to speculate about what they think the commodity's price will be in the future.

The use of commodity markets for financial speculation refers to buying and selling contracts with no intention to take physical possession of the underlying product. Each contract has a settlement date, however, at which point the holder is legally required to take possession. At that time the commodity's value depends on supply and demand for the physical product itself. The price of a futures contract can fluctuate before its expiration date but ultimately converges to the cash price for physical transactions on the contract's closing date. The price trajectory for a futures contract reflects evolving expectations about actual supply and demand on that closing date, starting from the contract's day of issue. Traders who expect scarcity of the commodity or inflation of prices in general will buy futures and call options, placing a bet that prices will rise. A group of such traders can bid up the futures price before its closing date, but if good harvests come in or inflation does not occur they will lose money when price at the closing date is lower than they predicted.

Aggregating the predictions of all market participants in a futures market provides useful but often unwelcome signals about future scarcity of a commodity, or inflation in general. For example, after a crop is planted, speculators who anticipate low yields based on crop growth and weather forecasts will buy contracts for delivery after harvest, bidding up the futures price. Market participants will respond with their own predictions, holding onto or buying up physical stocks, thereby raising the actual cash price in the pre-harvest period. Traders will also ship grain towards that destination. If the prediction is wrong and the harvest is normal, all of those market actors will lose money. Such mistakes do occur, where speculators are misled by erroneous predictions that cause a price swing which would not otherwise have occurred. But if the prediction is correct, the price rise after harvest will ultimately be smaller than otherwise, because market actors will have anticipated the problem, cutting back on consumption and bringing in grain from elsewhere. Economic analysis suggests that having a price forecast from the futures market is generally preferable to other ways to forecasting price, because each participant in the market has real money at stake.

A particularly dramatic aspect of commodity markets is the possibility that one or a group of participants can use contracts to buy up an entire harvest and hold it off the market to raise prices for what they sell, and also manipulate the timing of those sales. Gaining market power through financial instruments in this way is known as 'cornering' the market, by analogy to a boxing match. Efforts to corner commodity markets typically lose money in the end, because profits made on the initial high-priced sales are lost when the value of the remaining hoard declines as prices fall back to normal. For example, in 1989 a major soybean processor named Ferruzzi acquired a much larger share of Chicago futures contracts than it actually needed, leading to short-term profits when prices rose but large losses as prices dropped when Ferruzzi had to sell its remaining contracts.

A rare counterexample in which a trader exited their commodity contracts profitably occurred in the 1950s in the U.S. market for onions, a storable product with very inelastic demand whose prices can fluctuate greatly. Because fluctuating onion prices made both hedging and speculation attractive, the Chicago Mercantile Exchange introduced a futures market for onions in the 1940s. In 1955, a commodity trader and onion farmer named Vincent Kosuga partnered with a commodity trader named Sam Siegel to buy up a large fraction of all available onions in the U.S. They made some money from their initial long position, selling at high prices, and made even more by selling short and then provoking a sudden price crash. This rare example of successfully cornering a market was possible partly because of limited disclosure rules at the time about how much Kosuga and Siegel were buying or selling, and partly because high transport costs allowed Kosuga and Siegel to manipulate the market in Chicago with no competition from international trade. In response to the extreme price swing caused by Kosuga and Siegel having withheld supply and then flooded the market, U.S. legislators made onions the only commodity for which future trading is entirely banned, under the Onion Futures Act of 1958.

Industrialization and Farm Structure

Returning to the schematic diagram of the food system as a whole, both vertical and horizontal integration of value chains ultimately link back to agricultural production on farms, fisheries and livestock operations. As discussed in Section 2.2 on production systems, most field crops are grown by self-employed family farmers. Family farms differ widely in their land area and level of mechanization, the inputs they use and how they operate, including the use of forward contracts or other aspects of the business. What they have in common is self-employment of family members, typically living on or near their farm operation.

While nonfarm businesses that are often owned by outside investors and managed by full-time employees, the pattern of self-employment of farm families is remarkably consistent around the world as shown in Fig. 11.9.

The data in Fig. 11.9 come from national censuses of agricultural enterprises. Countries differ in how they define a farm, whether and how often they attempt a complete census or nationally representative survey of those farms,

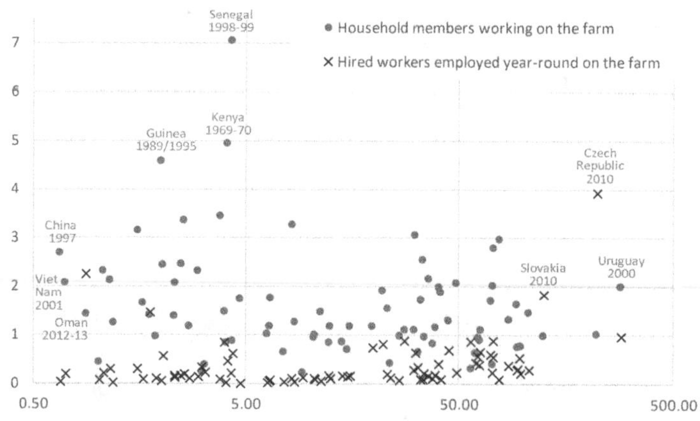

Fig. 11.9 Number of household members and year-round employees working on farms *Source*: Authors' chart of FAO data based on national governments' agricultural censuses, showing all 81 countries or territories for data are available on both household workers and employees. The earliest available is for Kenya in 1969–1970, followed by two in 1988 and 1989. Most are in the 1990s and 2000s, with the most recent in 2019 and 2020. The horizontal axis is farm size in hectares [log scale]. Countries shown have the three smallest and three largest average farm sizes, and the three largest family sizes. Updated datasets are available at https://www.fao.org/faostat/en/#data/WCAD

and what they ask about farms in those census or survey questionnaires. The data shown here are from the 81 countries for which the FAO's compilation of national census data includes both how many family members work on the farm, and also how many paid workers are employed for the entire year, in contrast to seasonal workers.

The horizontal axis shows farm size in hectares, using a log scale due to the exponential nature of variation. Circles show the number of family members, and X's show the number of employees. Most countries have an average of between 1 and 3 family members working on each farm, and an average of near-zero year-round employees.

The country names indicate the three smallest and three largest farm sizes, in terms of both farm size and number of family members. At the far-left, the smallest area of farms is China (surveyed in 1997) and Vietnam (in 2001) each had an average of 2–3 family members and almost no employees per farm. In contrast, the desert kingdom of Oman (surveyed in 2012–2013) had an average of 2.25 employees and 1.4 family members per farm, on just 0.9 hectares. Two other countries with year-round workers on farms are the formerly communist countries of Slovakia with 1.8 employees and 1 family member on 125 hectares, as well as the Czech Republic with 3.9 employees and 1 family member on 221 hectares. Having one or more year-round employees is clearly a result of unusual historical and political circumstances, not farm size.

Variation in the number of family members on each farm is also of interest, especially regarding large family sizes in the African countries shown. For Kenya and Guinea, these primarily reflect the large number of children as well as grandparents who may be listed as working on the farm. For Senegal, having an average of 7.1 working members arises due to the role of extended families living together in a single compound.

The relative absence of year-round employees does not mean a lack of hired workers. In fact almost all farming systems use labor exchange of some kind, typically for seasonal operations and tasks such as land clearing, building and repair of facilities, transportation, handling livestock and harvesting the crop. What those tasks have in common is that the farm owner can quickly observe whether the work was done, with some indication of how well the task was completed. In contrast, the management of field crops and tasks such as planting, weed and pest control or irrigation all influence the harvest in ways that are difficult to observe, so self-motivated workers can generally produce each crop at lower total cost than operations that rely on employees for those operations.

Farms where production operations are easier to supervise include greenhouses and horticultural operations, as well as many animal production systems. Those enterprises can often have several year-round employees. Another category of farm with many employees are plantation crops such as sugar, tea, rubber and oil palm which require immediate processing near the fields, using industrial machinery and facilities with large economies of scale. Sometimes these crops are grown by independent farmers around the central processing plant who are contracted for their crop, but such out-grower schemes typically give way to hired workers on a single plantation to ensure that harvests are tightly coordinated around their need for on-site processing. For plantation crops, processing plant operators need precise timing of delivery for each cart or truckload of raw material to the on-site factory. Furthermore there is only one buyer for the product, so if workers were operating their own farm on an out-grower basis they would be no less vulnerable to exploitation by plant owners. The geographic isolation of these workers, like those on commercial fishing boats, give them few alternatives and create risks of forced labor, wage theft, harassment and other forms of exploitation of concern to buyers and end-users of these products. Similar concerns arise regarding seasonal workers, and about child labor even on family farms.

Several important crops such as cocoa, coffee, cotton and tobacco had been grown on plantations in the eighteenth, nineteenth and early twentieth centuries, but those systems survived only as long as workers lacked civil rights and only a few owners had access to farmland. Across Africa, Asia, the Americas and elsewhere, once forced labor was ended most such plantations were no longer profitable. In some places, new governments actively subdivided land to accelerate the transition to more productive family farming. For cotton production in the U.S. after the Civil War, formerly enslaved people were given almost none of the land where they had been forced to work. They had to rent or buy it. The number of Black farm operators rose to a peak in the 1920 census, but the disenfranchisement and state-sanctioned violence of Jim Crow laws forced most of them off their land.

Beyond the number and average size of farms, how a country's land area is distributed among its population merits deep investigation. Land ownership and tenancy systems play an important role in how equitably, efficiently and sustainably the land is used. Land means much more to people than just the food it produces, and every country has its own unique history of possession and dispossession. For global comparison of land use distributions, the FAO compilation of agricultural census data is shown in Fig. 11.10.

The distributional data in Fig. 11.10 show the percentage of all farms in a country that are very small (0–1 hectare) on the left, and very large (over 500 hectares) on the right. In between there are three intermediate categories, small farms (1–5 hectares), medium-sized (5–50 hectares) and large (50–500 hectares). These thresholds and terminology are used here only for shorthand convenience. Whether a given area is adequate to provide a sufficient livelihood depends on many factors such as proximity to infrastructure and cities, soil quality and water management, availability of locally adapted seeds and farming methods. Even within a country, five hectares in a high-value location may be worth fifty hectares elsewhere. A farm of less than one hectare might be cultivated by hand, and could provide full-time employment above a country's poverty line only under very unusual conditions. In contrast, a farm

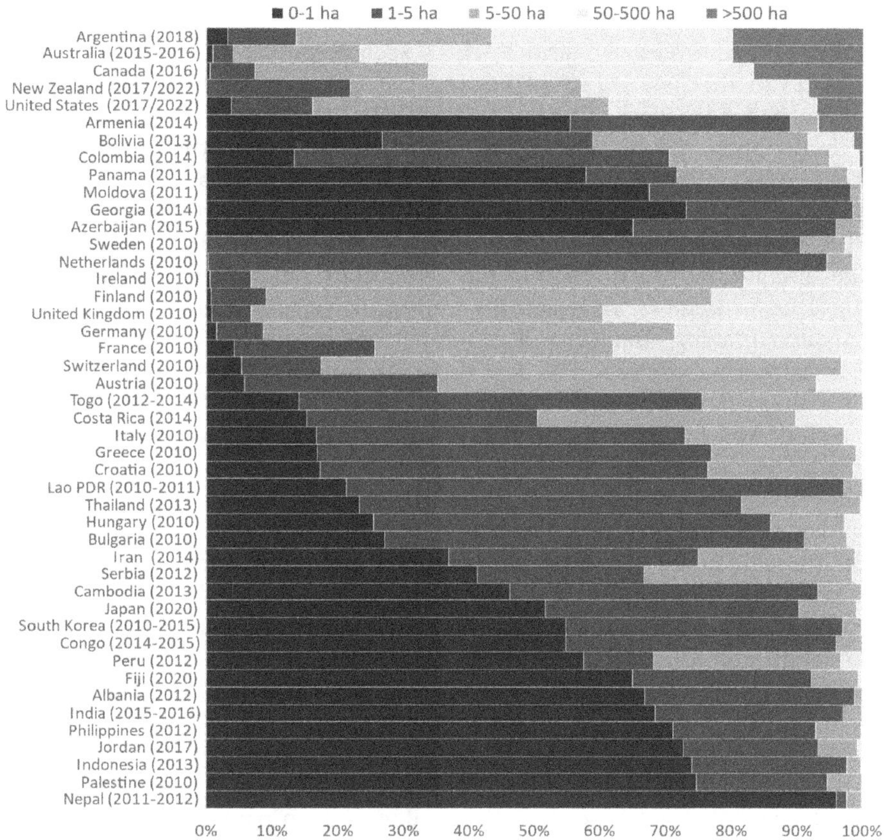

Fig. 11.10 Farm size distributions around the world *Source*: Authors' chart of FAO data based on national governments' agricultural censuses, showing all 46 countries or territories for which data are available on the number of farms by size category, in censuses conducted from 2010 to the most recent data from 2022. Countries are sorted by share of farms in the smallest and largest categories. Updated datasets are available at https://www.fao.org/faostat/en/#data/WCAD

of over 500 hectares might require a high degree of mechanization for one family to cultivate.

The chart shows all 46 countries for which the FAO compilation has an agricultural census conducted from 2010 to the most recent year of 2022, dropping the very small islands and territories with fewer than 50,000 farms. The countries shown vary greatly in terms of size, income level and location around the world. Sorting is done first on the percentage of very large farms at the top right, and then on the percentage of very small farms on the left.

Starting from the top of Fig. 11.10, Argentina and Australia both have about 20% of their farms in the very large category. In Canada that's 16%, and then New Zealand and the U.S. are at 8% and 7%. But the next country,

Armenia, also has 7% of its farms above 500 hectares. Like the unusually large number of employees per farm in the Czech Republic and Slovakia shown in Fig. 11.9, that is a legacy of Eastern European transition from socialism. Armenia had been part of the USSR until its dissolution in 1991, and the Czech Republic and Slovakia were formed in 1992 with the dissolution of Czechoslovakia. Previously those systems had consolidated land in state farms, in Armenia's case with 7% of farms each having more than 500 hectares. Meanwhile the privatization process left a majority of farms (55%) in the 0–1 hectare range, and another third (33%) in the 1–5 hectare range. It is possible that all of the land in large farms is actually unproductive mountain areas used only for limited grazing, but three Latin American countries also have some of this distributional pattern. The next three are Bolivia, Colombia and Panama, each with some very large farms over 500 hectares, and also many very small farms, followed by Moldova, Georgia and Azerbaijan that were formerly part of the USSR. Their large number of very small farms reflects limited access to employment opportunities, with a share of very small farms that is similar to much lower-income countries such as India.

In the middle of the chart are nine northern European and Scandinavian countries with almost all of their farms in the intermediate range. These farming systems are unusual in that regard. The bottom half of the countries, from Togo and Costa Rica down to Palestine and Nepal, have increasingly large fraction of farms in the 0–1 hectare category. Of those, Peru is an unusual case with 58% of farms in that very small category, but also 3% of farms with over 50 hectares, and also 29% in the 5–50 hectares category, revealing a high degree of inequality. Again these differences could simply reflect differences in land quality, so with measuring the value of each parcel we cannot know much about the significance of the land use disparities shown in the chart.

From the bottom of Fig. 11.10 we have Nepal, where 96% of recorded farms are in the 0–1 hectare range, Palestine at 75%, Indonesia at 74%, Jordan at 73%, then the Philippines and India at 71% and 69%. These are all quite different from each other, but the large number of very small farms implies a clear need to focus on that scale of production. Some high-income countries such as Japan and South Korea also have large number of such farms, although often managed as part-time activities. Only two African countries have census data of this type, both relatively small coastal countries in West Africa: Togo (about 8.6 million people) and Congo (about 5.7 million; this is the Congo whose capital is Brazzaville, not the very large D.R. Congo to its east whose population is about 96 million).

Full Cost Accounting for Nonmarket Costs and Benefits Along a Value Chain

The differences and similarities in various aspects in every aspect of the value chains, institutions and farm structures of each country discussed in this section lead many analysts to seek more complete accounting of the nonmarket costs and benefits of the activities in the food system. Section 6.2 introduced the basic framework of cost-effectiveness analysis, used to analyze nonmarket impacts of a project or program. For what is sometimes called 'true cost' accounting, the incremental costs of each market transaction are added up to see differences in the total externalities or other nonmarket costs and benefits are imposed on other people. A useful accounting framework for true or full cost accounting is shown in Fig. 11.11.

The accounting framework in Fig. 11.11 is built around the tools used for cost-effectiveness and social cost–benefit analysis described in Section 6.2, adapted for use by analysts looking to evaluate the incremental impact on society of expanding or shrinking private-sector activities along a value chain. The framework's purpose is to help readers keep track of what could potentially be measured, recognizing that actual measurements for each activity of interest will be available for only some of the variables shown. This specific framework borrows from the many different approaches currently being used in terms of social accounting, true cost accounting or full cost accounting. These ideas differ from similar-sounding term, the social accounting matrix (SAM), which refers to the flow of funds through the market economy as shown in the circular flow diagrams of Section 9.1, in an expanded version of Table 9.2.

The framework refers to each item of interest, denoted with the subscript *i*, starting with the observed market price of that item $\mathbf{P_i}$. Full cost accounting

Opportunity cost or social value for one additional unit of an item along a food value chain (the ith item)	**Impacts per unit of food**	**Valuation per unit of impact**	**Full cost or social value per unit of food**
Market price			$\mathbf{P_i}$
External costs			
Environmental (e.g. social cost of carbon emissions)	a_{ij}	c_j	$a_{ij} \cdot c_j$
Societal (e.g. social cost of underpaying workers)	a_{ij}	c_j	$a_{ij} \cdot c_j$
Health (e.g., social cost of a diet-related disease)	a_{ij}	c_j	$a_{ij} \cdot c_j$
			$\mathbf{C_i} = \Sigma_j (a_{ij} \cdot c_j)$
External benefits			
Environmental (e.g., social gains from ecosystem services)	a_{ik}	b_k	$a_{ik} \cdot b_k$
Societal (e.g., gains from food system amenities)	a_{ik}	b_k	$a_{ik} \cdot b_k$
Health (e.g., gains lower micronutrient deficiency risk)	a_{ik}	b_k	$a_{ik} \cdot b_k$
			$\mathbf{B_i} = \Sigma_k (a_{ik} \cdot b_k)$
Transfers between people in society			
Taxes paid on sales of products, e.g., VAT			t_i
Subsidies received for production, e.g., PSE			s_i
Markup due to market power, e.g., monopolies			m_i
			$\mathbf{T_i} = t_i - s_i + m_i$
Social value per unit (market price, plus or minus nonmarket impacts, in pesos/kg)			$\mathbf{SV_i} = P_i - C_i + B_i - T_i$
Social cost/benefit ratio (market price, plus or minus nonmarket impacts, as a unit-free ratio)			$\mathbf{SCB_i} = (P_i + C_i + s_i)/(P_i + B_i + t_i + m_i)$

Fig. 11.11 Social accounting for environmental, social and health impacts along a value chain *Source*: Authors' synthesis of social cost–benefit concepts applied to true cost accounting, full cost accounting and social accounting for enterprises, for example as part of environmental, social and governance [ESG] or health impact accounting

then asks what externalities and other nonmarket costs and benefits are associated with one more unit, above and beyond that market price. Interest in true cost accounting is driven primarily by the need to account for environmental externalities, including especially the first and usually most important example which is impact on climate change measured as the social cost of carbon-equivalent emissions. There might also be external costs associated with water or air pollution. The next line lists societal impacts that analysts could include, such as the harms to a community from having some workers along the value chain who are unjustly exploited. The third kind of externality is a set of health costs associated with one more unit of the item, such as increased risk of a diet-related disease.

Each specific kind of externality is given a subscript j, so as to look for evidence about the quantity of that externality from one more unit of i, and also the value per unit of that externality. By convention, the amount of damage is denoted as a_{ij} and the cost per unit of damage is denoted c_{ij}. For example, the manufacturing and distribution of an additional bottle of soda might be estimated to cause additional carbon-equivalent emissions of 0.5 kg CO_2-eq, so one bottle per day causes an annual amount of $a_{ij} = 0.5*365 = 182.5$ kg. The social cost of carbon was most recently estimated by the U.S. Environmental Protection Agency (EPA) at \$51 per ton, or roughly $c_j = \$0.05$ per kg. The resulting social cost per year of a daily soda is $a_{ij} \times c_j = 182.5 \times 0.05 = \$9.13$ per year.

One feature of this accounting framework is that it explicitly distinguishes between the amount of each harm or benefit and its cost per unit. The amount of CO_2-equivalent gases emitted per bottle produced would be estimated using life cycle analysis (LCA), while the social cost per ton of CO_2-equivalent emission would be obtained from cost–benefit analyses used by agencies such as the U.S. EPA. Each variable might change with new information, and the analysis can be updated accordingly.

Another feature of this accounting framework is that it shows how the exact same concept can be used to add up various other aspects of the value chain, including the external benefits from a socially desirable activities in the value chain. Many kinds of farming have environmental benefits, or create desirable amenities like urban green space, or generate health gains. In each case there would be an amount of that benefit denoted as a_{ik} and the gain per unit of that benefit of b_k.

A third aspect of the framework is to recognize that market prices do not represent society's opportunity cost when activities along the value chain pay taxes to fund other things in society, receive subsidies from other people in society or involve market power such that prices are not equal to marginal cost. If the market price of the ith item includes t_i taxes paid to other people within the country, the cost to society of one more unit is actually P_i minus t_i, and similarly for the other factors.

The net result of the framework is to recognize that each unit has a social value per unit equal to the sum of all costs minus benefits, and that can also be expressed as a unit-free social cost/benefit ratio as discussed for project and program analyses in Section 6.2. As with any real-world application, a central question is what data might actually be available for which of the variables. The accounting framework can be used with just one type of nonmarket impact, or many.

For the social value of products from a value chain to show the causal impact of one more unit, the amounts and costs of nonmarket impacts would have to show the marginal effect of just the one additional unit. In practice, real-world data generally refers to the total or average of all units, and estimating marginal cost is not feasible because it would require building a detailed simulation model of the entire value chain.

Social accounting reveals opportunities to improve outcomes by addressing each market failure that generates externalities or allows market power. The institutions that govern transactions between enterprises along the value chain, and govern the operations of each enterprise, are societal choices made through the policies and programs of government and other organizations. Reducing both market failure and policy failure aligns observed prices with societal needs, driving market outcomes towards more sustainable, inclusive and health-supportive food systems.

11.2.3 Conclusion

Each food item we might eat comes to us from a farmer through a value chain, with each link along that chain bringing connections to all other aspects of the interconnected food system. This section introduces ways of seeing the individual elements of every country's agriculture and food system as part of a larger whole, by tracing what is consumed back upstream to its origins, and tracing what is produced downstream to its destination. Every food value chain is shaped by a country's institutions, which include legal and civil rights as well as traditions and social conditions that drive land use, worker rights and the structure of food enterprises. Those institutions are social choices, which vary in response to the opportunities and constraints created by both natural resources and investments that create new opportunities.

Individual enterprises in the food system often seek horizontal integration across value chains and a wider geographic extent of their activity, diversifying to limit the risks they face and using any available economies of scale and scope to reduce their cost of production per unit of goods and services they supply. Horizontal integration by intermediaries in the food system creates opportunities for them to exercise market power against others upstream or downstream in each value chain where they work. In response to that, and also in response to their own risks and market opportunities, enterprises also seek vertical integration up and down the value chain, gaining more control over the sourcing and uses of what they buy and sell.

Economic analysis of value chains reveals the role of both horizontal and vertical integration in how value chains are organized, and the ways in which longer or shorter value chains with different structures pose different risks and offer different kinds of benefits. For items involving a standardized commodity, financial contracts such as futures and options provide continuously updated forecasts of future prices, reflecting both that commodity's relative scarcity and a forecast of inflation in general.

Value chain analysis is helpful not only to understand the price and quality of products being bought and sold, but also to measure the nonmarket costs and benefits that could be added up in an overall social accounting of that activity's net social cost/benefit ratio. We may not yet have all the data we need to reliably compare the social impact of all activities, but the insights from these analytical methods show us where to look and how to interpret what we see.

CHAPTER 12

The Future of Food: Meeting Human Needs with Systemic Change

12.1 Agribusiness and Agroecology: The Environment, Climate and Resources

12.1.1 Motivation and Guiding Questions

We start this chapter with agricultural production and food supplies. How can farms, fisheries and livestock systems adapt to meet growing needs on a rapidly changing planet? What can consumers, institutional decision-makers or government policies and programs do to facilitate resilience and help producers thrive in new environments?

Each farmer has a powerful incentive to be a careful steward of their own resources, such as the soil quality and moisture level of their own fields. They also have high stakes in collectively owned resources such as underground aquifers, but some effects of what they do are far away such as fertilizer runoff that causes downstream algae growth, or methane emissions than cause climate change. Agriculture both contributes to and is harmed by environmental change, playing a central role in the new green revolution towards decarbonization and resilience.

In this section we introduce the economics of innovation, including the role of public and private research and development, and farmer decisions about whether to adopt new methods. Innovations often involve new inputs that substitute for natural resources, using knowledge and capital to produce more with less.

By the end of this section, you will be able to:

W. A. Masters and A. B. Finaret, *Food Economics*,
Palgrave Studies in Agricultural Economics and Food Policy,
https://doi.org/10.1007/978-3-031-53840-7_12

1. Define and describe the principle of induced innovation for new technologies, policies and institutional arrangements in agriculture and other enterprises;
2. Use available data to describe intensification of input use, using the examples of total fertilizer use and yield of cereal grains around the world;
3. Use available data to describe changing use of natural resources, using the examples of cropland for cereals production and transition from wild-caught fish to aquaculture;
4. Describe how agriculture and food enterprises might change to meet food demand in ways that address climate change, demographic trends and societal needs around the world.

12.1.2 Analytical Tools

Agriculture and food play a leading role in humanity's relationship to the natural world, including longstanding concerns about land and water, and the urgent new priorities of mitigation, adaptation and resilience to climate change. Mitigation helps reduce future harms, adaptation responds to harms that are already occurring and resilience is the ability to recover and thrive despite setbacks.

Food production methods are among the most varied and diverse kinds of human activity, and can change rapidly when new opportunities arise. Variation and innovation in agriculture has been a distinctive strength of our species for over ten thousand years, enabling populations to survive and grow in every ecosystem on the planet. The pace of innovation has accelerated over time, as discoveries and technological developments in other domains provide new ways to improve agriculture itself.

One of the most important inputs to innovation is knowledge about what people are likely to need in the future, anticipating trends so that methods are adapted to future conditions. The principle of *induced innovation* says that new inventions can and should use resources that are increasingly abundant, and substitute away from resources that are increasingly scarce. In so doing, agricultural change advances through continuous interactions between people and the planet, altering the work of agriculture-related businesses in response to and in anticipation of changes in natural resources and agroecological conditions. What farmers do is influenced by government policies and programs as well as farmer organizations and civil society, but a convenient shorthand for how innovations scale up to reach all farm enterprises is *agribusiness*. Similarly, the environmental conditions under which farmers work involve many aspects of soils and water, climate and biodiversity, but a convenient shorthand for understanding the natural resources around farm enterprises is *agroecology*. The future of food depends on innovations in both domains, for agribusiness to work with agroecology in ways that meet each person's need for a healthy diet, decent work and resilience to shocks.

Induced Innovation, Agribusiness and Agroecology

Induced innovation applies to every scale of technical change. Most broadly, for most of the nineteenth and twentieth centuries, the increasingly abundant resource driving innovation was fossil fuels. Coal, oil and gas replaced the use of animals for power, and also replaced human labor, waterwheels and windmills. The direction of change turned in the 1970s, and induced innovation turned decisively towards electrification from renewable fuels with the rapidly declining cost of solar, wind, batteries and other means of decarbonization.

Within agriculture, the most fundamental change in resource scarcity driving innovation is population growth and land availability. When and where the labor-to-land ratio is rising, farmers need to intensify crop and livestock production for higher yields per acre. At other times and places, the labor-to-land ratio may be falling, so farmers are looking for ways to use more acres through livestock and mechanization. Induced innovation also applies to the mix of crops and foods produced. When the low-income population of the world is growing, the highest priority is to meet dietary energy needs with low-cost starchy staples and vegetable oils. As incomes rose priorities shifted towards more expensive foods including animal products, processed and packaged items and now with greater longevity priorities can shift towards foods for health.

The term agribusiness is most often used for companies that sell inputs and commercial services to farmers, while agroecology refers to how food is or can be produced using ecological principles and ecosystem services. Initiatives favoring agroecology typically advocate for less use of all industrially produced inputs, with food outputs sustained by closing the loop of nutrient cycling between plants, animals and the soil that sustains them. Initiatives favoring agribusiness typically favor more use of industrially produced inputs, despite runoff loss of nutrients and emissions that change the climate.

Global agriculture includes all kinds of farming. At one extreme, small farms using permaculture and similar techniques aim for closed-loop systems with no industrially produced inputs at all. The other extreme includes cattle operations in Brazil involved in illegal deforestation of the Amazon that are among the world's most environmentally harmful production systems. Most agriculture in each region evolves between those two extremes, using more or less agroecological principles with more or less inputs from agribusiness. Like the problem of dietary transition from inadequacy to excess and then just-right nutrition, agricultural production can and must avoid doing too little or too much of each thing, for a just-right balance of inputs to sustainable productivity growth.

Production Methods, Input Use and Intensification Within Resource Constraints

Many kinds of innovation and new investments will be needed for agriculture to meet humanity's need for healthier foods, produced in more inclusive and sustainable ways. To illustrate the range of innovations, a few examples that are used on many different crops and farms of all size include laser leveling, terracing or micro-catchments and reduced tillage for soil and water conservation; application of soil micronutrients like zinc, iron and boron to remedy deficiencies and improve crop yield and nutritional value; seed treatment and inoculation to improve germination and growth; and precision application of water and nutrients or plant protection techniques to reduce energy use, waste and runoff. Different kinds of innovation often complement each other, as alleviating one constraint on plant growth and farm operations makes alleviating the next constraint more valuable.

Which agricultural innovations are needed for each food product is specific to each place and time, but generally starts with selective breeding to alter the genetic potential of each species. Throughout history farmers have hand-selected their seeds and bred their own animals, producing crop varieties known as landraces that were well-suited to farmers' needs in the distant past. The development of randomized trials and statistical hypothesis testing in the early twentieth century occurred in large part to improve crop breeding, and was accompanied by systematic collection and cataloging of landraces from around the world to identify desirable traits from a wider range of backgrounds, improved techniques for crossing and selection from the full range of genetic potential and new methods for seed multiplication and distribution to farmers.

Throughout the twentieth century, crop breeders around the world worked in public and private institutions to improve dozens of commercially important species, creating many thousands of unique varieties suited to different purposes in each location. Tailoring the plant's genetic potential to local conditions improved its responsiveness to farm management and input use, making it worthwhile for farmers to invest in soil amendments, moisture control and plant protection against pests and weeds. Those investments to improve growing conditions set the stage for a next round of genetic improvement, again raising yield potential and responsiveness to additional nutrients, water and plant protection, potentially up to the ultimate yield ceiling for each species dictated by the total energy in sunlight.

As each round of innovation proceeds in any farming system, pathogens evolve to exploit the new agroecosystem. Pathogens would evolve even without agricultural innovation, but changing conditions creates new opportunities for all kinds of pests and weeds. Resistance to each pathogen is sometimes found from the existing catalog of genetic material collected from all around the world, and sometimes found using existing or new biochemical techniques for plant protection. New varieties and agronomic techniques are also needed to address changes in climate, water availability and other factors.

Productivity growth in crop production comes from the speed and accuracy with which new crop varieties and the accompanying management techniques can be tailored to changing agronomic conditions, and delivered to farmers on time and at scale in ways that are profitable for farmers to adopt. In settings with rapid increases in farm productivity, each new crop variety might be planted for just a few years before it is replaced by a better variety, and each successive new variety might be more narrowly tailored to a specific location, so the number of varieties in current use will grow over time. For some crops like corn and soybeans in the mid-western U.S., the plants' above-ground appearance is uniform but the genetic material underneath varies from in response to small differences in the environment, and varieties are quickly replaced over time.

From the entire universe of selective breeding and agronomic improvement over the twentieth century, a handful of species with breakthrough innovations emerged as the principal success stories. One fundamental step was to make the stalks of wheat and other crops shorter than the landraces selected by farmers. Landraces are often tall in part to shade out competing plants and weeds, but when planted simultaneously with sufficient weed control a short plant can concentrate energy in the grain. Another breakthrough was to make the leaves of corn plants stand up instead of spreading out, and then plant seeds closer together. Landrace varieties of corn were selected in part for yield per seed planted, whereas modern seeds produce less grain on each plant and are planted with many more seeds per field. These and other changes made other innovations more attractive, so that crop breeders could select for other traits such as pest resistance, efficiency in use of moisture and soil nutrients, and nutritional composition of the grain, and yield stability as well as average yield and for many other aspects of plant growth.

The steps needed for a flow of improved varieties and accompanying agronomic inputs to increase farm productivity start with a population of self-motivated family farmers who know their own needs better than anyone else, and a set of researchers in regional or national organizations able to conduct randomized trials and generate a flow of innovations tailored to those needs. The two are connected by education and extension to spread information and other public goods and services, and competitive rural markets or farmer-owned cooperatives through which farmers can buy and sell the products they need. Success stories can occur under almost any set of climatic and agronomic conditions, but the payoffs to innovation are greater where natural resources and infrastructure are more favorable. Innovation systems involve public goods dependent on government support, and therefore arise primarily in countries where governments have an interest and commitment to helping farmers grow more food.

Once farmers start increasing the yield harvested from a field they must replace the lost nutrients. Improved genetic potential, soil moisture management, plant protection and additional nutrients are all jointly needed for yield growth, but applying more nutrients typically follows rather than leads the sequence of innovations. One reason is that most crop improvement happens in places that were favorable to plant growth in the past, so their soils have a reservoir of nutrients that can be drawn down and then replaced with fertilizer. Two other reasons are that plant genetics selected in the past were not chosen to have higher yields when more fertilizer is applied, and nutrients are expensive while new seeds can be multiplied at low cost. Adding nutrients before genetic improvement therefore tends to have low returns and high costs, while new seed varieties can be adopted with fertilizer application rates that grow with the yields actually achieved.

Many different aspects of agricultural production are important for the future of food, but an especially useful starting point is the degree of intensification in soil nutrient use shown in Fig. 12.1.

The data on total fertilizer use per hectare in Fig. 12.1 are shown on a log scale, so that a straight line would be a constant percentage rate of growth. The horizontal guidelines from 1 to 10 kg/ha are in increments of one, the guidelines from 10 to 100 are in increments of ten and the guidelines above 100 are in increments of one hundred. Only selected regions are shown, but the data show clear patterns of change and difference between regions.

Starting at the top, the 27 countries forming today's European Union (EU) used around 100 kg/ha in 1960, far higher than North America at around 38 kg/ha. South Asia began with the lowest rate of fertilizer use but grew quickly to pass the world average in the 2000s, and a level above that of the EU and North America, partly because EU fertilizer use dropped back to levels observed in the 1960s. Africa's fertilizer use grew after independence in the 1960s and 1970s but stopped increasing in 1980 at a time of financial crisis, and fertilizer use growth did not resume until after 2005. One factor in

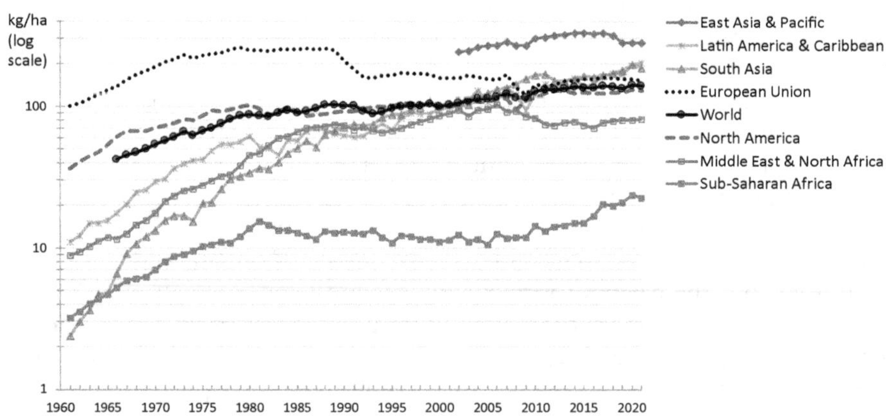

Fig. 12.1 Crop intensification as measured by fertilizer use, 1961–2021 *Source*: Authors' chart showing total nutrients, in kilograms per hectare of arable land, using FAO data as reported by the World Bank, World Development Indicators. Includes only major nutrients [nitrogenous fertilizers for N, potash for K, and phosphate for P, including ground phosphate rock], omitting other soil amendments [animal manure, plant residues and mulch or compost, lime for pH, zinc and other nutrients]. North America is the U.S., Canada and Bermuda. Other countries and regions and updated data are at https://databank.worldbank.org/Fert.-Use-and-Cereal-Yield/id/38545265

that trajectory is that the initial growth in Africa's fertilizer use was not done with limited rollout of new varieties and little pressure for intensification from population growth. In contrast, fertilizer use after 2005 occurred once new varieties had become more widely available, and rural population density was high and rising.

Fertilizer use is a very crude measure of intensification, and relates to productivity growth through a variety of other factors such as soil moisture, infrastructure and markets that determine which crops are grown. For the most basic and longstanding aspects of food production, a useful starting point is cereal grain yields per hectare. Different cereals have somewhat different price and nutritional value, and yield per hectare is driven by many different factors that influence production, but adding up total cereals produced per hectare of land used for cereals provides a simple and informative indicator of productivity.

Results for selected regions of the world are shown in Fig. 12.2.

Cereal grain yields are just one part of the world's agricultural production growth story, but the variability and trends shown in Fig. 12.2 are very revealing about the future of food. Again the vertical chart is in log terms so a straight line is a constant annual percentage rate of growth. Starting at the top left, North America had a slightly less growth and more variability in yields than the EU countries from 1961 through the 1980s, but EU yield growth

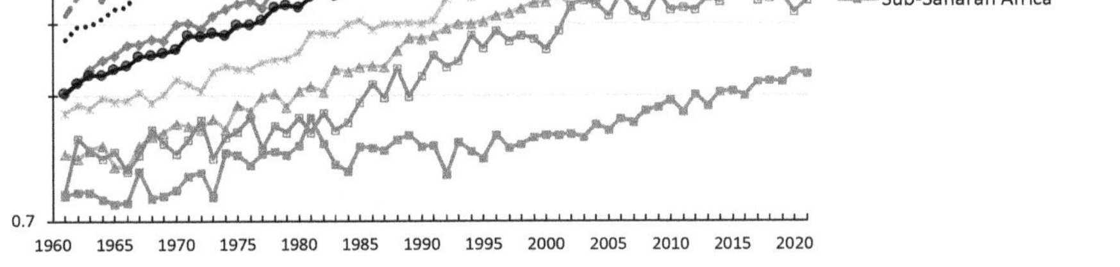

Fig. 12.2 Crop productivity as measured by average cereal yields, 1961–2021
Source: Authors' chart showing total yield, in metric tons per hectare harvested, using FAO data as reported by the World Bank, World Development Indicators. Cereals include wheat, rice, maize, barley, oats, rye, millet, sorghum, buckwheat, and mixed grains that are harvested for dry grain only, excluding crops harvested for hay, feed, or silage, used for grazing, or harvested green as fresh corn. Years refer to harvest, not utilization which may occur in the following year. Countries and other regions can be obtained with updated data at https://databank.worldbank.org/Fert.-Use-and-Cereal-Yield/id/38545265

slowed after 1990 while American yields have continued to rise at about the same annual rate to 2021. This reflects the very different circumstances of the two agricultural systems, as the EU's much higher initial level of fertilizer use and greater population density made further yield growth a low priority. Since the 1990s, European decision-makers have pursued other objectives, moving away from increased yield towards other ways to help farmers and improve rural environments.

East Asia and the Pacific had about the same cereal yields as the global average in 1961, then raised yields much faster than other regions until the early 1980s, after which their yield growth slowed when they too pursued other priorities. The Latin America and Caribbean region had the opposite trajectory, with their cereal yield growth rates below the world average from the 1960s through the 1980s, after which their yield growth accelerated to above the world average.

South Asia had about the same average yield level and growth as the Middle East and North Africa through the 1960s and early 1970s, but continued to raise yields at a roughly constant percentage rate to approach the world average, and also improved yield stability. Cereal yields in Sub-Saharan Africa grew but were highly variable in the 1960s and 1970s, then had no further growth until the 1990s. Prior to the African countries' independence in the 1960s, colonial governments had focused public-sector efforts on the export crops from which they derived tax revenue, and relied on land abundance for food supplies. Africa continued to have the world's most land-abundant agricultural systems through the 1970s, making yield per acre a low priority for national governments until the 1990s.

Sub-Saharan Africa's cereal yields since 1990 have grown roughly in parallel to South Asia, but at a much lower level. Since the 1990s, many African farmers and food consumers have benefited from the gradual rollout of new seed varieties and plant protection methods, accompanied by the increased fertilizer use per hectare shown in the previous chart, but by far the most important driver of yield growth has been increased labor use. That labor has been used to plant new fields which had been previously used for grazing and in some cases forestry, and to plant each field more often. Historically, many farming systems had so much land abundance that farmers would leave each field fallow for several years, building up soil nutrients from spontaneous growth of plants that they burned or cut before plowing and planting. Farmers in other regions had been forced into continuous cropping many decades earlier, using crop rotation and intercropping as well as manure and crop residue management to maintain fertility, and African farmers adopted those methods as well when their labor-to-land ratios rose in the 1980s.

Each region shown in these charts has great internal variation among and within countries, including differences in the accuracy of yield estimates. Each farmer's need and ability to measure their own crop yields, and each government's interest in building an agricultural statistics service capable of accurately estimating the country's total area and quantities harvested, is itself an important part of induced innovation in agriculture. For most of human history, the scarce input to cereals production was the seed. Putting grain into the ground instead of eating it was a painful decision, and yields were measured as the weight of grain obtained per seed planted. Even today, despite the scarcity of land and water, farmers have no need to accurately measure the area of each plot until it is profitable for them to apply expensive inputs like fertilizer in the precise quantities needed. Surveys show that farmers who are just starting to use purchased fertilizer make small but significant errors in measuring their own fields and choosing application rates, making it worthwhile to invest in more precise measurement.

Variation within regions and differences in the accuracy of measurement are important, but it is implausible for the total cereals production, area and average yield of entire regions to have been under- or over-estimated systematically in ways that changed enough to alter the trends shown in these charts. In fact the totals and averages for entire regions over many decades are important precisely because of the variation and measurement error affecting each location.

To help us understand the past and anticipate future changes, the shifting allocation of land to or from cereals, including the use of land that had been fallow or pasture and forestry in Africa as well as shifts in cropland allocation between cereals and other crops, is shown in the area data in Fig. 12.3.

The data shown in Fig. 12.3 are in millions of hectares, with guidelines in increments of 20 million hectares. Sub-Saharan Africa had some area expansion

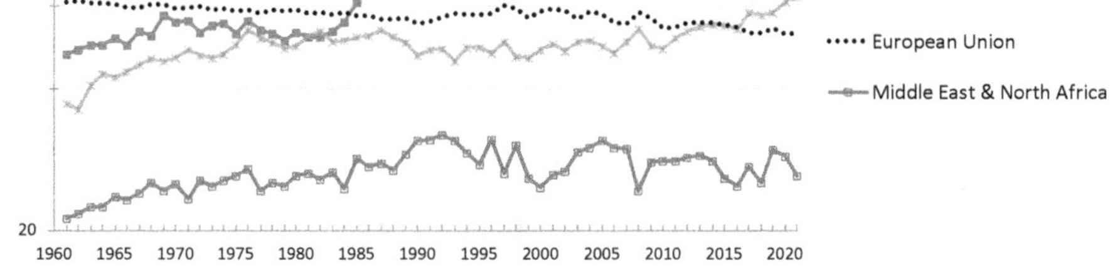

Fig. 12.3 Area used for cereal grains in selected world regions, 1961–2021 *Source*: Authors' chart of total area, in millions of hectares [log scale], using FAO data as reported by the World Bank, World Development Indicators. Land under cereal production refers to harvested area, although some countries report only sown or cultivated area. Countries and other regions can be obtained with updated data at https://databank.worldbank.org/Fert.-Use-and-Cereal-Yield/id/38545265

immediately after independence in the 1960s, then none until the mid-1980s, and is the only major region with large-scale expansion of cereals area since then. The total area of cereals in Africa is now close to that of South Asia, which had expanded in the 1960s and early 1970s but not since then. Cereals area in the North America has declined since 1980, and has declined in Europe since the 1960s.

The future of food will not be like the past. As shown by the trajectories of fertilizer use, cereals yield and cereals area in these charts, each region's agricultural technologies and land use changes with the changing priorities of farmers and national governments. When governments respond, and farmers are able to adopt valuable innovations, productivity per worker and per unit of natural resources can grow quickly.

Data about other crops and livestock systems could be used to chart trajectories similar to those shown for cereals, adding up to the changes in availability by food group that was shown in Section 10.2 on food system transformation. Cereals are important mainly because of their magnitude and comparability around the world.

To illustrate the magnitude of agricultural intensification and transition from natural resources to investment in innovations, another useful global picture to understand the future of food is the fisheries transition shown in Fig. 12.4.

As with cereal grains, the fish production estimates shown in Fig. 12.4 are the sum of national reports compiled by the FAO. Each country's data

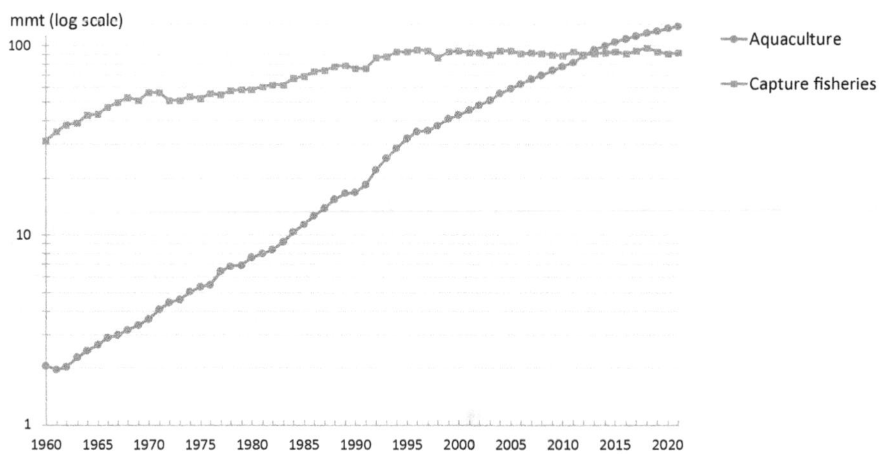

Fig. 12.4 The global transition from capture fisheries to aquaculture, 1960–2021
Source: Authors' chart showing total worldwide production, in millions of metric tons, using FAO data from the World Bank, World Development Indicators. Other regions, countries and updates are at https://databank.worldbank.org/From-Wild-Caught-Fish-to-Aquaculture/id/b567055f

are subject to measurement error, especially for the volume of captured fish which is systematically underestimated when international fleets violate catch limits. The data show rapid growth in wild-caught fish in the 1960s, slightly slower growth in the 1970s and 1980s, and no further growth in measured catch since then. Multiple factors contributed to that change, including overfishing that reduced the potential catch and hence profitability, but if that were the only story then volumes caught would have fallen. Instead, international treaties were used to establish 200-mile exclusive economic zones (EEZs) within which national governments could establish catch limits, and thereby slow down what remains the world's largest wild-animal hunt.

Even before government regulations slowed and perhaps ended growth in the pursuit and capture of wild fish, the world had exponential growth of aquaculture. That growth rate was roughly constant from 1960 through the 1980s, accelerated briefly in the 1990s, and has grown more slowly in recent years. The FAO's rough estimate of when the world reached half of its fish from cultivated sources is 2012.

The data shown in this section are totals per year, not per capita, to illustrate how food systems have shifted from more extensive using up of the world's natural resource to more intensive cultivation, through investment in innovations such as aquaculture. The techniques used for intensification are varied and complex, employing thousands of scientists in hundreds of public-sector institutions and private enterprises to identify opportunities, develop new methods and deploy them at scale among commercial food producers around the world. Experimentation generates countless new ideas, only some of which are sufficiently promising to attract investment for commercial delivery, and only some of those turn out to be sufficiently successful for widespread adoption.

Selected Examples of New Frontiers in Global Agriculture

Innovation in agriculture is not any one thing. Different growers need different things at each place and time, and all producers need a sequence of innovations to overcome the new problems that arise when previous problems are resolved. Individual farmers and private enterprises are constantly experimenting with alternative approaches to their work, drawing on public domain knowledge and other resources to adapt and adopt whatever methods and inputs turn out to work best under their circumstances. Studies have revealed some differences among people and enterprises in their degree of inventiveness and openness to new ideas, some of which are associated with long-lasting cultural and institutional differences, but surveys consistently reveal that new agricultural production methods are adopted to the extent that they actually meet farmers' needs. New techniques that work elsewhere or seem attractive from a distance often turn out to be poorly suited to local conditions, and even if an innovation works it may take a few harvests for the news to spread, but farmers who rely on agriculture for their livelihood have consistently been found to adopt whatever new inputs and production methods work best for them.

Because farmers and private enterprises are constantly experimenting with factors that are within their control, the driving force in the speed of innovation is whether government and philanthropic institutions provide a sufficient flow of new public goods and services tailored to evolving agricultural conditions. The future of food relies on farmers and other enterprises adapting and adopting those ideas, but history shows they have consistently done so. The variation we observe comes mostly from differences in government policies, such as the changes shown in this section for cereal grains and aquatic foods. To illustrate the variety of innovations needed in global agriculture, this section closes with just a few examples below.

Anti-spoilage Technology and Food Safety

Food preservation techniques are needed to protect against contaminants and pathogens for food safety, maintain or enhance nutritional values for health and limit the extent of food loss and waste. Ancient techniques include fermentation of grains and other starchy staples as well as dairy products and some vegetables such as cabbage for kimchi; drying and smoking especially for fish and meat or dehydration of fruit; and milling cereal grains to remove the oil and limit rancidity from oxidation. Techniques developed during the industrial revolution centered on canning, freezing and refrigeration, and the development of chemical preservatives. In the late twentieth century, innovation focused on anaerobic handling and packaging, including the use of nitrogen or other gases to protect foods from oxygen, or simply keeping a hermetically sealed bag or container closed so that additional oxygen cannot enter.

One modern frontier in food preservation of special interest for diet quality and nutrition is the use of edible films on the surface of produce. Moisture is locked inside the fruit or vegetable, and oxygen is prevented from entering. Edible films could potentially make fruits and vegetables more attractive to consumers than current forms of packaging and sale, and offer a new form of value added that helps reduce diet-related disease.

As in other fields, the success or failure of food safety innovations often depends on the incentives created by regulation, such as the U.S. Food Safety Modernization Act of 2011 and its gradual implementation by the Food and Drug Administration (FDA). The FDA was established through the Pure Food and Drugs Act of 1906, making it the world's first national agency with broad powers to regulate many kinds of food, but changes in the sector and limited funding for enforcement continue to attract interest in how best to limit foodborne illness. The need for further reform was highlighted by persistent infant formula shortages in 2021–2022 caused by bacterial contamination at poorly inspected manufacturing plants. In the U.S., food safety concerns from animal source foods are regulated by the USDA, and some issues such as antimicrobial resistance due to prophylactic antibiotic use in livestock or the improper use of pesticides are regulated by multiple agencies with overlapping jurisdictions.

Precision Agriculture and Information Technology

Precision agriculture is an umbrella term for adjusting the rate and timing of input use within each field, in contrast to uniform application over the entire plot. Variable-rate application typically reduces the total quantity of each input used, because prior methods had blanketed each field leading to more runoff, leaching and evaporation than when precision methods are used. Some precision application can be done by hand in very labor-intensive farming systems, but most relies on the combination of GPS positioning for farm equipment, optical and chemical or other sensors to map soil and plant conditions then measure the harvest from each location, and variable-rate applicators for water, fertilizer and chemicals for plant protection. Most of this is surface equipment, but airborne drones also play an increasing role, and some satellite imagery or other remote sensing and weather mapping is also involved.

A central challenge for precision farming, like any information technology, is what to do with the information. When GPS devices and variable-rate technology was first put on U.S. farm equipment in the 1990s, its most popular initial use was to steer the tractor more precisely. This reduced the degree of skipped or overlapping rows, and allowed farmers to work longer days despite low visibility and operator fatigue. Productivity gain from variable-rate application came later, once there was enough data to estimate input response from altering the level of each input for each grid cell across the field. Similar issues arise in lower-income, more labor-intensive settings where new machinery might be most valuable for seemingly simple tasks like measuring a field with drones, or using a laser to help level the surface of a field and control runoff.

Integrated Pest Management

Integrated pest management (IPM) is useful as an example of harm reduction rather than eradication. Agricultural pests can include insects, nematodes and mites as well as the pathogens that they transmit such as fungi and bacterial diseases. When pesticides were first developed, many users believed they might be used preventively to bring damage towards zero, in the same way that some human diseases can be mostly or even completely eradicated. High and frequent pesticide application rates that aimed for eradication were thought to be simple and cost-effective, but that led to very high levels of external harm including to the pesticide applicator and other farmers, and also turned out to be less cost-effective than a more management-intensive approach.

IPM starts with monitoring the level and growth of pest populations, and calculating the likely economic impact of the damage they cause. When the economic impact is high enough to justify the full costs—including environmental harms—application is justified. IPM can be seen as an early form of precision agriculture focused on the timing and level of input use, and it predates the development of electronic sensors. Even more information-intensive methods of pest control show considerable promise, including optical and other sensors to detect pathogens, and precision machinery to apply even more limited doses when and where they are needed.

Alternative Proteins and Indoor Agriculture

The practice of growing food indoors is as old as greenhouses, but access to capital for new ventures and the potential availability of low-cost renewable energy has led to many new efforts at growing food under increasingly controlled conditions. Traditional greenhouses give some ability to control temperature, moisture and other aspects of plant growth, but eliminating the soil through hydroponics can be helpful for even more precise control, and then stacking the plants in vertical racks for aeroponics can be helpful to make even more efficient use of energy and light. With both hydroponics and aeroponics the plant is held up on racks instead of its own root system, and nutrients are fed to the plant through water or mist in the air instead of the soil.

Historically the use of indoor farming was limited by the cost of capital and energy to build and operate them. High interest rates on loans for construction and start-up made it difficult to compete with existing farmers' open fields, especially given the relatively low cost and energy efficiency of transporting produce from farms to consumers. For macroeconomic reasons interest rates in the U.S. and other countries fell to zero from 2009 to 2016, offering an exceptionally long period in which many new ventures were funded by private investors seeking unusual opportunities, and the cost of solar and other renewable power sources was falling sharply. Indoor farming for high-value salad greens has been commercially successful in several instances, but even greater investment and interest has flowed into development of alternative proteins that could substitute for the vastly larger quantities of animal source foods.

Alternative protein is a term used broadly for new ways of making meat that replace the animal's metabolism with controlled processes developed through biological engineering. Older plant-based foods with somewhat similar texture and protein or fat content as meat include tofu and tempeh made from soybeans as well as fried foods like falafel. New alternatives developed in the 2000s used more advanced food science to process a plant food like yellow peas plus other ingredients into products that would look, taste and feel more like meat. Plant-based milks had long been made from coconuts and soybeans, but became much more popular when made from oats, almonds and other sources of nutrients, color and taste.

Through the 2010s three new approaches to making meats were of increasing interest: cellular agriculture, precision fermentation and precision photosynthesis. The cellular approach aims to replace the animal by multiplying their cells, feeding the nutrients from plants and protecting them from disease under very controlled conditions. The fermentation approach also uses nutrients from plants, but uses forms of yeast instead of animal cells to create new foods, while precision photosynthesis uses aquatic plants themselves (microalgae). All of these occur inside controlled environments, such as a fully enclosed bioreactor, with the resulting product potentially combined with other ingredients like the original plant-based meats.

Plant-based milks are commercially successful on a large scale, used primarily in coffee or tea and other beverages as well as breakfast cereals. The cost of ingredients and processing is relatively low, especially for oat and soy milk, and their texture or flavor profile is well adapted to beverages and breakfast cereals. Alternative meats may have technological breakthroughs that mimic the texture and flavor of meat, poultry or fish, and also reduce costs sufficiently to make the product attractive, especially if there are low real interest rates and low energy costs to build and operate these facilities.

Urban Agriculture and Community Gardens
Access to agriculture and gardening is a vital aspect of the human experience, and an important amenity for people everywhere. Plots of land reserved for school and community gardens are maintained in cities and towns around the world for that purpose, to ensure that people are able to connect with nature and join together for a common project even if they do not have land of their own. In temperate zones many people use those gardens for seasonal vegetables, and in tropical countries urban people can maintain kitchen gardens much of the year. In some settings, households are actively encouraged to expand them as in the use of Victory Gardens in wartime or when access to food from rural areas is limited for other reasons. In the U.S. and other countries, urban gardens intersect with issues of social justice and community, autonomy and self-reliance as well as use of the produce to promote healthy diets. In many settings the specific foods grown are of great significance, especially for communities that have been displaced and need to maintain continuity with foods of cultural importance to them. Urban gardens can be helpful even for people who do not use them personally, as a green space in the city.

12.1.3 Conclusion

Recent and ongoing changes in how food is grown demonstrate the potential for innovation to transform agricultural production. New production methods allow people to rely less on resources that are increasingly scarce or inputs found to be harmful, and produce healthier foods using inputs that are relatively abundant for those producers.

The shared priority for innovation globally is climate change mitigation and adaptation, building resilience to extreme weather and other climatic shocks. Agriculture plays a major role in that effort, calling for new production methods tailored to needs of each farming region. Agricultural innovation is much more location-specific than innovation for industry and services, not only because of each region's distinctive geography, ecosystems and infrastructure, but also because of differences in the levels and trends in the relative scarcity of different resources.

One of the few near-certainties about the twenty-first century is that the rural population of Sub-Saharan Africa will continue to rise, increasing the number of young workers who have few options other than to be farmers, while the rural populations of all other regions will decline or remain roughly constant and older in age. That difference ensures that young African farmers will be looking for and quickly adopting innovations adapted to a shrinking area of agricultural land per farm household, including higher input use to raise yields. Sustaining support for innovations that meet African farmers' need for intensification, even as governments elsewhere are no longer concerned about shrinking land area per farm in their own countries, is among the many challenges ahead that will shape the future of food.

12.2 Nutrition and Health: Food Environments, Retail Markets and Diet Quality

12.2.1 Motivation and Guiding Questions

Consumers have a strong interest in health for themselves and their loved ones, but the way that each food affects their future health is not usually visible from the food's appearance. Labeling requirements can provide some information, and dietary guidelines by food group can describe what a healthy diet would be, but consumers have many competing influences on their food choices leading to high rates of malnutrition and diet-related disease. Can the future of food be healthier than the past?

The future of groceries for meals at home and food service for meals away from home depends not only on individual choices and food businesses, but also on civic life and activism that influences government policies and programs. In this final section of the book, we address options for shaping the future of food for nutrition for health by returning to our analytical diagrams that distinguish between the roles of income, prices and preferences in food choice. That approach connects the discussion of human behavior in Chapter 8 with the fundamental principles introduced in Chapter 2 and the market failures from Chapters 4–6, providing a rich toolkit to guide intervention towards improved outcomes.

By the end of this chapter, you will be able to:

1. Distinguish among attributes of food and identify promising opportunities to improve diet quality for health and other goals;
2. Define credence goods, and identify attributes of food that are unobservable to consumers and therefore depend on independent quality assurance to be competitively supplied;
3. Describe and give examples of new initiatives and interventions intended to improve nutritional status, using analytical diagrams to predict their impacts; and
4. Compare economics to other ways of approaching agriculture, food and nutrition, including its strengths and limitations from your perspective.

12.2.2 Analytical Tools

An important insight allowing us to understand and potentially improve the food system is to distinguish among the many attributes of each food item and isolate its consequences. Some attributes are immediately visible, prior to purchase, from the outward appearance of an item. Other attributes are noticeable from the taste, smell or texture of a food soon after purchase.

The most basic attribute of a food is its energy content. On average each person on earth consumes just enough energy each day to sustain our body weight and physical activity level, plus enough for child growth and development starting in pregnancy, with some episodes of weight gain when energy intake overshoots those needs. On average our diets change relatively little in terms of total energy per day, but diet composition can vary enormously in ways that impair or improve our future health.

Obstacles to Dietary Change: Trust, Cost and Affordability and Collective Action

A central challenge for the food system is that each food's consequences for future health typically remain unknown even after consumption. These are examples of *credence attributes,* so called because they are a matter of faith. No amount of personal experience will provide convincing evidence about something like whether whole grains are protective against cardiovascular disease. Evidence for that is scientific in nature, coming from biochemistry and clinical studies as well as epidemiological data. Other attributes beyond health are also credence goods, including whether a food is helpful for environmental sustainability, decent work and livelihoods for farmers, or animal welfare. Credibly signaling credence attributes calls for an independent authority to set and enforce a quality standard, which can be voluntary for producers who wish to use that quality certification on their label, or mandatory for all producers in a given product category.

A second challenge for the future of food is access and affordability of foods with desired attributes. Diet cost analysis reveals whether foods with those attributes are not available or have unusually high costs, revealing a lack of access that could be remedied only by improving supply to deliver more of those foods at lower prices. Affordability analysis compares diet costs to a person's income available for food, thereby revealing whether it is even possible for a person with that income level to buy sufficient quantities of even the least expensive locally available items with attributes needed for health. When healthy diets are unaffordable, food choices could potentially improve diet quality but cannot reach international standards without transfer programs that provide additional resources or nutrition assistance. For many people, healthy diets are affordable and yet not chosen, as those items are displaced by other items that are more expensive per day but chosen because they meet needs other than health such as taste and aspirations, or saving time in meal preparation.

A third challenge for the future of food is the difficulty of collective action to remedy market failures and align incentives with the social costs and benefits of each product. Even after analysts have identified opportunities for public action to improve outcomes, it is not easy to interpret public opinion or even voting behavior for willingness to pay for public goods. For example, millions of Americans in California, Massachusetts and elsewhere have voted for referendums that would require all eggs sold in their state to be from hens raised under cage-free conditions. Before the vote they had the option to buy such eggs voluntarily but often did not do so, typically because of the higher cost. This contradiction between voting in a referendum and buying in a store could be a result of uncertainty, if it is not clear the laws would lead to higher egg prices, but can potentially be explained as an understanding of how free ridership affects collective action: these voters might truly be willing to pay more if others also do, but unwilling to take individual action that could be undermined by others' free riding on their choice. As of late 2023, only one-third of U.S. chickens used for egg production are housed in cage-free conditions layers, and it is not clear how animal welfare laws and practices will evolve in the years ahead.

Intervention to Improve Food Choice: The Three Mechanisms Again

In this final section of the book, we return to the basic principles of Section 2.1 that explained how interventions can alter food choices through three distinct mechanisms: price, income or preferences. Prices are influenced by food supply and trade, as part of the food environment that everyone has in common at a given place and time. Income available for food is an individual attribute of each person and their household, from earnings and wealth as well as transfers received. Preferences determine which of the person's affordable items are actually chosen, driven in part by constraints other than money such as time use, and by all the many other factors affecting behavior.

A standard analytical diagram showing interventions that target each of the three mechanisms is shown in Fig. 12.5.

The model used to explain food choice in Fig. 12.5 shows an individual person's consumption of fruits and vegetables on the horizontal axis, and their consumption of all other things projected onto the vertical axis. The diagonal straight lines show all combinations they can afford, with a vertical intercept where they have no fruits and vegetables at all. Food choice among those equally affordable options is explained as the highest attainable level of a indifference curve that is bowed in as shown, leading to the solid round point indicating this person's currently observed choice.

The set of three indifference curves shown by dotted lines below and to the right of the solid round point are drawn to represent this person's long-term best interests, meaning the preferences that their future self wishes they'd had at the time shown in the diagram. For example, a person might eat few fruits

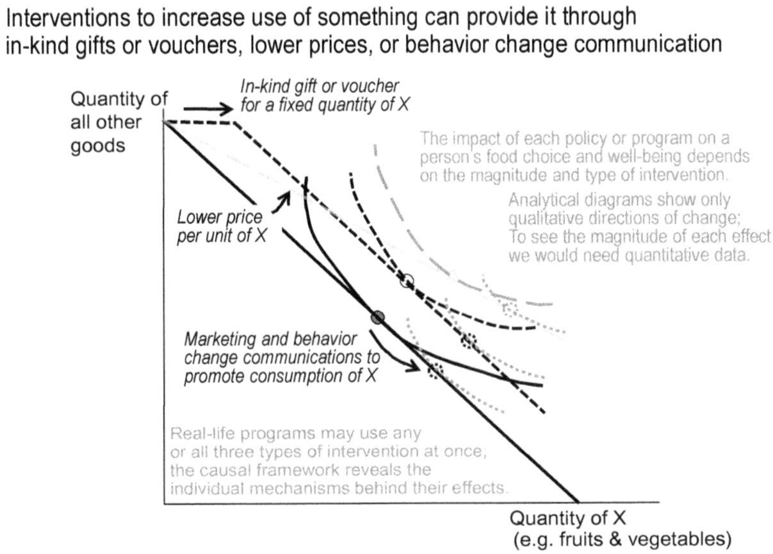

Fig. 12.5 Interventions can alter food choice through three main mechanisms

and vegetables in their 30s and 40s, but come to regret that in their 50s when it turns out that is a risk factor for colorectal cancer.

Intervening to help this person avoid regret—or more precisely, avoid the cancers that would cause regret—could be done purely through marketing and behavior change to alter their preferences. Marketing refers to what private enterprises do to sell their own products, and behavior change refers to public-sector or philanthropic efforts to change peoples' choices. Those marketing and behavior change efforts could focus just on persuasion, as in an advertising campaign, but fruit and vegetable sellers might adopt new more convenient forms of packaging the products, and a public health campaign might try things like teaching people how to cook or even providing them with kitchen equipment.

Efforts at persuasion, such as a behavior change communication campaign with advertisements to eat more vegetables, are generally the least expensive form of intervention per person. Similarly inexpensive interventions to change preferences include changing the placement of things in a store, altering language and imagery with which foods are described, and all of the other marketing activities of companies. Similar efforts to 'nudge' a person's choice in the desired direction might be taken by a school or employer regarding foods in their own cafeteria.

Each food vendor's advertising and marketing efforts, as well as the public and philanthropic efforts at behavior change communication and nudges, work (or don't work) by changing a person's mind about what they want. Altering aspirations in this way is sometimes possible but is difficult, especially given that the marketing and advertising efforts of food companies that influence the observed choice are many times larger in magnitude than any public effort at changing or nudging behavior in a different direction.

A more expensive but often needed intervention is shown with the dark dashed line, whose horizontal segment at the top indicates transfer of a voucher or card that can be used only for fruits and vegetables. In the example drawn, the voucher is for less than the recipient actually wants to consume after receiving the voucher, so they spend some of their own money in addition to the voucher to consume at the dashed circle.

A third kind of intervention that might sometimes be achievable is shown with the light dashed line, indicating a lower price of fruits and vegetables. That could be achieved by removing any policy interventions that raise their price, such as import restrictions or sales taxes on groceries. A lower price might also be achieved by innovation or investments in public infrastructure that lower the cost of production and distribution for competing fruit and vegetable suppliers.

When analysts say they want to 'subsidize' fruits and vegetables, what they usually mean is provide vouchers that cover all or part of the price for a limited quantity which would be drawn like the dark dashed line. The light dashed line refers to the price for everyone, and that cannot be reduced without changing the cost of supply or trade and distribution.

In practice, many interventions combine behavior change communication with a voucher for all or part of a product's price. That combination is a longstanding instrument of marketing, using the voucher to attract and retain attention and the communication to influence how the voucher is perceived and used. When vouchers or transfers are given without behavior change communication, the way they affect choice depends on whether or not the recipient spends some of their own money on the product in addition to the voucher.

Consumer response to a voucher program was discussed in Chapter 8 on food and health behavior, around three different panels in Fig. 8.7. Those concepts are repeated here in the form of a single diagram, as Fig. 12.6.

The choices shown in Fig. 12.6 start at the solid line and curve, and proceed with the dark dashed voucher for fruits and vegetables leading to the open circle. At that point the recipient is spending some of their own money in addition to the voucher. In economics jargon, the voucher is 'infra-marginal' to the person's choice, because the incremental last unit of fruits and vegetables bought by the person is purchased with their own money. This matters because some interventions are designed to be of this type. For example, if we had drawn the diagram with all food purchased at grocery stores along the horizontal axis, the U.S. SNAP benefit would have this type of effect. SNAP benefit cards are recharged once per month with an amount that is designed to supplement the recipient's own spending on food at home, so the recipient uses it until the month's electronic benefit is exhausted and then switch to their own spending. The recipient has no interest in using the benefits

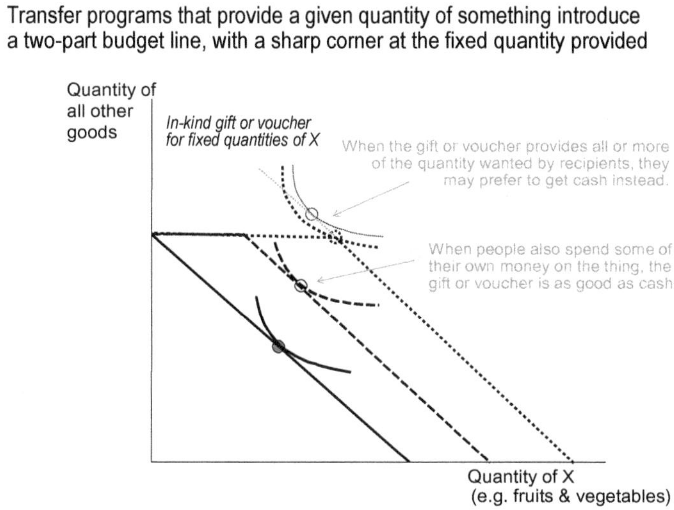

Fig. 12.6 How in-kind gifts or vouchers differ from cash transfers

card for anything other than groceries, because if they did so they would just need to start spending their own money earlier in the month. Keeping the program infra-marginal makes it very likely that recipients will want to use the program funds used as intended, because the voucher is as good as cash for the recipient.

The dotted line shows what would happen if the benefit is large enough that the recipient no longer wants to spend some of their own money on the item in addition to the voucher. Now the voucher is 'extra-marginal' to their spending, as shown by the dark dotted indifference curve, and the recipient could reach a higher indifference curve if they converted some of the benefit to cash and consumed less than the voucher amount of fruits and vegetables. This finding highlights the importance and relevance of accompanying voucher programs with behavior change communications to alter preferences.

12.2.3 Conclusion

This final section of the book is brief because the future of foods for health is up to you. Many different kinds of interventions are used to alter food choice, and all could be informed by the toolkit of economics introduced in this book. People want to be healthy, but choosing foods for health is challenging for at least three fundamental reasons: first of all healthiness is a credence attribute, for which the food's appearance itself conveys little information; then diet cost can be an insurmountable constraint if income available for food is insufficient; and finally each person's preferences, in addition to the prices they pay and the income they have, determine their choices from among affordable options. Those preferences are not easily changed, so interventions typically involve some combination of assistance and persuasion. Rapid changes in the market environment for food both at home and away from home create both the need and the opportunity to anticipate how each person might respond, and how each of us can do our part to form a healthier, more inclusive and sustainable food system.

Epilogue: The Price of Kiwifruit, Explained

Economists use abstract models to explain human affairs. This can be like explaining a joke, or dissecting a frog: it kills the thing you care about. Like comedians and biologists, our task as economists is to make the round trip back to real life. To complete our journey, here's an annotated version of the silly poem that William wrote for *Freakonomics:*

Why are kiwis so cheap?	
Damn supply and damn demand: Why cheap hogs and costly ham? Bargain wheat, expensive flour, the oldest villain's market power	*The first thing people don't like about food markets is farmers get too little, and consumers pay too much. A natural explanation is the behavior of big companies that stand between family farms and family kitchens*
Just one seller makes us nervous, like that U.S. Postal Service: They may offer bargain prices, but who disciplines their vices?	*The prompt for this poem from Freakonomics was that each kiwi cost the same as mailing a letter; at that time, the post office had a near monopoly and was widely criticized for poor performance*
Middlemen have long been blamed for every market that's inflamed, yet better explanations come from many a Hyde Park alum	*Since ancient times, food policy problems have been blamed on the companies that trade and distribute food. The Freakonomics style of explanation comes from the University of Chicago, located in Hyde Park*
Modern views from Chicago-Booth give a nuanced view of truth, Steven Levitt and John List made each of us a Freakonomist	*The 'Chicago School' of economic thought in the 1960s and 1970s was libertarian and ideological, but in the 1990s the university's business school became much more realistic and fun thanks to Levitt, List and others*

(continued)

W. A. Masters and A. B. Finaret, *Food Economics*,
Palgrave Studies in Agricultural Economics and Food Policy,
https://doi.org/10.1007/978-3-031-53840-7

(continued)

Why are kiwis so cheap?	
We let data speak its mind no matter what Friedman opined and find the price of fruit and veg to be driven by the market's edge	*Earlier economists focused on theory, but modern computing allows us to look more directly at lots of data. Unlike the free-market doctrine of Milton Friedman, we use marginal analysis to answer practical questions*
Like the tail that wags the dog, marginal thinking clears the fog: Sellers, buyers, traders too, interact and prices ensue	*Economics explains the price of all goods by focusing on the last unit being bought and sold. This idea helps clear up many puzzles as the result of interaction between many people, all along the chain from farm to fork*
A kiwi costs 33 cents simply because no one prevents another farm or New York store from entering and selling more	*The price of kiwifruit, like everything else, is set by the marginal cost of suppliers who might enter the market. The poem's prompt was prices in N.Y., where fruit is sold by small shops that compete with each other*
In contrast apples may be dear, for reasons that will soon be clear: Picking them's below our station, to lower costs we need migration	*The prompt compared kiwis to apples, which can be locally grown but are more expensive. One reason is the cost of labor for apple harvests, which is manual labor requiring physical skill but not formal education*
Bananas have a different story, seedless magic, breeder's glory, cheap to harvest and to ship, who cares if workers get paid zip?	*Bananas, unlike kiwis or apples, grow in the tropics. Almost all have identical genes, carefully selected to perform well under controlled conditions. In most banana-growing regions, workers are paid very little*
Each crop's method of production, where it grows and how it's trucked in, satisfies some needs quite cheaply while other costs will rise more steeply	*To understand food prices, we need to know something about farm technology and also transport or storage. Innovation makes some things surprisingly inexpensive while other things are difficult to make and sell*
A buyer's choices matter too, for nonsense stuff like posh shampoo, prices are not down to earth, the more you pay the more it's worth	*Food demand matters too, and depends on preferences. The shampoo example was prompted by a family debate; the last line is the title of a song by Don McLean that William knows from his childhood in the 1970s*
Behavior is as behavior does, maybe some things are just because much of life's a mystery, a habit due to history	*Many aspects of the food system are cultural in nature. They arise and persist for sociological or other reasons. The original cause may have been random, and can be understood only by tracing its origins back in time*

(continued)

(continued)

Why are kiwis so cheap?	
For prices, though, it's competition plus tariffs set by politicians, that determines whether we see such delightfully cheap kiwi	*Looking forward, we have choices. With innovative new entrants selling each thing from many locations, and limited restrictions that protect incumbents, we can have good things like year-round fruits and vegetables*

Index

W. A. Masters and A. B. Finaret, *Food Economics*,
Palgrave Studies in Agricultural Economics and Food Policy,
https://doi.org/10.1007/978-3-031-53840-7

N

Printed in the USA
CPSIA information can be obtained
at www.ICGtesting.com
CBHW071346200524
8819CB00003B/52

9 783031 538391